Perspectives on Bias in Mental Testing

PERSPECTIVES ON INDIVIDUAL DIFFERENCES

Series Editors

CECIL R. REYNOLDS, *Texas A&M University, College Station*
ROBERT T. BROWN, *University of North Carolina, Wilmington*

PERSPECTIVES ON BIAS IN MENTAL TESTING
Edited by Cecil R. Reynolds and Robert T. Brown

A Continuation Order Plan is available for this series. A continuation order will bring delivery of each new volume immediately upon publication. Volumes are billed only upon actual shipment. For further information please contact the publisher.

Perspectives on Bias in Mental Testing

Edited by

CECIL R. REYNOLDS

Texas A&M University
College Station, Texas

and

ROBERT T. BROWN

University of North Carolina
Wilmington, North Carolina

PLENUM PRESS • NEW YORK AND LONDON

Library of Congress Cataloging in Publication Data

Main entry under title:

Perspectives on bias in mental testing.

(Perspectives on individual differences)
Includes bibliographical references and indexes.
1. Psychological tests. 2. Educational tests and measurements. 3. Test bias. I.
Reynolds, Cecil R., 1952–   . II. Brown, Robert T. III. Series.
BF176.P47   1984   153.9′3   84-9800
ISBN 0-306-41529-1

©1984 Plenum Press, New York
A Division of Plenum Publishing Corporation
233 Spring Street, New York, N.Y. 10013

Printed in the United States of America

Contributors

ERNEST M. BERNAL, School of Education and Human Development, California State University, Fresno, California

ROBERT T. BROWN, Department of Psychology, University of North Carolina, Wilmington, North Carolina

H. J. EYSENCK, University of London, London, England

ROBERT A. GORDON, Department of Sociology, Johns Hopkins University, Baltimore, Maryland

GORDON M. HARRINGTON, Department of Psychology, University of Northern Iowa, Cedar Falls, Iowa

ASA G. HILLIARD III, Georgia State University, Atlanta, Georgia

LLOYD G. HUMPHREYS, Department of Psychology, University of Illinois, Champaign, Illinois

JOHN E. HUNTER, Department of Psychology, Michigan State University, East Lansing, Michigan

REX JACKSON, Applied Educational Research, Princeton, New Jersey

ARTHUR R. JENSEN, Institute of Human Learning, University of California, Berkeley, California

WINTON H. MANNING, Educational Testing Service, Princeton, New Jersey

JANE R. MERCER, Department of Sociology, University of California, Riverside, California

JOHN RAUSCHENBERGER, ARMCO Corporation, Middletown, Ohio

CECIL R. REYNOLDS, Department of Educational Psychology, Texas A & M University, College Station, Texas

FRANK L. SCHMIDT, U.S. Office of Personnel Management and George Washington University, Washington, D.C.

Preface

The cultural-test-bias hypothesis is one of the most important scientific questions facing psychology today. Briefly, the cultural-test-bias hypothesis contends that all observed group differences in mental test scores are due to a built-in cultural bias of the tests themselves; that is, group score differences are an artifact of current psychometric methodology. If the cultural-test-bias hypothesis is ultimately shown to be correct, then the 100 years or so of psychological research on human differences (or differential psychology, the scientific discipline underlying all applied areas of human psychology including clinical, counseling, school, and industrial psychology) must be reexamined and perhaps dismissed as confounded, contaminated, or otherwise artifactual. In order to continue its existence as a scientific discipline, psychology must confront the cultural-test-bias hypothesis from the solid foundations of data and theory and must not allow the resolution of this issue to occur solely within (and to be determined by) the political *Zeitgeist* of the times or any singular work, no matter how comprehensive.

In his recent volume *Bias in Mental Testing* (New York: Free Press, 1980), Arthur Jensen provided a thorough review of most of the empirical research relevant to the evaluation of cultural bias in psychological and educational tests that was available at the time that his book was prepared. Nevertheless, Jensen presented only one perspective on those issues in a volume intended not only for the scientific community but for intelligent laypeople as well. What is needed is a more thorough analysis of the issues of bias in mental testing that is written from a variety of perspectives, including interdisciplinary ones. Further, the field has been anything but static in recent years: Much research has been published since Jensen completed his book; new theoretical and conceptual issues have been raised; and new areas involving test bias have arisen, such as those concerning tests published by the Educational Testing Service. Finally, the issue of test bias has hardly been resolved in either its scholarly or its applied forms, as indicated by the opposing judicial verdicts handed down in the cases of *Larry P.* v. *Riles* and *PASE* v. *Hannon.*

This volume presents the views of several prominent authors in the fields of cultural test bias specifically and of individual differences generally. We have attempted to bring together proponents of the major views currently available, although space limitations have obviously prevented the presentation of all positions or all possible contributors. We have, however, tried to justify the use of the word *perspectives:* Our authors are from different academic disciplines, cultural backgrounds, and employment settings. They represent scholars, test publishers, private practitioners, and psychologists in private industry. Further, they have employed a variety of research approaches in addressing the issue of bias, from complex correlational approaches to those that are complex experimental. In dealing with this area, there are few simple approaches. Each author deals with a topic of specific relevance to a full evaluation of the cultural-test-bias hypothesis. Competing views have been purposely presented so as to make clear where the areas of disagreement lie. The request to the authors was simple and straightforward: They were asked to focus on the empirical, scientific evaluation of the cultural-test-bias hypothesis and to avoid emotional issues. The responses to this request, the authors' chapters, are presented with minimal editorial alteration, so that readers can clearly see the positions of experts in the field at this time and can find the basis for an evaluation of the viability of their views.

Some notes on the organization and content of the book follow. The first two chapters provide background information. The first chapter, an introduction to the issues by the editors, is an overview of the scientific and emotional issues surrounding the test bias hypothesis and provides a historical perspective that acts as a context for the rest of the book. The chapter by Hunter, Schmidt, and Rauschenberger is a sophisticated presentation of the methodological and statistical considerations that may lead to problems in interpreting research in the area, as well as of the ethical considerations that must guide that research.

Chapters 3 through 10 present specialized areas of research or topics of interest relevant to test bias. As can be seen, these chapters cover a diversity of topics from a diversity of perspectives, and by design, there has been no attempt to bring unity or any particular organization to them. They well represent the variety of methodological and theoretical approaches that characterizes the field at this time. Harrington, in Chapter 3, offers an unusual perspective on test bias: a true experimental model that has attempted, through the use of animal subjects, to test the assumptions that underlie standardized psychological tests. As might be expected, his approach is not universally accepted, but it is certainly thought provoking. Bernal, in Chapter 5, describes a new research project using different types of instructions to evoke different levels of performance on intelligence tests by different cultural groups. Manning and Jackson discuss the charges of test bias that have been leveled against tests produced by the Educational Testing Service and describe research that they feel successfully answers those charges. Eysenck, in Chapter 8, faces head-on one of the issues that underlies the current interest in the cultural-test-bias hypothesis: racial differences in intelligence test performance.

The other chapters are more theoretically oriented. Hilliard (Chapter 4) and Mercer (Chapter 9) criticize present intelligence tests from, respectively, a black and a sociological perspective. Both believe that the cultural-test-bias hypothesis is basically correct. Gordon (Chapter 10) provides a sociological perspective that is not only opposed to but highly critical of Mercer's. Humphreys (Chapter 7) discusses the issue of test bias in the larger context of the theoretical construct of general intelligence. In the last chapter, Jensen updates his position as presented in *Bias in Mental Testing* and critiques the other chapters in this volume. Among his criticisms is a statistical reevaluation of Bernal's results that leads to questions concerning Bernal's interpretation. In a postscript at the end of the book, Bernal replies to Jensen's criticism.

We suffer under no illusion that the test bias issue will be resolved to the satisfaction of all for some time to come. Our hope is that this book will clarify the positions and the supporting data of various camps. We hope that the volume will expose areas where little evidence has been gathered and where additional research is needed. We hope additionally that the volume will demonstrate that even areas of considerable emotional impact and political and social implications will benefit from scientific evaluation.

There are many to whom we owe thanks for assistance in the preparation of this book. We appreciate the cooperation of the authors in the timely submission of their contributions. The cooperation and the encouragement of Leonard R. Pace, formerly of Plenum Press, has helped to smooth the development of this volume and the series on individual differences of which it is the initial volume. The patience and the support of our wives, Brenda and Sue, and our families has contributed in a major way to the successful completion of this book. Finally, the invaluable assistance of the office staff at University of North Carolina at Wilmington (Martha Jo Clemmons and Eleanor Martin), University of Nebraska at Lincoln (Linda Weber), and Texas A & M University (Lori Powell) is gratefully acknowledged.

CECIL R. REYNOLDS
ROBERT T. BROWN

Contents

CHAPTER ONE

Bias in Mental Testing
An Introduction to the Issues

CECIL R. REYNOLDS
and
ROBERT T. BROWN

Public controversy deals with stereotypes, never in subtle-
ties. The Luddites can smash up a device, but to improve a
system requires calm study. . . . Sound policy is not for tests
or against tests, but how tests are used. But all the public
hears is endless angry clamor from extremists who see no
good in any test, or no evil.

Cronbach, 1975, p. 1

Cultural bias in mental testing has been a recurring issue since the beginning of the testing movement itself. From Binet to Jensen, many professionals have addressed the problem, with varying and inconsistent outcomes. Unlike the pervasive and polemical nature–nurture argument, the bias issue has been until recently largely restricted to the professional literature, except for a few early discussions in the popular press (e.g., Freeman, 1923; Lippmann, 1923a,b). Of some interest is the fact that one of the psychologists who initially raised the question was the then-young Cyril Burt (1921), who even in the 1920s was concerned about the extent to which environmental and motivational factors affect performance on intelligence tests. Within the last few years, however, the question of cultural test bias

CECIL R. REYNOLDS ● Department of Educational Psychology, Texas A & M University, College Station, Texas 77843.   ROBERT T. BROWN ● Department of Psychology, University of North Carolina, Wilmington, North Carolina 28401.

1

has burst forth as a major contemporary problem far beyond the bounds of scholarly academic debate in psychology. For approximately the last decade, the debate over bias has raged in both the professional and the popular press (e.g., Fine, 1975). Entangled in the larger issues of individual liberties, civil rights, and social justice, the bias issue has become a focal point for psychologists, sociologists, politicians, and the public. Increasingly, the issue has become a political and legal one, as reflected in numerous court cases and passage in the state of New York and consideration elsewhere of "truth-in-testing" legislation. The magnitude—and the uncertainty—of the controversy and its outcome is shown in two highly publicized recent federal district court cases. The answer to the question "Are the tests used for pupil assignment to classes for the educably mentally retarded biased against cultural and ethnic minorities?" was "Yes" in California (*Larry P.*, 1979) and "No" in Chicago (*PASE*, 1980).

Unfortunately, we are all prisoners of our language. The word *bias* has several meanings, not all of which are kept distinct. In relation to the present issue, bias as "partiality towards a point of view or prejudice" and bias as "a statistical term referring to a constant error of a measure in one specific direction as opposed to random error" frequently become coalesced. If the latter meaning did not drag along the excess baggage of the former, the issue of bias in mental testing would be far less controversial and emotional than it is. However, as indicated in the *Oxford English Dictionary*, bias as partiality or prejudice can be traced back at least to the sixteenth century and clearly antedates the statistical meaning. We are likely ourselves to be biased toward the meaning of partiality whenever we see the word *bias*. The discussion of bias in mental testing as a *scientific* issue should concern only the statistical meaning: whether or not there is systematic error in the measurement of mental ability as a function of membership in one or another cultural or racial subgroup (Reynolds, 1982b).

As would be expected, Jensen's *Bias in Mental Testing* (1980a) has hardly stilled the controversy. Since his now-classic "How Much Can We Boost IQ and Scholastic Achievement?" (1969), virtually anything with Jensen's name on it has had earthquake impact, some publications evoking higher Richter-scale readings than others. Whatever its actual effect, *Bias in Mental Testing* was intended to be a scholarly presentation of the statistical concepts and the empirical research concerning test bias. After an exhaustive evaluation of the literature, Jensen concluded that the charge of bias in mental tests could not be substantiated. Although virtually all scholars respect

Jensen's scholarship and integrity, by no means do all accept his conclusions. Other recent independent, extensive reviews of the empirical literature have also generally come to the same conclusion as has Jensen (e.g., Reynolds, 1982a; Vernon, 1979). Jensen's book has been subjected to peer evaluation not only in multiple individual book reviews, but in a recent issue of *Behavioral and Brain Sciences* (1980b), in which his position was strongly supported by some professionals and just as strongly attacked by others. The present book is designed to provide a more extensive presentation of a variety of views on bias than is available elsewhere. It is not intended as a critique of Jensen, but as an original scholarly contribution to the literature on bias. For that reason, authors have been chosen who have a variety of opinions on the issue, but who, for the most part, share an interest in an empirical as opposed to an emotional resolution of the issue. Unfortunately, it was not possible to include all those qualified to write on the issue. As the acknowledged authority in the field, Jensen was invited to comment on the other papers.

At the outset, we would like to make our position as editors clear: In order to maintain its scientific integrity, psychology must treat the cultural-test-bias hypothesis as a serious scientific question, to be argued and resolved on the basis of empirical research and theory rather than on one or another of our many politicosocial *Zeitgeister.* The history of genetics under T. D. Lysenko in Stalinist Russia should be a warning to us all of the danger of political resolutions to scientific questions. However impossible full objectivity is in science (e.g., Kuhn, 1962) and however much we are trapped by our metatheoretical views, as well as by our language, we must view all socially, politically, and emotionally charged issues from the perspective of rational scientific inquiry. Moreover, we must be prepared to accept scientifically valid findings as real—even if we do not like them. Otherwise, we risk psychology's becoming an impotent field whose issues will be resolved not by scholars in courts of scientific inquiry but by judges in courts of law, and whose practitioners will be viewed as charlatans with opinions of no more validity than the claims of patent-medicine-pushing quacks. Further, it behooves us as social scientists to be aware of and sensitive to the historical perspective from which some concerned groups may view an issue.

The need for an objective answer to the question "Is there bias in mental testing?" is as manifest as the need to eliminate any such bias found.

THE CONTROVERSY: WHAT IT IS AND WHAT IT IS NOT

Systematic group differences on standardized intelligence and aptitude tests occur as a function of socioeconomic level, race or ethnic background, and other demographic variables. Black-white differences on IQ measures have received extensive investigation over the past 50 or 60 years. The preponderance of these studies has been reviewed by Shuey (1966) and Tyler (1965). Jensen (1980a) and Willerman (1979) have reviewed several more recent studies. Although the results occasionally differ slightly, depending on the age groups under consideration, random samples of blacks and whites show a mean difference of about one standard deviation, with the mean score of the whites consistently exceeding that of the black groups. The differences have persisted at relatively constant levels for quite some time and under a variety of methods of investigation. When a number of demographic variables are taken into account (most notably socioeconomic status), the size of the mean black-white difference reduces to .5 to .7 standard deviations (e.g., Kaufman, 1973; Kaufman & Kaufman, 1973; Reynolds & Gutkin, 1981) but remains robust in its appearance. All studies of racial and ethnic group differences on ability tests do not show higher levels of performance by whites. Although not nearly as thoroughly researched as black-white groups, Oriental groups have been shown to perform consistently as well as, or better than, white groups (Pintner, 1931; Tyler, 1965; Willerman, 1979). Depending on the specific aspect of intelligence under investigation, other racial and ethnic groups show performance at or above the performance level of white groups. There has been argument over whether any racial differences in intelligence are real or even researchable (e.g., Schoenfeld, 1974), but the reliability across studies is very high, and the existence of the differences is now generally accepted. It should always be kept in mind, however, that the overlap among the distributions of intelligence test scores for the different races is much greater than the degree of differences between the various groups. There is always more within-group variability than between-group variability in performance on mental tests. The differences are nevertheless real ones and are unquestionably complex (e.g., Reynolds & Jensen, 1983).

The issue at hand is the explanation of those group differences. It should be emphasized that both the lower scores of some groups and the higher scores of others need to be explained, although not necessarily, of course, in the same way. The problem was clearly stated by Eells in his classic study of cultural differences (Eells, Davis, Havighurst, Herrick, & Tyler, 1951):

> Do the higher test scores of the children from high socioeconomic backgrounds reflect genuine superiority in inherited, or genetic, equipment? Or do the high scores result from a superior environment which has brought about real superiority of the child's "intelligence"? Or do they reflect a bias in the test materials and not any important difference in the children at all? (p.4)

Eells *et al.* also concisely summarized the cultural-test-bias hypothesis as it applied to differences in socioeconomic status (SES):

> If (a) the children from different social-status levels have different kinds of experiences and have experiences with different types of material, and if (b) the intelligence tests contain a disproportionate amount of material drawn from the cultural experiences with which pupils from the higher social-status levels are more familiar, one would expect (c) that children from the higher social-status levels would show higher I.Q.'s than those from the lower levels. This argument tends to conclude that the observed differences in pupil I.Q.'s are artifacts dependent upon the specific content of the test items and do not reflect accurately any important underlying ability in the pupils. (p. 4)

Eells was aware that his descriptions were oversimplifications and that it was unlikely that all of the observed group differences could be explained by any one of the three factors alone. More recently, Loehlin, Lindzey, and Spuhler (1975) concluded that all three factors were probably involved in racial differences in intelligence. In its present, more complex form, the cultural-test-bias hypothesis itself considers other factors than culture-loaded items, as will be seen below. But the basics of Eell's summary of the cultural-test-bias hypothesis still hold: Group differences stem from characteristics of the tests or from aspects of test administration. Because mental tests are based largely on middle-class white values and knowledge, they are more valid for those groups and are biased against other groups to the extent that these groups deviate from those values and knowledge bases. Thus, ethnic and other group differences result from flawed psychometric methodology and not from actual differences in aptitude (Harrington, 1975, 1976). As is described in some detail below, this hypothesis reduces to one of differential validity, the hypothesis of differential validity being that tests measure intelligence more accurately and make more valid predictions about the level of intellectual functioning for individuals from the groups on which the tests are mainly based than for those from other groups. Artifactually low scores on an aptitude test could lead to pupil misassignment to educational programs and unfair denial of admission to college, graduate school, or other programs or occupations in which such test scores are an important decision-making component. This is the issue over which most of the recent court cases have been fought. Further, there would be dramatic implications for whole areas of psychological research and practice if the cultural-test-bias hypothesis is correct: The principal research of the last century in the psychology of human differences would have to be dismissed as confounded and largely artifactual because much of the work is based on standard psychometric theory and testing technology. The result would be major upheavals in the practice of applied psychology, as the foundations of clinical, school, counseling, and industrial psychology are strongly tied to the basic academic field of individual differences. The issue, then, is one of the most crucial facing psychology today (Reynolds, 1980c).

On the other hand, if the cultural-test-bias hypothesis is incorrect, then group differences are not attributable to the tests and must be due to one of the other factors mentioned by Eells *et al.* (1951) or to some combination of them. That group differences in test scores reflect real group differences in ability should be admitted as a possibility, and one that calls for scientific study.

The controversy over test bias should not be confused with that over the etiology of any obtained group differences in test scores. Unfortunately, it has often seen inferred that measured differences themselves indicate genetic differences, and therefore the genetically based intellectual inferiority of some groups. Jensen has himself consistently argued since 1969 that mental tests measure, to a greater or lesser extent, the intellectual factor g, which has a large genetic component, and that group differences in mental test scores may then reflect group differences in g. Unless one reads Jensen's statements carefully, it is easy to overlook the many qualifications that he makes regarding these differences and conclusions.

But, in fact, Jensen or anyone else's position on the basis of actual group differences should be seen as irrelevant to the issue of test bias. However controversial, etiology is a separate issue. It would be tragic to accept the cultural-test-bias hypothesis as true if it is, in fact, false. In that case, measured differences would be seen as not real, and children might be denied access to the educational environment best suited to them. Further, research on the basis of any group differences would be stifled, as would implementation of programs designed to remediate any deficiences. Further, from our perspective, the most advantageous position for the true white racist and bigot would be to *favor* the test bias hypothesis! Acceptance of that hypothesis *inappropriately* would eventually result in inappropriate pupil assignment, less adaptive education for some groups, and less implementation of long-range programs to raise intellective performance. Inappropriate confirmation of the test bias hypothesis would appear to maintain, not break down, the poverty cycle (Birch & Gussow, 1970).

The controversy is also not over the blatantly inappropriate administration and use of mental tests. The administration of a test in English to an individual for whom English is a second language and whose English language skills are poor is inexcusable, regardless of any bias in the tests themselves. It is of obvious importance that tests be administered by skilled and sensitive professionals who are aware of the factors that may artifactually lower an individual's test scores. That should go without saying, but some court cases involve just such abuses. Considering the use of tests to assign pupils to special-education classes or other programs, a question needs to be asked: What would one use instead? Teacher recommendations are notoriously less reliable and less valid than standardized-test scores. As to whether special-education programs are of adequate quality to meet the needs of children, that is an important educational question, but distinct from the test bias one. This distinction is sometimes confused (e.g., Reschly, 1980).

The controversy over the use of mental tests is further complicated by the fact that resolution of the cultural-test-bias question in either direction will not resolve the problem of the role of nonintellective factors that may influence the test scores of *individuals* from any group, minority or majority. Regardless of any group differences, it is individuals who are tested and whose scores may or may not be accurate. Similarly, it is individuals who are assigned to classes and who are accepted or rejected. As indicated by Wechsler (1975) and others, nonintellective factors frequently influence performance on mental tests. As suggested by Zigler and Butterfield (1967), at least two nonintellective factors, informational content and emotional-motivational conditions, may be reflected in performance on mental tests. The extent to which these factors influence individual as opposed to group performance is difficult to determine. Perhaps with more sophisticated multivariate designs, we will be better able to identify individuals with characteristics that are likely to have an adverse effect on their performance on mental tests. Basically outside the major thrust of the issue of bias against groups, potential bias against individuals is a serious problem itself and merits research and analysis. Sternberg (1980), also concerned about individual performance, observed that research on bias has concentrated on "status variables" such as ethnicity rather than on "functional variables" such as cognitive styles and motivations.

A different aspect of the test bias hypothesis concerns the effects of practice on performance on the standard aptitude tests used in decisions regarding college and graduate and professional school admissions. Such tests, many produced by the Educational Testing Service (ETS), include the Scholastic Aptitude Test (SAT), Graduate Record Examination (GRE), Medical College Admissions Test (MCAT), and Law School Admissions Test (LSAT). The ETS has consistently maintained that relatively short periods of practice have little effect on performance on these tests, but a dispute has recently developed around the question of how much effect such practice may have and under what conditions. On the other hand, Slack and Porter (1980a, b) have maintained that training can significantly raise scores on these tests and that the tests themselves are not valid measures of intellective ability. They have gone so far as to say that students who have interpreted low scores on the tests as an indication of their aptitude have been misled: "We hope that students will remember that the scores are *unrelated* to the quality of their minds" (Slack & Porter, 1980b, p. 399, emphasis added). On the other hand, a representative of ETS has defended the use of the tests and has differentiated between the effects of short-term "coaching," claimed to be ineffective, and long-term "educational programs" in the skills required on the test, which may be effective in raising scores (Jackson, 1980). As with other issues, the same data serve as the basis for quite different interpretations by people holding opposite positions. This is not the place for a discussion of practice effects *per se*, but the issue becomes relevant to questions of test bias in the following way: Programs claiming success in raising scores on the ETS-type exams have multiplied in the last few years and have become commonplace in some metropolitan centers. Given the spotty distribution of these programs and their high cost, members of low SES and rural groups may be effectively excluded from participation in programs that would raise their scores. In addition, the low income level of many ethnic and racial minorities may differentially deprive members of such groups of the opportunity to participate in such training programs. The most effective programs are also the longest and most expensive; the relationship between time in training and score improvement is a geometric one, with score increments becoming progressively more expensive (Messick & Jungeblut, 1981). Thus, economic and other factors may result in the scores of members of some groups being lower than they would have been with the benefit of training. The resulting bias, it should be emphasized, would be attributable not to differential validity, but to the differential access to programs that help to develop the skills tapped by the tests.

The conflicting claims, the emotional overtones, and the extreme positions taken (as indicated in the quotation from Slack and Porter above) ensure that the controversy over ETS-type tests will continue for some time.

EMOTIONAL AND POLITICAL ASPECTS OF THE CONTROVERSY

Discussions of test bias are frequently accompanied by heavily emotional polemics decrying the use of tests with any minority and considering all tests inherently biased against individuals who are not members of the middle-class white majority. Mercer (1973, 1976) has contended that current intelligence tests such as the Wechsler Intelligence Scale for Children-Revised (WISC-R; Wechsler, 1974) measure not aptitude or intelligence, but the Anglocentrism (degree of adherence to white middle-class values and culture) of the home. Unfortunately, some critics have imputed malevolent intentions to test developers and test uses. Williams (1974) has "declared war" on the use of standardized tests with minority group members and has indicated that his purpose is "to expose the white pimp and hustler type psychologists who have been agents in the abuse and dehumanization of black people by employing an instrument called the psychological test." In presenting the response of the Association of Black Psychologists to the American Psychological Association (APA) committee report on the use of educational and psychological tests with minority and disadvantaged students (Cleary, Humphreys, Kendrick, & Wesman, 1975), Jackson (1975) contended that "under the guise of scientific objectivity, it [the committee] has provided a cesspool of intrinsically and inferentially fallacious data which inflates the egos of whites by demeaning black people and threatens to potentiate black genocide" (p. 88).

But the polemics are not all on one side. Some of America's well-known psychologists have adopted stridently racist positions:

You can no more mix the two races and maintain the standards of civilization than you can add 80 (the average I.Q. of Negroes) and 100 (average I.Q. of Whites), divide by two and get 100. What you would get would be a race of 90s, and it is that 10 percent that spells the difference between a spire and a mud hut; 10 percent—or less—is the margin of civilization's "profit"; it is the difference between a cultured society and savagery.

Therefore, it follows, if miscegenation would be bad for White people, it would be bad for Negroes as well. For if leadership is destroyed, all is destroyed. (Garrett, undated)

We are incorporating the negro into our racial stock, while all of Europe is comparatively free from this taint. . . . The steps that should be taken . . . must of course by dictated by science and not by political expediency. . . . The really important steps are those looking toward the prevention of the continued propagation of defective strains in the present population. (Brigham, 1923)

I have seen gatherings of the foreign-born in which narrow and sloping foreheads were the rule. . . . In every face there was something wrong—lips thick, mouth coarse . . . chin poorly formed . . . sugar loaf heads . . . goose-bill noses . . . a set of skew-molds discarded by the Creator. . . . Immigration officials . . . report vast troubles in extracting the truth from certain brunette nationalities. (Hirsch, 1926)

These quotations are taken from Karier (1972) and Kamin (1976). Brigham later retracted his statements, and other psychologists argued strongly for other interpretations of group differences in behavior. But the dominant pioneers of the testing movement in the United States held strongly hereditarian beliefs that, at the least, had racist implications, and they cited "data" to support their positions. The emotional and seemingly irrational reactions of some blacks and other minorities to the present controversy over test bias may better be understood from a historical perspective.

WHY THE CONTROVERSY EXISTS: HISTORY OF SCIENTIFIC RACISM

History: An account mostly false, of events mostly unimportant, which was brought about by rulers mostly knaves, and soldiers mostly fools.
                              Ambrose Bierce, *The Devil's Dictionary*

From the early nineteenth century until recently, many of the foremost European and American biologists, anthropologists, and psychologists have held racist positions. All cited "scientific data" to support their positions, data that are now frequently seen as baseless. Several recent books have chronicled aspects of the history of scientific racism in general (Chase, 1977), of racism in evolutionary theory (Gould, 1977), and of the misuse of IQ test data (Block & Dworkin, 1976; Eckberg, 1979; Kamin, 1974). Scientists' personal/political views have frequently determined their scientific positions. Unfortunately, both Chase and Kamin are themselves guilty of excesses in the opposite direction, demonstrating again that history may not exist separately from the historian.

Scientific racism has been traced by Chase back to Malthus, who proposed early in the 19th century that steps should be taken not to alleviate poverty, but to encourage disease among the poor. As chronicled by Gould (1978), at approximately the same time in the United States, Morton began to acquire what eventually became an extraordinary collection of human skulls, representing as many different "races" as possible. Using cranial capacity as a measure of brain size, Morton reported in 1849 that the capacity of Nordic Caucasians was largest, of Semitic and Chinese intermediate, and of American Indians and Negroes smallest. (This ordering bears a certain resemblance to that based on the IQ studies done on World War I inductees and at Ellis Island.) According to Gould (1978), Morton's data was widely cited and reprinted as objective anthropometric support for the existence of inherent racial differences in intellectual capability. Through a reanalysis of Morton's data, however, Gould (1978) found that widespread and systematic—although apparently unconscious—errors in Morton's methods and calculations accounted for *all* the supposed racial differences in cranial capacity. Gould's conclusion concerning Morton may apply to many scientists who in the past have offered scientific support of racist doctrine: "All I [Gould] discern is an a priori conviction of racial ranking so powerful that it directed his tabulations along preestablished lines. Yet Morton was widely hailed as the objectivist of his age" (p. 509).

Many other nineteenth- and early-twentieth-century biologists and anthropologists were equally adept at bending empirical data to suit their preconceived theoretical wills. Louis Agassiz, among the foremost naturalists of the nineteenth century, believed that blacks were a separate and inferior species. Further, he claimed that the cranial sutures of blacks closed in mid-childhood, and that the result was a rigid cranium. Too much education for blacks, therefore, was dangerous because their brains might swell too much, and their skulls might burst (Gould, 1977). Haeckel and other supporters of the "ontogeny recapitulates phylogeny" doctrine offered recapitulationist support for northern European white superiority: Blacks, Indians, and other nonwhite groups were inferior because their adult features and characteristics are evolutionarily primitive. However, recapitulationist theory collapsed in the 1920s for a variety of reasons, to be replaced partly by the opposing theory of neoteny that humans had evolved by retaining into adulthood what had been the juvenile characteristics of our ancestors. As Gould pointed out, this new view should have elevated blacks to the top of the *scala naturae*, but scientists simply discarded the earlier recapitulationist data and seized new evidence to support the traditional racial hierarchy. Thus, Bolk in 1926 claimed that blacks pass prenatally through stages that are the final ones for whites and thus mature early. As Gould (1977) concluded; "The litany is familiar: cold, dispassionate, objective, modern science shows us that races can be ranked on a scale of superiority. . . . But the data were worthless" (p. 127).

That many psychometricians, from Galton on through Pearson, Goddard, Terman, Yerkes, and others, have also held what appear to be racist and/or eugenic positions based on questionable data is so familiar as to need no retelling here (Block & Dworkin, 1976; Kamin, 1974).

Given this background, it should come as no surprise that blacks and other minorities view present evidence of racial differences, particularly any that imply inherent differences, as just another of the wolves of preconceived racist beliefs masquerading in the sheep's clothing of pseudoscientific evidence. History does not justify the vilification and the interference with free speech and inquiry that have confronted Jensen, Herrnstein, and others. This legacy, however, does call for extraordinary care on the part of present-day researchers and theoreticians and for a greater than normal degree of scientific skepticism. One of our greatest responsibilities as scientists investigating sensitive issues is to ensure that we will not repeat the errors of the past, but that we will correct for them.

WHY THE CONTROVERSY EXISTS: THE NATURE OF PSYCHOLOGICAL TESTING

The question of bias in mental testing arises largely because of the nature of psychological processes and the measurement of those processes. Psychological processes, by definition internal and not directly subject to observation or measurement, must be inferred from behavior. Theoretically, in the classic discussion by MacCorquodale and Meehl (1948), a psychological process has the status of an "intervening variable" if it is used only as a component of a system that has no properties beyond those that operationally define it, but it has the status of a "hypothetical construct" if it is thought actually to exist with properties beyond the defining ones. A historical example of a hypothetical construct is *gene*, which had meaning beyond its use to describe the cross-generational transmission of characteristics. Intelligence, from its treatment in the professional literature, has the status of a hypothetical construct.

As even beginning psychology students know, it is difficult to determine one-to-one relationships between observable events in the environment, the behavior of an organism, and hypothesized underlying mediational processes. Many classic controversies over theories of learning have revolved around constructs such as *expectancy*, *habit*, and *inhibition* (e.g., Hilgard & Bower, 1975; Kimble, 1961; Goldstein, Krantz, & Rains, 1965). Disputes among different camps in learning have been polemical and of long duration. Indeed, there are still disputes about the nature and the number of processes such as emotion and motivation (e.g., Bolles, 1975; Mandler, 1975). One of the major areas of disagreement has been over the measurement of psychological processes. It should be expected that intelligence, as one of the most complex psychological processes, involves definitional and measurement disputes that prove difficult to resolve.

Assessment of intelligence, like that of many other psychological processes in humans, is accomplished by standard psychometric procedures that are the focus of the bias issue. These procedures, described in detail in general assessment texts (e.g., Anastasi, 1976; Thorndike, 1971b), are only briefly summarized here in relation to the issue of bias. The problems specific to validity are discussed in a separate section.

Similar procedures are used in the development of any standardized psychological test. First, a large number of items are developed that for theoretical or practical reasons are thought to measure the construct of interest. Through a series of statistical steps, those items that best measure the construct in a unitary manner are selected for inclusion in the final test battery. The test is then administered to a sample, which should be chosen to represent all aspects of the population on whom the test will be used. Normative scales based on the scores of the standardization sample then serve as the reference for the interpretation of scores of individuals tested thereafter. Thus, as has been pointed out numerous times, an individual's score is meaningful only relative to the norms and is a relative, not an absolute, measure. Charges of bias frequently arise from the position that the test is more appropriate for the groups heavily represented in the standardization sample. Whether bias does, in fact, result from this procedure is one of the specific questions that must be empirically addressed.

As has also been frequently pointed out, there are few charges of bias of any kind relating to physical measures that are on absolute scales, whether interval or ratio. Group differences in height, as an extreme example, are not attributed by anyone we know of to any kind of cultural test bias. There is no question concerning the validity of measures of the height or weight of anyone in any culture. Nor is there any question about one's ability to make cross-cultural comparisons of these absolute measures.

The whole issue of cultural bias arises because of the procedures involved in psychological testing. Psychological tests measure traits that are not directly observable, that are subject to differences in definition, and that are measurable only on a relative scale. From this perspective, the question of cultural bias in mental testing is a subset—obviously of major importance—of the problems of uncertainty and of possible bias in psychological testing generally. Bias may exist not only in mental tests but in other types of psychological tests as well, including personality, vocational, and psychopathological tests. Making the problem of bias in mental testing even more complex is the fact that not all mental tests are of the same quality: Like Orwell's pigs, some may be more equal than others. There is a tendency for critics and defenders alike to overgeneralize across tests, lumping virtually all tests together under the heading "Mental Tests" or "Intelligence Tests." As reflected in the *Mental Measurements Yearbook* (Buros, 1978), professional opinions of mental tests vary considerably, and some of the most used tests are not well respected by psychometricians. Thus, unfortunately, the question of bias must eventually be answered on a virtually test-by-test basis.

MINORITY OBJECTIONS TO STANDARDIZED PSYCHOLOGICAL TESTING

In 1969, the Association of Black Psychologists (ABP) adopted the following official policy on educational and psychological testing:

The Association of Black Psychologists fully supports those parents who have chosen to defend their rights by refusing to allow their children and themselves to be subjected to achievement, intelligence, aptitude and performance tests which have been and are being used to A. Label black people as uneducable. B. Place black children in "special" classes and schools. C. Perpetuate inferior education in blacks. D. Assign black children to educational tracts. E. Deny black students higher educational opportunities. F. Destroy positive growth and development of black people. (quoted in Reynolds, 1982a, p.179)

Since 1968, the ABP has sought a moratorium on the use of all psychological and educational tests with the culturally different (Samuda, 1975, and Williams, Dotson, Dow, &. Williams, 1980, have provided a more detailed history of these efforts). The ABP carried its call for a moratorium to other professional organizations in psychology and education. In direct response to the ABP call, the Board of Directors of the American Psychological Association (APA) requested its Board of Scientific Affairs to appoint a group to study the use of psychological and educational tests with disadvantaged students. The committee report (Cleary et al., 1975) was subsequently published in the official journal of the APA, American Psychologist.

Subsequent to the ABP's policy statement, other groups have adopted policy statements on testing. These groups included the National Association for the Advancement of Colored People (NAACP), the National Education Association (NEA), the National Association of Elementary School Principals (NAESP), the American Personnel and Guidance Association (APGA), and others (Committee on Testing, 1974; Williams et al., 1980). The APGA called for the Association for Measurement and Evaluation in Guidance (AMEG), a sister organization, to

> develop and disseminate a position paper stating the limitations of group intelligence tests particularly and generally of standardized psychological, educational, and employment testing for low socioeconomic and underprivileged and non-white individuals in educational, business, and industrial environments.

The APGA also resolved that, if no progress was made in clarifying and correcting the current testing of minorities, it would also call for a moratorium, but only on the use of group intelligence tests with these groups.

The NAACP adopted a more detailed resolution and joined in the call for a moratorium on standardized testing of minority groups at its annual meeting in 1974. The text of the NAACP resolution was:

> Whereas, a disproportionately large number of black students are being misplaced in special education classes and denied admissions to higher educational opportunities,
>
> Whereas, students who fail to show a high verbal or numerical ability, score low on the Scholastic Achievement Test (SAT), the Law School Admissions Test (LSAT), the Graduate Record Examination (GRE), etc., and are routinely excluded from college and graduate or professional education,
>
> Be it resolved, that the NAACP demands a moratorium on standardized testing wherever such tests have not been corrected for cultural bias and directs its units to use all administrative and legal remedies to prevent

the violation of students' constitutional rights through the misuse of tests, and

Be it further resolved, that the NAACP calls upon the Association of Black Psychologists to assert leadership in aiding the College Entrance Examination Board to develop standardized tests which have been corrected for cultural bias and which fairly measure the amount of knowledge retained by students regardless of his or her individual background.

Be it finally resolved, that the NAACP directs its units to use all administrative remedies in the event of violation of students' constitutional rights through the misuse of tests and directs National Office staff to use its influence to bring the CEEB and ABP together to revise such tests.

Also in 1974, the Committee on Testing of the ABP issued a position paper on the testing of blacks that described their intent as well as their position:

(1) To encourage, support and to bring action against *all* institutions, organizations and agencies who continue to use present psychometric instruments in the psychological assessment of Black people;

(2) To continue efforts to bring about a cessation of the use of standard psychometric instruments on Black people until culturally specific tests are made available;

(3) To establish a national policy that in effect gives Black folk and other minorities the right to demand that the psychological assessment be administered, interpreted, and supervised by competent psychological assessors of their own ethnic background;

(4) To work toward and encourage efforts to remove from the records of all Black students and Black employees that data obtained from performance on past and currently used standard psychometric, achievement, employment, general aptitude and mental ability tests;

(5) To establish a national policy that demands the appropriate proportional representation of competent Black psychologists on all committees and agencies responsible for the evaluation and selection of tests used in the assessment of Black folk;

(6) To establish a national policy that demands that all persons engaged in the evaluation, selection and placement of Black folks undergo extensive training so they may better relate to the Black experience;

(7) To demand that all Black students improperly diagnosed and placed into special education classes be returned to regular class programs;

(8) To encourage and support all suits against any public or private agency for the exclusion, improper classification and the denial of advancement opportunities to Black people based on performance tests.

It should be noted that the statements by these organizations have *assumed* that present tests are biased, and that what is needed is the removal of that assumed bias.

WHAT ARE THE POSSIBLE SOURCES OF BIAS?

Many potentially legitimate objections to the use of educational and psychological tests with minorities have been raised by black and other minority psychologists. Unfortunately, these objections are frequently stated as facts on rational rather than empirical grounds (e.g., Council for Exceptional Children, 1978; Chambers, Barron, & Sprecher, 1980; Hilliard, 1979). The most frequently stated problems fall into one of the following categories:

(1) *Inappropriate content.* Black and other minority children have not been exposed to the material involved in the test questions or other stimulus materials. The tests are geared primarily toward White middle-class homes, vocabulary, knowledge, and values.

(2) *Inappropriate standardization samples.* Ethnic minorities are underrepresented in standardization samples used in the collection of normative reference data. Williams (Wright & Isenstein, 1977) has criticized the WISC-R (Wechsler, 1974) standardization sample for including Blacks only in proportion to the United States total population. Out of 2200 children in the WISC-R standardization sample, 330 were minority. Williams contends that such small actual representation has no impact on the test. In earlier years, it was not unusual for standardization samples to be all White (e.g., the 1937 Binet and 1949 WISC).

(3) *Examiner and language bias.* Since most psychologists are White and speak only standard English, they may intimidate Black and other ethnic minorities. They are also unable accurately to communicate with minority children—to the point of being insensitive to ethnic pronounciation of words on the test. Lower test scores for minorities, then, may reflect only this intimidation and difficulty in the communication process, not lower ability.

(4) *Inequitable social consequences.* As a result of bias in educational and psychological tests, minority group members, already at a disadvantage in the educational and vocational markets because of past discrimination and thought unable to learn, are disproportionately relegated to dead-end educational tracks. Labelling effects also fall under this category.

(5) *Measurement of different constructs.* Related to (1) above, this position asserts that the tests measure different attributes when used with children from other than the White middle-class culture on which the tests are largely based, and thus do not measure minority intelligence validly.

(6) *Differential predictive validity.* Although tests may accurately predict a variety of outcomes for White middle-class children, they do not predict successfully any relevant behavior for minority group members. Further, there are objections to use of the standard criteria against which tests are validated with minority cultural groups. That is, scholastic or academic attainment levels in White

> middle-class schools are themselves considered by a variety of
> Black psychologists to be biased as criteria. (Reynolds, 1982a, pp.
> 179–180)

Contrary to the situation a decade ago, when the current controversy began, research now exists that examines each of the above areas of potential bias in assessment. This evidence has been reviewed elsewhere (Jensen, 1980a; Reynolds, 1982a) and is also dealt with throughout this volume. Except for the still unresolved issue of labeling effects, the least amount of research is available on the long-term social consequences of testing, although some data are now becoming available (Lambert, 1979). But both of these problems are aspects of testing in general and are not limited to minorities. The problem of the social consequences of educational tracking is frequently lumped with the issue of test bias. Those issues, however, are separate. Educational tracking and special education should be treated as problems of education, not assessment. This point becomes especially clear in examining the *Larry P.* (1979) decision.

THE ETHICAL MANDATE AGAINST BIAS

Many legal cases mandate the elimination of bias in psychological assessment (Bersoff, 1979, 1982; Connolly & Connolly, 1978). Recent federal legislation also requires that tests be valid for all purposes to which they are applied and that fairness be maintained (Education for All Handicapped Children Act of 1975; Section 713 of Title 7 of the Civil Rights Act of 1964; Section 504 of the Vocational Rehabilitation Act of 1973). Such mandates to eliminate bias have been extensively reported in the professional literature. Less frequently discussed is the ethical mandate to eliminate bias in psychological assessment.

Psychologists involved in testing and assessment must remain objective regarding the use and the interpretation of test results or other information gathered about any individual (or group of individuals). Information about tests and individuals' performance on tests must be communicated so as to guard against any misuse or misinterpretation of the information. Where bias against any group or any single individual occurs, it must be so indicated, and corrective measures must be taken. However, claims of bias must be based on objective evidence, just as claims of validity and reliability must be substantiated by empirical investigation. Both positions require proof. Psychological and educational test publishers and authors share in this ethical mandate regarding the potential bias of tests. It is incumbent on test authors and publishers to conduct test bias research with their instruments, to report the results of these studies in professional journals, and to eliminate any observed bias from tests to ensure nonbiased measurement. Such empirical research and test modification should obviously be part of the standard procedure in test design and should be carried out *before* the publication of new tests.

ASPECTS OF THE TEST BIAS ISSUE

The definition of test bias has produced considerable and unresolved debate among measurement and assessment experts. It is necessary to define the term *bias* independently of tests or other issues. *Bias* is an accepted, well-defined, statistical term denoting constant or systematic error rather than random, patternless error. As stated above, this use of the term is quite distinct from either its legal or its common "lay" usage. The academic debates occurring over the proper definition and evaluation of test bias have generated a number of models from which to examine the issues (e.g., Cleary *et al.*, 1975; Darlington, 1971; Humphreys, 1973; Thorndike, 1971a).

PRIMARY SELECTION MODELS

Primary selection models do not typically focus on the test itself; rather, they focus on the decision-making system. The primary selection models from which bias is usually viewed are critically examined in the next chapter of this volume by Hunter, Schmidt, and Rauschenberger; they have also been reviewed elsewhere by Jensen (1980a), and Petersen and Novick (1976). Which decision-making system is chosen must ultimately be a societal decision (especially as regards educational decision-making) that will depend to a large extent on the value system and goals of the society. Thus, prior to choosing a model for test use in selection, one must decide whether the ultimate goal is equality of opportunity, equality of outcome, or representative equality (these concepts are discussed in more detail in Nichols, 1978).

Equality of opportunity is a competitive model wherein selection is based on ability. The higher the level of ability possessed by an individual, the greater the probability that the individual will be afforded opportunities, advancement, specialized training, and so on.

With fair and unbiased tests, in an otherwise fair and equal society, equality of opportunity is a superlative democratic model. This would appear to be the model envisioned by Herrnstein (1973) in his "meritocracy." Equality of outcome is a selection model that is based on ability deficits. Compensatory and remedial education programs are typically constructed on the basis of the equality-of-outcome selection models. Children either of low ability or at high risk for academic failure are selected for remedial, compensatory, or other special education-programs. In a strictly predictive sense, tests are used in a similar manner in both of these models. However, in the equality-of-opportunity model, selection is based on the prediction of a high level of criterion performance, whereas under equality of outcome, selection is determined by the prediction of "failure" or a pre-selected low level of criterion performance in the absence of intervention. It is worth noting that the apparent initial failure of compensatory and remedial programs to raise the performance of disadvantaged children to "average" levels led to many of the current charges of test bias. Of course, it now appears that considerable change in IQ can be effected by intensive intervention programs (Heber, 1978) and that the Head Start programs had greater impact than was initially apparent (Lazar, Hubbell, Murray, Rosche, & Royce, 1977; Zigler, 1976).

The representative equality model also relies on selection, but selection that is proportionate to the numerical representation of subgroups in the population under consideration. Representative equality is typically thought to be independent of the level of ability within each group. However, models can be constructed that select from each subgroup the desired proportion of individuals relative to the ability level of the group, independent of the ability of the group, or on any gradient between these two extremes. Even under the conditions of representative equality, it is imperative to employ a selection device (test) that will rank-order individuals within groups reliably and validly.

The only way to ensure fair selection in *any* of these models is to employ tests that are of equal reliability and validity for all groups concerned. Of course, the tests should be the most reliable and valid for those groups.

TEST BIAS VERSUS TEST MISUSE

The issue of test bias reduces to one of test validity. Test use, on the other hand, in terms of the applications of the results of psychological tests, is fair or unfair only in relation to societal value systems. At present, this value system leans strongly toward the representative-equality selection model. As noted above, all models are made more valid through the use of nonbiased tests. That is, the use of a test with equivalent cross-group validities results in the most parsimonious selection model. Test bias, again, is a statistical term: systematic error in the estimation of some "true" value for a group of individuals. Test misuse, on the other hand, is a political-social problem: the inappropriate application of a test in some decision-making process so as to make unfair or prejudiced selection or assignment.

Unfortunately, test bias and test misuse are often confused, or worse, collapsed into the same issue. Although related, the two issues deal with separate questions, both concerning validity. Bias concerns differential validity, particularly predictive validity, for different groups. Misuse, on the other hand, leads to low predictive validity for *all* individuals, regardless of group membership. Misuse occurs when a test is used for selection purposes for which it is invalid generally. The hierarchical relation between bias and misuse is similar to the traditional one between test reliability and validity. Reliability is needed for validity but does not ensure it. Similarly, a test must be unbiased in order to be generally fair, but "unbiasedness" does not ensure fairness in any given application.

For the purpose of empirical analysis and decision making, it is important to keep the issues separate. Intertwining questions of misuse with those of bias only makes it difficult to answer satisfactorily—and unemotionally. Worse, an acceptable resolution of one issue might, most inappropriately, be taken as a resolution of both.

CONCEPTS OF VALIDITY

It has been popular in the general literature on test bias to provide definitions and to research test bias either from the paradigm of the traditional tripartite conceptualization of validity (content, construct, and predictive or criterion-related validity) or from the dyadic model of internal and external validity. These models of validity are typically adopted out of tradition or for the purposes of clarity and convenience in discussion, and both have problems (Berk, 1980; Messick, 1980; Shepard, 1980). The greatest difficulty in breaking down validity into subcategories is the danger of fragmenting or pigeonholing the larger context of *test validity*, thus losing sight of the more comprehensive picture. This approach can, inappropriately, lead to a narrow examination of potential bias in a given test, with the decision on bias being based on a single study of only one facet of the test's validity. Messick (1980), for example, listed 17 different types of validity, any or all of which may be applicable to any given test or testing problem. A scientific model of validity would almost certainly have as one of its requirements the hierarchical arrangement of the subsets of validity. A scientific model would necessarily require content validity prior to construct validity and construct prior to predictive validity or internal prior to external validity. Purely actuarial models would require only predictive validity.

In any scientific, tripartite, dyadic, or other fasciated conceptualization of validity, it is difficult to distinguish where one type of validity ends and another begins. It is particularly difficult, especially with regard to test bias, to distinguish where content validity ends and construct validity begins. The problem is principally one of distinguishing how we measure from what we measure and how we interpret and apply those measurements. Boring's classic position (1923) that intelligence is what intelligence tests test is a striking statement of this dilemma. The editors of this volume are essentially in agreement with Messick (1980) and Guion (1976) that construct validity is the unifying concept of any nomothetical presentation or evaluation of test validity. In the present chapter, validity is considered under the tripartite model of content, construct, and predictive (criterion-related) validity. This approach is used for clarity and convenience and with a recognition of the caveats discussed above and elsewhere (Berk, 1980; Cronbach, 1971; Shepard, 1980).

Also frequently encountered in test bias research are the terms *single-group validity* and *differential validity*. *Single-group validity* refers to a test's being valid for *only* one group and invalid for others. *Differential validity* refers to a test's being somewhat valid for all groups concerned but having a varying degree of validity as a function of group membership. Although these terms have been most often applied to predictive or criterion-related validity (regression systems are then examined for significance and are compared across groups), the concepts of single-group and differential validity are equally applicable to content and construct validity.

Before examining the "test bias" definitions of content, construct, and predictive validity and the corresponding research methodology of each, we give some attention to the concept of culture-free testing and the definition of test bias as mean differences in test scores between groups. Bias as mean differences has been the popular lay definition for some time, has had periodic credibility with the courts, and is advocated by Williams and other minority psychologists.

CULTURE-FAIR TESTS, CULTURE LOADING, AND CULTURE BIAS

Culture loading and *culture bias* are not synonymous terms, though the concepts are frequently confused even in the professional literature (e.g., Alley & Foster, 1978; Chinn, 1979). A test or a test item can be culturally loaded without being culturally biased. *Culture loading* refers to the degree of cultural specificity present in the test or in individual items of the test. Certainly, the greater the cultural specificity of a test item, the greater the likelihood of the item's being biased against those outside the central culture. The test item "Who was the first president of the United States?" represents a culture-loaded item. However, the item is general enough to be potentially useful with *most* children in the United States. Yet, the cultural specificity of the item is too great to allow the item to be used on an aptitude measure for 10-year-old children from Paraguay, though it could possibly serve appropriately on an American history test with such children. Virtually all mental tests in current use are bound in some way by their cultural specificity—in fact, because of psychometric standardization procedures, they may inevitably be so bound (Harrington, 1975; 1976; Chap. 3). Culture loading must be viewed on a continuum from general (defining the culture in a broad, liberal sense) to specific (defining the culture in narrow, highly distinctive terms).

A variety of attempts have been made to develop a culture-fair intelligence test (Cattell, 1979). The reliability and validity of these tests are characterized as inadequate from a psychometric perspective (Anastasi, 1976; Ebel, 1979). The difficulty in developing a culture-fair measure of intelligence lies in the problem of developing a test that is independent of intellectual behavior within the culture under study. Intelligent behavior is defined within human society, in large part, on the basis of behavior judged to be of value to the survival and the improvement of the culture and the individuals within that culture. This, of course, was one of Piaget's (1952) defining characteristics of intelligence. A test that is "culture-blind" cannot be expected to predict intelligent behavior within a cultural setting. Once a test has been developed within a culture (a culture-loaded test), its generalizability to other cultures or subcultures within the dominant societal framework becomes a matter for empirical investigation.

MEAN SCORE DIFFERENCES AS TEST BIAS

Differences in mean levels of performance on cognitive tasks between whites and ethnic minorities are, in and of themselves, mistakenly believed to constitute evidence of test bias by a number of writers (Alley & Foster, 1978; Chinn, 1979; Hilliard, 1979; Jackson, 1975; Mercer, 1976; Williams, 1974; Wright & Isenstein, 1977). Those who support this definition of test bias correctly state that there is no valid *a priori* scientific reason to believe that intellectual or other cognitive performance levels should differ across race. What is fallacious is the inference that tests demonstrating such a difference are inherently biased because there *can* in reality be no differences. Just as there is no *a priori* basis for deciding that differences exist, there is no *a priori* basis for deciding that differences do not exist. From the standpoint of the objective methods of science, *a priori* or premature acceptance of either hypothesis (differences exist vs. differences do not exist) is untenable. As indicated above, the history of the area of group differences is tainted by *a priori* judgments—almost all of them to the effect that differences do exist and are genetic. It would be as tragic for those who believe that differences do not exist to twist data to suit their ends. Some adherents to the "mean difference demonstrates bias" definition also require that the distribution of test scores in each population or subgroup be identical before concluding that the test is nonbiased, regardless of its validity: "Regardless of the purpose of a test *or its validity for that purpose*, a test should result in distributions that are statistically equivalent across the groups tested in order for it to be considered nondiscriminatory for those groups" (Alley & Foster, 1978, p. 2; emphasis in original). Portraying a test as biased regardless of its purpose or validity conveys an inadequate understanding of the psychometric construct and issues of bias. It also equates nondiscriminatory with nonbiased. The mean difference concept and the equivalent distribution concept of test bias have been uniformly rejected as criteria for test bias by sophisticated psychometricians involved in investigating the problems of bias in assessment. Group differences in scores on mental tests, or any other kind of test, *per se* give no directly applicable information regarding test bias. Jensen (1980a) discussed this point extensively under the rubric of the egalitarian fallacy.

BIAS IN DIFFERENT ASPECTS OF VALIDITY

BIAS IN CONTENT VALIDITY

Bias in the item content of intelligence tests is a common charge of those who decry the use of standardized tests with minorities (e.g.,

Hilliard, 1979; Jackson, 1975; Williams, 1974; Wright & Isenstein, 1977). Typically, critics review the items of a test and single out specific items as being biased on at least one of these bases: (1) the items ask for information that minority or disadvantaged children have not had equal opportunity to learn; (2) the items are scored improperly because the test author has arbitrarily decided on the only correct answer, and minority children are inappropriately penalized for giving answers that are correct in their own culture but not in that of the test maker; or (3) the wording of the question is unfamiliar, and a minority child who may "know" the correct answer is unable to respond because she or he did not understand the question. Each of these three criticisms, when accurate, has the same basic empirical result: The items become relatively more difficult for minority group members than for the majority population. This result leads directly to the empirically defined, testable definition of content bias for aptitude tests provided by Reynolds (1982):

> An item or subscale of a test is considered to be biased in content when it is demonstrated to be relatively more difficult for members of one group than another when the general ability level of the groups being compared is held constant and no reasonable theoretical rationale exists to explain group differences on the item (or subscale) in question. (p. 188)

With regard to achievement tests, the issue of content bias is considerably more complex. Exposure to instruction, the general ability level of the groups, and the accuracy and specificity of the sampling of the domain of items are all important variables in determining whether the content of an achievement test is biased. Research into item (or content) bias in achievement tests has typically, and perhaps mistakenly, relied on methodology appropriate for determining item bias in aptitude tests. The methodology appropriate to the evaluation of content bias under the above proffered definition is questionable in examining for bias in achievement test items whenever more than one classroom, or especially more than one school or school district, is employed, unless there is nearly perfect, proportionate representation of all groups in all classrooms.

The above definition also recognizes that bias is a two-way phenomenon: It may operate against or for certain minorities. Most individuals assume that bias must always adversely affect the minority group. In an analysis of content bias in the items of the Boehm Test of Basic Concepts (BTBC), a test Williams (see Wright & Isenstein, 1977) pointed to as an example of a test with item content inappropriate for minorities, Piersel, Plake, Reynolds, and Harding (1980) found the item bias to be equally distributed "against" whites and minorities. Of 10 biased items, 5 were biased in a direction favoring minorities and 5 in a direction favoring the white group. As is representative of results in studies of bias in item content, however, the effect of bias in the BTBC was small, accounting for only about 1% of the variance of any random observation.

A variety of methods has been employed for examining content or item bias (see especially Berk, 1982; Jensen, 1980a,b; Reynolds, 1982b) by which researchers have attempted to determine a set of common characteristics of test items that cause the items to be biased. Thus far, such efforts have met with total failure. Panels of expert judges from both minority and majority groups have also proved to be no better than chance in *a priori* predictions of which items on a test will ultimately be found to be biased. Although the search for common item traits contributing to bias will continue, the clue to this mechanism remains unknown and, unfortunately, may lie in the extreme power of the statistical methodology typically employed in studies of item bias. Cross-validation studies are needed to confirm the external validity of findings in studies of item bias.

BIAS IN CONSTRUCT VALIDITY

There is no single method for the accurate determination of the construct validity of educational and psychological tests. The definition of bias in construct validity, then, requires a general statement that can be researched from a variety of viewpoints with a broad range of methodologies. A definition has been offered by Reynolds (1982a):

> Bias exists in regard to construct validity when a test is shown to measure different hypothetical traits (psychological constructs) for one group than another or to measure the same trait but with differing degrees of accuracy. (p. 194)

As befits the concept of construct validity, many different methods have been employed to examine psychological tests and test batteries for potential bias in construct validity. One of the more popular and necessary empirical approaches to investigating construct validity is factor analysis (Anastasi, 1976; Cronbach, 1970). Factor analysis, as a procedure, identifies clusters of test items or clusters of subtests of psychological or educational tests that correlate highly with one another, and less so or not at all with other subtests or items. Factor analysis allows one to determine patterns of interrelationships of performance among groups of individuals. For example, if several subtests of an intelligence scale load highly on (are members of) the same factor, then individuals scoring highly on one of these subtests would be expected to score highly on other subtests that load highly on that factor.

Psychologists attempt either to determine through a review of the test content and correlates of performance on a given factor what psychological trait underlies performance or, in a more hypothesis-testing approach, to predict the pattern of factor loadings. Hilliard (1979), a persistent critic of IQ testing with minorities, has pointed out one potential area of bias dealing with the comparison of factor analysis of tests across race:

> If the IQ test is a valid and reliable test of "innate" ability or abilities, then the factors which emerge on a given test should be the same from one population to another, since "intelligence" is asserted to be a set of *mental* processes. Therefore, while the configuration of scores of a particular group on the factor profile would be expected to differ, logic would dictate that the factors themselves would remain the same. (p. 53)

Identical factors across populations may or may not reflect the innateness of the abilities being measured. However, the factor analysis of test results across populations provides consistent evidence that whatever is being measured by the instrument is measured in the same manner and is, in fact, the same construct in each group. Over the past decade, a number of factor-analytic studies have compared the factor structure of a cognitive test or battery of tests for children across diverse cultural groups. These studies have invariably supported the consistency of factors across groups (Reynolds, 1982a). The information derived from comparative factor-analysis studies across populations is directly relevant to the use of educational and psychological tests for diagnosis and other kinds of decision making. In order to make consistent interpretations of test score data, psychologists must be certain that the test measures the same variable across populations.

Other techniques must be employed to adequately assess construct validity, however. Reynolds's (1982a) definition requires equivalent internal consistency estimates across groups. Multitrait, multimethod test validation matrices must also be examined across groups if one is to determine consistency of outcome prior to concluding that a test is measuring the same construct for all concerned. With tests for children, the relationship between increases in chronological age and raw scores on the test should be essentially equivalent. Methodology for and outcome research on these and other problems bias in construct validity have been reviewed in several sources Jensen, 1976, 1980a; Reynolds, 1980a, 1982a,b).

The evaluation of cultural bias in construct validity is crucial to the entire issue of cultural test bias, not only for the practical application of psychometric methods and tests, but for theoretical research; if there is cultural bias in the construct validity of a test, all research outcomes of studies wherein the test has been employed with the groups for which bias exists must be entirely recast in light of the evidence of bias and must potentially be discarded altogether.

BIAS IN PREDICTIVE OR CRITERION-RELATED VALIDITY

Evaluating bias in the predictive validity of educational and psychological tests is less related to the evaluation of group differences in mental test scores than to the evaluation of individual test scores in a more absolute sense. This is especially true of aptitude (as opposed to diagnostic) tests where a primary purpose of administration is the prediction of some specific future outcome or behavior. Internal analyses of bias in content and construct validity are less confounded than analyses of bias in predictive validity, however, because of the potential problems of bias in the criterion measure. Predictive validity is also strongly influenced by the reliability of criterion measures, which frequently is poor. The magnitude of the problem is made clearer by the following relationship: The degree of the relation between a predictor and a criterion is restricted as a function of the square root of the product of the reliabilities of the two variables.

Arriving at a consensual definition of bias in predictive validity is also a difficult task, as has already been discussed. Yet, from the standpoint of the traditional practical applications of aptitude and intelligence tests in forecasting probabilities of future performance levels, predictive validity is the most crucial form of validity in relation to test bias. Much of the discussion in professional journals concerning bias in predictive validity has centered on the models of selection discussed previously in this chapter. Looking directly at bias as a characteristic of a test and not of a selection model, the definition of test fairness of Cleary *et al.* (1975), as restated by Reynolds (1982a), is a clear, direct statement of test bias with regard to criterion-related or predictive validity:

> A test is considered biased with respect to predictive validity when the inference drawn from the test score is not made with the smallest feasible random error or if there is constant error in an inference or prediction

as a function of membership in a particular group. (Reynolds, 1982a, p. 201)

The evaluation of bias in prediction under the Cleary *et al.* (1975) definition (the regression definition) is quite straightforward. With simple regressions, predictions take the form of

$$\hat{Y}_i = aX_i + b$$

where *a* is the regression coefficient and *b* is some constant. When this equation is graphed (forming a regression line), *a* represents the slope of the regression line and *b* the Y-intercept. Given our definition of bias in predictive validity, nonbias requires errors in prediction to be independent of group membership, and the regression line formed for any pair of variables must be the same for each group for whom predictions are to be made. Whenever the slope or the intercept differs significantly across groups, there is bias in prediction if one attempts to use a regression equation based on the combined groups. When the regression equations for two (or more) groups are equivalent, prediction is the same for those groups. This condition is referred to variously as *homogeneity of regression across groups, simultaneous regression,* or *fairness in prediction.* Whenever homogeneity of regression across groups does not occur, separate regression equations should be used for each group concerned.

In actual clinical practice, regression equations are seldom generated for the prediction of future performance. Rather, some arbitrary, or perhaps statistically derived, cutoff score is determined, below which "failure" is predicted. For school performance, a score of two or more standard deviations below the test mean is used to infer a high probability of failure in the regular classroom if special assistance is not provided for the student in question. Essentially, then, clinicians are establishing prediction equations about mental aptitude that are assumed to be equivalent across race, sex, and so on. Although these mental equations cannot be readily tested across groups, the actual form of criterion prediction can be compared across groups in several ways. Errors in prediction must be independent of group membership. If regression equations are equal, this condition is met. If one wants to test the hypothesis of simultaneous regression, the slopes and the intercepts must both be compared. An equally acceptable alternative method, especially with multiple independent measures, is the direct examination of residuals through ANOVA or a similar design (Reynolds, 1980b, 1982b).

In the evaluation of slope and intercept values, two basic techniques have been most often employed. Gulliksen and Wilks (1950) and Kerlinger and Pedhazur (1973) have described methods for separately testing regression coefficients and intercepts for significant differences across groups. Using separate, independent tests for these two values considerably increases the probability of a decision error and unnecessarily complicates the decision-making process. Potthoff (1966) has described a useful technique that allows simultaneous testing of the equivalence of regression coefficients and intercepts across K-independent groups with a single F ratio. If a significant F results, one may then test the slopes and intercepts separately for information concerning which value differs. When homogeneity of regression does not occur, there are three basic conditions that can result: (1) the intercept constants differ; (2) the regression coefficients (slopes) differ; or (3) the slopes and the intercepts differ.

When the intercept constants differ, the resulting bias in prediction is constant across the range of scores. That is, regardless of the level of performance on the independent variable, the direction and the degree of error in the estimation of the criterion (systematic over- or underprediction) remain the same. When the regression coefficients differ and the intercepts are equivalent, the direction of the bias in prediction remains constant, but the amount of error in prediction varies directly as a function of the distance of the score on the independent variable from the origin. With regression coefficient differences, then, the higher the score on the predictor variable, the greater the error of prediction for the criterion. When both slopes and intercepts differ, the situation becomes even more complex: Both the degree of error in prediction and the direction of the "bias" vary as a function of the level of performance on the independent variable. The results of these various conditions are presented in detail in Reynolds (1982a). Generally, research on predictive bias with preschool, school-aged, and college-aged individuals has shown either no bias in prediction or an intercept-only bias that has resulted in constant *overprediction* of minority performance on the criterion (Reynolds, 1982a).

BIAS IN THE EVALUATION OF PSYCHOPATHOLOGY

The potential for cultural bias in personality measures, both objective and projective techniques, has not received nearly the same attention as cognitive tests. Personality and overt behavior are almost certain to be more culturally determined than are one's intellectual skills. Cross-racial studies of personality scales typically have not been cast in the paradigm of bias but have looked at differential responding as reflecting differences in a given personality dimension. Whether the same dimensions of personality and overt behavior exist cross-racially has been little researched. Evidence is now being brought to light, however, that there may be a significantly greater likelihood of cultural bias in personality assessment than in cognitive assessment (e.g., Reynolds & Paget, 1983; Reynolds, Plake, & Harding, 1983). The methodology of research on bias for cognitive measures is equally applicable to standardized personality measures: The question of cultural bias in personality assessment is in dire need of investigation and need not await any further methodological refinements, though some paradigmatic shifts in thinking will need to occur.

Several interesting studies of bias in the diagnosis and evaluation of psychopathology and behavior have recently appeared, though they do not examine the tests in use. Lewis, Balla, and Shanok (1979) recently reported that when black adolescents were seen in community-mental-health settings, behaviors symptomatic of schizophrenia, paranoia, and a variety of psychoneurotic disorders were frequently dismissed as only "cultural aberrations" appropriate to coping with the frustrations created by the antagonistic white culture. Lewis *et al.* further noted that white adolescents exhibiting similar behaviors were given psychiatric diagnoses and were referred for therapy and/or residential placements that were not provided blacks. Lewis *et al.* contended that this failure to diagnose mental illness in the black population acts as a bias in the denial of appropriate services. Another study (Lewis, Shanok, Cohen, Kligfeld, & Frisone, 1980) found that "many seriously psychiatrically disturbed, aggressive black adolescents are being channeled to correction facilities while their equally aggressive white counterparts are directed toward psychiatric treatment facilities" (p. 1216). The expressed "failure" of mental health workers to diagnose these black adolescents as emotionally disturbed may be attributed to the critics of the psychological testing of minorities. These workers have been told repeatedly that behaviors that are unacceptable in the society at large are not only acceptable in the black culture but adaptive and in some cases necessary.

Plaintiffs' witnesses in *Larry P.* (1979) and *PASE* (1980) indicated, for example, that, although it might be appropriate for a white middle-class child to respond to a much smaller child who starts a fight by not fighting and by seeking other solutions, black children must respond by fighting back because any other response would be nearly suicidal in the black ghetto culture. Through such criticisms, psychologists are led (1) to believe that aggression and violence are not pathological among certain groups and (2) to interpret the behavior and personality test scores of members of these groups differently. Reynolds (1982a) reviewed a number of studies from the cognitive realm that indicate a similar phenomenon with regard to special class placement. When faced with obtained IQs, practicing clinicians tend to overestimate the "true IQ" of blacks relative to that of whites. Further, when IQ *and* achievement in the classroom are held constant, black children are *less likely* to be recommended for special class placement than their white counterparts. This particular type of bias works consistently to keep blacks and other minorities out of treatment programs, whether the treatment programs are viewed as desirable (psychiatric treatment vs. prison) or undesirable (regular classroom vs. a classroom for mentally retarded persons). Test interpretations should not be modified on the basis of an externally perceived desirability of programming for one or another group. How can tests be considered biased in the case of regular versus special-education placement and not biased in the case of incarceration versus mental health treatment? Whether the existing interpretive bias is viewed as "discriminatory" depends on whether one regards the contemplated services as being beneficial or harmful to the individual involved.

As noted earlier, however, modifications in test interpretation cannot ethically be undertaken on the basis of anecdotal or "expert witness" testimony. The decision to modify test score interpretations must ultimately be guided by empirical data. Much has been done in the cognitive arena, but bias in noncognitive measures is a recent consideration. The discussions that follow in this volume should shed considerable light on the existing data and on the many viewpoints from which they can be seen.

CONCLUSION

The issues regarding cultural bias in psychological and educational assessment are complex and are not given to simple resolution. The number and variety of polemic as well as rational statements made by otherwise objective professionals is certainly one indication of the different levels—scientific, educational, legal, sociopolitical, and emotional—involved in the issue of bias. The controversy over bias may remain with psychology and education as long as has the ubiquitous and perpetual nature–nurture controversy. It is the editors' conviction, however, that an empirical resolution of the test bias controversy is possible. At present, only scattered, inconsistent evidence of bias exists, and only of bias in support of disadvantaged ethnic minorities. The few findings of bias do suggest several guidelines that should be followed in order to ensure nonbiased assessment: (1) Assessment should be conducted with the most reliable instrumentation available, and (2) multiple abilities should be assessed. In other words, psychologists need to view multiple sources of accurately derived data before making decisions concerning individuals. One hopes that this is what has actually been occurring in the practice of psychological assessment, although one continues to hear isolated stories of grossly incompetent placement decisions' being made. This is not to say that psychologists should be blind to an individual's cultural or environmental background. Information concerning the home, the community, and the school environment must all be evaluated in individual decisions. Yet, the psychologist cannot ignore the fact that low-IQ, ethnic, disadvantaged children are just as likely to fail academically as are white, middle-class, low-IQ children, provided that their environmental circumstances remain constant. Indeed, it is the purpose of the assessment process to beat the prediction and to provide insight into hypotheses for environmental interventions that will prevent the predicted failure.

Test developers are also going to have to become more sensitive to the issues of cultural bias to the point of demonstrating whether their tests have differential content, construct, or predictive validity across race or sex prior to publication. Test authors and publishers need to demonstrate factorial invariance across all groups for whom the test is designed in order to make the instrument more readily interpretable. Comparisons of predictive validity are also needed across race and sex during the test development phase. With the exception of some recent achievement tests, this has not been common practice, yet it is at this stage that tests can be altered through a variety of item analysis procedures to eliminate any apparent racial or sexual bias.

A number and variety of criteria need to be explored further before the question of bias is empirically resolved. Many different achievement tests and teacher-made, classroom, specific tests need to be employed in future studies of predictive bias. The entire area of the differential validity of tests in the affective domain is in need of exploration. With the exception of a few limited studies of differential construct validity (e.g., Katzenmeyer & Stenner, 1977; Ozehosky & Clark, 1971; Reynolds & Paget, 1983), little work has been done evaluating the validity of psychologists' interpretations of objective personality-test data across race and sex. This is an important area for examination, as more objective determinations of emotional disturbance are required. It will also be important to stay abreast of methodological advances that may make it possible to resolve some of the current issues and to identify common characteristics among findings of bias that are now seen as irregular or random and infrequent.

In the pages that follow, many different views toward bias are expressed. It is noteworthy that all are scholarly and nonpolemic and directed toward a resolution of the issue. Obviously, the fact that such different views are still held indicates that resolution lies in the future. The editors' hope is that, in the reader's coalescing of the information and the positions regarding bias that follow, new approaches to the question will arise. As far as the present situation is concerned, clearly all the evidence is not in. Were a scholarly trial to be held, with a charge of cultural bias brought against mental tests, we feel that the jury would return not a verdict of "guilty" or "innocent," but the verdict that is allowed in British law: "Not proven."

REFERENCES

Alley, G., & Foster, C. Nondiscriminatory testing of minority and exceptional children. *Focus on Exceptional Children*, 1978, 9, 1–14.

American Psychological Association. *Ethical standards of psychologists*. Washington, D.C.: Author, 1979.

Anastasi, A. *Psychological testing* (4th ed.). New York: Macmillan, 1976.

Berk, R. A. *Conference introduction.* Paper presented to the Johns Hopkins University National Symposium on Educational Research: Test Item Bias Methodology—The State of the Art, Washington, D.C., November 1980.

Berk, R. A. (Ed.). *Handbook of methods for detecting test bias*. Baltimore: Johns Hopkins University Press, 1982.

Bersoff, D. N. Regarding psychologists testily: Legal regulation of psychological assessment in the public schools. *Maryland Law Review*, 1979, 39, 27–120.

Bersoff, D. N. The legal regulation of school psychology. In C. R. Reynolds & T. B. Gutkin (Eds.), *The handbook of school psychology*. New York: Wiley, 1982.

Birch, H. G., & Gussow, J. D. *Disadvantaged children: Health, nutrition, and school failure*. New York: Grune & Stratton, 1970.

Block, N. J., & Dworkin, G. (Eds.). *The IQ controversy: Critical readings*. New York: Pantheon, 1976.

Bolles, R. C. *Theory of motivation* (2nd ed.). New York: Harper & Row, 1975.

Boring, E. G. Intelligence as the tests test it. *New Republic*, 1923, *35*, 35–37.

Buros, O. K. (Ed.). *Eighth mental measurements yearbook*. Highland Park, N.J.: Gryphon Press, 1978.

Burt, C. *Mental and scholastic tests*. London: P. S. King, 1921.

Cattell, R. B. Are culture fair intelligence tests possible and necessary? *Journal of Research and Development in Education*, 1979, *12*, 3–13.

Chambers, J. S., Barron, F., & Sprecher, J. W. Identifying gifted Mexican-American students. *Gifted Child Quarterly*, 1980, *24*, 123–128.

Chase, A. *The legacy of Malthus: The social costs of the new scientific racism*. New York: Knopf, 1977.

Chinn, P. C. The exceptional minority child: Issues and some answers. *Exceptional Children*, 1979, *46*, 532–536.

Cleary, T. A., Humphreys, L. G., Kendrick, S. A., & Wesman, A. Educational uses of tests with disadvantaged students. *American Psychologist*, 1975, *30*, 15–41.

Committee on Testing, National Association of Black Psychologists. *A position paper on psychological testing of black people*. Washington, D.C.: Author, 1974.

Connolly, W. B., & Connolly, M. J. Equal employment opportunities: Case law overview. *Mercer Law Review*, 1978, *29*, 677–744.

Council for Exceptional Children. Minorities position policy statements. *Exceptional Children*, 1978, *45*, 57–64.

Cronbach, L. J. *Essentials of psychological testing* (2nd ed.). New York: Harper and Row, 1970.

Cronbach, L. J. Test validation. In R. L. Thorndike (Ed.), *Educational measurement* (2nd ed.). Washington, D.C.: American Council on Education, 1971.

Cronbach, L. J. Five decades of public controversy over mental testing. *American Psychologist*, 1975, *30*, 1–14.

Darlington, R. B. Another look at "cultural fairness." *Journal of Educational Measurement*, 1971, *8*, 71–82.

Ebel, R. L. Intelligence: A skeptical view. *Journal of Research and Development in Education*, 1979, *12*, 14–21.

Eckberg, D. L. *Intelligence and race: Origins and dimensions of the IQ controversy*. New York: Praeger, 1979.

Eells, K., Davis, A., Havighurst, R. J., Herrick, V. E., & Tyler, R. W. *Intelligence and cultural differences: A study of cultural learning and problem-solving*. Chicago: University of Chicago Press, 1951.

Fine, B. *The stranglehold of the I.Q.* Garden City, N.Y.: Doubleday, 1975.

Freeman, F. N. A referendum of psychologists. *Century Illustrated Magazine*, 1923, *107*, 237–245.

Goldstein, H., Krantz, D. L., & Rains, J. D. (Eds.). *Controversial issues in learning*. New York: Appleton-Century-Crofts, 1965.

Gould, S. J. *Ontogeny and phylogeny*. Cambridge: Harvard University Press, 1977.

Gould, S. J. Morton's ranking of races by cranial capacity. *Science*, 1978, *200*, 503–509.

Guion, G. M. Recruiting, selection, and job placement. In M. D. Dunnette (Ed.), *Handbook of industrial and organizational psychology*. Chicago: Rand McNally, 1976.

Gulliksen, H., & Wilks, S. S. Regression tests for several samples. *Psychometrika*, 1950, *15*, 91–114.

Harrington, G. M. Intelligence tests may favour the majority groups in a population. *Nature*, 1975, *258*, 708–709.

Harrington, G. M. *Minority test bias as a psychometric artifact: The experimental evidence.* Paper presented to the annual meeting of the American Psychological Association, Washington, D.C., September 1976.

Heber, F. R. Sociocultural mental retardation—A longitudinal study. In D. Forgays (Ed.), *Primary prevention of psychopathology: Vol. 2. Environmental influences.* Hanover, N.H.: University Press of New England, 1978.

Herrnstein, R. J. *IQ in the meritocracy.* Boston: Little & Brown, 1973.

Hilgard, E. R., & Bower, G. H. *Theories of learning* (4th ed.). Englewood Cliffs, N.J.: Prentice-Hall, 1975.

Hilliard, A. G. Standardization and cultural bias as impediments to the scientific study and validation of "intelligence." *Journal of Research and Development in Education,* 1979, *12,* 47–58.

Humphreys, L. G. Statistical definitions of test validity for minority groups. *Journal of Applied Psychology,* 1973, *58,* 1–4.

Jackson, G. D. Another psychological view from the Association of Black Psychologists. *American Psychologist,* 1975, *30,* 88–93.

Jackson, R. The scholastic aptitude test: A response to Slack and Porter's "Critical appraisal." *Harvard Educational Review,* 1980, *50,* 382–391.

Jensen, A. R. How much can we boost IQ and scholastic achievement? *Harvard Educational Review,* 1969, *39,* 1–123.

Jensen, A. R. Test bias and construct validity. *Phi Delta Kappan,* 1976, *58,* 340–346.

Jensen, A. R. *Bias in mental testing.* New York: Free Press, 1980. (a)

Jensen, A. R. Correcting the bias against mental testing: A preponderance of peer agreement. *The Behavioral and Brain Sciences,* 1980, *3,* 359–368. (b)

Kamin, L. J. *The science and politics of I.Q.* Potomac, Md.: Lawrence Erlbaum, 1974.

Kamin, L. J. Heredity, intelligence, politics, and psychology: II. In N. J. Block & G. Dworkin (Eds.), *The IQ controversy: Critical readings.* New York: Pantheon, 1976.

Karier, C. Testing for order and control in the corporate liberal state. *Educational Theory,* 1972, *22,* 154–180.

Katzenmeyer, W. G., & Stenner, A. J. Estimation of the invariance of factor structures across sex and race with implications for hypothesis testing. *Educational and Psychological Measurement,* 1977, *37,* 111–119.

Kaufman, A. S. Comparison of the performance of matched groups of black children and white children on the Wechsler Preschool and Primary Scale of Intelligence. *Journal of Consulting and Clinical Psychology,* 1973, *41,* 186–191.

Kaufman, A. S., & Kaufman, N. L. Black-white differences on the McCarthy Scales of Children's Abilities. *Journal of School Psychology,* 1973, *11,* 196–206.

Kerlinger, F. N., & Pedhazur, E. J. *Multiple regression in behavioral research.* New York: Holt, Rinehart, & Winston, 1973.

Kimble, G. A. *Hilgard and Marquis' conditioning and learning* (2nd ed.). New York: Appleton-Century-Crofts, 1961.

Kuhn, T. S. *The structure of scientific revolutions.* Chicago: University of Chicago Press, 1962.

Lambert, N. M. *Adaptive behavior assessment and its implications for educational programming.* Paper presented to the Fourth Annual Midwestern Conference on Psychology in the Schools, Boys Town, Neb., October 1979.

Larry P. *et al.* v. Wilson Riles *et al.,* C 71 2270 (United States District Court for the Northern District of California, October 1979, slip opinion).

Lazar, I., Hubbell, V., Murray, H., Rosche, M., & Royce, J. *The persistence of preschool effects: A long-term follow-up of fourteen infant and preschool experiments.* Final report of the Consortium on Developmental Continuity. Washington, D.C.: U.S. Department of Health, Education, and Welfare, 1977.

Lewis, D. O., Balla, D. A., & Shanok, S. S. Some evidence of race bias in the diagnosis and treatment of the juvenile offender. *American Journal of Orthopsychiatry,* 1979, *49,* 53–61.

Lewis, D. O., Shanok, S. S., Cohen, R. J., Kligfeld, M., & Frisone, G. Race bias in the diagnosis and disposition of violent adolescents. *American Journal of Psychiatry,* 1980, *137,* 1211–1216.

Lippmann, W. A judgment of the tests. *New Republic,* 1923, *34,* 322–323. (a)

Lippmann, W. Mr. Burt and the intelligence tests. *New Republic,* 1923, *34,* 263–264. (b)

Loehlin, J. C., Lindzey, G., & Spuhler, J. N. *Race differences in intelligence.* San Francisco: W. H. Freeman, 1975.

MacCorquodale, K., & Meehl, P. E. On a distinction between hypothetical constructs and intervening variables. *Psychological Review,* 1948, *55,* 95–107.

Mandler, G. *Mind and emotion.* New York: Wiley, 1975.

Mercer, J. R. *Labeling the mentally retarded.* Berkeley: University of California Press, 1973.

Mercer, J. R. *Cultural diversity, mental retardation, and assessment: The case for non-labeling.* Paper presented to the Fourth International Congress of the International Association for the Scientific Study of Mental Retardation, Washington, D.C., August 1976.

Messick, S. Test validity and the ethics of assessment. *American Psychologist,* 1980, *35,* 1012–1017.

Messick, S., & Jungeblut, A. Time and method in coaching for the SAT. *Psychological Bulletin,* 1981, *89,* 191–216.

Multiple book review of A. R. Jensen, *Bias in mental testing. Behavioral and Brain Sciences,* 1980, *3,* 325–371.

Nichols, R. C. Policy implications of the IQ controversy. In L. S. Schulman (Ed.), *Review of research in education* (Vol. 6). Itasca, Ill.: F. E. Peacock, 1978.

Ozehosky, R. J., & Clark, E. T. Verbal and nonverbal measures of self-concept among kindergarten boys and girls. *Psychological Reports,* 1971, *28,* 195–199.

PASE: Parents in action on special education *et al.* v. Hannon *et al.* No. 74 C 3586 (United States District Court for the Northern District of Illinois, Eastern Division, July 1980, slip opinion).

Petersen, N. S., & Novick, M. R. An evaluation of some models for culture fair selection. *Journal of Educational Measurement,* 1976, *13,* 3–29.

Piaget, J. *The origins of intelligence in childhood.* New York: International Universities Press, 1952.

Piersel, W. C., Plake, B. S., Reynolds, C. R., & Harding, R. D. *Conceptual development and ethnic group membership: Item bias on the Boehm Test of Basic Concepts.* Paper presented at the annual meeting of the Iowa Educational Research Association, Iowa City, December 1980.

Pintner, R. *Intelligence testing.* New York: Holt, Rinehart & Winston, 1931.

Potthoff, R. F. *Statistical aspects of the problem of biases in psychological tests.* Institute of Statistics Mimeo Series No. 479. Chapel Hill: University of North Carolina Department of Statistics, 1966.

Reschly, D. J. School psychologists and assessment in the future. *Professional Psychology*, 1980, *11*, 841–848.

Reynolds, C. R. Differential construct validity of intelligence as popularly measured: Correlation of age and raw scores on the WISC-R for blacks, whites, males, and females. *Intelligence: A Multidisciplinary Journal*, 1980, *4*, 371–379. (a)

Reynolds, C. R. An examination for test bias in a preschool battery across race and sex. *Journal of Educational Measurement*, 1980, *17*, 137–146. (b)

Reynolds, C. R. In support of "Bias in Mental Testing" and scientific inquiry. *The Behavioral and Brain Sciences*, 1980, *3*, 352. (c)

Reynolds, C. R. The problem of bias in psychological assessment. In C. R. Reynolds & T. B. Gutkin (Eds.), *The handbook of school psychology*. New York: Wiley, 1982. (a)

Reynolds, C. R. Construct and predictive bias. In R. A. Berk (Ed.), *Handbook of methods for detecting test bias*. Baltimore: Johns Hopkins University Press, 1982. (b)

Reynolds, C. R., & Gutkin, T. B. A multivariate comparison of the intellectual performance of blacks and whites matched on four demographic variables. *Personality and Individual Differences*, 1981, *2*, 175–180.

Reynolds, C. R., & Jensen, A. R. *Patterns of intellectual performance among blacks and whites matched on "g."* Paper presented to the annual meeting of the American Psychological Association, Montreal, September 1983.

Reynolds, C. R., & Paget, K. National normative and reliability data for the Revised-Children's Manifest Anxiety Scale. *School Psychology Review*, 1983, *12*, 324–336.

Reynolds, C. R., Plake, B. S., & Harding, R. D. Item bias in the assessment of children's anxiety: Race and sex interaction on items of the Revised Children's Manifest Anxiety Scale. *Journal of Psycho-Educational Assessment*, 1983, *1*(1), 17–24.

Samuda, A. J. *Psychological testing of American minorities: Issues and consequences.* New York: Dodd, Mead, 1975.

Schoenfeld, W. N. Notes on a bit of psychological nonsense: "Race differences in intelligence." *Psychological Record*, 1974, *24*, 17–32.

Shepard, L. A. *Definitions of bias.* Paper presented to the Johns Hopkins University National Symposium on Educational Research: Test Item Bias Methodology—The State of the Art, Washington, D.C., November 1980.

Shuey, A. M. *The testing of Negro intelligence* (2nd ed.). New York: Social Science Press, 1966.

Slack, W. V., & Porter, D. The Scholastic Aptitude Test: A critical appraisal. *Harvard Educational Review*, 1980, *50*, 154–175. (a)

Slack, W. V., & Porter D. Training, validity, and the issue of aptitude: A reply to Jackson. *Harvard Educational Review*, 1980, *50*, 392–401. (b)

Sternberg, R. J. Intelligence and test bias: Art and science. *Behavioral and Brain Sciences*, 1980, *3*, 353–354.

Thorndike, R. L. Concepts of culture-fairness. *Journal of Educational Measurement*, 1971, *8*, 63–70. (a)

Thorndike, R. L. (Ed.). *Educational measurement* (2nd ed.). Washington, D.C.: American Council on Education, 1971. (b)

Tyler, L. E. *The psychology of human differences.* New York: Appleton-Century-Crofts, 1965.

Vernon, P. E. *Intelligence: Heredity and environment.* San Francisco: W. H. Freeman, 1979.

Wechsler, D. *Wechsler Intelligence Scale for Children–Revised.* New York: The Psychological Corporation, 1974.

Wechsler, D. Intelligence defined and undefined: A relativistic appraisal. *American Psychologist,* 1975, *30,* 135–139.

Willerman, L. *The psychology of individual and group differences.* San Francisco: W. H. Freeman, 1979.

Williams, R. L. From dehumanization to black intellectual genocide: A rejoinder. In G. J. Williams & S. Gordon (Eds.), *Clinical child psychology: Current practices and future perspectives,* New York: Behavioral Publications, 1974.

Williams, R. L., Dotson, W., Dow, P., & Williams, W. S. The war against testing: A current status report. *Journal of Negro Education,* 1980, *49,* 263–273.

Wright, B. J., & Isenstein, V. R. Psychological tests and minorities. Rockville, Md.: NIMH, DHEW Publication No. (ADM) 78-482, 1977 (reprinted 1978).

Zigler, E. Head Start: Not a program but an evolving concept. In J. D. Andrews (Ed.), *Early childhood education: It's an art? It's a science?* Washington, D.C.: National Association for the Education of Young Children, 1976.

Zigler, E., & Butterfield, E. C. Motivational aspects of changes in IQ test performance of culturally deprived nursery school children. *Child Development,* 1967, *39,* 1–14.

CHAPTER TWO

Methodological, Statistical, and Ethical Issues in the Study of Bias in Psychological Tests

JOHN E. HUNTER,
FRANK L. SCHMIDT,
and
JOHN RAUSCHENBERGER

TEST FAIRNESS VERSUS ETHNIC IMBALANCE

The hypothesis that tests are biased against minority groups asserts that scores on psychological tests may be accurate estimates of the ability of majority white test-takers but they are poor estimates of the ability of minority persons. This hypothesis can be tested empirically with data from any domain. If tests are biased, then evidence of bias should be found in every domain in which tests are used. If the evidence in any domain shows ability tests to be unbiased, then the hypothesis of bias must be abandoned. Findings suggesting bias in another domain would have to be explained by some other hypothesis that is specific to that domain.

An analogy can be drawn with physical measurement. If someone hypothesized that a certain yardstick actually was 38 rather than

The opinions expressed herein are those of the authors and do not necessarily reflect the policies of the organizations with which they are affiliated.

JOHN E. HUNTER ● Department of Psychology, Michigan State University, East Lansing, Michigan 48823. FRANK L. SCHMIDT ● U.S. Office of Personnel Management and George Washington University, Washington, D.C. 20052. JOHN RAUSCHENBERGER ● ARMCO Corporation, Middletown, Ohio 45042.

36 inches long, then that hypothesis could be tested in any laboratory with proven instruments. If one lab found the measurement to be 36 rather than 38 inches long, the hypothesis of bad measurement need not be tested in other labs.

This chapter focuses primarily on the employment domain, where ability tests are used to predict job performance. The massive data now available from test validation studies in that domain show clearly and unequivocally that tests have no bias in measuring ability. In particular, a minority person with a low ability-test score will, on the average, perform just as poorly on the job as would a majority worker with the same low score.

Because tests are not biased in the employment domain, they cannot be biased in any other domain. Evidence suggesting bias would have to have some other explanation. However, we know of no domain where there has been cumulative evidence suggesting bias. For example, we have read three extensive reviews of the empirical studies in education, and all three find overwhelming evidence disconfirming the bias hypothesis (Reynolds, 1981; Gordon & Rudert, 1979; Jensen, 1980).

Any discussion of the racial or ethnic impact of testing must sharply distinguish between two questions: (1) Is the test fair to minority group members? and (2) Does the use of the test produce a racially or ethnically unbalanced work force? To say that a test is fair is to say that the score on the test is an accurate estimate of the ability of a person in any racial or ethnic group. Those who hypothesize that tests are unfair to minorities believe that the test scores underestimate the ability of minority members. This is a scientific question that can be answered empirically. The first section of this chapter reviews the now-massive amount of data gathered on this question. This review presents the scientific proof that tests are fair to minority groups.

To say that test use produces an unbalanced work force is to say that selection based on a test results in hiring a smaller percentage of minority applicants than of majority applicants. The extent of disparity in hiring rates depends on the difference between group means on the test scores. These differences vary drastically from test to test. For example, U.S. Employment Service data (USES, 1970, p. 281) show that Mexican-Americans have a mean on cognitive ability (e.g., intelligence, verbal ability, numerical ability) that is about one half of one standard deviation below the majority mean. Thus, for a high-complexity job where optimal test use calls for cognitive ability, an employer selecting the top half of majority applicants would hire only the top 31% of the Mexican-American applicants. However, the mean for Mexican-Americans on psychomotor ability is .18 standard deviations higher than that for the majority. On low-complexity jobs where psychomotor ability would be used alone as a predictor, an employer hiring the top half of majority applicants would hire 57% of the Mexican-American applicants. Thus, the same employer could have an imbalance in hiring rates going in opposite directions for different jobs.

Multiple regression shows that performance on high-paying white-collar jobs can be best predicted by means of a cognitive-ability composite score (Ghiselli, 1973; Hunter, 1980b; Pearlman, Schmidt, & Hunter, 1980; Schmidt, Hunter, Pearlman, & Shane, 1979). Thus, the selection of an optimally productive work force would mean under-representation of blacks, Mexican-Americans, and Indians. Any scheme that uses tests in such a way as to reduce the ethnic imbalance in hiring rates necessarily reduces the average productivity of the applicants hired. If tests were unfair to minority applicants, then it would be possible to create new tests to resolve this problem. But tests are fair, and the differences in ability between ethnic groups are real. If these differences stem from cultural disadvantage, then the differences may disappear over the next several generations. However, at present, there is no way to avoid the trade-off between high productivity and ethnic imbalance in hiring.

The choice between high productivity and ethnic balance can be treated as an ethical decision. Hunter and Schmidt (1976) showed that the so-called statistical models of test fairness discussed in the professional literature are actually different ways of introducing quotas into hiring. The second section of this chapter reviews this literature.

However, the ethical discussions of test "fairness" have mostly ignored the economic costs that result from the nonoptimal use of tests. If the employer has increased labor costs because of the use of quotas of some sort, then these costs must be passed on. Manufacturers pass the costs on in the form of higher prices. These result in lower sales and hence in lower employment, especially in cases where the American firm is in direct competition with foreign manufacturers. This increase in unemployment hits hardest among minority workers. Thus, jobs gained by some minority workers are lost for other minority workers, and the economy as a whole suffers severely.

The situation is even more dramatically complicated in the public sector. Hunter (1979) estimated that the abandonment of a cognitive ability test for the selection of police officers in Philadelphia would result in increased labor costs of $180 million over a 10-year period. Philadelphia cannot further increase its business taxes without a massive exodus of businesses, and hence employers, to the suburbs. Thus, the $180 million can be paid in only one of two ways: (1) by a reduction in the quality of police protection or (2) by a reduction in city services in other areas. Police protection is most important in the high-crime areas. Minority citizens are heavily overrepresented in high-crime areas. Thus, the ultimate cost of reduced police protection is borne largely by minority citizens. Reduction in city services in other areas would mean reduction in social services such as subsidized medical services. Again, these services are most heavily used by minority citizens. Thus, the ultimate cost of reduced city services would be borne largely by minority citizens. That is, ethnic balance in police hiring results in little economic benefit to minority citizens and results in reduced city services for all.

The economic costs of various schemes for achieving ethnic balance can be estimated. Hunter, Schmidt, and Rauschenberger (1977) analyzed utility differences for the various statistical models of fair test use. These results were recently replicated and extended by Cronbach, Yalow, and Schaeffer (1980). The third section of this chapter reviews this work. Under most conditions, the use of quotas along with valid tests to achieve ethnic balance results in a loss of the economic benefits of selection of 15% or less.

However, the Equal Employment Opportunity Commission has been urging employers to use a radically different method of achieving ethnic balance: the low cutoff method. In this procedure, the test is used only to screen out the extremely poor prospects, usually the bottom 10% to 20%. Applicants are then hired randomly from among those above this very low cutoff score. Hunter (1979, 1981) and Mack, Schmidt, and Hunter (1984) have shown the cost of the low cutoff procedure to be disastrous. At least 85% of the reduction in labor costs due to selection is lost by use of the low cutoff method. This 85% loss should be compared with a 15% (or less) loss resulting from the use of population quotas in a comparable situation.

But the low cutoff procedure not only is a disaster economically, it does not even achieve its racial and ethnic aims. The number of minority members hired is higher for quotas than for the low cutoff method. Thus, by any criterion, the low cutoff method is somewhat worse for minority applicants and disastrously worse for employers (and for those who pay the ultimate bill).

THE SCIENTIFIC PROOF THAT TESTS ARE FAIR TO MINORITIES

Fifteen years ago, industrial psychologists became generally aware of the large difference between blacks and whites in mean cognitive-ability test scores. Because most psychologists believed at that time that there could be no real difference between racial groups in cognitive ability, many assumed that the differences in test scores might mean that the tests were biased against blacks. The theory behind this hypothesis was this: Tests are developed by middle-class white psychologists in terms of their own culturally determined ways of thinking and perceiving. Black culture is so different from white culture that items that have one meaning to white applicants might have a different meaning (or no meaning) to black applicants. Thus, test scores for black applicants would underestimate their actual ability level. Many pointed to the known differences between black and white English dialects as the basis for a linguistic bias in tests written by whites.

Actually there was much evidence available even 15 years ago to show that the cultural bias hypothesis was false, although the evidence had not yet been collated. In particular, there are many nonverbal tests of cognitive ability, and the mean differences between blacks and whites are just as high or higher on the nonverbal tests (Reynolds & Jensen, 1980). However, there was little evidence bearing on this question within the employment area at that time. Since then, hundreds of data sets have been accumulated. These studies show that tests are just as valid for blacks as for whites, and that the test scores do *not* underestimate the ability of blacks. Similar evidence has also been accumulated for Hispanic applicants. This evidence is reviewed below.

The key to testing the hypothesis of test bias is to state the hypothesis in terms that can be assessed empirically. This has been done in three ways. The most extreme form of the test bias hypothesis is the assertion that black culture is so alien to white culture that a test might be completely meaningless to blacks. Thus, a test that is a valid predictor of job performance in some setting for whites might be completely invalid for blacks. This is known as the hypothesis of *single-group validity*. A less extreme version of this hypothesis is the assertion that a test is less meaningful for blacks than for whites. Thus, any given test would be less valid for blacks than for whites. This is the hypothesis of *differential validity*. Finally, there is the mildest form of the hypothesis: *Some* items on a test are meaningless for blacks. Thus, although the rank order of scores for black applicants is correct and hence the test is just as valid for blacks as for whites considered separately, the scores for blacks are systematically lower than the scores for whites of equal ability because the blacks have missed the biased items. This is the hypothesis of *underprediction of black performance*. All three hypotheses have been extensively tested, and all three have been found false.

The empirical assessment of the test bias hypothesis is greatly complicated by the statistical sampling error in studies based on fewer than 1,000 workers. For example, if the population correlation between the ability test and job performance were .20 for both black and white workers, then a validation study with several thousand workers would show unequivocally that the test was equally valid for both groups. However, if the study is done with 100 workers from each group, then the two correlations will vary from the population value of .20 because of chance fluctuations in the sample drawn. For a population correlation of .20 and a sample of 100 workers, the observed correlation would vary randomly over a region from .01 to .39. In fact, 1 in 40 such studies will even get a value below 0, and 1 in 40 such studies will show a value greater than .40. Thus, even though the population validity might be .20 for both racial groups, a study with 100 workers of each race might well show observed correlations of .35 for white workers and .05 for black workers. The author would then falsely conclude that tests are biased against black applicants. The truth would be found only when other studies showed the reverse finding with equal frequency. Alas, the number of workers at a given job in a given organization is usually fewer than 100, and hence, small samples are all that is available for study. Lent, Aurbach, and Levin (1971) found that the median sample size in 1,500 validation studies was only 68. This problem is particularly acute in racial and ethnic studies because the number of minority workers is usually even smaller.

The presence of large sampling errors means that the results of single studies have little meaning taken by themselves. The effects of sampling errors can be eliminated only when enough individual studies have been done to permit a cumulative analysis of results across studies. Thus, there have been two phases in the empirical study of the test bias hypothesis: an early phase in which some authors of individual validation studies claimed to have found evidence of test bias, whereas others claimed to have disconfirmed the hypothesis, followed by a later phase of cumulative studies that have produced unequivocal evidence disconfirming the test bias hypothesis. That is, the cumulative studies have shown that the findings suggesting test bias have been chance level fluctuations in correlations due to sampling errors produced by small sample sizes.

EVIDENCE AGAINST THE SINGLE-GROUP VALIDITY HYPOTHESIS

If a test is a valid predictor of job performance for whites, then will it also be valid for blacks? At one point, there seemed to be evidence that tests valid for white job applicants were sometimes not valid for black applicants. However, this evidence has subsequently been shown to be an artifact of the statistical procedure used. Because most studies have data for many more white workers than black workers, a given correlation between test results and job performance is much more likely to be statistically significant for whites than for blacks. For example, suppose that a study found a correlation of .25 for both groups, 100 white workers and 30 black workers. Then, the correlation of .25 would be statistically significant for the white workers, whereas the same correlation of .25 would not be statistically significant for black workers. An unwary investigator might claim this finding as evidence confirming the test bias hypothesis. Even if sample sizes were equal, Humphreys (1973) noted that separate significance tests should be used not alone but in conjunction with a significance test checking to see if the two correlations were significantly different from each other. This procedure would eliminate the error in the example above, though there would still be a sampling error in the significance for differences between correlations. Only cumulative evidence can tell the full story.

The first statistically correct study in this area was done by Schmidt, Berner, and Hunter (1973). A number of studies had reported significant correlations for whites but not for blacks (apparent single-group validity). However, these researchers noted that in such studies there was typically a vast disparity in the sample sizes for the two racial subgroups. Thus, the same sized correlation would be significant for whites but not significant for blacks. They devised a procedure for cumulating evidence across studies in such a way that it would control for differences in sample size. They applied this cumulative analysis to 410 sets of validity data: 249 studies using supervisor ratings as the job performance measure and 161 studies in which a job sample test or production records were used to measure job performance. This cumulative analysis showed that findings of single-group validity are entirely an artifact of differential sample size. In fact, this cumulative analysis suggested that there might be no differences in validity between blacks and whites at all. The Schmidt, Berner, and Hunter single-group validity-cumulation has been subsequently replicated three times (O'Connor, Wexley, & Alexander, 1975; Boehm, 1977; Katzell & Dyer, 1977).

EVIDENCE DISCONFIRMING THE DIFFERENTIAL VALIDITY HYPOTHESIS

The Schmidt *et al.* (1973) procedure does not have great statistical power against the gentler hypothesis that tests are less valid for blacks than for whites. Thus, although this study did show that there is no single-group validity, it did not conclusively show that there is no differential validity. Humphreys (1973) showed that doing separate significance tests is an inappropriate way of assessing differences in validity between races. He suggested testing the difference between the correlations for statistical significance. In 1974, the American Psychological Association *Standards* for tests expressly endorsed the Humphreys position.

Katzell and Dyer (1977) and Boehm (1977) have claimed to have found evidence of differential validity using a cumulative form of the Humphreys procedure. They applied the Humphreys test to a cumulation of data across many studies and counted the number of times that they found statistical significance. They found more than 5% significant findings and therefore concluded that they had found evidence of differential validity. However, there was a conflict between their findings and the hypothesis of differential validity. When they compared correlations, both studies found that the validity coefficient for blacks was larger than the coefficient for whites just as often as the reverse. That is, they found validity for blacks to be just as high as validity for whites, on the average. The discrepancy between these findings was explained by Hunter and Schmidt (1978), who noted that both studies had preselected the pairs of correlations to be tested. Hunter and Schmidt showed mathematically that this preselection would have the effect of producing a spuriously high (i.e., as much as 20%) number of significant differences among the subsample of considered studies. If preselection led to the false identification of differences, then the direction of the difference would be random. Thus, the analyses of Katzell and Dyer (1977) and of Boehm (1977) are actually consistent with the hypothesis that there are *no* differences in validity between races.

In a nonpreselected sample of 1,190 pairs of regression lines, Bartlett, Bobko, Mosier, and Hannan (1978) found a chance level 5.21% differences in slopes. Hunter, Schmidt, and Hunter (1979) have used a variety of more powerful cumulation procedures with the same result: Differences in validity between racial groups are the statistical artifact of the use of small sample sizes.

A cumulative study of differential validity for Hispanic workers was done by Schmidt, Pearlman, and Hunter (1980). They located 1,323 data sets in which test/criterion correlations are given for both majority and Hispanic workers. The initial analysis showed that 11% of the correlations were significantly different and that the cumulative chi-square test was statistically significant. However, a further check showed that over half of the significant differences occurred in one small study with very small sample sizes, namely, the Rosenfeld and Thornton (1976) study at Site 4. At this one site, the average validity for the sample of 62 majority workers was a minus .16, whereas the average for the sample of 49 Hispanic workers was plus .16. That is, most of the significant differences were from one study in which the test was apparently valid for Hispanic workers and not valid for the majority. However, these results for the majority group are highly suspect because they contradict the results found at the other three sites in the Rosenfeld and Thornton (1976) study and contradict a large number of studies done on similar tests in other settings for the same job. If the data from this one suspect study are deleted, then there are 1,128 data sets left. The number of significant differences is less than 6%, well within the range of chance expectation.

The results of these cumulative studies are clear. The validity of a test in the employment area is the same for blacks as for whites. The validity of the test is the same for Hispanics as for majority white workers. Thus, in any given setting, the validity of a given test in predicting job performance is the same for white, for black, and for Hispanic workers. There is no differential validity.

EVIDENCE DISCONFIRMING THE HYPOTHESIS THAT TESTS UNDERPREDICT MINORITY JOB PERFORMANCE

The least extreme form of the hypothesis that tests are unfair to minorities is the claim that only certain items on each test are biased. If only certain items were biased, then the test as a whole would still be as valid for blacks as for whites considered separately. However, the test scores of blacks would be systematically lower than those of whites of the same ability level because blacks would miss the biased items. If it were true that tests underestimate black ability, then it would follow that test scores would underpredict black performance on the job. This, in turn, leads to the prediction that if tests were biased against blacks, then the regression line for blacks would lie above the regression line for whites. The data show just the reverse to be true.

We will first derive the test bias prediction about regression lines. Consider a typical validation study. Each worker has two scores: a test score and a job performance score. Plot this pair of scores as a point on a two-dimensional graph such as that shown in Figure 1. The set of such points is called a *scatterplot*, and the tightness of the scatter shows the strength of the relationship between the test score and the job performance in that study. The points on the scatter plot do not fall perfectly on a line because no test perfectly predicts job performance. However, a number of cumulative studies (see Hunter & Schmidt, 1982; Schmidt, Hunter, McKenzie, & Muldrow, 1979, for a review of these studies) have shown that, in the employment literature, these scatter plots each lie about a straight line. That straight line is called the *regression line* of the scatter plot. The regression line is defined in terms of the mean performance of subgroups based on test scores. That is, the height of the regression line above each test score is the mean job performance for all those workers with that test score. Thus, the regression line shows mean performance on the job as a function of test score.

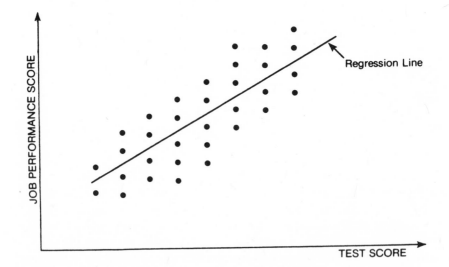

FIGURE 1. A hypothetical scatterplot showing the relationship between test scores and job performance scores in a validation study.

What, then, is the meaning of the differences in mean test scores for different ethnic groups? Are they evidence of hereditary differences, or could they be the result of cultural disadvantage? These questions cannot be answered on the basis of the evidence cited here. Studies relevant to test fairness start at the time of taking the test and predict forward in time. Thus, the finding of test fairness means that a test score represents the person's ability at the moment that the test is taken and predicts future events that depend on ability at that moment. On the other hand, questions about the origins of test differences start from the moment of taking the test and work backward in time. Thus, evidence bearing on heredity must come from different sources. For example, the evidence from twin studies suggests that heredity accounts for, at most, 75% of the variance in adult test scores. This finding suggests that adult ability levels can be far distant from the level of hereditary potential. On the other hand, adult ability levels are very resistant to training (see, for example, USES, 1970, pp. 275–276). Thus, the environmental effects on ability scores may not be cultural. Noncultural environmental factors that may be important include chemical disturbances during embryonic development; trauma, disease, and maturational disturbance during childhood; and trauma and disease during adult life. Some of these may be related to cultural lifestyle. For example, poor people get poorer prenatal care than rich people. Thus, even if the differences between ethnic groups are due to environmental factors, those factors may not be cultural in the psychological sense.

ETHICAL AND STATISTICAL IMPLICATIONS OF VARIOUS DEFINITIONS OF TEST BIAS

In the last decade, there has been a series of articles devoted to the question of the fairness of employment and educational tests to minority groups (Cleary, 1968; Darlington, 1971; Thorndike, 1971). Although each of these articles came to an ethical conclusion, the basis for that ethical judgment was left unclear. If there were only one ethically defensible position, then this would pose no problem. But such is not the case. The articles that we review have a second common feature. Each writer attempts to establish a definition on purely statistical grounds, that is, on a basis that is independent of the content of test and criterion and that makes no explicit assumption about the causal explanation of the statistical relations found. We argue that this approach merely makes the substantive consider-ations implicit rather than explicit.

In this section, we first describe three distinct ethical positions. We next examine five statistical definitions of test fairness in detail and show how each is based on one of these ethical positions. Finally, we examine the technical, social, and legal advantages and disadvantages of the various ethical positions and statistical definitions.

THREE ETHICAL POSITIONS

Unqualified Individualism

The classic American definition of an objective advancement policy is giving the job to the person "best qualified to serve." Couched in the language of institutional selection procedures, this means that an organization should use whatever information it pos-sesses to make a scientifically valid prediction of each individual's performance and should always select those with the highest pre-dicted performance. From this point of view, there are two ways in which an institution can act unethically. First, an institution may knowingly fail to use an available, more valid predictor; for example, it may select on the basis of appearance rather than scores on a valid ability test. Second, it may knowingly fail to use a more valid predic-tion equation based on its available information; for example, it may administer a more difficult literacy test to blacks than to whites and then use a cutoff score for both groups that assumes that they both took the same test. In particular, if, in fact, race, sex, or ethnic group membership were a valid predictor of performance in a given situ-ation over and above the effects of other measured variables, then the unqualified individualist would be ethically bound to use such a predictor.

Quotas

Most corporations and educational institutions are creatures of the state or city in which they function. Thus, it has been argued that they are ethically bound to act in a way that is "politically appropri-ate" to their location. In particular, in a city whose population is 45% black and 55% white, any selection procedure that admits any other ratio of blacks and whites is "politically biased" against one group or the other. That is, any politically well-defined group has the "right" to ask and receive its "fair share" of any desirable product or position that is under state control. These fair-share quotas may be based on population percentages or on other factors irrelevant to the predicted future performance of the selectees (Darlington, 1971; Thorndike, 1971).

Qualified Individualism

There is one variant of individualism that deserves separate discussion. This position notes that America is constitutionally opposed to discrimination on the basis of race, religion, national origin, or sex. A qualified individualist interprets this constitutional precept as an ethical imperative to refuse to use such qualities as race or sex as a predictor even if it were, in fact, scientifically valid to do so. Suppose, for example, that race were a valid predictor of some criterion; that is, assume that the mean difference between the races on the criterion is greater than would be predicted on the basis of the best measures of ability available. This would mean that the use of race in conjunction with the ability test would increase the multiple correlation with the criterion. That is, prediction would be better if separate regression lines were used for blacks and whites. To the unqualified individualist, on the other hand, failure to use race as a predictor would be unethical and discriminatory because it would result in a less accurate prediction of the future performance of applicants and would "penalize" or underpredict the performance of individuals from one of the applicant groups. The qualified individualist recognizes this fact but is ethically bound to use one overall regression line for ability and to ignore race. Thus, the qualified individualist relies solely on measures of ability and motivation to perform the job (e.g., scores on valid aptitude and achievement tests, assessment of past work experiences, and so on).

DEFINITION OF DISCRIMINATION

There is one very important point to be made before leaving this issue: The word *discriminate* is *not* ambiguous. Qualified individualists interpret the word *discriminate* to mean "treat differently." Thus, they will not treat blacks and whites differently even if such treatment is statistically warranted. However, unqualified individualists also refuse to discriminate, and they use a different definition of that word. Unqualified individualists interpret *discriminate* to mean "treat unfairly." Thus, unqualified individualists would say that if there is, in fact, a valid difference between the races that is not accounted for by available ability tests, then to refuse to recognize this difference is to penalize the higher performing of the two groups. Finally, the person who adheres to quotas will also refuse to discriminate, but she or he will use yet a third definition of that word. The person who endorses quotas interprets *discriminate* to mean "select a higher proportion of persons from one group than from the other group." Thus, the adherents of all three ethical positions accept a constitutional ban against discrimination, but they differ in their views of what the ban is and how it is to be put into effect.

THREE ATTEMPTS TO DEFINE TEST FAIRNESS STATISTICALLY

In this section, we briefly review three attempts to arrive at a strictly statistical criterion for a fair or unbiased test. For ease of presentation, the discussion uses a comparison of blacks and whites. However, the reader should bear in mind that other demographic classifications, such as social class or sex, could be substituted with no loss of generality.

The Cleary Definition

Cleary & Hilton (1968) defined a test as being unbiased only if the regression lines for blacks and whites are identical. The reason is brought out in Figure 4, which shows a hypothetical case in which

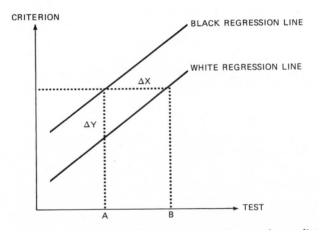

FIGURE 4. A case in which the white regression line underpredicts black performance.

the regression line for blacks lies above the line for whites and is parallel to it. Consider a white and a black subject, each of whom has a score of A on the test. If the white regression line were used to predict both criterion scores, then the black applicant would be underpredicted by an amount, Δy, the difference between his expected score's making use of the fact that he is black and the expected score assigned by the white regression line. Actually, in this situation, in order for a white subject to have the same expected performance as a black whose score is A, the white subject must have a score of B.

That is, if the white regression line underpredicts black performance, then a white and a black are truly equal in their expected performance only if the white's test score is higher than the black's by an amount related to the amount of underprediction. Similarly, if the white regression line always overpredicts black performance, than a black subject has equal expected performance only if his test score is higher than the corresponding white subject's score by an amount related to the amount of overprediction. Thus, if the regression lines for blacks and whites are not equal, then each person will receive a statistically valid predicted criterion score only if separate regression lines are used for the two races. If the two regression lines have exactly the same slope, then the use of regression lines can be accomplished by predicting performance from two separate regression equations or from a multiple-regression equation with test score and race as the predictors. If the slopes are not equal, then either separate equations must be used or the multiple-regression equation must be expanded by the usual product term for moderator variables. Thus, we can view Cleary's definition of an unbiased test as an attempt to rule out disputes between qualified and unqualified individualism.

If the predictors available to an institution are unbiased in Cleary's sense, then the question of whether to use race as a predictor does not arise. But if the predictors are *biased,* the recommended use of separate regression lines is clearly equivalent to using race as a predictor of performance. Thus, although Cleary may show a preference for tests that meet the requirements of both unqualified and qualified individualism, in the final analysis her position is one of unqualified individualism.

A Cleary-defined unbiased test is ethically acceptable to those who advocate quotas only under very special circumstances. In addition to identical regression lines, blacks and whites must have equal means and equal standard deviations on the test, which implies equal means and standard deviations on the performance measure. Furthermore, the proportion of black and white applicants must be the same as their proportion in the relevant population. These are conditions that rarely occur.

Linn and Werts (1971) have pointed out an additional problem in Cleary's definition, the problem of defining the fairness when using less than perfectly reliable tests. Suppose that a perfectly reliable measure of intelligence were, in fact, an unbiased predictor in Cleary's sense. Because perfect reliability is unattainable in practice, the test used in practice will contain a certain amount of error variance. Will the imperfect test be unbiased in terms of the regression equations for blacks and whites? If black applicants have lower mean IQs than white applicants, then the regression lines for the imperfect test will *not* be equal. This situation is illustrated in Figure 5. In this figure, we see that if an imperfect test is used, then that test produces the double regression line of a biased test in which the white regression line overpredicts black performance; that is, by Cleary's definition, the imperfect test is biased against whites in favor of blacks.

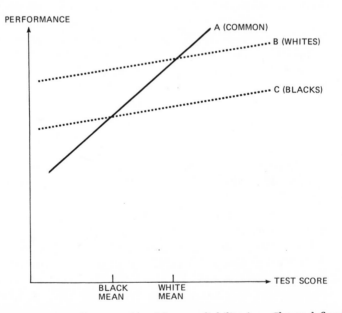

FIGURE 5. Regression artifacts produced by unreliability in a Cleary-defined "unbiased" test. A is the common regression line for a perfectly reliable test. B and C are the regression lines for whites and blacks, respectively, for a test of reliability .50.

Cleary's critics have questioned whether the failure to attain perfect reliability (impossible under any circumstances) should be adequate grounds for labeling a test as biased. But suppose we first consider this question from a different viewpoint. Suppose there were only one ethnic group—whites, for example. Assume that Bill has a true ability level of 115 and Jack has a ability of 110. If ability is a valid predictor of performance in this situation, then Bill has the higher expected performance; and if a perfectly reliable test is used, Bill will invariably be admitted ahead of Jack. But suppose that the reliability of the ability test is only .50. Then, each of the two obtained scores will vary randomly from their true values, and there is some probability that Bill's will be randomly low when Jack's is randomly high; that is, there is some probability that Jack will be admitted ahead of Bill. If the standard deviation of the observed ability scores is 15, then the difference between their observed scores has a mean of 5 and a standard deviation of 21. The probability of a negative difference is then .41. Thus, the probability that Bill will be admitted ahead of Jack drops from 1.00 to .59.

This imperfect test is, in fact, sharply biased against better qualified applicants. This bias, however, is not directly racial or cultural in nature. It takes on the appearance of a racial bias only because the proportion of better qualified applicants is higher in the white group. Thus, the bias created by random error works against more applicants in the white group, and thus, on balance, the test is biased against that group as a whole. But at the individual level, such a test is no more biased against a well-qualified white than against a well-qualified black. The question, then, is whether Cleary's (1968) definition is defective in some sense in labeling this situation as biased. If so, it may perhaps be desirable to modify the definition to apply only to bias beyond that expected on the basis of test reliability alone.

While on the topic of reliability, we should note that as the reliability approaches .00, the test becomes a random selection device and is hence utterly reprehensible to an individualist of either stripe. On the other hand, a totally unreliable test would select blacks in proportion to the number of black applicants and hence might well select in proportion to population quotas. Ironically, the argument that tests are biased against blacks because they are not perfectly reliable is not only false; it is exactly opposite to the truth.

Let us consider in detail the comparison of whites and blacks on an imperfectly reliable test. We first remark that it is a fact that, on the average, whites with a given score have a higher mean performance than do blacks who have that same score. Thus, the use of a single regression line will, in fact, mean that whites near the cutoff will be denied admission in favor of blacks who will, on the average, not perform as well. Cleary's (1968) definition would clearly label such a situation biased. Furthermore, in this situation, the partial correlation between race and performance with observed ability held constant is not zero. Thus, race makes a contribution to the multiple regression because, with an imperfect ability test, race is, in fact, a valid predictor of performance after ability is partialed out. That is, from the point of view of unqualified individualism, the failure to use race as a second predictor is unethical. If the test is used with only one regression line, then the predictors are, in fact, biased against whites. If two regression lines are used, then each person is being considered solely on the basis of expected performance.

Thus, in summary, we feel that Cleary's critics have raised a false issue. To use an imperfect predictor is to blur valid differences between applicants, and an imperfect test is thus, to the extent of the unreliability, biased against people or groups of people who have high true scores on the predictor. Thus, from the point of view of an unqualified individualist, a test is indeed biased. On the other hand, a qualified individualist would object to this conclusion. Use of separate regression lines is statistically optimal because the imperfect test does not account for all the real differences on the true scores. But the qualified individualist is ethically prohibited from using race as a predictor and therefore can employ only a single regression equation. He can, however, console himself with the fact that the bias in the test is not specifically racial in nature. And, of course, he can attempt to raise the reliability of the test.

In practice, unreliability is a minor issue. Only a small portion of the difference between regression lines for single tests is due to less-than-perfect reliability. Most of the difference is due to missing abilities. If the appropriate ability composite is used for prediction, then the composite has a higher reliability than single tests. Often, the reliability of the composite score is so high as to render the effect of unreliability undetectable (especially in the face of the massive sampling error present in most local validation studies).

Thorndike's Definition

Thorndike (1971) began his discussion with the simplifying assumption that the slope of the two regression lines is equal. There are then three cases. If the regression lines are identical, then the test satisfies Cleary's (1968) definition. If the regression line for blacks is higher than that for whites (as in Figure 4), then Thorndike would label the test "obviously unfair to the minor group." On the other hand, if the regression line for whites is higher than that for blacks, then he would *not* label the test as obviously unfair to whites. Instead, he made an extended argument that the use of two regression lines would be unfair to blacks. Clearly, there must be an inconsistency in his argument, and indeed, we ultimately show this.

Thorndike noticed that whereas using two regression lines is the only ethical solution from the point of view of unqualified individualism, it need not be required by an ethic of quotas. In particular, if the black regression line is lower, then blacks will normally show a lower mean on both predictor and criterion. Suppose that blacks are one standard deviation lower on both and that validity is .50 for both groups. If we knew the actual criterion scores and set the cutoff at the white mean on the criterion, then 50% of the whites and 16% of the blacks would be selected. If the white regression line were used for both groups, then 50% of the whites and 16% of the blacks would be selected. However, if blacks are selected by use of the black regression line, then, because the black regression line lies .5 standard deviations below the white regression line, blacks will have to have a larger score to be selected (i.e., a cutoff two sigmas, instead of one, above the black mean) and hence, fewer blacks will be selected. Thus, if the predictor score is used with two regression lines, then 50% of the whites but only 2% of the blacks will be admitted. Thorndike argued that this selection process would be unfair to blacks as a group. He then recommended that we throw out individualism as an ethical imperative and replace it with a specific kind of quota. The quota that he defined as the fair share for each group is the percentage of that group that would have been selected had the criterion itself been used or had the test had perfect validity. In the above situation, for example, Thorndike's definition would consider the selection procedure fair only if 16% of the black applicants were selected.

What Thorndike rediscovered has long been known to biologists: Bayes's law is cruel. If one of two equally reproductive species has a probability of .49 for survival to reproduce and the other species has a probability of .50, then ultimately the first species will become extinct. Maximization in probabilistic situations is usually much more extreme than most individuals expect (Edwards & Phillips, 1964).

What, then, was Thorndike's contradiction? He labeled the case in which the black regression line was higher than the white line as "obviously unfair to the minor group." But his basis for this state-ment was presumably unqualified individualism. In effect, he said that if blacks perform higher than whites over and above the effects of measured ability, then this fact should be recognized and blacks should have a correspondingly higher probability of being selected. That is, if the black regression line is higher, then separate regression lines should be used. But if separate regression lines are used, then the number of whites selected would ordinarily be drastically reduced. In fact, the number of whites selected would be far below the Thorndike-defined fair share of slots. The mathematics of unequal regression lines (i.e., of Bayes's law) is the same for a high black regression line as for a high white regression line: The use of a single regression line lowers the validity of the prediction but tends to yield selection quotas that are much closer to the quotas that would have resulted from clairvoyance (i.e., much closer to the selec-tion quotas that would have resulted had a perfectly valid test been available). Thus, Thorndike's inconsistency lies in his failure to apply his definition to the case in which the white regression line under-predicts black performance. The fact that, because of a technicality (i.e., racial equality on the performance measure), this effect would not manifest itself in Thorndike's (1971) Case 1 should not be allowed to obscure this general principle.

If only one regression line is to be used, then a test will meet the Thorndike quotas only if the mean difference between the groups in standard score units is the same for both predictor and criterion. For this to hold for a Cleary-defined unbiased test, the validity of the test must be 1.00—a heretofore unattainable outcome.

Once Thorndike's position is shown to be a form of quota setting, then the obvious question is, Why his quotas? After all, the statement that 16% of the blacks can perform at the required level would not apply to the blacks actually selected and is in that sense irrelevant. In any event, it seems highly unlikely that this method of setting quo-tas would find support among those adherents of quotas who focus on population proportions as the proper basis of quota determina-tion. Thorndikean quotas would generally be smaller than popula-tion-based quotas. On the other hand, Thorndike-determined quotas may have considerable appeal to large numbers of Americans as a compromise between the requirements of individualism and the social need to upgrade the employment levels of minority group members.

There is another question that must be raised concerning Thorn-dike's position: Is it ethically compatible with the use of imperfect selection devices? We will show that Thorndike's selection rule is contradictory to present test usage, that is, that, according to Thorndike, we will fill N vacancies not by taking the top N applicants but by making a much more complicated selection. Consider the following example: Assume that one is using a test score of 50 ($\overline{X}$ = 50, SD = 10, r_{XY} = .50) as a cutoff and that the data show that 50% of those with a test score of 50 will be successful. Applicants with a score of 49 would all be rejected, though for r_{XY} = .50 about 48% of them would have succeeded had they been selected (a score of 49 is $-.1$ sigmas on X and implies an average score of $-.05$ on the criterion with a sigma of .87). Thus, applicants with a test score of 49 can correctly state, "If we were all admitted, then 48% of us would succeed. Therefore, according to Thorndike, 48% of us should be admitted. Yet, we were all denied. Thus, you have been unfair to our group, those people with scores of 49 on the test." That is, strictly speaking, Thorndike's ethical position precludes the use of any predictor cutoff in selection, no matter how reasonably determined. Instead, from each predictor category one must select the percentage that would fall above the criterion cutoff if the test were perfectly valid. For example, if one wanted to select 50% of the applicants and the validity were .60, then one would have to take 77% of those who lie 1 SD above the mean, 50% of those within 1 SD of the mean, and 23% of those who fall 1 SD below the mean. And Thorndike's definition could be interpreted, of course, as requiring the use of even smaller intervals of test scores.

There are several problems with this procedure. First, one must attempt to explain to applicants with objectively higher qualifications why they were not admitted—a rather difficult task and, from the point of view of individualism, an unethical one. Second, the general level of performance will be considerably lower than it would have been had the usual cutoff been used. In the previous example, the mean performance of the top 50% on the predictor would be .48 standard score units, whereas the mean performance of those selected by the Thorndike ethic would be .29. That is, in this example, using Thorndike's quotas has the effect of cutting the usefulness of the predictor by about 60%.

One possible reply to this criticism would be that Thorndike's definition need not be interpreted as requiring application to all definable groups. The definition is to be applied only to "legitimate minority groups" and would exclude groups defined solely by obtained score on the predictor. If agreement could be reached that, for example, blacks, Chicanos, and Indians are the only recognized minority groups, the definition might be workable. But such an agreement is highly unlikely. On what grounds could we fairly exclude Poles, Italians, and Greeks, for example?

Perhaps an even more telling criticism can be made. In a college or university, performance below a certain level means a bitter tragedy for a student. In an employment situation, job failure can often be equally damaging to self-esteem. In the selection situation described above, the percentage of failure would be 25% if the top half were admitted, but one-third if a Thorndikean admission rule were used. Furthermore, most of the increase in failures comes precisely from the poor-risk admissions. Their failure rate is two-thirds. Thus, in the end, a Thorndikean rule may be even more unfair to people with low ability than to people with high ability.

Darlington's Definition

Darlington's (1971) first step was a restatement of the Cleary (1968) and Thorndike (1971) criteria for a "culturally" fair test in terms of correlation rather than regression. Let X be the predictor, Y the criterion, and C the indicator variable for culture (i.e., $C = 1$ for whites, $C = 0$ for blacks). He made the empirically plausible assumption that the groups have equal standard deviations on both predictor and criterion and that the validity of the predictor is the same for both groups (hence, parallel regression lines). Darlington then correctly noted that Cleary's (1968) criterion for a fair test could be stated,

$$r_{CY \cdot X} = 0$$

That is, there is no criterion difference between the races beyond that produced by their difference on X (if any). If all people are selected by means of a single regression line, then Thorndikean quotas are guaranteed by Darlington's Definition 2, that is,

$$r_{CX} = r_{CY}$$

That is, the racial difference on the predictor must equal the racial difference on the criterion in standard score units. However, if people are selected by means of multiple regression or separate regression lines, then this equation would not be correct. Instead there are two alternate conditions:

$$R_{Y \cdot CX} = 1$$
$$r_{CY} = 0$$

That is, if *separate* regression lines are used, then the percentages selected would match Thorndike's quotas only if the test had perfect validity or if there were no differences between the groups on the criterion.

Darlington then attacked the Cleary definition on two very questionable bases: (1) the reliability problem raised by Linn and Werts (1971), which was discussed in depth above, and (2) the contention that race itself would be a Cleary-defined fair test. Actually, if race were taken as the test, then there would be no within-groups variance on that predictor and hence no regression lines to compare. Thus, Cleary's definition cannot be applied to the case in which race itself is used as the predictor test. The nontrivial equivalent of this is a test whose sole contribution to predicting Y is the race difference on the mean of X, but for such a test, the regression lines are perfectly horizontal and grossly discrepant. That is, in a real situation, Cleary's definition would rule that a purely racial test is biased.

Darlington's Definition 3 and Cole's Argument

Darlington (1971) proposed a third definition of test fairness, his Definition 3. This definition did not attract a great deal of attention until Cole (1972, 1973) offered a persuasive argument in its favor. We first present Darlington's definition, his justification of it, and our critique of that justification. We then consider Cole's argument.

If X is the test and Y is the criterion, and if C, the variable of culture, is scored 0 for blacks and 1 for whites, then Darlington's Definition 3 can be written as follows: The test is fair if

$$r_{XC \cdot Y} = 0$$

His argument for this definition went as follows: The ability to perform well on the criterion is a composite of many abilities, as is the ability to do well on the test. If the partial correlation between test and race with the criterion partialed out is not zero, then it means that there is a larger difference between the races on the test than would be predicted by their difference on the criterion. Hence, the test must be tapping abilities that are not relevant to the criterion but on which there are racial differences. Thus, the test is discriminatory.

Note that Darlington's argument makes use of assumptions about causal inference. If those assumptions about causality are, in fact, false, then his interpretation of the meaning of the partial correlation is no longer valid. Are his assumptions so plausible that they need not be backed up with evidence? Consider the time ordering of his argument. He is partialing the criterion from the predictor. In the case of college admissions, this means that he is calculating the correlation between race and entrance exam score, with grade point average (GPA) four years later being held constant. This is looking at the causal influence of the future on the past and is valid only in the context of very special theoretical assumptions. The definition would, in fact, be inappropriate even in the context of a concurrent validation study because concurrent validities are typically derived only as convenient estimates of predictive validity. Thus, even when there is no time lag between predictor and criterion measurement, one is operating implicitly within the predictive validity model.

Other problems with Darlington's argument will be brought out in our general discussion relating to statistical models and causal processes.

Darlington's Definition 3 received little attention until a novel and persuasive argument in its favor was advanced by Cole (1973). Her argument was this: Consider those applicants who would be "successful" if selected. Should not such individuals have equal probability of being selected regardless of racial or ethnic group membership? Under the assumption of equal slopes and standard deviations for the two groups, the answer to her question is in the affirmative only if the two regression lines of the test on criterion are the same (and hence, $r_{XC.Y} = 0$). That is, Cole's definition is the same as Cleary's, with the roles of the predictor and the criterion reversed. However, this similarity of statement does not imply compatibility—just the reverse. If there are differences between the races on either test or criterion, then the two definitions are compatible only if the test validity is perfect, so the two definitions almost invariably conflict.

Although Cole's argument sounds reasonable and has a great deal of intuitive appeal, it is flawed by a hidden assumption. Her definition assumes that differences between groups in probability of acceptance, given later success if selected, are due to discrimination based on group membership. Suppose that the two regression lines of criterion performance as a function of the test are equal (i.e., the test is Cleary-defined unbiased). If a black who would have been successful on the criterion is rejected and a white who fails the criterion is accepted, this need not imply discrimination. The black is not rejected because he is black but because he got a low score on the ability test. That is, the black is rejected because his ability at the time of the predictor test was indistinguishable from that of a group of other people (of both races) who, on the average, have low scores on the criterion.

To make this point more strongly, we note that according to Cole's definition of a fair test, it is unethical to use a test of less-than-perfect validity. To illustrate, consider the use of a valid ability test to predict academic achievement in any one group—say, whites—applying for university admission. If the university decides to take only the people in the top half of the distribution of test scores, then applicants in the bottom half, acting under Cole's definition, may well file suit charging discriminatory practice. According to Cole, an applicant who would be successful if selected should have the same probability of being selected regardless of group membership. That is, among the applicants who would have been successful had they been selected, there are two groups. One group of applicants has a probability of selection of 1.00 because their scores on the entrance exam are higher than the cutoff point. The other group of potentially successful applicants has a selection probability of .00 because their exam scores are lower than the cutoff point. According to Cole, we should ask: Why should a person who would be successful be denied a college berth merely because he had a low test score? After all, it's success that counts, not test scores. But the fact is that for any statistical procedure that does not have perfect validity, there must always be incorrect prediction of low performance for some people; that is, there will always be successful people whose predictor scores were down with the generally unsuccessful people instead of up with the generally successful people (and vice versa). In that sense, anything less than a perfect test will always be "unfair" to the potentially high-achieving people who were rejected. It can be seen that lack of perfect validity functions in exactly the same way as test unreliability, discussed earlier.

As noted earlier in the case of Thorndike's definition, this problem could be partly overcome in practice if social consensus restrictions could be put on the defining of bona fide minority groups. But given the almost unlimited number of potentially definable social groups, it is unlikely that social or legal consensus would be reached limiting the application of this definition to blacks, Chicanos, American Indians, and a few other groups.

Basically, Cole noted the same fact that Thorndike noted: In order for a test with less-than-perfect validity to be fair to individuals, the test must be unfair to groups. In particular, in our example, the group of applicants who score below average on the test will have none of their members selected despite the fact that some of them would have shown successful performance if selected. The test is thus unfair to this group. However, it is fair to each individual because each is selected or rejected based on the best possible estimate of his or her future performance. It is perhaps important to note that this is not a problem produced by the use of psychological tests; it is a problem inherent in reality. Society and its institutions must make selection decisions. They are unavoidable. Elimination of valid psychological tests usually means their replacement with devices or methods with less validity (e.g., the interview), thus further increasing the unfairness to individuals and/or groups.

Darlington's Definition 4

The fourth concept of test bias discussed by Darlington (1971) defines a test as fair only if $r_{cx} = 0$. That is, by this definition, a test would be unfair if it showed any mean difference between the races at all, regardless of the size of the difference that might exist on some criterion that is to be predicted. If the same cutoff score is to be used for blacks and whites, then this statistical criterion corresponds to the use of population-based quotas. If separate regression lines and hence separate cutoff scores are to be used, then mean differences on the test are irrelevant to the issue of quotas.

A Fifth Definition of Test Fairness

After defining and discussing four different statistical models of test fairness, Darlington (1971) turned to the commonly occurring prediction situation in which there is a difference favoring whites on both the test and the criterion and the black regression equation falls below that for whites. This situation is shown in Figure 6A. Noting that the use of separate regression equations (or the equivalent, the use of multiple-regression equations with race as a predictor), as required by Cleary's 1968 definition, would admit or select only an extremely small percentage of blacks, Darlington introduced his concept of the "culturally optimun" test. Darlington suggested that admissions officers at a university be asked to consider two potential graduating seniors, one white and the other black, and to indicate how much higher the white's GPA would have to be before the two candidates would be "equally desirable for selection" (p. 79). This number is symbolized K and given a verbal label, such as *racial adjustment coefficient*. Then, in determining the fairness of the test, K is first subtracted from the actual criterion scores (GPAs) of each of

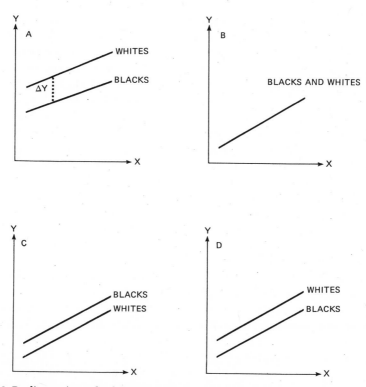

FIGURE 6. Darlington's method (1971) of altering the data to define a "culturally optimal" test. (A) The original test. (B) The altered data when $K = \Delta Y$. (C) The altered data when $K > \Delta Y$. (D) The altered data when $K < \Delta Y$.

the white subjects. If these altered data satisfy Cleary's 1968 definition of a fair test, the test is considered culturally optimum.

Figure 6 illustrates the geometrical meaning of Darlington's doctored criterion. If the admissions officer chooses a value of K that is equal to ΔY in Figure 6A, then the altered data will appear as in Figure 6B; that is, there will be a single common regression line and the test as it stands will be culturally optimum. If, however, an overzealous admissions officer chooses a value of K greater than ΔY, the doctored data will appear as in Figure 6C; that is, the test will appear to be biased against blacks according to Cleary's definition and will thus not be culturally optimum. Similarly, should an uncooperative admissions officer select a value of $K < \Delta Y$, the altered data would look like Figure 6D and would thus appear to be biased against whites by Cleary's criterion and hence show the test *not* to be culturally optimum.

Thus, a cynic might well assume that in practice Darlington's definition of *culturally optimum* would simply lead to the selection of a value of K that would make whatever test was being used appear to be culturally optimum. But suppose that admissions officers were willing to choose K without looking at the effect that their choices would have on the data. How, then, are the nonoptimum tests to be used? One might suppose that, because Darlington was eager to doctor the criterion data, he would also be willing to doctor the predictor data as well. For example, the situation in Figure 6D could be remedied by simply subtracting a suitable constant from each black's test score. However, Darlington permitted the doctoring only of criterion scores; he was opposed to doctoring the predictor scores.

If the predictor scores are not manipulated by a direct mathematical rescoring, then the same effect must be obtained by constructing a new test. Consider, then, the situation shown in Figure 6D. The new test must have the ultimate effect of giving blacks lower scores than they would have got on the original test, while leaving white scores untouched. Thus, the test constructor is in the awkward position of adding items that are biased against blacks in order to make the test fair!

Darlington was not unaware of this problem. He would not label the test fair unless the two regression lines using the doctored criterion were equal. But what if we do not yet have a culturally fair test? What did Darlington recommend as an interim procedure for using an unfair test? He stated that the unfair test can be *used* in a fair way if it is combined with race in a multiple-regression equation based on the doctored criterion (i.e., if separate, doctored regression lines are used). Thus, he used the unequal doctored regression lines in much the same way as Cleary recommended use of the unequal regression lines for undoctored regression lines. What does this procedure come to, in which the administrator has chosen a value of K that is too low to label the existing test culturally optimum? If the doctored regression line for blacks is still below the doctored regression line for whites, then the beta weight for blacks will still be negative, and the multiple-regression equation will implicitly subtract that weight from each black's score.

What would an administrator do if this were pointed out to her or him? We believe that she or he would react by increasing the value of K to make the doctored regression lines equal. That is, we think that the actual consequence of Darlington's recommendation for the fair use of an unfair test would be to further increase the likelihood of using a value of K that makes the doctored regression lines equal. That is, we believe that Darlington's definition of *fair use*, like his definition of *fair test*, is most likely to result in a harried administrator's choosing K to eliminate the difference between the doctored regression lines. If we are right, then Darlington's recommendations for fair use will lead in practice to simply labeling existing tests culturally optimum.

What is the upshot of Darlington's suggestion? From a mathematical point of view, adding a constant to or subtracting it from the criterion is exactly equivalent to adding constants to or subtracting them from the predictor, and this, in turn, is equivalent to using different cutoff scores for the two groups. Thus, in the last analysis, Darlington's method is simply an esoteric way of setting quotas, and hence, the expense of constructing culturally optimum tests to set quotas is a waste of time and money.

Variations and Decision Theory

There have been a number of variations on the previous themes. These are summarized in Novick and Peterson (1976), who eventually opted for Darlington's last definition. However, they explicitly recognized that new tests need not be written because differential cutoff procedures do the same thing. They called their position the "decision theory" position because they linked their differential evaluation of people to the differential evaluation of outcomes in a decision-theoretic scheme. A similar position was adopted by Cronbach (1976). Darlington (1978) even claimed that this decision-theoretic approach was a reconciliation of the argument about quotas versus merit. However, Hunter and Schmidt (1978) pointed out that decision theory merely restates the problem in an esoteric form. Rather than arguing that blacks deserve a certain proportion of the admissions or jobs, one must argue that a black person is worth 2 (or 1.8 or 2.2 or . . .) times as much as a white person. Indeed, one difficulty of the decision theory approach is the difficulty of computing the exact ratio of differential worth required to yield population quotas as the desired result.

Statistical Models versus Causal Processes

We believe that statistical equations cannot be considered in the abstract. The ethical implications of a given statistical result depend on the substantive meaning of that result, and that meaning depends on a causal theory linking the variables to the way in which race enters the relationship. We will now consider several examples in detail. Across the set of examples, we will show weaknesses in all of the definitions, though the Darlington–Cole definition fares worst.

First, consider a pro football coach attempting to evaluate the rookies who have joined the team as a result of the college draft. Because the players have all come from different schools, there are great differences in the kind and the quality of training that they have had. Therefore, the coach cannot rely on how well they play their positions at that moment in time; they will undergo considerable change as they learn the ropes over the next few months. What the coach would like to know is exactly what their athletic abilities are without reference to the way they've learned to play to date. Suppose he decides to rely solely on the 40-yard dash as an indicator of football ability, that is, as a selection test. It is possible that he would then find that he was selecting a much larger percentage of blacks than he had expected, using his judgment of current performance. Would this mean that the test is discriminatory against whites? That depends on the explanation for this outcome. Consider the defensive lineman on a passing play. His ability to reach the quarterback before he throws the ball depends not only on the speed necessary to go around the offensive lineman opposing him but also on sufficient arm strength to throw the offensive lineman to one side. Assume, for the sake of this example, that blacks are faster, on the average, than whites but that there are no racial differences in upper body strength. Because the 40-yard dash represents only speed and does not measure upper body strength, it cannot meet Darlington's substantive assumptions. That is, the 40-yard dash taps only the abilities on which there are racial differences and does not assess those that show no such differences.

How does the 40-yard dash behave statistically? If speed and upper body strength were the only factors in football ability, and if the 40-yard dash were a perfect index of speed, then the correlations would satisfy $r_{YC \cdot X} = 0$. That is, by Cleary's definition, the 40-yard dash would be an unbiased test. Because $r_{YC \cdot X} = 0$, $r_{XC \cdot Y}$ cannot be zero, and hence, according to Darlington's definition, the 40-yard dash is culturally unfair (i.e., biased against whites). (Because the number of whites selected would be less than the Thorndike quota, Thorndike, too, would call the test biased.) If the coach is aware that upper body strength is a key variable and is deliberately avoiding the use of a measure of upper body strength in a multiple-regression equation, then the charge that the coach is deliberately selecting blacks would seem quite reasonable. But suppose that the nature of the missing predictor (i.e., upper body strength) is completely unknown. Would it then be fair to charge the coach with using an unfair test?

At this point, we should note a related issue raised by Linn and Werts (1971). They, too, considered the case in which the criterion is affected by more than one ability, one of which is not assessed by the test. If the test assessed only verbal ability and the only racial differences were on verbal ability, then the situation would be like that described in the preceding paragraph: The test would be unbiased by the Cleary definition, but unfair according to Darlington's Definition 3. However, if there are also racial differences on the unmeasured ability, then the test is not unbiased by Cleary's definition. For example, if blacks are also lower, on the average, in numerical ability and numerical ability is not assessed by the entrance test, then the black regression line and the test would be biased against whites by Cleary's definition. According to Darlington's Definition 3, on the other hand, the verbal ability test would be fair if, and only if, the racial difference on the numerical test were of exactly the same magnitude in standard score units as the difference on the verbal test. If the difference on the missing ability were less than the difference on the observed ability, then Darlington's definition would label the test unfair to blacks, whereas if the difference on the missing ability were larger than the difference on the observed ability, then the test would be unfair to whites. Furthermore, if the two abilities being considered were not the only causal factors in the determination of the criterion (i.e., if personality or financial difficulties were also correlated), then these statements would no longer hold. Rather, the fairness of the ability test under consideration would depend not only on the size of racial differences on the unknown ability, but on the size of racial differences on the other unknown causal factors as well. That is, according to Darlington's Definition 3, the fairness of a test cannot be related to the causal determination of the criterion until a perfect multiple-regression equation on known predictors has been achieved. That is, Darlington's definition can be statistically but not substantively evaluated in real situations.

For the purpose of illustration, we now consider a simplified theory of academic achievement in college. Suppose that the college entrance test were, in fact, a perfect measure of academic ability for high school seniors. Why is the validity not perfect? Consider three men of average ability. Sam meets and marries "Wonder Woman." She scrubs the floor, earns $200 a week, and worships the ground Sam walks on. Sam carries a B average. Bill dates from time to time, gets hurt a little, turns off on girls who like him once or twice, and generally has the average number of ups and downs. Bill carries a C average. Joe meets and marries "Wanda the Witch." She lies around the house, continually nags Joe about money, and continually reminds him that he is "sexually inadequate." As Joe spends more and more time at the local bar, his grades drop to a D average, and he is ultimately thrown out of school. In a nutshell, the theory of academic achievement that we wish to consider is this: Achievement equals ability plus luck, where luck is a composite of few or no money troubles, sexual problems, automobile accidents, deaths in the family, and so on. There are few known correlations between luck and ability and few known correlations between luck and personality, but for simplicity of exposition, let us assume that luck is completely independent of ability and personality. Then, luck in this theory is the component of variance in academic performance that represents the *situational* factors in performance that arise after the test is taken and during the college experience. Some of these factors are virtually unpredictable: just what woman he happens to sit beside in class, whether he arrives at the personnel desk before or after the opening for the ideal part-time job is filled, whether he gets a good adviser or a poor one, and so on. Some of these factors may be predicted: family financial support in case of financial crisis, probable income of spouse (if any), family pressure to continue in college in case of personal crisis, and so on. However, even those factors that may be predicted are potentialities and are not actually relevant unless other, nonpredictable events occur. Thus, there is inevitably a large random component to the situational factors in performance that is *not* measurement error, but that has the same effect as measurement error in that it sets an upper bound on the validity of any predictor test battery even if it includes biographical information on family income, stability, and the like.

According to this theory, a difference between the black and white regression lines (over and above the effect of test unreliability) indicates that blacks are more likely to have bad luck than are whites. Before going on to the statistical questions, we note that because we have assumed a perfect ability test, there can be no missing ability in the following discussion. And because we have assumed that nonability differences are solely determined by luck, the entity referred to as *motivation* is in this model simply the concrete expression of luck in terms of overt behavior. That is, in the present theory, *motivation* is assumed to be wholly determined by luck and hence already included in the regression equation.

Now, let us consider the statistical interpretations of the fairness of our hypothetical, perfectly valid (with respect to ability), and perfectly reliable test. Because on the average blacks are assumed to be unlucky as well as lower in ability, the racial difference in college achievement in this model will be greater than that predicted by ability alone, and hence the regression lines of college performance compared with ability will not be equal. The black regression line will be lower. Thus, according to Cleary, the test is biased against whites. According to Thorndike, the test may be approximately fair (perhaps slightly biased against blacks). According to Darlington, the test could be either fair or unfair: If the racial difference in luck were about the same in magnitude as the racial difference on the ability test, then the test would be fair; but if the race difference in luck were less than the difference on the ability test, then the test would be unfair to blacks. That is, the Darlington assessment of the fairness of the test would depend not on the validity of the test in assessing ability, but on the relative harshness of the personal-economic factors determining the amount of luck accorded the two groups. Darlington's statistical definition thus does not fit his substantive derivation in this context—unless one is willing to accept luck as an "ability" inherent to a greater extent in some applicants than in others.

The problem with Darlington's definition becomes even clearer if we slightly alter the theory of the above paragraph. Suppose that the world became more benign and that the tendency for blacks to have bad luck disappeared. Then, if we make the same assumption as above (i.e., a perfect test and our theory of academic achievement), the regression curves would be equal, and $r_{YC \cdot X} = 0$. Thus, according to Cleary's definition, the test would be unbiased against whites. Darlington's Definition 3 would then label the test unfair to blacks. This last statement is particularly interesting. In our theory, we have assumed that exactly the same ability lay at the base of performance on both the test and later GPA. Yet, it is not true in our theory that $r_{XC \cdot Y} = 0$. Thus, this example has shown that Darlington's substantive interpretation of $r_{XC \cdot Y}$ does not hold with our additional assumption (of a nonstatistical nature), and hence, his argument about the substantive justification of his definition is not logically valid.

We note in passing that this last example poses a problem for Cleary's definition as well as for Darlington's. If the difference between the regression lines were, in fact, produced by group differences in luck, then would it be proper to label the test biased? And if this model were correct, how many unqualified individualists would feel comfortable using separate regression lines to take into account the fact that blacks have a tougher life (on the average) and hence make poorer GPAs than their ability would predict? In the case of both definitions, this analysis points up the necessity of substantive models and considerations. Statistical analyses alone can obscure as much as they illuminate.

ETHICAL POSITIONS, STATISTICAL DEFINITIONS, AND PROBLEMS

In this section, we briefly relate each ethical position to its appropriate statistical operation and point out some of the advantages and disadvantages of each approach.

UNQUALIFIED INDIVIDUALISM

The ethical imperative of individualism is to apply to each person the prediction procedure that is most valid for that person. Thus, white performance should be predicted by the test that has maximum validity for whites. Black performance should be predicted by means of the test that has maximum validity for blacks. The person with the highest predicted criterion score is then selected. If there are differences in the regression lines, then separate regression lines would be used.

Empirical research has shown that most of the problems in this position cited by Hunter and Schmidt (1976) do not exist. Research has shown that validity is the same for all major ethnic groups. Thus, the test with maximum validity for whites is the test with maximum validity for blacks. Research has shown that regression lines have the same slope and that differences in intercepts vanish for composite ability scores (i.e., those with maximum validity). Thus, the unqualified individualist argues for the use of standard tests (i.e., ranking) in whatever combination is known to have optimal validity.

QUALIFIED INDIVIDUALISM

The qualified individualist argues for the predictor combination that maximizes validity, so long as race is not part of the predictive system. Hunter and Schmidt (1976) noted that such a choice could create severe logical problems if differences in test regression lines were found, as additional predictors could be indirect indicators of race. However, research has now shown that differences in regression lines are an artifact of considering tests one at a time. The regression lines become essentially identical once an optimally valid composite ability score is considered.

Given the cumulative research findings available today, there is no longer any separation between qualified and unqualified individualism that is empirically relevant. That is, although the positions can be separated philosophically, the empirical situations that would result in a difference in outcome do not occur.

QUOTAS

The main technical question for an adherent of quotas is, Whose? Once the quotas have been set, the only remaining ethical question is how to select from within each group. Although some would use random selection within groups, most would invoke individualism at this point. With this assumption, the optimal strategy for filling quotas can be stated: For each group, obtain predicted criterion performance using the test that has maximum validity for the given group. If the test with maximum validity for blacks is not the test with maximum validity for whites, then it is unethical to use the same test for both.

The major problem in a quota-based system is that the criterion performance of selectees as a whole can be expected to be considerably lower than in unqualified or even qualified individualism. In college selection, for example, the poor-risk blacks who are admitted by a quota are more likely to fail than are the higher scoring whites who are rejected because of the quota. Thus, in situations in which low-criterion performance carries a considerable penalty, being selected on the basis of quotas is a mixed blessing. Second, there is the effect on the institution. The greater the divergence between the quotas and the selection percentages based on actual expected performance, the greater the difference in mean performance in those selected. If lowered performance is met by increased rates of expulsion, then the institution is relatively unaffected, but (1) the quotas are undone, and (2) there is considerable anguish for those selected who don't make it. On the other hand, if the institution tries to adjust to the candidates selected by quotas, there may be great cost and inefficiency.

The situation in industry is even more complicated. First, low-ability workers are, on the average, the low-performance workers. If the organization fires low-performance workers, then the quotas are undone. If the poor-performance workers are kept on, then they become known as "affirmative action" workers. This approach is demoralizing for the poor worker and creates considerable resentment among the better workers, who view themselves as "carrying" the poor worker. There is also great cost for the high-performance black worker because there is no recognition that the high-ability black worker is there on merit.

Second, if higher positions within the organization are filled from within, then using lowered standards for minority workers at the entry level produces severe problems for later promotion. If promotion is done on the basis of high performance on the entry-level job, then merit promotion quickly produces an entry-level worker population that is heavily weighted with low-ability, low-performance workers. Thus, new high-ability hires (largely white) will be promoted ahead of low-performance workers who have been in the job for some time. This pattern may appear to be even more unfair than using merit hiring for the entry-level job in the first place.

Third, the promotion problem is even worse if the higher order jobs require more cognitive ability than the lower level job. Now, maximum validity promotion would call for the use of tests as well as performance as a basis for promotion. The dilemma of merit versus quotas is then moved en masse from entry-level hiring to promotion.

Fourth, there is the loss in productivity that results from hiring low-ability workers. As noted earlier, this loss in productivity must be paid for by the consumer, by the company in terms of reduced sales and a poorer competitive market position, and ultimately by minority workers in terms of reduced employment.

Concluding Remarks on Ethics

We have presented three ethical positions in regard to the use of tests or other selection devices for hiring, and we have shown that these positions are irreconcilable. We have also shown that various attempts to construct statistical definitions of "fairness" have been linked to these ethical positions rather than to scientific questions about the meaning of test scores. Thus, we feel that we have shown that none of these statistical procedures can be accepted as scientific definitions of fairness.

The problem in all these definitions is that they confuse two separate issues: the fairness of test scores with the fairness of racially or ethnically unbalanced work forces. The fairness of test scores is a scientific question that can be and has been answered by empirical study. Test scores are fair to minority groups; test scores are just as indicative of ability among minority applicants as among majority applicants. However, the question of how many minority workers should be hired is an ethical question and has no scientific resolution.

PRODUCTIVITY INCREASE VERSUS MINORITY HIRING RATES FOR FOUR STRATEGIES OF SELECTION USING TESTS

Because there are no differences in the slopes of regression lines for different ethnic groups, tests can always be scored so as to be consistent with any of the models of fair test use defined in the previous section. That is, by adding a certain number of points to the test score for each black applicant, the effective test score can be made to be "fair" by different definitions. The number of points to be added is least for the Cleary definition (Cleary, 1968), then higher for Thorndike (1971), higher yet for Darlington–Cole (Darlington, 1971; Cole, 1973), and highest of all for population quotas. These formulas are given in the appendix.

If tests can be scored to produce any desired definition of fairness, then one can mathematically calculate the consequences of such test use. We will calculate two important bases for evaluating different test-use models: the economic benefits in terms of increased average productivity and the minority hiring rate. The two aspects turn out to be negatively correlated. The Cleary model yields the highest productivity but the lowest minority hiring rate. Quotas maximize the minority hiring rate but minimize productivity. The trade-off between the two is quantified by these computations, though the resolution of the conflict must be settled by considerations beyond the computations.

The present section has two purposes. The first is to assess as accurately as possible on a continuous interval scale the utility loss that one can expect in practice in moving from the Cleary through the Thorndike and the Darlington models to the quota model of fairness. That there will be losses is known a priori. Tests meeting the Cleary definition provide maximum utility because the definition is based on a least-squares prediction of the criterion; Thorndike's definition moves away from this principle, and Darlington's definition even more so.

The second purpose of this section is to assess the impact of the four models on minority selection rates under varying conditions of overall selection ratio, validity, and minority base rate in the applicant pool, thus allowing direct comparison of gains in minority hiring rates with losses in selection utility. As noted previously, there has been increasing recognition by selection psychologists that the choice of a fairness model cannot satisfactorily be made solely on statistical bases; questions of social policy and social values necessarily enter into the choice (Cronbach, 1976; Hunter & Schmidt, 1976). In fact, some have recommended the application of decision-theoretic models, with explicit and potentially different utilities being assigned to minority and majority selection outcomes (Gross & Su, 1975; Novick & Peterson, 1976). If one is to intelligently weight social value considerations in this decision process, he or she must first understand the properties of competing models—specifically, a model's implications for minority selection rates and for selection utility.

METHOD

Assessment of Selection Utility

It has been demonstrated (Brogden, 1946; Cronbach & Gleser, 1965, Chap. 4) that gain in employee performance due to selection (assuming fixed jobs) is a direct linear function of test validity (r_{ZY}) *per se*, and not of r_{ZY}^2 (the coefficient of determination), or of

$$1 - \sqrt{1 - r_{ZY}^2} \text{ (the index of forecasting efficiency)}$$

The validity coefficient itself is the proportion of maximum utility attained, where maximum utility is what would be attained if, holding the selection ratio and the quality of the applicant pool constant, one could select on a perfectly valid test. Attained gain in utility is typically expressed as $\overline{Z}_Y$ of those selected, $\overline{Z}_Y$ (selectees). $\overline{Z}_Y$ (selectees) $= r_{XY}\overline{Z}_X$ (selectees). This gain is actually a difference score, and thus, on a ratio scale of performance, $\overline{Z}_Y$ (selectees) $= \overline{Z}_Y$ (selectees) $- \overline{Z}_Y$ (applicants). But $\overline{Z}_Y$ (applicants) $= 0$. (The z-score scale used is that of the total group.) In the terms of the economist, $\overline{Z}_Y$ (selectees) is the marginal utility of the selection test. This principle, however, holds only when X and Y are identically distributed (Brogden, 1946) and there is a single regression line for all subgroups. In subgroup validation studies, if X and Y are normally distributed within both groups and if the mean difference on X is not equal to the mean difference on Y, the composite distributions of X and Y differ in shape.

In addition, the regression lines for the two groups may differ (in this study, the intercepts are often unequal). Therefore, the usual equation for computing selection utility could not be used; instead, $\overline{Z}_Y$ (selectees) $- \overline{Z}_Y$ (applicants), the marginal utility, was computed directly by means of the procedure described in the Appendix. It should be noted that our analysis, like that of Brogden (1946), assumes a linear relation between job performance and the value or utility of that performance. Under most circumstances, this would appear to be a quite reasonable assumption.

Finally, it should be emphasized that the term *utility* is used in this chapter to indicate both gain (in standard score form) in average employee performance due to selection and the dollar value of this gain. *Utility*, as the term is used by Cronbach and Gleser (1965), refers to the dollar value of this gain minus the cost of testing. Our analysis assumes, in effect, that the cost of testing is zero. This assumption has no effect at all on obtained *differences* in dollar utility among the various models because the cost of testing is common to all models and thus drops out. (Even the quota model requires selection, within groups, on test score.) The assumption does, however, have a slight effect on ratios of utilities, as noted below.

Independent Variables

In addition to the four models of test fairness, the three other independent variables were within-group validities (r_{XY}, varied from .00 through 1.00 in steps of .10); minority base rate in the applicant pool (BR_{min}, varied from .00 to 1.00 in steps of .10); and the overall selection ratio (SR, values of .10 and .50).

The Model and the Program

A careful review of the subgroup employment-test validation literature revealed an average majority–minority difference on the criterion of approximately .5 standard deviation *(SD)* units favoring the majority group. Variation around this figure is not great; on the one hand, there is almost always some difference, and, on the other, it is seldom as great as, say, one standard deviation (although test score differences are frequently one standard deviation or greater). Accordingly, group differences on Y were held constant at .5 standard deviation units throughout the study. A computer program was written that, for each level of r_{XY}, adjusted the mean minority test score to produce a fair test under the requirements of the special model of test fairness. Majority test means were held constant across models and levels of r_{XY}. Both subgroups' standard deviations and r_{XY}'s were assumed equal. Conceptually, this procedure is identical to either revising a test to alter subgroup differences (holding validity constant) or adjusting the cutoff on X so that the proportion of the total group above the cutoff equals the desired overall selection ratio. The procedure explained in the Appendix was then used to compute the marginal utility of selection, as explained above. Marginal utilities for the Thorndike, Darlington, and quota models were expressed as percentages of maximum attainable utility, that is, the utility of the Cleary model. The selection ratio for the minority group under each condition was also determined. (This is the proportion of the minority applicants that were selected, not the proportion of selectees who were minority. The latter figure can be quite deceptive because of its direct dependence on the minority base rate in the applicant pool.)

RESULTS AND DISCUSSION

Tables 1 and 2 present the standard-score marginal utilities of the four fairness models for the overall selection ratios of .10 and .50, respectively. These figures represent the increase, in within-group standard-deviation units, in mean performance level attributable to the use of the selection test. It can be seen that, as noted earlier, when there is only one applicant subgroup (i.e., when $BR_{min} = 1.00$ or .00), utilities are a linear function of validity. With two subgroups present in the applicant pool, this function becomes somewhat nonlinear: a mildly positively accelerated monotonically increasing function of validity. As would be expected, marginal utilities increase with validity and decrease with selection ratio. When the overall selection ratio is .50, marginal utilities are always greatest when minority group members comprise half the applicant pool. When the overall selection ratio is .10, higher minority base-rate values provide maximum marginal utilities at low validities, but the optimal minority base rate moves toward .50 as validity increases.

It can be seen in Tables 1 and 2 that the four fairness models are ranked in utility as expected. Tables 3 and 4 show utilities for the three statistically nonoptimal models as percentages of Cleary-model utility. It can be seen that the relative utility loss is greatest at low validities and decreases as validity increases. The lower the validity, the greater the departure from the regression model required by the Thorndike, Darlington, and quota models, as validity approaches

TABLE 1
Marginal Utility of a Selection Test for Four Models of Fairness $(SR = .10)^a$

BR_{min}	Model[b]	Validity									
		.10	.20	.30	.40	.50	.60	.70	.80	.90	1.00
1.00	C	176	351	527	702	878	1.053	1.229	1.404	1.580	1.755
	T	176	351	527	702	878	1.053	1.229	1.404	1.580	1.755
	D	176	351	527	702	878	1.053	1.229	1.404	1.580	1.755
	Q	176	351	527	702	878	1.053	1.229	1.404	1.580	1.755
.90	C	451	504	623	770	930	1.095	1.263	1.434	1.606	1.778
	T	222	395	568	741	914	1.087	1.259	1.432	1.605	1.778
	D	180	359	539	718	897	1.075	1.253	1.429	1.604	1.778
	Q	176	351	527	702	878	1.053	1.229	1.404	1.580	1.755
.80	C	480	563	672	809	962	1.122	1.287	1.454	1.624	1.794
	T	253	424	596	767	938	1.109	1.281	1.452	1.623	1.794
	D	183	365	548	730	911	1.091	1.270	1.447	1.622	1.794
	Q	176	351	527	702	878	1.053	1.229	1.404	1.580	1.755
.70	C	459	569	689	827	978	1.137	1.300	1.466	1.634	1.804
	T	271	441	612	782	952	1.123	1.293	1.463	1.634	1.804
	D	185	370	554	737	920	1.101	1.280	1.458	1.632	1.804
	Q	176	351	527	702	878	1.053	1.229	1.404	1.580	1.755
.60	C	427	540	687	830	983	1.142	1.305	1.471	1.639	1.809
	T	278	448	618	788	958	1.128	1.298	1.469	1.639	1.809
	D	186	372	557	741	925	1.106	1.285	1.463	1.637	1.809
	Q	176	351	527	702	878	1.053	1.229	1.404	1.580	1.755
.50	C	390	522	673	822	978	1.139	1.303	1.470	1.639	1.809
	T	275	446	616	786	957	1.127	1.298	1.468	1.638	1.809
	D	186	372	558	742	925	1.106	1.285	1.462	1.637	1.809
	Q	176	351	527	702	878	1.053	1.229	1.404	1.580	1.755
.40	C	350	495	651	822	967	1.130	1.296	1.464	1.634	1.804
	T	266	437	608	786	950	1.121	1.291	1.462	1.633	1.804
	D	186	371	556	742	922	1.102	1.281	1.458	1.632	1.804
	Q	176	351	527	702	878	1.053	1.229	1.404	1.580	1.755
.30	C	308	463	625	786	950	1.116	1.285	1.454	1.625	1.797
	T	250	422	593	765	937	1.109	1.281	1.453	1.625	1.797
	D	185	369	552	734	915	1.095	1.273	1.449	1.624	1.797
	Q	176	351	527	702	878	1.053	1.229	1.404	1.580	1.755
.20	C	265	428	594	761	929	1.098	1.269	1.441	1.613	1.785
	T	229	402	575	748	921	1.094	1.267	1.440	1.612	1.785
	D	182	364	545	726	905	1.084	1.261	1.437	1.612	1.785
	Q	176	351	527	702	878	1.053	1.229	1.404	1.580	1.755
.10	C	220	390	562	733	905	1.077	1.250	1.424	1.597	1.772
	T	204	378	552	726	901	1.075	1.249	1.423	1.597	1.772
	D	179	358	537	715	893	1.070	1.246	1.422	1.597	1.772
	Q	176	351	527	702	878	1.053	1.229	1.404	1.580	1.755
.00	C	176	351	527	702	878	1.053	1.229	1.404	1.580	1.755
	T	176	351	527	702	878	1.053	1.229	1.404	1.580	1.755
	D	176	351	527	702	878	1.053	1.229	1.404	1.580	1.755
	Q	176	351	527	702	878	1.053	1.229	1.404	1.580	1.755

[a] All utilities are expressed in within-group SD units. For $r_{XY} \leq .50$, decimals have been omitted.
[b] C = Cleary (1968); T = Thorndike (1971); D = Darlington (1971, 1978); Q = Quota.

TABLE 2

Marginal Utility of a Selection Test for Four Models of Fairness $(SR = .50)$[a]

BR_{min}	Model[b]	Validity									
		.10	.20	.30	.40	.50	.60	.70	.80	.90	1.00
1.00	C	080	160	239	319	399	479	559	638	718	798
	T	080	160	239	319	399	479	559	638	718	798
	D	808	160	239	319	399	479	559	638	718	798
	Q	080	160	239	319	399	479	559	638	718	798
.90	C	121	192	265	340	416	493	571	649	728	807
	T	096	175	254	333	412	491	570	649	728	807
	D	082	163	244	326	407	487	568	648	728	807
	Q	080	160	239	319	399	479	559	638	718	798
.80	C	161	222	287	356	430	505	581	658	736	814
	T	109	188	266	344	422	501	579	657	735	814
	D	083	165	248	331	413	494	575	655	735	814
	Q	080	160	239	319	399	479	559	638	718	798
.70	C	198	246	303	369	440	513	588	664	741	819
	T	119	197	274	352	430	508	585	663	741	819
	D	084	168	251	335	417	499	581	661	740	819
	Q	080	160	239	319	399	479	559	638	718	798
.60	C	230	264	314	377	446	518	592	668	745	822
	T	125	202	280	357	435	512	589	667	744	822
	D	085	169	253	337	420	502	584	664	744	822
	Q	080	160	239	319	399	479	559	638	718	798
.50	C	250	270	318	380	448	520	594	669	746	823
	T	127	204	281	359	436	513	591	668	745	823
	D	085	169	254	337	421	503	585	665	745	823
	Q	080	160	239	319	399	479	559	638	718	798
.40	C	230	264	314	377	446	518	592	668	745	822
	T	125	202	280	257	435	512	589	667	744	822
	D	085	169	253	337	420	502	584	664	744	822
	Q	080	160	239	319	399	479	559	638	718	798
.30	C	198	246	303	369	440	513	588	664	741	819
	T	119	197	274	352	430	508	585	663	741	819
	D	084	168	251	335	417	499	581	661	740	819
	Q	080	160	239	319	399	479	559	638	718	798
.20	C	161	222	287	356	430	505	581	658	736	814
	T	109	188	266	344	422	501	579	657	735	814
	D	083	166	248	331	413	494	575	655	735	814
	Q	080	160	239	319	399	479	559	638	718	798
.10	C	121	192	265	340	416	493	571	649	728	807
	T	096	175	254	333	412	491	570	649	728	807
	D	082	163	244	326	407	487	568	648	728	807
	Q	080	160	239	319	399	479	559	638	718	798
.00	C	080	160	239	319	399	479	559	638	718	798
	T	080	160	239	319	399	479	559	638	718	798
	D	080	160	239	319	399	479	559	638	718	798
	Q	080	160	239	319	399	479	559	638	718	798

[a] All utilities are expressed in within-group SD units. All decimals have been omitted.
[b] C = Cleary (1968); T = Thorndike (1970); D = Darlington (1971, 1978); Q = Quota.

TABLE 3

Marginal Utility as Percentage of Cleary-Model Utility for Three Fairness Models
$(SR = .10)$[a]

BR_{min}	Model[b]	Validity									
		.10	.20	.30	.40	.50	.60	.70	.80	.90	1.00
.90	T	49.2	78.4	91.2	96.2	98.3	99.3	99.7	99.9	99.9	100
	D	39.9	71.2	86.5	93.3	96.5	98.2	99.2	99.7	99.9	100
	Q	39.0	69.6	84.6	91.2	94.4	96.2	97.3	99.9	98.4	98.7
.80	T	52.7	75.3	88.7	94.8	97.5	98.8	99.5	99.9	99.9	100
	D	38.1	64.8	81.6	90.2	94.7	97.2	98.7	99.5	99.9	100
	Q	36.7	62.3	78.4	86.7	91.3	93.9	95.5	96.6	97.3	97.8
.70	T	59.0	77.5	88.8	94.6	97.3	98.8	99.5	99.8	99.9	100
	D	40.3	65.0	80.4	89.1	94.1	96.8	98.5	99.5	99.9	100
	Q	38.3	61.7	76.5	84.9	89.8	92.6	94.5	95.8	96.7	97.3
.60	T	65.1	83.0	90.0	94.9	97.5	98.8	99.5	99.9	99.9	100
	D	43.6	68.9	81.1	89.3	94.1	96.9	98.5	99.5	99.9	100
	Q	41.2	65.0	76.7	84.6	89.3	92.2	94.2	95.5	96.4	97.0
.50	T	70.5	85.4	91.5	95.6	97.9	99.0	99.6	99.9	99.9	100
	D	47.7	71.3	82.9	90.3	94.6	97.1	98.6	99.5	99.9	100
	Q	45.1	67.2	78.3	85.4	89.8	92.5	94.3	95.5	96.7	97.0
.40	T	76.0	88.3	93.4	96.5	98.2	99.2	99.6	99.9	99.9	100
	D	53.1	75.0	85.4	91.7	95.4	97.5	98.8	99.6	99.9	100
	Q	50.3	70.9	81.0	87.0	90.8	93.2	94.8	95.9	96.7	97.3
.30	T	81.2	91.1	94.9	97.3	98.6	99.4	99.7	99.9	99.9	100
	D	60.1	79.7	88.3	93.4	96.3	98.1	99.1	99.7	99.9	100
	Q	57.2	75.8	84.3	89.3	92.4	94.4	95.6	96.6	97.2	97.7
.20	T	86.4	93.9	96.8	98.3	99.1	99.6	99.8	99.9	99.9	100
	D	68.7	85.0	91.8	95.4	97.4	98.7	99.4	99.7	99.9	100
	Q	66.4	82.0	88.7	92.3	94.5	95.9	96.8	97.4	98.0	98.3
.10	T	92.7	96.9	98.2	99.1	99.5	99.8	99.9	99.9	99.9	100
	D	81.4	91.8	95.6	97.5	98.7	99.4	99.7	99.9	99.9	100
	Q	80.0	90.0	93.8	95.7	97.0	97.8	98.3	98.6	98.9	99.0

[a] All fairness models produce equal utility when $BR_{min} = 1.00$ or .00.
[b] T = Thorndike (1971); D = Darlington (1971, 1978); Q = Quota.

1.00, and the Thorndike and Darlington definitions converge with the regression model. The quota model, however, does not fully converge at $r_{XY} = 1.00$. (This reflects the fact that the quota model is the only standard that does not respond at all to differences in mean criterion scores. In each of the other three models, the emphasis on the mean criterion difference increases as validity increases.) The reader

TABLE 4

Marginal Utility as Percentage of Cleary-Model Utility for Three Fairness Models $(SR = .50)^a$

		Validity									
BR_{min}	Model[b]	.10	.20	.30	.40	.50	.60	.70	.80	.90	1.00
	T	79.3	91.2	95.9	97.9	99.0	99.6	99.8	99.9	99.9	100
.90	D	67.7	84.9	92.1	95.9	97.8	98.8	99.5	99.9	99.9	100
	Q	66.1	83.3	89.8	93.8	95.9	97.2	97.9	98.3	98.6	98.9
	T	67.7	84.7	92.7	96.6	98.1	99.2	99.7	99.9	99.9	100
.80	D	51.6	74.3	86.4	93.0	96.1	97.8	99.0	99.5	99.9	100
	Q	49.7	72.1	83.3	89.6	92.8	94.9	96.2	97.0	97.6	98.0
	T	60.1	80.0	90.4	95.4	97.7	99.0	99.5	99.9	99.9	100
.70	D	42.4	68.3	82.8	90.8	94.8	97.3	98.8	99.5	99.9	100
	Q	40.4	5.0	78.9	86.5	90.7	93.4	95.1	96.1	96.6	97.4
	T	54.4	76.5	89.2	94.7	97.5	98.8	99.5	99.9	99.9	100
.60	D	37.0	64.0	80.6	89.4	94.2	96.9	98.7	99.4	99.9	100
	Q	34.8	60.1	76.1	84.6	89.5	92.5	94.4	95.5	96.4	97.1
	T	50.8	75.6	88.4	94.5	97.3	98.7	99.5	99.9	99.9	100
.50	D	34.0	62.6	79.9	88.7	94.0	96.7	98.5	99.4	99.9	100
	Q	32.0	59.3	75.7	84.0	89.1	92.1	94.1	95.4	96.3	97.0
	T	54.4	76.5	89.2	94.7	97.5	98.8	99.5	99.9	99.9	100
.40	D	37.0	64.1	80.6	89.4	94.2	96.9	98.7	99.4	99.9	100
	Q	34.8	60.1	76.1	84.6	89.5	92.5	94.4	95.5	96.4	97.1
	T	60.1	80.0	90.4	95.4	97.7	99.0	99.5	99.9	99.9	100
.30	D	42.4	68.3	82.8	90.8	94.8	97.3	98.8	99.6	99.9	100
	Q	40.4	65.0	78.9	86.5	90.7	93.4	95.1	96.1	96.9	97.4
	T	67.7	84.7	92.7	96.6	98.1	99.2	99.7	99.9	99.9	100
.20	D	51.6	74.3	86.4	93.0	96.1	97.8	99.0	99.5	99.9	100
	Q	49.7	72.1	83.3	89.6	92.8	94.9	96.2	97.0	97.6	98.0
	T	79.3	91.2	95.9	97.9	99.0	99.6	99.8	99.9	99.9	100
.10	D	67.7	84.9	92.1	95.9	97.8	98.8	99.5	99.9	99.9	100
	Q	66.1	83.3	89.8	93.8	95.9	97.2	97.9	98.3	98.6	98.9

[a]All fairness models produce equal utility when $BR_{min} = 1.00$ or .00.
[b]T = Thorndike (1971); D = Darlington (1971, 1978); Q = Quota.

should remember that the utility ratios shown in Tables 3 and 4 are in terms of mean gain in performance due to selection and do not include the cost of testing. But as a practical matter, these ratios would be little changed given realistic estimates of the cost of testing. The effect of considering the cost of testing would be to reduce all of the ratios slightly.

When the overall ratio is .50, the loss in utility, moving from Cleary through Thorndike and Darlington to the quota model, is always greatest at a minority base rate of .50. When the overall selection ratio is .10, maximum utility loss occurs at higher minority base-rate values at low r_{XY}; and as r_{XY} increases, the point of maximum loss moves toward a minority base rate of .50.

Tables 5 and 6 present the minority-group selection ratios (MSRs) for the four fairness models when overall selection ratios are .10 and .50, respectively. It can be seen that the minority selection ratio increases with validity under the Cleary model and decreases with validity under the Darlington model. In Thorndike's model, the minority selection ratio is independent of validity, being determined solely by the subgroup difference on the criterion, the minority base rate, and the overall selection ratio. Differences between the models in minority selection ratio are greater, on a relative basis, than utility differences and, in fact, are quite substantial. Given overall selection ratios of .10 or .50 and a known payoff standard deviation (SD_Y), r_{XY}, and minority base rate, Tables 1, 2, 5, and 6 provide the information necessary to compute trade-offs between utility and the minority selection ratio.

To compute economic savings in dollar terms, we need two more numbers: the number of persons to be hired and the standard deviation of performance in dollar terms. The standard deviation in dollar terms varies from job to job. The value to be used here is an average value based on a review of the literature by Hunter and Schmidt (1982; see also Schmidt, Hunter, McKenzie, & Muldrow, 1979). They found that the standard deviation in dollar terms is typically about 40% of the mean wage. The large known deviations are in the direction of being much larger than 40% of the mean wage. Thus, the use of this base rate may underestimate utility differences for certain critical jobs. The average annual wage in 1980 for nonsupervisory and nonagricultural workers was $13,540. Thus, for this group, the standard deviation in dollar terms would average $5,416 on an annual basis. But a person is not hired just for one year; the benefits or losses associated with a particular hire extend over the entire time that the employee is with the organization. Median tenure in 1978 was 3.6 years. Thus, we estimate the average standard deviation in dollar terms to be approximately $20,000 over the tenure of the worker hired (3.6 × $5,416 = $19,497).

Consider now the more commonly occurring combinations of r_{XY} and the minority base rate. In Table 1, it can be seen that when the overall selection ratio is .10, the minority base rate (BR_{min}) is .30;

TABLE 5

Minority Group Selection Ratios under Four Fairness Models (Overall $SR = .10)^a$

BR_{min}	Model[b]	Validity									
		.10	.20	.30	.40	.50	.60	.70	.80	.90	1.00
.90	C	002	030	053	067	075	080	083	086	088	089
	T	089	089	089	089	089	089	089	089	089	089
	D	099	098	097	096	095	094	093	092	090	089
.80	C	000	005	026	044	056	064	069	074	077	080
	T	080	080	080	080	080	080	080	080	080	080
	D	098	096	094	092	090	088	086	084	082	080
.70	C	000	002	014	030	042	052	059	064	068	071
	T	071	071	071	071	071	071	071	071	071	071
	D	097	095	092	089	086	083	080	077	074	071
.60	C	000	005	009	021	033	042	050	056	060	064
	T	064	064	064	064	064	064	064	064	064	064
	D	096	093	089	086	082	078	075	071	068	064
.50	C	000	003	006	016	026	035	043	049	054	058
	T	058	058	058	058	058	058	058	058	058	058
	D	096	091	087	083	078	074	070	066	062	058
.40	C	000	002	004	012	021	030	037	043	048	053
	T	053	053	053	053	053	053	053	053	053	053
	D	095	090	085	080	075	070	066	061	057	053
.30	C	000	001	003	010	018	026	032	038	044	048
	T	048	048	048	048	048	048	048	048	048	048
	D	094	088	082	077	071	066	061	057	052	048
.20	C	000	001	002	008	015	022	029	035	040	044
	T	044	044	044	044	044	044	044	044	044	044
	D	093	087	080	074	068	063	058	053	048	044
.10	C	000	001	002	007	013	019	026	031	036	041
	T	041	041	041	041	041	041	041	041	041	041
	D	092	085	078	072	066	060	054	049	045	041

[a] SR for quota model = .100 in all cells. When $BR_{min} = 1.00$, $MSR = .100$ for all models and levels of r_{XY}. All decimals have been omitted.
[b] C = Cleary (1968); T = Thorndike (1971); D = Darlington (1971, 1978).

r_{XY} is .30; and the utility difference between the Cleary and Thorndike models is .032 standard deviation units (Thorndike utility = 94.9% of Cleary utility). If the payoff standard deviation is \$20,000, this represents \$640 per selectee. If there are 2,000 selectees, this is \$1,280,000. Against this gain, Table 5 shows a reduction of the minor-

TABLE 6

Minority Group Selection Ratios (MSR) under Four Fairness Models (Overall $SR = .50)^a$

BR_{min}	Model[b]	.10	.20	.30	.40	.50	.60	.70	.80	.90	1.00
						Validity					
	C	444	445	451	458	465	469	473	476	479	481
.90	T	481	481	481	481	481	481	481	481	481	481
	D	498	496	494	492	490	488	486	484	482	481
	C	375	379	395	413	427	437	447	452	457	461
.80	T	461	461	461	461	461	461	461	461	461	461
	D	496	492	488	484	480	476	472	469	465	461
	C	286	296	332	364	388	404	417	427	435	441
.70	T	441	441	441	441	441	441	441	441	441	441
	D	494	488	482	476	470	464	458	453	447	441
	C	167	199	266	314	348	371	389	402	413	421
.60	T	421	421	421	421	421	421	421	421	421	421
	D	492	484	476	468	460	452	444	437	429	421
	C	006	106	202	266	309	338	360	377	391	401
.50	T	401	401	401	401	401	401	401	401	401	401
	D	490	480	470	460	450	440	431	421	411	401
	C	000	049	149	222	271	307	333	353	369	382
.40	T	382	382	382	382	382	382	382	382	382	382
	D	488	476	464	452	440	428	417	405	393	382
	C	000	025	109	183	238	277	307	330	348	363
.30	T	363	363	363	363	363	363	363	363	363	363
	D	486	472	458	444	430	417	403	389	376	363
	C	000	014	081	152	207	250	282	307	327	344
.20	T	344	344	344	344	344	344	344	344	344	344
	D	484	468	452	436	421	405	389	374	359	344
	C	000	009	061	126	181	225	259	286	308	326
.10	T	326	326	326	326	326	326	326	326	326	326
	D	482	464	446	429	411	393	376	359	342	326

[a] SR for quota model $= .500$ in all cells. When $BR_{min} = 1.00$, MSR $- .500$ for all models and levels of r_{XY}. All decimals have been omited.
[b] C = Cleary (1968); T = Thorndike (1971); D = Darlington (1971, 1978).

ity selection ratio from .048 to .003; that is, only about one-sixteenth as many minority group members are hired (18 vs. 288).

Another realistic cell in Tables 1 and 5 is that where $r_{XY} = .40$ and $BR_{min} = .20$. Here the utility difference between the Cleary and the Thorndike models in standard score form is .013. If the payoff standard deviation is $20,000 and 2,000 new employees are to be hired, the Cleary model saves $520,000 more than the Thorndike model. But less than one-fifth as many minority group members are hired (32 vs. 176).

In Tables 2 and 6, where the overall selection ratio is .50, consider the cell in which $r_{XY} = .30$ and $BR_{min} = .30$. The utility edge of the Cleary model over the Thorndike model is .029 in standard score units. Assuming again that the payoff standard deviation is $20,000 and there are 2,000 hires, the Cleary model saves $1,160,000 more than the Thorndike model. But the minority selection ratio is .109 versus .363 for the Thorndike model; this means $(.363 - .109) [(4,000) (.30)]$ or 305 fewer minority group members will be hired. When $r_{XY} = .50$ and $BR_{min} = .20$, and continuing the above assumptions, the advantage of the Cleary over the Thorndike model is $320,000, but the minority selection ratio is only .207 versus .344 with Thorndike's definition. Approximately 110 fewer minority group members will be hired.

If the payoff standard deviation is taken to be $40,000, probably a reasonably accurate lower-bound estimate for middle-level jobs, utility differences between the Thorndike and the Cleary models are doubled for all cells examined. If more than 2,000 applicants are selected, both utility losses and utility gains in numbers of minority members hired are greater; if fewer than 2,000 applicants are selected, both are less. Both utility losses and utility gains in the minority selection ratio due to choice of the Darlington or quota models over the Cleary model will be greater than in the case of the Thorndike model. And, of course, comparisons not involving the Cleary model can be made. One can, for example, compute the loss in utility and the gain in the minority selection ratio that would be occasioned by moving from the Thorndike to the quota model. The reader is invited to make the comparisons he or she desires, substituting his or her own values for the dollar standard deviation of job performance and the number hired.

Analysis of this kind makes clear, for a given selection situation, the trade-offs between these two presumably desirable outcomes. Such clarity may contribute to more informed decisions, but it is not sufficient, at present, to actually make such decisions.

If a method could be devised for expressing increases in the minority selection ratio in utility units, the choice of a fairness model would be a simple task: The model would be chosen that has the highest sum of the two utilities. In all probability, however, there will be great disagreement about the specific economic utility of increases in the minority selection ratio. And some on both sides of the question will maintain that moral values (the "evil" of reverse discrimination and a "moral obligation" to atone for past discrimination) are involved and that therefore increases in the minority selection ratio cannot be evaluated on a purely economic scale. It therefore appears that what one sees as the implications of these findings will be to a great extent determined by his or her personal values. Supporting this conclusion is the additional fact that legal limitations on the choice of a fairness model are not yet clearly defined. Despite its association with lower minority selection ratios, the Cleary model is clearly legal. In fact, it is the model endorsed in the Uniform Guidelines on Employee Selection Procedures (U.S. Equal Employment Opportunity Commission *et al.*, 1978; Ledvinka, 1979; cf. also Hunter, 1980, 1981). On March 11, 1975, Federal Judge Spencer Williams, U.S. District Court, Northern District of California, ruled in *Cortez* v. *Rosen* that the Cleary model is the "only one which is historically, legally, and logically required." This ruling, which sustained the use of a police examination shown to meet Cleary-model requirements, was the first to address the question of the relative legal merits of alternative fairness models. The quota model, of course, invites charges of reverse discrimination. Although it may eventually be declared illegally discriminatory, it has not yet been. The legal status of the Thorndike and Darlington models is even less clear.

Nothing in this analysis in intended to suggest that the minority selection ratio and the expected utility are or should be the sole criteria employed in choosing a fairness model. Other factors (for example, the possibility of reverse discrimination charges and lawsuits) must also be considered. Nevertheless, expected utility and the minority selection ratio will usually (and should) weigh heavily in such decisions, and in order to weigh each in a way consistent with one's personal values, one must have accurate estimates of their numerical values in specific situations.

SUMMARY

The hypothesis that cognitive tests are unfair to minority testtakers has been repeatedly subjected to empirical test in studies of job performance. Massive empirical evidence has now accumulated showing that tests are fair to minority members; the mean job performance of minority and majority members is the same when people are matched on the composite-ability test score that best predicts performance. For hiring purposes, this means that minority applicants with low ability-test scores later have the same low job performance as majority applicants with the same ability scores. Massive evidence in the educational domain not reviewed in this paper shows the same thing; minority students with low ability scores do just as poorly in learning situations as do majority students with the same low scores.

This means that the goals of merit and ethnic balance are empirically incompatible in selection. If applicants are hired on the basis of ability or predicted performance on the job, then there will be ethnic imbalance in the resulting work force. Any system that achieves ethnic balance must reject some majority applicants in favor of minority applicants who will do more poorly on the job. That is, even though minority applicants with high ability scores will perform on the job just as well as majority workers with the same high ability scores, there are just not enough high-ability minority applicants to go around. Those who offer the highest wage may be able to obtain the desired number of minority workers, but everyone else will fall short accordingly.

If an employer chooses to hire for ethnic balance rather than for merit, then there will be a reduction in the labor savings that result from selection on the basis of ability. The size of the economic loss is always large in dollar terms, though it varies in percentage terms, depending on the method used to define ethnic balance. Three methods have been derived from unsuccessful attempts to define test bias in terms of regression equations: the Cleary model, the Thorndike model, and the Darlington–Cole model. Use of the Cleary model results in no loss to the employer (though few would be willing to use separate regression lines as required by the model in some cases). The other two regression models result in losses of less than 10% in labor savings. On the other hand, neither model provides the degree of ethnic balance desired by civil rights zealots.

Two blatantly antimerit procedures for obtaining ethnic balance have been proposed: the use of quotas and the use of low cutoff scores as a screen only. The optimal quota system is to select from the top test scores down within each group separately until the same percentage of applicants is hired in each group. This quota method provides the full degree of ethnic balance desired by civil rights advocates with minimal loss of economic benefit; the losses are about 10% –15% in typical cases. The low cutoff method is a disaster by either reckoning. The low cutoff does not achieve ethnic balance, and it results in an 85% or greater loss in labor savings. In the low cutoff method, the employer matches his or her hiring of a small number of substandard minority applicants by the hiring of a very large number of substandard majority applicants as well.

APPENDIX

GENERAL PROCEDURE

Assume that the standard deviations on both predictor and criterion are the same for whites and for blacks. Assume also that the validity is the same for each group. Then, the fairness of a given test is solely a function of whether the mean difference on the test is commensurate with the difference on the criterion. The various definitions of test bias can be stated in terms of the definition of *commensurate*.

Once this is done, test use can be made fair by adding or subtracting some number from the score for each black. This number differs from one definition to the next.

Because the standard deviations are the same for both groups, we can express all scores in terms of white standard scores. Thus, $\sigma_X = \sigma_Y = 1$ for both groups, and $E(X) = E(Y) = 0$ for whites. The validity for both groups is the same and is denoted r. The mean on the criterion for blacks is assumed to be Δ less than that for whites (where Δ is negative if the black mean-criterion performance is greater than the mean performance for whites). The test is then fair if the mean test score for blacks is

$E(X_B) = -\Delta/r$ by the Cleary definition,

$E(X_B) = -\Delta$ by the Thorndike definition,

$E(X_B) = -r\Delta$ by the Cole–Darlington definition, and

$E(X_B) = 0$ to yield population-based quotas.

From this, the formulas for the amount to be added to the test score for black applicants are easily derived. For convenience in actual use, these formulas are given in raw score form. In these formulas, $\overline{X}_B$ and $\overline{X}_W$ are the predictor means for blacks and whites, $\overline{Y}_B$ and $\overline{Y}_W$ are the criterion means for blacks and whites, S_X and S_Y are the majority standard deviations for predictor and criterion. The symbol Δ refers to mean differences for blacks and whites, that is,

$$\Delta X = \overline{X}_W - \overline{X}_B$$
$$\Delta Y = \overline{Y}_W - \overline{Y}_B$$

The raw-score formulas for the amount to add to the minority score are:

$$\text{Cleary: } \Delta X \to X + \Delta_x - \frac{S_x \Delta_Y}{r_{XY} S_Y}$$

$$\text{Thorndike: } X \to X + \Delta_x - \frac{S_x \Delta_Y}{S_Y}$$

$$\text{Darlington–Cole: } X \to X + \Delta_x - \frac{r_{XY} S_x \Delta_Y}{S_Y}$$

$$\text{Quotas: } X \to X + \Delta_x$$

For the rest of the Appendix, we return to majority standard-score formulas. For example, suppose that $r = .50$, $\Delta = .50$, and the actual test mean for blacks is $-.75$. Then, the adjustment to each black score required by test fairness would be as follows:

$$X \rightarrow X - .25 \text{ according to Cleary}$$
$$X \rightarrow X + .25 \text{ according to Thorndike}$$
$$X \rightarrow X + .50 \text{ according to Cole and Darlington}$$
$$X \rightarrow X + .75 \text{ to yield population-based quotas}$$

The utility of the test can then be calculated by assuming that the appropriate adjustment in scores is made for each definition in turn. There are four steps in the calculation of the utility for each method of using test scores. First, the selection cutoff score must be calculated so as to yield the given overall selection ratio. Second, the expected performance score is calculated for each group separately. This calculation is made in two parts. First, the expected test score for those selected in each group is calculated from the cutoff score. Then, the expected test score is converted to an expected criterion score by using the regression line for that group. The regression equation for whites is always $E(Y/X) = rX$, but the regression equation for blacks is different for each bias definition because of the different adjustment made for each definition. Third, the overall mean criterion performance for those selected is obtained by combining the separate group means. If the number of selectees who are white is N_W and the number of selectees who are black is N_B, then the overall mean performance is

$$E(Y/\text{selected}) = \frac{N_W E(Y_W/\text{selected}) + N_B E(Y_B/\text{selected})}{N_W + N_B}$$

The fourth step is the computation of the utility. If people are selected at random, and if the proportion of applicants who are white is denoted P, then

$$E(Y/\text{random selection}) = PE(Y_W) + QE(Y_B) = -Q\Delta$$

where $Q = 1 - P$ is the proportion of applicants who are black. Hence, the marginal utility of the test is

$$U = E(Y/\text{selected}) - E(Y/\text{random selection})$$

REFERENCES

Bartlett, C. J., Bobko, P., Mosier, S. B., & Hannan, R. Testing for fairness with a moderated multiple regression strategy: An alternative to differential analysis. *Personnel Psychology*, 1978, *31*, 233–241.

Boehm, V. R. Differential prediction: A methodological artifact? *Journal of Applied Psychology*, 1977, *62*, 146–154.

Brogden, H. E. On the interpretation of the correlation coefficient as a measure of predictive efficiency. *Journal of Educational Psychology*, 1946, *37*, 65–76.

Campbell, J. T., Crooks, L. A., Mahoney, M. H., & Rock, D. A. An investigation of sources of bias in the prediction of job performance: A six-year study. Final Project Report No. PR-73-37. Princeton, N.J.: Educational Testing Service, 1973.

Cleary, T. A., & Hilton, T. I. Test bias: Prediction of grades of Negro and white students in integrated colleges. *Journal of Educational Measurement*, 1968, *5*, 115–124.

Cole, N. S. *Bias in selection*. ACT Research Report No. 51, May, 1972. Iowa City, Iowa: American College Testing Program, 1972.

Cole, N. S. Bias in selection. *Journal of Educational Measurement*, 1973, *10*, 237–255.

Cronbach, L. J. Equity in selection—Where psychometrics and political philosophy meet. *Journal of Educational Measurement*, 1976, *13*, 31–42.

Cronbach, L. J., & Gleser, G. C. *Psychological tests and personnel decisions*. Urbana: University of Illinois Press, 1965.

Cronbach, L. J., Yalow, E., & Schaeffer, G. A mathematical structure for analyzing fairness in selection. *Personnel Psychology*, 1980, *33*, 693–704.

Darlington, R. B. Another look at "cultural fairness." *Journal of Educational Measurement*, 1971, *3*, 71–82.

Darlington, R. B. Cultural test bias: Comment on Hunter and Schmidt. *Psychological Bulletin*, 1978, *85*, 673–674.

Edwards, W., & Phillips, L. D. Man as transducer for probabilities in Bayesian command and control systems. In M. W. Shelley II & G. L. Bryan (Eds.), *Human judgments and optimality*. New York: Wiley, 1964.

Gael, S., & Grant, D. L. Employment test validation for minority and non-minority telephone company service representatives. *Journal of Applied Psychology*, 1972, *56*, 135–139.

Gael, S., Grant, D. L., & Ritchie, R. J. Employment test validation for minority and non-minority clerks with work sample criteria. *Journal of Applied Psychology*, 1975, *60*, 420–426.(a)

Gael, S., Grant, D. L., & Ritchie, R. J. Employment test validation for minority and non-minority telephone operators. *Journal of Applied Psychology*, 1975, *60*, 411–419.(b)

Ghiselli, E. E. The validity of aptitude tests in personnel selection. *Personnel Psychology*, 1973, *26*, 461–477.

Gordon, R. A. Examining labeling theory: The case of mental retardation. In W. R. Gove (Ed.), *The labeling of deviance: A perspective*. Beverly Hills, Calif.: Sage/Halstead, 1975.

Gordon, R. A., & Rudert, E. E. Bad news concerning IQ tests. *Sociology of Education*, 1979, *52*, 174–190.

Grant, D. L., & Bray, D. W. Validation of employment tests for telephone company installation and repair occupations. *Journal of Applied Psychology*, 1970, *54*, 7–14.

Gross, A. L., & Su, W. Defining a "fair" or "unbiased" selection model: A question of utilities. *Journal of Applied Psychology*, 1975, *60*, 345–351.

Humphreys, L. G. Statistical definitions of test validity for minority groups. *Journal of Applied Psychology*, 1973, *58*, 1–4.

Hunter, J. E. *An analysis of validity, differential validity, test fairness, and utility for the Philadelphia Police Officers Selection Examination prepared by the Educational Testing Service*. Report to the Philadelphia Federal District Court, *Alvarez v. City of Philadelphia*, 1979.

Hunter, J. E. *Test validation for 12,000 jobs: An application of synthetic validity generalization to the General Aptitude Test Battery (GATB).* Washington, D.C.: U.S. Employment Service, U.S. Department of Labor, 1980.

Hunter, J. E. *The economic benefits of personnel selection using ability tests: A state of the art review including a detailed analysis of the dollar benefit of U.S. Employment Service placements and a critique of the low cutoff method of test use.* Washington, D.C.: U.S. Employment Service, U.S. Department of Labor, 1981.

Hunter, J. E., & Schmidt, F. L. A critical analysis of the statistical and ethical implications of five definitions of test fairness. *Psychological Bulletin,* 1976, *83*(6), 1053–1071.

Hunter, J. E., & Schmidt, F. L. Differential and single group validity of employment tests by race: A critical analysis of three recent studies. *Journal of Applied Psychology,* 1978, *63,* 1–11.

Hunter, J. E., & Schmidt, F. L. Fitting people to jobs: Implications of personnel selection for national productivity. In M. D. Dunnette & E. A. Fleishman (Ed.), *Human performance and productivity: Human capability assessment.* Hillsdale, N.J.: Lawrence Erlbaum Associates, 1981.

Hunter, J. E., Schmidt, F. L., & Hunter, R. Differential validity of employment tests by race: A comprehensive review and analysis. *Psychological Bulletin,* 1979, *86,* 721–735.

Hunter, J. E., Schmidt, F. L., & Rauschenberger, J. M. Fairness of psychological tests: Implications of four definitions for selection utility and minority hiring. *Journal of Applied Psychology,* 1977, *62,* 245–260.

Jensen, A. R. *Bias in mental testing.* New York: Free Press, 1980.

Katzell, R. A., & Dyer, F. J. Differential validity revived. *Journal of Applied Psychology,* 1977, *62,* 137–145.

Ledvinka, J. The statistical definition of fairness in the Federal selection guidelines and its implications for minority employment. *Personnel Psychology,* 1979, *32,* 551–562.

Lee, R., & Booth, J. M. A utility analysis of a weighted application blank designed to predict turnover of clerical employees. *Journal of Applied Psychology,* 1974, *59,* 516–518.

Lent, R. H., Aurbach, H. A., & Levin, L. S. Research design and validity assessment. *Personnel Psychology,* 1971, *24,* 247–274.

Linn, R. L. Fair test use in selection. *Review of Educational Research,* 1973, *43,* 139–161.

Linn, R. L. Test bias and the prediction of grades in law school. *Journal of Legal Education,* 1975, *27,* 293–323.

Linn, R. L., & Werts, C. E. Considerations for studies of test bias. *Journal of Educational Measurement,* 1971, *8,* 1–4.

Mack, M. J., Schmidt, F. L., & Hunter, J. E. *Dollar implications of alternative models of selection: A case study of park rangers.* Technical Report, Personnel Research and Development Center, Office of Personnel Management, Washington, D.C., 1984.

Novick, M. R., & Peterson, N. S. Towards equalizing educational and employment opportunity. *Journal of Educational Measurement,* 1976, *13,* 77–88.

O'Connor, E. J., Wexley, K. N., & Alexander, R. A. Single-group validity: Fact or fallacy? *Journal of Applied Psychology,* 1975, *60,* 352–355.

Pearlman, K. *The validity of tests used to select clerical personnel: A comprehensive summary and evaluation.* U.S. Office of Personnel Management, Personnel Research and Development Center, TS-79-1, August 1979.

Pearlman, K., Schmidt, F. L., & Hunter, J. E. Validity generalization results for tests used to predict success and job proficiency in clerical evaluations. *Journal of Applied Psychology*, 1980, *65*, 373–406.

Powers, D. E. *Comparing predictions of law school performance for black, Chicano, and white law students.* Law School Academic Council, LSAC-77-3, 1977.

Reilly, R. R. A note on minority group test bias studies. *Psychological Bulletin*, 1973, *80*, 130–132.

Reynolds, C. R. An examination for bias in a preschool test battery across race and sex. *Journal of Educational Measurement*, 1980, *17*, 137–146.

Reynolds, C. R. The problem of bias in psychological assessment. In C. R. Reynolds & T. B. Gutkin (Eds.), *A handbook for school psychology*. New York: Wiley, 1981.

Reynolds, C. R., & Jensen, A. R. *Patterns of intellectual abilities among blacks and whites matched on "g."* Paper presented to the annual meeting of the American Psychological Association, Montreal, 1980.

Rosenfeld, M., & Thornton, R. F. *The development and validation of a multijurisdictional police examination.* Princeton, N.J.: Educational Testing Service, 1976.

Ruch, W. W. *A re-analysis of published differential validity studies.* Paper presented at the symposium "Differential Validation under EEOC and OFCC Testing and Selection Regulations," American Psychological Association, Honolulu, Hawaii, 1972.

Schmidt, F. L., & Hoffman, B. Empirical comparison of three methods of assessing the utility of a selection device. *Journal of Industrial and Organizational Psychology*, 1973, *1*, 13–22.

Schmidt, F. L., & Hunter, J. E. Racial and ethnic bias in psychological tests: Divergent implications of two definitions of test bias. *American Psychologist*, 1974, *29*, 1–8.

Schmidt, F. L., Berner, J. G., & Hunter, J. E. Racial differences in validity of employment tests: Reality or illusion? *Journal of Applied Psychology*, 1973, *53*, 5–9.

Schmidt, F. L., Hunter, J. E., McKenzie, R., & Muldrow, T. The impact of valid selection procedures on workforce productivity. *Journal of Applied Psychology*, 1979, *64*, 609–626.

Schmidt, F. L., Hunter, J. E., Pearlman, K., & Shane, G. S. Further tests of the Schmidt-Hunter Bayesian validity generalization procedure. *Personnel Psychology*, 1979, *32*, 257–281.

Schmidt, F. L., Pearlman, K., & Hunter, J. E. The validity and fairness of employment and educational tests for Hispanic Americans: A review and analysis. *Personnel Psychology*, 1980, *33*, 705–724.

Tenopyr, M. L. *Race and socio-economic status as moderators in predicting machine-shop training success.* Paper presented at the American Psychological Association Meeting, Washington, D.C., 1967.

Thorndike, R. L. Concepts of culture-fairness. *Journal of Educational Measurement*, 1971, *8*, 63–70.

U.S. Employment Service. Section III of the *Manual for the USES General Aptitude Test Battery*. U.S. Department of Labor, 1970.

U.S. Equal Employment Opportunity Commission, U.S. Civil Service Commission, U.S. Department of Labor and U.S. Department of Justice. Adoption by four agencies of Uniform Guidelines on Employee Selection Procedures. *Federal Register*, 1978, *43*, 38290–38315.

CHAPTER THREE

An Experimental Model of Bias in Mental Testing

GORDON M. HARRINGTON

The necessary condition for test bias in the psychometric sense is the existence of group membership by test-item statistical interactions. To my knowledge, there is no disagreement on this point and the rationale has been fully developed elsewhere (Jensen, 1980). Attention here is focused on such statistical interactions and on bias as defined in this specific psychometric context.

The concept of interaction originated with R. A. Fisher and can be traced to his classic analysis of heredity (Fisher, 1918). That paper proved to be the cornerstone both of modern quantitative genetics and of modern statistical analysis. The concepts presented there and their subsequent development had little, if any, influence on psychometric thought or practice. That lack of influence is unfortunate because the concepts remain relevant today. In fairness to our psychometric predecessors, I should digress to observe that it was entirely appropriate that they were not influenced by Fisher's concepts. Statisticians of the stature of Neyman, Wilks, and Wishart misunderstood or disagreed with Fisher through the 1930s (Box, 1978), and the most relevant genetic concepts were still open to debate during World War II ('Espinasse, 1942). Thus, it took some time for statisticians and geneticists to resolve the issues in their own specialties. It is seldom either common or appropriate for members of one specialty to adopt concepts from another specialty in advance of their

GORDON M. HARRINGTON • Department of Psychology, University of Northern Iowa, Cedar Falls, Iowa 50614.

general acceptance within that specialty. On the other hand, all specialties exist in a common general milieu, so that there is much interdisciplinary commonality on the cutting edges of different fields, though the relevant parallels may be evident only in retrospect. In the case of Fisher's early work, a retrospective review of key concepts is instructive.

In 1918, the dominant genetic view of individual differences was that of Galton and Pearson (see Dunn, 1965). Humans were characterized by continuous variation in multiple characteristics. These characteristics were fully or partially a product of heredity, which involved an additive blending of parental characteristics. The characteristics of populations could thus be represented by the correlation matrix. Genetic structure could be arrived at inductively from an analysis of the correlation matrix. Fisher's seminal paper demonstrated that, if variables interact, one can deduce the characteristics of the correlation matrix from a knowledge of underlying structure, but one cannot infer underlying structure from a knowledge of the correlation matrix. Genetic dominance is an instance of interaction. Fisher's analysis showed that the data of the correlationists must follow from Mendelian structure, including dominance (Dunn, 1965; Mather, 1951). The eventual effect of this paper was the displacement of the Galton–Pearson "blended inheritance" model by the Mendelian model for quantitative genetics and the replacement of correlational analysis by analysis of variance as the statistical method.

It is of more than passing interest to observe that continuous variation in genetic characteristics is polygenic under the Mendelian model. With the natural selection of polygenic characteristics, correlated responses are "inevitable" (Mather, 1942). Hirsch (1967) pointed out in a behavioral context the relevance of such accidental correlations. That is, not only does correlation not imply causation, but with polygenic inheritance, correlations between continuous variables will occur that are devoid of any causal linkages other than accidents of natural selection. The origin of psychometric correlation analysis was the Galton–Pearson model of hereditary variation. By the time that Mendelian genetics was fully accepted in quantitative genetics, psychology had moved from a strong hereditarianism to a strong environmentalism. The Fisher arguments were derived from a specific theory of genetics that entailed interaction. The fundamental issues were substantive, so that the issue of correlational versus variance components methodology was simply a matter of which statistical model fitted the data of heredity. The critiques of correlational analysis of genetic data were not relevant to, and thus did not influence, an environmentalistic psychology.

The other major creative contribution in the 1918 paper was the introduction of the term *variance* and the concept of the analysis of variance into its components. The first analysis-of-variance table, complete with an interaction term, appeared in 1923 (Fisher & Mackenzie, 1923). Fisher originated conceptualization in terms of sample space, and by 1925, he had expanded his thinking to the multivariate case with the introduction of what today would be called the *general linear model*. This he applied to a number of analytic problems, including analyses of variance and regression (Fisher, 1925). That statistical contribution also contributed to correlation analysis because, in multivariate sample space, the correlation coefficient is the cosine of the angle between two vectors. It is interesting that the use of dummy variables, introduced in that paper, has recently engaged behavioral scientists as though the idea were new (Kerlinger & Pedhazur, 1973). The ensuing analyses established the entire system of regression analysis, including analysis of variance, to replace correlation analysis. As Fisher (1950) was later to point out, many techniques of the times "misapplied" the term *correlation* (e.g., point-biserial correlation) to regression models. Many contemporary statistics texts in the behavioral sciences fail to make clear the major distinction between correlation models, which have meaning only as measures of the strength of linear association in bivariate normal distributions, and regression models, which predict the relationships between independent and dependent variables without restriction as to the form of the relationship and under conditions of great generality as to the distribution of the independent variables. Clear, brief presentations have been provided in various editions of the well-known texts of Ezekiel and of Snedecor (Ezekiel & Fox, 1959; Snedecor & Cochran, 1980).

With the introduction of the first ANOVA table in 1923, Fisher also introduced the concept of randomization. This led to a reconceptualization of research methodology in terms of "experimental designs" built on randomization (Fisher, 1935). Though behavioral scientists tend to be quite sensitive to the necessity for randomization in experimental methodology, its relevance to the ensuing statistical analysis is not so clearly understood. Fisher saw that his 1918 assumption of normality and independence of errors in the analysis of variance was not necessary, given randomization in the experimental design. Robustness in the analysis of variance in practical applications is achieved through the symmetry of errors achieved by the process of experimental randomization, rather than through intrinsic statistical properties of the analytic procedure (Fisher, 1925). The importance of randomization was later demonstrated in a paper that flew in the face of the intuition and the common sense of the day (Fisher & Barbacki, 1936). This paper considered the precision of systematic, compared with randomized, experimental designs in the assignment of plots in a field with a fertility gradient. The common expectation was that systematic assignment along the gradient to balance the fertility variation would show maximum precision. Contrary to expectation, the empirical results showed no gain—and, in fact, a loss—in precision. Thus, systematic designs showed no empirical gain, yet at the same time, they sacrificed the theoretical capability for probabilistic generalization that comes from randomization. Randomization is central to experimental methodology and to a meaningful interpretation of results. This central principle has been developed here at some length because test items are selected systematically.

Because of the close historical relationships between experimental design and the analysis of variance, there has been a continuing tendency to confuse sampling design with analytic design. It is important to keep in mind that "experimental design" governs the means of selection of subjects, and that one important factor in selection is whether treatment conditions are assigned as independent variables or are taken as they naturally occur as dependent variables. That is, it is sampling design that differentiates correlational from experimental methodology. Analytic design governs the means of examination of the numbers produced in the research. The question of whether those numbers should be subjected to correlational analysis or to analysis of variance is independent of the question of whether the numbers are a product of correlational or of experimental methodology.

Given Fisher's demonstration that correlational methods do not provide a basis for inference in the presence of interactions, coupled with the fact that interactions are the touchstone for test bias, it follows that an experimental design is needed for the examination of test bias. This chapter sets forth an experimental approach. Problems of randomization and sampling design in item selection and effects of failures of assumptions are examined. Because ethical considerations do not permit experimental control of the relevant variables with human subjects, an experimental animal model was developed to assess the empirical effects of conventional item-selection procedures. It is shown that standard psychometric-item procedures lead to bias in multiple-factor tests.

THE EXPERIMENTAL METHOD

The burgeoning of the sciences in the nineteenth and twentieth centuries can be attributed to the rise of the experimental method. For many years philosophers of science perceived the essence of the experimental method to be reductionism (Windelband, 1901/1958). Reducing a problem to simple elementary units allowed precise examination of those units in the laboratory. In the process of reducing problems to more elementary units, investigators found *inter alia* that simple units were often more tractable and thus susceptible to direct manipulation in the laboratory. Eventually, the pragmatists (Dewey, 1938; James, 1907) introduced an epistemology based on actions of the seeker of knowledge. In effect, they pointed out that an explanation of a phenomenon that is backed by the actual creation of that phenomenon under controlled conditions carries far more weight than an explanation based solely on an examination of the phenomenon as it occurs naturally, no matter how precise that examination.[1] Thus, only in the twentieth century did it become clear that the power of the experiment is attributable more to the manipulation of variables than to reductionism. *Experiment* came to be defined as research in which the experimenter controlled variation in *experimental variables* or, in current terminology, *independent variables* (Woodworth & Schlosberg, 1954). The modern scientist is well aware that correlation is not causation and thus prefers, where possible, research designed with independent variables.

Fisher's approach to experimentation by randomization lies in the category of knowledge gained by the action of the experimenter. The experimental procedures—in other words, the actions of the experimenter—are designed to enable particular analyses. That is, analyses of the data derive from the conduct of the experiment. The statistical model is inherently a model of the procedure as much as it is of the data. This approach based on the experimenter's actions (randomization) is quite different from an approach taking the data

[1]The idea of the scientist as an actor, and not simply a passive receiver, is Kantian, of course. Professor Fred W. Hallberg has pointed out to me that Kant (1791/1933) was the first to suggest the superiority of knowledge based on the actual creation of events, but that neither he nor his immediate successors pursued the idea further.

as given and regarding the statistical model as inherently a model of the phenomena under investigation. The first edition of what is widely considered the leading statistics textbook for the behavioral sciences was cast entirely in the latter, abstract-model framework (Hays, 1963). In its second edition, passing mention is made to "actual randomization performed in the experiment" as an alternative ratio-nale to that presented in the text (Hays, 1973). Hays identified his book as representing a "classical" or "normal-theory" model and implied that a randomization approach is an emerging new concept, when, in fact, randomization preceded the "normal-theory" model. This is not to criticize a minor passage but rather to observe that Hays is representative of the mainstream of American statistics in develop-ing statistical procedures from abstract mathematical models. There is a long history in statistics of confusion leading to controversy because of failure to distinguish between statistical usages motivated from abstract models and statistical usages motivated from concrete research operations (Box, 1978). Randomization is not a property of a mathematical model but a technique of experimental method that has certain desirable consequences for the interpretation of results. For example, with a random assignment of subjects to the levels of an independent variable, one can meaningfully interpret a standard-ized regression coefficient without assuming normality in either the independent or the dependent variable. Different and more stringent restrictions on interpretation apply if one assumes an underlying sta-tistical model and draws (rather than actively assigning) samples of subjects at selected levels of the independent variable. To meaning-fully interpret a standardized regression coefficient as a correlation coefficient requires the very specific mathematical model of bivariate normality and a population-sampling procedure in which both var-iates are dependent variables (by definition, a nonexperimental design).

In many research problems, experimentation is not possible, or at least, not feasible. In some fields, such as astronomy, this limitation is absolute. However, in many areas of interest, research strategies can be developed linking experimental studies with correlational studies. The best known general strategy is that of biomedical research, where experimentation is carried out with animal models until results are well established. Then, the results are extended with a combination of limited human experimentation and targeted nat-uralistic observation.

The vital issues that surround the problems of test bias relate to the nature and the explanation of observed group differences. Group differences, such as ethnic differences, are not susceptible to experimental manipulation in a free society. Yet there is a near infinitude of variables possibly correlated with group membership. Thus, definitive answers to questions about the nature of group differences cannot be obtained in the absence of experimental data—data that cannot practicably and ethically be obtained. Though definitive answers may be beyond reach, the practical problems are the same ones faced by the biomedical community. The strategy of using animal models has proved fruitful in advancing understanding in biomedicine, and here, the animal model strategy is applied to the problem of test bias.

ORIGINS OF ANIMAL TESTING

In its origins and early history, experimental animal psychology was an integral part of the rise of mental testing. Cattell (1890) was, of course, the originator of the term *mental test* and the leading figure in the early development of mental testing. It may be recalled that he was also the supervisor of the first experimental animal research, as systematic behavioral experimentation with animals is usually regarded as having begun with his student, E. L. Thorndike, and Thorndike's dissertation, *Animal Intelligence: An Experimental Study of the Associative Processes in Animals* (1898). Cattell suggested to Thorndike that he might try to apply the animal testing methods to the testing of children. Thorndike accepted the challenge, and the resulting work led ultimately, six years later, to his publication of *An Introduction to the Theory of Mental and Social Measurements* (1904), which established the field of educational measurement. Of course, it is well known that Thorndike's interest continued and that he became a leader in the mental test movement. Thus, psychometrics and animal experimental psychology share common roots and, in the early days of testing, shared common interests and common objectives. In early differential psychology, directions in human testing were suggested by results of animal research as much as animal studies were suggested from the study of human phenomena.

In many respects, Thorndike's early animal work was characterized by the same level of simplicity of test task as was promulgated by Galton. That simplicity typified the work of Cattell and testing in general at the turn of the century. However, while Thorndike was working on the translation of animal methods to humans, Small

(1900, 1901) introduced the use of the maze and the rat. This provided a technique for measuring complex problem-solving ability just at the time when it was becoming clear that the accumulation of a series of simple sensorimotor test results did not adequately characterize human intelligence. As a result, maze tests were developed for humans as well as for animals. The development of a complex solving test procedure was a harbinger of a trend in testing that would crystallize around Binet's scale, to usher in the modern era in testing.

The effectiveness of mazes in human testing reinforced confidence in their use for animal testing as a measure of intelligence. Accordingly, in the succeeding four decades until World War II, many of the issues concerning individual differences became prime topics for laboratory investigation with animals, just as they were prime topics for study in human populations. However, though animals were used for the study of substantive issues concerning individual differences, animal studies ceased to be major sources of influence on psychometric methodology.

The main theme of animal research, from Thorndike's dissertation until World War II, became the nature–nurture issue. The principal lines of application to investigations of learning are too well known to require repetition. On the nature side, investigators such as Bassett (1914) examined the relationship between genetic variation and maze performance. Tolman (1924) seems to have been the first to recognize that animal studies provided the opportunity for experimental analysis as distinct from correlational analysis. In attempting to carry through with manipulating individual variation as an independent variable rather than observing it as a dependent variable, Tolman encountered acute maze-reliability problems. This was a common state of affairs in maze studies up until that time. In retrospect, it is perhaps unfortunate that these reliability problems did not generate significant psychometric interest.

Tolman's work did stimulate two major lines of research. The first of these (McDougall, 1927, 1930, 1938; Rhine & McDougall, 1933), puporting to prove the Lamarckian position (inheritance of acquired characteristics), has passed into utter oblivion. The studies are of passing interest, however. Water mazes were used as tests. Animals that completely failed to learn in the mazes drowned and therefore were not progenitors of succeeding generations. Thus, the results were biased because data for those subjects that did not learn were excluded from analysis. The exclusion proved to be correlated with Mendelian genetic factors. Natural selection (drowning) eliminated the poorest maze learners, so that the mean performance of the offspring of the survivors was higher than the mean of those not exposed to the maze. The conduct of the experiment eliminated negative cases so that subject assignment could not be considered random. Exclusion of negative instances would open the same investigators to sampling criticisms when they later turned to extrasensory perception. Such studies do illustrate the problems of maintaining the randomization conditions required for experimental designs. Because a failure to meet the randomization requirements leaves only correlational data, these studies also illustrate the problems of interpretation of correlational data.

It was Tryon (1940, 1942) who finally produced a successful experimental study of hereditary influence by breeding lines of "maze-bright" and "maze-dull" rats. However, Tryon did note that the differences tended to be specific to the mazes used, and Searle (1949) provided extensive evidence showing lack of correlation with performance on other measures. Although the implications of such specificity for the understanding of individual differences did attract some attention, no one seems to have considered the possibility that the results might also have psychometric implications. Only later did the early problems of maze reliability and the specificity of selective breeding results suggest some alternative approaches.

Methodologically, in this period, the development and refinement of animal tests proceeded in two directions, reflecting different objectives and different uses. Investigations of "nurture" became studies of "learning." In accord with principles of experimental methodology, procedures were refined and simplified to isolate the relevant units for manipulation and analysis. Complex mazes were reduced to T or Y form or to the ultimate simplication of the maze: the single alley or runway. These simplifications enabled analysis of the structure of the individual response. Analysis of function was facilitated by shortening the alley to the point where successive responses could be made with minimal locomotion—the operant chamber. Studies of individual differences, the majority of which were directed to "nature" questions, tended to focus more on complex problem-solving tests. A number of variations of complex mazes were developed.

Immediately after World War II, Hebb and Williams (1946) described the development of two forms of a maze test. Each form consisted of a series of problems. Each problem was a maze with multiple choice points. Each form is loosely referred to as a *maze*, though properly each was a series of mazes. One of the forms was an elevated maze. The other form was a series of patterns using movable partitions in a closed field. Each showed good reliability and validity. The Hebb–Williams closed-field test and revisions thereof (Rabinovitch & Rosvold, 1951) became the standard complex problem-solving test for differential studies using the laboratory rat. This test came to occupy much the same place in animal testing as has the Stanford–Binet in human testing and has been broadly accepted as the animal analogue of human intelligence tests because of demonstrable validity in a variety of applications (Davenport, Hagquist, & Rankin, 1970; Livesey, 1966).

For the purposes of examining an experimental model of test bias, the Hebb–Williams type of maze provides an appropriate test instrument. The fact that such mazes are widely accepted as animal analogues of human intelligence tests is not, however, necessary to those purposes. Maze tests are a measure of performance in a complex problem-solving situation. The use of mazes with rats has been popular in part because the behavior is natural to the species. Thus, the test content has ecological validity. It is irrelevant to the general problem of bias whether this is an aptitude, an ability, or an achievement test. It is a test of complex behavior. Maze performance is known to depend on multiple factors. The maze is used as a test instrument in the present context solely for the psychometric property of being a multiple-factor test as distinguished from a unidimensional test. No further substantive characteristics of the test instrument are implied in the experimental design. The psychometric properties of multiple-factor tests are examined here under conditions of experimental control. Thus, any direct generalizations are to the psychometric domain, that is, to the characteristics of multiple-factor tests. Whether animal intelligence is an analogue of human intelligence and the behavioral implications of the data are both beyond the scope of this analysis.

SAMPLING AND ITEM SELECTION

It has long been known that test-item difficulties are different for different groups (Jones, Conrad, & Blanchard, 1932; Shimberg, 1929). Such variations in item difficulty appear as group-by-item interactions in an anlysis of variance. A test is considered biased if, and only if, the effects of such interactions lead to group differences in means, in predictive validities, or in standard errors of estimate of the test (Jensen, 1980).

In constructing the 1937 revision of the Stanford–Binet test, items were selected to balance for interactions of sex with item difficulty to ensure that the the tests would not show any group differences based on sex (McNemar, 1942). It should be obvious that, if one has selected items to eliminate group differences, then it is absurd to use the resulting test to show that there are no group differences. As a corollary, if items were selected to enhance group differences, it would be meaningless to use the resulting test to show that there were group differences. If group membership has been a factor in item selection for a test, then group differences cannot be evaluated with those items! If group membership has been a factor in item selection for a test, then group differences cannot be evaluated with that test!

Because group-by-item interactions represent difference evaluations at the item level, it follows that one cannot evaluate the extent of bias in item selection by examining the end product of selection. In fact, if randomly drawn items show group-by-item interactions, selection to balance items to equalize groups would tend to increase observed interactions in the resulting test, whereas selection to enhance group differences would tend to reduce interactions in the resulting test. This fact can be illustrated by considering selection from a universe of items to be used to test a population of two groups of individuals where there are group differences (G) in individual item difficulties (D), but the mean population difference between groups is zero when measured over all items in the item universe.

For the first illustration, select a set of items for a test minimizing group differences by the following strategy: (1) Draw an item from the universe; (2) select an item with the same magnitude of group difference but of opposite sign; and (3) repeat Steps 1 and 2 until a sufficient number (N) of item pairs has been selected. The resulting test will show absolutely no group difference. Because there is indeed no difference in the population, the test is unbiased. Now, a common recommended index of bias is the correlation of item difficulties between groups (Jensen, 1980). From the preceding example there are $2N$ items or N pairs. For each pair, the mean group scores for the paired items would be, respectively, $D_{n1} + G_n$ and $D_{n2} - G_n$ for one group, and $D_{n1} - G_n$ and $D_{n2} + G_n$ for the other group. The item difficulty correlation between the two groups would be

$$r = \frac{\sigma_D^2 - \sigma_G^2}{\sigma_D^2 + \sigma_G^2}$$

(in practice, Spearman's rho is usually used for convenience, but this has no effect on the theory). Clearly, σ_G^2 is nonzero, so $r < 1.00$. Yet, the test is unbiased. The correlation of item difficulties depends only on the relative magnitude of variance in item difficulty and not on bias.

Consider next the selection of items from the same population of individuals and the same item universe using a different strategy: (1) Select an item that shows a large group difference; (2) select an item showing a group difference of the same magnitude and sign; and (3) repeat Step 2 until a sufficient number of items (N) has been selected. For any given item, the item score for one group will be $D_n + G$ and for the other group, $D_n - G$. The resulting test will show a group difference, $2NG$. Because there is no difference in the population, the test is biased. In this case σ_G^2 vanishes and $r = \sigma_D^2/\sigma_D^2 = 1.00$. The item difficulties are perfectly correlated. Thus, with the selection of items, a high correlation of item difficulties is found in the biased test and a low correlation is found in the unbiased test. High correlations have been considered evidence of lack of bias and low correlations evidence of bias. Item selection can completely reverse the implications of item difficulty correlations.

It is also relevant to consider the underlying statistical assumptions in using the analysis of variance to assess group-by-item interactions. One alternative is a random effects model; that is, the items are drawn at random. They are not selected. The other alternative is a fixed effects model; that is, the items are fixed. They are selected. In fixed-effects models, results have no implied generality beyond the specific items. Yet, implicit in any test situation is prediction or inference beyond the test to some criterion. Hence, a test that has no generality beyond the specific items of which it is composed can have no validity. An analysis of variance of item characteristics is appropriate only if one can assume that the items were sampled, that is, randomly drawn from a universe. If the items are selected, rather than sampled, then the analysis of variance does not meet the necessary conditions for probabilistic inference.

Test bias can arise in the process of selecting items. It cannot be adequately assessed by examining the end product, the selected items. An appropriate experimental model must address the item selection process itself, not simply the resulting test. To accomplish this objective, any research design to examine bias must include actual item-selection operations under experimentally controlled conditions. The null hypothesis is that none of the item selection operations lead to test bias. The specification of alternative hypotheses depends on the specific design and the choice of the independent variables for experimental manipulation. Using an animal model, the experiments to be described later examined some consequences of using standard psychometric methods for item selection with experimental control of minority group membership as the independent variable.

CRITERION BIAS

Jensen's (1980) book is the most recent summary of the literature showing possible representations of group differences in regression of criterion on test scores. As Anastasi (1976) pointed out, the classic concept of bias is one in which the test score is lower than it should be, so that the true regression line for the minority is displaced to the left of the combined regression and of the nonminority regression. The result of such displacement would be a higher intercept for the minority regression. Use of the minority regression for the minority would correctly predict a higher performance for a given test score than would the combined regression. The combined regression would underpredict the performance of the minority, favoring the nonminority.

Reilly (1973) examined the statistical consequences if performances on both criterion and test are correlated with a third variable, which is correlated with group membership. He showed that, with reasonable statistical assumptions, this underlying "sociocultural" variable would lead to parallel regression lines with a lower intercept for the minority. He demonstrated that, under these circumstances, the use of the common regression line overpredicts (i.e., favors) the performance of the minority and underpredicts the performance of the nonminority. Jensen developed this point further at considerable length and rightly observed that such a regression pattern characterizes much of the available data on race differences and test performance. That is, the data are generally consistent with the hypothesis that racial differences reflect some third causal variable, such as a "sociocultural" disadvantage (or genetic variation), affecting both the test performance and the criterion performance of the individual.

An alternative hypothesis also fits the data. The third variable may be a biasing variable. Both the test and the criterion measures may be biased. Though this bias would lead to the same pattern of lower minority intercept as would a "sociocultural" variable, the common regression would not favor the minority as it would on the "sociocultural" hypothesis. A criterion-measurement-bias hypothesis leads to an entirely different interpretation from a "sociocultural" disadvantage hypothesis, and both fit the data. The criterion bias problem is therefore another relevant element in creating an experimental model.

ITEM SELECTION AND TEST THEORY

Nineteenth-century mental testing foundered on its reliance on isolated measurements of simple sensorimotor behaviors. The tests of that era were single-task—that is, single-item—tests. Spearman (1904) solved the problem by showing the advantages of pooling items to produce a multiple-item test, and in the process, he demonstrated that the problem with nineteenth-century testing was the low reliability of single-item tests. This work founded classical test theory, with a conceptual basis in the concept of reliability and a procedural basis in the pooling of items.

With his intelligence scale, Binet put this theory into practice— with a significant addition. He had concluded that complex mental function might better be measured by the use of complex tasks than by the use of simple sensorimotor tasks. The combination of these two ideas into a multiple complex-item scale was, as is well known, extremely successful. The test movement was provided with strong, pragmatic support for its new theoretical basis.

In revising Binet's scale for use in the United States, Terman (1916) expended a great deal of time and effort in evaluating and selecting items in terms of relative difficulty and relationship to overall test results. It was this careful attention to item analysis that caused the Standford–Binet to sweep the field and to become the standard intelligence scale. Terman's criterion of internal consistency became a cardinal principle of classical test methodology. Though the internal consistency criterion was originally a contribution to the reliability problem of classical test theory, it would later take on an even broader significance. Advances in the conceptualization of validity following World War II gave rise to the concept of construct validity. The requirement of internal consistency became an aspect of construct validity (Cronbach & Meehl, 1955) as well as of reliability. It is now referred to as a "necessary" condition for construct validity (Nunnally, 1978).

Selection of items is, of course, based first on considerations of content validity. This phase of the test construction process rests essentially on expert analysis and judgment. No matter how carefully done, this process contains an unavoidable element of subjectivity. Thus, there is always a possibility of bias in that judgment. For the reasons cited earlier, such sources of bias may not be detectable by analysis. If items must initially be devised and screened subjectively, then one can never be assured that those items resemble a random sample from an appropriate item universe.

After a collection of items has been devised, the next steps in test construction are to try out the items, to carry out an item analysis, and to select a subset for retention in the test. It is at this point that the internal consistency criterion comes into play. There are objective procedures for selecting a subset of items. In classical test theory, several alternative indices are available to provide a basis for choice among items (Gulliksen, 1950). All of the indices used in practice are based on the item–test correlation or on the related item–test or test–item regressions. This chapter specifically examines the consequences of classical test-theory use of the item–test correlation as a criterion for item selection.

Although they are beyond the scope of the empirical studies covered here, it is appropriate for the purposes of context and completeness to mention other procedures in item selection. In classical test theory, one may, in principle, select items not only for reliability but for validity as indicated by item–criterion correlations. In practice, it is seldom that an independent criterion is directly available for such an approach to item selection. In achievement and personality tests, validity is almost invariably content- or construct-based. Independent criterion measurements are often somewhat more readily defined for ability tests but still present problems. Ability tests are intended for assessment or prediction in more than one situation. Thus, the test criteria for differing situations differ, with resulting differences in validities. As a result, item selection for item validity may contribute little, if anything, to the general usefulness of a test. In practice, therefore, item selection is usually based on reliability on the internal consistency criterion, a practice bolstered by the fact that validity generally tends to increase with reliability. Moreover, because criterion measurement is usually subject to error of measurement, just as is test measurement, the criterion measurement used for item–criterion correlation item-selection is only an estimate. For item–test correlation item-selection, the test is being used to estimate a trait. If the possession of that trait is the criterion, then, given good content and construct validity, the test often seems the best practical estimate of the criterion.

Conceiving of the test under item analysis as an estimator of the trait also provides a framework for an alternative to classical test theory. Latent trait theory assumes that each item in a test is characterized by its difficulty and by the extent to which it measures the trait underlying the test. An individual's response to an item is therefore a stochastic function of the item's difficulty and the individual's trait level. Of several alternatives available, the current preference is to follow Rasch (1966) and Birnbaum (1968) and to assume that the trait–difficulty relationship is a logistic function. The individual-by-item score matrix and the adjoined test-score column matrix define a set of simultaneous logistic equations. The maximum likelihood solution yields trait estimates for individuals and difficulty estimates for items. These can be used to obtain the statistical operating characteristic of each item. This is the latent-trait theoretic item-characteristic curve (ICC). Because the procedure leads to estimates of the absolute parameters of the ICCs, it is presumably sample-independent. Items thus can be selected for a test on the basis of their absolute characteristics. At the moment, there is no evidence, in terms of test characteristics, that item selection based on latent trait theory offers any practical advantages over classical test methods (Douglass, Khavari, & Farber, 1979). Classical methods are much simpler and less laborious. Presumably, the added labor of latent trait methods becomes cost-effective in the construction of item banks where the items can be used for the construction of multiple forms. However, the use of such fixed-item banks raises, and leaves unanswered at this time, the very questions of randomization and selection considered by Fisher half a century ago and examined earlier here. Currently, then, there are problems yet to be explored in latent trait methods, and those methods seem to offer most promise to larger scale test developers. Thus, most test development still rests on classical test theory.

Although the studies to be discussed here rest only on classical test-theory item-selection, the present focus is not based solely on the fact that most tests are constructed by classical methods. Indeed, its sample independence gives latent trait theory strong theoretical advantages that might ultimately point toward better methodology. On the other hand, latent trait theory rests on a set of assumptions different from those that underlie classical test theory. The assumption of most relevance to the empirical work is that the items of a test measure a unitary trait. This assumption of unidimensionality underlies most latent trait methodology. In principle, a multidimensional latent-trait model is possible with only slightly less restrictive assumptions, but at the price of a substantial increase in the complexity of an already-complex system of item analysis. In the studies reported here, it is not assumed that the items are unidimensional, and thus, the data are not appropriate for currently used methods of latent trait analysis.

Jensen (1980) suggested that similarity of within-group ICCs is evidence of lack of bias. It should perhaps be pointed out that the ICCs he showed were those of classical test theory and not those of latent trait theory. For classical test theory, the ICC is the regression (curvilinear) of the item score (or probability of passing for dichotomous scoring) on the test score. For latent trait theory, the ICC is the regression of the item score (or probability of passing) on the estimated trait level.

For an experimental model, we turn to the development of a test to predict maze performance. To this end, the construction of an item pool to serve as the item universe from which items are selected is described. Populations of individuals are experimentally defined in terms of homogeneous groups within those populations. The effects of the use of classic test-theory methodology for item selection are examined with differing populations.

PROCEDURES

Six genetically homogeneous groups were chosen from six inbred strains of rats listed in the Fourth International Listing of Strains (Festing & Staats, 1973). Standard nomenclature is described in that reference. Detailed descriptions of the strains have been reported elsewhere (Harrington, 1981). The groups were males from INR/Har, IR/Har, and MNR/Har, and females from A35322/Har, MNRA/Har, and WAG/Har. All animals were bred and maintained under standard conditions (Harrington, 1968). For Experiment 1, there were 366 subjects, 61 animals from each of the six defined groups. For Experiment 2, there was an independent sample of 146 subjects from these same groups numbering from 20 to 31 from each group. At the beginning of Experiment 1 and Experiment 2, the subjects were 90–108 days of age. Experiment 3 used the same subjects used in Experiment 2.

All data were based on the use of Hebb–Williams-type closed-field maze tests in configurations with well-established reliability and validity (Davenport *et al.*, 1970; Hebb & Williams, 1946; Livesey, 1966;

Rabinovitch & Rosvold, 1951). This was a square field 72.5 cm on each side with walls 10 cm high. The floors and walls were painted a uniform background color, except that the floor was divided into 36 squares by stripes of a contrasting color 1.9 cm wide. A start box and a goal box were in opposite corners with gates that could be raised or lowered. Movable partitions the width of the stripes provided the means for creating varying problem configurations. For the first two experiments, the fields were either white or black and the partitions were either white or black. This arrangement provided four possible combinations of partition color and field color. For Experiment 3, both field and partitions were an intermediate gray.

The most used version of this procedure consists of six "pretraining" configurations and 12 "test" configurations (Rabinovitch & Rosvold, 1951). However, all were used here for test purposes, so that that differentiation is not applicable. A total of 19 configurations was obtained by adding another configuration to the set. With a problem defined as a specific configuration combination, 4 different black and white color combinations and 19 (XIX) configurations provided a total of 76 problems.

For both Experiment 1 and Experiment 2, the subjects were tested on all 76 problems. The testing sequence was fixed for the first 28 problems. The animals were tested on a sequence of seven configurations (I–VII) first with the white-on-white maze. The same sequence of configurations was repeated with black-on-white combinations, then again with white-on-black, and finally with the black-on-black maze. After completing 28 problems, the animals were tested on Problems 29–76, going through the standard configuration sequence (VIII–XIX) four times. Though the configuration order was fixed for these problems, the color combinations were randomized from problem to problem for each animal individually. Thus, each animal encountered a random color sequence that differed from subject to subject, and the patterns recurred every 12th problem. The testing sequence is shown in Table 1. (The rather complex sequencing was derived from other research objectives not relevant to these studies.)

A different maze was used (Davenport et al., 1970) for Experiment 3. The standard procedure was used with this maze: 4 unscored practice problems followed by 12 test problems in standard sequence.

The testing provided 15 trials on each problem at the rate of one problem a day. The reinforcement was a 45-mg Noyes pellet in the goal box for each trial. The animals were maintained at 85% of *ad libitum* body weight. For each trial, the following data were

TABLE 1
Item-Pool Testing-Sequence

Problem	Configuration	Color	Item
1	I	White on white	1–5
.	.	.	.
.	.	.	.
7	VII	White on white	31–35
8	I	Black on white	36–40
.	.	.	.
.	.	.	.
14	VII	Black on white	66–70
15	I	White on black	71–75
.	.	.	.
.	.	.	.
21	VII	White on black	101–105
22	I	Black on black	107–110
.	.	.	.
.	.	.	.
28	VII	Black on black	136–140
29	VIII	Randomized	141–145
.	.	for	.
.	.	each	.
40	XIX	subject	196–200
41	VIII	for	201–205
.	.	each	.
.	.	problem	.
52	XIX	.	256–260
53	VIII	.	261–265
.	.	.	.
.	.	.	.
64	XIX	.	316–320
65	VIII	.	321–325
.	.	.	.
.	.	.	.
76	XIX	.	376–380

recorded: (1) the time from the opening of the start gate until the animal's head passed through the gate; (2) the time required to pass completely through the gate and out of the start box; (3) the time from leaving the start box to entering the goal box; and (4) the number of errors.

DATA ANALYSIS

For each problem, five measures were constructed from the data obtained. For each trial, the reciprocals of the three time measures were used as measures of speed. Averaging over the 15 trials for each measure for each problem yielded start speeds, exit speeds, and goal speeds. The fourth measure was the total number of errors over 15 trials. The fifth measure was the trials to criterion. The criterion was both (1) four errorless trials out of five sequential trials and (2) a maximum of 10 seconds' goal latency in four out of five sequential trials. Failures to reach criterion were rare. Where they occurred, the animal was arbitrarily assigned a score for that problem from 16 to 19, based on the minimum number of trials in which criterion could have been achieved. Each of these derived measures was considered an item score. Thus, there were 5 different test items associated with each of the 76 problems. This is a total of 380 items in all. For all measures, in order that higher achievement levels would be reflected by higher scores, the signs of the error scores and the trial-to-criterion scores were changed. This procedure resulted in a covariance matrix in which over 90% of the elements were positive. This is a desirable precondition for internal consistency analysis (Nunnally, 1967).

All item scores were transformed to standard normal deviates by subtracting the mean for that item over all subjects and dividing by the standard deviation. Thus, all items were equally weighted. This normalization was done separately for each of the three experiments. Inspection of the data revealed no unusual characteristics in the score distributions. To check the data, skew and kurtosis were calculated for each item score and were well within the limits of sampling variability for normal distributions. In a preliminary analysis (Harrington, 1975), all item scores were standardized empirically to yield an absolutely normally distributed data matrix. No substantive difference was detected between the results of analysis based on empirically standardized scores and the conventional analysis that follows.

Experiment 1: Construction of Parallel Tests

For the design of Experiment 1, six experimental "populations" of subjects were formed. The 61 animals within each genotype (strain) were randomly assigned to one of six minority groups consisting of 22, 15, 11, 8, 5, and 0 animals. The resulting six minority groups of each genotype were then randomly assigned to experimental populations subject to the condition that each genotypic minority group appeared once and only once in each population and subject to the condition that each population was composed of every size of group. The result was six populations each made up of six minority groups of the same genotypes but differing in the proportional representation of each of these minorities in the population. It will be noted that this is a 6 × 6 Latin square in which one dimension identifies populations; the other dimension represents the representation of the minority in the population, namely, 22 (36%), 15 (25%), 11 (18%), 8 (13%), 5 (8%), and 0 (0%); and the cells represent the assignment of genotypes. The design is shown in Figure 1. All assignment of subjects was done by computer by means of a random number-generating subroutine in the context of the actual data analysis. Thus, the assignment of subjects was unknown to the experimenters throughout the process of data collection, was unknown during analysis, and, in fact, remains unknown.

Each of the six populations was then considered independently as a base population. The data from the subjects within a population were used for item analysis for the construction of a maze performance test. Within each population, the 50 items showing the highest correlation with the total of the items were selected as the maze performance test for that population. Selection of items on the basis of correlation with total test score is the conventional procedure for applying the internal consistency criterion in selecting items from a larger item pool (Guilford, 1954; Nunnally, 1967).

The resulting six sets of 50 items each constituted six nominally parallel test forms of maze performance, each constructed on the

Representation of Each Minority in Each Test-Base Population
(Percentage of Base Population)

		36%	25%	18%	13%	8%	0%
	A	I	II	III	IV	V	VI
	B	II	III	I	VI	IV	V
Test Base Population (or Test)	C	III	I	II	V	VI	IV
	D	IV	V	VI	I	II	III
	E	V	VI	IV	III	I	II
	F	VI	IV	V	II	III	I

FIGURE 1. Latin-square experimental design for assignment of individuals from homogeneous groups (Roman numerals) to test base populations (letters) for test development. (Example of interpretation: Group I comprised 36% of test base population used to develop Test A. Group VI comprised 18% of population used to develop Test D.)

same criteria from the same item pool. They differed only in that the item selection was based on an item analysis from a different population. Each of these six test-base populations used for item analysis was comprised of the same six genotypes, but in differing proportions.

EXPERIMENT 2: MINORITY GROUP PERFORMANCE

Logically, given the experimental design, it is sufficient to analyze the data of Experiment 1 to determine whether the experimental manipulations affect item selection. On the other hand, if the experiment is considered a model of psychometric procedure, then there is justification for following psychometric practice further. It is standard psychometric procedure to cross-validate any consequences of test construction on an independent sample. Experiment 2 was that independent validation. The subjects in Experiment 2 were tested with the same procedures and the same 380 items as in Experiment 1. It was possible, therefore, to obtain the scores of each animal on each of the six tests constructed in Experiment 1 simply by scoring each animal on each set of 50 items comprising those tests. It is self-evident that this procedure provided complete experimental control of any error variance associated with order effects or multiple testing.

The mean of test scores for each test was then obtained for each genotype. Thus, there were six means of scores for each genotype. The only experimental variable differentiating the tests was that each genotype represented a different proportion of the base population for item analysis for each test in Experiment 1. Though the experimental operations were simple and clear-cut, the properties of the data are complicated by the fact that cell frequency as an independent variable does not readily fit standard parametric statistical models. It is straightforward, however, to look at the order statistics for that independent variable. That is, the data can be ordered on the basis of representation in the base population as shown in Figure 2. For each genotype, it was convenient and appropriate to rank the mean scores on the six tests. With six genotypes and six levels of representation, analysis called for a nonparametric analogue of the analysis of variance against an ordered hypothesis. Page's L (1963) was appropriate. As can be seen from Table 2, $L = 500$, $p < .001$. The data were unequivocal in showing that for these homogeneous

Representation of Minority in Test Base Population
(Percentage of Base Population)

	36%	25%	18%	13%	8%	0%
I	M_A	M_C	M_B	M_D	M_E	M_F
II	M_B	M_A	M_C	M_F	M_D	M_E
III	M_C	M_B	M_A	M_E	M_F	M_D
IV	M_D	M_F	M_E	M_A	M_B	M_C
V	M_E	M_D	M_F	M_C	M_A	M_B
VI	M_F	M_e	M_D	M_B	M_C	M_A

FIGURE 2. Design for test mean (M) comparisons on each $(N = 20–31)$ group (Roman numerals) on each test (letters). (Example of interpretation: Group I represented 36% of the base population used to develop Test A, and M_A is the group performance on that test; Group VI were 18% of the population used to develop Test D, and M_D is the group performance on that test.)

TABLE 2
Rankings of Means of Test Scores on Nominally Parallel Tests

Source	Representation of minority group in test base population (percentage)						Rank statistics
	36	25	18	13	8	0	
	Within groups						Rho
Group							
I	2	1	6	3	4	5	.60
II	4	3	1	2	6	5	.43
III	2	1	5	6	3	4	.49
IV	4	1	2	6	3	5	.43
V	2	5	1	3	6	4	.43
VI	1	2	3	4	5	6	1.00
	Groups combined						Page's L
Sum	15	13	18	24	27	29	
(Order)	(1)	(2)	(3)	(4)	(5)	(6)	
Product	15	26	54	96	135	174	
							500*

*$p < .001$.

groups there was a significant positive association between the test performance of a group and representation in the population used for item analysis and the ensuing item selection.

Each group (G) has some mean performance M_g for all items in the item universe. With item selection effects (S) related to level (L) of representation in the item analysis population, the expected group mean performance on any test is

$$E(Mg_l) = Mg + S_l.$$

The data analysis used ordinal estimates of S_l and demonstrated that S_l is ordered and not random. An index of the magnitude of selection effects can be obtained for graphic representation by obtaining, at each level, the mean value of S_l. It is immediately obvious that this is identical with the mean of the ranks of test score means at each level. Figure 3 utilizes this index to display the increasing test scores with an increasing representation in the item analysis population. Because all levels of representation are less than 50% (a minority), the data speak only to minority group representation.

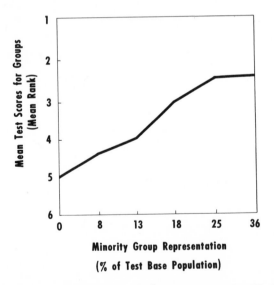

FIGURE 3. Mean rank of samples from six homogeneous groups, each ranked on scores on six nominally parallel tests as a function of the proportional representation of the groups in the six independent base-populations used for development of the six tests.

EXPERIMENT 3: MINORITY EFFECTS ON TEST VALIDITY

Experiment 3 investigated the predictive validity of the tests. Performance on the 60 items of the test problems of the gray maze was defined as the criterion to be predicted by the test constructed in Experiment 1. Thus, the sum of the 60 standardized item scores was the criterion score. The predictive validity of each test was then the correlation between the score on that test and the criterion score. It should be particularly noted that the initial set of items in the item pool used to construct the predictive tests consisted of identically the same kinds of items in identically the same proportions as did the criterion. Therefore, the predictive item pool met the standard criteria for content validity. Both the application of the internal consistency criterion and the close and obvious relationship between test items and criterion items established construct validity.

The predictive validities are the product–moment correlations between each of the tests and the criterion that were calculated for each group. There was necessarily item overlap between the various tests. Therefore, the distribution function of the correlation coefficients is unknown. One of the reasons is that, in this experiment, the variance of the coefficients is necessarily substantially less than for independent samples. A nonparametric analysis is again indicated. Ranking the coefficients and ordering the data for each group on the basis of representation in the item-selection-base population also led to Page's nonparametric analogue of the analysis of variance with an ordered hypothesis. For the ranking of validity coefficients, as shown in Table 3, $L = 495$, $p < .001$ (one-tailed). A one-tailed test was the only proper one for these data. (The use of a two-tailed test would assume the possibility of results on the other tail. This possibility would require that validity increase with decreasing information, an absurdity.)

The data were unequivocal in indicating that for these homogeneous groups the predictive validity of the tests was associated with representation in the population on which the item analysis of the test was based. Following the same reasoning and procedures used in Experiment 2, mean ranks of predictive validities were obtained at each level of representation. The increasing predictive validity with increasing minority-group representation is displayed graphically in Figure 4.

The data from all subjects in Experiment 2 and 3 were pooled and examined with a variety of procedures. No anomalies were

TABLE 3
Rankings of Predictive Validities of Nominally Paralled Tests

Source	Representation of minority group in test base population (percentage)						Rank statistics
	36	25	18	13	8	0	
	Within groups						Rho
Group							
I	1	2	4	5	6	3	.66
II	1	4	2	3	6	5	.77
III	2	1	6	4	5	3	.43
IV	1	4	5	2	6	3	.37
V	1	3	6	4	2	5	.43
VI	2	5	1	3	6	4	.43
	Groups combined						Page's L
Sum	8	19	24	21	31	23	
(Order)	(1)	(2)	(3)	(4)	(5)	(6)	
Product	8	38	72	84	155	138	
							495*

*$p < .001$ (one-tailed).

detected, and the six tests gave every indication of being six closely parallel forms for a population with approximately equal numbers of each genotype.

THE INTERNAL CONSISTENCY CRITERION

What is tested by analogy depends on the soundness of the analogy. What is tested directly can be generalized directly. These experiments directly tested the effects of using standard psychometric procedures. Therefore, generalization to those procedures is direct. First, the mean performance of homogeneous groups on tests tends to vary directly with the extent of the representation of the groups in the population used for the psychometric construction of the tests. Second, the predictive validity of tests for members of homogeneous groups tends to vary with the representation of the groups in the population used for the psychometric construction of the tests. The effects occurred experimentally solely as a result of applying standard methods. Because these effects are a product of a methodology, they are, by definition, artifacts. Thus, two different forms of

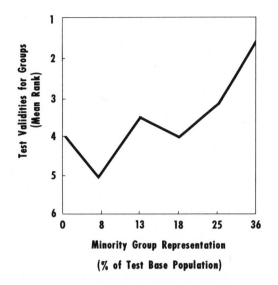

FIGURE 4. Mean rank of samples from six homogeneous groups, each ranked on predictive validities of six nominally parallel tests as a function of the proportional representation of the groups in the six independent base populations used for the development of the six tests.

minority test bias occur as psychometric artifacts from the use of standard psychometric procedures.

These artifacts occurred despite the fact that the tests met conventional psychometric standards (American Psychological Association, 1966). In the experimental procedures, the pool of predictor items provided a properly balanced sample of items matching the criterion both in the types of items and in the proportions of each type. Therefore, the criteria for content validity were fully met. Because the items also clearly sampled the types of behavior being predicted, they also offered some degree of construct validity. Clearly, the observed effects are attributable to the use of the internal consistency criterion. The application of that criterion led to the selection of a set of items that did not have the characteristics of a sample randomly drawn from the item universe.

GROUP-BY-ITEM INTERACTIONS

Nothing in the empirical scientific literature suggested such possibilities. Experiment 1 showed that minority group membership affected item selection. Experiment 2 showed that the item selection effect was not random error and resulted in test bias. Experiment 3 showed that this minority effect also affects the predictive validity of the test. No evidence was to be found for one of those unusual sampling events that statistical theory says can occur, though with a high degree of improbability. On the contrary, a detailed examination of the data and the procedures indicated no significant deviations from normality in distributions.

Could these minority effects be an instance of the phenomenon represented in the "Chitlin'," or Dove, test or its more recent version, the Black Intelligence Test of Cultural Homogeneity (BITCH test) (Dove, 1968; Kifner, 1968; Williams, 1972)? Almost everyone is now familiar with this test, which contains a series of ghetto, welfare-oriented items of which the upper-middle-class white would purportedly be totally ignorant. At first glance, it seems very reasonable to draw this analogy. There are some items that are just not predictive for some groups because their cultural background may not include any experience related to the item. After all, Binet's test had to be translated into English to be used in this country, and American children would do very badly on the original French version. For them, it would have near-zero validity.

However, this analogy fails to fit the experimental conditions. The whole idea behind the "Chitlin'" test was that it shifted the criterion from survival in a professional white suburb to survival in an unemployed black ghetto. The school-administered "intelligence" test and the "Chitlin'" test are not designed to predict the same things. Any perceived commonality rests on the assumption that both indirectly measure some unobservable underlying psychological entity that we label *intelligence*, which is reflected in adaptations to one's environment. In short, any commonality derives from perceiving both as indirect measures of a common trait not directly measurable. However, in the present experiments, the criterion was objectively defined, and the question being asked of the data was a question of the validity of the test for minority groups in predicting the same common criterion. The "Chitlin'" test calls into question both the relevance of the items and the relevance of the criteria. The data reported here show that, even when items are relevant and the criteria are common, standard psychometric procedures result in a reduction in validity for homogeneous minorities.

Now, what are the conditions under which group membership could influence item selection and validity? Obviously, the data show group-by-item interactions in the psychometric sense and genotype-by-environment interactions in the biological sense. The results suggest that the observed differences in group means could be attributed to disordinal interactions. The differences in test validities must be attributed to disordinal interactions. Jensen (1980) has shown at some length that disordinality is a necessary condition for differential group validities. Disordinality is present if items exist that are positively correlated with the criterion for some groups and that are negatively correlated with that criterion for other groups. However, though this is a sufficient condition, it is not evident that it is a necessary condition except for the case of unidimensional tests, which is the case to which Jensen's analysis is devoted. Further work on item selection is in progress. Although neither the empirical nor the theoretical aspects of that work are complete, it now appears that such negative correlations in item factor scores, rather than raw item scores, are sufficient to affect validity. Whatever the case, with disordinality there are simply no mathematical manipulations that can be used to adjust the data to compensate for the effects and to render the tests equally valid for all. There is a minority effect that depresses both test scores and test validity in a way that cannot be corrected simply by using different norms. The evidence shows that the real world is not fully consonant with psychometric assumptions. The result is a psychometric artifact.

FROM RATS TO HUMANS

What are the limits for generalization from an animal model? Generalization depends on the similarity or difference in the phenomena or processes studied. The experiments tested standard psychometric procedures, and therefore, the generalization is to those procedures. There is nothing in the experimental design or the hypotheses tested that is specific to rats. What was tested was the method of test development. The statistical principles on which psychometric methods rest do not change in the presence or absence of humans. From this viewpoint, the results are universal. They apply to those differences on the Minnesota Multiphasic Personality Inventory that necessitate separate norms for blacks and for whites in assessing psychopathology in exactly the same way that they apply to differences on an employment aptitude test, a school achievement examination, or the Wechsler Intelligence Scale for Children.

Some may grant the applicability to personality assessment, but not to IQ. Are the results applicable to human intelligence? The

Hebb–Williams test is commonly regarded as an analogue of human intelligence tests. Note, though, that the data imply a far more complex structure for intellective behavior than is commonly proposed in explanation of human intelligence. The results obtained are, however, consistent with the detailed analysis of McGuire and Hirsch (1977). The behavior measured clearly is multifactorial. To suggest that such results are true only for animals and not for humans is to argue that the rat is intellectually a much more complicated creature than is the human being. Yet this, it seems to me, is the implication of the g hypothesis. In most behavioral matters, humans are more complex than infrahuman species, and the burden of proof would seem to lie with those who would contend that intelligence is a striking contrary instance.

Turning from the psychological to the biological, consider the proposition that genetic-environmental interactions are characteristic of lower species or inbred strains but not of humans. The theory of evolution posits that environmental circumstances tend to select out those genotypes best adapted to survival in the specific environment and that, in different environmental circumstances, different genotypes are selected. The theory is that different genes fit different environments better. This theory exactly defines the term *genetic-environmental interaction*. Different genotypes respond differently in different environments. The existence of such interactions is a necessary precursor to natural selection in the evolution of species. If, in fact, one concludes that such interactions do not exist for humans, the implication would be that humans are not a product of evolution. This is more nearly a nineteenth-century theological point of view than a view of contemporary science. Alternatively, one could suggest that, for humans, all interactions have been selected out. This viewpoint would imply that humans have reached the end of the evolutionary road and that further evolution is biologically impossible. This is a profoundly novel biological idea. It would be a stunning scientific discovery if empirically demonstrated.

There is no substantial documented evidence pro or con on the existence of genetic-environmental interactions in intelligence. Evolutionary theory requires the existence of such interactions for natural selection for fitness. It is possible that whatever intelligence tests measure is devoid of evolutionary significance or survival value. In that case, there might be no observed interactions. Such a possibility is not to be summarily dismissed. It is not at all clear that intelligence tests measure anything of significant long-term survival value for the human species.

CORRELATION AND CAUSATION

The present data do speak to some classic problems in testing. The animal behavior cannot be represented with a single general factor such as Spearman's g (1904). The experimental design used to generate the present data involved random permutations of minority group size for six minority groups. Every permutation produced significantly different results. Only a multiple-factor interpretation can account for the differentiation of the groups. Because six distinct orderings were actually obtained, the lower bound for the number of factors is of the order of 6.

On the other hand, the data also are not consistent with a model of complete behavioral specificity. Complete specificity is tantamount to an infinite number of factors. Systematic variation in validity coefficients was found in Experiment 3. Such results can occur only if there are systematic intragroup vis-à-vis intergroup dependencies. The intergroup variation in means showed a lower bound of the order of six factors for the differentiation of groups in means of test scores. The intergroup variation in validity coefficients shows a lower bound on the order of six factors for the differentiation of groups in covariation between test and criterion. The data do not reveal whether the same factors govern differentiation of means as govern differentiation of validity. On the other hand, there were 50 items on the tests and 60 items on the criterion. If the number of factors were very large or there were complete specificity, 50 items would not afford a sufficient number of degrees of freedom to differentiate the group covariations. Thus, the upper bound to the number of factors is on the order of 50.

These factor bounds have an important consequence. It follows that the data can be explained by a finite number of variables. (See McGuire & Hirsch, 1977, for an explanation of how polygenic inheritance may permit description of the effects of an infinite number of possible genetic combinations in terms of a finite number of multiple factors.) This offers substantial hope for the future. If the realm is finite, it can be brought within the boundaries of understanding.

These observations have another consequence. Bias arises as a result of the item selection procedures in the presence of multiple factors. Consider a test devised by standard psychometric procedures for purposes of prediction. Let us label it an "aptitude" test. The test may be biased. Consider a criterion that is measured by a test that has also been developed by standard psychometric procedures. Let us label it an "achievement" test. The item selection for the criterion test is then subject to the same item selection procedures and the same multiple factors as was the predictor test. Thus, it is subject to the same underlying interactions. Both tests will be biased. Both tests will be biased in the same way. Similar disordinalities will have been selected against on both predictor and criterion. Therefore, the groups will tend to show the same magnitude of difference on both the predictor and the criterion. Selection against the disordinalities on the predictor and the criterion will also select against the disordinalities in covariation. It is those disordinalities that account for the validity coefficient differences in Experiment 3. Thus, selection on both predictor and criterion tends to eliminate differences in calculated validities.

Because the experimental validities represent true validities, the experimental procedures provided power not ordinarily available in the testing situation. In the experiment, the criterion (the criterion test) was established by experimental definition. By definition, the criterion was measured without error because the defined purpose of the tests was to predict each animal's performance in that specific set of mazes. With a criterion measured without error, it was possible to see that the true predictive validities varied with representation in the predictor-test item-selection population. As the preceding analysis shows, if there is item selection leading to bias for a predictor test, and if such item selection procedures are also applied to the criterion test, then (1) the criterion test will be biased; (2) the group means will differ in the same way on both predictor and criterion; and (3) the apparent group validities will be spuriously equal.

Because the obtained experimental validities were the true validities, it is evident that the correlation between the predictor tests and any nonrandom subset of the criterion is not a true validity. Item selection on the criterion would increase the estimated validity for groups in proportion to the disordinalities in the true covariation while decreasing the true validity. It follows that if there is item selection leading to group bias in a predictor test, and if such item selection procedures are also applied to the criterion test, then, subject to random variation, (1) the criterion test will be biased; (2) the group means will be biased in the same way in both predictor test and criterion test; (3) the observed group validities will be equal; and (4) the observed group validities will be greater than the true validities. That is, if a predictor is biased on the basis of item selection as found in the present experiments, and if similar item selection procedures are used in constructing a criterion test, then it follows that (1) the observed regression of criterion on predictor will be the same for all groups and (2) group-by-item interactions will be minimal in the tests. Bias in both tests will result in common intercepts and common slopes.

The full implications of these results are not yet clear. Experimentally, it proved to be convenient to create homogeneous groups by controlling genotype. Many psychologists are inclined to believe that environmental factors have a more profound impact than do genetic factors in the final determination of individual characteristics. There is every reason to believe that comparable results would have occurred had the groups been differentiated by environmental manipulation rather than by genetic manipulation. Such an experiment needs to be done. It would be amazing if the results could not be replicated if environmental manipulation were used in lieu of genetic differences.

A completely unanswered question in terms of the generalization of results lies in the problem of defining a homogeneous group. Experimentally, such a definition has been made possible by breeding control and by environmental control. That control has defined the similarity of one white rat to another and of one black rat to another. The results show that there is a bias with respect to homogeneous minority groups, but the results do not indicate the essential factors differentiating those minority groups. Breeding control has established only that all members of a group have essentially the same genealogy and its associated expectation, that they have essentially the same genes. It does not tell what has been controlled that is relevant.

In human affairs, one of the errors of racism has been to assume that, because one can identify the skin color gene, it is necessarily in any way biologically associated with other genes that may be affecting the behavior of concern. From a population-genetic perspective, races are not characterized by genes common to all members. Races differ genetically only in the relative frequency with which different genes are found among members of the race. The same genes are found in all races. Thus, any racial differences in characteristics affected by those genes occur solely as a result of differences in frequency. Consider as a hypothetical example a racial minority (A) showing a very high frequency—say, 85%—of a gene, m_a, with the alternative, m_b, at 15%. Let this be a gene that interacts with test items so that m_a carriers do better on one type of item and m_b on another. Let another racial minority (B) show the reverse frequencies. Let a racial majority (C) show 60% m_a. Then, item selection will tend to bias tests in terms of the majority of m_a. The majority, A, will show mean scores higher than the majority, C, which, in turn, will be higher than those of another minority, B. The test will favor $.85^2$ $(.85 \times .85$, since genes are paired) of the members of A, $.60^2$ of C, and $.15^2$ of B. On the other hand, the test will disfavor $.15^2$ of A, $.40^2$ of C, and $.85^2$ of B. The observed group differences arise only through a gene frequency correlation with the irrelevant variable of race. Therefore, tests standardized on natural racial groupings do not resolve the bias problem. Not only may there be accidental correlations with race, but it is abundantly clear that there can be accidental correlations within races (Hirsch, 1967).

Developing different tests for different groups defined on an irrelevant though correlated variable, as compared with using a single test, may reduce bias somewhat for some but may increase it for others. By no means would it necessarily remove bias for the population as a whole. Elimination of the bias first requires an identification of the relevant variables and a description of the individual in terms of those relevant variables. To achieve the elimination of bias by the use of alternative tests requires tests appropriate to the individual's characteristics.

The data of this research program provide one explanation of minority group differences in test performance. The results are applicable to all forms of tests. They imply a general tendency for tests to be biased against minorities and to have less validity when used with minorities. They imply that the effects of the biases are not fully removable by the development of separate norms. One possibility is the development of separate tests. At the same time, it is clear that a superficial definition of minority membership is likely to tap not relevant variables but only correlated variables without causal relationship. Therefore, the results do not support simplistic approaches to developing alternative tests. Rather, they suggest a search for the relevant variables. The data do imply that such variables exist in finite number, so that the task is not impossible. A multiplicity of variables implies that useful tests must be multifactorial, not global. This, in turn, implies a test battery structure oriented toward differential prediction or diagnosis and not toward assessment of level. Moreover, the data do not encourage hope for a fixed test system as a single frame of reference. Rather, they may imply a relativistic system necessitating a sequential, subject–response dependent approach to differential assessment.

The data do, of course, indicate that the bias arises from the fact that items are selected, not sampled, from the item universe. Thus, the means of item selection tends both to bias the tests and to negate the statistical assumption underlying most psychometric analyses, that is, that the items behave as if drawn at random. Accordingly, there is a clear need for systematic study and creative thinking to improve the processes of item selection.

Both of the above approaches seem necessary. If we could construct an ideal item universe, we could randomize item choice to obtain a valid, unbiased test. If there existed a significant number of interactions in that ideal item universe, we would require a relatively large number of items to achieve adequate universal validity. For many purposes, it may be more efficient and effective to develop and use shorter alternative tests. This approach seems most likely in diagnostic applications. It might be well to emulate the medical model here and to develop a large armamentarium of highly focused tests. On the other hand, global tests may well have a place that would justify a greater length and associated costs to examiners and examinees. Competitive examinations come to mind immediately. Strategically, a systematic attack on both fronts to determine the relevant variables promises understanding, and understanding is always the best route to practical problem solution.

The test bias controversy has been fueled by issues of race. Half a century has been devoted to polemics over whether heredity or environment is the determinant of groups' differences on tests. The data suggest that the debate was irrelevant and that it diverted attention from a search for the relevant. Asking wrong questions yields wrong answers. The right questions appear to be those directed toward individual diversity rather than group homogeneity.

REFERENCES

American Psychological Association. *Standards for educational and psychological tests and manuals.* Washington, D.C.: Author, 1966.

Anastasi, A. *Psychological testing* (4th ed.). New York: Colber & Macmillan, 1976.

Barbacki, S., & Fisher, R. A. A test of the supposed precision of systematic arrangements. *Annals of Eugenics,* 1936, 7, 189–193.

Bassett, G. C. Habit formation in a strain of albino rats of less than normal brain weight. *Behavior Monographs,* 1914, 2(4).

Birnbaum, A. Some latent trait models and their use in inferring an examinee's ability. In F. M. Lord & M. R. Novick, *Statistical theories of mental test scores.* Reading, Mass.: Addison-Wesley, 1968.

Box, J. F. *R. A. Fisher: The life of a scientist.* New York: Wiley, 1978.

Cattell, J. M. Mental tests and measurements. *Mind,* 1890, 15, 373–380.

Cronbach, L. J., & Meehl, P. E. Construct validity in psychological tests. *Psychological Bulletin,* 1955, 52, 281–302.

Davenport, J. W., Hagquist, W. W., & Rankin, G. R. The symmetrical maze: An auto-
    mated closed-field test series for rats. *Behavior Research Methods and Instrumen-
    tation*, 1970, 2, 112–118.
Dewey, J. *Logic, the theory of inquiry*. New York: Holt, 1938.
Douglass, F. M., IV, Khavari, K. A., & Farber, P. D. A comparison of classical and latent
    trait item analysis procedures. *Educational and Psychological Measurement*, 1979,
    39, 337–352.
Dove, A. Soul story. *New York Times Magazine*, December 8, 1968, pp. 82–96.
Dunn, E. C. *A short history of genetics*. New York: McGraw-Hill, 1965.
'Espinasse, P. G. The polygene concept. *Nature*, 1942, 149, 732.
Ezekiel, M., & Fox, K. A. *Methods of correlation and regression analysis*. New York:
    Wiley, 1959.
Festing, M., & Staats, J. Standardized nomenclature for inbred strains of rats. 4th listing.
    Transplantation, 1973, 16, 221–245.
Fisher, R. A. The correlation between relatives on the supposition of Mendelian inher-
    itance. *Transactions of the Royal Society of Edinburgh*, 1918, 52, 399–433.
Fisher, R. A. Applications of "Students" distribution. *Metron*, 1925, 5, 90–104.
Fisher, R. A. *The design of experiments*. London: Oliver & Boyd, 1935.
Fisher, R. A. *Contributions to mathematical statistics*. New York: Wiley, 1950.
Fisher, R. A., & Mackenzie, W. A. Studies in crop variation: II. The manurial response
    of different potato varieties. *Journal of Agricultural Science*, 1923, 13, 311–320.
Guilford, J. P. *Psychometric methods*. New York: McGraw-Hill, 1954.
Gulliksen, H. *Theory of mental tests*. New York: Wiley, 1950.
Harrington, G. M. Genetic-environmental interaction in "Intelligence": Biometric
    genetic analysis of maze performance of *Rattus norvegicus*. *Developmental Psy-
    chobiology*, 1968, 1, 211–218.
Harrington, G. M. Intelligence tests may favour the majority groups in a population.
    Nature, 1975, 258, 708–709.
Harrington, G. M. The Har strains of rats: Origins and characteristics. *Behavior
    Genetics*, 1981, 11, 445–468.
Hays, W. L. *Statistics for psychologists*. New York: Holt, Rinehart & Winston, 1963.
Hays, W. L. *Statistics for the social sciences* (2nd ed.). New York: Holt, Rinehart & Win-
    ston, 1973.
Hebb, D. O., & Williams, K. A method of rating animal intelligence. *Journal of Genetic
    Psychology*, 1946, 34, 59–65.
Hirsch, J. Behavior-genetic, or "experimental" analysis: The challenge of science ver-
    sus the lure of technology. *American Psychologist*, 1967, 22, 118–130.
James, W. *Pragmatism, a new name for some old ways of thinking*. New York: Long-
    mans-Green, 1907.
Jensen, A. R. *Bias in mental testing*. New York: Free Press, 1980.
Jones, H. E., Conrad, H. S., & Blanchard, M. B. Environmental handicap in mental test
    performance. *University of California Publications in Psychology*, 1932, 5(3), 63–
    99.
Kant, I. *Critique of pure reason*. London: Macmillan, 1933. (Originally published, 1791.)
Kerlinger, F. N., & Pedhazur, E. J. *Multiple regression in behavioral research*. New
    York: Holt, Rinehart & Winston, 1973.
Kifner, J. The "Chitlin' Test" for Negroes. *Chicago's American*, July 3, 1968, p. 5.
Livesey, P. M. The rat, rabbit, and cat in the Hebb-Williams closed field test of animal
    intelligence. *Australian Journal of Psychology*, 1966, 18, 71–79.
Mather, K. The polygene concept. *Nature*, 1942, 149, 731–732.

Mather, K. The progress and prospect of biometrical genetics. In L. C. Dunn (Ed.), *Genetics in the 20th century.* New York: Macmillan, 1951.

McDougall, W. An experiment for the testing of the hypothesis of Lamarck. *British Journal of Psychology,* 1927, *17,* 267–304.

McDougall, W. Fourth report on a Lamarckian experiment. *British Journal of Psychology,* 1938, *28,* 321–345, 365–395.

McDougall, W. Second report on a Lamarckian experiment. *British Journal of Psychology,* 1930, *20,* 201–318.

McGuire, T. R., & Hirsch, J. General intelligence (g) and heritability (H^2, h^2). In I. C. Uzgiris & F. Weizmann (Eds.), *The structuring of experience.* New York: Plenum Press, 1977.

McNemar, Q. *The revision of the Stanford-Binet scale: An analysis of the standardization data.* Boston: Houghton-Mifflin, 1942.

Nunnally, J. C. *Psychometric theory.* New York: McGraw-Hill, 1967.

Nunnally, J. C. *Psychometric theory* (2nd ed.). New York: McGraw-Hill, 1978.

Page, E. B. Ordered hypotheses for multiple treatments: A significance test for linear ranks. *Journal of the American Statistical Association,* 1963, *58,* 216–230.

Rabinovitch, H. S., & Rosvold, H. E. A closed-field intelligence test for rats. *Canadian Journal of Psychology,* 1951, *5,* 122–128.

Rasch, G. An item analysis which takes individual differences into account. *British Journal of Mathematical and Statistical Psychology,* 1966, *19,* 49–57.

Reilley, R. R. A note on minority group test bias studies. *Psychological Bulletin,* 1973, *80,* 130–132.

Rhine, J. B., & McDougall, W. Third report on a Lamarckian experiment. *British Journal of Psychology,* 1933, *24,* 213–235.

Searle, L. V. The organization of hereditary maze-brightness and maze-dullness. *Genetic Psychology Monographs,* 1949, *39,* 279–325.

Shimberg, M. E. An investigation into the validity of norms with special reference to urban and rural groups. *Archives of Psychology,* 1929, No. 104.

Small, W. S. An experimental study of the mental processes of the rat. *American Journal of Psychology,* 1900, *11,* 133–165.

Small, W. S. Experimental study of the mental processes of the rat: II. *American Journal of Psychology,* 1901, *12,* 206–239.

Snedecor, G. W. & Cochran, W. G. *Statistical methods* (7th ed.). Ames: Iowa State University Press, 1980.

Spearman, C. "General intelligence," objectively determined and measured. *American Journal of Psychology,* 1904, *15,* 201.

Terman, L. M. *The measurement of intelligence.* Boston: Houghton-Mifflin, 1916.

Thorndike, E. L. Animal intelligence. *Psychological Monographs,* 1898, *2* (4, Whole No. 8). (Originally titled *Psychological Review, Monograph Supplements.*)

Thorndike, E. L. *An introduction to the theory of mental and social measurements.* New York: Teachers College, 1904.

Tolman, E. C. Inheritance of maze learning ability in rats. *Journal of Comparative Psychology,* 1924, *4,* 1–18.

Tryon, R. C. Genetic differences in maze-learning ability in rats. In *39th Yearbook of National Society for Study of Education* (Vol. 1). Bloomington, Ill.: Public School Publishing Company, 1940.

Tryon, R. C. Individual differences. In F. A. Moss (Ed.), *Comparative psychology.* New York: Prentice-Hall, 1942.

Williams, R. C. *The BITCH test (Black Intelligence Test of Cultural Homogeneity)*. St. Louis: Williams (Robert L.) & Associates, 1972.

Windelband, W. *A history of philosophy*. New York: Harper, 1958. (Originally published, 1901.)

Woodworth, R. S., & Schlosberg, H. *Experimental psychology*. New York: Holt, 1954.

CHAPTER FOUR

IQ Testing as the Emperor's New Clothes

A Critique of Jensen's *Bias in Mental Testing*

ASA G. HILLIARD III

One day there came two swindlers; they claimed to be weavers and said that they knew how to weave the most wonderful cloth imaginable. Not only were the colors and patterns something uncommonly beautiful to see, but also clothes sewn from their cloth had the extraordinary quality of being invisible to anyone either badly suited for his position or unforgivably stupid.

Hans Christian Anderson, "The Emperor's New Clothes"

I, for one, was very happy to see the publication by Arthur Jensen, *Bias in Mental Testing* (1980), not for the reason, as some have suggested, that it provides a "final definitive answer" to the critics of standardized IQ tests. I am happy because *Bias in Mental Testing*, as Jensen's attempt to be comprehensive, actually covers so much territory that the soft underbelly of key arguments in support of IQ testing in general and IQ testing for "minority populations" in particular is easily exposed. Presumably, this book is Arthur Jensen's tour de force. He has done a distinct service to education measurement by his articulation of common practice in test construction, experimental design, and statistical methodology. I can think of few references that treat these topics quite so clearly and comprehensively. On the other hand, Arthur Jensen has *listed* most of the major criticisms in

---

ASA G. HILLIARD III ● Georgia State University, Atlanta, Georgia 30303.

the IQ-testing controversy but has failed to deal with the data that are presented in support of the criticisms by others. Jensen has claimed that he has made an exhaustive review of all the literature that pertains to the IQ argument. In this critique, we will look precisely at that claim.

The bulk of the Jensen book contains material that can be accepted on its face without much difficulty, in particular material that clarifies traditional practice in test construction, experimental design, and statistical methodology. However, it is with the smaller part of Jensen's book that the major difficulty lies. In particular, the difficulty lies with those parts of the book where traditional statistical methodology, experimental design, and test construction are applied in discussions about cultural bias. These traditional procedures were never designed to illuminate the presence or absence of cultural bias. Indeed, the basic assumptions underlying these procedures imply the nonexistence of culture. This critique is limited to Jensen's treatment of cultural bias.

By *culture*, I mean the shared creativities of a group of people, including such things as language, values, experiences, symbols, tools, and rules. The existence of culture can be described and demonstrated for specific groups of people (Hilliard, 1976). In America, there are both strong tendencies toward a common culture and strong tendencies toward unique cultural forms. There is no universal American vocabulary, general information, or set of value. Some of these things are shared, but many cultural groups exhibit uniqueness as well. Intelligence is reflected in both common and unique cultural behavior. These matters have been verified empirically (Labov, 1970; Lévi-Strauss, 1966).

It is a commonplace now to assert that *intelligence* has no common definition among the community of scholars who study it. It is also quite usual to find among those who study intelligence the stated position that a common definition of intelligence is unnecessary and that the wide variety of operational definitions, as represented by diverse IQ tests, is quite acceptable in the measurement of intelligence because the intercorrelation among these tests tends to be fairly high. Analogies are sometimes drawn between "intelligence" and certain things in the physical science area, such as electricity, which was accepted as "real" before it could be defined. And yet the analogy does not quite hold because, in the physical science realm, even though the construct associated with the thing being measured may not be defined in precise terms conceptually, at the operational level it is almost always the case that a common instrument and measuring procedure exist. Electrical meters or thermometers must provide the same results, no matter what the make. IQ tests differ widely and have merely an association with each other, as they do with many other things, such as socioeconomic status.

Arthur Jensen (1980) made the following comment about criticisms of psychological tests:

> Psychological tests and the theories underlying them are surely not exempt from criticism. Yet, if tests as such are to be subjected to *real* critical scrutiny, it will have to come from psychometric and statistical analysis coupled with psychological theory. The verbal fulmination type of criticism carries no weight scientifically, although as propaganda its effects in the public sphere are undoubtedly considerable. Antitest propaganda has been energetically promoted by various political action organizations, most notably the National Educational Association and the Association of Black Psychologists. (p. 24, italics in original)

Although Jensen reduced the position of the National Education Association and the Association of Black Psychologists to "verbal fulmination" and "propaganda," he did so without treating with precision either their conclusions or the data that are used to support their conclusions. Thus, his own comments in this regard bear more of the character or propaganda than do those that he chose to castigate. There can be no question that the National Education Association and the Association of Black Psychologists have been involved in the political as well as the professional arena. However, the same may be said of organizations that have given historical support to IQ testing, such as the American Psychological Association. In fact, the title of Leon Kamin's book, *The Science and Politics of* IQ (1974), illustrates the essentially political nature of the position that IQ psychologists have taken in support of IQ testing. The role of IQ psychologists in the eugenics movement and the role of IQ psychologists in lobbying for eugenics goals with legislative and policymaking bodies has been amply documented (Chase, 1976; Kamin, 1974). Notably, Jensen's "exhaustive review" of the relevant data completely ignores or overlooks Kamin's historic and devastating critique of his own work and the work of other important IQ scholars. The exhaustive review fails to treat the role of Cyril Burt (Hearnshaw, 1979; Kamin, 1974) as politician or his full role in science, though Burt is quoted extensively as a scientist. However, the issues before us are not resolved by name calling by either side in the controversy. The issue of cultural bias in mental testing must be resolved by appeal to data and criteria.

UNRESOLVED ISSUES IN THE TEST BIAS CONTROVERSY

SEPARATING BIAS ISSUES FROM MEASUREMENT ISSUES

In dealing with Jensen's material, it is necessary to point out at the outset that there are really two separate issues contained under the one heading of *Bias in Mental Testing*. First, there is the issue of whether IQ tests *measure* mental functions at all for anyone; and second, there is the issue of whether IQ testing is biased for different cultural groups. By *bias*, I mean a condition in which the same mental process is not being measured in two or more cultural groups whose standardized IQ test scores are being compared. The tests may be biased and at the same time may or may not be a measure of mental functions. The test may or may not be a measure of mental functions, and we would still be left with the question of whether it is biased. Jensen seems to be able to recognize the difficulty with IQ testing but does not appear to be able to follow up on that recognition:

> The American Association of Mental Deficiency has recommended that the borderline of mental retardation be set at between IQ 70 to 85, defining as "subnormal" IQ deviations of more than one standard deviation below the general mean of the population. *But this is a matter of statistical definition and does not agree with the general practice of basing classification as retarded not only on IQ but on various criteria of the individual's social adjustment and adaptive behavior.* The majority of adults with IQs between 70 and 85 are not retarded by ordinary criteria of social adjustment. In one large study, for example, it was found that 84 percent of such persons had completed at least eight years of school, 83 percent had held a job, 65 percent had a semiskilled or higher occupation, 80 percent were financially independent or a housewife, and almost 100 percent were able to do their own shopping and travel alone. (p. 109, italics mine)

IQ or intelligence testing should identify mental functions, not statistical rank, on culturally specific experiences from a single cultural group.

THE LIMITS OF IQ IN THE DESCRIPTION OF MENTAL FUNCTIONS

Almost all of the arguments in the IQ controversy center on the psychometric properties of IQ tests. In practical, everyday school operations, for example, it appears that practitioners favor the use of IQ test scores as evidence of a person's inherent capacity. And yet, as Jensen's observation indicates, social adjustment and adaptive behavior might well lead us to make conclusions about inherent ability quite at variance with those that IQ tests would seem to suggest. The operational definition of IQ must be rendered in terms of mental functions that can be recognized, rather than in terms of gross scores, if they are to be of any real value in professional practice. The closest that Jensen came to discussing this point was in his explanation of Spearman's definition:

> But, if the items are to measure intelligence, they must all possess certain abstract properties, described by Spearman as presenting the possibility for *eduction of relations and correlates*. This has much the same meaning as inductive ("relations") and deductive ("correlates") reasoning. *Eduction of relations* means inferring the general rule from specific instances (i.e., induction). *Eduction of correlates* means making up or recognizing a specific instance when given one other specific instance and the general rule (i.e., deduction). Later we shall see how Spearman's principle of "eduction of relations and correlates" applies to a great variety of specific items. (p. 127, italics in original)

The hypothesized mental *functions* that are identified are deduction and induction. Of course, then, the question is whether IQ tests are "measures" of induction and deduction, or any other mental function. And even if they are, the major question is, Are they uniquely so? In other words, do IQ tests really provide an opportunity for the demonstration of a culturally specific instance of induction or deduction? If subjects fail to get a question right, can we be certain that they are unable to perform *the same mental function* if they utilize familiar cultural material? IQ tests are devised so that only one set of cultural material can be utilized for such a demonstration. Feuerstein's important work (1979), which was overlooked in Jensen's exhaustive review, provides the empirical data to destroy the fallacy of using unfamiliar cultural material as a vehicle for mental measurement.

FINESSING THE BASIC ISSUES

In some ways, Jensen's book is intellectual sleight of hand. On the one hand, by listing criticisms of IQ tests meticulously at the beginning of the book, but failing to deal with the data that are used to support those criticisms, Jensen offered *the appearance of handling the criticisms*, most of which he ignored. On the other hand, by manipulating the definition of *bias* so as to arbitrarily restrict that definition to traditional statistical, experimental design, or psychometric procedures, Jensen has ruled as off limits entire categories of empirical data, especially those of cultural linguistics and cultural anthropology:

> This term [*bias*] is henceforth used also in a strictly statistical sense. As such, the term "bias" is to be kept distinct from the concept of fairness-unfairness.
>
> In mathematical statistics, "bias" refers to a *systematic* under- or overestimation of a population parameter by a statistic based on samples drawn from the population. In psychometrics, "bias" refers to systematic errors in the *predictive validity* or the *construct validity* of test scores of individuals that are associated with the individual's group membership. "Bias" is a general term and is not limited to "culture bias." It can involve any type of group membership—race, social class, nationality, sex, religion, age. The assessment of bias is a purely objective, empirical, statistical and quantitative matter entirely independent of subjective value judgments and ethical issues concerning fairness or unfairness of tests and the uses to which they are put. *Psychometric bias is a set of statistical attributes conjointly of a given test and two or more specified subpopulations.* As we shall see in terms of certain criteria of fairness, unbiased tests can be used unfairly and biased tests can be used fairly. Therefore, the concepts of bias and unfairness should be kept distinct. The main purpose of this chapter is to explicate the statistical meaning of test bias and to examine various criteria of fair use of tests. (p. 375, italics in original)

By drawing a distinction between test bias and test fairness, Jensen clouded the issue. *Test bias*, in his terms, seems to refer to psychometric analysis, whereas *test fairness*, in his terms, does not really apply to the science of measurement so much as to the *use* to which valid instruments are put. It is a traditional article of faith with test makers that tests themselves generally cannot be faulted, although the *use* to which they are put may be. This shift takes the tests themselves away from the area of scientific criticism. Once we restrict the definition of test bias to statistical bias and classify anything that is left over as test "fairness" or "unfairness," the argument is virtually over. The rest of the discussion is merely a cleanup operation. Indeed, that is precisely the way Jensen proceeded. And yet, the real cultural-bias problem lies in the area that Jensen arbitrarily chose to treat as a "fairness" matter.

Assuming That Particular Language Is Universal

There are some lingering problems where Jensen failed to deal with "fairness" as bias. Some of them are revealed in Jensen's observations:

> It is important to understand the principle enunciated by the English psychologist Charles E. Spearman (1923), known as "the indifference of the indicator" (or "the indifference of the fundaments"). It means that in an intelligence test the specific content of the item is unessential, *so long*

as it is apprehended in the same way by all persons taking the test
italics mine)

The question here is, Can we be certain that items are apprehended or perceived in the same way by all persons taking the test? At present, Jensen's way of making this determination is simply to examine, by item analysis, the pattern of response for a given group and to compare that to the pattern of response for another group. Jensen has made the implicit assumption that two groups responding to the same item with the same pattern on the multiple-choice option test are reflecting a common understanding of the item. Yet, in presenting this principle, no appeal was made to data from cultural anthropology or from cultural linguistics. Certainly, if such an appeal was made, it is absent from Jensen's discussion and also absent from the references that are cited in his book. Cultural linguists and cultural anthropologists are scientists who have developed a systematic study of particular cultural groups and who are in a position to interpret the behavior of cultural groups from the perspective of the history and the cultural norms of that group. In general, persons with such expertise and the data that they have developed have not been a part of the IQ debate at all. It is for this reason that some critics of IQ testing who allege cultural bias in the tests may do so with inadequate preparation. However, the matter of cultural bias can and must still be analyzed. It seems obvious that Jensen either does not understand or does not accept empirical demonstrations of the existence of culture and cultural varieties. His discussions in responses to charges of cultural bias are quite naive:

> Critics often try to ridicule tests by pointing to a specific test item as an example of culture bias or whatever point the critic wants to make. The implication to most readers is that the test as a whole measures no more than what the selected item seemingly measures. It is usually assumed that no other information than that of holding up the item itself is needed to evaluate the item or the test from which it was selected. Attention is directed entirely to the "face validity" of specific items. Yet no competent psychometrist would attempt to criticize or defend specific test items out of context. The importance of the "face validity" of an item depends, first, on the nature and purpose of the test in which it is included and, second, on certain "item statistics" that are essential to the psychometrist in evaluating any test item. Without such information, criticism of individual test items can carry no weight. Rarely does a test constructor attribute much importance to whether or not any given person knows the specific information content of any single item; rather, the chief concern is with the measurement of whatever is common to a number of quite diverse items. This is determined by summing the "rights" and "wrongs" over a large number of such items to obtain a total score.

The specific features of single items thus average out, and the total score is a measure of whatever ability is common to the whole set of items. The more diverse the items, the more general is the ability measured by the total score. For this reason, criticism of item content, outside a context of essential psychometric information, is the weakest criticism of all. (p. 4)

Clearly, Jensen appears to have assumed that items have unique and universal linguistic meanings. Further, he appears to have assumed that essential meaning is in the item rather than in the person! There can be no objection to Jensen's statement that the discussion of item content must take place within the context of what he has called "essential psychometric information." However, to discuss item content in the context of essential information without also making reference to specific cultural information is to leave basic issues poorly treated and to commit a scientific error. Jensen's point that "face validity" is insufficient is one with which I agree. However, it is incorrect to assume that all critics approach the determination of cultural bias only through face validity. For example, Chomsky's (1957) formulation of deep and surface structure in language has been extended in the work of more recent cultural linguists, such as Shuy (1976), who have pointed out clearly the measurement error of using language while confusing deep and surface structures in semantics or grammar. Anthropologists, such as Lévi-Strauss (1966), have illustrated the culturally specific nature of intellectual manifestations. Linguists, such as Shuy (1976), who study the language of test items point out that semantic meanings vary among individuals and among groups of individuals. Further, the approach of the cultural linguists to the discovery of semantic meaning among individuals or among groups is seldom through a statistical analysis of responses to multiple-choice items. Unless Jensen is willing to reject the work of cultural linguists out of hand, it is important that he, as a scientist, deal with the meaning of that work in his own conclusions. It would be beyond the scope of this paper to deal with that meaning here. I merely point out that Jensen's "exhaustive review of relevant literature" fails to exhaust or even to touch certain highly relevant empirical data. It is especially important that a review of *relevant literature* be done because, as Jensen indicated that

the most g-loaded tests [on the Wechsler Intelligence Scale for Children—Revised] are Information, Similarities, and Vocabulary. But the relative sizes of the factor loadings are not meaningful in any general psychological sense unless they have been corrected for attenuation. Because the various subtests differ in reliability, the relative sizes of the loadings reflect, in part, the reliabilities of the tests. (p. 216)

The most important point here is that information, similaritie vocabulary are heavily culturally loaded. Vocabularies vary, therefore, a vocabulary test or vocabulary similarities that are de ﹍n- dent on a common vocabulary meaning should be expected to vary by cultural group. Similarly, "general information" varies by cultural group. It seems interesting, therefore, that the most g-loaded tests may also be the most culturally loaded tests. Donaldson (1978) has shown how the change in a given test of a single equivalent word can sometimes produce major changes in children's achievement on tests.

ASSUMING THAT RACE IS A BIOLOGICAL REALITY

Like *intelligence, race* is undefined in operational terms. As Jensen has been noted for his idea that "races" differ in mental ability as measured by IQ tests, it is instructive to note how he has used the term:

> We see that race and SES [socioeconomic status] together contribute only 22 percent of the total IQ variance. (In this context "race" refers to the variance associated with classification as black or white, independent of any variance associated with SES as measured by the Duncan index. *Thus the term "race" here is not exclusively a biological factor but some combination of all the factors associated with the racial classification* except whatever socioeconomic factors are measured by the SES index.) (p. 43, italics mine)

In other words, *race*, though generally understood in biological terms, is undefined in operational terms, or it is so broadly defined that an investigator can commute between genetic and logical categories without being held accountable for either. Jensen has indicated that he believes that there is a *genetic* basis for the IQ differences between "racial" groups. Yet, as is indicated above, he does not use the term *race* in a biological sense. In fact, one wonders whether any scientists would agree with the definition of race that is expressed or implied in the quotation above. One certainly would wonder how geneticists would accept such a definition. Under such circumstances, how do IQ researchers select "black" or "white" samples for comparison? Perhaps there is a secret method of selection, as no method has been publicly described. This is a vital matter for test construction because it is related to the selection of populations for "norming" the tests.

DETERMINING CULTURAL BIAS IN IQ TESTING

Jensen has stated:

> I have not found in the literature any defensible proposal for a purely objective set of criteria for determining the *culture-loadedness* of individual test items, and perhaps none is possible. This is not the same as saying there are not objective measures for determining test *bias*, a topic to be taken up shortly. As we shall see, one can determine with objective statistical precision how and to what degree a test is *biased* with respect to members of particular subpopulations. But no such objective determination can be made of the degree of *culture-loadedness of a test*. That attribute remains a subjective and, hence, fallible judgment. Because there is no *a priori* basis for assuming that all subpopulations are equal in the ability that a particular test is intended to measure, items cannot be ordered on the culture-loading continuum simply according to how much they discriminate among various subpopulations. (p. 375, italics in original)

Once again, Jensen has mistaken the distinction between determining cultural bias statistically and determining cultural bias in other ways for a distinction between objective and subjective data. Although it may be true that there are few commonly used procedures for determining cultural bias in testing objectively, it is certainly not the case that descriptions of culture are merely subjective. Once again, in order to come to such a conclusion, one must rule out years of systematic work by cultural linguists and cultural anthropologists.

In the past, the mere existence of differential averages in IQ between cultural groups or "races" has resulted in charges of cultural bias on the presumption that there should be no difference among cultural or "racial" groups in basic mental capacity. Indeed, this is the precise argument that was used in the *Larry P. v. Wilson Riles* IQ-testing case in California. Judge Robert F. Peckham (1979) ruled that without compelling data to the contrary from sources other than the IQ tests themselves, the court would assume that the true difference between "racial" or cultural groups is zero. Even so, Jensen was quite correct in stating that items cannot be ordered along a continuum of cultural loading simply because psychometrically obtained results discriminate among various cultural or "racial" subpopulations. However, although the "discrimination" that exists *may* signal cultural bias, it does not define cultural bias. The definition must come from much more sophisticated and empirical methods, methods that are well beyond the expertise of traditional psychometricians and that do exist in related behavioral-science disciplines. For example, content analysis, participant observation, and ethnography are tools that can be used to establish the unique cultural experiences of particular groups.

THE QUESTION OF TEST NORMS

Some critics of IQ testing have suggested that separate norms be provided for different cultural populations. Jensen's response is as follows:

> Merely rescaling or renorming a given test on a sample from a different population than the one on which the test was originally standardized accomplishes nothing of fundamental significance. It merely assigns different numerical values of the mean and standard deviation of the standardized scores of a particular group. It does not change the relative positions of persons within the groups or the relative difference between the groups. It merely puts these differences on a different numerical scale without essentially changing them, like shifting from a Fahrenheit to a Celsius thermometer. (p. 372)

Jensen was correct in taking this position, up to a point. For example, it would do absolutely no good to renorm an IQ test that is written in English for a population that speaks only French by placing more French speakers in the norming sample in relationship to their numbers in the general population. This kind of cultural difference in populations requires much more than "shifting from a Fahrenheit to a Celsius thermometer," or, put another way, a change in scale of measurement. Quite clearly, the test is linguistically inappropriate for French speakers. So I see that Jensen was right for the wrong reasons: This is not simply a problem in scoring or scaling; it is clearly a problem of the cultural appropriateness of the measures. The problem here is with the cultural content of the items. Jensen was also right for the wrong reasons on the same norm topic:

> Critics of mental testing often argue that IQs or other derived test scores should be based on separate racial and ethnic norms. In other words, an individual's score essentially would represent his deviation from the mean of his own racial or ethnic group. Hence, with separate norms, the same raw score on a test, reflecting a certain absolute level of performance, would result in different standardized scores for different groups. It is hard to see any practical utility in this proposal. It would greatly complicate the interpretation of test scores, since, if one were to use the scores for prediction of some criterion such as grades or job performance, or as an indication of relative standing in the knowledge or skills measured by the test, one would have to know the subject's group membership and make the necessary statistical adjustments for the scores to have the same meaning and predictive validity across groups. Also, an

individual could raise his or her standardized score merely by claiming membership in a group with lower norms. There is also the problem of how many different sets of norms there should be; every ethnic group and religious group and every geographical region of the country could insist on its own norms.

Common sense as well as psychometric and statistical considerations dictate that test scores should have the same scale for everyone of a given age. That is, all scores should be scaled on homogeneous age groups within a single normative population. How well the normative sample was chosen is a separate consideration and depends in part upon the nature and purpose of the test and the populations in which it is to be used. The psychometrist aims to maximize the theoretical meaningfulness and practical usefulness of tests and the scores derived from them. Scores scaled to separate norms for different groups would solve no real problems and would create a practical nuisance, much like having to contend with different currencies and exchange rates in going from one country to another. If tests are biased for some groups in the population, the bias should be recognized rather than obscured by having separate norms for that group. (p. 95)

When Jensen argued that separate norms would complicate interpretations, or would allow subjects to manipulate the meaning of scores, or would be complicated and uneconomical to administer because too many groups might require the same treatment, his arguments are not so much academic as economic or managerial in their orientation. The academic issue is whether a real population is being represented accurately (regardless of the expense or inconvenience) or whether a variety of real populations are being represented equally accurately.

Jensen called for an empirical determination of cultural variation:

> The presumption is that certain groups in the population have experienced different cultural backgrounds that do not include these kinds of knowledge. . . . The fallacy is not in the possibility that some test items may discriminate between different cultural groups because of the groups' differences in experience but that such items can be identified or graded as to their degree of culture boundness merely by casual inspection and subjective judgment. . . . The determination of bias must be based on objective psychometric and statistical criteria. (p. 371)

The pity is that, with his claimed exhaustive review of the relevant literature, Jensen overlooked such empirical approaches as do exist. It is possible to gain a more accurate empirical estimate of the "normal vocabulary" of a particular cultural group. It is also possible to give a better empirical description of the "normal general information" to which particular cultural groups are exposed. As mentioned earlier, ethnographic observation, participant observation, and content analysis are just three of the scientific tools that can be used for such investigations. Quite clearly, it would be expensive to do this; however, the issue for the science of measurement is whether an empirical approach to the development of cultural norms *can* be taken, not whether test makers can afford to take it.

CULTURAL BIAS GOES BEYOND PREDICTOR AND CRITERION

Jensen also attempted to link the question of test bias to the relationship between a predictor and its criterion:

> In the most general terms, bias exists when the method of selection discriminates individuals differently than does the criterion measure of performance. (This leaves out of the question for the moment the adequacy and possible bias in the criterion itself.) This may be stated in a number of ways. A predictor is biased if it either overestimates or underestimates an individual's criterion performance depending upon his group membership. A predictor is biased if it correlates more with group membership than with the criterion it is intended to predict.... Bias enters into the testing aspect of selection when the test does not measure the same trait or ability when applied to different groups, or does not measure with the same reliability in different groups.... Bias is essentially a form of error: it is error of measurement (unreliability) and error of prediction (invalidity) that are related to the individual's group membership. (p. 48)

Apparently, Jensen failed to see that bias may be thought of in at least three, rather than simply in two, major ways. The predictor may be biased; the criterion may be biased; and the treatment that occurs between the predictor and the criterion may also be biased. In fact, this is precisely what has been asserted by critics of IQ testing in particular. At no point in Jensen's presentation has he examined the empirical evidence of differential treatment among groups in education or evidence of bias in criterion measures of performance. Yet, both are critically important if the validity of the predictor is to be established beyond question (Feuerstein, 1979; Fuller, 1977). It is really puzzling how Jensen, in his "exhaustive review" of the relevant literature, could have overlooked 25 years of empirical research by Feuerstein (1979) in Israel. This work turns Jensen's interpretations upside down, since low-performing students ("retarded performers") can be shown to make dramatic and permanent changes in school learning.

CULTURAL REALITY AND PSYCHOMETRICS

Many basic psychometric terms carry confounded or multiple meanings. These have led to a great deal of ambiguity in discussions of test bias. For example,

> the *difficulty* of an item is objectively defined as the proportion of subjects in a given population (or sample from a population) that passes the item (i.e., gets it "right"). Difficulty is indexed by the symbol p (for proportion passing). Note that an item's p value is specific to a particular group of persons or sample to whom the test was administered. (p. 66, italics in original)

Apparently, this definition of *difficulty* is based on the assumption that the "harder" the item is, the fewer will be the people who get it correct, or that the easier the item is, the more will be the people who get it correct, and that nothing else is needed to account for the difference in the proportions of people who get items either correct or incorrect, other than error. Yet, a person may get an item correct in part because she or he has had an opportunity to become familiar with the item through experience, such as knowing the name of a particular shape (*square, triangle,* or *rectangle*). On the other hand, a person may find an item difficult because the concept or construct is hard to grasp, such as *justice* or *difficulty*. In such a case, where confounding is so evident, it is important to explicate the assumptions that allow for a solely statistical definition of difficulty. This is also a point where the expertise of cultural linguists should be used. Further, there ought to be some method of distinguishing between the subject who has heard a particular word over and over and who may not remember, and a subject who has heard a word only once and may not remember. At present, there is no control for the amount or type of experience that a given subject has had as a basis for interpreting the differences in performance among subjects.

CULTURAL VARIATION, ITEM DIFFICULTY, AND THE INTERVAL SCALE

Though Jensen seems to have recognized the necessity of developing an interval scale in order for measurement to take place, he has been more convincing about the need for such a scale than about its existence:

> Each of the physical measurements just mentioned constitutes an *absolute* scale; that is, the measuring instrument in each case has a true zero point and the units of measurement are equal intervals throughout the entire scale. The measurements therefore have two important prop-

erties: (1) they are additive and (2) they can yield meaningful ratios. (Thus an absolute scale is also called a *ratio* scale.) *Unless the units of measurement are equal intervals at every part of the scale, they cannot be called additive* [italics mine]. If our yardstick did not have equal intervals, 4 inches plus 5 inches would not necessarily total the same actual length as 3 inches plus 6 inches, and the distance between the 2-inch and 12-inch marks would not necessarily be the same as the distance between the 20-inch and 30-inch marks. Also, if there were no true zero point on the scale, our measurements could not form meaningful ratios; the ratio of 2 inches to 1 inch would not be the same as the ratio of 8 inches to 4 inches. Without a true zero point on our scale for measuring weight, we would not be sure that a 200-pound man is twice as heavy as a 100-pound man. All we would know is that the 200-pound man is 100 pounds heavier than the 100-pound man; but we could not say he is twice as heavy.... An *interval* scale has equal units but no *true* zero point. The zero point on such a scale is arbitrary.... Measurements on an ordinal scale can only represent "greater than" or "less than"; but we cannot know *how much* "greater than" or "less than." Thus the measures only denote rank order. (p. 74)

One thing that is not clear is how psychometrists can claim to have an interval scale and can reconcile that notion with the notion of a test made up of items graduated in "difficulty." On an interval scale, one would suppose that each item represents an equal amount of the same type of data. By introducing the concept of "difficulty," there is the intention that items at the beginning of a test are quite different in quantity or quality of intelligence that they measure from items at the end. But the matter is even more grave than that. Psychometrists can demonstrate neither an interval nor an ordinal scale except within traditional psychometric definitions, and only by avoiding cultural linguistics data (Cole & Scribner, 1974; Lévi-Strauss, 1966; Shuy, 1976; Smith, 1978; Turner, 1949; Whorf, 1956).

The Normal Distribution as Subjective Data

Ignorance of cultural data will cause a basic error in psychometry to be obscured:

We simply *assume* what the distribution of scores should look like if we had an ideal test that measured the trait or ability in question on a perfect interval scale. Then, if we can construct an actual test that in fact yields a score distribution like the one we have assumed, we can be absolutely certain that the scores are on an equal-interval scale—provided, of course, that we are correct in our initial assumption about the true shape of the distribution. For most mental abilities, and particularly general intelligence, psychologists have *assumed* that the true distribution is the normal distribution. *Ipso facto*, any test of intelligence that yields a normal distribution of scores must be an interval scale. The logic boils down to the one crucial question: What is the justification for the assumption of normality? (p. 75, italics in original)

Is intelligence, whatever that may be, distributed normally in the population at large? Are a culturally specific vocabulary and a culturally specific general information pool—the presumed indices of intelligence—also distributed normally within the American population? Jensen and others make that assumption as they attempt to justify the creation of tests that presume such a distribution:

> It is claimed that the psychometrist can make up a test that will yield any kind of score distribution he pleases. This is roughly true, but some types of distributions are much easier to obtain than others. However, the fact that the form of the distribution is merely a function of the item difficulties and item intercorrelations, as explicated previously, and the fact that these properties are rather easily manipulated by means of item selection, which is an important aspect of the whole process of test construction, surely means that there is nothing inevitable or sacred about any particular form of distribution with regard to mental test scores. (p. 71)

It must be pointed out that the argument in support of a normal distribution of IQ test scores is a rational argument and not an empirical argument. It is hard to imagine the type of empirical test that could be conducted to determine if, independent of IQ tests, intelligence and/or its presumed indices are distributed according to the normal distribution. However, my purpose for bringing up this matter is neither to seek an answer nor to suggest an answer. Rather, it is to highlight the fact that Jensen's arguments are based on speculation and a subjective substructure of the type that he has abhorred in others. Clearly, a leap has been made. Jensen has stated that, even when psychologists are not attempting to construct tests in order to make them fit the normal curve, they discover an approximately normal distribution. He has stated that the original Wechsler Bellevue Intelligence Scale in 1944 yielded an approximately normal distribution, as did the Pittner Ability Test of 1923 and the original Binet and Stanford-Binet Intelligence Tests. And yet, as Jensen has indicated:

> The simple fact is that a test unavoidably yields a near-normal distribution when it is made up of: (1) a large number of items, (2) a wide range of item difficulties, (3) no marked gaps in item difficulties, (4) a variety of forms, and (5) items that have a significant correlation with the sum of all other item scores, so as to insure that each item in the test measures whatever the test as a whole measures. (pp. 72–73)

As Jensen has indicated, these are "commonsense" features of tests that inevitably lead to a closer approximation of the normal distribution. And yet, as was indicated in an earlier discussion, the core of these commonsense notions revolves around a statistical definition of item "difficulty." Are items "difficult" in the sense that they are complex mentally? Or are items "difficult" only in the sense that they may be unfamiliar? Given the way that Jensen has treated other complex matters, it is not surprising that he did not ask such questions. For example:

> As we move on to even more intellectually loaded performances that can be measured on an absolute or interval scale, we find that the distribution of measurements still approximates the normal curve. For example, vocabulary is highly correlated with other measures of intelligence. The size of a person's vocabulary constitutes an absolute scale, with the word as the unit. Some vocabulary tests are made up by selecting words at random from a dictionary, and scores on such vocabulary tests should be distributed approximately the same as the distribution of total vocabulary. It is consistently found that vocabulary so measured is approximately normally distributed within any given age group. (p. 77)

Jensen's views here reflect a particularly limited and naive notion of what vocabulary is. There is no dictionary that contains the whole of human vocabulary. Is the random selection of words from a selected dictionary vocabulary in English a measure of any given individual's total vocabulary? This certainly is not a definition of vocabulary that a cultural linguist could accept. Words and meanings do exist that are not in any dictionary and yet are normal or typical for some cultural groups. Although such words and meanings may not be useful or valued in the mainstream of American culture, nevertheless, they are no less evidence of intellect than are words that fail more within the so-called mainstream. In other words, is a random sample of a particular dictionary's listing of words equivalent to a random sample of any group's vocabulary? It is when such issues are ignored in the construction of IQ tests, and when such "neutral" techniques as defining item difficulty in statistical terms are utilized, that artifacts of the measurement process come to be viewed as an adequate representation of reality itself.

GETTING AT THE ROOT OF CULTURAL BIAS

Every group of people develops ways of working with its environment. It develops a set of rules that are widely shared within the culture. These may be rules about talking, rules about making tools, or rules about the use of symbols. Makers of standardized IQ tests operate as if there is only one set of rules for all cultural groups. Otherwise, it would be foolish to speak of something such as "general knowledge" when thinking of a general population that consists of diverse cultural groups. Jensen appears to agree in part:

> The range of a person's general knowledge is generally a good indication of that individual's intelligence, and tests of general information in fact correlate highly with other noninformational measures of intelligence. For example, the Information subtest of the Wechsler Adult Intelligence Scale [WAIS] correlated .75 with the five nonverbal performance tests among 18- to 19-year-olds.
>
> Yet information items are the most problematic of all types of test items. The main problems are the choice of items and the psychological rationale for including them. It is practically impossible to decide what would constitute a *random* sample of knowledge; no "population" of "general information" has been defined. The items must simply emerge arbitrarily from the heads of test constructors. No one item measures *general* information. Each item involves only a specific fact, and one can only hope that some hypothetical general pool of information is tapped by the one or two dozen information items that are included in some intelligence tests.
>
> Information tests are treated as *power* tests: time is not an important factor in administration. Like any power test, the items are steeply graded in difficulty. The twenty-nine Information items in the WAIS run from 100 percent passing to 1 percent passing. Yet how can one claim the items to be *general* information if many of them are passed by far fewer than 50 percent of the population? Those items with a low percentage passing must be quite specialized or esoteric. Inspection of the harder items, in fact, reveals them to involve quite "bookish" and specialized knowledge. The correlation of information with the total IQ score is likely to be *via* amount of education, which is correlated with intelligence but is not the cause of it. A college student is more likely to know who wrote *The Republic* than is a high school dropout. It is mainly because college students on the average are more intelligent than high school dropouts that this information gains its correlation with intelligence. The Information subtest of the WAIS, in fact, correlates more highly with the amount of education than any other subtest. (pp. 147–148, italics in original)

In this passage, Jensen seems to have been making the very argument that his critics make: "General knowledge" is culturally specific, and its correlation with "school success" can be explained in large measure because it is related to the amount of education that a person receives. Even Jensen has recognized the fact that we are unable to define a population of "general information" from which a random sample may be drawn. The same may be said of vocabulary. Thus, any selection of items is both basically arbitrary and culturally specific. In other words, there is a basic principle in cultural areas that we may refer to as *variation*, without any implication of subordinate or superordinate. Given this condition, what is its meaning in IQ measurement? Jensen has offered no adequate treatment of this question. Indeed, there is little evidence from his writing that he can.

It is hard to tell just how much Jensen understands in the cultural area. At certain points, he appears to be able to take cultural dimensions into account:

> Verbal IQ tests given in English afford about as good validity for the short-range prediction of scholastic achievement in the case of bilingual children as for other children from exclusively English-speaking homes. The verbal test scores of bilingual children, however, should not be interpreted beyond their function as merely a short-term predictive index of the pupil's probable achievement in a typical school setting where English is the medium of instruction. For bilingual children, never should long-term (i.e., more than a year) educational predictions or placement in special classes, particularly classes for the educably mentally retarded or the educationally subnormal, be based on standard verbal tests administered in English. Nonverbal and performance tests (in addition to social adjustment criteria) are essential and should be primary considerations in making placement recommendations or diagnoses of educational problems. If the results of testing are of importance to the individual, the bilingual child should be tested in *both* languages by an *E* [examiner] who is fluent in the *S*'s [subject's] primary language and its particular localisms, and the test should be scored in terms of the total number of correct responses in *either* language, with proper corrections for guessing, if the answers are multiple choice. School psychologists who have made this a general practice in testing bilingual children report that the maximum score obtained in both languages is usually not more than 5 to 10 points higher than in either language alone, but occasionally the difference is considerably greater, thus making this precaution worthwhile if any important decision concerning the individual child is to be based on the test results. (pp. 606–607, italics in original)

Unfortunately, Jensen's limited understanding of linguistic principles seems to suggest that he can accept certain foreign-language vocabulary differences as evidence of linguistic differences but fails to see that language is much more than that. Language is a total communication system that uses vocabulary—as well as paralinguistic features, such as symbols and body language—variously and in varying combinations of rule-governed ways to make and receive meaning. Moreover, the reduction of the number of verbal items in a test is not equivalent to the reduction of culture in items because all items, both verbal and nonverbal, represent particular cultural material that is dependent on particular experience. Therefore, it is the nature of language itself that renders its surface features inappropriate as a universal vehicle for communication and, therefore, for standardized testing.

One can see something of the theoretical statistician in the Jensen statement that follows; however, one does not see a person who understands linguistic principles:

> The best vocabulary test limited to, say, one hundred items would be that selection of words the knowledge of which would best predict the total vocabulary of each person. A word with wide scatter would be one that is almost as likely to be known by persons with a small total vocabulary as by persons with a large total vocabulary, even though the word may be known by less than 50 percent of the total population. Such a wide-scatter word, with about equal probability of being known by persons of every vocabulary size, would be a poor predictor of total vocabulary. It is such words that test constructors, by statistical analyses, try to detect and eliminate. (p. 147)

One wonders to what linguistic expertise Jensen has appealed. His bibliography is mute on this question. Such statements as the one above are typical of the absence of empirical grounding for Jensen's linguistic explanations. Let's look again at Jensen as linguist:

> Word knowledge figures prominently in standardized tests. The scores on the vocabulary subtest are usually the most highly correlated with total IQ of any of the other subtests. This fact would seem to contradict Spearman's important generalization that intelligence is revealed most strongly by tasks calling for the eduction of relations and correlates. Does not the vocabulary test merely show what the subject has learned prior to taking the test? How does this involve reasoning or education?
>
> In fact, vocabulary tests are among the best measures of intelligence because the acquisition of word meanings is highly dependent on the *eduction* of meaning from the contexts in which the words are encountered. Vocabulary for the most part is not acquired by rote memorization or through formal instruction. The meaning of a word most usually is acquired by encountering the word in some context that permits at least some partial inference as to its meaning. By hearing or reading the word in a number of different contexts, one acquires, through the mental processes of generalization and discrimination and eduction, the essence of the word's meaning, and one is then able to recall the word precisely when it is appropriate in a new context. Thus the acquisition of vocabulary is not as much a matter of learning and memory as it is of generalization, discrimination, eduction, and inference. Children of high intelligence acquire a vocabulary at a faster rate than children of low intelligence, and as adults they have a much larger than average vocabulary, not primarily because they have spent more time in study or have been more exposed to words, but because they are capable of educing more meaning from single encounters with words and are capable of dis-

criminating subtle differences in meaning between similar words. (pp. 145–146, italics in original)

Did Jensen make such descriptive statements based on observation or speculation? We cannot tell from his references. Even assuming that all that Jensen has described is true, we are still left with the question, Do all highly intelligent children acquire the same vocabulary? Is a standardized IQ vocabulary test a test of a subject's known vocabulary or of a subject's eduction of vocabulary? Regardless of the answer, one is struck that Jensen's entire bibliography may be combed for references to linguistic evidence to support such assertions as he has made, and none will be found. We have only Jensen's testimony or speculation.

A special word must be said about Jensen's treatment of the data on the measurement of the IQ of African-American children. Jensen is well known for his interpretation of the "15-point difference" in average IQ between "blacks" and "whites." He has attributed the difference in scores not to cultural differences, but to genetic differences. Neither Jensen nor anyone else he has cited who has conducted studies of the IQs of African-American children has exhibited an academic knowledge of the history and culture of African-American people. Out of Jensen's approximately 757 references, only approximately 11 pertain directly or indirectly to the matter of African-American language:

Bean, K. L. Negro responses to verbal and nonverbal test material. *Journal of Psychology*, 1942, *13*, 343–353. (p. 748)

Crown, P. J. *The effects of race of examiner and standard versus dialect administration of the Wechsler Preschool and Primary Scale of Intelligence on the performance of Negro and White children.* Doctoral dissertation, Florida State University, 1970. (p. 752)

Eisenberg, L., Berlin, C., Dill, A., & Sheldon, F. Class and race effects on the intelligibility of monosyllables. *Child Development*, 1968, *39*, 1077–1089. (p. 753)

Hall, V. C., & Turner, R. R. The validity of the "different language explanation" for poor scholastic performance by black students. *Review of Educational Research*, 1974, *44*, 69–81. (p. 757)

Harms, L. S. Listener comprehension of speakers of three status groups. *Language and Speech*, 1961, *4*, 109–112. (p. 757)

Marwit, S. J., & Neumann, G. Black and white children's comprehension of standard and nonstandard English passages. *Journal of Educational Psychology*, 1974, *66*, 329–332. (p. 763)

Peisach, E. C. Children's comprehension of teacher and peer speech. *Child Development*, 1965, *36*, 467–480. (p. 766)

Quay, L. C. Language, dialect, reinforcement, and the intelligence test performance of Negro children. *Child Development*, 1971, *42*, 5–15. (p.
767)

Quay, L. C. Negro dialect and Binet performance in severely disadvantaged black four-year-olds. *Child Development*, 1972, *43*, 245–250. (p.
767)

Quay, L. C. Language, dialect, age, and intelligence test performance in
disadvantaged black children. *Child Development*, 1974, *45*, 463–468.
(p. 767)

Weener, P. D. Social dialect differences and the recall of verbal messages.
Journal of Educational Psychology, 1969, *60*, 194–199. (p. 773)

No discussion of "black–white" differences in IQ is adequate in
absence of a professionally adequate treatment of the data on African-American language. Even in the minimal literature that is cited
by Jensen on this matter, there is one review article in the *Review of
Educational Research* (Hall & Turner, 1974) that covers slightly more
territory, primarily on the matter of scholastic performance. However, there is no evidence that Jensen has dealt with the substance of
the material presented in even that article. His primary citations are
three articles by Quay. Jensen's observations are as follows:

> The consensus of a number of studies, however, indicates that,
> although black children produce somewhat different speech, they com-
> prehend standard English at least as well as they comprehend their own
> nonstandard dialect and that they develop facility in understanding the
> standard language at an early age. . . . The effect of black dialect as com-
> pared with standard English on the IQs of black lower class children was
> investigated in three studies by Quay (1971, 1972, 1974), who had the Stan-
> ford–Binet translated into black ghetto dialect by a linguistics specialist in
> black dialect. No significant difference (the difference actually amounts to
> less than 1 IQ point) was found between the nonstandard dialect and stan-
> dard English forms of the Stanford–Binet when administered by two
> black *E*s to one hundred black children in a Head Start Program in Phil-
> adelphia. (p. 604)

It is not clear just what Jensen meant when he referred to the translation of Stanford–Binet tests into "black ghetto dialect." There are,
in fact, many variations in African-American language (not black
ghetto dialect) in America, just as there are many variations in
English as spoken by Europeans. Certainly, in a matter as important
as this, Jensen would see the need to give more care to a determination of precisely what was done even in the few studies that he
cited. Whatever it is that distinguishes the language of African-Americans, it is not the fact that some live in "ghettoes." The language that
is spoken by large numbers of African-Americans is an amalgam of

African linguistic antecedents with American modifications of English. English is itself a type of nonstandard German, which is an amalgam of an essentially Germanic grammar and an essentially Romance vocabulary (Hilliard, 1970). We are able to demonstrate that there are certain regular features of phonology, grammar, tone, and rhythm; but even more important for IQ testing, the large majority of African-American people, most of the group that does poorly on IQ tests, share an environment that, although it may be characterized by poverty, is nevertheless made up of relatively homogeneous linguistic communities. Thus, vocabulary and semantics tend to be unique to the locations where large number of African-Americans find themselves over time. Cultural linguists who are qualified to study this phenomenon have not been as amply supported in their research efforts as have psychometrists who develop standardized IQ tests. Therefore, even though cultural linguistics data are highly significant, they are not abundant. These data certainly amount neither to rhetoric nor to propaganda. Yet, what can be said for those who hold opinions about "black ghetto speech" without having any particular preparation for understanding what they are describing?

In general, the attention of linguists has not focused on the application of their discipline to the development and refinement of standardized IQ tests. In fact, much of the applied technology of linguists is so new that it has not been applied in a number of areas where it would seem able to make a distinct contribution. Linguists have a great deal to offer in the field of psychometry. There are two areas in which linguistic contributions are particularly appropriate. On the one hand, they can clarify, sharpen, and assist in the formulation of certain important constructs that are used by psychometrists. The most notable instances where psychometrists are sorely in need of professional help is with the constructs *vocabulary* and *word difficulty*. The second area where cultural linguists have a great deal to offer is in the provision of tools for the analysis of the use of language. One of the best examples of the relevance and the necessity of the field of linguistics for psychometry is provided in a very brief paper that was done by Shuy (1976). In this paper, Shuy integrated theoretical and applied material from sociolinguistics. As he dealt with the question of the possibility of quantifying linguistic data, Shuy presented (see Figure 1) a succinct diagram of linguistic phenomena. Based on his work as a linguist, he cautioned that only those things that appear at the peak of the diagram are readily amenable to quantification techniques. As we move to the deeper structures on the dia-

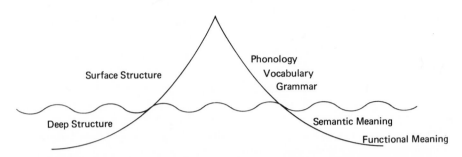

FIGURE 1. Diagram of the structure of language and of key linguistic parameters.

gram, specifically to the level of semantic meaning, traditional quantification techniques become considerably less appropriate, especially across cultural groups.

Undoubtedly, had cultural linguists been included in the development of psychometrics over the past few decades, there would be a body of appropriate linguistic technology for testing. But even though cultural linguists have been slow in realizing the implications of their field for psychometry, and even though their contributions to this area have not yet been fully developed, psychometric instrumentation that is dependent on linguistic phenomena will be scientifically inadequate until such time as these instruments can be brought up to date in cultural linguistic science. It is the psychometrists's lack of an academically adequate sense of linguistic phenomena that is responsible for a slavish insistence on the use of parochial English as if it were a universal language. This insistence can be forgiven in achievement testing, where the objective of instruction may well be to teach a parochial English for the purpose of establishing a common vehicle of efficient mass communication. However, it is unforgivable in that psychometry which is devoted to the revelation of mental functions. Although language is a prerequisite of thought, parochial English is not. Psychometrists who are responsible for the development of standardized tests of intelligence have been guilty of a particularistic "Level 1" type of thinking about the use of language. Either Jensen does not have such linguistic knowledge as is indicated by Shuy, or he may be aware of it but rejects its applicability to psychometry, or he is aware and realizes its applicability but chooses to ignore it. No matter which, his psychometry—and that of any other psychometrist so limited—is inadequate.

THE USE OF IQ TESTING

Critics of IQ testing have received a frequent response from advocates: "The tests as they exist are the best that we have." That may be true; however, the real question is, Is the best that we have even a slight contribution to the improvement of instruction? IQ tests are used currently as an applied rather than a simply experimental tool; and yet, it cannot be shown that the use of IQ testing results has improved educational achievement outcomes for children. Once again, there is a place to agree with Jensen:

> The only justification for placement is evidence that the alternative treatments are more beneficial to the individuals assigned to them than would be the case if everyone got the same treatment, with the slight variations in instruction that occur informally in the ordinary class. The supposed benefits of placement are often highly debatable. They are difficult to evaluate and are often undemonstrated. Placement is a complex matter, to say the least. (p. 46)

Too often, there is a presumption that unique pedagogy exists to which well-diagnosed learning "cases" may be assigned, with significant improvement in learning as a result. If that is the case, that unique pedagogy has yet to be described.

A more frequent use of IQ has been to predict future school achievement. To describe the known relationship between existing IQ test scores and grade-point averages or future standardized-achievement-test scores is a far cry from explaining either the scores or the relationship. Schools should be interested first and foremost in how to help children to learn, and yet, IQ testing, according to Jensen and others, may be quite unrelated to learning:

> One still occasionally sees intelligence defined as learning ability, but for many years now, since the pioneer studies of Woodrow, . . . most psychologists have dropped the term "learning ability" from their definitions of intelligence. To many school teachers and laymen this deletion seems to fly in the face of common sense. Is not the "bright," or high-IQ, pupil a "fast learner" and the "dull," or low-IQ, pupil a "slow learner"? Simple observations would seem to confirm this notion.
> The ability to learn is obviously a mental ability, but it is not necessarily the same mental ability as intelligence. Scientifically the question is no longer one of whether learning ability and intelligence are or are not the same thing, but is one of determining the conditions that govern the magnitude of the correlation between measures of learning and measures of intelligence.
> The Woodrow studies showed two main findings. (1) Measures of performance on a large variety of rather simple learning tasks showed

only meager intercorrelations among the learning tasks, and between learning tasks and IA. Factor analysis did not reveal a general factor of learning ability. (2) Rate of improvement with practice, or gains in proficiency as measured by the difference between initial and final performance levels, showed little or no correlation among various learning tasks or with IQ. Even short-term pretest–posttest gains, reflecting improvement with practice, in certain school subjects showed little or no correlation with IQ. Speed of learning of simple skills and associative rote learning, and rate of improvement with practice, seemed to be something rather different from the g of intelligence tests. (pp. 326–327)

I would wager that most teachers and administrators would be surprised by the conclusions that are presented in the quotation from Jensen above. I expect that most practicing educators, if they see any benefit in IQ tests at all, would be interested in their relationship to learning, and yet, that relationship is either weak and tenuous or obscure, to the extent that it exists at all. Jensen has shown that some learning and memory tasks are related to IQ, in what he regards as going from simple to complex learning. For example, he has indicated that learning is more highly correlated with IQ when it is intentional and when the task calls for conscious mental effort and is paced in such a way as to permit the subject to "think." He has also stated that learning is more highly correlated with IQ when the material to be learned is hierarchical in the sense that the learning of the later elements depends on the mastery of early elements. Jensen has written that learning is more highly correlated with IQ when the material to be learned is meaningful in the sense that it is in some way related to other knowledge or experience already possessed by the learner. He has written that learning is more highly correlated with IQ when the nature of the learning task permits a transfer from somewhat different but related past learning, and that learning is more highly correlated with IQ when it is insightful, that is, when the learning task involves catching on or getting the idea and the like. Although none of these statements are accompanied by specific material indicating more precisely the magnitude of the relationship between IQ test scores and learning, or just how these results can be applied in teaching, it becomes clear at once that few teachers or administrators use test results for that type of determination. If tests are used at all, they are used only to justify labels and placement.

SUMMARY AND CONCLUSIONS

Mental measurement, as far as its application to education is concerned, has been the phlogiston of the twentieth century, at least until the recently reported work of Feuerstein (1980). IQ testing is the naked emperor who badly needs new clothes. Jensen may be the leader of the cult of intelligence. The true believers in this cult do not demand that IQ test results to be used to improve the quality of education. The true believers ask only to be included in the IQ ritual. Psychometrists, the high priests of the IQ ritual, are distinguished not as educational problem-solvers, but as murmurers of incantations, as comforters of the flocks, as salespeople of academic indulgences, practicing numerology and calling it science; at present, they are education's parasites. This need not be the case (Feuerstein, 1980).

Jensen's book *Bias in Mental Testing* could have a very subtle effect on the IQ controversy over and beyond the effect that may be produced by an examination of the issues that he has treated. Because there is no other book quite like this one in the field, this subtle effect may be to establish a way of thinking about test bias, as separate and distinct from taking any side on the issues in the controversy. The subtle effect of Jensen's book may be to establish or to limit the parameters of the domain within which discussion can proceed. In a way, this has already happened through the establishment of traditional approaches in psychometry. Jensen's contribution has been to treat these traditional things comprehensively, but comprehensively only with reference to existing procedures. As indicated before, however, the basic weakness of existing procedures is that they are incapable of handling the types of issues that fall under the heading of cultural bias or, more precisely, cross-cultural validity. Present psychometric procedures are built on the implicit presumption of a universal cultural norm in an era of ethnocentrism and cultural chauvinism in science. They have yet to be purged or reconstructed so as to take into account a knowledge of the real world.

At a basic level, the question of test bias is important only in relation to its meaning in test validity. When we look closely at the validity of standardized tests of intelligence, we find that the tests are invalid in the sense that they do not describe accurately either the mental functions or the potential achievement levels of many learners. In addition, there are basic inadequacies in psychometric models for test validation when these models are applied to pluralistic cultural populations. These inadequacies have little to do with the type of statistical procedures involved, such as the type of factor-analytic method that is applied (e.g., matrix rotation). The inadequacies have little to do with refinements and methods of calculating reliability coefficients or with standard error in predictive validity coefficients. The problem is much more basic than any of these things. Existing psychometric predictive validity models fail to describe, to control for, or to account for intervening variables between IQ testing and measures of achievement. In particular, variations in the quality of instruction and variations in relevant life experiences are totally ignored. Does the negative differential treatment that minority cultural groups receive in the public schools need further documentation? Does the negative differential experience of these minority cultural groups need documentation? At present, psychometrists fail to deal with this issue at all. Test manuals that report validity studies do not reflect attention to intervening variables. Tests certainly do not allow various cultural groups to use their own experiences as a vehicle for the expression of the intelligent mental operations that they possess. I have discovered no evidence to indicate that the inadequacy in the models for validity study is being examined. Indeed, I have found almost no evidence in the psychometric literature that this inadequacy is even recognized.

The IQ debate has not been a real scientific engagement at all; or if it has, it has been on issues that are quite peripheral to what should be the primary matter of concern: The mass use of IQ testing in education must be called into question for several very special reasons, none of which are included in the debate over IQ testing:

1. IQ tests are not scientific measuring devices and do not measure the mental functions of "white" children or "black" children.
2. The cultural bias of IQ tests can be demonstrated by an appeal to empirical data from cultural linguistics and from cultural anthropology.
3. The use of IQ tests cannot be shown to result in the improvement of educational performance of any students.

It is a pity that in the ponderous book by Arthur Jensen, as in the discussions and writings on the IQ question in general, there is from minimal to no treatment at all of the specific issues listed above. Supporters of IQ testing and critics alike have chosen instead to struggle over the safer questions (for mass-production test makers) of the face validity of items and the possibility of devising (mass-produced) culture-free or culture-fair tests.

IQ test belief is a catechism, an ideology, that at present offers little or nothing to education. The important empirical demonstration that is needed is not an empirical demonstration regarding test bias. It is an empirical demonstration of test *utility*. None of the discussion over the presence or absence of bias should be allowed to obscure that central matter.

Jensen was right when he said that, before the use of tests is rejected outright, one must consider the alternatives to testing: whether decisions based on less objective means of evaluation (usually educational credentials, letters of recommendation, interviews, and biographical inventories) would guarantee less bias and greater fairness for minorities than would result from the use of tests. He was absolutely right in saying that bias may exist in any of those alternatives—perhaps, bias even greater than that found in the test itself. However, the measurement question at issue is whether the tests measure intelligence, not whether they reduce inequity, though this is certainly an objective. In fact, it is Jensen's own interpretation that has produced mischievous results by suggesting a genetic difference in ability between "white" and "black" populations.

Jensen's book is not presented as a book about the inequities that result from bias in tests or in the other criteria; it is an attempt to establish the validity of IQ tests for the purpose of measuring mental functions. In fact, as he indicated, it is primarily a book about the psychometric methods for objectively detecting what he has called bias in mental tests. Jensen issued a disclaimer: "In the terminology of genetics, test scores—*all* test scores—are measures of *phenotypes,* not of *genotypes.* The study of test bias, therefore, concerns only bias in the measurements of phenotypes" (p. xi). These two things are not separated in the minds of readers. Genotypes are inferred from phenotypes where IQ testing has been concerned and where Jensen in particular has been concerned.

Jensen's book does list objections to and criticism of standardized IQ testing in the first chapter. Arthur Jensen's book does not deal fully with the majority of these criticisms; rather, by restricting the definition of test bias and by ignoring whole categories of relevant empirical data, Jensen's response to criticism is more finesse than substance.

Jensen's "exhaustive review of the empirical research" is really an exhausting review of highly selected empirical research. It is not the book for the century. It merely exposes the weakness of IQ ideology to a wider audience.

> *And so the Emperor walked in the procession under the lovely canopy, while all the crowds in the street and all the people at their windows said, "Heavens! How marvelous the Emperor's new clothes look! Such a beautiful train on those*

*robes! How exquisitely it fits!" No one wanted it thought that
he could not see anything, as that would make him some-
body who was either very stupid or badly fitted for his
position. None of the Emperor's clothes had ever before
been such a success.*

*"But he has nothing on!" said a little child. "Good heav-
ens, listen to the voice of innocence!" said the father, and
the child's remark was whispered from one to another. "He
has nothing on! That's what a little child is saying: 'He has
nothing on!'"*

*"He has nothing on!" shouted everybody in the end.
And the Emperor cringed inside himself, for it seemed to
him that they were right; but he thought like this: "I shall
have to go through with the procession."*

*And then he held himself even more proudly erect, and
the chamberlains walked on behind him carrying the train
that was not there at all.*

Hans Christian Anderson, "The Emperor's New Clothes"

REFERENCES

Chase, A. *The legacy of Malthus: The social costs of the new scientific racism.* New York: Knopf, 1976.

Chomsky, N. *Syntactic structure.* The Hague: Mouton, 1957.

Cole, M., & Scribner, S. *Culture and thought.* New York: Wiley, 1974.

Donaldson, M. *Children's minds.* New York: W. W. Norton, 1978.

Feuerstein, R. *The dynamic assessment of retarded performers.* Baltimore: University Park Press, 1979.

Feuerstein, R. *Instrumental enrichment.* Baltimore: University Park Press, 1980.

Fuller, R. *In search of the IQ correlation.* Stonybrook, N.Y.: Ball-Stick-Bird Publications, 1977.

Hall, V. C., & Turner, R. R. The validity of the "differential language explanation" for poor scholastic performance by black students. *Review of Educational Research,* 1974, 44, 69–81.

Hearnshaw, L. S. *Cyril Burt, psychologist.* Ithaca, N.Y.: Cornell University Press, 1979.

Hilliard, A. G. *Language, culture and assessment.* Paper presented at the National Institute of Education Conference on the Ann Arbor Decision, Ann Arbor, Michigan, 1970.

Hilliard, A. G. *Alternatives to IQ testing: An approach to the identification of gifted minority students.* Final Report, Special Education Support Unit, California State Department of Education. ED 146-009, ERIC Clearinghouse on Early Childhood Education, 1976.

Jensen, A. R. *Bias in mental testing.* New York: Free Press, 1980.

Kamin, L. J. *The science and politics of IQ.* Potomac, Md.: Lawrence Erlbaum, 1974.

Labov, W. The logic of nonstandard English. In F. Williams (Ed.), *Language and poverty.* Chicago: Markham Publishing, 1970.

Larry P, by his guardian *ad litem,* Lucille P. *et al.* v. Wilson Riles, Superintendent of Public Instruction for the State of California *et al.,* C 71 2270 RFP (United States District Court for the Northern District of California, 1979).

Lévi-Strauss, C. *The savage mind.* Chicago: University of Chicago Press, 1966.

Quay, L. C. Language, dialect, reinforcement and the intelligence test performance of Negro children. *Child Development,* 1971, *42,* 5–15.

Quay, L. C. Negro dialect and Binet performance in severely disadvantaged black four-year-olds. *Child Development,* 1972, *43,* 245–250.

Quay, L. C. Language, dialect, age, and intelligence-test performance in disadvantaged black children. *Child Development,* 1974, *45,* 463–468.

Shuy, R. Quantitative language data: A case for and some warnings against. *Anthropology and Education Quarterly,* 1977, 78–82.

Smith, E. A. *Paper No. 43: The retention of the phonological, phonemic, and morphophonemic features of Africa in Afro-American ebonics.* Department of Linguistics, California State University, Fullerton, 1978.

Spearman, C. *The nature of "intelligence" and the principles of cognition.* London: Macmillan, 1923.

Turner, L. *Africanisms in the Gullah dialect.* New York: Arno Press and the New York Times, 1949.

Whorf, B. L. *Language, thought and reality,* ed. by J. B. Carroll. Cambridge: MIT Press, 1956.

CHAPTER FIVE

Bias in Mental Testing

Evidence for an Alternative to the Heredity–Environment Controversy

ERNEST M. BERNAL

Jensen, in his *Bias in Mental Testing* (1980) and other publications, has carefully documented a corpus of research on general intelligence (g) spanning some 75 years. His work, however, is perhaps best known for its exploration of minority–majority group differences in mental abilities (Jensen, 1969a,b,c), which, through the applications of genetic theory and heritability indices to a plethora of test data, he has interpreted to be for the most part genetically determined (Jensen, 1970). This basic finding, furthermore, cannot, according to Jensen (1980), be rationalized away by any extant studies of cultural or racial bias in professionally acceptable (i.e., well constructed) achievement, academic aptitude, or intelligence tests.

Jensen has characterized learning tasks or test items as tapping abilities that lie on a continuum from Level I to Level II. Level I involves tests that measure such abilities as short-term memory for digits and serial learning. Level II abilities include "education," concept attainment, symbolic manipulation, and problem solving. In general, Level II abilities transform stimuli, as in the case of tasks that educe verbal mediation prior to the production of observable responses.

This Level I–Level II continuum is central to understanding Jensen's discussion of ethnic and racial group differences in average

ERNEST M. BERNAL ● School of Education and Human Development, California State University, Fresno, California 93740.

scores on mental tests, for although all groups are equally capable of Level I tasks (Jensen, 1969b) or can be trained to perform equally well (see Jensen & Rohwer, 1963a, b), the groups generally become progressively more distinguishable as the tasks they are performing approach Level II. Level I and Level II abilities are genetically independent—that is, they are determined by different gene combinations—although they may become correlated (or functionally dependent) through such mechanisms as assortative mating and geographic isolation (Jensen, 1968, 1969a). Thus, for Jensen, these Level II abilities are most resistant to practice or coaching, although some psychologists (see Cronbach, 1969) disagree with him on this basic point. Environment is, for Jensen, a threshold variable only (1969b): Extreme deprivation can cause children not to realize their full genotypic potential, but enrichment cannot produce any phenotypic surprises, as it were.

Most of the arguments against Jensen's hereditarian position have involved variant philosophical contentions, criticisms of his studies' oversights, alternative genetic-environmental interaction theories, or different interpretations of the evidence (Bereiter, 1970). Jensen's *Bias in Mental Testing* was no doubt meant, in part, to answer many—but not all—of his critics, in part to reveal the misunderstandings about tests that abound in the popular press and that are assumed to be true even by otherwise knowledgeable professionals. The sum impact of his book is clearly that he is a scholar well versed in psychometrics and determined to link mental measurements to the science of genetics. As in his previous works, Jensen continued to use selected studies to broaden the data base that supports his basic contentions.

But in one important respect, his book adds nothing new to the controversy. Like the ambiguities that exist in research linking cigarette smoking to lung cancer, Jensen's analyses of more of the same kinds of data are still not entirely satisfying. Matarazzo (1972) documented the difficulty of the heredity–environment controversy in the psychological domain, to wit, that two equally competent scholars can review the same sets of data and reach contrary conclusions. It appears that considerable ambiguity continues to plague this issue, and that Jensen's *Bias in Mental Testing* is not a definitive treatise but merely an alternative interpretation of the "facts." This book, *Perspectives on Bias in Mental Testing*, may at last bring all of the issues together simultaneously, so that the reader may determine independently how Professor Jensen deals with the evidence presented and which issues remain unaddressed or ambiguous.

What is needed is empirical research that (1) addresses the issue with fewer assumptions about g; (2) recasts the nature–nurture problem into more directly testable hypotheses; (3) incorporates the socioeconomic, cultural, and linguistic variables of potential interest in the research design (Carter, 1970); and (4) has practical (Boyer & Walsh, 1968) and theoretical implications for improving the science of psychological measurement. Such research might permit a new assessment of the basic hereditarian conclusions about the antecedents of intelligence and might influence research generally on majority–minority group differences in test performance.

ASSUMPTIONS AND HYPOTHESES

Over the years, this writer has personally tested and observed children from different ethnic and racial groups taking group and individually administered standardized tests of various kinds, and he has noted the anxiety and the apparent lack of motivation and attention that many of them evidence in engaging in the tasks posed by the instruments. Rapport building and maintenance and the need for constant encouragement are problems that would seem subjectively to be more frequently encountered in testing minorities than in testing majority subjects, and these occur among all age groups, not just among those who have endured previous testing frustrations. Even tests of vocational interest or preference are often adversely affected, so that the internal validity checks of such instruments indicate the questionable utility of the results.

Thus, this writer feels that many tests are biased in a more basic or quintessential sense than has heretofore been investigated. It is a question not just of items, subtests, or directions—issues that Jensen has discharged effectively—but of the entire testing ambience (Bernal, 1975), the total experience, which probably is qualitatively different from the sum of its parts. Most lower socioeconomic minority children very likely have some intuition about tests, that somehow they are being "put on the spot" to perform as whites do (Katz, Epps, & Axelson, 1964) on tasks that are of no relevance to them, that what they answer will reveal something about themselves, that they have little control over what is happening or what will be asked of them next, and that they are slowly being pressed to perform increasingly difficult tasks by an authority figure whose behavior has suddenly turned cold or whose motives are not exactly known or who uses ambiguous phrases intended to keep them trying even in the face of obvious failure on the previous few tasks. These perceptions are in many instances discontinuous with their expectations (Burger, 1972; Cole & Brunner, 1971). In contrast, most majority children understand testing in a way that is not disabling, that seems, in fact, to enhance or facilitate their performance. These differences in perceptions may be sufficiently large and important to bring about the noted discrepancies in scores on which the hereditarian interpretation of the phenomenon is based.

There have been numerous studies over the years on attempts to facilitate the tested performance of minority groups. Test practice, test coaching, variations in the sex and ethnicity of the examiner, variations in the dialect or level of the language of the items (i.e., standard-nonstandard, formal-informal) or directions, timed and untimed testings—all these have been used singly or in certain (but not all) combinations (Bernal, 1977). The results, which Jensen has reviewed (and summarized) in his most recent book (1980), are mixed, and not infrequently, they interact with race/ethnicity and social class.

Yet, none of these studies has fully addressed the ambience issue in testing that is posed here. First, rarely have three or more of the factors presumed to facilitate minority-group test performance been taken into account in the same study. Second, many studies have been conducted with minority students of high school age or older, groups that, on the one hand, had survived the modal dropout age in the educational system, and that, on the other hand, probably included significant proportions of persons whose prior frustrations with tests would make the facilitating interventions less efficacious than they might have been. Third, socioeconomic status (SES) has not always been accounted for in the research designs. This third point presents an important and difficult issue, for without such control, the main effects of treatment on race or ethnicity could be swamped by the influence of SES background on test performance; yet, the inclusion of SES, if improperly handled, could partial out what hereditarians would claim to be a true source of variance brought about by assortative mating on g, the consequences of which might influence social stratification in the long run and, as a further consequence, the average levels of ability in the resultant social classes (see Jensen, 1973).

If this deeper or more pervasive form of test bias exists, anchored, as it were, in the total testing ambience with which members of diverse cultural backgrounds are differentially prepared to cope, then certain inferences may be drawn and converted into testable hypotheses. First, the test bias results from the exercise of the test maker's culturally influenced judgments about what constitutes an adequate measure of a construct and what are the appropriate circumstances for educing the test performance that reflects that construct. Second, the resultant test will have considerable overlap with the culturally learned examination "expectations" of the vast majority of persons who share the test maker's culture and will thus be appropriate for them. Other cultural/racial groups, even those that superficially seem quite similar or distinct from the test maker's group, will be prepared to engage in the examination only to the extent that they share these deeper expectations—cognitive and motivational elements—with the test maker. Thus, blacks may not have much overlap with whites in this realm of behavior, although they speak English (see Hall & Turner, 1974) and share native-born citizenship status with whites, whereas foreign-born Orientals who have learned English as a second language may actually have quite a bit in common with whites insofar as test-taking behaviors are concerned and may thus perform roughly on a par with them and outperform blacks.

Third, these expectations are learned behaviors and thus should be amenable to teaching. How much can be learned, however, would be in part a function of how much one still needs to learn. Whites should, on the average, learn little, so that, with teaching, their scores should improve only a small amount or not at all. Blacks and Hispanics, on the other hand, should improve quite a bit, thereby diminishing the differences that exist between them and whites and perhaps reducing a source of error variance (see Ginther, 1978; Jensen, 1980) in their scores. Level I abilities are measured by tests that pose tasks that are not unfamiliar to many different ethnic groups, and thus their performance levels are similar. Level II tasks, however, are more likely to be culturally loaded, and even culturally reduced tests of Level II abilities probably involve the establishment of a testing ambience that is more-or-less inappropriate for certain ethnic or racial groups.

Accordingly, a number of hypotheses are presented. The first hypothesis is that an appropriate and efficacious treatment designed to facilitate the test performance of minority students on Level II tasks can be devised. The result should be higher average scores for these groups on such tests.

Another hypothesis is that the average test performance on whites on Level II tasks cannot be significantly altered by current facilitation strategies. Jensen (1980) has found that test practice, although effective for naive subjects, is of little value much beyond the early elementary grades in school, as most schools provide sufficient practice on standardized tests in the normal course of events to ensure that their students will develop test sophistication.

Jensen (1980) also reviewed the studies on coaching and concluded that the results of such interventions are, on the whole, not worth the effort or the cost, as most of the same gains can be effected through test practice alone.

If the test performance of whites were affected positively, their higher scores would damage the assumption of a close match between the demand characteristics of the test and the expectations of white examinees, on which this study is predicated. A decrement in white test performance, on the other hand, although unlikely (see Jensen, 1980), would indicate that the facilitation strategy is inappropriate for whites. If minority students' scores were increased and majority students' scores decreased significantly by this intervention, then the possibility of a fundamental psychometric incompatibility between majority and minority students would have to be investigated.

Finally, if this investigator's contention that racial and ethnic differences in Level II test scores are due to an artifact created by the testing ambience is true, then an appropriate facilitating intervention should virtually eliminate these differences: The minority and majority groups would no longer be significantly different. Such a finding would, furthermore, obviate the need for genetic explanations of traits that are clearly amenable to environmental intervention.

METHOD

This experiment compared the effects of two testing conditions—a standard test administration and a complex facilitation strategy—on the tested Level II performance of white (W), black (B), Mexican-American monolingual English-speaking (M1), and Mexican-American bilingual (M2) eighth-grade students, who were further classified by SES. The M2 subjects in the facilitation condition, furthermore, were treated bilingually, and the B subjects were treated bidialectically.

The Mexican-American subjects were divided into M1 and M2 groups on the basis of demographic information in order to account for possible differential effects of English language skills (or other environmentally or genetically related factors) and bilingualism on tested performance. The influence of bilingualism in cognitive functioning is well documented, though at times contradictory, especially as it relates to IQ (e.g., see Kittell, 1959; Peal & Lambert, 1962). Cummins (1979), in reviewing this literature, has postulated that a certain type of bilingualism, additive bilingualism, produces high cognitive effects. No Spanish monolinguals were included in this experiment because the Level II tests selected were in English and could thus confound (Jensen, 1980) the results.

SUBJECTS AND GROUPS

The subjects were all eighth-grade students from three public and six private schools in south-central Texas. At each school, the subjects initially completed a brief demographic questionnaire. Each subject was then assigned to either the standard or the facilitating testing condition. Because of the time constraints imposed by several of the schools, optimal randomization procedures could not be used on site; instead, subjects' demographic questionnaires were collected, grouped by race/ethnicity and language, and alternately sorted into two stacks, one for each condition, and marked appropriately. The testing commenced almost immediately thereafter. Later, the questionnaires and the tests were matched by name and stapled together. The demographic information then permitted each student to be further categorized by sex and SES. The few Spanish monolinguals (usually recent immigrants from Mexico) who were identified through the cooperation of teachers and counselors were excluded from participation, but the M2 group did include some students with limited English proficiency. Unfortunately, time again dictated that the English proficiency levels of M2 students not be directly assessed. SES was determined by the occupational status of the head of household. Three classifications were used: lower class (LC), lower middle class (MC), and upper middle, or upper, class (UC).

Altogether, 308 students were tested, but not all were used in the analyses. The factorial design contemplated would assign students by treatment, ethnicity, and SES, yielding a $2 \times 4 \times 3$ matrix. Because of the possible confounding effect of subjects' sex on the results and because sex was not a pivotal issue in this research, it was decided to control this variable by including males and females in each cell in the matrix in constant ratio. An examination of the demographic tabulations indicated that the M1-LC group was, not surprisingly, the least numerous, and that of the two treatment groups the smallest number was 8, 4 males and 4 females. Accordingly, the students for every other category were numbered and selected through the use of a table of random numbers to yield a sample of 192 subjects, 4 males and 4 females per cell, 96 subjects in each treatment group.

INSTRUMENTS

The subjects in this experiment were administered adaptations of the Letter Sets Test (LST) (French, Ekstrom, &. Price, 1963) and the Number Series Test (NST), instruments that involve higher order cognitive operations in the correct solution of their items. The order of the items in each of these tests appears to be based, at least roughly, on item difficulty. Modifications were made by taking out every third item, thereby reducing the total number of items in each test to 20. The remaining 10 items constituted the practice sets for the LST and the NST under the facilitation treatment. The time limit for each test was proportionately reduced, so that the modified LST was administered in 10 minutes (two parts, each 5 minutes) and the NST in 9 minutes.

The LST has two practice items that are given as part of the standard directions, which illustrate the nature of the test:

| 1. NOPQ | DEFL | ABCD | HIJK | UVWX |
| 2. NLIK | PLIK | QLIK | THIK | VLIK |

The subjects are asked to find the rule that makes four of the five sets of letters alike and to x out the set that is different. This is a multiple-choice test. In Item 1, the second set should be marked; in Item 2, the fourth set.

The NST presents a series of numbers that follow each other according to some rule. Two examples from the standard directions follow:

| A. 15 | 18 | 21 | 24 | 27 | 30 | _____ |
| B. 24 | 48 | 12 | 24 | 6 | 12 | 3 | _____ |

Item A illustrates the rule of "+3"; item B's rule is "$\times 2, \div 4$." Students are cautioned to be parsimonious, that is, not to repeat a rule or any part of it in writing the rule in the blank, for such repetition causes the item to be scored as incorrect. The items used here to illustrate the LST and the NST are relatively simple compared with most of the items on the actual tests.

Although the placement of tests on the culture-loaded–culture-reduced continuum is a fallible, subjective judgment (Jensen, 1974, 1980), the NST would probably favor the culturally loaded side because it depends heavily on mathematics achievement through multiplication and division. The LST, on the other hand, would probably fall on the culture-reduced side for students who know the alphabets of the languages of many Western nations. The LST would probably not show much cultural loading among eighth-grade students in the United States, for example.

EXAMINERS

Several female and male examiners of black, white, and Mexican-American background were employed as examiners on this experiment. All were seniors in a teacher education program at a local university, and they were selected because of their enthusiasm and seeming ability to relate well to students. The black examiners were bidialectal, and the Mexican-Americans could speak the nonstandard dialect of the *barrio*. They were taught to administer the LST and the NST rigorously, and they practiced the facilitation strategies to be employed in the experimental (i.e., facilitative) group setting among themselves under the supervision of the author, who later supervised their work in the schools to ensure that the desired test conditions were fulfilled.

These examiners, however, were incompletely briefed on the purpose of the experiment. Because both instruments were in typed form, copied and stapled, and because both were unfamiliar to the examiners, the examiners were told only that the efficacy of the standard instructions was being compared with maximally facilitating practice and coaching so that recommendations could be made about testing conditions for these groups.

TREATMENTS

The control condition consisted of a standard administration of the adapted NST and LST in groups that ranged in size from 10 to 30 students. The subjects were simply read the instructions aloud while they read them silently, and immediately thereafter, the subjects took the test. The order of NST and LST was varied at each school site. A white examiner administered the tests to the control subjects.

Under the experimental condition, the subjects were matched by ethnicity or race and organized into small groups (not less than two nor more than five) to work with an examiner of the same background. Rapport was established by the examiners through informal exchanges or by answering the students' questions about who they were, what they planned to do in life, and the like. The subjects were then introduced to the testing by practicing on one of the 10-item sets abstracted from the original NST or LST instruments, and after completing their work, they scored their own answer sheets. The subjects were asked individually which answer they had marked and were given feedback as to their accuracy. The subjects who answered an item correctly were asked to explain the problem, and if no one was correct or if all had omitted a particular item, the examiner provided the correct answer and explained it, often with the use of a chalkboard. After this exercise, which never lasted more than 20 minutes for either test, the students were told that they would be timed on the "real" test and were encouraged to work quickly and accurately; then, the corresponding test was administered in standard fashion, including the reading of the directions. The testing of students with two different tests effected a quasi-replication. The order of NST and LST administration, as in the standard condition, was changed at each site.

The M1 and W subjects were treated exclusively in English. The B and M2 subjects in the experimental group were facilitated in linguistically appropriate ways (after Matluck & Mace, 1973). The black examiners frequently used black dialect, and the Mexican-American examiners often used code switching to communicate with the M2 subjects. This author's subjective impressions gathered while observing these sessions are that they were lively and on task.

The facilitation condition combined several facilitation strategies designed to educe task-related, problem-solving mental sets that cannot be assumed to occur spontaneously in all subjects (see Rapier, 1967) and that seem to assist in concept attainment (Prehm, 1966; Rohwer, 1968; Zimmerman & Rosenthal, 1972). Some of the known score-enhancing techniques were omitted (see Jensen, 1980, for a detailed discussion), but this was by design. These techniques for developing test sophistication are—to this author's mind, at least— best taught only after the issues of test ambience have been addressed, particularly after students feel confident that they have "caught on" to the demands of the test and can at least "make a showing" on their own merits.

RESULTS

The control testing-condition was designed to provide a contrast to the experimental, or facilitating, condition and to show if the generally predictable results of differential performance by racial and ethnic and SES groups would be obtained on the NST and the LST under standard testing conditions. Tables 1 and 2 present the results and the analyses of the NST and LST standard administrations, respectively.

The effects of race/ethnicity and SES were significant on both tests. For the NST, the significance of race/ethnicity was less than .01; of the SES, less than .05. For the LST, the p for both variables was .05 or less. The W subjects outperformed the minority subjects in both instances. The order of the results for the NST was W, M1, B, M2; for the LST, the order was W, B, M1, M2. No significant interactions between race/ethnicity and SES occurred; hence, the differences seem to have obtained at all SES levels.

The performance of these groups under facilitation is presented in Tables 3 and 4. The effects of race/ethnicity on both tests did not reach statistical significance. For the NST, the p of race/ethnicity was .24; for the LST, .48. There were no interaction effects.

The SES effects on the NST approached significance ($p = .07$) but were clearly nonsignificant for the LST ($p = .59$). The comparatively higher performance scores of the LC-M2, MC-W, LC-W, and LC-B sub-

TABLE 1

Analysis of Variance of Number Series Test: Standard Administration (Control) Group ($N = 96$, or 8 per Cell)

		M1	M2	W	B	SES averages
UC	$\overline{X}$	5.25	3.12	6.25	4.2	5.36
	SD	(3.81)	(0.64)	(4.03)	(2.75)	
MC	$\overline{X}$	4.62	3.88	5.38	3.88	4.86
	SD	(2.00)	(3.04)	(3.46)	(2.95)	
LC	$\overline{X}$	2.75	2.25	5.38	1.75	3.55
	SD	(2.60)	(1.28)	(2.77)	(1.16)	
Ethnic averages	$\overline{X}$	4.21	3.08	5.67	3.25	Grand mean 4.05
	SD	(2.98)	(1.98)	(3.33)	(2.56)	(2.90)

Source	SS	DF	MS	F	p
Main effects	152.135	5	30.427	4.053	.002
Race/ethnic	101.115	3	33.705	4.490	.006
SES	51.021	2	25.510	3.398	.04
Interactions	17.979	6	2.997	.399	.88
Explained	170.115	11	15.465	2.060	.03
Residual	630.625	84	7.507		
Total	800.740	95	8.429		

TABLE 2

Analysis of Variance of Letter Sets Test: Standard Administration (Control) Group ($N = 96$, or 8 per Cell)

		M1	M2	W	B	SES averages
UC	$\overline{X}$	10.75	8.88	11.38	10.12	10.28
	SD	(2.60)	(3.56)	(3.02)	(4.32)	(3.40)
MC	$\overline{X}$	10.75	10.00	11.38	10.62	10.69
	SD	(3.28)	(4.04)	(1.51)	(3.74)	(3.17)
LC	$\overline{X}$	6.12	8.62	12.25	7.50	8.62
	SD	(3.76	(4.69)	(3.15)	(3.34)	(4.27)
Ethnic averages	$\overline{X}$	9.21	9.17	11.67	9.42	Grand mean 9.86
	SD	(3.82)	(3.99)	(2.58)	(3.91)	(3.72)

Source	SS	DF	MS	F	p
Main effects	181.177	5	36.235	2.942	.02
Race/ethnic	104.781	3	34.927	2.835	.04
SES	76.396	2	38.198	3.101	.05
Interactions	95.437	6	15.906	1.291	.27
Explained	276.615	11	25.147	2.042	.03
Residual	1034.625	84	12.317		
Total	1311.240	95	13.803		

TABLE 3

Analysis of Variance of Number Series Test: Facilitation Administration (Experimental) Group ($N = 96$, or 8 per Cell)

		M1	M2	W	B	SES averages
UC	$\overline{X}$	7.50	5.38	5.12	6.12	6.03
	SD	(3.51)	(1.51)	(3.36)	(2.53)	(2.86)
MC	$\overline{X}$	6.62	4.75	6.12	3.62	5.28
	SD	(5.58)	(2.92)	(3.91)	(3.81)	(4.14)
LC	$\overline{X}$	4.75	4.88	3.38	3.25	4.06
	SD	(3.45)	(3.64)	(2.72)	(2.38)	(3.04)
Ethnic averages	$\overline{X}$	6.29	5.00	4.88	4.33	Grand mean 5.12
	SD	(4.27)	(2.72)	(3.42)	(3.13)	(3.45)

Source	SS	DF	MS	F	p
Main effects	112.771	5	22.554	1.934	.10
Race/ethnic	49.583	3	16.528	1.417	.24
SES	63.187	2	31.594	2.709	.07
Interactions	40.229	6	6.705	.575	.75
Explained	153.000	11	13.909	1.193	.30
Residual	979.500	84	11.661		
Total	1132.500	95	11.921		

TABLE 4
Analysis of Variance of Letter Sets Test: Facilitation Administration
(Experimental) Group (N = 96, or 8 per Cell)

		M1	M2	W	B	SES averages
UC	$\overline{X}$	13.38	11.25	10.38	13.50	12.12
	SD	(5.29)	(2.31)	(3.96)	(4.00)	(4.07)
MC	$\overline{X}$	11.62	10.62	14.38	9.38	11.50
	SD	(4.37)	(2.45)	(3.16)	(3.42)	(3.75)
LC	$\overline{X}$	11.00	11.12	12.38	10.25	11.19
	SD	(2.83)	(3.98)	(2.50)	(4.95)	(3.60)
Ethnic averages	$\overline{X}$	12.00	11.00	12.38	11.04	Grand mean 11.60
	SD	(4.22)	(2.89)	(3.54)	(4.38)	(3.79)

Source	SS	DF	MS	F	p
Main effects	48.958	5	9.792	.706	.62
Race/ethnic	34.375	3	11.458	.826	.48
SES	14.583	2	7.292	5.26	.59
Interactions	151.000	6	25.167	1.815	.11
Explained	199.958	11	18.178	1.311	.23
Residual	1165.000	84	13.869		
Total	1364.958	95	14.368		

jects on the LST almost resulted in an interaction between race/ethnicity and SES (p = .11).

But before any conclusions can be reached, let us remember that these hypothesized results are predicted on a null effect on the W subjects. Accordingly, one-way ANOVAs were conducted for the NST and the LST. For the NST, the W means were 5.67 under standard (control) and 4.88 under facilitation (experimental) conditions (p = .57). For the LST, the means, respectively, were 11.67 and 12.38; the p in this instance was .56.

Tables 5 and 6 present the three-way ANOVAs for this study: treatment × race/ethnicity × SES. The NST and the LST showed strong treatment effects. No significant interactions were detected.

The results can be summarized as follows. First, the minority groups scored significantly higher under the facilitation condition than under the standard condition on both tests. Second, the white subjects' performance was essentially unchanged from one condition to the other. Third, under the facilitation condition, the racial/ethnic and SES group differences, reliably detected under standard testing conditions, were no longer in evidence. The hypotheses were all verified.

TABLE 5

Analysis of Variance of Number Series Test: Treatment $\times$ Race/Ethnicity $\times$ SES (N = 192, or 8 per Cell)

Source	SS	DF	MS	F	p
Main effects					
Treatment (A)	55.255	1	55.255	5.765	.02
Race/ethnic (B)	88.182	3	29.394	3.067	.03
SES (C)	112.166	2	56.083	5.852	.004
Interactions					
A $\times$ B	62.517	3	20.839	2.174	.09
A $\times$ C	2.042	2	1.021	.106	.90
B $\times$ C	26.334	6	4.389	.458	.84
A $\times$ B $\times$ C	31.872	6	5.312	.554	.77
Explained	378.373	23	16.451		
Residual	1610.112	168	9.584		
Total	1988.485	191	10.411		

TABLE 6

Analysis of Variance of Letter Sets Test: Treatment $\times$ Race/Ethnicity $\times$ SES (N = 192, or 8 per Cell)

Source	SS	DF	MS	F	p
Main effects					
Treatment (A)	145.255	1	145.255	11.094	.001
Race/ethnic (B)	112.824	3	37.616	2.873	.04
SES (C)	66.218	2	33.109	2.529	.08
Interactions					
A $\times$ B	26.307	3	8.769	.670	.57
A $\times$ C	24.760	2	12.380	.946	.61
B $\times$ C	145.824	6	24.304	1.856	.09
A $\times$ B $\times$ C	100.614	6	16.769	1.121	.27
Explained	621.802	23	27.036		
Residual	2199.624	168	13.093		
Total	2821.426	191	14.772		

DISCUSSION

This experiment was designed to study the effects of the testing ambience on the Level II performance of white, black, and Mexican-American groups, with a view to examining the viability of an alternative interpretation to the heredity–environment controversy. The findings in this study suggest that, to a much greater extent than the hereditarian position would indicate, tested performance differences between white and certain minority groups are an artifact of conditions that favor the repertoire of whites and that are clearly amenable to learning by minority groups. It would appear that the culture-loaded–culture-reduced continuum, as defined by Jensen, is of little value in the practical realm, as in either or both cases, the NST and LST instruments showed no significant differences among the racial and ethnic groups studied under conditions of facilitation. Were one or both tests culturally loaded, then circumstances would seem to be able to "unload" them considerably; if unloaded, then group differences can be explained by their differential readiness to engage in the tasks.

Possibly the most important limitations of this study lie in the fact that the groups were small in number and were not proportionately representative of SES categories. These limitations notwithstanding, the impact of the intervention on minority groups—even those at the lowest SES levels—cannot be overlooked.

The SES effects of the intervention are also interesting but should come as no surprise. Haggard (1954) had earlier demonstrated positive effects on lower- and middle-SES children on IQs after having coached them intensively for three days. Lower-SES children increased their IQ by 15–20 points. Haggard believed that these children, although they may have taken many tests, had not developed the requisite test-taking skills (contrary to Jensen's assumption), lacked motivation to engage the tasks, had a distant relationship with the examiner, and were generally fearful of the experience.

For this study to have practicable test-design implications, it should be expanded and replicated with other types of tests and more ethnic and language minority groups; various strategies should be used singly and in combination to determine if an optimal mix can be found. The challenge to psychometricians is to empirically discover and sedulously implement multiculturally appropriate testing conditions in tests that require maximal performance.

The conclusion seems inescapable that the heredity–environment controversy should be reexamined not on its extant merits but from the perspective that there could easily be a fundamental problem with our instrumentation or with the conditions under which test data are acquired. Typically designed and established standardized-testing conditions may be directly contributing to the depression of minority groups' test scores (see Zirkel, 1972), a phenomenon that may or may not be detectable through ordinary procedures for determining or calculating test reliability and validity, but that may be seen when the testing ambience is altered.

The findings reported in this chapter indicate that certain tests of higher order cognitive abilities are heavily biased against minorities, but in a more quintessential way than Jensen and other hereditarians have considered. Moreover, the score differences among the groups in these cognitive skills—scores like those on which genetic heritability theories have been founded—have been shown to be amenable to procedures such as pretraining. Before continuing to expend our energies debating a problem that as yet seems to have no solution, we should first satisfy ourselves that the problem exists, that it is not an artifact created by the limitations of our measurement instruments.

REFERENCES

Bereiter, C. Genetics and educability: Educational implications of the Jensen debate. In J. Hellmuth (Ed.), *Disadvantaged child: Vol. 3. Compensatory education: A national debate.* New York: Brunner/Mazel, 1970.

Bernal, E. M. Comment: A response to educational uses of tests with disadvantaged subjects. *American Psychologist*, 1975, *30*, 93–95.

Bernal, E. M. Assessment procedures for Chicano children: The sad state of the art. *Aztlán*, 1977, *8*, 69–81.

Boyer, W. H., & Walsh, P. Are children born unequal? *Saturday Review*, 1968, *51*(42), 61–78.

Burger, H. G. Ethno-lematics: Evoking "shy" Spanish American pupils by cross-cultural mediation. *Adolescence*, 1972, *6*, 61–76.

Carter, T. P. Mexican Americans: How the schools have failed them. *College Board Review*, Spring 1970, pp. 5–11.

Cole, M., & Brunner, J. Cultural differences and inferences about psychological processes. *American Psychologist*, 1971, *26*, 867–876.

Cronbach, L. J. Heredity, environment, and educational policy. In *Environment, heredity, and intelligence.* Cambridge: Harvard Educational Review, 1969.

Cummins, J. Linguistic interdependence and the educational development of bilingual children. *Review of Educational Research*, 1979, *49*, 222–251.

French, J. W., Ekstrom, R. G., & Price, L. A. *Manual for kit of reference tests for cognitive factors* (rev. ed.). Princeton, N.J.: Educational Testing Service, 1963.

Ginther, J. R. Pretraining Chicano students before administration of a mathematics predictor test. *Journal for Research in Mathematics Education*, 1978, *9*, 118–125.

Haggard, E. A. Social status and intelligence. *Genetic Psychology Monographs*, 1954, *49*, 141–186.

Hall, V. C., & Turner, R. R. The validity of the "different language explanation" for the poor scholastic performance by black students. *Review of Educational Research*, 1974, *44*, 69–81.

Jensen, A. R. The culturally disadvantaged and the heredity-environment uncertainty. In J. Hellmuth (Ed.), *Disadvantaged child: Vol. 2. Head start and early intervention.* New York: Brunner/Mazel, 1968.

Jensen, A. R. Heredity, environment, and educability. *Encyclopedia of education.* New York: Macmillan, 1969. (a)

Jensen, A. R. How much can we boost IQ and scholastic achievement? *Harvard Educational Review,* 1969, *39,* 1–123. (b)

Jensen, A. R. Reducing the heredity-environment uncertainty: A reply. *Harvard Educational Review,* 1969, *39,* 449–483. (c)

Jensen, A. R. Can we and should we study race differences? In J. Hellmuth (Ed.), *Disadvantaged child: Vol. 3. Compensatory education: A national debate.* New York: Brunner/Mazel, 1970.

Jensen, A. R. *Educational differences.* London: Methuen, 1973.

Jensen, A. R. How biased are culture-loaded tests? *Genetic Psychology Monographs,* 1974, *90,* 185–244.

Jensen, A. R. *Bias in mental testing.* New York: Free Press, 1980.

Jensen, A. R., & Rohwer, W. D., Jr. The effect of verbal mediation on the learning and retention of paired-associates by retarded adults. *American Journal of Mental Deficiency,* 1963, *68,* 80–84. (a)

Jensen, A. R., & Rohwer, W. D., Jr. Verbal mediation in paired associate and serial learning. *Journal of Verbal Learning and Verbal Behavior,* 1963, *1,* 346–352. (b)

Katz, I., Epps, E. G., & Axelson, L. J. Effect upon Negro digit-symbol performance of anticipated comparison with Whites and with other Negroes. *Journal of Abnormal and Social Psychology,* 1964, *69,* 77–83.

Kittell, J. E. Bilingualism and language–non-language intelligence scores of third-grade children. *Journal of Educational Research,* 1959, *52,* 263–268.

Matarazzo, J. D. *Wechsler's measurement and appraisal of adult intelligence* (5th ed.). Baltimore: Williams & Wilkins, 1972.

Matluck, J. H., & Mace, B. J. Language characteristics of Mexican American children: Implications for assessment. *Journal of School Psychology,* 1973, *11,* 365–386.

Peal, E., & Lambert, W. E. The relation of bilingualism to intelligence. *Psychological Monographs,* 1962, *76* (27, Whole No. 546).

Prehm, H. J. Concept learning in culturally disadvantaged children as a function of verbal pretraining. *Exceptional Children,* 1966, *32,* 599–604.

Rapier, J. L. Effects of verbal mediation upon the learning of Mexican American children. *California Journal of Educational Research,* 1967, *18,* 40–48.

Rohwer, W. D., Jr. Mental mnemonics in early learning. *The Record,* 1968, *70,* 213–226.

Zimmerman, B. J., & Rosenthal, T. L. Observation, repetition, and ethnic background in concept attainment and generalization. *Child Development,* 1972, *43,* 605–613.

Zirkel, P. A. Spanish-speaking students and standardized tests. *Urban Review,* 1972, *5–6,* 32–40.

CHAPTER SIX

College Entrance Examinations
Objective Selection or Gatekeeping for the Economically Privileged

WINTON H. MANNING
and
REX JACKSON

Although arguments concerning the usefulness of tests in education are not new (Cronbach, 1975), the last few years have seen two changes that should be noted. First, there has been a significant escalation in the intensity of the criticism directed at tests, so that a large proportion of those concerned with education—teachers, legislators, administrators, parents, and students—are disturbed, if not bewildered, by the vehemence and persistence of the attacks on tests. Second, the testing controversy has been increasingly centered on the public journalistic domains of newspapers, television, and popular magazines, rather than within the traditional scientific framework of educational research and professional literature. This has led inevitably to a reduction in the quality and the intellectual depth of the debates, as the most extreme critics are largely unfamiliar not only with the empirical research on testing but with the methodology of social science generally. Furthermore, the public has little understanding of and less patience for technical and scientific argument and is easily misled by superficial stereotypes, at least in the short run.

WINTON H. MANNING ● Educational Testing Service, Princeton, New Jersey 08541.   REX JACKSON ● Applied Educational Research, Princeton, New Jersey 08542.

What is important in the controversy about testing—especially admissions testing—is the insight it provides into the ways in which testing has become invested with the social tensions arising from deep value conflicts within our society. Over the past 50 years, increasing use has been made of tests in education because they have been seen by policymakers as useful instruments for attaining social and educational objectives. Public and institutional policies that incorporate the use of examinations have developed because these policies are the means by which certain admirable ideals could be realized. At the heart of these ideals stands the belief that individual merit—not wealth, social class, influence, gender, or social background—should be the touchstone of enlightened educational and social policy. Although this commitment to the fair and objective appraisal of individual merit has deep roots in the religions and the political and economic beliefs of our society, attacks on testing arise partly from more recent uncertainties about the social consequences of a meritocratic philosophy and partly out of the ubiquitous tendency to find easy solutions to complicated problems.

In recent years, many thoughtful persons have also been disillusioned and angered by the contrasts between the ideal and the actuality of schooling, between the expressed goals of education and the seeming intransigence of the disparities between our intentions and our outcomes. Testing, as the most visible expression of the commitment to individual merit, is also the vehicle by which our failures to educate are most starkly revealed, and this revelation makes us very uncomfortable.

It is therefore understandable that hostility towards testing would become, perhaps irrationally, one important means of dealing with this larger conflict of values, indeed, with the guilt and frustration that have arisen over the failures of education. A campaign to abolish testing in education thereby becomes an escape from persevering in the effort to understand the reasons that the fruits of our educational policies have fallen so short of our social expectations.

Writing some years ago, Gallagher (1975) described the low estate of educational research in government circles in terms that may be paraphrased to apply to the situation in testing today:

> While decision makers still have a basically favorable attitude towards educational testing in general, that is now tempered by some new anger and disillusionment. The entire profession of measurement is held accountable for the manifest inability of education to do better with the economically poor and culturally different child. . . . Testing displays the

major requisites of a good scapegoat: it is visible, there are reasons to be mad at it, and it cannot effectively strike back. (p. 13)

Neither debate nor polemic nor even litigation in the courts can resolve issues that are fundamentally problems of inadequate human knowledge. However, with respect to the usefulness of tests in college admissions, there exists a very substantial body of research findings that are useful in evaluating the strengths and limitations of tests, and that can also serve as a foundation for finding solutions to some of our vexing problems. The purpose of this chapter is not to review the criticisms of testing in general, nor even to examine the attacks on college admissions testing in particular. However, in examining such questions as the validity and the fairness of college admissions tests, it is inevitable and desirable that some of the facets of the attacks on admissions tests should be addressed.

Inevitably, the authors have drawn primarily on the substantial body of research studies on the Scholastic Aptitude Test (SAT) of the College Board. With more space and time, a detailed presentation of research could be provided on the American College Test (ACT) assessment program, and on admissions tests for graduate schools, law schools, business schools, and medical schools. On the whole, the research findings concerning various college admissions tests are very, very similar, and for that reason, our examination of research on the SAT is largely generalizable. For a useful and more detailed presentation of the relevant research and typical practices in admissions at both the undergraduate and the graduate levels, the reader is referred to the report of the Carnegie Council entitled *Selective Admissions in Higher Education* (1977), and especially to the section of that report on "The Status of Selective Admissions" by Willingham and Breland in association with Ferrin and Fruen.

HOW IMPORTANT ARE TESTS IN ADMISSIONS?

From one standpoint, at least, there is little support for the argument that test scores play a crucial role in the admission of students to college. It is known, for example, that only about 1 college in 10 accepts less than half the students who apply, and about one-third of U.S. colleges and universities accept more than 90% of their applicants (Hartnett & Feldmesser, 1980). The typical secondary-school student applying to college makes application to only a single college, and the vast majority are accepted by the college to which they have applied.

For example, in a 1972 survey (Hilton & Rhett, 1973), 87.5% of the students who had applied to one or more colleges had been admitted to some college by the end of their senior year of high school. Even more telling is the result of a 1978 survey by the American Council on Education (ACE), which indicated that 75% of all freshmen were attending their first-choice college, and nearly 95% were attending the college that was either their first or second choice (Astin, King, & Richardson, 1978, p. 18).

Furthermore, in a 1979 study of admissions officers conducted by the College Board and the American Association of Collegiate Registrars and Admissions Officers, the report was that less than 2% of admissions officers regard scores on college admissions tests as the most important determiners of who is accepted at their own institution (College Entrance Examination Board, 1980). These facts are at considerable variance with the imagery conjured up by the term gatekeepers; rather, they suggest that test scores may be less crucial than is commonly supposed. There are many doors to a higher education; they are mostly open (as a consequence, especially, of demographic changes); and where tests do play an explicit role in admissions decisions, this role is far less salient than is widely believed to be the case.

However, these arguments are relevant but rightfully unconvincing in evaluating the usefulness of college admissions tests. First, the point that most colleges are unselective fails to take account of the fact that there is a small number of very prestigious institutions that *are* selective, and they enjoy reputations for conferring on their graduates not only the stamp of a high-quality education but an additional incremental advantage in the marketplace of jobs because of the lustre attached to their degree. Hence, on practical as well as ideological grounds, access to this relatively small number of prestigious colleges is a matter of general concern, albeit somewhat exaggerated in the public's eye. Certainly, to the extent that tests play a salient role in these highly selective institutions, it is important to examine carefully the validity and the fairness of the tests.

Second, the process of *self-selection*, whereby students themselves choose the colleges to which they apply, exerts a far more profound influence on the distribution of students from the nation's secondary schools to its colleges than does the process of explicit selection by a particular college of those whom it will admit from among its applicants. To a degree, students tend to sort themselves across colleges in a manner that reflects—at least partially—their own *perceived ability* in relation to the *perceived demands* of the college program. Our knowledge of this process is quite primitive. To some extent, students' self-perceptions are related to the kinds of abilities assessed by college admissions tests, but the vast majority of students form impressions of themselves and of colleges, which together shape their intentions long before they take college admissions tests as juniors or seniors in high school. Indeed, one of the benefits of admissions tests, many feel, has been the discovery of "hidden" talent—of students whose aspirations and self-concepts have been limited by parents or teachers who have failed to recognize the level of a student's abilities until the tests provided new evidence.

Third, what is generally true for the majority of students may not necessarily be true for those racial and ethnic groups that have historically been denied equal opportunity in our society. There is considerable evidence to suggest that, on an individual basis, admissions tests have been crucially helpful in searching out talented minority persons who, but for the tests, would have been barred from or neglected by higher education. But critics of testing often point to the disparities in average performance between majority and minority groups as presumptive evidence of a test bias that produces unequal opportunities for education and thereby undermines upward social mobility. This is the problem of individual *versus* group equity that lies at the root of so much recent social strife, that triggered the *Bakke* debate, and that enormously complicates the pursuit of fairness in admissions (Manning, 1977).

The justification of the use of college admissions tests necessarily depends on a far wider range of data than research evidence alone. One must evaluate the effects of the tests on individual students, on schools, and on colleges. The productivity of our society, for example, depends not only on the capacity of education to recruit, train, and deploy those whose task is the creation of knowledge, but also on those who will apply, disseminate, and operate the products of new knowledge for the benefit of society. In assisting institutions in meeting the demands of society for educated people, admissions tests are asked to support institutional productivity by communicating standards of preparation from colleges to schools that are engaged in preparing students for successful transition and entry, by providing a means of monitoring the outcomes of education at each level against some expected standard of quality, and by reducing barriers to equality of opportunity. Correspondingly, tests, aside from providing estimates of future performance, are expected to motivate students to strive for rewards, to certify types and levels of competency, and to provide alternative, second-chance mechanisms for those whose careers have been derailed by adverse circumstances.

Whether admissions testing programs, as now constituted, are sufficiently broad and flexible to sustain the substantial burden placed on them by these various institutional and individual functions is an important concern, which can be addressed only in a limited way within the scope of this chapter. Our principal concern is with a prior question: whether present tests are valid predictors of an appropriate criterion of success in college, and whether the degree of relationship between admissions test scores and criterion measures is generalizable across various social class and racial groups. However, in addressing whether college admissions tests are invalid and racially biased, it is well to remember that even if the evidence is overwhelmingly in support of tests, there remain numbers of other important and complex issues concerning the benefits or disadvantages of admissions testing. These questions also need to be seriously studied and debated.

WHY ARE TESTS NEEDED?

In contrast to the situation in many countries, the philosophy underlying much of education in the United States today places great stress on providing students with a broad base of general education and on delay of academic or professional specialization until a relatively late age. Students throughout high school and college are encouraged to acquire a broad acquaintance with the liberal arts and the sciences. Considerable emphasis is placed on exploration, flexibility, and choice. There is no national syllabus. Both the curriculum and the standards of secondary schools are under substantial local control. Similarly, institutions of higher education offer a wide array of educational options.

This situation creates a need for common examinations taken by students at the point of transition to college, and at the same time, it delimits the form that these examinations may appropriately take. Fairness to students from schools with varying academic standards requires that certain common measures (such as admissions test scores) be evaluated along with the students' school records in reaching admissions decisions. However, this same diversity among secondary schools and the fact that there is no closely prescribed course of preparation for college studies argue against the use of highly specific subject-matter achievement tests as a principal component of admissions.

Accordingly, the most widely used college admissions tests—the College Board's Scholastic Aptitude Test and the American College Tests—place heavy emphasis on developed abilities, on highly general educational outcomes, and on skills that are relevant to success in a wide variety of postsecondary programs. The SAT, for example, is made up principally of problems that test reading comprehension, verbal reasoning and vocabulary, and quantitative reasoning. It is accompanied by a test of English usage. Many colleges ask applicants to take the College Board Achievement Tests as well as the SAT, and these achievement tests are designed, insofar as possible, to test an understanding of certain core concepts and bodies of knowledge common to high school courses in particular disciplines. But the SAT is much more widely used by colleges to obtain common assessments of students' levels of development in certain abilities (such as reading comprehension) that are fundamental to further academic work.

ARE ADMISSIONS TESTS VALID?

As noted, admissions tests are designed to provide a common basis for evaluation, supplementary to students' prior academic records. Their appropriateness and utility for this purpose may be evidenced in several ways. At the foundation is an informed judgment by the designers and developers of the tests that the tasks sampled by the tests require skills that are important to competent academic performance—that the tests are, in fact, academic work samples and hence possess content relevance, an important constituent of test validity. This judgment is guided by experience with particular types of questions or problems in other settings and by research showing a relationship between performance on these tasks and academic success. In addition, this judgment is subject to the review of independent educators, particularly those in the institutions that use the tests. The practice of publishing sample test forms with answer keys for each of the major admissions testing programs further encourages the widest possible scrutiny of test content. There is considerable agreement among those using the tests that the abilities assessed by the reading, verbal reasoning, and mathematical problems contained in college admissions tests are relevant to successful academic work in their institutions. The prevailing view of the SAT, for example, is the one expressed by William Ambler, Dean of Admissions at Haverford College (as quoted by Sewell, Carey, Simons, & Lord, 1980): "The test reflects the words and symbols that students must deal with in courses every day" (p. 97).

In another context, the president of Harvard University (Bok, 1974) discussed the purpose of undergraduate education, giving primary place to the objective of acquiring information and knowledge:

> The most obvious function of a college education is to help students acquire information and knowledge by acquainting them with a body of fact, theories, generalizations, and ideas of every sort. This purpose scarcely requires justification. Information provides the raw material for discourse, inquiry, choice, reflection—indeed, for almost every form of intellectual activity. For some students, especially in the sciences, the knowledge gained in college provides a necessary foundation for graduate study. For almost all students, a liberal arts education helps to create a web of knowledge that can illumine experience and enlighten judgment throughout life. (p. 162)

Other important objectives delineated by Bok include the acquisition of skills and habits of thought, such things as the ability to write effectively; to read with comprehension; to analyze problems, identifying issues and selecting relevant information; to understand quantitative methods—the language of quantitative reasoning—and, indeed, even to understand an academic discipline well enough to gain a sense of what it means to master at least one subject in depth.

The stuff of which admissions tests are constructed is in no way mysterious or arcane. Rather, the test items and materials are constructed to assess the verbal and quantitative skills that students require in order to make effective progress in achieving the objectives of undergraduate education described by Bok.

Judgments of content relevance, although central to the rationale supporting the use of admissions tests, are subject to at least partial verification by research that examines the relationship of test scores to other measures of educational preparation, development, or achievement. The major admissions testing programs offer services to colleges and graduate schools using the tests that are supportive of an institutional evaluation of the tests' validity in predicting academic outcomes. These studies constitute an enormous body of knowledge pertaining to the predictive validity of college admissions tests. It is doubtful that any other kind of test or even any other body of test validation research approaches the number of studies in which college admissions test scores are related to future academic performance. The studies have been repeated thousands of times, and the results quite consistently support the conclusion that admissions tests are generally valid, in the sense that the higher the test scores the more successful, on the average, the students are in college or graduate study. Not surprisingly, it is also true that the prediction is imperfect, and that the usually employed criterion of grades is not all-encompassing. However, the data clearly support the assertion that admissions tests are valid predictors of important criteria of success in college.

Typical results of prediction studies based on test scores and grades of enrolled students are shown in Table 1. The correlations reported are median values; for several reasons, these values are conservative estimates.

First, validity studies are conducted on restricted groups of admitted, enrolled, and persisting students. Selective institutions use test scores and other academic information to identify the students who are likely to do well. To a large extent, these institutions are successful, and the great majority of admitted students are capable of meeting the demands of these institutions' academic programs. Because validity studies in many colleges are necessarily performed on such relatively homogeneous student groups, the observed correlations of test scores and grades are lower than would be obtained in studies of student groups reflecting the full range of applicant abilities.

Second, the criterion most often used in validity studies (grade point average, or GPA) is an imperfect measure of academic performance. Students take different courses and programs of study. Grading standards vary from program to program and from instructor to instructor, and even the grade that a student receives from a partic-

TABLE 1

Characteristic Validity Coefficients of Admissions Test Scores and Previous Grade Record (GPA) for Predicting Subsequent Grades

Admissions test	Type of school	No. of studies	Median validity coefficients		
			Test scores	Previous GPA	Both predictors combined
SAT	Undergraduate	827	.41	.52	.58
GRE	Graduate arts and sciences	24–30	.33	.31	.45
LSAT	Law	116	.36	.25	.45
GMAT	Graduate management	67	.29	.21	.38

ular instructor in a particular course is generally a matter of judgment. Lack of precision and consistency in grades as a measure of academic outcomes similarly depresses the apparent validity of test scores and other variables used in prediction.

Although formulas are available (and are sometimes used) to correct for the attenuating affects of range restriction and criterion unreliability on validity coefficients, we will not use them here, because such corrections are based on assumptions about the nature of the selection process and about the properties of grades that cannot be verified. Instead, we will use the unadjusted and conservative estimates.

Despite problems in interpretation, what do the results of validity studies tell us about the usefulness of tests for selection purposes? A number of authors have addressed the problem of interpreting validity coefficients in terms of utility or benefits—a body of work treated comprehensively by Cronbach and Gleser (1965). Each of these approaches, however, is based on the simplifying assumption that selection is based exclusively on test scores (or test scores combined with other quantitative measures), whereas the selection process in most institutions is, in fact, based on human judgment informed by a body of quantitatively expressed and other information collected for each applicant. Thus, the true role of test scores in the admissions process and the utility attributable to their use is not readily assessible in quantitative terms.

Figure 1 displays the average grades that would be expected at a college typical of those conducting validity studies through the College Board's Validity Study Service in 1974.[1] This illustration of average grades conditional on test scores is consistent with the conception of utility as an incremental gain in a measure of outcomes. Without attempting to reduce this gain to a single number, the figure illustrates that the use of the SAT as one component of admissions can be of significant help in assuring that the admitted students will be those who are likely to go on to obtain satisfactory grades.

The usefulness of a test can also be evaluated in "percentage correct" terms through the use of tables developed by Taylor and Russell (1939). As an illustration of this method, consider a college with 1,000 applicants, but only 900 places. It has to deny admission to 100

[1]This figure is a composite illustration of the regression of grades on test scores based on the distribution of test scores and grades for colleges conducting validity studies in 1974 and on a correlation of .40, which is just below the characteristic validity of the SAT.

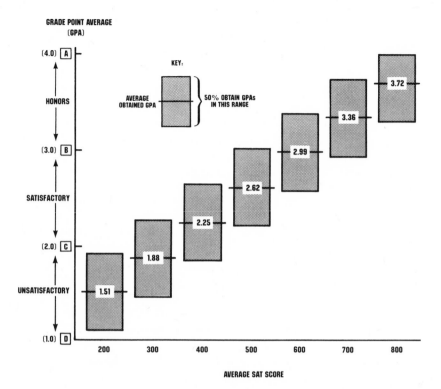

FIGURE 1. Average college grades for students with different SAT scores. Typical SAT score/college GPA correlation = 0.40. (Based on data from 159 validity studies in 1974.)

students. If these students were chosen at random, about 50 of the students denied admission would have ranked in the top half of the class in terms of later grades. The Taylor–Russell tables indicate that the use of a test with a validity of .41 to select these students would reduce the number of incorrect decisions to 21. The use of test scores and previous grades with a combined validity of .58 would reduce the number to 11. In the former case, we have reduced our errors by 58%; in the latter, by 78%. Other illustrations could be developed based on different selection ratios and different assumptions about the desired criterion levels. In general, illustrations based on realistic assumptions similarly show a meaningful improvement in selection decisions due to use of the test.

Generally, test scores and prior grades are used together in making academic forecasts. One way to assess the contribution of several variables to prediction is to examine the weights that must be applied to each variable to obtain optimum overall prediction. Consider a college at which SAT scores alone have their typical validity of .41 and where high school grades alone have their typical validity of .52. In using these predictors together to obtain a typical overall predictive validity of .58, the test scores would be given 39% of the weight and the grades would be given 61% of the weight. At the graduate and professional school level, the validity study results would lead one to place even more weight on tests than on grades in order to obtain optimum prediction. From this perspective also, the tests make a useful contribution to improving decisions.

The weights given to different kinds of information in arriving at admissions decisions, however, should not be based solely on the results of validity studies. Prior grades reflect the pooled judgment of a number of instructors who have evaluated students' work on tests, term papers, class projects, recitations, and other aspects of academic work. Admissions tests reflect student performance on a carefully selected sample of intellectual tasks, scored in a highly consistent way across individuals. Students' prior academic records are properly given great weight in admissions. Likewise, scores on the tests are properly weighted in these decisions. Although tests measure a narrower range of abilities than grades, they are also valid. Because test scores have a consistent meaning for all students, they help to redress the unfairness that would occur if the grades from a variety of sending schools with different grading standards were used alone. It is very largely this fairness, as well as a desire to select students who will perform well academically, that motivates institutions to use the tests.

Deciding on admissions criteria is fundamentally a matter of judgment. These judgments take into account the relevance, dependability, comparability across individuals, comprehensiveness, and validity of the information considered for use. The weight to be given to various factors in admissions is not a matter that should be decided in simple, absolute terms, with a reliance entirely on the results of limited statistical studies. If the admissions decision were made in these terms, test scores would probably be given greater weight than is typically the case currently, for the studies show them to be nearly as valid as or, in many cases, more valid than grades. Fortunately, admissions officers and admissions committees generally use considerable judgment and discretion in weighing other kinds of evidence.

Despite the substantial judgmental and research evidence supporting the use of tests in admissions, a number of critics of such tests have questioned whether studies of test validity provide evidence of

TABLE 2b
Predicted and Actual Law School Grades for Black
Students[a]

Study/school	Predicted average grade[b]	Actual average grade	Amount of overprediction
II-A	39	36	3
II-B	42	37	5
II-C	40	38	2
II-D	40	36	4
II-E	40	38	2
III-D	36	33	3
III-E	39	36	3
III-F	39	37	2
III-G	44	42	2
III-H	40	36	4
III-1	38	33	5
III-J71	40	35	5
III-J72	40	36	4

[a]The predictions are based on UGPA and LSAT using the combined group consisting of the total black sample and the proportional white sample. Table adapted from Linn (1975).
[b]Grades were scaled to have a mean of 50 and a standard deviation of 10 for the combined group of students within each school. Predictions are for UGPA and LSAT scores at the mean of black students within each school.

consideration, and somewhat higher for longer term cumulative GPA than for shorter term GPA, inconsistent with the late bloomer hypothesis. (p. 23)

Writing in 1980, Linn stated:

It is simply not the case that test scores give a misleading low indication of the likely performance of blacks whether that performance is measured in terms of freshman GPA in college, first year grades in law school, outcomes of job training, or job performance measures. (p. 20–21)

Where does this leave us? Certainly, the bulk of research evidence runs counter to the view that admissions tests contain sources of significant difficulty for minority students that are irrelevant to future academic performance.[2] There are other factors to consider, however. Thorndike (1971) demonstrated that, even when an admissions process is "fair" (in that it is based on a composite of assessments that neither systematically over- or underpredict criterion

[2]However, Richard Duran (1983) has recently completed a critical analysis of studies of the performance of Hispanic students in college. He concludes that "high school grades and admissions test scores were not as good predictors of U.S. Hispanics' college grades as they were of white non-Hispanics' college grades" (p. 102).

performance for members of a subgroup), decisions based on a ranking of individuals on this composite tends to result in a lower representation of the lower scoring groups than if they had been selected
on the criterion itself. Others (e.g., Cole, 1973) have explored this
seeming paradox and have proposed models involving different decision rules for subgroups that are intended to result in greater group
parity. Petersen and Novick (1976), however, offered a compelling
argument that none of the group parity models offers a comfortable
escape from value choices. That is, a departure from procedures that
are individually "fair" and that are intended to optimize the criterion
performance of the admitted groups involves (explicitly or implicitly)
the imputation of value to an increased representation of individuals
who are members of the groups favored by the new set of rules, a
value that must be traded off against an expected decrement in overall performance.

Although these models bear only a partial resemblance to the
realities of admissions, their implications and other considerations
compel us—and those in charge of our institutions—to examine the
goals and objectives of the institution's admissions policy, with a
view to the significant underlying issues that should guide a university in this area: its values, its philosophy, and the overarching goal
of equity.

Without hiding in the shadows of presumed cultural bias, there
are reasons enough to consider the preferential admission of minority students (see also Manning, 1977). Such reasons might include

1. Justification in terms of the benefits of including in a student
body persons of widely varying cultural and ethnic background.
This argument is rooted in the awareness that education is nothing
more than shared experience, that students learn much about
human values and social responsibility through interaction with culturally different peers, and that these larger educational goals
require an "organic" rather than a "mechanistic" admissions policy—one that sets aside maximizing the goal of higher grades in favor
of attaining other desired educational objectives.

2. Justification because classifications based on race can be conceived of as a temporary remedy necessary to rectify past injustices
that have stemmed from overt or covert policies of racial discrimination. Although injustices may appear to be visited on particular
nonminority persons, in given situations, such persons "are or have
been the willing or unwilling beneficiaries of a fundamentally racist
society" (Redish, 1974) and hence must pay a price for past and present wrongs.

3. Justification on the grounds that the needs of society for educated leadership in the professions, sciences, and humanities are so compelling, and the representation of minorities in these cadres is so disproportionally low, that accommodation must be made for this overreaching priority within the field of higher education, at least until parity among races is attained.

4. Justification because there is now no adequate basis for determining in a fully satisfying way any final order of merit among candidates for admission. The apparent issue of "cultural bias" simply distracts attention from the more fundamental limitations of the present methods of quantifying human diversity. Turnbull (1974) expressed this position well when he stated:

> From the standpoint of anyone familiar with the technical aspects of measurement as embodied in both tests and grades, there is one salient point that I think needs to be made. That is that the technology is too weak to bear the weight that many would place upon it. The assumption is made that scores and grades, properly combined, constitute an adequate or sufficient basis for defining relative merit. The facts simply don't support that assumption. Major areas of human characteristics and functioning, directly relevant to the likelihood of academic and career success, are omitted from those two useful but incomplete sources of data about a student. It is not only proper for, but incumbent on an institution to use additional information if it is seeking those applicants most likely to use limited places to best advantage. (p. 16–17)

ARE ADMISSIONS TESTS BARRIERS TO UPWARD SOCIAL MOBILITY?

Perfect social mobility is never attainable in practice, but democratic societies must continue to hold forth to all citizens the hope of progress and must strive to create conditions that are conducive to its attainment. Davis (1962) observed that two conditions are essential to social mobility: (1) inequality of rewards and (2) equality of opportunity in their pursuit. The increasingly differentiated hierarchy of occupational roles is more and more evident in our society, and in principle, unequal rewards should lead the members of society to strive to attain for themselves and their children (and those bound to them by ties of race, ethnicity, or religion) the rewards attainable from higher occupational status.

Sociologists are divided as to whether social mobility in the United States is increasing or decreasing, just as political scientists and economists are divided over whether so-called classless societies can exist or, if they can, whether the motivation for work can be sustained under those conditions. In American society, education is nevertheless seen as the principal means of attaining upward social mobility, and, indeed, as the stratification and differentiation of education itself have evolved, questions about admission to what kind and how much education have come to mirror all the problems of social mobility in the larger society.

Admissions tests are seen, therefore, as important "gates" in the endless game of upward striving. Even a cursory examination of the issue suggests that a number of factors influence what might be called socioeducational mobility. Wolfle (1954) identified the following factors:

- Developed academic abilities
- Previous accomplishment in school or college
- Desire on the part of the student
- Money to pay for education
- Sex-related attitudes and values
- Geographic location
- Cultural background
- Ethnic, racial, and religious background

The effect of these factors is manifold; that is, they may influence the degree to which the inequalities in rewards are recognized and the consequences of actions (or inactions) are anticipated, the extent to which striving to attain the rewards is present, and the resiliency with which setbacks can be tolerated or accommodated.

For many, however, the main influence of these factors on social mobility is in relation to equality of opportunity. As noted above, this is particularly true for racial and ethnic minorities who have current and historical reasons to doubt whether anything approximating an equal chance to compete will be afforded them. Increasingly, as the costs of higher education have mounted, students from lower income families have also begun to raise these same questions about the degree to which they are locked in an endless cycle of poverty.

Indeed, many young people and their parents now see the American dream of success as questionable. The American dream may never have been a reality: There is no consensus among those who have intensively studied social mobility in America about the degree to which we now have social mobility or about whether it is increasing or decreasing. What may be new, however, is that an ever-growing number of people, rightly or wrongly, perceive that we do not have enough social mobility to be tolerable, and that the state of affairs is getting worse rather than better.

Admissions tests are therefore seen by some as an indispensable tool in the battle to achieve greater social mobility. For others, these tests are seen as barriers to upward striving. The widespread support of testing found in the Gallup Poll and similar surveys (Lerner, 1980) supports the view that the former group is in the majority. Similarly, many people see tests as an indispensable tool in assuring educational productivity, including school effectiveness, accountability, and minimum-competency assessment. The widespread public concern about the decline of SAT scores, the broad-based movement toward minimum-competency tests in the states, and even the interesting clash of viewpoints between Albert Shanker and the American Federation of Teachers (who support tests), on the one hand, and Terry Herndon and the National Education Association (who oppose tests), on the other, testify to the perceived impact of tests on educational productivity.

What is also evident, however, is that there is widespread frustration and bitterness about admissions testing at a time when—as a consequence, mainly, of demographic changes—the selectivity of colleges is diminishing.

The data in Table 3 are instructive with respect to understanding the shifts in college-going rates over the past 25 years or so. It is evident that there is a substantial difference in the college-going rates for students of both sexes, depending on the socioeconomic status of the family. Equally salient, however, is the sharply different college-

TABLE 3
Percentage of High School Graduates Attending 2- or 4-Year Colleges[a]

Sex/ ability quarter	1st SES quarter (low)				2nd SES quarter				3rd SES quarter				4th SES quarter (high)			
	1957	1961	1968	1972	1957	1961	1968	1972	1957	1961	1968	1972	1957	1961	1968	1972
Men																
1st (low)	6	9	14	16	12	14	18	16	18	16	33	20	39	34	40	30
2nd	17	16	29	22	27	25	55	31	34	36	47	35	61	45	62	41
3rd	28	32	48	36	43	38	57	47	51	48	61	57	73	72	70	69
4th (high)	52	58	75	53	59	74	78	70	72	79	86	81	91	90	88	85
Women																
1st (low)	4	8	17	14	9	12	16	13	16	13	29	21	33	26	55	38
2nd	6	13	25	22	20	12	29	25	26	21	48	29	44	37	66	44
3rd	9	25	41	28	24	30	51	46	31	40	67	50	67	65	77	65
4th (high)	28	34	67	66	37	51	67	66	48	71	79	75	76	85	88	85

[a] 1957 data are from Sewell and Shah (1967); 1961 data are from Schoenfeldt (1968); 1968 data are from Norris and Katz (1970); 1972 data are from Peng (1977).

going rates for students of differing ability, particularly among students from below-average SES families. Over time, we can also see that the rates of college going increased steadily until, perhaps, about 1970, after which they declined slightly. The decline, however, has been largely undifferentiated with respect to SES or ability level. These data do not offer direct evidence on the question of whether admissions tests have encouraged or diminished college-going rates, but it is relevant to note that the period of the most rapid growth in the use of admissions tests corresponded roughly to the period of rapid increases in college going among lower-SES students, as well as upper-level-SES students.

Perhaps more pertinent to the question of the possible deterrent effects of tests on college going are the data in Table 4, which has been adapted from Peng (1977). These data reveal that by 1972 the rates of college going for black students by ability level exceeded those of whites entering four-year colleges. It is the four-year colleges that are typically more selective, and that constitute a disproportionate number of the institutions that require admissions tests. It is difficult to reconcile these data with the argument that tests are a gatekeeper that so dominates admissions decisions as to constitute a severe barrier to admission to college for blacks and others who are heavily represented in lower-SES groups.

TABLE 4
Percentage of High School Graduates Going on to College
by Group and Ability Quarters, 1972[a]

Group	Ability quarter	4-year college	2-year college	Other postsecondary education
Black	1st (low)	15.5	10.0	14.0
	2nd	42.2	11.3	9.1
	3rd	54.7	10.5	5.1
	4th (high)	73.8	4.6	8.0
White	1st (low)	6.4	10.7	11.8
	2nd	15.0	17.4	11.8
	3rd	33.7	18.9	10.2
	4th (high)	61.3	13.2	5.8
Hispanic	1st (low)	9.6	19.4	11.3
	2nd	20.2	30.2	6.8
	3rd	33.8	26.4	5.9
	4th (high)	52.1	26.3	0.0

[a] Adapted from Peng (1977).

TABLE 5
1973–1974 College-Bound Seniors Classified by SAT Average and
Family Income[a]

SAT average	Reported family income				Average Income[b]
	$0–5,999	$6,000–11,999	$12,000–17,999	$18,000+	
750–800	17	117	169	415	$24,124
700–749	239	1,172	1,725	3,252	$21,980
650–699	686	3,994	5,683	9,284	$21,292
600–649	1,626	9,352	12,187	17,992	$20,330
550–599	3,119	17,042	20,822	28,151	$19,481
500–549	4,983	26,132	29,751	37,400	$18,824
450–499	6,663	33,209	35,193	41,412	$18,122
400–449	8,054	34,302	33,574	37,213	$17,387
350–399	8,973	29,762	25,724	26,175	$16,182
300–349	9,622	21,342	14,867	13,896	$14,355
250–299	7,980	10,286	5,240	4,212	$11,428
200–249	1,638	1,436	521	325	$ 8,639
Total number	53,600	188,146	185,483	219,727	
Average SAT score	403	447	469	485	

[a]The total number of students in this table (646,956) is very slightly smaller than the number (647,031) included in the analyses reported in *College Bound Seniors, 1973–74* (College Entrance Examination Board, 1974). Students in this table must have had both SAT verbal and SAT mathematical scores and must have reported family income on the Student Descriptive Questionnaire. Students with only one SAT score were included in *College Bound Seniors, 1973–74*.
[b]From College Entrance Examination Board, 1974.

In their attacks on admissions tests as biased in favor of the economically advantaged, critics have fastened on the finding that a positive relationship exists between test scores and reported family income. Indeed, it is frequently charged that test scores rank individuals according to their family incomes with few exceptions. In fact, the relationship is far more moderate than the critics suggest. Table 5 shows average SAT scores and reported family incomes for several hundred thousand college-bound seniors (College Entrance Examination Board, 1974). Students from each income level obtained the full range of SAT scores. Many students from the top income group ($18,000 and over) earned low scores. For example, 8% scored below 350. Many students from the low-income group (less than $6,000) earned high scores, 5% scored above 600. About one-third of the students in the lowest income category obtained above-average scores.

The correlation of test scores and family incomes (as reported by students) for the nearly 650,000 students shown in Table 5 was .23. Because the questionnaires in use when these data were obtained had a limited number of categories for reporting family income, it is

. this correlation coefficient understates the true relation-
...alysis by the authors of test scores and self-reported fam-
...e reported on a finer scale for a more recent group showed
...lation of .29, a figure that may also be somewhat low because
...perfections in the measurement of family income.

What level of relationship may be expected between measures of students' educational development and their family's income? It is well known that, in relation to students from low-income families, students from middle- and upper-class families usually have more highly educated parents, have home and community environments that provide more support for educational attainment, and attend better schools, to name only a few of the relevant factors. To deny that valid measures of educational attainment may be related to the economic circumstances of students' families is to ignore the realities of social and educational inequality.

In fact, the relationships of educational attainment to socioeconomic status have been widely studied. Charters (1963) summarized the general findings of the sociological and educational research literature as follows:

> To categorize youth according to the social class position of their parents is to order them on the extent of their participation and degree of "success" in the American educational system. This has been so consistently confirmed by research that it now can be regarded as an empirical law. It appears to hold, regardless of whether the social class categorization is based upon the exhaustive procedures used in Elmtown (Hollingshead, 1949) or upon more casual indicators of socioeconomic status such as occupation or income level. It seems to hold in any educational institution, public or private, where there is some diversity in social class, including universities, colleges, and teacher-training institutions as well as elementary and secondary schools. Social class position predicts grades, achievement and intelligence test scores, retentions at grade level, course failures, truancy, suspensions from school, high school drop-outs, plans for college attendance, and total amount of formal schooling.
>
> The predictions noted above are far from perfect. Inasmuch as social class position rarely accounts for more than half the variance of school "success," the law holds only for differences in group averages, not for differences in individual success. The relationship in some instances may be curvilinear rather than linear, but the data rarely have been assembled to test this possibility. Finally, there are a few cases in the literature in which the expected relationships have failed to emerge. Nevertheless, positive findings appear with striking regularity.[3] (pp. 739–740)

---

[3]From "The Social Background of Teaching" by W. W. Charters in *Handbook of Research on Teaching*, N. L. Gage (Ed.). Copyright 1963 by American Educational Research Association, Washington, D.C. Reprinted by permission.

More recently, a meta-analysis by White (1976) showed an average correlation of .25 between family socioeconomic status and various indicators of educational achievement, based on 489 analyses and some 100 separate studies. The average of 41 correlations of socioeconomic status and school grades was .24. When SES was defined solely in terms of family income, the average of 19 correlations between income and measures of educational achievement was .32. The correlation found between SAT scores and income (of about .30) is consistent with more general research findings on the relationship of educational achievement to family circumstances and with the everyday experience of teachers in schools and colleges.

Even so, the data in Table 5 tend to obscure the fact that a disproportionate share of low-income families are also minority families. As discussed earlier, the test scores of black students, on the average, are about one standard deviation below the average for white students. Under these circumstances, it becomes of interest to ascertain whether there is a different relationship between self-reported family income and SAT scores for white students as compared with minority students.

Table 6 reports the correlations for the representative samples of the 1979–1980 SAT population between SAT verbal and SAT mathematical scores, respectively, and reported family income. Most striking is the substantially lower correlation between SAT scores and income for majority (white) students, as compared with minority students. It is evident that a substantial portion of the observed relationship between test scores and income, as shown in Table 5, is actually associated with the disproportionate number of low-scoring and low-income students who are minority persons, rather than deriving from a more homogeneous, general relationship. The median correlation between family income and test scores for white

TABLE 6
Correlations between Self-Reported Income and SAT Scores for Various Ethnic Groups

		Black	Chicano	Oriental	Puerto Rican	White
Verbal	Male	.23	.18	.21	.21	.07
	Female	.26	.23	.30	.27	.08
Math	Male	.20	.14	.14	.25	.06
	Female	.22	.23	.21	.34	.11
Average income		15.1	18.4	25.4	16.5	30.5

students is only about .08, a very weak relationship. Indeed, the correlations between income and test scores for minority students are also quite low and are noteworthy primarily for the differences in the strength of the relationship between majority and minority groups.

The reasons for these differences in correlations and for corresponding group differences in the slopes of the regression lines of SAT scores on reported family income are not conclusively known, but plausible hypotheses are not difficult to formulate. It seems likely that a variety of factors related to income could underlie this difference—some exogenous to the family, and some endogenous. Among the former is the tendency for poor minority students to be enrolled in schools offering inferior programs, often located in underfinanced and overburdened urban school systems. As family income increases, the options available to the minority family become wider, including residence in more affluent communities or the purchase of higher quality independent education. Other factors seem equally obvious, namely, that as discretionary income increases, the opportunities for the cultural enrichment of family life are larger. To a certain extent, these factors operate for all families, but these data are consistent with the suggestion that, for a given increment in family income, minority families are able to convert the increase into proportionately larger gains in scholastic aptitude (and school achievement) than are white families.

Ogbu (1978) has suggested that the widespread perception of education as a major means of access to highly rewarding adult roles has been overemphasized in interpreting the historical experience of blacks and other "caste minorities" who are burdened with the consequences of profound and lengthy discrimination. At the same time, it seems reasonable to believe that even if Ogbu's main hypothesis is correct, the striving for upward mobility through education is, to some degree, a factor. A synthesis of both of these points of view seems consistent with the data on test scores and family income. On the one hand, differences between minority and majority students on the SAT become narrower as family income increases, but they do not completely disappear. This finding is consistent with the observations of Ogbu and others (Carter & Segura, 1979; Kardiner & Ovesey, 1951) on the role of caste as distinct from social class. On the other hand, the stronger relationship (albeit weak) between family income and test scores for minority students suggests that there is an increasing emphasis on educational attainment—and a proportionately greater one—as family income increases. If such a relationship exists, it is a remarkable testimony to the resiliency and resourcefulness of the minority families whose upward striving may underlie the observed interaction between race and family income in explaining variances in scores on tests of developed ability.

The mechanisms by which racial and socioeconomic status are translated into differential educational attainment are complex and difficult to identify. Careful observation and analysis of classroom and teacher–student interactions led Rist (1970) to carry out a seminal study of kindergarten children, in which he searched for these mechanisms. Rist stated:

> When a teacher bases her expectations of performance on the social status of the student, and assumes that the higher the social status, the higher the potential of the child, those children of low socioeconomic status suffer a stigmatization outside of their own choice and will. Yet there is a greater tragedy than being labeled as a slow learner, and that is being treated as one. The differential amounts of control-oriented behavior, the lack of interaction with the teacher, the ridicule from one's peers, and the caste aspects of being placed in lower reading groups all have implications for the future life style and value of education for the child.

Rist went on to say:

> It should be apparent, of course, that if one desires this society to retain its present social class configuration and the disproportionate access to wealth, power, social and economic mobility, medical care and choice of life styles, one should not disturb the methods of education as presented in this study. This contention is made because what develops as "caste" within classrooms appears to emerge in the larger society as "class." . . . It appears that the public school system not only mirrors the configurations of the larger society, but also significantly contributes to maintaining them. Thus the system of public education in reality perpetuates what it is ideologically committed to eradicate—class barriers which result in inequality in the social and economic life of the citizenry.[4] (pp. 448–449)

Modern day polemicists of the antitesting movement have sought to displace the responsibility for public miseducation (which Rist so poignantly described) onto educational tests. Lacking either the fortitude or the commitment to change education, they have sought to deny the source problem by attributing it to bias in the tests. It is a paradox of tragic proportions that so many well-intentioned persons have failed to grasp the consequences of blaming the tests, which reflect educational experience, rather than the educa-

---

[4]From "Student Social Class and Teacher Expectations: The Self-Fulfilling Prophecy in Ghetto Education" by R. Rist, *Harvard Educational Review*, 1970, *40*(3), 411–451. Copyright 1970 by President and Fellows of Harvard College. Reprinted by permission.

tional system that has unintentionally fostered the barriers of class and caste.

A careful reading of some critics indicates that, although alleging test bias, they do not, in fact, challenge the reality of the relationship of students' family incomes and educational achievement. Their fundamental thesis is that the use of the tests, which help to disclose the effects of unequal resources and prior learning opportunities on the education of children of different classes, should be terminated or, at the least, modified. For example, Nairn and Associates (1980) wrote:

> In terms of action it should be remembered that many aspects of class discrimination will only change when the fundamental rules of the current economic system change. But the use of ETS aptitude scores to influence advancement, while rooted in the economic system, . . . has its impact on people's lives through a practice which is more immediate, specific, and subject to rapid change. . . . The effects of a change in the test system on class opportunities could be considerable. (p. 454)

Even if there were agreement that the best approach to expanding access to higher education is to eliminate evidence of unequal educational preparation, it is doubtful that the course of action advocated by Nairn and other critics would have the effects that he predicted.

First, the relationship of SAT scores to family income is more modest than the statement implies and is not peculiar to the SAT.

Second, admissions do not occur in the way in which the critics suggest. Many colleges are not selective and admit nearly all applicants. Those colleges that are selective base their admissions decisions on many different kinds of information, not test scores alone. In many cases, these colleges take into account the obstacles that disadvantaged students have overcome in reaching their present levels of achievement. Indeed, they seek out such students and provide them financial aid and other kinds of assistance. The image of a system of admissions based on test scores that is designed to discriminate unfairly against low-income groups is remarkably at variance with the facts.

Third, history indicates that selective admissions to higher education were far more a matter of class and economic status before the use of national admissions tests than they have been since then. In the absence of a uniform and dependable indicator of a student's abilities, admissions officers gave far more weight to grades and recommendations of students from a select group of well-known schools. The introduction of tests resulted in a substantial increase in the opportunities for educational advancement of low-income students by providing a credible demonstration that many such students from schools without reputations for educational excellence could succeed in the demanding academic programs of the most selective institutions. Before rushing into radical surgery on the current system of admissions tests, we should carefully consider whether alternative systems would serve widely held social values as well.

UPSHOT

Admissions programs in selective colleges, and in many graduate and professional schools, are based on a balancing of values. These institutions place importance not only on achievement, accomplishment, demonstrated ability, and special talents, but also on more elusive personal qualities, such as creativity and motivation. In their admissions procedures, many of these institutions also seek to redress the effects of past inequality and to admit groups of students that are diverse in terms of geography, family economic background, race, and other characteristics. They do so not only to serve egalitarian principles, but also to accomplish their own educational objectives.

Because the admissions and financial aid policies of higher education institutions are designed in large part to promote increased access to disadvantaged students, and because the relationships of test scores and other educational indicators to family income are moderate, there are reasons to judge that the net effect of current admissions practices is to promote greater social mobility. Indeed, there are reasons to fear that the elimination of objective measures of ability would result in a greater use of criteria that have a more substantial and direct link to social class.

More fundamentally, the evidence on the relationships of achievement to social class demonstrates clearly that educational inequality is real and not simply a function of how achievement is assessed. The failure of society to provide the best education possible to all its citizens has an impact on the capacity of individuals to lead satisfying and productive lives. This reality presents a challenge to society as a whole. The challenge might be obscured by abandoning tests, but the underlying problems would be worsened.

The proposal to eliminate evidence of inequality before "constructing a society with a new definition of economic justice" is one that has its advocates. But there are many who favor a more balanced response to this challenge: first, seeking, through broadly based efforts, to reduce real inequality in children's educational achievement; and second, recognizing within systems of advancement both the values of educational achievement and accomplishment *and* the need to expand the access of all groups in the society to educational and occupational opportunities.

Admissions tests have played and will continue to play an important role in fostering the attainment of these goals.

REFERENCES

Astin, A. W., King, M. R., & Richardson, G. T. *The American freshman: National norms for Fall 1978.* Los Angeles: University of California at Los Angeles and the American Council on Education, 1978.

Bayley, N. Comparison of mental and motor test scores for ages 1–15 months by sex, birth order, race, geographical location, and education of parents. *Child Development*, 1965, *36*, 379–411.

Bok, D. On the purposes of undergraduate education. *Daedalus*, Fall 1974, *103*(4), 159–172.

Breland, H. M. *Population validity and college entrance measures.* Research Monograph No. 8. New York: The College Board, 1979.

Carnegie Council on Policy Studies in Higher Education. *Selective admissions in higher education.* San Francisco: Jossey-Bass, 1977.

Carter, T. P., & Segura, R. D. *Mexican American schools: A decade of change.* New York: The College Board, 1979.

Charters, W. W. The social background of teaching. In N. L. Gage (Ed.), *Handbook of research on teaching.* Chicago: Rand McNally, 1963.

Cole, N. S. Bias in selection. *Journal of Educational Measurement*, 1973, *10*, 237–255.

College Entrance Examination Board, *College-bound seniors, 1973-1974: Admissions testing program of the College Entrance Examination Board.* New York: Author, 1974.

College Entrance Examination Board. *Undergraduate admissions: The realities of institutional policies, practices, and procedures.* New York: Author, 1980.

Cronbach, L. J. Five decades of public controversy over mental testing. *American Psychologist*, 1975, *30*, 1–14.

Cronbach, L. J., & Gleser, G. C. *Psychological test and personnel decisions.* Urbana: University of Illinois Press, 1965.

Davis, K. The role of class mobility in economic development. *Population Review*, 1962, *6*, 67–73.

Duran, R. *Hispanics' education and background: Predictors of college achievement.* New York: College Entrance Examination Board, 1983.

Gallagher, J. The prospects for governmental support of educational research. *Educational Researcher*, July–August 1975, *4*(7), 12.

Hartnett, R. T., & Feldmesser, R. A. College admissions testing and the myth of selectivity: Unresolved questions and needed research. *AAHE Bulletin*, 1980, *32*, 3–6.

Hilton, T. L., & Rhett, H. *Final report: The base-year survey of the national longitudinal study of the high school class of 1972, Appendix B, Part II.* Washington, D.C.: National Center for Educational Statistics, 1973.

Hollingshead, A. B. *Elmtown's youth.* New York: Wiley, 1949.

Kardiner, A., & Ovesey, L. *The mark of oppression.* Cleveland: World, 1951.

Klineberg, O. An experimental study of speed and other factors in "racial" differences. *Archives of Psychology,* 1928, No. 93.

Lerner, B. The war on testing: David, Goliath and Gallup. *The Public Interest,* 1980, *60,* 119–147.

Linn, R. L. Fair test use in selection. *Review of Educational Research,* 1973, *43,* 139–161.

Linn, R. L. Test bias and the prediction of grades in law school. *Journal of Legal Education,* 1975, *27,* 293–323.

Linn, R. L. *Admissions testing on trial.* Paper presented at the Annual Meeting of the American Psychological Association, Quebec, Canada, September 1980.

Lorge, I. Differences or bias in tests of intelligence. In A. Anastasi (Ed.), *Testing problems in perspective.* Washington, D.C.: American Council on Education, 1966.

Manning, W. H. The pursuit of fairness in admissions to higher education. In Carnegie Council on Policy Studies in Higher Education, *Selective admissions in higher education.* San Francisco: Jossey-Bass, 1977.

Nairn, A., & Associates. *The reign of ETS: The corporation that makes up minds.* Washington, D.C.: Ralph Nader, 1980.

Norris, L., & Katz, M. R. *The measurement of academic interests, Part II: The predictive validities of academic interest measures* (ETS RB-70-67). Princeton, N. J.: Educational Testing Service, 1970.

Ogbu, J. *Minority education and caste: The American system in cross cultural perspective.* New York: Academic Press, 1978.

Peng. S. S. Trends in the entry to higher education: 1961–1972. *Educational Researcher,* 1977, *6*(1), 15–19.

Petersen, N. S., & Novick, M. R. An evaluation of some models for culture-fair selection. *Journal of Educational Measurement,* 1976, *13,* 31–41.

Powers, D. E. Comparing predictors of law school performance for black, chicano, and white law students. Report #LSAC-77-3. In Law School Admission Council, *Reports of LSAC Sponsored Research, Vol. 3: 1975–1977.* Princeton, N.J.: Law School Admission Council, 1977.

Redish, M. *Preferential law school admissions and the equal protection clause: An analysis of the competing arguments.* Princeton, N.J.: Law School Admissions Council, 1974.

Rist, R. Student social class and teacher expectations: The self-fulfilling prophecy in ghetto education. *Harvard Educational Review,* 1970, *40*(3), 411–451.

Ruch, W. W. *A re-analysis of published differential validity studies.* Paper presented at the symposium on: Differential validation under EEOC and OFCC testing and selection regulations. American Psychological Association, Honolulu, Hawaii, September 1972.

Schoenfeldt, L. F. Education after high school. *Sociology of Education,* Fall 1968, 351–369.

Sewell, G., Carey, J., Simons, P. E., & Lord, M. How good—and fair—are tests? *Newsweek,* Feb. 18, 1980, 97–104.

Sewell, W. H., & Shah, V. P. Socioeconomic status, intelligence, and the attainment of higher education. *Sociology of Education,* 1967, *40*(1), 1–23.

Taylor, H. C., & Russell, J. T. The relationship of validity coefficients to the practical effectiveness of tests in selection: Discussion and tables. *Journal of Applied Psychology,* 1939, *23,* 565–578.

Thorndike, R. L. Concepts of culture-fair. *Journal of Educational Measurement*, 1971, *8*, 63–70.

Turnbull, W. W. *On educational standards, testing and the aspirations of minorities.* Address before the Conference on Academic Standards and their Relationship to Minority Aspirations by the American-Jewish Congress, Columbia University, December 1974.

White, K. R. *The relationship between socioeconomic status and academic achievement.* Unpublished doctoral dissertation, University of Colorado, 1976.

Willingham, W. W., Breland, H. M., Ferrin, R. I., & Fruen, M. The status of selective admissions. In Carnegie Council on Policy Studies in Higher Education, *Selective admissions in higher education.* San Francisco: Jossey-Bass, 1977.

Wilson, K. M. The performance of minority students beyond the freshman year. *Research in Higher Education*, 1980, *13*(1), 23–47.

Wolfle, D. (Ed.). *America's resources of specialized talents.* New York: Harper & Bros., 1954.

CHAPTER SEVEN

General Intelligence

LLOYD G. HUMPHREYS

Both the theory of intelligence and its measurement have been confused by failure to follow a scientifically acceptable definition of intelligence. In good part, the problem arises from the folk definition of intelligence that involves the innate fixed capacity of a person to solve problems. This folk definition differs in only one important respect in its usage by environmentalists as opposed to hereditarians. The former tend to minimize the importance of individual differences in this fixed capacity, holding that any normal person has the fundamental capacity to achieve at a high level. Environmentalists are also strongly convinced that intelligence tests do not measure this capacity.

One can agree wholeheartedly with the environmentalists that intelligence tests do not measure intelligence as defined in this way, but this agreement does not lead to the rejection of intelligence tests. Instead, it leads to the rejection of the folk definition. No matter how firmly entrenched the folk definition is, and no matter how firmly entrenched it may be in a particular subset of a population (e.g., psychologists), it is necessary to define the construct in a fashion that allows it to enter into theory and research. A construct that cannot be measured directly or estimated from measurements at present or in the foreseeable future cannot be tolerated in either science or technology. The nature of the concept of gravitation changed markedly from Aristotle to Newton to Einstein, but there are probably no more

This research was supported by National Institute of Mental Health Grant MH 23612-06, Studies of Intellectual Development and Organization.

LLOYD G. HUMPHREYS • Department of Psychology, University of Illinois, Champaign, Illinois 61820.

than a handful of know-nothings who criticize physicists for the change in the meaning. A scientist has not merely a right but a duty to define concepts in a way compatible with measurement operations and with the data resulting from those operations.

INTELLIGENCE AS PHENOTYPE

Jensen stated in his recent book (1980) that intelligence, in his usage, is a phenotypic trait. He also stated that a person's genotype can be estimated from the phenotype. The latter requires an estimate of the heritability of the trait. I applaud Jensen's way of phrasing the problem for definition and theory, but I differ with him in two respects. He is not consistent in his discussion of intelligence with the requirements of the definition of phenotype; he also believes that present data support a firmer and higher estimate of heritability than I do. This latter difference may be settled in the future by the accumulation of more and better data. The first difference requires logical analysis.

Phenotypic traits are observable. If observable, they are also measurable. In certain cases, the measurements may be relatively crude (e.g., at the nominal level). Many traits of physique, however, are measured with ratio scales. Height and weight are prime examples of such phenotypic traits. Both have genetic and environmental components in their variance, and the presumption is strong that these components are not the same for the two traits. The heritability of a phenotypic trait, as a matter of fact, can vary from zero to unity. Head shape in a cultural group that practices head binding in infancy in order to achieve certain socially desirable head shapes may have zero heritability. Adult weight is probably less highly heritable than adult height.

Behavioral traits are also observable and measurable. Intelligence can be measured by obtaining ratings from persons who know the individuals to be measured. The rating made is obviously abstracted from observations of a great deal of behavior. The ratings will agree more closely if the judges have equal opportunities to observe. Equal opportunity requires not merely adequate time of acquaintance but a similar sample of occasions. Two primary teachers will show more agreement than one primary teacher and one music teacher. Coaches will not agree well with either the classroom teacher or the music teacher. Just how general intelligence is is determined, however, by finding some minimal degree of agreement in widely divergent kinds of activities. Once the limits of generality have been determined, furthermore, the most valid ratings of intelligence will be obtained from raters who have been able to observe the persons rated in the full gamut of activities.

Ratings as measurement scales have a good many undesirable attributes. The zero point on a rating scale not only is arbitrary but varies from one rater to another. The units of measurement are also arbitrary and vary from one rater to another. These variations from rater to rater are confounded by the relationships between the rater and the ratees. One rater may rate a docile child higher than an active one whereas a second rater may do the reverse. It is known that teachers confound ratings of intelligence with the occupation and the social status of parents as well as with race, religion, ethnic origin, and physical appearance.

The solution to the problems or ratings is to sample behavior in a variety of situations in an objective manner. Binet and Simon accomplished this by starting with a pool of items that they believed would sample intelligent behavior, especially as it was manifested in school rooms, and by demonstrating that the score on their test showed sufficient agreement with ratings of intelligence to be a reasonable substitute for those ratings. It has been shown many times since that scores on intelligence tests are correlated with ratings of intelligence, with academic grades, with educational and occupational placement, and with job performance in industry and in the military. The items in intelligence tests are positively intercorrelated, indicating that the limits of generality set are not too broad. The items are correlated with chronological age during the period of rapid learning and maturation, as are measures of height and weight. These item characteristics are essential for the construct of general intelligence.

Present standard tests of intelligence, such as the Stanford–Binet and the Wechsler, have types of content nearly identical with the original scales published by Binet and Simon. There is currently no consensus among researchers about whether it would be advantageous to broaden the types of items (problem-solving situations) contained in these tests. The standard test may be overly academic, in part neglecting the problem-solving situations that can be generically labeled *mechanical*. The inclusion of Piagetian tasks, an innovation for which there is a sound statistical basis, would broaden intelligence tests in a desirable fashion (Humphreys & Parsons, 1979).

Practically all human behavior is acquired, and all intelligent behavior that is sampled by an intelligence test involves acquired behavior. This is as true for nonverbal performance tests as it is for verbal tests. Learning requires motivation and opportunities to learn. There is no way in which a behavioral test can measure an unobservable capacity. An intelligence test designed for use in a preliterate culture would necessarily be different from one of our standard tests, but a behavioral trait of intelligence could still be measured by the appropriate design of test items. There is no assurance, however, that one can merely substitute the Wechsler performance scale or a matrices-reasoning test for the preliterate group. Comprehension of the analogies, series, and classification formats so common in nonverbal reasoning tests may have strong cultural determinants.

A recognition of the importance of prior learning does not, however, require an assumption that prior learning has been equal. The measurement of phenotypic height does not require an assumption that everyone has had equal nutrition and freedom from disease. A person who might have been six inches taller if he had had adequate nutrition pre- and postnatally will still play basketball at his phenotypic height. Intelligence as a phenotypic construct requires exposure to the kinds of situations incorporated in the items, but not equality of opportunity to learn.

There is one difference between the measurement of phenotypic height and intelligence or any other behavioral trait that requires comment. Measures of height do not vary from one well-constructed measurement scale to another when the measurements are taken nearly simultaneously in time, except for some small degree of error of measurement. Intelligence tests are typically less reliable than measures of height when both are administered under equally careful conditions, but the reliability of intelligence tests scores could be increased to equal the reliability of the measurement of height by increasing the number of items. The more fundamental difference is that variability is introduced between measures of intelligence from the sampling of the items. There is no recognized population of items, and test constructors do not sample randomly from even an arbitrarily defined item pool. Differences from test to test, going beyond the differences attributable to measurement error are inevitable. Fortunately, there is sufficient communality among different types of problem-solving items so that this error of "sampling" can be kept relatively small by selecting items of sufficient heterogeneity of content and by including a sufficient number of such items. The communality of the heterogeneous test with the construct of general intelligence will approach the reliability of the test as the number of items increases. The correlation with the construct will be higher than the correlation with an equally good test of intelligence.

Actually, there are more similarities than differences between height and intelligence, as phenotypic traits. What differences there are are matters of degree rather than kind. Height is more readily observable than intelligence. Height is also less frequently confused with other traits than intelligence. It can be confused with weight judgmentally, but not when measured by physical scales. Both height and intelligence have genetic substrates; both have environmental substrates. There is no more reason to assume some sort of entity underlying intelligence than there is for height. Height at age 6 is not a measure of aptitude for attaining adult height. Height in feet and inches changes from year to year during development, but standard scores for height based on groups homogeneous in chronological age also change from year to year and in either direction. The change in standard scores from one year to the next is relatively small, but the change over longer periods of time can be quite large. The same statements can be made concerning mental ages, which increase from year to year, and standard scores or IQs, which may change in either direction from year to year.

In reading Jensen, as mentioned earlier, one infers that he assumes an entity underlying the behavioral repertoire sampled by the test. One chapter discusses whether intelligence tests really measure intelligence. Another chapter drastically overinterprets the forms of distributions of test scores. More significant is the emphasis on the "education of relations and correlates," Spearman's phrase (1914), which Jensen has quoted frequently and, on the Ravens test, as pure measure of general intelligence. Closely related is the sharp distinction he has attempted to draw between intelligence and achievement tests. He used the argument that the circumference and the diameter of a circle are different concepts even though they are perfectly correlated. Although this statement is true, there is only the most superficial relationship to the measurement of intelligence. Intelligent behavior is observed in numerous situations. By the time a population of children has been exposed to the curriculum of the first six grades, a test covering all of the varieties of school achievement is as highly correlated with one standard test of intelligence as the latter is with a second standard test. Also, if one measures a wide enough variety of nonacademic information, an excellent test of intelligence is obtained in terms of the functional characteristics of the total score. One cannot distinguish between intelligent behavior and achievement behavior.

The relatively minor differences between intelligence and achievement tests have been described on several occasions (Cleary, Humphreys, Kendrick, & Wesman, 1975; Humphreys, 1962b). The most important difference is the breadth of coverage of the intelligence test. Intelligence or so-called aptitude items also tend to reflect older learning. The eight-grade problem arithmetic that occurs in most batteries of achievement tests becomes an aptitude test in the Graduate Record Examination. Achievement tests are more closely tied to curriculum content than intelligence tests, but this difference matters little when the population tested has been exposed to basically the same curriculum. Finally, if a test is used to predict future performance, it is an aptitude test, but if it is used to measure past attainments, it is an achievement test. Both the data and the logic require rejection of all variations, such as Jensen's, of the folk definition.

INTELLIGENCE AS GENOTYPE

Given conditions of experimental control of mating and of the environment, one can compute the heritability of a trait, either in physique or of behavior, in a given population in a given environment. Without experimental control, one can estimate heritability in a population in an environment from observations of the correlations among relatives of given categories. If the correlations fit the genetic model, heritability may be high. Family relationships in intelligence do fit the genetic model approximately, but there is a convenient "fudge" factor. The model requires knowledge of the degree of assortative mating that has taken place and the number of generations during which that degree has held in order to be precise in determining the degree of correlation expected from the model.

In addition to the lack of experimental control and the required information concerning assortative mating, family relationship data are not as good or as complete as they should be. The problem is not primarily with Cyril Burt's data. As Jencks (1972) pointed out, before there was a general agreement to reject those data, a principal problem is the difference between the correlation in the median study of a particular relationship and the weighted mean from all studies of that relationship. A second important problem is that the several different ways of estimating heritability from different family relationships also lead to rather divergent results.

It does not seem to be generally recognized with respect to family relationship correlations that they depend on the reliability of the test and the range of talent of the population being sampled. One rarely sees any reference to these parameters in the literature on family resemblance coefficients. It is not surprising, therefore, that a more subtle problem is missed by authors reporting these correlations: They are also a function of the narrowness of focus of the measuring instrument. A test of general intelligence shows presumptive evidence of higher heritability than a narrow achievement test not because there is a fundamental difference between intelligence and achievement but because the achievement test covers a narrower gamut of problem-solving behavior (Humphreys, 1970).

Because heritability is the amount of common variance between phenotype and genotype, if the heritability of intelligence were known with any reasonable degree of confidence in our population, its square root would be the correlation between phenotype and genotype. This correlation could be entered in an ordinary regression equation to estimate an individual's genotype from phenotype. Attached to each such estimate would be its standard error. As long as heritability is less than 1, the estimation of an individual's heritability by means of a regression equation is entirely probabilistic. Even high heritability leads to a substantial amount of uncertainty.

If the heritability of intelligence were known with confidence in the adult, there would be other problems. It is entirely possible that the estimate of heritability would vary with the chronological age of the child. Jensen reported, for example, that the correlation between parent and child changes with chronological age. In addition, a child's phenotypic standard score varies from age to age. The intercorrelations of intelligence tests from age to age form a simplex matrix in which the correlations are gradually reduced in size from those between adjacent occasions to those involving the most remote occasions. If the estimate of heritability were constant during development, many children would require a different estimate of genotype at every age. The assumption of a constant genotype during the period of maturation may represent a logical inference from genetic theory, but a construct that cannot be estimated is useless in any scientific theory, and nothing is gained in the prediction of a practical behavioral criterion by bringing in an estimate of genotype. An estimate of genotype is similar in this respect to an estimate of true score. I have stated elsewhere (Humphreys, 1971) that acceptance of evolutionary continuity in both function and structure is a rational basis for the acceptance of a genetic component of variance in intelligence, but this approach does not lead to a specific estimate of heritability.

For some personnel decisions, a test user may wish to turn the estimation problem around. It is hypothesized that Individual A might have had a higher level of phenotypic intelligence if it had not been for certain conditions of environmental deprivation. How does one estimate phenotype from an unknown genotype? Clearly, this is impossible. The motivation to do this also avoids the principal issue. How much, if any, can the phenotype be changed? Does the answer to this question depend on the person's chronological age? How much effort and how much expense are required to effect a given amount of change? If we do not know how to effect change in phenotypic intelligence at a given age, should we not be supporting research on methods to do so? After all, every serious and thoughtful hereditarian allows a sizable environmental component of variance.

Even if one could solve the problem of estimating phenotype from an unknown genotype, it is clear that the essential factor in how one performs in society is the phenotype. Genotypic potential must be realized in phenotypic performance. Even if the contribution to the variance of individual differences in intelligence were 100% environmental, there is not the slightest assurance that low phenotypic performance at a given age can be quickly and readily increased. Some environmental contributions to variance may not be reversible; others may be very resistant to change, particularly in the adult; others may require more motivation than is now being applied to the problem.

The possibility that heritability might he high within a group has been a bogeyman for many critics of intelligence tests. This negative attitude is based quite largely on a lack of information concerning the mechanisms of polygenic inheritance and the definition of heritability. Heritability is the contribution to phenotypic variance of genotype. One minus the coefficient or heritability represents, in the simple additive model, the contribution to variance of environmental causes. If heritability is high in the United States, it is a tribute to our democratic society and its educational system in equalizing the environmental contribution. Heritability of intelligence would be lower in a rigidly stratified society.

An important attribute of the genetic mechanism is that it produces variability in phenotype from one generation to another. It is highly supportive of the democratic ideal that each person should be evaluated as an individual. For example, the expected correlation between one parent and one child, given lack of assortative mating, is .50. The obtained correlation is also about .50. Thus, the expected value of the child's intelligence is halfway back toward the population mean from the parent. Very intelligent parents have children who are above average on average, but who are not as intelligent as their parents. Similarly, parents who are below average in intelligence have children who are below average on average, but who are more intelligent than their parents. In both cases, there is a great deal of variability of the children around the expected value.

These expectations do not require that intelligence be highly heritable. The correlation between parent and offspring of .50 is the important datum. It does not matter whether this degree of resemblance is produced by polygenic inheritance or by the multitude of environmental similarities and differences between parent and child. Again, whether the causes are environmental or genetic, the correlation between a grandparent and a grandchild is only about .25.

The children of highest ability in any one generation have parents who are also halfway back toward the population mean from the children. The correlation between parent and child can be used in either of two regression equations: to estimate the child's intelligence when one knows that of the parent and to estimate the parent's intelligence when one knows that of the child. The largest *number* of children of high intelligence in any one generation have parents who are just a small amount above the population mean. On the other hand, the parents who have the largest *proportion* of very bright children are those who are very bright themselves. Even so, in a highly fluid society in which education, occupation, and status are highly dependent on measured ability, there is no permanence of social classes. High ability tends to dissipate in fewer generations than do wealth and prestige, both of which are supported by law and by custom, not by the biological nature of the human being.

A parent's intelligence is more highly correlated with his or her child's intelligence than is the parent's socioeconomic status or income. The correlation between excellent measures of SES and intelligence in ninth-grade boys in Project Talent is about .40 (Humphreys & Dachler, 1969). This correlation is noteworthy because it represents almost the full range of talent; most high school dropouts occur in the later grades. This correlation is also a good deal lower in a population of applicants for admission to college, who represent a narrower range of talent. In the wide range of talent, the expectation of the child's intelligence is only four-tenths as far away from the population mean as is the parent's socioeconomic status when both are represented by standard scores. The child's intelligence is estimated with even less accuracy from family income alone. The claim that intelligence tests measure only middle-class learning is patently nonsense. The learning may be more valued by the middle class, although even this is doubtful. In a highly technologically oriented society, it is very difficult to dismiss reading, listening, arithmetic, and mathematics as unimportant, but some critics have tried to do so. The 16% of common variance of a child's intelligence and family SES also does not necessarily represent common environmental variance.

PHENOTYPIC AND GENOTYPIC INTELLIGENCE IN BLACKS AND WHITES

Blacks, on average, are lower in phenotypic intelligence than whites. It should by now be clear that this means difference represents more than a lower mean on an intelligence test. Blacks are lower in the behavioral repertoire sampled by an intelligence test. This intellectual repertoire is also basic to performance in school and to occupational level attained. If intelligence is general, as our data indicate, criterion performance is simply another way of assessing general intelligence. There is also no evidence to date that a low-scoring black will show more improvement following increased opportunities than a white at the same level.

The evidence for the preceding generalizations has been reviewed quite completely by Jensen (1980) in his discussion of bias in predictive validity. If there is any bias in the predictive validity of intelligence tests, it lies in the direction of an underprediction of criterion performance for whites and an overprediction for blacks, in racially mixed groups for whom a single regression equation has been used. Overprediction of the criterion performance of blacks based on their scores on intelligence—and related—tests is not found in all samples, but sample size and sampling error are sufficient reasons for most of the variability. An explanation of overprediction does not require that blacks also be lower on the nonintellectual dimensions of criterion performance. If both the test and the criterion performance are measures of the general factor, but if each is fallible, the deficit in both can be explained without resort to other possible differences.

Given that there is, on average, no bias against blacks in the predictive validity of intelligence tests, it is not surprising to find that studies of item bias show much less bias than armchair critics of the tests have claimed. Difficulty-by-race interactions on test items tend to be small and can be reduced in size by controlling for total score, as Jensen has done. If items are difficult for blacks, they are also difficult for whites. Some items are much easier for blacks than one would expect if the items were as far removed from the black culture as critics have concluded.

It must also be realized that a goal of zero item bias as measured by any currently available methodology is not attainable. For one thing, statistically significant differences of any kind can always be obtained if the sample size is sufficiently large. There are no zero differences in nature. One must always impose a criterion of social as well as statistical significance. Also, if item bias is measured by the difficulty-by-race interaction, some degree of interaction is expected when items differ in their construct validity as measures of general intelligence, and if the two races also differ on the general factor. This expectation requires matching of groups on the general factor before computing an analysis of variance. Jensen's method of comparing older blacks with younger whites is an effective way of accomplishing such a match.

There is conflicting evidence concerning the estimated heritability, based on family relationships correlations, of intelligence within the black group. Loehlin, Lindzey, and Spuhler (1975) have summarized the evidence and concluded that there is probably little difference between blacks and whites in this regard. Because the body of information is less complete for the black population than for the white, and because there is at least the same degree of confounding of possible genetic and environmental influences, caution concerning the degree of heritability for whites should be doubled for the black population.

When one moves from heritability within groups to possible genetic differences between groups in the substrate for intelligence, the degree of caution to be exercised in drawing conclusions should probably be increased by a factor of 10. In addition to the usually adduced possible effects of years of segregation and discrimination, there are cultural differences in child rearing that may have substantial effects on the development of intelligence. At least one of these cultural differences, the proportion of black families headed by lone women, is very large (Children's Defense Fund, 1982). According to the 1980 census, 43.8% of black children are in families with a mother only; another 11.5% are in families without either parent. One can infer that a substantial proportion of black children without either parent are also in households headed by a lone woman because 40% of all black families are so structured. Median family income in lone-woman families, both white and black, is less than half that of married-couple families, and a large proportion of the children in these families are supported by Aid for Families with Dependent Children. The second cultural difference, as reported by Clarke-Stewart (1973), is in infant–mother and child–mother interactions. The different pattern of interactions appears to extend to two-parent families. These environmental factors may affect the development of intelligence in whites and blacks.

It should be apparent that the preceding discussion is almost pure speculation. There is no acceptable evidence at present that allows one to reject the genetic explanation for the race difference in intelligence. By the same token, there is no acceptable evidence that allows one to reject the environmental explanation. The nature–nurture controversy with respect to the development of intelligence is similar in many ways to the ESP controversy. John Edgar Coover (1927) once characterized the supporters of psychic belief (ESP had not yet come into our language) as persons who accepted the "fagot theory" of scientific evidence. A fagot is composed of a very large number of slender twigs, each one of which could easily be broken in one's hands, but bound together the fagot is unbreakable by the direct application of human force. Coover evaluated the evidence for psychic belief as composed of many observations, each one flawed experimentally, but supposedly invulnerable as a whole. The positions of hereditarians and environmentalists are highly similar. Scientific evidence is indeed accumulated in small amounts, but each component must stand alone.

A genetic contribution to the mean difference in intelligence of blacks and whites is also something of a bogeyman. For example, the genetic hypothesis does not assume that there are special Negroid genes that are defective. There is a strong presumption that the gene pools for both blacks and whites contain the same genes providing the genetic substrate for the development of intelligence. The difference, if there is one, is in the frequency distribution of the genes for intelligence in the two gene pools.

As the genetic hypothesis is developed, the overlapping frequency distribution of the many genes responsible for the development of intelligence produces the overlapping frequency distribution of measured intelligence. To the extent that there is a genetic basis for the mean difference in phenotypes, that basis is *quantitative*. Though the data of cultural anthropology have frequently been adduced in support of racial equality, those data are relevant only to the *qualitative* identity of black and white intelligence. Genes for high intelligence are as important and valuable to our society in blacks as in whites or, more generally, in any member of our species.

The possible consequences for social policies of a genetic contribution to the difference between blacks and whites in intelligence—and the absence of such consequences—have been discussed both thoroughly and rationally by Loehlin *et al.* (1975). There is no need for me to repeat their evaluation, especially as the genetic hypothesis is in the "what if" category. There is too little known about human intellectual development, including, and perhaps especially, during the prenatal and early postnatal periods, to concern ourselves with a bogeyman even though he does not look so scary when closely examined.

PRIMARY MENTAL ABILITIES AND GENERAL INTELLIGENCE

In any large set of cognitive tests, it is easy to show that there are multiple factors defined by the correlation matrix. Thurstone (1938) christened the first-order factors obtained in such matrices as the primary mental abilities, but it is very easy to misinterpret multiple group factors. It is also easy to misinterpret Thurstone's use of *primary* to describe them, and when they are rotated orthogonally, it is easy to misinterpret the use of *orthogonal* and even of *independent* to describe them. Factors rotated obliquely are also frequently described as *independent factors* when *different* would be a more accurate description.

The basic evidence for multiple group factors is that the correlations among the measures defining the factor are higher than correlations of those measures with the measures defining a second factor. If the mean correlation within each of two clusters is .90 and that between clusters is .89, and if these correlations are population values and thus not subject to sampling error, the measures will define two factors. The unrotated factors will be orthogonal, the factors after orthogonal rotation will be orthogonal, and the factors after oblique rotation will be perceptibly different.

The preceding example is, of course, extreme, but consider a more realistic situation. A battery of 60–80 tests that would define 20 factors would not be highly unusual today. If the mean correlation within clusters is about .70 and that between clusters is .50, following orthogonal rotations the factor loadings defining the first-order factors will be between .60 and .65 in size, and the near zero loadings of all other variables on these factors will be between .10 and .15. The small loading would not be quite zero, but the factor analyst would congratulate himself or herself on obtaining a very good rotated structure and would be very likely to stress the fact that the 20 factors were orthogonal and independent. Everyone disregards factor loadings smaller than .20. Yet, the most striking and important aspect of the basic data is that the 60–80 variables have a great deal in common. The intercorrelations of oblique first-order factors will define a single factor in the second order, and use of the Schmid–Leiman transformation (1957) will reveal a very large general factor defined by loadings of about .70, as well as much smaller group factor loadings of about .45. This final rotated factor matrix is hierarchical.

Intercorrelations of the size just described may not commonly occur in samples of college undergraduate populations, but they do commonly occur among tests of imperfect reliability in samples from wide ranges of talent. School psychologists and military psychologists have much more understanding of the extent of human variability and the generality of ability from task to task than those psychologists who gather their data from classes in introductory psychology. Even the latter miss important information when they look at and interpret only their first-order factors.

The basic evidence for a general factor in human cognitive performance does not require factoring in orders beyond the first. One needs to look only at the smallest correlations in the matrix. One must look long and hard to find zero or negative correlations among supposedly cognitive tasks or tests in large samples from a wide range of talent. In the intercorrelations of tests from Project Talent (Flanagan, Davis, Dailey, Shaycoft, Orr, Goldberg, & Neyman, 1964), there are small negative correlations between the number of attempts on highly speeded tests containing very simple items and the number of items right on assorted information, achievement, and aptitude tests. (I use the traditional names only in order to communicate.) There are a smaller number of near-zero correlations, both positive and negative, involving the number of right answers on these highly speeded tests. When a formula score that penalizes wrong answers is applied, the correlations become appreciably positive. One is also likely to find small negative correlations involving highly speeded fluency-type tests that are not scored in terms of the appropriateness of the responses. It is difficult to see much cognitive content in the variance of the scores on such tests, and the generality of general intelligence is restricted very little by rejecting these measures as components of a test of general intelligence. Mere speed of responding without regard to accuracy is not very intellectual.

With the exceptions noted in the preceding paragraph, intercorrelations of cognitive measures are positive, and most are sufficiently high in a wide range of talent so that a large general factor can be readily defined. The general factor defined in this way does not produce negative residuals among test intercorrelations. Large numbers of residual correlations are reduced to zero, however, in a very heterogeneous battery of cognitive tests by holding constant the factor of general intelligence. This means that neither the first principal component (extracted from variances and covariances) nor the first principal factor (extracted with communalities replacing variances) is ever a complete substitute for the theoretical general factor. If a battery of tests is assembled and the different types of tests are weighted in accordance with their loadings on the general factor, either the first principal component or the first principal factor becomes a reasonably accurate surrogate for the general factor in terms of the rank ordering of the tests on that factor. Loadings, however, are too large. On the other hand, if the tests are weighted very differently from their general factor loadings, neither the first component nor the first unrotated factor is an acceptable substitute. As substitutes, they are especially inaccurate when measures are included that do not load on the general factor.

A standard test of intelligence is thus not a pure measure of the general factor. Instead, it is the equivalent of the first component in a properly selected set of tests; that is, each item type is included with its full variance, whereas some part of that variance in the hierarchical rotation is on a small group factor. There is no way to avoid this difficulty. Even the best of intelligence tests will include several sources of unwanted variance. The problem of the test constructor is to minimize the size of these sources of variance. He or she is not forced to reject the construct of general intelligence because small unwanted sources of variance are present.

GENERAL INTELLIGENCE AND LATENT-TRAIT TEST THEORY

The last section ended with the statement of a problem for the constructor of intelligence tests. The problem is now described more fully. Tests of high homogeneity have been the goal of test constructors for many years. Guilford's model of the structure of intellect (1967) is based on the conception of factor-pure tests, each of high homogeneity. Present developments in latent trait theory assume unidimensionality of the items in a test. Each of the present models requires unidimensionality. Jensen, in his most recent book (1980), stated that one must compromise with the characteristics expected in a good test in order to construct an intelligence test. One might well conclude that the intelligence test is an outmoded concept, but there is another approach to test theory.

The development of an alternate theoretical basis for the construction of all tests, not merely intelligence tests, starts with an outright rejection of the goal of high homogeneity. There is no basis for believing that a moderately homogeneous test acclaimed today as factor-pure will not give way tomorrow to several tests in the same area, each more homogeneous than the predecessor and each now acclaimed as factor-pure. If Guttman's perfect scale (1944) is taken as the goal, there is a long way to go in constructing factor-pure tests to achieve that goal. I described a good many years ago (Humphreys, 1962a) how a test of mechanical information could give way to tests in carpentry, plumbing, and electricity, and how each of these could be further broken down into still narrower areas, for example, carpentry cutting tools. One might possibly achieve something approaching a Guttman scale by further narrowing the focus by constructing a short scale concerning information about the crosscut saw.

A critic might protest at this point that the preceding examples are all concerned with information, but so-called verbal aptitude is measured by information concerning word knowledge. A general vocabulary test can be "splintered" into many tests of word knowledge. In a similar fashion, an arithmetic reasoning test can also be reconstituted as several tests, each measuring a particular subset of arithmetical reasoning problems. In all of these examples, it would be possible to show with careful work and samples of sufficient size that the correlations among the narrow tests would be lower than their respective reliabilities would allow. This relationship of intercorrelations to reliability, incidentally, is the basic definition of multiple factors.

More recently, I have expanded Guilford's structure of intellect model by describing dimensions or facets beyond those of content, operations, and products (Humphreys, 1981). The facet of timing, for example, requires at least three elements: highly speeded, moderately speeded, and unspeeded. At least, these three levels are now used in various so-called primary mental ability tests, and there is no law of nature that requires a particular combination of content, operation, and product to be administered in one way or another. By adding facets such as timing, directions concerning guessing, the sensory modality of the examinee, the use of both right and wrong scores, and the intrinsic difficulty of the items, one increases markedly the number of primary mental abilities. A Cartesian space of more then 8,000 cells can be achieved. This is clearly absurd. Although there are some empty cells in the space described—right and wrong scores furnish identical information in an unspeeded test, and very simple items will not discriminate among examinees under those same conditions—there are too many highly homogeneous, factor-pure tests having high, though not complete, levels of redundancy with the other tests for any useful purpose.

There is a second major criticism of the factor-pure test. Whether a given cell in the Cartesian space is defined by three or n dimensions, the highly homogeneous test in that cell is inextricably complex psychologically. In Guilford's model, each test measures a combination of content, operation, and product. One can, however, obtain a relatively pure measure of one element of a particular facet (e.g., verbal content) by including verbal items covering all elements of operations and products. By making the verbal test as heterogeneous as possible with respect to facets other than content, the contribution of each of the many sources of variance contributed by operations and products is minimized. In return, verbal variance is maximized. Given enough verbal items, also, the sum of these other contributions to variance is also minimized.

An intelligence test is broader than a verbal test and involves the selection of items representing all of the cells in Guilford's model. If the number of cells is larger than the number of items that one can feasibly include in the intelligence test, stratified sampling of the space is indicated. The general rule is that, once the scope of the test has been determined, the selection of items requires maximizing the heterogeneity of the test within the limits set by the desired scope. As long as these heterogeneous items remain positively correlated with each other, no matter how low those positive correlations may be, the test is acceptable theoretically. It remains to be determined, however, whether that test will be useful in applied situations or in a theory concerning individual differences in behavior. A well-constructed test of general intelligence containing seemingly very heterogeneous items is still homogeneous with respect to the latent trait of general intelligence. In the full range of talent, the first-order factors in such a test constitute minor aberrations, but in behavioral measures, there is no way in which the aberrations can be eliminated.

Based on the preceding analysis, it is immaterial that different examinees can obtain the same total score on an intelligence test from different item-response patterns as long as the test is sufficiently heterogeneous so that differential skills and information average out. Given these conditions, equal scores on the test will, on average, be equal on the general factor. Likewise, in a well-constructed test, examinees who differ in total score can also be expected to have different scores on the general factor, no matter what the patterns of scores on the profile of subtests may be.

If good tests of intelligence are not quite unidimensional just because specific content, operation, and product variance can only be minimized rather than eliminated, it is probable that current latent-trait models can be applied to intelligence tests only in an approximate fashion, if at all. This is not a matter of serious concern. Mathematical models must be designed to meet the needs of psychologists and the requirements of their data. An oversimplified and misleading model should not be allowed to dictate the design of tests.

It is fitting to close this section with a short discussion of the implications of the test theory presented here for research on the component analysis of reasoning. From the point of view of what might be termed *controlled-heterogeneity test theory*, a test of analogical reasoning based on figural materials is not a pure test of reasoning. It contains a combination of reasoning, figural, and analogical variance. A more valid reasoning test can be constructed by systematically varying the content used in reasoning and the operations called for by the format of the test. A component analysis of the variance of the revised test would reveal a good deal more about the nature of reasoning than a component analysis of a highly homogeneous test in which different sources of variance are confounded.

IMPORTANCE OF THE GENERAL FACTOR

The importance of the general factor in human affairs does not depend on the applications of intelligence tests in such areas as selection and diagnosis. The data of selection and diagnosis are used because they are related to the construct validity of a test of general intelligence, but the case for the importance of the construct does not depend on the practical applications of tests of the construct.

An occupational title is frequently assigned to persons showing a rather wide diversity in job duties. *Engineer*, for example, is used for Ph.D.'s in engineering and for persons who might more accurately be labeled *technicians.* Yet, in spite of this ambiguity in terminology, there is a very substantial relationship between intelligence and membership in occupational groups. This relationship is also, as Jensen has most recently pointed out, highly related to the prestige ratings of occupations. It is also highly relevant that most of these data underestimate the relationship between intelligence and occupation because the intelligence data are frequently obtained in grade school and high school. There are changes that take place in the phenotype between measurement occasions. The normal measurement of occupational placement, particularly in the occupations showing the higher scores, takes place many years after the person has left the public school system. These very real changes produce some of the variability around the larger means.

It is also instructive in this regard that there is a good deal more variability around the smaller than around the larger means. For whatever reason, including the possibility that key adults did not take intelligence test results seriously, there are large numbers of persons with high intelligence in unskilled and semiskilled occupations. On the other hand, the presence of low-scoring individuals in high-scoring occupations is explained in part by ambiguous job titles, low quality of job performance, measurement error in the test, and the difference in time between test and criterion.

By explaining away some part of the variability at the low end of the distribution of high-scoring occupations, I do not mean to belittle the importance of other human qualities. Intelligence is not the end-all of human existence. Motivational dispositions, traits of character, sensitivity to interpersonal relationships, and emotional maturity are also important, as are the special abilities required in musical, dramatic, artistic, and athletic performance. The importance of other qualities is illustrated very well indeed by the trait rating of effective intelligence that we used in a good deal of research in the U.S. Air Force during the 1950s. Peer ratings of this trait during officer training are substantially correlated with scores on tests that measure general intelligence, but the trait ratings are better predictors of later officer effectiveness than the test scores, although it is necessary to keep in mind that there is direct selection on the latter. Persons high on the trait rating are described as those who consistently use their ability to the fullest. They are well organized; they are in charge of events. These are qualities that would seem to be important in any field of endeavor.

Some critics have claimed that the relationship between intelligence and occupational role is produced spuriously by the academic hurdles that persons must overcome to become members of many occupations. Statements of this sort question implicitly the importance of evaluating academic learning and even its content. If academic hurdles are artificial, then how well material is learned and even the content of the material learned are artificial as well. A conclusion of Jencks (1972) is relevant in this regard. If we had a system in the United States that made entrance into higher education and into occupations entirely dependent on test scores and academic grades, the present educational and occupational advantage of white middle-class children over white working-class children would be reduced by one-third. That is, in a more fluid society that paid more attention to merit than our present one, the relationship between intelligence and occupational membership would be *increased.*

Correlations between individual differences in intelligence and various criterion performances are also highly relevant to the importance of the construct in human affairs. Although qualifications have to be introduced, particularly with respect to the size of the correlations, one can support a very broad generalization about prediction of criterion performances. If the scores on an intelligence test are correlated with scores representing proficiency in the criterion performance, and if this proficient performance has an appreciable cognitive content, the population correlation will be nonzero. High criterion performance will accompany high test performance to some degree under these circumstances.

The preceding statement rules out proficiency criteria that are very largely sensory or motor in nature. It also rules out criteria such as satisfaction with work, absenteeism, and turnover that do not reflect proficiency. Correlations based on small samples that contradict the generalization are not satisfactory as evidence. The sizes of the correlations obtained are also functions of all relevant measurement parameters.

Most authors who report correlations know that relationships are attenuated by measurement error, but the reliability of the test is more often reported than the reliability of the criterion measurement. On *a priori* grounds, the latter is more often suspect. The reliability of a grade point average for a single semester of college work in an institution that is not highly selective among high school graduates is probably about .70. Grades must also be valid indicators of proficiency. One cannot safely assume such validity. The "A for effort" is quite common at all levels of education.

A different sort of error is introduced by assembling samples from several sources, such as different schools or industrial departments, into one large sample when the criterion measure has both a zero and units of measurement that differ from one group to another. Most persons know vaguely that different high schools and colleges differ in the mean level of ability of their students at the time of entrance to the institution, but they do not realize how large those differences are. In the state of Illinois, for example, there are high schools whose means for intelligence are below the 10th and above the 90th percentiles of individual differences norms. There are colleges that differ almost as much. Throwing academic grades into a single sample can substantially attenuate correlations with intelligence tests. The desired procedure is to compute a correlation for each group and to obtain a sample of adequate size by obtaining a weighted (by sample size) average of the within-group correlations. Even within a single institution, an investigator is frequently faced with the same problem when a number of different curricula are involved. On a large, heterogeneous campus, the highest grades are very likely to be given by the faculties of those units admitting the students of lowest ability.

A systematic study of the variability of high schools along four different dimensions, including one of general intelligence, has been published by Humphreys, Parsons, and Park (1979). The first noteworthy finding for a random sample of high schools in the Project Talent data of 1960 was that there was huge variability among the nation's high schools. The variance of high school means of tenth-grade students on a talent composite used as a measure of general intelligence was more than one-third of the variance of the individual students in those schools. A second important finding was that the causes for students being in one high school rather than another were reflected more directly by a test of intelligence than by the socioeconomic status of the children's families. Selection appeared to be more directly on the general factor in intelligence than on socioeconomic status. As a matter of fact, 6% to 9% of the variance of mean SES scores was related to a factor identified as urban versus rural schools. The one good measure of the general factor whose loading on the rural/urban difference was outside the range of zero $\pm.04$ was arithmetic reasoning. The sign of the latter placed it on the rural school end of the continuum, whereas SES was on the urban end. It is also of interest that the usual listing of the attributes of a quality education by educators, such as class size, days in the school year, teaching experience, dollar expenditure per pupil, and even books in the library, had very little relationship to the general factor of intelligence in the range of values of each variable in high schools in 1960. Yet, two of the best measures of the general factor, reading comprehension and arithmetic reasoning, had loadings of .90–.95 in the school means data.

One of the least understood effects on the size of correlations is that of restriction of range. Nonpsychological critics, such as the uninformed members of the Ralph Nader organization, seem to be completely oblivious to the effects of restriction of range. For example, to conclude that correlations of .30 between test scores and academic grades in highly selective undergraduate and graduate schools indicate that test scores generally have little validity is simply ludicrous. A test that can discriminate this well in the highest 10% of our population in general intelligence is very valid indeed.

Even well-trained psychologists neglect the total impact of selection on correlations and, in particular, do not distinguish between the effects of direct restriction of range on the test and the effects of indirect restriction on the test. A drop in variability on the test from a less restricted range to a more restricted range when the restriction occurs on the criterion (e.g., by firing unsatisfactory employees or dropping unsatisfactory students from the university) indicates much more attentuation of the correlation between test and criterion than when the same decrease in variability is the result of selection on the test itself.

A great deal of self-selection takes place in application for jobs and for college admission. It is highly probable that this takes place primarily on the general factor of intelligence, although not on the fallible measure of the general factor used by the institution for selection purposes. This and other types of selection that take place before application are not taken into account in the selection research literature. The definition of the unrestricted range of talent that typically occurs in the literature is the variance of the applicant group. The restricted range of talent is the variance of the selected group.

It may be useful to summarize the major restrictions of range of talent that occur between the public school period and entrance into a profession that requires graduate or professional school training. We graduate less than 80% of our youth from high school. Only about one-half apply for admission to a four-year college. Not all are accepted. Of those who enter, not all receive degrees. Of those who receive degrees, not all apply for admission to graduate or professional school. Of those who apply, not all are admitted. Of those admitted, not all receive advanced degrees. Of those who receive advanced degrees, not all enter the profession. Of those who enter initially, not all stay. Selection on general intelligence takes place at every hurdle, but in some cases, the direct selection is on the general factor itself; in some, on a test of the general factor; and in others, on the criterion measure that is also a measure of the general factor. The size of the standard deviation of intelligence tests along the way is a fallible guide to the amount of attenuation one might expect for validity coefficients.

The preceding discussion documents the need for calibrating tests used for selection in education, industry, or the military to measures of general intelligence in the unrestricted range of talent. There appears to be little realization of how much selection takes place as students move up the educational ladder. I referred to tests making discriminations in the upper 10% of our population. Highly selective private colleges do have student bodies who are drawn almost 100% from the highest decile of general intelligence. Graduate and professional school students in selective institutions are even more highly selected. This selection appears to be primarily on the general factor in intelligence, but its extent is not generally known. This lack of knowledge contributes to a good many of the misconceptions about general intelligence that are held by many persons in our population. It would be useful to test users if the major publishers of tests designed to be used on restricted populations would routinely calibrate those tests against the Stanford–Binet or the Wechsler norms. This procedure would also be useful from the public relations point of view; it would document the importance in human affairs of the concept of general intelligence.

DEFINITION AND THEORY OF GENERAL INTELLIGENCE

There is only one change that I would make today in the definition of intelligence that I have been espousing for a number of years. I shall first repeat the original definition (Humphreys, 1971):

> Intelligence is defined as the entire repertoire of acquired skills, knowledge, learning sets, and generalization tendencies considered intellectual in nature that are available at any one period of time. An intelligence test contains items that sample the totality of such acquisitions. . . . The definition of intelligence here proposed would be circular as a function of the use of intellectual if it were not for the fact that there is a consensus

among psychologists as to the kinds of behaviors that are labeled intellectual. Thus, the Stanford–Binet and the Wechsler tests can be considered
examples of this consensus and define the consensus. (p. 31–32)

When an attorney for plaintiffs who wished to bar the use of
intelligence tests for the purpose of placement in special classes
asked whether the preceding definition was the consensus of all psychologists, I had to state that it was not. One cannot get the members
of the American Psychological Association to agree on anything psychological. The definition should be modified by the addition of an
adjective such as *cognizant* before the word *psychologists* in the
next-to-the-last sentence quoted.

It is also useful to repeat a description of the processes that are
involved in the development and the utilization of the intellectual
repertoire (Humphreys, 1979): " Intelligence is the resultant of the
processes of acquiring, storing in memory, retrieving, combining,
comparing, and using in new contexts information and conceptual
skills; it is an abstraction" (p. 115). Intelligence is abstracted from the
many kinds of behaviors that we are willing to label *intellectual*.

There is no need to assume, as many psychologists do, an entity
underlying the behavior sampled by an intelligence test. Spearman
(1914) called his entity "mental energy." When Jensen (1980) used
"g," he meant a real intelligence that is something other than the
behavior sampled by the test. For an explanation, one needs nothing
more than the basic approach originally described by Thomson
(1919). One might prefer a different terminology today, but the concept of large numbers of overlapping bonds still provides the right
emphasis. To the extent that intelligence is genetically determined,
many genes are involved. To the extent that intelligence is environmentally determined, many environmental causes are required. The
combination of genetic and environmental factors is responsible for
individual differences in the structure and function of the many components in the central nervous system. Intelligent behavior covers a
wide range of activities. I have used the terms (most of them coined
for the purpose) *polygenic, polyenvironmental, polyneural,* and
polybehavioral to characterize the construct.

This characterization of intelligence is highly congruent with
the content of this chapter. In the beginning, I stressed that intelligence is a phenotypic trait. As such, it is observable and measurable.
The observations are of behavior, not of an underlying thing or
entity. Judgments concerning intelligence are inherently faulty,
however, because ratings are inadequate measuring instruments.
Both the zero point of the scale and the units of measurement vary

from rater to rater. Other characteristics of the ratee are frequently confounded with intelligence. In addition, raters who observe only a limited segment of behavior lack the breadth of experience with the ratee to make highly valid judgments. The intelligence test samples broadly and in an objective manner the kinds of problem-solving behaviors that characterize the construct of intelligence. The limits of the trait are not as clearly established as the limits of height and weight, but a reasonable consensus has developed concerning those limits.

As with any phenotypic trait, it is theoretically possible to estimate the correlation with genotype of persons in a particular population. A valid estimate depends on experimental control that is lacking in human data. The mere fact that there are many elements in the central nervous system and that these are determined by many genes suggests a genetic component to the variance of the phenotypic trait of intelligence. The genetic mechanism par excellence is a producer of individual differences. Central nervous system structures are also determined by environmental influences, but the mere fact that intelligence is a behavioral trait requires a substantial environmental contribution to variance. Behavior, after all, is acquired during development. No test is independent of the learning that has taken place in a human environment.

With intelligence defined as a phenotypic behavioral trait, it is possible to assert without possibility of debate that American blacks have a lower mean intelligence level than American whites at this point in our history. The available data, however, do not permit any conclusion about a possible difference in the genotype for intelligence. For a phenotypic difference, there is no requirement that opportunities for blacks be equal to those for whites, just as there is no requirement in describing group differences in height and weight that the groups be equal in their nutritional histories. A person functions in school or in occupations at his or her level of phenotypic intelligence. This is not to say that the phenotype does not change. The important questions concern the extent to which the phenotype can be modified at a given stage of development, with a given amount of time and effort, and with what techniques of behavior modification. The evidence to date indicates that the phenotypic intelligence of blacks has changed very little in comparison to that of their white counterparts, after age 18, as a consequence of a special admission to college, to a graduate school, to a professional school, or to an occupation.

There is no doubt that the intercorrelations of a large set of tests of cognitive abilities will define multiple orthogonal factors in the first order, but the measures of these factors are far from being mutually orthogonal. The orthogonality of the factors is a function of the mathematics, not of the nature of human abilities. The substantial level of positive intercorrelations among these tests in a wide range of talent furnishes a firm empirical basis for the general factor in intelligence.

Tests of intelligence, even in a wide range of talent, do not fit the latent trait models that are so popular in test theory today. The nature of the construct of general intelligence requires a set of very heterogeneous items that may be unidimensional with respect to the latent trait of intelligence but that also define a large number of small group factors. The latter are more appropriately termed *unavoidable noise*, arising from the characteristics of behavioral traits, than *primary mental abilities*. If measures of general intelligence are insufficiently unidimensional to fit present latent-trait models, the latter should be modified, not the test.

The first-order factors, mistakenly called *primary* and connoting psychological importance, constitute in a wide range of talent relatively minor perturbations in the measurement of general intelligence. They are primary only in the limited sense that the factor-analytic methodology requires that they be extracted first. Properly defined in terms similar to the overlapping bonds of Godfrey Thomson (i.e., the repertoire of skills and knowledge labeled *intellectual* by cognizant psychologists), general intelligence is better considered primary.

There is a great deal of evidence, some of which I have reviewed in this chapter, that intelligence is an important trait in human affairs, but there are other important traits as well. Although it is not essential that social policies be based in a one-to-one fashion on the importance of individual and group differences in intelligence, social policies that are based on the supposed lack of importance of these differences are highly suspect. White middle-class liberals have been traumatized by the mean difference in intelligence between blacks and whites, but the irrational reactions to this trauma have not been helpful. Sophisticated environmentalists should have been the first to accept the reality of the phenotypic difference. Sophisticated hereditarians have a more difficult task to explain the relatively large differences in the frequency distributions of the intellectual genes in the respective gene pools of two subgroups of a single species.

REFERENCES

Children's Defense Fund. America's children and their families: Key facts, 1982. (Available from author [1520 New Hampshire Avenue, N.W., Washington, D.C. 20036]).

Clarke-Stewart, A. Interactions between mothers and their young children: Characteristics and consequences. *Monograph of the Society for Research in Child Development*, 1973, *38* (6–7).

Cleary, T., Humphreys, L., Kendrick, S., & Wesman, A. Educational uses of tests with disadvantaged students. *American Psychologist*, 1975, *30*, 15–41.

Coover, J. E. Metapsychics and the incredulity of psychologists. In C. Murchison (Ed.), *The case for and against psychic belief.* Worcester, Mass.: Clark University Press, 1927.

Flanagan, J., Davis, F., Dailey, J., Shaycoft, M., Orr, D., Goldberg, I., & Neyman, C. *The American high school student.* Pittsburgh: University of Pittsburgh, 1964.

Guilford, J. P. *The nature of human intelligence.* New York: McGraw-Hill, 1967.

Guttman, L. A basis for scaling qualitative data. *American Sociological Review*, 1944, *9*, 139–150.

Humphreys, L. The nature and organization of human abilities. In M. Katz (Ed.), *19th Yearbook of the National Council on Measurement in Education.* Ames, Iowa: Author, 1962. (a)

Humphreys, L. The organization of human abilities. *American Psychologist*, 1962, *17*, 475–483. (b)

Humphreys, L. Analytical approach to the correlation between related pairs of subjects on psychological tests. *Psychological Bulletin*, 1970, *74*, 149–152.

Humphreys, L. Theory of intelligence. In R. Cancro (Ed.), *Intelligence: Genetic and environmental influences.* New York: Grune and Stratton, 1971.

Humphreys, L. The construct of general intelligence. *Intelligence*, 1979, *3*, 105–120.

Humphreys, L. The primary mental ability. In M. P. Friedman, J. P. Das, & N. O'Connor (Eds.), *Intelligence and learning.* New York: Plenum, 1981, 87–102.

Humphreys, L., & Dachler, H. P. Jensen's theory of intelligence. *Journal of Educational Psychology*, 1969, *60*, 419–426.

Humphreys, L., & Parsons, C. Piagetian tasks measure intelligence and intelligence tests assess cognitive development. *Intelligence*, 1979, *3*, 369–382.

Humphreys, L., Parsons, C., & Park, R. Dimensions involved in differences among school means of cognitive measures. *Journal of Educational Measurement*, 1979, *16*, 63–76.

Jencks, C. *Inequality: A reassessment of the effect of family and schooling in America.* New York: Basic Books, 1972.

Jensen, A. *Bias in mental testing.* New York: Free Press, 1980.

Loehlin, J., Lindzey, G., & Spuhler, J. *Race differences in intelligence.* San Francisco: W. H. Freeman, 1975.

Schmid, J., & Leiman, J. The development of hierarchical factor solutions. *Psychometrika*, 1957, *33*, 53–61.

Spearman, C. The theory of two factors. *Psychological Review*, 1914, *21*, 101–115.

Thomson, G. On the cause of hierarchical order among correlation coefficients. *Proceedings of the Royal Society* (A), 1919, *95*.

Thurstone, L. *Primary mental abilities.* Chicago: University of Chicago Press, 1938. (Psychometric Monograph No. 1)

CHAPTER EIGHT

The Effect of Race on Human Abilities and Mental Test Scores

H. J. EYSENCK

Theories concerning racial differences in intelligence are age-old and antedate empirical studies by thousands of years; Greek and Roman writers in the centuries preceding and following the birth of Christ had much to say about the weak intellects of "barbarians." The development of IQ tests made possible more experimental investigations, and we now have a plethora of results from such studies. Unfortunately, these results are not easily interpreted, and diametrically opposite views have been expressed by different writers. Some are clearly writing outside the scientific tradition (Lawler, 1978; Liungman, 1972; Gillie, 1976), and such works only contribute to the popular suspicion that psychologists are not scientists evaluating empirical evidence, but prophets mouthing environmental or genetic shibboleths. But agreement is not noticeably closer when we turn to more academic works, ranging from Kamin (1974), who denied that there is any evidence of genetic causes of IQ differences even within a given racial group, through Block and Dworkin (1976), Flynn (1980), Eckberg (1979), Halsey (1977), and Loehlin, Lindsey, and Spuhler (1975), to Eysenck (1971) and Jensen (1972, 1973, 1980). The writers involved in the dispute acknowledge that those whose views they criticize have important points to make, and none suggest that sufficient data are available, or that the available data are of sufficient quality, for a final decision to be made on the question(s) raised in the title of this chapter. In this chapter, an effort is made to eschew the

H. J. EYSENCK ● University of London, London, England.

personal and political arguments that have served to muddy the scene, and to draw attention to the weaknesses of the various positions taken by advocates of strong environmentalistic and strong hereditarian positions. If the outcome of the examination of probabilistic studies falls short of certainty, then that does not indicate a failure of the scientific method but an indication that the methodology will have to be improved in order to produce agreed-upon conclusions. Suggestions for such improvement are made in the final paragraphs.

When there are violently opposing views on an emipirical issue, it is usual in science to look for confusion in definition, terminology, and conceptualization. It seems clear that there is much evidence of such confusion. Some of this confusion is discussed in the course of the chapter, but some must be dealt with immediately if we are to get clear the meaning at least of the terms included in the chapter heading.

RACE

Race is a term so emotion-laden—due in no small measure to the racial teachings and policies of Hitler, leading as they did to genocide and war—that many writers would prefer to discard the term altogether as "meaningless" and unscientific. This is not a tenable argument, and readers who wish to see what modern anthropology has to say on this subject may consult Baker's excellent book (1974) on the topic. The objection to the concept of *race* is, of course, well taken if it is directed against the absurd notion of "pure" races, whether in the olden days, or at present; all races are to some extent hybrids, including American blacks. This fact does not invalidate the possibility that groups of people forming ethnic subgroups clearly differentiated in skin color, type of hair, shape of nose, or any combination of these and other characteristics may differ from each other in mental ability; this must remain an empirical question. However, there is a very important consideration that tends to invalidate any comparison between large racial groups, such as the usual comparison of blacks and whites. To make sense, such a comparison assumes that all blacks and all whites have a mean IQ that varies randomly within races, so that any reasonable sample of blacks and whites can be used to stand for all the remaining blacks and whites. Such an assumption is demonstrably false, as we shall see, and consequently, all comparisons that have been made are *not* between black and white, but between, for example, U.S. whites and blacks

selected in certain ways and representing certain sharply demar-
cated larger groups; they do not and cannot represent all blacks and
all whites. This point should be too obvious even to mention, but it
seems to have been largely neglected in many of the debates on this
issue.

The most obvious exemplification of this principle is the well-
known difference in IQ between blacks (and whites!) in the northern
and southern United States (Shuey, 1966). Where the average IQ of
blacks in the United States is approximately 85%, that of southern
blacks is around 80 and that of northern blacks is around 90. Thus,
the difference between whites and northern blacks is no greater than
that between northern blacks and southern blacks; clearly it is
doubtful if we can regard blacks in the United States as a homogeneous group in any meaningful scientific sense. It is possible to argue
that the difference has arisen through emigration, or through better
educational facilities in the North, or for some other reasons; that is
not the point at issue. In comparing "blacks" (as a whole) with
"whites" (as a whole), we are grouping together widely different
components of some arbitrary "unitary" group that may be differentiated into many ethnic subgroups, not all of which are likely to
be genetically or otherwise similar with respect to IQ. This fact
becomes even more evident when we compare American blacks
with African blacks, or one tribe of African blacks with another.
There may be uniformity, but unless and until that uniformity is
proven, it is inadmissible to use the scores obtained by *particular*
black and white groups to make statements about blacks and whites
in general.

Documentation about differences between northern and southern whites is plentiful, and the results (which parallel those for
blacks) are well known. It may be more interesting to consider differences within a much more homogeneous country, such as the
United Kingdom (Lynn, 1979) or France (Lynn, 1980). In the first of
these studies, Lynn presented evidence to show that there are differences in mean population IQ in different regions of the British Isles.
The mean population values are highest in London and southeast
England and tend to drop with distance from this region. Mean population IQs are highly correlated with measures of intellectual
achievement, per capita income, unemployment, infant mortality,
and urbanization. The regional differences in mean population IQ
appear to be due to historical differences, which are measured back
to 1751, and to selective migration from the provinces into the Lon-

don area. Figure 1 gives the standard regions of England, Wales, Scotland, and Ireland, showing mean population IQs.

Similar results are reported for France; here, too, there appears to have been a "brain drain" from the provinces to Paris. The mean population IQs are significantly correlated with migration since 1801, "and it is suggested that internal migration has been an important factor leading to contemporary differences in intelligence" (Lynn, 1980, p. 325). Figure 2 shows a path model indicating the hypothesized chain linking historical net migration to contemporary mean population IQs, and to four economic and social output variables.

FIGURE 1. Standard regions of England, Wales, Scotland, and Ireland showing mean population IQs (from Lynn, 1979).

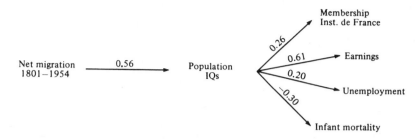

FIGURE 2. Path model showing hypothesized causal chain linking historical net migration to contemporary mean population IQs and to four economic and social output variables. (Significance levels: 0.21 < 5%; 0.28 < 1%.) (From Lynn, 1980.)

These investigations are of outstanding importance, although not entirely free of possible flaws (Kirby, 1980); it is possible that the rather arbitrary administrative regions for which data are available may themselves be heterogeneous. This possibility does, of course, exist, but the general gradients found by Lynn cover many regions and undoubtedly suggest the existence of clear-cut differences in IQ between different white groups living within the same country. As to causation, Lynn's suggestion of emigration finds strong support in his detailed study of the decline of intelligence in Scotland (Lynn, 1977b), and in an earlier study in which Thomson (1953) showed that, within Scotland, the rural areas near big towns had the most emigration and the lowest IQs; outlying country districts not near towns had little emigration, and IQs significantly higher than in the emigration areas. The low mean IQ level in Ireland (e.g., Byrt & Gill, 1975) and the very high prevalence of mental defect there (MacKay, 1971) may also be due to selective emigration (MacKay & McCoy, 1975).

The incredibly high IQ of British Jews (Davies & Hughes, 1927; Vincent, 1966) poses another problem for anyone attempting to group all "whites" together as a somewhat homogeneous group; Vincent found Jewish children in Glasgow as much superior to their non-Jewish but white contemporaries as American blacks are inferior to American whites in points of IQ! But even Jews are certainly not homogeneous racially (Baker, 1974); we discriminate Sephardic from Ashkenazic Jews, and many European Jews are very likely the offspring of the Aryan-language group called the Khazars, a polydeistic people that, surrounded by Muslims on the south flank and Christians on the western side, was persuaded by its leaders to adopt the Jewish religion. Pushed westward later on by Tartar hordes, they constituted the majority of Jews in Russia, Hungary, Poland, and in countries even further west (Koestler, 1976). Truly, Europeans as well as American white groups are too heterogeneous to be characterized by a mean IQ figure.

INTELLIGENCE

The term *intelligence* is often used as if it had a universally agreed-upon meaning, as if it were synonymous with IQ, and as if different measures of it could readily be substituted for each other. All these notions are false. The orthodox meaning of intelligence is related to three different conceptions, sometimes referred to as Intelligence A, Intelligence B, and Intelligence C (Vernon, 1979). Intelligence A is the genotype, that is, the (hypothetical) genetic substratum that underlies differences in cognitive performance on IQ-type tests and in problem-solving behavior in everyday life. Some psychologists (e.g., Kamin, 1974) still seem to dispute the evidence concerning the existence of such a genotype, but almost all other writers on the topic agree that genotypic factors do exist that predispose people in different degrees toward good or poor performance in the cognitive field; disagreement arises primarily in regard to the amount of heritability found in this field. Hardly anyone would be likely to estimate heritability in Western countries as being below 50% to 60%, or above 80%, but some would still maintain that quantitative estimates make too many assumptions to be admissible at the present time. A survey of the available literature on the topic, using the relatively new methods of biometrical genetical analysis, gave an estimate of 70% for the narrow heritability of intelligence, plus 10% for dominance and assortative mating effects; after measurement error in the tests used had been removed statistically, an estimate of broad heritability of 80% was arrived at (Eysenck, 1979). This estimate is, of course, subject to the usual estimation errors and is a population estimate; that is, it has no universal validity. However, it rests on a surprisingly good agreement of figures derived from many different types of evidence (e.g., monozygotic twins brought up in isolation; comparisons of monozygotes and dizygotes; regression effects; adopted children; and intrafamilial correlations). Heritability of intelligence seems rather similar for blacks and whites in the United States (Osborne, 1980).

Intelligence B refers to the expression of the genotype in interaction with environmental factors such as socioeconomic status (SES), in everyday life behavior, and when problem-solving, cognitive, or academic tasks are involved. Thus, an individual's standing in school and university, success in dealing with occupational problems and tasks, and general way of dealing with the problems thrown up in the course of his or her life, insofar as his or her reactions are not emotional in nature, would be considered relevant to Intelligence B, which might thus be identified with "intelligence" as it is understood by the proverbial person in the street. Clearly, Intelligence B is phenotypic, combining hereditary and environmental effects in producing individual differences in effective intelligence. Intelligence C is the attempted measurement of Intelligence B by means of IQ tests. Although this attempt has been quite successful, the types of intelligence (A and B) can not be clearly identified (Eysenck, 1979; Vernon, 1979). It may be surmised that IQ is closer to Intelligence A than is Intelligence B, if only because Intelligence B is more likely to be affected by emotional and other irrelevant factors (anxiety is an obvious example). Ordinarily, the methods of IQ testing at least attempt to eliminate such emotional and other irrelevant factors.

Although this subdivision of "intelligence" into three different kinds of intelligence is useful, it does not go far enough. Thus, Intelligence C can itself be subdivided into "fluid" and "crystallized" intelligence (Cattell, 1971). Thurstone (1938) further divided it into a set of primary mental abilities, and finally, Guilford and Hoepfner (1971) eliminated "intelligence" completely and substituted their "structure-of-intellect" model, consisting of some 120 different and independent abilities. This gradual elimination of intelligence as a concept has clearly gone too far (McNemar, 1964; Reynolds, 1982; Vernon, 1965), and such positions as Guilford's cannot be sustained in the face of the evidence of a "positive manifold," that is, a well-nigh universal tendency for performances on all cognitive tasks to correlate positively with each other. There is no doubt about the existence of primary or group factors in addition to a general factor (g) of intelligence, but all the data point to the predominance of such a general factor in the cognitive field (Eysenck, 1979). Nevertheless, the existence of many group factors, as well as the fact that different types of tests have different g loadings, presents difficulties for anyone who wishes to generalize over different tests and populations; it also, however, offers interesting possibilities of meaningful analyses of data comparing the performance of different races.

Tests differ in the degree of "culture fairness" they show; this dimension is related to but not identical with the concepts of fluid and crystallized ability. Culture-fair tests are usually nonverbal (for obvious reasons), and they tend to be abstract, that is, to contain reference to learned concepts, but to be built on perceptual relations between simple lines (as in Raven's matrices test), simple numerical relations (as in the dominoes test), or simple alphabetical relations (as in the letter series test). The least culture-fair tests are vocabulary and general knowledge tests, because they obviously depend on a particular culture and a particular schooling system. Other tests are intermediate. These judgments are based on common sense; they may lead, particularly in fairly homogeneous countries like England, to erroneous conclusions. Thus, one might imagine that culture-fair tests like the dominoes test has a higher heritability than a culture-bound test like a vocabulary test; this is not necessarily true. In his study of monozygotic (MZ) twins brought up together or in isolation, Shields (1962) found that on the dominoes test, the intraclass correlations for twins brought up together or in separation were .71 and .76; on vocabulary tests, the values were .74 and .74. Thus, there is no real difference between the two tests; one might have expected that, compared with the separated twins, twins brought up together would have been much more alike on the vocabulary test than on the dominoes test. In a less homogeneous population than that characteristic of England, quite different figures might have been obtained.

Different IQ tests are used for different purposes, and a test suitable for selection by a school in a homogeneous country (homogeneous as far as education is concerned) may be quite unsuitable in another country. Tests in educational and industrial practice are often used for specific purposes that lead to the construction of measures that confound fluid intelligence and acquired knowledge (like the Army Alpha); such tests may give better prediction than pure IQ tests, but the usual practice of calling these hybrids "IQ tests" makes discussion difficult. Often, items from such "practical-purpose" tests are quoted to illustrate the culture-dependence of IQ tests, but this practice disregards the purpose for which the particular tests were constructed. It might be better to call IQ tests only those tests that were constructed simply for the purpose of obtaining as pure a measure as possible of the general factor of intelligence. However, it is clear that the term *intelligence* is used in so many different senses, and that IQ tests appear in so many quite different guises, it is necessary in discussion to be quite specific about what meaning of *intelligence* and what type of IQ test one may be referring to. Many arguments in this field have continued because the participants used identical terms to refer to quite distinct concepts, tests, and theories.

RACIAL DIFFERENCES

This topic has often been reviewed, a recent and very competent account being that of Lynn (1978); as the facts are not really in dispute, we will summarize only the main findings. In this section, we deal, of course, only with measured IQ, that is, "Intelligence C"; the interpretation of the findings is to be based on more specialized studies and is taken up later. It is important at this stage not to overinterpret data that by themselves are ambiguous; observed differences may be due to many causes, and the existence of the difference does not by itself suggest which of these causes may have been active in producing the observed differences.

We have noted that, even within a given country with a relatively homogeneous population (e.g., England or France), there may be stable IQ differences from one section of the country to another. Much the same is true when we look at different European countries, although the differences are somewhat more pronounced. As Lynn (1978) pointed out, "It has generally been found that populations of Northern European extraction have mean IQs of approximately 100" (p. 268). This has been found to be so of large and well-selected samples of Scottish children tested in 1932 and 1947 (Scottish Council for Research in Education, 1933, 1949); a New Zealand sample of 26,000 children of European extraction, who obtained a mean IQ of 98.5 (Redmond & Davies, 1940); an Australian sample of 35,000 children with a mean IQ of approximately 95 (McIntyre, 1938); a Belgian sample of children giving a mean IQ of 104 (Goosens, 1952); a French children's sample obtaining a mean IQ of 104 (Bourdier, 1964); an East German study giving a mean of 100 (Kurth, 1969); and a representative sample of Danish children obtaining a mean score on Raven's Matrices almost identical with the original British standardization sample (Vejleskov, 1968). The analysis carried out by Garth (1931) in his review of American Army Alpha Test data from World War I immigrants showed Scots, English, and Northern Europeans at the top of the scale.

IQs in Southern European countries appear somewhat lower (Hirsch, 1926), with the possible exception of Italy (Tesi & Young, 1962). (The results from this small-scale Italian study conflict with the results obtained by Garth, 1931, in his review of the IQs of Italian immigrants to the United States between the two world wars, who averaged about one standard deviation lower on individual Binet tests, as well as on a nonlanguage group test.) In Spain, a very large sample of 113,749 army conscripts was tested on Raven's Matrices in

1965 and obtained an IQ of 87 (Nieto-Alegre, Navarro, Santa Cruz, & Domínguez, 1967). A Yugoslavian sample of schoolchildren obtained a mean IQ of 89 (Sorokin, 1954), and a sample of Greek children a mean IQ of 89 (Fatourous, 1972). These results bear out the Army Alpha studies of immigrants into the United States, which showed immigrants from Southern European countries to have IQs below those of immigrants from Northern European countries (if we can count the Army Alpha as a proper IQ test!).

Lynn (1978) argued that the Caucasoid race extends eastward from Europe into the Near East and India, and consequently, he discussed Iraqi and Iranian children in his section on "Caucasoids"; children tested there have IQs around the 80 mark (Alzobaie, 1965; Mehryar, Shapurian, & Bassiri, 1972). For India, the findings are rather diverse, ranging from a sample of students with a mean IQ of 95 (Maity, 1926) to mean IQs from 81 to 94 obtained from 17 samples of children aged 9–15 (Sinha, 1968). The overall mean of the children was around 86. Thus, the mean scores of Indians, Iranians, and Iraqi is about the same as that of American blacks. When we turn to blacks, we find that a very large number of studies (Shuey, 1966, reviewed 382 studies, employing 81 different tests of mental ability) agree on the fact that the mean IQ of American blacks is approximately 85, and that they score somewhat higher on verbal tests than on nonverbal tests. Blacks from the southeastern states tend to have lower IQs and smaller standard deviations than those living in the North, averaging perhaps 81 with a standard deviation of around 12. As already pointed out, blacks from the United States should not be considered representative of all blacks; they are descended from slaves, who were either purchased or captured from selected areas in Africa, and who may have been selected in various ways (Darlington, 1969). Furthermore many Afro-Americans have some Caucasoid ancestry, with an average admixture of between 20% and 30% (Reed, 1969).

Studies of blacks in Africa and other parts of the world do not give very dissimilar results. Silvey (1972) reported a mean IQ of 88 for a group of almost 500 children in Uganda, but these were selected for educational achievement, so that the mean for the total population is probably lower. Vernon (1969) found a mean of approximately 80 for a group of 50 boys aged 12 in Kampala, the capital of Uganda. In Jamaica, the average level of intelligence as judged by IQ tests was around 80 (Vernon, 1969). As in the United States, the children tended to do better on verbal and educational tests than on nonverbal and spatial tests. Klingelhofer (1967) found a mean IQ of 88 for almost

3,000 Negroid children in Tanzania; a group of Asian children in the same country had a mean IQ of 98. In Jahoda's (1956) study, children in Ghana scored at a level of IQ somewhat below 80, as did various samples of African children in South Africa (quoted by Lynn, 1978).

We next turn to the Mongoloids, in whom the picture is quite different. Quite generally, they do at least as well as whites, and they often do significantly better. Much of the work has been done on Chinese and Japanese immigrants to the United States. An example is the work of Jensen (1973), who found that on the Gesell Figure Copying Test, Mongoloid children had better scores than Caucasoids or other racial groups. Studies of immigrants like these are, of course, somewhat inconclusive because immigrants are not necessarily typical of the populations of which they are a self-selected sample. However, studies in their native countries tend to bear out these general findings.

Lynn (1977a) surveyed the intelligence of the Japanese and also (Lynn, 1977b) the intelligence of the Chinese and the Malays in Singapore. These studies, as well as one by Chan (1974) in Hong Kong, confirm that by and large Mongoloids in their home countries are something like half a standard deviation above the white IQ mean on nonverbal tests.

Again, one should not generalize from the Japanese and the Chinese to all Mongoloids. A study by Thomas and Sjah (1961) of Mongoloids in Indonesia gave a mean IQ of 96, which was probably an overestimate because of poor sampling. Eskimos, a Mongoloid subrace living above the Arctic Circle, gave a mean IQ approximately the same as Scots in Scotland (Berry, 1966), but this claim was discounted by Lynn (1978) for good reasons. Vernon (1969) obtained a mean IQ of 85, whereas McArthur (1969), using Raven's Matrices, found his Arctic Eskimoes at or above Caucasoid norms for Canada. Some of the contradictions in these findings may be due to different tests' being used, but it would seem that no certain conclusions about Eskimos can be made at present.

Another group for whom a certain amount of evidence is available are Amerinds living on reservations in the United States. Early work was summarized by Garth (1931) and Pintner (1931) and more recent work has been done by Tyler (1965) and Coleman (1966). Most studies agree that Amerinds have a mean verbal IQ of about 90 and a mean nonverbal IQ of approximately 96. There appears to be a correlation of about .4 between IQ and degree of Caucasoid admixture among Amerinds; the interpretation of this finding is not unambiguous (Garth, 1931).

Australoids (i.e., the full-sized Aborigines of Australia) were one of the earliest groups to be studied by Porteus with his newly created maze test (Porteus, 1937, 1965, 1967), and many others have since obtained IQs from this group, using various other tests. A recent study by McElwain and Kearney (1973) gives a mean of 85 for the IQ of children going to school with European Australians and brought up in an advanced Western culture. Maoris in New Zealand have done rather better, obtaining a mean IQ of 94 (St. George 1972; St. George &. St. George, 1975; Du Chateau, 1967). Other smaller groups of Australoids have been studied with similar results.

We may briefly summarize the frequently replicated findings from the literature. The highest IQs in different parts of the world have been obtained by Mongoloid populations, particularly the Japanese and the Chinese, both in their own countries and in emigrated samples studied in the United States. They are followed by Caucasoid populations in Northern Europe or emigrated from there to the United States, Australia, and elsewhere. Caucasoid groups in Southern Europe come next, followed by Caucasoid peoples in the Middle and Near East. Amerinds and Mexican-Americans come next, followed by Afro-Americans, African Negroids, and Australoids. As Baker (1974) has noted, the mean IQs of different races are mostly related to per capita incomes and to cultural achievements. These facts are not really in dispute; their explanation, however, is. We must next turn to a survey of possible interpretations of the observed results.

CAUSES OF RACIAL IQ DIFFERENCES

Lynn (1978) listed five possible positions that have been taken by responsible writers and that deserve consideration. The first of these is that, "despite possible appearances to the contrary, all ethnic groups have much the same innate intelligence" (p. 277). As Lynn also pointed out, "It is not easy to find evidence to support this position" (p. 277). The point has been argued by Comas (1961) and Garth (1931). In a sense, this is a view often considered orthodox because it was enshrined in a statement issued by UNESCO (1951) to the effect that "According to present knowledge there is no proof that the groups of mankind differ in their innate mental characteristics, whether in respect of intelligence or temperament. The scientific evidence indicates that the range of mental capacities in all ethnic groups is much the same" (p. 58). A counterresolution, signed by 50 scientists, was published in the *American Psychologist* (Resolution, 1972), but of course, neither resolution is scientifically very relevant. Certainly, the UNESCO view finds no direct support in the figures quoted in the last section; for support, it would have to rely on special arguments and experiments.

A second point of view maintains that intelligence tests do not give valid measures of mental ability beyond the culture for which they were designed, and that hence mean IQs are not necessarily valid and meaningful measures of intelligence. There are obvious difficulties in this position, as Lynn (1978) has noted. If American and British IQ tests show Belgian, Danish, French, East German, New Zealand, and Australian populations to score at approximately the Anglo-American mean, why should not Spaniards, Yugoslavs, or Greeks do the same? How can it be that Mongoloids do better on Anglo-American IQ tests than Anglo-American populations? We shall return to a consideration of this argument later on.

A third position acknowledges the validity of IQ tests but explains the observed differences in IQ in terms of various environmental factors, such as standard of living, quality of education, general intellectual sophistication, and level of nutrition. There certainly are such correlations both within and between nations, but it still remains a moot point whether it is intelligence that causes a differential level of culture and income, or whether differences in income and culture cause variations in IQ.

The fourth position, taken by many who find the evidence insufficient in favor of the notion that environmental differences of the kind suggested above account for observed IQ differences, is that there may be unknown and perhaps quite subtle environmental differences that are responsible; climatic factors are sometimes suggested, or simply the consciousness of being a member of a minority race. Adherents of this view regard the question as completely open and incapable of being solved by existing techniques (Bodmer, 1972).

The fifth position would hold that no convincing environmentalistic explanations exist for the differences observed, and that consequently genetic factors should be appealed to for at least part of the observed differences. Jensen (1969, 1972, 1973) is perhaps the best-known exponent of this view, which, however, has a respectable ancestry (Woodworth, 1910; Porteus, 1917, 1937). These are the major competing views, and the continuing controversy suggests that none of them has clearly succeeded in convincing the majority.

We may perhaps reject some of the views stated above as being contrary to the evidence, or scientifically unhelpful. An appeal to hitherto unknown causes is not helpful because it is essentially untestable; we can never rule out environmental causes that are not specified sufficiently to be made the subject of an experimental enquiry. The view that intelligence tests are not valid is subject to investigation, and as stated above, the evidence does not suggest that this view can be taken very seriously. It does, however, serve to suggest certain possible tests of the environmental and the genetic views; if tests may be partly invalid because they are culture-bound, then differences between the results given by culture-bound and culture-fair tests may throw some light on the question of the environmental or the genetic determination of racial differences.

The first position described by Lynn (1978) may be amalgamated with this third position, namely, that differences in observed IQ means are due to specified environmental factors, without any genetic contributions; this may be contrasted with the fifth position, namely, that genetic factors do, in part, account for the observed IQ differences. The effective argument, therefore, is between a purely environmentalist explanation, which would account for existing differences in terms of educational, socioeconomic, and cultural factors, and a partly genetic explanation, which, although admitting the importance of such environmental factors, would also add genetic factors as contributory causes. We shall refer to these as the *environmental* and the *genetic hypotheses*, respectively, but it should always be remembered that the "genetic" hypothesis does, in fact, admit environmental causes as being at least partly responsible for observed differences. Furthermore, the "genetic" hypothesis postulates not that all observed differences are (partly) genetic, but only that some may be so; it is perfectly possible that genetic factors may account for some of the observed differences between American whites and blacks, but that the differences between Chinese and Malays in Singapore may be due to environmental factors entirely. Each observed difference must be judged in terms of the relevant evidence. It is to this evidence that we must next turn.

SPECIAL STUDIES

Theoretically, it might be thought that we have two ways of conducting specialized studies to decide between our two major hypotheses. One of these sets of studies might be genetic, looking at direct genetic evidence for or against the contribution of heredity to racial IQ differences. The other would be environmental, that is, conducting crucial studies of the influence of alleged environmental factors in the causation of such IQ differences. Unfortunately, we are effectively restricted to studies of the second kind; it is difficult, if not impossible, to think of or to conduct direct studies of a genetic nature in this field. The fact that differences in IQ within racial groups are largely determined by heredity is a necessary but not a sufficient reason for arguing in favor of heredity as a factor in cultural differences; it is clearly possible for differences *within* given cultures to be largely due to heredity, but for differences *between* cultures to be entirely due to environmental factors. Perhaps such a position would be unlikely, but the possibility cannot be ruled out.

Asking the question "Can we ... argue that genetic studies ... give *direct* support to the hereditarian position?" I have pointed out in my book *Race, Intelligence and Education* that "the answer must, I think, be in the negative. The two populations involved (black and white) are separate populations, and none of the studies carried out, such as twin studies, are feasible" (Eysenck, 1971, p. 117). This statement may not be entirely correct; thus, it has been suggested that possibly we could compare non-Caucasoid populations having different admixtures of Caucasoid heredity (De Lemos, 1969; Garth, 1931); a correlation between IQ and the degree of Caucasoid admixture might suggest a genetic determination of cross-cultural intellectual differences. Such a test would have to be controlled for environmental effects of racial characteristics, such as skin color, and in any case, we cannot rule out the possibility that those whites who crossbred with nonwhite partners differed in IQ from the mean for their own group. Thus, such a test would not be decisive.

Another alternative might be to test for heterosis, or "hybrid vigor"; on a genetic basis, one would expect that, if children were produced as the offspring of a marriage between partners belonging to two different races, the children should have a higher IQ than children produced from parents of the same racial stock and of the same mean intelligence as the cross-breeding parents. Unpublished work suggests that heterosis does in fact exist, and its existence would prove a powerful argument that the genetic determination of interracial differences in IQ is based on genetic factors. However, even here, it might be possible to advance environmentalist hypotheses, although these would, of course, be susceptible to direct study. Probably, heterosis is the only genetic effect that would provide powerful direct evidence of the existence of genetic factors in the causation of IQ differences, but apart from that, the existing evidence relies almost exclusively on direct studies of hypothetical environmental factors.

In the nature of the case, these can be only circumstantial; they can disprove specific environmentalist hypotheses, but they cannot establish directly the existence of genetic factors. The postulation of such factors must remain a residual assumption, based on the failure of alternative hypotheses of an environmentalist kind.

The obvious difficulty with this kind of argument is that the hypotheses put forward by environmentalists tend to be vague and imprecise; thus it is very difficult to disprove them. It is easy to appeal to such factors as underfeeding, but this can be broken down into innumerable subelements, including specified vitamin deficiencies and other defects that may occur even on the most ample European or American diet. Additionally, one can specify many different periods during which starvation may affect performance on IQ tests: *in utero*, immediately postnatally, in the first year, in the first five years, after long-continued malnutrition, and so on. A monograph edited by Lloyd-Still (1976) discusses many of the complexities of the problem. What often makes discussion difficult is the transfer of results from one universe of discourse to another, mediated simply by the single term *malnutrition*. Thus, the effects of defective glycos-aminoglycin concentrations due to kwashiorkor may be inadvertently transferred to a slightly subnormal food supply in American blacks because both may be grouped under the generic term *malnutrition*. In appealing to any single environmental cause, it should always be specified as clearly as possible just what it is that is being invoked. Long-continued malnutrition at starvation levels, which afflicts many underdeveloped areas of the world, may have effects that are strikingly absent from the slight degree of malnutrition found in advanced countries.

SOCIOECONOMIC STATUS AND EDUCATION

The first argument to be considered relates to a simple deduction from the environmentalist hypothesis. If differences in IQ between American blacks and whites are due entirely to such differences as socioeconomic status, schooling, housing, then a *relative improvement* on the part of the blacks over a number of years should reduce the observed difference. This argument was first presented in detail by McGurk (1953a), whose analysis of the data purported to show that improving the socioeconomic status of blacks *increased* the racial difference in intelligence performance. The same writer returned to the subject some 20 years later (McGurk, 1978) and analyzed the available literature in considerable detail. He was concerned with the differences in IQ between representative samples of blacks and whites, taken at various times between the 1917–1919 war and the present time, and with the percentage overlap between the races observed during these years. (*Overlap* is defined as that proportion of black subjects whose individual IQs equal or exceed the mean IQ of the white group with which the blacks are being compared.) The comparison is between black overlap shown in the publications of the past 20 years with black overlap in the World War I era. The studies were divided into two groups, Category A and Category B studies, with the Category B studies based more reasonably on representative data than those in Category A. The overlap in category B studies was 11%: in Category A studies, it was 23%. With a weighted mean of both groups together, the overlap was 16%. These figures, taken for the period 1951–1970, show no support of any change in overlap from the time of World War I, in spite of the tremendous improvement in the status of blacks documented by McGurk. He concluded by saying that

> at this moment, from the evidence since 1917–1919, it seems clear that there has been no measurable improvement in either the absolute or the relative intelligence of the negro.... Intellectually, the negro of today bears the same relationship to the contemporary white as did the negro of the World War One era to the white of that time. Socioeconomic changes have not resulted in a higher relative intellectual status for the negro. (pp. 33, 35)

It is, of course, open to environmentalists to argue along two lines. One is that the changes that occurred during the 30 years intervening between the original period of testing and the later period were not relevant to intellectual improvements of blacks. This is not an argument that can be regarded as very strong because it does not specify precisely what the changes should have been that might have had the effect of making the gap smaller. It should be remembered that in the World War I period, blacks were limited to certain specified residential sections of most cities, usually in undesirable parts of the town. Generally, blacks were congregated in rural areas, and the available schools were underequipped, understaffed, and often difficult to get to. Blacks were limited in general social participation; they were limited economically because there were only certain jobs open to them even when they lived in the city, and these jobs were mostly menial. The income of blacks was therefore markedly restricted, and compared with the present, there was undoubtedly strong cultural deprivation. Conditions have changed markedly since then, blacks now being mainly city dwellers, schools being completely accessible to them, and their attendance indeed being required under compulsory school-attendance laws. Neither is black employment any longer restricted; indeed, employment laws are now biased in favor of the black through "affirmative action" programs. If these changes, asked McGurk, have not produced any narrowing in the gap between black and white IQs, the environmentalist hypothesis certainly has a difficult task of explanation.

The second line open to environmentalists is to argue that many of the tests used were verbal, and that blacks are at a disadvantage in culturally biased tests of this kind. This argument is a very important one, and it is dealt with below. As far as this first deduction from the environmentalist hypothesis is concerned, we must conclude that the data tend to falsify it.

The second argument to be taken up here relates to the differences between American blacks and American whites observed on culture-bound, verbally weighted types of tests, as compared with nonverbal, "culture-fair" types of tests. If it is true that economic circumstances related to such factors as educational disadvantages as well as cultural deprivation generally, are responsible for the poor showing of blacks, then it would seem to follow inexorably that when whites and blacks are compared on culture-bound and culture-fair tests, blacks should do comparatively better on the culture-fair than on the culture-bound tests. McGurk analyzed results relevant to this question (1953b, 1978) and showed that verbally weighted test questions improved the blacks' test-scoring ability, as compared with whites. He listed a large number of relevant investigations, using many different tests. Table 1 gives an extract summary from McGurk, showing that, for each test or type of test used, there is greater overlap on the verbal than on the nonverbal subtests, the

TABLE 1
Degree of Overlap between Blacks and Whites on a Variety of Tests[a]

| | | Percentage overlap | | |
	N	Verbal	Nonverbal	Significance (%)
WISC data	1,692	18	14	1
WAIS data	506	19	16	10
Wechsler–Bellevue data	279	21	16	20
Miscellaneous data	1,202	19	14	1
Total	3,639	19	15	1

[a]From McGurk (1978), Table 7.

total for all different types of tests being 19% overlap for verbal and 15% overlap for nonverbal tests.

Describing the results in his Table 7, McGurk (1978) stated that

> for no test is the overlap for the non-verbal questions equal to or higher than the overlap for the verbal questions ... superiority of the negro's *verbal* scores over his non-verbal scores is significant beyond the 1% level. This is an absolute denial of the contention of many social scientists that verbal test material penalises the negro in his psychological test performance. (p. 161)

In another study, McGurk (1951) asked a panel of 78 judges, well qualified in psychology and sociology, to classify 226 items from a number of well-known standarized tests of general intelligence into one of three categories according to their degree of involvement of cultural factors. The 184 items on which there was the highest agreement among the judges as to their being most or least cultural were administered as a test to large numbers of white and black highschool pupils. It was found that the mean white–black difference on the test comprised of items classified as "least cultural" was almost twice as great as the mean white–black difference on the test comprised of items classified as "most cultural." Clearly there must be some property on which these two classes of items differed, besides their judged cultural loadings, that would account for this unexpected result. It can hardly be argued that the blacks were the more culturally advantaged group with respect to the item content of these traditional test items.

A similar result was reported by Jensen (1973), who administered two tests to white, black, and Mexican-American children from 6–12 years of age. One was the Peabody Picture Vocabulary Test (PPVT), a typical culture-bound test; the other was the Progressive Matrices, a typical culture-fair test. According to their socioeconomic status, the Mexican-Americans were bottom, the blacks intermediate, and the whites top. This ordering appeared in the PPVT IQ but not in the matrices scores; on the former, the blacks were clearly superior; on the latter, the Mexicans.

When children were equated with respect to their PPVT scores, then Mexican-Americans scored higher on the matrices than did the white or the black children; this scoring was consistent with the cultural deprivation hypothesis. But the blacks went in exactly the opposite direction: they scored lower than Mexican or whites. In other words, this combination of tests made it possible to demonstrate cultural effects on IQ (as shown by the results achieved by the Mexicans) but failed to demonstrate any such effects in the case of the blacks. Black pupils do better, relative to whites and Mexican-Americans, on the more culture-loaded than on the culture-fair test. It would seem very difficult to account for these findings about black children in purely environmental terms. Other studies reported by Jensen (1980a) give similar results; they suggest strongly that, although cultural and socioeconomic factors disadvantage Chicanos, they do not disadvantage blacks and may even have the opposite effect on the test scores of blacks. This deduction from the environmentalist hypothesis, too, therefore fails to make the correct predictions.

In a study by Reynolds and Gutkin (1981) to be described in detail later, blacks and whites were matched on four demographic variables, including SES. The results from a multivariate analysis of variance indicate that a significant discrepancy still existed between the performance of the black and the white groups on the WISC-R. Significant differences were found on every subtest with the exception of digit span, as well as on the more global indices (verbal, performance, and full-scale IQs). Whites exceeded blacks in each instance. The differences quite consistently ranged from .5 to .7 standard deviations. This finding again speaks against the environmentalist hypothesis because the study effectively equated black and white children on important demographic variables that, according to the environmentalist hypothesis, should account for most, if not all, of the observed differences. Yet, differences of around 9–10 points of IQ still remained even after such equalization.

Other investigators (e.g., Kaufman, 1973) have found similar results; summaries are given in Shuey (1966) and Tyler (1965). It is clear that equating for socioeconomic status and other important demographic differences only reduces black–white IQ differences by something like one-third of a standard deviation. In the Reynolds and Gutkin (1981) study, for instance, the full-scale IQ of the blacks was 87 and that of the whites 99, leaving a difference of 12 points instead of 15. This finding suggests that environmental changes bringing up the socioeconomic status of blacks to the level of whites would reduce the IQ difference by only 3 points.

It may, of course, be objected that the variables on which the groups were matched are not the truly important environmental variables, but such an objection encounters two difficulties. The first one is that traditionally it was precisely socioeconomic status—and all that follows from it by way of educational disadvantages and so on—that was cited as the main environmental cause of the black IQ deficit. The data fairly decisively disprove this original hypothesis.

Any alternative hypotheses would have to be much more precise than simply to vaguely suggest alternative environmental factors of a more subtle kind; the hypothesized factors would have to be indicated sufficiently clearly to make testing possible.

The other difficulty in such a view is that the observed change in IQ difference with socioeconomic status matching is in good accord with other indicators of the relative lack of importance of environmental factors in determining IQ differences. A good example is the study by Firkowska, Ostrowska, Sokolvoska, Stein, Susser, and Wald (1978), in which they studied the effects of IQ variability of the political decisions made in Poland with respect to the rebuilding of Warsaw after World War II. Completely egalitarian principles were used in allocating housing, educational, and medical facilities, in the hope that such policies would lead to a less varied distribution of intelligence. The outcome showed that these policies had little effect on the variability of IQ. The study is important because, in interpreting it, we are not faced with the difficulties of having to incorporate a rather imprecise variable, namely, racial consciousness; if strict equalization of opportunities and socioeconomic, educational, and medical background has little effect on the variance of IQ test scores, then clearly we should not have expected any very different results from the Reynolds and Gutkin study. The data, whichever way we look at them, can be accommodated within an environmentalist framework only by *ad hoc* hypotheses of a relatively imprecise and nontestable kind.

THE NATURE OF BLACK–WHITE IQ DIFFERENCES

The next argument is not unrelated to the preceding one and may be regarded in some ways as a generalization of it. It fundamentally concerns what Jensen (1980b) has called "Spearman's hypothesis." Spearman (1927) commented on a study involving 10 different mental tests administered to large samples of black and white American children, and he noted that the blacks, on the average, obtained lower scores than the whites on all 10 tests; he also noted, however, that the mean difference "was most marked in just those [tests] which are known to be most saturated with *g*" (p. 379). As Jensen (1980b) pointed out:

> Spearman's hypothesis that magnitudes of white-black mean differences on various mental tests are directly related to the tests' g loadings, if substantiated by subsequent studies, would be an important and unifying dis-

covery in the study of race differences in mental abilities. The Spearman hypothesis, if true, would mean that the white-black difference in test scores is not essentially attributable to idiosyncratic cultural or linguistic peculiarities in this or that test, but to a *general* factor that all mental tests measure in common, but which some tests measure to a greater degree than others.

Such a view would stand in marked contrast to findings that indicate that racial groups differ from one another in such a way that different mean profiles or patterns of measured abilities are obtained by different groups on batteries of different tests. An earlier study by Lesser, Fifer, and Clark (1965) showed distinctly different patterns of ability for 6- to 8-year-old Chinese, Jewish, black, and Puerto Rican children in New York City on tests of verbal, reasoning, number, and spatial abilities. The literature on the topic was summarized by Willerman (1979), and Jensen (1980a, pp. 729–736) discussed some of the inherent methodological problems involved in such studies. The main one of these is, of course, that if groups differ on general ability, and if different tests have different loadings on this general ability, the apparently differential patterning may reduce to nothing but an overall difference in *g*.

Jensen (1980b) has subjected this hypothesis to a statistical study, drawing on published data by others, as well as data collected by him and his students. In each of these studies, groups of blacks and whites were administered batteries of tests or test items; Jensen carried out factor analyses to determine the loadings of tests or items on the general factor for each test with the degree to which each test was able to differentiate the white and the black subject tested[1]. Table 2 gives a summary of Jensen's findings. In many cases, he was able to carry out independent factor analyses for the white and the black subjects, and in some cases, it was possible to do only a joint factor analysis. Fortunately, whenever factor analyses were done separately for whites and blacks, the results showed very high agreement; this finding speaks strongly against the second hypothesis given by Lynn (1978) to account for racial differences, namely, that tests give different results for members of different cultures. At least as far as American blacks and whites are concerned, the general finding is that factor analyses give practically identical results for these two groups.

[1]The method used by Jensen (and by Reynolds & Jensen, 1980, and Reynolds & Gutkin, 1981) is essentially an adaptation of the method of *criterion analysis* originally introduced by the writer (Eysenck, 1950) to aid in the testing of explicit hypotheses regarding the nature of a given factor and its relation to observed group differences.

TABLE 2
Correlation between g Loading and Black and White Differences on a
Variety of Intelligence Tests[a]

	Whites	Pooled	Blacks
Nichols (1972)	.69		.71
Hennessy and Merrifield (1976)		.74	
Osborne (1980) g_f	.56		.42
g_c	−.24		−.02
Veroff, McClelland, and Marquis (1971)	.66		.60
Jensen (1977)	.47		.62
Jensen (1980b): Children		.78	
Jensen (1980b): GATB		.88	

[a]From Jensen (1980b).

It will be seen that, for all the groups tested, the results were in favor of Spearman's hypothesis, with some very high correlations between g loading and the ability to differentiate between the racial groups. The only difference from this general pattern is found in the crystalized ability tests administered by Osborne, where no relationship was found. Jensen commented on the unsatisfactory nature of the tests used by Osborne, and in any case, Spearman's hypothesis applies to fluid rather than to crystalized ability. (It should be noted that the environmentalist hypothesis predicts the opposite relationship, that is, a positive correlation for crystallized ability tests and a zero correlation for fluid ability tests.) Thus, the data summarized by Jensen strongly support Spearman's hypothesis.

Two recent studies by Reynolds and Jensen (1980) and by Reynolds and Gutkin (1981) are relevant to this hypothesis. In the Reynolds and Jensen study, the WISC-R standardization sample of 2,200 children between the ages of 6 and 16½ years was used, a sample that contained 305 blacks. An attempt was made to match each of these children with a white child on the basis of age, sex, and full-scale IQ. Two hundred and seventy exact matches were made; thus, the matching procedure provided a more accurate, overall level-free picture of the differences in *pattern* of performance between whites and blacks. Each of the subtests of the WISC-R, in addition to measuring a general factor of ability, also reliably measured certain more distinct abilities: broad group factors and narrow abilities that are specific to each subtest (Kaufman, 1975).

Table 3 shows the means and standard deviations of the scaled scores of the matched white and black groups on each of the subtests of the WISC-R, the mean group difference ($D = $ white $\overline{X}$ − black $\overline{X}$,

TABLE 3

Performance on WISC-R Subtests of Groups of Blacks and Whites Matched
on WISC-R Full-Scale IQ[a]

| WISC-R variable | Whites | | Blacks | | | |
	$\overline{X}$	SD	$\overline{X}$	SD	D^b	F^c
Information	8.24	2.62	8.40	2.53	−.16	0.54
Similarities	8.13	2.78	8.24	2.78	−.11	0.22
Arithmetic	8.62	2.58	8.98	2.62	−.36	2.52*
Vocabulary	8.27	2.58	8.21	2.61	+.06	0.06
Comprehension	8.58	2.47	8.14	2.40	+.44	4.27**
Digit Span	8.89	2.83	9.51	3.09	−.62	6.03***
Picture Completion	8.60	2.58	8.49	2.88	+.11	0.18
Picture Arrangement	8.79	2.89	8.45	2.92	+.34	1.78*
Block Design	8.33	2.76	8.06	2.54	+.27	1.36
Object Assembly	8.68	2.70	8.17	2.90	+.51	4.41**
Coding	8.65	2.80	9.14	2.81	−.49	4.30**
Mazes	9.19	2.98	8.69	3.14	+.50	3.60**
Verbal IQ	89.61	12.07	89.63	12.13	−.02	0.04
Performance IQ	90.16	11.67	89.29	12.22	+.87	0.72
Full-Scale IQ	88.96	11.35	88.61	11.48	+.35	0.13

[a]From Reynolds and Jensen (1980).
[b]White $\overline{X}$ − black $\overline{X}$.
[c]$df. = 1,538.$
 *p ≤ .10.
 **p ≤ .05.
 ***p ≤ .01.

and the univariate F tests of the significance of the differences. Accuracy of the matching is indicated by the verbal, performance, and full-scale IQs, which are also shown in the table. A multivariate analysis of variance revealed with the patterns of the subtests' means differed significantly between whites and blacks. Blacks, it will be seen, did not earn significantly higher scores on the verbal subtests, contrary to the conclusions of Lesser *et al.* (1965) and Vance, Hankins, and McGee (1979); this finding indicates the need for controlling general level of intelligence. The data also fail to support claims of greater cultural bias in the verbal subtests of the WISC-R (Williams, 1974).

G factor loadings were obtained, although, because whites and blacks were intentionally matched on Wechsler full-scale IQ in this study, the Spearman hypothesis obviously cannot be completely tested with these data. However, one prediction was made from the Spearman hypothesis, namely, that for white and black samples so matched there should be a *negative* correlation between the absolute (i.e., unsigned) mean white–black differences on the subtests and their g loadings. The correlation turned out to be −.67, which is significant at the 1% level on a one-tailed test. Correction for unreliability lowered this correlation to −.64. The data therefore bear out Spearman's hypothesis.

Reynolds and Jensen drew attention to two further aspects of the data relevant to the environmentalist hypothesis regarding black–white differences. As they pointed out, the WISC-R information, vocabulary, and comprehension subtests are frequently singled out for accusations of blatant cultural bias against blacks, yet of these three subtests, only comprehension is relatively more difficult for blacks: "The three subtests on which blacks had the highest level of performance (arithmetic, digit span, and coding) also form a triad that is frequently referred to in the clinical literature as freedom from distractibility." Numerous studies (see Kaufman, 1979) indicate that performance on these three subtests is adversely affected by an increase in the subject's anxiety level. Many critics of intelligence testing contend that black children, because of their unfamiliarity with such situations, become inordinately anxious during the administration of an indivudual intelligence test, and that this anxiety partially accounts for the lower overall scores for these groups.[2] That black children earn their highest scores on those tests known to be the most disrupted by high anxiety levels argues strongly against the existence of any such effective mechanisms of bias against black children.

Reynolds and Gutkin's 1981 study matched 285 pairs of black and white chilren on the WISC-R on four demographic variables (sex, socioeconomic status, region of residence, and urban versus rural residence). Again, the Spearman hypothesis was tested by correlating g loadings against test differences between blacks and whites on each subtest, and a correlation of .53 was found, which is not dissimilar from the correlations given in the Reynolds and Jensen study. The authors concluded "the differences in g account for a substantial proportion of the observed differences in test performance of blacks and whites" (p. 119). It is apparent from these studies that g differences are not the only ones that occur; the Reynolds and Jensen study makes it clear that there is a strong black deficit in spatial visualization skills, for instance. What the studies do not support, how-

---

[2]The hypothesis that black children are more affected by anxiety than whites, and that this anxiety lowers their scores on tests of intellectual skills has been advocated by Minton and Schneider (1980) and Samuda (1975), among others.

ever, is the usual belief that the verbal subtests inappropriately penalize blacks; the data from Reynolds and Gutkin

> are clearly inconsistent with such an hypothesis. When rank-ordered by difficulty or degree of black-white score differences, the sub-tests show an almost perfect alternation of verbal test and non-verbal test. After correction for unreliability, four of the five most difficult tests were from the performance scale. (p. 179; see also Jensen & Reynolds, 1982)

The studies summarized here seem to indicate on the whole that, as Jensen (1980a) suggested, "with our present evidence and lack of any proper profile studies ... it would be difficult to make a compelling argument that blacks and whites differ on any abilities other than g in both its fluid and crystallised aspects" (p. 732). This statement could be reworded so as to say that whites and blacks show relatively small or nonexistent differences in Jensen's Level 1 ability, and marked differences in his Level 2 abilities. In other words, compared with whites, blacks show little impairment in associative learning ability, but considerable disability in conceptual learning and problem solving. Such a generalization, if true, is difficult to reconcile with an environmentalist hypothesis of the causation of the differences.

STUDIES FAVORING THE ENVIRONMENTALIST VIEW

The next argument has been presented by Eyferth (1959, 1961) and Eyferth, Brandt, and Hawel (1960). It has been accorded great weight by Flynn (1980), who argued as follows:

> Let us imagine what would constitute an ideal test of whether the I.Q. gap between black and white is environmental. Imagine that: a random selection of black men from America were transported to Germany, fathered children with a random sample of German women, and then were removed from the environment entirely, and a random sample of white men from America fathered children under exactly the same conditions. If the offspring of the black fathers and the offspring of the white fathers were found to have the same mean I.Q., this would constitute powerful evidence for an environmental hypothesis. (p. 84)

The Eyferth studies of the offspring of black and white occupation forces in Germany after World War II, born from late 1945 through 1953, were based on approximately 4,000 children of black fathers born during this period and constituted a reasonably representative sample of 5% of these children. These children were matched with a larger population in terms of age, sex, socioeconomic status of the mother or the foster parents, the number of siblings, the number of black children in the locale, type of schooling, and skin color. The total sample numbered 181, almost all of whom were from the lower class. They were compared with a control group of 83 white occupation children; one white child was included for every two black children in a particular locale. Eyferth also attempted to control for relevant variables, in particular the socio-economic circumstances of the mother and family.

A German version of the WISC was used, with the following results. White boys had a mean IQ of 101, white girls of 93; the overall mean was 97.2. Black boys had a mean IQ of 97, and black girls of 96; the overal mean was 96.5. Thus, the mean IQs of the two groups of children were virtually identical. These data, as they stand, do not suggest any important influence of the race of the father on the IQ of the offspring. Flynn noted a number of possible objections. The mothers were not a random sample of German women; the American fathers were not a random sample of American whites and blacks because the U.S. Armed Forces had used selection tests that had a much higher failure rate for blacks than for whites; a minority of the fathers were of French rather than of American origin. Flynn made a strong case to show that these objections are not, in fact, insuperable and do not damage the experiment sufficiently to make the results meaningless. On the face of it, therefore, the Eyferth studies constitute evidence that supports an environmentalist hypothesis.

One possible objection to taking these results too seriously, however, is Flynn's and Eyferth's failure to take into account heterosis, that is, the well-known "hybrid vigor" that increases the score of the offspring of interracial matings on traits or features involving dominant and recessive genes. IQ is known to involve almost complete dominance (Eysenck, 1979), and consequently, heterosis is a factor that would have increased the IQ of the children with black fathers but would have failed to do so for the children of white fathers. It is difficult to put this argument into a quantitative framework; the numbers involved are too small, in any case. It will be remembered that the difference in IQ between white boys and white girls in the Eyferth sample was 8 points and would almost certainly have arisen completely by chance. This means, conversely, that the failure of a large difference between black and white children to appear is compatible with a "true" difference of several points. The standard errors involved are simply too large to make any quantitative argument possible. We must conclude that the argument in favor of an environmental factor is strong but far from conclusive. What would be required to put it on a stronger footing would be (1) a testing of the total available population, rather than a small subsample, and (2) an investigation of the strength of heterosis effects as far as black–white marriages are concerned. Until such investigations are done, the argument remains inconclusive.

Flynn asked us to look at this study in conjunction with such other studies as those of Witty and Jenkins (1936), in which little relationship was found between IQ and degree of white admixture, and of Scarr, Pakstis, Katz, and Barker (1977), which shows the absence of a relationship between degree of white ancestry and intellectual skills within a black population. Flynn was aware of the objections to both studies, and until the former is replicated and the latter can deal with the objections raised by Loehlin, Vandenberg, and Osborn (1973), we can only regard these studies as equally inconclusive.

ADOPTION STUDIES

Adoption studies give us another example of what Flynn (1980) regarded as "direct" evidence in the nature–nurture controversy, as opposed to the "indirect" evidence presented in the first four arguments listed here. He put particular stress on the Scarr and Weinberg (1976) study of 101 families living in the state of Minnesota who collectively had 321 children 4 years of age and older, of whom 145 were natural children and 176 were adopted children. All the adoptive parents were white, and all had adopted at least one nonwhite child. The major results of the study are given in Table 4.

The aim of the study was to assess the development of the IQ of black children raised in white home environments, and as Flynn pointed out, "therefore, this study falls within our category of direct

TABLE 4
Comparison of Adopted Children by Race[a]

Race of parents	N	IQ	Age at adoption (months)	Time in adoptive home (months)
Black–black	29	96.8	32.3	42.2
Asian and Indian	21	99.9	60.7	63.8
Black–white	68	109.0	8.9	60.6
White–white	25	111.5	19.0	104.2

[a]From Scarr and Weinberg (1976).

evidence on race and I.Q. although we must remember that it cannot simulate a total shift of environments for a variety of reasons" (p. 89). The data undoubtedly show a shift upward in the I.Q. of the black–black (both parents black) and black–white (one parent black: one, white) children, due no doubt to the excellence of the adoptive homes: the adoptive parents were above average in level of education and had a mean IQ of 120.

As regards the black–black children, the most likely expected IQ would be something like 89, thus suggesting that the adoption raised their IQ by about 8 points. The black–white children did appreciably better, and Flynn focused his argument on them. It is doubtful whether the data can bear the burden of his argument, however. The possibility that the admixture of white ancestry could have had a positive effect cannot be ruled out, and the possibility of heterosis is an ever-present one; hybrid vigor could have raised the black–white IQ level significantly above the black–black level. Nevertheless, one has to agree that the data suggest strong environmental effects, as the black–white figures are fairly close to the white–white figures. (The natural children of the adoptive parents had a mean IQ of 116.7.)

Studies along similar lines, on which Flynn placed much confidence, are by Tizard (1974), Tizard, Cooperman, Joseph, and Tizard (1972), and Tizard and Rees (1974). These deal with children of West Indian parents in England who were sent to long-stay residential nurseries. The first group of children tested were aged from 24 to 59 months, lived in the nursery at least 6 months, had a healthy medical record, and were not considered handicapped by their doctors. There were 85 of these children, all illegitimate, and most had been admitted to the residential nursery as infants, 86% of them before the age of 24 months. The second group tested were all the available children aged 4.5 years who had been admitted to any of the residential nurseries of three voluntary societies by the age of 4 months and had remained there until at least the age of 2 years. There were 64 of these, and at the time of testing, 25 were still living in the nurseries, 24 had been adopted, and 15 had been restored to their natural mothers.

The general findings can be summarized by saying that, in the first group, the white–white children did less well than the black–white and black–black children, who had essentially similar scores on the Reynell Comprehension, the Reynell Expression, and the Minnesota Non-Verbal Tests. The scores were rather variable, with the differences between the groups averaging about 4 or 5 points. In the second group also, the white–white children did less well than the black–white or the black–black children. Flynn suggested that the good quality of the institutions in question and their equalizing influence were responsible for the results. It is difficult to see why these factors should produce higher IQs among black–white and black–black children, but above all, it must be very doubtful whether so-called IQ tests adapted for children under the age of 6 really measure anything we would call *intelligence;* the prediction of adult IQ from baby tests is notoriously poor (Eysenck, 1979), and this fact must undermine any interpretation of these data. It is to be hoped that the children will be retested at the age of 10 or older; these figures should tell us a great deal about the actual effects of early nursery education. Failing such follow-up, one can regard the data as intriguing and challenging, at best; they certainly fail to disprove the possibility of genetic differences.

MISCELLANEOUS ARGUMENTS

We must now turn to a miscellaneous group of arguments that have often been made, but that are now of little interest because they seem to have been fairly decisively settled. The first of these is the question of the race of the tester: It has been suggested that blacks may do poorly on IQ tests because white testers may make them nervous, produce inferiority feelings, reduce motivation, and in other ways sabotage their efforts. There are now some 30 studies to show that, although the personality of the examiner may have some slight effect, he or his color does not; in the overall results, there is no evidence that white examiners cause black children to do less well than black examiners, or that black examiners cause white children to do less well then white examiners (Jensen, 1980a).

Another effect that has been suggested as producing racial differences is the so-called Pygmalion effect. In their book, *Pygmalion in the Classroom*, Rosenthal and Jacobson (1968) suggested that low performance of pupils on IQ tests resulted from teachers' expectations; these in turn came from considerations of the pupils' race or social class and other sociological and biological background variables. This hypothesis has achieved wide acceptance, but these authors' method of collecting data and their analysis of these data have been discredited by competent critics, and many studies carried out to replicate their findings have failed to do so. On the basis of present evidence, we must disregard the Pygmalion effect on IQ as unproven (Eysenck, 1979).

We have already referred to the frequent suggestion that black children may be unduly anxious in taking IQ tests, and that this anxiety may be reflected in low scores. The evidence quoted above from the Reynolds and Jensen (1980) study, showing that black children earn their highest scores on those tests known to be the most disrupted by high anxiety levels, argues strongly against the existence of any such affective mechanisms of bias against black children. This hypothesis, too, must therefore be rejected as being contrary to the evidence. The Reynolds and Gutkin (1981) study, giving similar results, further supports this conclusion.

Another argument often put forward is that the well-known Heber studies, in which extraordinary efforts were made to upgrade the IQs of prospectively low IQ black babies, demonstrate the absence of genetic racial effects (Garber & Heber, 1981). The many criticisms made of this study (Eysenck, 1979) would make such a conclusion impossible, and in any case, the amount of improvement achieved was just within the limits of the 20% environmental influence allowed for by the genetic-environmental interaction hypothesis.

Another argument frequently put forward is that populations in deprived cultures lack test practice or test sophistication. Lloyd and Pidgeon (1961) attempted to test this hypothesis using European, Negroid and Indian children in South Africa. They found that, after coaching on the principles of the tests, the European children gained 10.6 points, the Negroid children 14.6 points, and the Indian children 6.1 points. The authors believe that these differences showed that the tests were not culture-fair, but as Lynn (1978) pointed out:

> This inference does not seem to follow. It is not part of the theory of culture-fair tests that the principles involved in the problems cannot be acquired by coaching. In this study, on first testing, the European children obtained a mean IQ of 103, and the Negroid and Indian children a mean I.Q. of 87. The point here is that the European children were better at seeing the principles of the tests for themselves when the test was first given. And even after the principles of the test had been explained, the European children still scored substantially higher on the test, and the gap was hardly diminished. One conclusion indicated by this study is that neither practice nor coaching do [sic] much to reduce the superiority of children of Northern European origin on intelligence tests. (p. 279)

Many other alleged sources of bias are discussed in Jensen's book (1980a), and it would be a task of supererogation to repeat his arguments. On the whole, it must be said that the biases alleged so frequently to exist and to make comparison between blacks and whites impossible have not been demonstrated in actual experimental studies, and that, until they are, such comparisons must remain meaningful and interpretable.

FUTURE RESEARCH

Having now surveyed the major arguments in favor of the different positions, we may ask ourselves some questions about the direction of future research. There are two major ways in which such research may be conducted. The first, and the most obvious, is of course the continuation of research along the lines already pioneered, but with improvements of the kind occasionally suggested during the discussion of the various lines of research. For example, many of the studies could benefit greatly by having larger numbers of subjects, although the difficulty of obtaining the proper subjects must be freely acknowledged. Another desirable improvement would be for researchers to obtain far more information on environmental factors related to socioeconomic status, particularly the actual intellectual atmosphere within given families and the amount of verbal interaction between mother and child. Another improvement would be for researchers to take into account factors such as heterosis and, if possible, to obtain quantitative estimates of the amount of heterosis actually present in given black–white or other cross-culture matings. The list of such improvements is almost endless, and no doubt future reserach will benefit from the criticisms made of past work. However, something more is clearly needed if we are to have any semblance of consensus on these matters.

What is needed most of all, as has been pointed out several times before, is for the environmentalists to state their hypotheses in a clear, concise, and testable manner. In the past, what has happened has been that faith has been placed in such factors as socioeconomic status and educational facilities. As research demonstrated that these factors were of relatively minor importance, *ad hoc* alternative hypotheses were suggested, often in so nebulous a form that no proper testing could be carried out. It seems desirable for those who maintain a 100% environmentalist hypothesis to realize that the burden of proof is on them, and that it is they who are required not only to state hypotheses, but also to demonstrate that these can carry the burden put upon them. The complete rejection of any form of genetic hypothesis on the basis of hypothetical and rather nebulous environmental factors is not the best way to carry out a scientific attack on this very complex and difficult problem. Both sides of the controversy must recognize that there are anomalies and difficulties attached to to their positions and must attempt to resolve these, in harmonious joint research, if possible. Taking up adversary positions, as has so often been done in the past, is appropriate to legal, not scientific, disputes.

Although fully agreeing that such improvements in present-day types of research would be useful and desirable and would undoubtedly throw much light on the subject, the present author feels that an alternative approach has even more to offer. In the nature of things, the use of tests that are inevitably culture-laden, even if to varying degrees, must lead to very complex experimental designs and statistical arguments, and whether agreement can ever be reached on such a basis has seemed doubtful to many knowledgeable observers. An alternative might be to search for noncognitive tests of cognitive ability, that is, tests that are not subject to the limitations of orthodox IQ tests, but that measure fundamental and possibly genotypic properties of the nervous system directly. There is a long history of such tests, beginning with Sir Francis Galton, who suggested the use of simple reaction times. The writer (Eysenck, 1981) has given a brief account of such measures and has in particular suggested the use of psychophysiological measures of intelligence, basing this suggestion on the obvious corollary of the genetic determination of individual differences in intelligence, namely, that such differences must ultimately be based on anatomical, physiological, and biochemical differences in the CNS.

In contrast to earlier studies, more recent work has shown that measures of reaction times (particularly complex reaction-time measures and measures of variability of reaction time) can give good correlations with IQ and that the use of inspection time measures (using backward masking techniques) has given spectacularly high correlations of .80 or thereabouts with IQ (Eysenck, 1981). Similar work has been reported by Lehr (1980), Lehr, Gallwitz, and Blaha (1980), and Lehr, Straub, and Straub (1975), on a different kind of inspection task. Such tests could form the basis of a study of cross-cultural differences independent of educational and cultural factors or of socioeconomic status.

The early studies of Bastendorf (1960) on palmar skin conductance, of Barratt, Clark, and Lipton (1962) on critical flicker frequency, and of Ertl and Schafer (1969) on latency of evoked potentials all have given positive results that indicate that significant correlations between psychometric intelligence and physiological measures exist.

None of these approaches has proved practically useful because the correlations, although interesting, are not high enough so that any of these measures can be used directly in cross–cultural studies (inspection time techniques excepted). Furthermore, there is little in the way of theory to integrate them with what is known about intelligence. The situation has changed through the work of Hendrickson and Hendrickson (1980), who proposed a theory of information processing through the cortex, and who derived from it a physiological measure, using the auditory evoked potential, which differs from the usual latency and amplitude measures. Essentially, the theory maintains that, when information is processed through the cortex, errors occur (probably at the synapse), and that there are individual differences in error-proneness that lead to differences in IQ in the sense that the higher the IQ, the lower the error-proneness of the individual. Because evoked potentials (because of their poor signal-to-noise ratio) tend to be averaged over a number of time-locked trials, individuals who are error-prone tend to produce averaged potentials (AEP), which lose some of the complexity that is preserved by subjects who are less error-prone; consequently, the measure of compexity (or of intrasubject variability) could be used as a direct index of error-proneness, and hence of IQ.

A recent study of 219 schoolchildren by Hendrickson (1982) gave a correlation of the WISC with evoked potential measures of .83 and a factor analysis of the 11 Wechsler subtests, together with the evoked-potential measures, showed that, on the general factor of intelligence, the evoked potential had a loading of .91, much higher than any of the individual Wechsler scales. Tests of adult subgroups gave similar results, and it would seem that we have here a physiological measure that measures intellectual ability better than traditional tests, and without contamination by educational, cultural, or social factors of the kind that partly determine success on traditional IQ tests (Eysenck, 1981, Eysenck & Barrett, in preparation).

The use of such tests together, perhaps, with inspection time and some reaction time measures, would give us an index of intelligence much closer to the genotype than traditional IQ tests, and such a battery of tests could therefore be used with great advantage to settle some of the questions that have been raised about cross-cultural differences. The writer has suggested a paradigm that would govern such research (Eysenck, 1981). Consider two populations, differing in race or socioeconomic status. Let us suppose that the difference between the two groups is one standard deviation on the Wechsler, Binet, or some other IQ test. Let us now test the two groups by means of the AEP, the inspection time, or the reaction time paradigm. Assuming that variance on the Wechsler test is contaminated to the extent of 20% by environmental factors, whereas the AEP is a pure measure of genotype (or almost so), we should be able to predict the observed difference on the AEP, all differences, of course, being expressed in standard scores. We would predict a *reduction* in standard score difference on the AEP, corresponding to the loss of enviornmental determination present in the traditional test, and the loss could be quantitatively predicted with some degree of accuracy. In a preliminary study (Eysenck, 1982), the writer has indeed found that a predicted reduction in differentiation between two SES groups occurred at a high level of significance. No work on different racial groups has as yet been reported.

Such a design should enable us to test directly the conclusions derived by Jensen (1973) from his study of 1,703 white, Mexican-American, and black schoolchildren in California, using the culture-fair Raven's Matrices and the culture-biased Peabody Picture Vocabulary Test. Jensen argued that "California Orientals bear a similar relationship to whites as the Mexicans bear to the Negroes, that is, a higher average genotype and lower average environmental advantages" (p. 312). Translated into the terms of a comparison of group differences on IQ and AEP measures, this suggests that as compared to whites, Orientals and Mexicans would show *smaller* differences on AEP than on IQ, whereas Negroes would show *larger* differences. Such a study, given a proper selection of cases, would be well within the realm of possibility at the present time, and it would undoubtedly throw new light on this whole controversy.

SUMMARY AND CONCLUSIONS

It is difficult, if not impossible, to summarize a discussion that is itself a summary of a very large and disputatious literature. However, certain generalizations may be made with some confidence:

1. There is no doubt that differences in IQ exist between different racial groups, and also within single racial or even national groups.

2. Some of these differences, particularly insofar as they occur within fairly homogeneous national groups, are probably due to

emigration, but this theory is less likely to account for cross-cultural differences.

3. There is a general decline of IQ mean scores, ranging from the Mongoloid races, particularly the Chinese and the Japanese, through Northern European Caucasoids and their descendants, to Southern European Caucasoids and Indians, to Malays and Negroid groups. In each case, it should, of course, be remembered that, even within a given racial group, there may be, and frequently are, differences between one subgroup and another.

4. There is a close correlation between the IQ level of given groups, their socioeconomic status, and their degree of cultural achievement. Neither the fact of the observed differences nor the correlation with SES and cultural achievement tells us anything directly about the direction of the causal arrow: that can only be determined by special experimental studies.

5. The major hypotheses in the field are the environmental hypothesis (which states, essentially, that all human races, ethnic subgroups, and nations are genetically equal in intelligence, and that all observed differences are due to environmental factors of one kind or another) and the interactionist hypothesis (which states that genetic as well as environmental causes are active in producing differences in IQ between different groups).

6. Direct experimental evidence regarding genetic factors is lacking and may be impossible to obtain. The observation of heterosis effects (hybrid vigor) might constitute an exception to this rule, but other suggested methods have not been found acceptable by competent critics.

7. We are thus left with circumstantial evidence, depending largely on the testing of specific environmental hypotheses, such as the effects of the race of the examiner, of socioeconomic status, of nutrition, of educational facilities, or of other environmental factors. Insofar as these can be shown to be effective in producing differences, the environmentalist hypothesis is strengthened; insofar as they can be shown to be inoperative, or less powerful then expected, the interactionist hypothesis is strengthened. Clearly, a quantitative analysis of effects is of the essence; the interactionist would expect, like the environmentalist, that these factors have some effect; he or she would merely expect that the effect does not account for all of the observed differences.

8. Some of the facts that seem to contraindicate a purely environmentalist hypothesis are that there seems to have been no change in overlap between American blacks and whites over the last 50 or 60

years, in spite of a relative improvement of the educational and socio-economic position of the blacks; that blacks do better, or at least not worse, on verbal and culture-bound tests than they do on culture-fair tests; that the differentiation between American blacks and whites seems to be highest on tests having the highest g loadings and poorest on those having the lowest g loading; that even matching for socioeconomic status leads to only a slight lessening of the differences between American blacks and whites; and that, on tests made by white middle-class psychologists, nonwhite, non-middle-class populations of Chinese or Japanese origin actually do better than the white populations for whom the tests were originally made. Thus, Chinese children in Singapore had a mean score of 110 IQ points on the British-made Matrices Test, although the average per capita income in Singapore was less than half that in Great Britain, and less than a fifth that in the United States (at the time the children were born). At the same time, Malays attending the same schools had an IQ of 96, although not apparently differing from the Chinese in educational facilities or SES (Lynn, 1977a).

9. The environmentalists' position is difficult to support because it requires proof of the absence of genetic effects, which is methodologically an extremely difficult thing to obtain. Thus, even studies that have been cited as supporting the environmentalist position, such as studies of children fathered by black and white American groups in Germany, or studies of adopted children of black and white parentage, show only that there is some environmental effect; they cannot exclude genetic effects.

10. This methodological difficulty is compounded by the fact that environmentalist hypotheses are seldom stated in an unambiguous, specific, and testable manner. Such precision of statement is a *sine qua non* of the proper scientific investigation of a given theory.

11. It is suggested that, although no certain conclusions can be drawn from the evidence so far available, the trend of the results reported is, on the whole, in favor of some form of genetic differentiation between racial groups, responsible for some but certainly not all of the observed differences. Quantitative estimates of the degree of genetic involvement are hazardous in the extreme, and none are attempted here.

12. It is suggested that future work follow two lines. One is to improve the existing paradigms, to use larger numbers, to improve the rigor of the design, and to collect more detailed and relevant data. The alternative (or, more likely, complementary) method would be to make use of the recent studies that directly measure the underly-

ing physiological properties of the CNS closely related to IQ. The burden of the discussion is that those who declare the problem to be ultimately insoluble are wrong, and that methods exist that could give us a satisfactory answer if they were applied with sufficient rigor. The fact that at present no definitive answer exists does not contradict this belief. Perhaps the best final word at the moment is a quotation from Sir Francis Bacon: "If a man will begin with certainties he shall end in doubts; but if he will be content to begin with doubts, he shall end in certainties."

REFERENCES

Alzobaie, A. J. The validity of the Goodenough Draw-a-Man Test in Iraq. *Journal of Experimental Education*, 1965, *33*, 331–335.

Baker, J. R. *Race*. London: Oxford University Press, 1974.

Barratt, E. S., Clark, M., & Lipton, J. Critical flicker frequency in relation to a culture fair measure of intelligence. *American Journal of Psychology*, 1962, *75*, 324–325.

Bastendorf, W. L. *Activation level, as measured by palmar conductance, and intelligence in children*. Unpublished Ph.D. thesis, Claremont Graduate School, 1960.

Berry, J. W. Temne and Eskimo perceptual skills. *International Journal of Psychology*, 1966, *1*, 207–229.

Block, N. J., & Dworkin, G. (Eds.). *The I.Q. controversy*. New York: Pantheon, 1976.

Bodmer, W. F. Race and I.Q.: The genetic background. In K. Richardson & D. Spears (Eds.), *Race, culture and intelligence*. Harmondsworth, England: Penguin Books, 1972.

Bourdier, G. Utilisation et nouvel étalonnage du PM47. *Bulletin de Psychologie*, 1964, *235*, 39–41.

Byrt, E., & Gill, P. *The standardization of a non-verbal reasoning test and vocabulary test for the Irish population aged 6–12 years*. Report to the Minister of Education, 1975.

Cattell, R. B. *Abilities: Their structure, growth and action*. Boston: Houghton Mifflin, 1971.

Chan, J. Intelligence and intelligence tests in Hong Kong. *New Horizon*, 1974, *15*, 82–88.

Coleman, J. S., *et al. Equality of educational opportunity*. Washington, D.C.: U.S. Office of Education, 1966.

Comas, J. "Scientific" racism again? *Current Anthropology*, 1961, *2*, 303–314.

Darlington, C. D. *The evolution of man and society*. New York: Simon & Schuster, 1969.

Davies, M., & Hughes, A. G. An investigation into the comparative intelligence and attainments of Jewish and non-Jewish school children. *British Journal of Psychology*, 1927, *18*, 134–146.

De Lemos, M. The development of conservation in aboriginal children. *International Journal of Psychology*, 1969, *4*, 253–269.

Du Chateau, P. Ten point gap in Maori aptitudes. *National Education*, 1967, *49*, 157–158.

Eckberg, D. L. *Intelligence and race*. New York: Praeger, 1979.

Ertl, J. P., & Schafer, E. W. P. Brain response correlates of psychometric intelligence. *Nature*, 1969, *223*, 421–422.

Eyferth, K. Eine Untersuchung der Neger-Mischlingskinder in Westdeutchland. *Vita Humana*, 1959, *2*, 104–105.

Eyferth, K. Leistungen verschiedener Gruppen von Besatzungskindern im Hamberg-Wechsler Intelligenztest für Kinder (HAWIK). *Archiv für die Gestamte Psychologie*, 1961, *113*, 223–231.

Eyferth, K., Brandt, V., & Hawel, W. *Farbige Kinder in Deutschland*. Munich: Juventa Verlag, 1960.

Eysenck, H. J. Criterion analysis—An application of the hypothetic-deductive method to factor analysis. *Psychological Review*, 1950, *57*, 38–53.

Eysenck, H. J. *Race, intelligence and education*. London: Temple Smith, 1971. (U.S. title: *The I.Q. Argument*. New York: The Library Press.)

Eysenck, H. J. *The structure and measurement of intelligence*. London: Springer, 1979.

Eysenck, H. J. The psychophysiology of intelligence. In C. D. Spielberger & J. N. Butcher (Eds.), *Advances in personality assessment*. Hillsdale, N.J.: Lawrence Erlbaum, 1981.

Eysenck, H. J. (Ed.). *A model for intelligence*. New York: Springer, 1982.

Eysenck, H. J., & Barrett, P. Psychophysiology and the measurement of intelligence. In C. R. Reynolds & V. L. Willson (Eds.), *Methodological and statistical advances in the study of individual differences*. New York: Plenum Press, in preparation.

Fatouros, M. The influence of maturation and education on the development of mental abilities. In L. J. Cronback & P. J. D. Drenth (Eds.), *Mental tests and cultural adaptation*. The Hague: Mouton, 1972.

Firkowska, A., Ostrowska, A., Sokolvoska, M., Stein, Z., Susser, M., & Wald, I. Cognitive development and social policy. *Science*, 1978, *200*, 1357–1362.

Flynn, J. R. *Race, I.Q. and Jensen*. London: Routledge & Kegan Paul, 1980.

Garber, H. L., & Heber, R. Preventing mental retardation in children at risk. In C. R. Reynolds & T. B. Gutkin (Eds.), *The handbook of school psychology*. New York: Wiley, 1981.

Garth, T. R. *Race psychology*. New York: McGraw-Hill, 1931.

Gillie, O. *Who do you think you are?* New York: Saturday Review Press, 1976.

Goosens, G. Une application du test d'intelligence de R. B. Cattell. (Echelle 2, Forme A). *Revue Belge de Psychologie et de Pedagogie*, 1952, *14*, 115–124.

Guilford, J. P., & Hoepfner, R. *The analysis of intelligence*. New York: McGraw-Hill, 1971.

Halsey, A. H. (Ed.). *Heredity and environment*. London: Methuen, 1977.

Hendrickson, E. The biological basis of intelligence. Part II: Measurement. In H. J. Eysenck (Ed.), *A model for intelligence*. New York: Springer, 1982.

Hendrickson, D. E., & Hendrickson, A. E. The biological basis of individual differences in intelligence. *Personality and Indivdual Differences*, 1980, *1*, 3–33.

Hennessy, J. J., & Merrifield, P. R. A comparison of the factor structures of mental abilities in four ethnic groups. *Journal of Educational Psychology*, 1976, *68*, 754–759.

Hirsch, N. D. M. A study of natio-racial mental differences. *Genetic Psychology Monographs*, 1926, *1*, 231–406.

Johoda, G. Assessment of abstract behaviour in a non-Western culture. *Journal of Abnormal and Social Psychology*, 1956, *53*, 237–243.

Jensen, A. R. How much can we boost IQ and scholastic achievement? *Harvard Educational Review*, 1969, *39*, 1–123.

Jensen. A. R. *Genetics and education*. London: Methuen, 1972.

Jensen, A. R. *Educability and group differences*. London: Methuen, 1973.

Jensen, A. R. An examination of culture-bias in the Wonderlic Personnel Test. *Intelligence*, 1977, *1*, 51–64.

Jensen, A. R. *Bias in mental testing*. New York: Free Press, 1980. (a)

Jensen, A. R. *The nature of the average difference between white and blacks on psychometric tests: Spearman's hypothesis*. Unpublished paper, 1980. (b)

Jensen, A. R., & Reynolds, C. R. Race, social class and ability patterns on the WISC-R. *Personality and Individual Differences*, 1982, *3*, 423–438.

Kamin, L. J. *The science and politics of I.Q.* London: Wiley, 1974.

Kaufman, A. S. Comparison of the performance of matched groups of black children and white children on the Wechsler Preschool and Primary Scale of Intelligence. *Journal of Consulting and Clinical Psychology*, 1973, *41*, 186–191.

Kaufman, A. S. Factor analysis of the WISC-R at eleven age levels between 6½ and 16½ years. *Journal of Consulting and Clinical Psychology*, 1975, *43*, 135–143.

Kaufman, A. S. Intelligence Testing with the WISC-R. New York: Interscience, 1979.

Kirby, A. A critical comment on "The social ecology of intelligence in the British Isles." *British Journal of Social and Clinical Psychology*, 1980, *19*, 333–336.

Klingelhofer, E. L. Performance of Tanzanian secondary school pupils on the Raven Progressive Matrices Test. *Journal of Psychology*, 1967, *72*, 205–215.

Koestler, A. *The 13th tribe*. London: Hutchinson, 1976.

Kurth, E. von. Erhöhung der Leistungsnormen bei den farbigen progressiven Matrizen. *Zeitschrift für Psychologie*, 1969, *177*, 86–90.

Lawler, J. *Intelligence, genetique, racisme*. Paris: Editions Sociales, 1978.

Lehr, S. Subjectives Zeitquant als missing link zwischen Intelligenz-psychologie und Neurophysiologie? *Grundlegenstudien aus Kybernetik und Geisteswissenschaften*, 1980, *21*, 107–116.

Lehr, S., Straub, B., & Straub, R. Infornationspsychologische Elementarabzugsteine der Intelligenz. *Grundlagenstudien aus Kybernetik und Geisteswissenschaften*, 1975, *16*, 41–50.

Lehr, S., Gallwitz, A., & Blaha, L. *Kurztest für allgemeine Intelligenz KAI: Manual*. Munich, Vless, 1980.

Lesser, G. S., Fifer, G., & Clark, D. H. Mental abilities of children from different social-class and cultural groups. *Monograph of the Society for Research in Child Development*, 1965, *30*(4).

Liungman, C. *What is I.Q.?* London: Anchor Press, 1972.

Lloyd, F., & Pidgeon, D. A. An investigation into the effects of coaching on non-verbal test material with European, Indian and African children. *British Journal of Educational Psychology*, 1961, *31*, 145–151.

Lloyd-Still, J. D. (Ed.). *Malnutrition and intellectual development*. Lancaster: M.T.P., 1976.

Loehlin, J. C., Vandenberg, S. G., & Osborne, R. T. Blood group genes and Negro-white ability differences. *Behavior Genetics*, 1973, *3*, 263–270.

Loehlin, J. C., Lindzey, G., & Spuhler, J. N. *Race differences in intelligence*. San Francisco: W. H. Freeman, 1975.

Lynn, R. The intelligence of the Chinese and Malyas in Singapore. *Mankind Quarterly*, 1977, *18*, 125–128.(a)

Lynn, R. Selective emigration and the decline of intelligence in Scotland. *Social Biology*, 1977, *24*, 173–182.(b)

Lynn, R. Ethnic and racial differences in intelligence: International comparisons. In R. T. Osborne, C. E. Noble, N. Weyl (Eds.), *Human variation*. New York: Academic Press, 1978.

Lynn, R. The social ecology of intelligence in the British Isles. *British Journal of Social and Clinical Psychology*, 1979, *18*, 1–12.

Lynn, R. The social ecology and intelligence in France. *British Journal of Social and Clinical Psychology*, 1980, *19*, 325–331.

MacArthur, R. S. Some cognitive abilities of Eskimo, white, and Indian-Metis pupils aged 9 to 12 years. *Canadian Journal of Behavioral Sciences*, 1969, *1*, 50–59.

MacKay, D. N. Mental subnormality in Northern Ireland. *Journal of Mental Deficiency Research*, 1971, *15*, 12–19.

Mackay, D., & McCoy, M. Long-term emigration and subnormality: A connection? *The Journal of Psychological Research in Mental Subnormality*, 1975, *1*, 47–57.

Maity, H. A report on the application of the Stanford adult test to a group of college students. *Indian Journal of Psychology*, 1926, *1*, 214–222.

McElwain, D. W., & Kearney, G. E. Intellectual development. In G. E. Kearney *et al.* (Eds.), *The psychology of Aboriginal Australians*. New York: Wiley, 1973.

McGurk, F. C. J. *Comparison of the performance of Negro and white high-school seniors on cultural and non-cultural psychological test questions*. Washington, D.C.: Catholic University Press, 1951 (microcard).

McGurk, F. C. J. On white and Negro test performance and socio-economic factors. *Journal of Abnormal and Social Psychology*, 1953, *48*, 448–450. (a)

McGurk, F. C. J. Socioeconomic status and culturally-weighted test scores of Negro subjects. *Journal of Applied Psychology*, 1953, *37*, 276–277. (b)

McGurk, F. C. J. Race differences—20 years later. Torrance, Calif.: Noontide Press (International Association for the Advancement of Ethnology and Eugenics), 1978.

McIntyre, G. A. *The standardisation of intelligence tests in Australia*. Melbourne: University Press, 1938.

McNemar, Q. Lost our intelligence: Why? *American Psychologist*, 1964, *19*, 871–882.

Mehryar, A. H., Shapurian, R., & Bassiri, T. A preliminary report on a Persian adaptation of Heim's AH4 test. *Journal of Psychology*, 1972, *80*, 167–180.

Minton, H. L., & Schneider, F. W. *Differential psychology*. Monterey, Calif.: Brooks/Cole, 1980.

Nichols, P. L. *The effects of heredity and environment on intelligence test performance in 4 and 7 year old white and Negro sibling pairs*. Unpublished doctoral dissertation, University of Minnesota, 1972.

Nieto-Alegre, S., Navarro, L., Santa Cruz, G., & Domínguez, A. Diferencias regionales en la medida de la inteligencia con el test M.P. *Revista de Psicologia General y Aplicado*, 1967, *22*, 699–707.

Osborne, R. T. *Twins: Black and white*. Athens, Ga.: Foundation for Human Understanding, 1980.

Pintner, R. *Intelligence testing*. New York: Holt, 1931.

Porteus, S. D. Mental tests with delinquents and Australian aboriginal children. *Psychological Review*, 1917, *24*, 32–42.

Porteus, S. D. *Primitive intelligence and environment*. New York: Macmillan, 1937.

Porteus, S. D. *Porteus Maze Test*. Palo Alto, Calif.: Pacific Books, 1965.

Porteus, S. D. Ethnic groups and the Maze Test. In R. E. Kuttner (Ed.), *Race and modern science*. New York: Social Science Press, 1967.

Redmond, M., & Davies, F. R. *The standardisation of two intelligence tests*. Wellington: New Zealand Council for Educational Research, 1940.

Reed, T. E. Caucasian genes in American Negroes. *Science*, 1969, *165*, 762–768.

Resolution. *American Psychologist*, 1972, *7*, 660–661.

Reynolds, C. R. The neuropsychological basis of intelligence. In G. W. Hynd & J. E. Obrzut (Eds.), *Neuropsychological assessment of the school aged child: Issues and procedures.* New York: Grune & Stratton, 1982.

Reynolds, C. R., & Gutkin, T. B. A multivariate comparison of the intellectual performance of black and white children matched on four demographic variables. *Personality and Individual Differences,* 1981, *2,* 175–180.

Reynolds, C. R., & Jensen, A. R. *Patterns of intellectual abilities among blacks and whites matched on "g."* Paper read at American Psychological Association meeting in Montreal, 1980.

Rosenthal, R., & Jacobson, L. *Pygmalion in the classroom.* New York: Holt, Rinehart & Winston, 1968.

St. George, R. Tests of general cognitive ability for use with Maori and European children in New Zealand. In L J. Cronbach & P. J. Drenth (Eds.), *Mental tests and cultural adaptation.* The Hague: Mouton, 1972.

St. George, R., & St. George, A. The intellectual assessment of Maori & European school children. In P. D. K. Ramsey (Ed.), *The family and the school in New Zealand society.* London: Pitman, 1975.

Samuda, R. J. *Psychological testing of American minorities: Issues and consequences.* New York: Dodd, Mead, 1975.

Scarr, S., Pakstis, A. J., Katz, S. N., & Barker, W. Absence of a relationship between degree of white ancestry and intellectual skills within a black population. *Human Genetics,* 1977, *39,* 73–77, 82–83.

Scarr, S., & Weinberg, R. A. I.Q. test performance of black children adopted by white families. *American Psychologist,* 1976, *31,* 726–739.

Scottish Council for Research in Education. *The intelligence of Scottish children.* London: London University Press, 1933.

Scottish Council for Research in Education. *The trend of Scottish intelligence.* London: London University Press, 1949.

Shields, J. *Monozygotic twins.* London: Oxford University Press, 1962.

Shuey, A. M. *The testing of Negro intelligence.* New York: Social Science Press, 1966.

Silvey, J. Long range prediction of educability and its determinants in East Africa. In L. J. Cronbach & P. J. D. Drenth (Eds.), *Mental tests and cultural adaptation.* The Hague: Mouton, 1972.

Sinha, U. The use of Raven's Progressive Matrices in India. *Indian Educational Review,* 1968, *3,* 75–88.

Sorokin, B. *Standardisation and analysis of Progressive Matrices Test by Penrose and Raven.* Unpublished manuscript, 1954.

Spearman, C. *The abilities of man.* London: Macmillan, 1927.

Tesi, G., & Young, H. B. A standardisation of Raven's Progressive Matrices. *Archivio Psicologia Neurologica Psiquiatra,* 1962, *5,* 455–464.

Thomas, R. M., & Sjah, A. The Draw-a-Man test in Indonesia. *Journal of Educational Psychology,* 1961, *32,* 232–235.

Thomson, G. H. (Ed.). *Social implications of the 1947 Mental Survey.* London: University of London Press, 1953.

Thurstone, L. L. *Primary mental abilities.* Chicago: University of Chicago Press, 1938.

Tizard, B. I.Q. and race. *Nature,* 1974, *247*(5439), 316.

Tizard, B., & Rees, J. A comparison of the effects of adoption, restoration to the natural mother, and continued institutionalization on the cognitive development of four-year old children. *Child Development,* 1974, *45,* 94.

Tizard, B., Cooperman, O., Joseph, A., & Tizard, J. Environmental effects on language development: A study of young children in long-stay residential nurseries. *Child Development*, 1972, *43*, 342–343.

Tyler, L. E. *The psychology of human differences*. New York: Appleton-Century-Crofts, 1965.

UNESCO. *Statement of the nature of race and race differences*. Paris: United Nations, 1951.

Vance, H. B., Hankins, N., & McGee, H. A preliminary study of black and white differences on the revised Wechsler Intelligence Scale for Children. *Journal of Clinical Psychology*, 1979, *35*, 815–819.

Vejleskov, H. An analysis of Raven matrix responses in fifth grade children. *Scandinavian Journal of Psychology*, 1968, *9*, 177–186.

Vernon, P. E. Ability factors and environmental influences. *American Psychologist*, 1965, *20*, 723–733.

Vernon, P. E. *Intelligence and cultural environment*. London: Methuen, 1969.

Vernon, P. E. *Intelligence: Heredity and environment*. San Francisco: W. H. Freeman, 1979.

Veroff, J., McClelland, L., & Marquis, K. *Measuring intelligence and achievement motivation in surveys*. Final Report to U.S. Department of Health, Education, and Welfare, Contract No. OEO-4180. Ann Arbor: Survey Research Center, Institute for Social Research, University of Michigan, 1971.

Vincent, P. The measured intelligence of Glasgow Jewish school children. *Jewish Journal of Sociology*, 1966, *8*, 92–108.

Willerman, L. *The psychology of individual and group differences*. San Francisco: W. H. Freeman, 1979.

Williams, R. L. From dehumanization to black intellectual genocide: A rejoinder. In G. J. Williams & S. Gordon (Eds.), *Clinical child psychology: Current practices and future perspectives*. New York: Behavioral Publications, 1974.

Witty, P. A., & Jenkins, M. D. Inter-race testing and Negro intelligence. *Journal of Psychology*, 1936, *1*, 188–191.

Woodworth, R. S. Race differences in mental traits. *Science*, 1910, *31*, 171–186.

CHAPTER NINE

What Is a Racially and Culturally Nondiscriminatory Test?
A Sociological and Pluralistic Perspective

JANE R. MERCER

INTRODUCTION

Public Law 94-142 (Section 612[5] [C] of the Education of the Handicapped Act) mandated, for the first time, racially and culturally nondiscriminatory assessment procedures in the identification of "handicapped" children to be served by federally funded programs. Each state is to establish

> procedures to assure that testing and evaluation materials and procedures utilized for the purposes of evaluation and placement of handicapped children will be selected and administered so as not to be racially or culturally discriminatory. Such materials or procedures shall be provided and administered in the child's native language or mode of communication, unless it clearly is not feasible to do so, and no single procedure shall be the sole criterion for determining an appropriate educational program for a child.

Ancillary documents, such as the Senate Report (No. 94-168, Education for All Handicapped Children Act, June 2, 1975, pp. 26–29), indicate that the law is concerned with the "erroneous classification" of children variously described as "non-English-speaking," "poor," "minority," and "bilingual."

JANE R. MERCER ● Department of Sociology, University of California, Riverside, California 92521.

The term *nondiscriminatory* is not defined explicitly in the statute or the *Federal Register,* which provides the guidelines for implementing the law (Tuesday, August 23, 1977, Part II). The clearest definition of the concept available in the government documents appears in the discussion of the "erroneous" classification of children with physical handicaps:

> Tests are selected and administered so as best to ensure that when a test is administered to a child with impaired sensory, manual, or speaking skills, the test results accurately reflect the child's aptitude or achievement level of whatever other factors the test purports to measure, rather than reflecting the child's impaired sensory, manual, or speaking skills (except where those skills are the factors which the test purports to measure). (*Federal Register,* 121a.532 [C])

This statement can be rephrased to apply to racial and cultural factors as well. It would read:

> Tests are selected and administered so as best to ensure that when a test is administered to a child *from a cultural background markedly different from the background assumed by the test,* the test results accurately reflect the child's aptitude or achievement level or whatever other factors the test purports to measure, rather than reflecting the child's *cultural background* (except where that *background* is the factor which the test purports to measure).

In short, is the test measuring what it purports to measure or is the test measuring, to some extent, the child's physical impairment and/ or cultural background?

In addition, the *Federal Register* specified that tests and other evaluation materials shall "have been validated for the specific purposes for which they are used." The term *validation,* however, is undefined, and the procedures for validating any particular measure for a specific purpose are not specified. The purpose of this chapter is to propose, explicitly, a general definition of a "racially and culturally nondiscriminatory" test and to propose the set of criteria that a test ought to meet to be considered nondiscriminatory. It is perhaps unfortunate that the framers of the legal code used the term *nondiscriminatory* because the purpose of any set of testing procedures is, precisely, to "discriminate." Nevertheless, their intent is quite clear. A test should "discriminate" along those dimensions that it purports to measure but should not differentiate or discriminate students along dimensions that the test does not purport to measure, such as the extent of a student's visual or auditory impairment or the particular linguistic and sociocultural setting in which the student is being reared.

GENERAL DEFINITION OF "RACIALLY AND CULTURALLY NONDISCRIMINATORY" ASSESSMENT

Jensen (1980) did not use the phrase "racially and culturally non-discriminatory." Instead, he wrote of test "bias" and test "fairness," and he differentiated them as follows:

> In psychometrics, "bias" is a general term and is not limited to "culture bias." It can involve any type of group membership—race, social class, nationality, sex, religion, or age. The assessment of "bias" is a purely objective, empirical, statistical and quantitative matter entirely independent of subjective value judgments and ethical issues concerning fairness and unfairness and the uses to which they are put. Psychometric bias is a set of statistical attributes conjointly of a given test and two or more specified subpopulations. As we shall see in terms of certain criteria of fairness, unbiased tests can be used unfairly and biased tests can be used fairly. (p. 375)

Jensen sees "bias" as a statistical attribute of a test that relates to its "predictive validity and construct validity" as concepts that are somehow divorced from the uses made of a test, which may be "fair" or "unfair" according to a separate set of criteria. The law makes no such distinction when it states that evaluation materials shall "have been validated for the specific purposes for which they are used." Validity and use are linked, inextricably, in the legal mandate. They are also linked logically in the assessment process as it operates in the real world. Hence, the distinction between *bias* and *fairness* is not utilized here in the proposed working definition; rather, the concepts are integrated into a single model. This model formulates a set of operational definitions for the concepts of "racially and culturally nondiscriminatory" and of test "validation," that reflect the accumulated wisdom of the psychometric tradition but are also attuned to the complexities of the cultural pluralism that currently characterizes American society and the social context in which tests are used to make decisions about individual life trajectories. The purpose of this chapter is to propose a set of working definitions and to illustrate their operation by applying them to data collected for the Wechsler Intelligence Scale for Children (WISC-R—Wechsler, 1974).

The proposed working definition of a "racially and culturally nondiscriminatory test" includes most of the elements discussed by Jensen under the rubrics of test bias and test fairness but adds other elements that he did not include. It reorganizes these elements into a general framework that more closely approximates the intent of the law and specifies precisely the statistical criteria that I believe should be met before a test can be considered "racially and culturally nondiscriminatory." Whenever possible, traditional terminology has been preserved. However, as noted by Messick (1980), the term *validity* has been used in so many different contexts that it has become relatively meaningless as a generic term and derives its content from the adjective used to describe the type of validity intended. For this reason, this discussion uses the term only when accompanied by a specific modifier and in relation to the particular purpose for which a test is being used.

The definition of a racially and culturally nondiscriminatory test proposed in this paper is as follows:

Testing procedures are racially and culturally nondiscriminatory when they have (1) equal internal integrity and (2) equal external relevance for the groups on whom the procedures are to be used. *Equal internal integrity* requires that a test have (a) equivalent reliabilities; (b) equivalent stability; (c) equivalent item patterning; and (d) equivalent intercorrelational and/or factor patterns for all the groups on which it is to be used. *Equal external relevance* requires that a test have similar relevance to the purpose for which it is being used for all groups on which it is to be used. There are four major purposes for testing: (a) When a test is being used to measure organic functions, it should have equal biological relevance for all groups; (b) when a test is used to measure the level of knowledge or skill the individual has in a particular area, the test must have equivalent content relevance for all groups; (c) when used to predict future performance in an academic, job, professional, or other role, the test must have equivalent pragmatic/predictive relevance for all groups; and (d) when used to measure an abstract construct or a theoretical trait, the test must have equivalent construct relevance for all groups, and the form taken by the construct validation must be congruent with theoretical and working definitions of the construct purportedly being measured.

After a brief description of the research procedures used to collect the WISC-R data used to illustrate the above definition, the discussion proceeds to a point-by-point elucidation of the proposed criteria. Each section indicates the similarities of and the differences between the proposed working definition and the position proposed by Jensen (1980).

RESEARCH DESIGN

A parent was interviewed and a WISC-R was administered to 627 black, 617 Hispanic, and 669 white students 5 through 11 years of age who were selected on a random probability basis from the California public-school population during the 1973–1974 school year. Each ethnic sample was independently selected to be representative of that ethnic group in the school population. Identical three-stage sampling procedures were used: individual students within elementary school within school districts. All examiners had been trained in regular university courses designed to train persons to administer individual tests and were also given additional training by the project to assure standard procedures. About half were fully credentialed, working school psychologists. The other half were in advanced graduate training in school psychology. All but one of the psychologists was white. Hence, the tests were administered under conditions similar to those that currently prevail in most American public schools. All tests were administered in English. After interacting with each Hispanic student, the psychologist made a clinical judgment concerning the adequacy of the student's mastery of English for the purposes of testing. If judged inadequate, the student was not tested. To discourage testing students having a marginal comprehension of English, the psychologists were paid for testing the student, even if the student was not actually tested. Less than 30 students were dropped from the Hispanic testing sample because of insufficient command of English. Details of the sample design and field procedures are described elsewhere (Mercer, 1979b).

EQUAL INTERNAL INTEGRITY

The first set of criteria used to determine if a test is racially and culturally nondiscriminatory relates to the extent to which the test procedures have equivalent internal integrity for all the groups on whom the procedures are to be used. *Internal integrity* refers to the robustness, the stability, and the coherence of the testing procedures as a measurement instrument. Traditionally, there have been four basic approaches to measuring scale integrity: (1) determining scale reliability and the standard error of measurement of scaled scores; (2) determining scaled score stability, usually by test–retest procedures; (3) determining item patterning by looking at difficulty levels and increments in difficulty levels between items; and (4) ascertaining item consistency by examining intercorrelations among items, between subscales and total scores, and between items and total scores and/or by conducting a factor analysis of the items. Operationally, to have equivalent internal integrity for two or more groups, a test must have (1) equivalent reliability for all groups on which it is to be used; (2) equivalent stability; (3) equivalent item patterning; and (4) equivalent coherence. We will now examine our data for the WISC-R on the three samples.

CRITERION 1: EQUIVALENT RELIABILITY

The *WISC-R Manual* (Wechsler, 1974, Table 9) presents reliability coefficients for 11 age groups obtained by the split-half technique, with correction for the full length of the test by the Spearman–Brown formula, for each subtest except Coding and Digit Span. Whites and nonwhites were included in the sample in the same proportion found in the 1970 Census for each age range tested. Nonwhites were defined by Wechsler (Wechsler, 1974, p. 17) as "blacks and also other nonwhite groups such as American Indians and Orientals. Puerto Ricans and Chicanos were categorized as white or nonwhite in accordance with visible physical characteristics." No separate analysis is presented for the "white" and "nonwhite" groups.

Table 1, Column 1, presents the average reliability coefficient for all 11 age groups reported by Wechsler for each subtest, except Coding and Digit Span. Columns 2, 3, and 4 present the reliability coefficients for the white, Hispanic, and black students in our samples based on Cronbach's alpha. The reliabilities for the three groups are

TABLE 1

Reliability Coefficients[a] for WISC-R Subscales for Black, Hispanic, and White Elementary-School Students

Scale	WISC-R sample Average[b]	Elementary-school students		
		White	Hispanic	Black
Verbal				
Information	.85	.89	.84	.85
Similarities	.81	.85	.84	.82
Vocabulary	.86	.89	.88	.87
Comprehension	.77	.85	.82	.81
Arithmetic	.77	.86	.86	.97
Performance				
Picture Arrangement	.73	.81	.85	.87
Picture Completion	.77	.86	.86	.85
Block Design	.85	.77	.77	.79
Object Assembly	.70	.72	.68	.72
Mazes	—	.77	.80	.81

[a] Reliability coefficients based on Cronbach's alpha.
[b] Average reliability coefficient over age reported in Wechsler (1974), Table 9.

of approximately the same magnitude. They range from .68 to .97 and are well within the usual limits of acceptability. They are comparable to the reliabilities reported by Jensen (1980, Tables 7.2, 7.3, 7.4, and 7.5) for the Standford Binet, Wechsler Preschool and Primary Scale of Intelligence (WPPSI), Wechsler Intelligence Scale for Children (WISC), Wechsler Adult Intelligence Scale (WAIS), and a wide variety of group "mental ability" tests and standard achievement tests. We conclude, therefore, that the WISC-R passes the first criterion for equal internal integrity: It has equivalent reliabilities for the white, Hispanic, and black students in the California populations that were sampled. This conclusion, of course, does not mean that the test necessarily has equivalent reliability for black, Hispanic, or white groups living outside California or living outside the United States. Nor does it necessarily imply that there would be equivalent reliabilities for recent immigrants to the United States or for persons who speak another language or for translated versions of the test. Data from 1100 public school students in Mexico City using the *WISC-R Mexicano* show reliabilities ranging from .69 to .89 (Gomez-Palacio, Margarita, Rangel-Hinojosa, Elena, Padilla, & Eligio, 1982).

CRITERION 2: EQUIVALENT STABILITY

Jensen (1980) distinguished between *reliability* and *stability*, reserving the latter term for measures of the "consistency of test scores over time" (p. 261). Stability is usually measured by means of test–retest procedures. Unfortunately, we do not have test–retest data for the students in our three samples at the present time. However, such retesting is now in progress as part of a six-year follow-up study of the three samples that is being conducted by Richard Figueroa (Department of Education, Grant 13.4430). Because the size of the stability coefficient is a function of the amount of time separating the two testings, the coefficients will probably be relatively low for all three samples. The study will provide information on important questions: Are the scores for any of the three groups sufficiently stable to warrant drawing long-range conclusions about any student's likely test performance in secondary school based on tests administered in elementary school? Is there differential stability, and if so, which groups have the greatest stability? Do the scores of minority students change more than the scores of white students and, if so, in what direction? If the stability coefficients are lower for minority students than for white students because scores for minority students are increasing more over time, such a finding would lend support to the hypothesis that exposure to the culture of the school has a greater impact on the test performance of minority than of majority students. Jensen did not present data on the stability of test scores for different ethnic groups. A test of this criterion must await further study.

CRITERION 3: EQUIVALENT ITEM PATTERNING

Several years ago, Jensen (1974) proposed a third criterion for ascertaining bias in tests, evidence of groups $\times$ items interaction. He argued that, when there is no groups $\times$ items interaction, the test is not "biased." This criterion is another way of looking at the robustness of a test when the test is used on different populations, and it fits comfortably within the rubric of internal integrity. In general, two types of evidence are used to determine if there is a significant groups $\times$ items interaction: (1) calculating the rank order of item difficulty, as indicated by the percentage passing each item, to determine if the rank order is similar for the populations under consideration, and (2) determining whether the increments between items (the differences between the percentage passing adjacent items) is similar.

The rank order of difficulty of items in a test is related to the characteristics of the cultural system that the test covers, to the hierarchy of the knowledge system being covered, and to the number and complexity of elements to be processed. Words, information, and concepts that are widely used in the cultural system are easier because more persons are likely to have encountered them than less widely used materials. Because the patterning of item difficulty is related to the cultural system covered in the test and not to the cultural background of the persons taking the test, we would anticipate that item patterning for vocabulary and information type tests will remain relatively stable, regardless of the background of the test taker. Further, we would anticipate that persons who have had less exposure to the vocabulary and information in the test will have more difficulty on all the items than persons with greater overall cultural exposure. We would not expect items to reverse their relative difficulty so that a person with less exposure to the language is more familiar with rarely used words and less familiar with commonly used words than a native speaker.

The other major elements determing the difficulty level of items are the hierarchy of knowledge and the number and complexity of the elements to be processed. The hierarchy of knowledge is readily illustrated in the arithmetic test in the WISC-R. The child must be able to count (low-difficulty items) before adding and subtracting (medium-difficulty items) and must be able to add and subtract before multiplying and dividing (high-difficulty items). This hierarchy of skills exists quite independently of the cultural background of the child taking the test. We would not anticipate that, because a child has been reared in Mexico, he will somehow be able to pass items involving multiplication and division but will fail items that involve counting. It would be illogical to expect a reshuffling of the relative difficulty levels. What could logically be expected is that, if the arithmetic questions are given orally in English, the child reared in Mexico might have more difficulty with all the items than a child from an English-speaking background because of greater difficulty in understanding the language. The Mexican child's score would be depressed on all items because the test would be measuring not only what it purports to measure (knowledge of arithmetic) but also a factor extraneous to the purpose for testing, the child's command of English.

Block Design, Picture Arrangement, and Object Assembly illustrate the use of an increasing number of elements to increase difficulty level. Reproducing a design with 4 blocks (low-difficulty level) is easier than reproducing a design with 6 blocks (medium-difficulty level) or one with 9 blocks (high-difficulty level). A puzzle with 4 pieces (low-difficulty level) is easier than one with 6 pieces (medium-difficulty level or one with 8 pieces (high-difficulty level). Such rank orders of complexity exist in the nature of the task. We would not anticipate a reordering of item difficulties in which one group of children, however different their cultural background, would find it easier to reproduce a block design using 9 blocks than one using 4 blocks or would find it easier to put an 8-piece puzzle together than a 4-piece puzzle. What we would anticipate is that a group of children who have had no experience with blocks and have had no opportunity to play with puzzles will find all the tasks somewhat more difficult than children who have played with blocks and puzzles, but this increased difficulty will appear in all the items, whereas the rank order of relative difficulty will remain unchanged.

Not surprisingly, there are several studies that show that the rank order of item difficulties and the differences in the p values of adjacent items are almost identical for different populations being tested over the same cultural material (Miele, 1979; Cleary & Hilton, 1968; Angoff & Ford, 1973). Sandoval (1979) did an extensive analysis of items $\times$ groups interaction on a subset of the black, Hispanic, and white students tested with the WISC-R in our California samples. He reported rank-order correlations for item difficulties ranging upward from .88 and correlations of differences in difficulty level for adjacent items ranging upward from .73, except for the Vocabulary subtest on which the correlation dropped inexplicably to .49 in the white versus black analysis. He conducted an analysis of variance on the data matrix race × socioeconomic status × items × subjects, and he found a statistically significant items × group interaction in 9 of 10 analyses for blacks versus whites and in 5 of 10 analyses for Hispanics versus whites. However, Sandoval argued that the amount of the variance explained by the interaction, less than 1% in 19 of 20 tests, is trivial. Jensen (1980, p. 554) also reported on items × race interaction "significant beyond the .01 level for every subtest at every age" on the WISC. He concluded that "most of the item × race interaction is due to unequal intervals between the various item difficulties in the two groups" and cannot be interpreted as evidence of bias.

It is, of course, important to differentiate between statistical significance and substantive importance. Most reasonable persons would probably agree that an interaction that accounts for less than 1% of the total variance does not represent a very serious threat to the internal integrity of the test, even if it is statistically reliable.

Table 2 presents a reanalysis of the data for our three California samples controlling for age. The table presents the rank-order correlation of item difficulties on the WISC-R subtests for white, Hispanic, and black students 6, 8, and 10 years of age, correlating white with Hispanic, white with black, and Hispanic with black. The correlations, when age is controlled for, are even higher than those reported by Sandoval.

There are only two situations in which a test might fail to meet Criterion 3, and each of those situations would be gross deviations from acceptable testing practice. If a test were simply translated into another language and the items were modified to fit another cultural milieu without a change in the order or the scoring of the items, an items × groups interaction might emerge. Information presumed to be equivalent to that asked in the English version of the test might be more or less common knowledge in the other cultural system. Certainly, vocabulary words cannot simply be translated into their nearest equivalent in another language because the best equivalent in another language may be more or less frequently used in that linguistic system, and the item difficulties would vary accordingly. In such a circumstance, the internal integrity of the test would be lost, and the items would need to be reordered to fit the other cultural system. The standardization of the *WISC-R Mexicano* required sig-

TABLE 2

Rank-Order Correlations of Item Difficulties on the WISC-R Subtests for White, Hispanic, and Black Elementary-School Students 6, 8, and 10 Years of Age[a]

	6-year-olds			8-year-olds			10-year-olds		
	White/Hispanic	White/Black	Black/Hispanic	White/Hispanic	White/Black	Black/Hispanic	White/Hispanic	White/Black	Black/Hispanic
Verbal									
Information	.94	.98	.96	.88	.99	.97	.97	.94	.97
Similarities	.98	.94	.93	.99	.97	.96	.97	.94	.97
Arithmetic	.96	.97	.97	.98	.95	.98	.97	.98	.98
Vocabulary	.98	.98	.99	.98	.99	.98	.98	.98	.97
Comprehension	.96	.97	.97	.99	.98	.98	.99	.99	.99
Digit Forward	.97	1.00	.97	1.00	1.00	1.00	1.00	1.00	1.00
Digit Backward	.94	.94	1.00	.97	.97	1.00	.99	.96	.97
Performance									
Picture Completion	.99	.98	.98	.99	.98	.99	.97	.96	.97
Picture Arrangement	.93	.98	.90	.95	.97	.99	.95	1.00	.95
Block Design	1.00	.98	.98	.99	.98	.99	1.00	.98	.98
Object Assembly	.95	.80	.95	1.00	1.00	1.00	1.00	1.00	1.00

[a]Coding and mazes have been omitted because the format of those subscales is not appropriate for this analysis.

nificant modification and reordering of items in the Vocabulary sub-test (Gomez-Palacio, Margarita, Padilla, Eligio, Roll, & Samuel, 1982).

The only other circumstance in which there might be items × groups interaction would be a situation in which the members of one group have little or no knowledge of the language or content of the test and are responding at random. It is highly unlikely that random responses could generate any type of meaningful pattern in an individually administered test such as the WISC-R because the format is open-ended rather than fixed-response. Because items × groups interaction is unlikely to occur except in the most unorthodox testing situations, Criterion 3 contributes little to operationalizing a definition of a "racially and culturally nondiscriminatory" test.

Criterion 4: Equivalent Internal Consistency

There are two standard procedures for determining the internal consistency of tests: (1) studying the intercorrelations of items with each other, of items with total scores, of subscale scores with each other, and of subscales with total scores and (2) using factor analysis to examine item and scale clusters. Jensen (1980) suggested that, "In an unbiased test, ideally, the item × score correlations for any given item should be the same in the major and minor groups" (p. 445). Although he did not present any data showing intercorrelational patterns for students from differing ethnic groups, equivalent internal consistency is a sensible criterion.

It would be beyond the scope of this paper to present the intercorrelation matrices for items and subtest scores for each of the three groups in our samples. Instead, Tables 3, 4, and 5 present the intercorrelations of subtests with each other and with verbal, performance, and full-scale scores. The latter correlations have been corrected for contamination; that is, the subtest score has been removed from the total prior to calculating the correlation between that subtest and the total. Wechsler (1974) presented similar information for the standardization sample for each year of age and for the total sample, but he did not provide information on black, Hispanic, or white children separately.

Even a cursory comparison of the three tables reveals a marked similarity in the intercorrelations for the three ethnic groups. The average range in differences across the three groups is about .07. The correlation matrices are also very similar to those published by Wechsler for the standardization sample (Wechsler, 1974, Table 14).

TABLE 3
Intercorrelations of WISC-R Subscales for White Elementary Students ($N = 668$)[a]

	Infor	Simil	Arith	Vocab	Comp	Digit	Pict Comp	Pict Arr	Block	Obj Assem	Code	Mazes	Verbal
Similarities	.50												
Arithmetic	.49	.46											
Vocabulary	.59	.56	.47										
Comprehension	.45	.49	.40	.58									
Digit Span	.38	.34	.42	.33	.27								
Picture Completion	.31	.32	.27	.31	.30	.21							
Picture Arrangement	.33	.37	.33	.37	.33	.33	.34						
Block Design	.31	.32	.38	.34	.31	.27	.37	.36					
Object Assembly	.30	.30	.31	.29	.26	.22	.40	.36	.53				
Coding	.26	.19	.22	.22	.24	.24	.15	.19	.21	.19			
Mazes	.27	.16	.23	.23	.22	.25	.21	.22	.32	.37	.22		
Verbal[b]	.65	.63	.60	.69	.58	.45							
Performance[b]							.44	.44	.56	.58	.28	.40	
Full scale[b]	.63	.59	.59	.64	.57	.45	.46	.50	.54	.51	.34	.40	.57

[a]Pairwise deletion was used.
[b]Correlations corrected for contamination.

TABLE 4
Intercorrelations of WISC-R Subscales for Hispanic Elementary-School Students ($N = 613$)[a]

	Infor	Simil	Arith	Vocab	Comp	Digit	Pict Comp	Pict Arr	Block	Obj Assem	Code	Mazes	Verbal
Similarities	.54												
Arithmetic	.56	.46											
Vocabulary	.65	.64	.45										
Comprehension	.53	.50	.34	.65									
Digit Span	.48	.41	.49	.43	.37								
Picture Completion	.40	.31	.37	.40	.27	.32							
Picture Arrangement	.37	.37	.36	.35	.30	.35	.32						
Block Design	.39	.30	.34	.36	.28	.30	.41	.32					
Object Assembly	.36	.33	.29	.36	.29	.33	.33	.30	.44				
Coding	.28	.20	.33	.28	.19	.22	.23	.28	.30	.20			
Mazes	.30	.19	.30	.22	.28	.34	.28	.26	.36	.36	.23		
Verbal[b]	.72	.67	.57	.75	.63	.53							
Performance[b]							.46	.43	.54	.49	.33	.44	.59
Full scale[b]	.70	.61	.59	.70	.59	.54	.49	.49	.52	.49	.35	.43	

[a]Pairwise deletion was used.
[b]Correlations corrected for contamination.

Table 5

Intercorrelations of WISC-R Subscales for Black Elementary-School Students ($N = 619$)[a]

	Infor	Simil	Arith	Vocab	Comp	Digit	Pict Comp	Pict Arr	Block	Obj Assem	Code	Mazes	Verbal
Similarities	.49												
Arithmetic	.50	.40											
Vocabulary	.60	.52	.47										
Comprehension	.53	.50	.40	.61									
Digit Span	.33	.28	.44	.30	.29								
Picture Completion	.43	.32	.41	.42	.35	.28							
Picture Arrangement	.42	.33	.41	.40	.33	.33	.33						
Block Design	.35	.30	.40	.35	.30	.30	.37	.44					
Object Assembly	.31	.29	.35	.36	.28	.29	.39	.42	.53				
Coding	.26	.22	.34	.28	.21	.28	.30	.28	.28	.24			
Mazes	.23	.23	.27	.27	.21	.22	.29	.35	.41	.38	.19		
Verbal[b]	.67	.58	.59	.68	.62	.41							
Performance[b]							.47	.53	.60	.57	.36	.45	
Full scale[b]	.64	.54	.62	.66	.56	.46	.54	.57	.57	.54	.40	.42	.61

[a]Pairwise deletion was used.
[b]Correlations corrected for contamination.

Factor analysis is a more rigorous examination of the intercorrelation matrix. Jensen (1980, p. 533 ff.) presented data for the WISC, the WISC-R, and various other tests and concluded that the factor structures are stable across groups. Kaufman (1979a,b) reported the results of separate factor analyses on white and nonwhite subjects in the standardization sample for the WISC-R and for samples of children referred for psychiatric problems, for mental retardation, and for other clinical symptoms. He found that

> Regardless of the factor analytic technique employed, the age or ethnic background of the children tested, or the nature of the sample (normal vs exceptional), factor analysis of the WISC-R has yielded one consistent and recurrent finding: the emergence of robust Verbal Comprehension and Perceptual Organization factors. . . . When principal components or principal factor analysis is performed, Verbal Comprehension and Perceptual Organization factors emerge first, usually followed by a distractibility factor. (Kaufman, 1979b, p. 6)

Reschly (1978) reported the emergence of the same three factors for Anglo and Hispanic samples selected from first- through ninth-grade students in Pima County, Arizona, but found only two factors (Verbal Comprehension and Perceptual Organization) when he analyzed data for black and Papago Indian samples from the same county. The Verbal Comprehension factor consisted of Information, Similarities, Vocabulary, and Comprehension. The Perceptual Organization factor consisted of Picture Completion, Picture Arrangement, Mazes, Block Design, and Object Assembly. These two factors parallel the basic division of the test into verbal and performance scales. Arithmetic, Digit Span, and Coding formed the third factor.

Table 6 presents the results of two factor-analytic approaches to the subtests of the WISC-R for the black, Hispanic, and white students in our samples. The orthogonal (uncorrelated) factor matrix derived by means of the varimax procedure yielded two factors that parallel the verbal and performance subtests of the WISC-R. No third factor emerged when we used this procedure. In every case, the verbal factor accounts for an overwhelming percentage of the variance. The factor loadings are similar for all three groups and also are similar to those reported by Kaufman (1979b). He found loadings for Information, Similarities, Vocabulary, and Comprehension of .53 or higher on Verbal Comprehension; our loadings were .61 or higher. Kaufman reported loadings for Block Design and Object Assembly of .56 or higher on Perceptual Organization; ours were .55 or higher. Kaufman found loadings for Picture Arrangement, Picture Completion, and Mazes of .31 or higher, with most in the range of .50–.60; ours

TABLE 6
Factor Analysis of the Subtests of the WISC-R for Black, Hispanic, and White
Elementary Students Using Orthogonal and Oblique Rotations

Scales	Orthogonal factor matrix[a]						First principal component		
	White		Hispanic		Black		White	Hispanic	Black
	I	II	I	II	I	II			
Verbal									
Information	.69	.25	.68	.40	.70	.29	.70	.77	.71
Similarities	.67	.24	.70	.25	.61	.24	.67	.69	.60
Vocabulary	.76	.21	.81	.28	.74	.28	.72	.79	.74
Comprehension	.62	.23	.66	.22	.70	.19	.63	.66	.64
Arithmetic	.58	.31	.46	.47	.51	.44	.65	.62	.66
Digit Span	.43	.24	.43	.43	.33	.37	.49	.58	.48
Performance									
Picture Arrangement	.36	.41	.31	.44	.34	.54	.54	.51	.61
Picture Completion	.28	.46	.27	.53	.40	.43	.50	.53	.58
Block Design	.26	.65	.20	.63	.21	.70	.59	.55	.62
Object Assembly	.15	.76	.24	.55	.20	.66	.58	.53	.58
Mazes	.20	.42	.16	.52	.52	.52	.42	.45	.45
Coding	.26	.23	.16	.40	.26	.35	.35	.36	.42
Eigenvalue	4.07	.72	4.47	.65	4.39	.71	4.0	4.34	4.30
Percentage of Variance	85	15	87	13	86	14	85	87	86

[a]The table presents the varimax rotated-factor matrix and the first principal component using the Statistical Package for Social Science (SPSS). Pairwise deletion was used.

were .41 or higher, with most in the range of .40–.50. Arithmetic, Digit Span, and Coding had somewhat lower loadings than other subtests in their factors. When the analysis was redone, specifying three factors, the third factor (consisting of Arithmetic, Digit Span, and Coding) did emerge but accounted for only about 7% of the total variance.

Jensen (1980) insisted that the varimax approach to factor analyses, "as applied to factor extraction in the abilities domain" is

> flatly *wrong*, not mathematically, but psychologically and scientifically. In the abilities domain, either oblique rotation would be done to permit hierarchical extraction of *g*, or the *g* factor should be extracted (as the first principal factor) prior to rotation of the remaining factors. (p. 675)

Table 6 also presents the first principal component, which Jensen called *g*. The loadings are similar in magnitude to those reported by Jensen in Table 11.3 (p. 536) for white and black 7-year-olds. Regardless of the approach used, the factor structure is similar for the black, white, and Hispanic students in our three samples. When we used an oblique rotation, two factors emerged that paralleled the verbal and performance scales of the WISC-R. Hence, we conclude that the internal consistency of the scales is stable across groups. They maintain their internal integrity when used on these three populations because they have the following characteristics:

1. Subscale–subscale and subscale–total correlations were similar for all the groups on whom the test was used and were of sufficient magnitude to warrant treating the subtests as an integrated scale.

2. Factor analyses, whether by means of Kaiser's varimax approach, the hierarchical extraction of the principal component, or an oblique rotation, yielded similar results for all the groups on whom the test was used.

Summary of Findings on the Internal Integrity of the WISC-R

Based on our findings, we conclude that the WISC-R meets three of the criteria for internal integrity for the black, Hispanic, and white students in our public-school samples. It has equivalent reliabilities, equivalent item patterning, and equivalent internal consistency. We have no data on score stability over time, and Jensen did not report any data on this question. Such studies are needed because present practice tends to assume high, equivalent stability for all groups, and decisions made on the basis of test scores tend to be long-term decisions. For example, the federal guidelines require a comprehensive reassessment only every three years. If the scores of minority groups are less stable, this factor needs to be taken into account when establishing reassessment schedules.

The internal integrity of the WISC-R and similar tests has not been a major issue in the controversy over nondiscriminatory assessment. For example, the question was not even raised by the plaintiffs in *Larry P.* versus *W. Riles* (1979), nor was it discussed in Judge Peckham's opinion. Findings from our California sample are in essential agreement with Jensen's position in Chapters 8 and 11 (1980). Major differences arise, however, in defining and operationalizing external relevance.

EQUAL EXTERNAL RELEVANCE

In addition to having internal integrity, tests administered to identify handicapping conditions must have "been validated for the specific purpose for which they are used" (*Federal Register*, 121a.532 [2]). The determination of a test's validity is directly related to its intended use, that is, its relevance to the task(s) at hand.

The guidelines list many different purposes for testing and insist that multiple purposes be addressed in a comprehensive assessment, such as that required for identifying handicapping conditions under P.L. 94-142: "No single procedure is used as the sole criterion for determining an appropriate educational program for a child," and tests and evaluation materials must include materials "tailored to assess specific areas of educational need and not merely those which are designed to provide a single general intelligence quotient" (*Federal Register*, 121a.532 [3b,d]). The child is to be assesed in all areas related to the suspected disability. Areas specifically mentioned are

> health, vision, hearing, social and emotional status, general intelligence, academic performance, communicative status, and motor abilities ... psychological, physical, or adaptive behavior ... aptitude and achievement tests, teacher recommendations, physical condition, social or cultural background, and adaptive behavior. (*Federal Register*, 121a.532 [3f] and 121a.533 [1])

Clearly, the federal guidelines envision the use of tests for many differing purposes in the assessment process, and presumably, tests used for each purpose need to be validated for that purpose.

The legal mandate provides a solid basis for addressing the issue of equal external relevance because it focuses on real-world decisions and is quite specific about the various "purposes" that tests may serve. The purposes implied in the law are equally appropriate for testing at any age and can be grouped into four broad questions:

1. Is the child an intact organism? Has the test been validated for the purpose of identifying a particular organic anomaly? Is it equally valid for all groups on which it is being used?

2. Has the child mastered particular areas of knowledge or acquired particular skills and competencies? Has the test been validated for its content relevance to the domain of knowledge or skills it is presumably measuring? Is it equally valid for all groups on which it is being used?

3. How will the child perform in some future program or social role? Has the pragmatic-predictive relevance of the test been determined in relation to the programs and/or the social roles that it presumably predicts? Is it an equally accurate predictor for all groups on which it is being used?

4. What is the child's current condition in relation to some "trait" or "state" that is presumed to exist in the child, such as "emotional status" or "general intelligence"? Does the test have construct validity in relation to the "trait" presumably being measured? Does it have equal construct validity for all the groups on which it is being used?

The criterion for external relevance that a test must meet depends on the purpose for which the test is being used. A test that meets the criterion for one type of use may or may not meet the criterion for another use. Hence, we must first determine the purpose of testing before we can decide on the proper criterion to apply in judging whether the test has equal external relevance for each group on which it is being used. We will discuss each purpose, in turn.

Criterion 5: Equal Biological Relevance

When the purpose of the testing is to answer the question, "Is this child an intact organism?" the assessment uses the framework of the medical assessment model. Because a comprehensive assessment should include evaluations of "vision," "hearing," "motor abilities," "health," and "physical condition," schools are heavily involved in conducting preliminary medical screening for biological anomalies. The validity of testing instruments for this purpose is determined by the extent to which scores accurately reflect the state of the organism in relation to the biological function being measured. The criterion for test validity is direct observation and medical examination. For example, the ultimate criterion for the validity of a tuberculin test is an autopsy to verify lesions in the lungs. The norms for organismic functioning are biologically determined and universal to the species. They do not vary with the language or the culture of a particular group. Hence, measures of the physical condition of an organism have equal biological relevance in various sociocultural, racial, and ethnic groups. Questions of racial and cultural discrimination do not arise in connection with the testing devices used to measure vision, hearing, blood type, and so forth.

A common fallacy in educational assessment is interpreting scores on tests that measure learned behaviors as if the scores were direct evidence of organic pathology. The medicalizing of behavioral assessment has been particularly widespread in the area of so-called mental testing. When asked directly, most educational psychologists agree with Cleary, Humphreys, Kendrick, and Wesman (1975) that there "are *no* measures of innate capacity" (p. 17). Nevertheless, the testing literature is replete with medical, biological, and physical analogies. For example, Clarizio (1979) compared the IQ with air temperature as measured by a thermometer, and also with a tuberculin test. Flaugher (1978) likened the IQ test to a scale that measures a child's weight to detect malnutrition. Macmillan and Meyers (1977) compared it to a measure of height. Gordon (1975, p. 87) compared the IQ test to a situation in which height is used to predict the broad jump. He reasoned that, just as a measure of height would predict broad jumping ability in a Pygmy population as accurately as in the population of the United States, IQs are equally valid for inferring the intelligence of persons in different linguistic and sociocultural groups. Indeed, he even went so far as to talk about "verbal ability genes" and "nonverbal ability genes," treating Wechsler subtest scores as if they have genetic equivalents. Needless to say, "mental tests" have not been validated against unambiguous *biological* signs, nor were they intended to be used for biological screening by the persons who developed them.

It has also become popular practice to interpret profiles of subtest scores, especially on the Wechsler, as evidence of specific biological anomalies. It is beyond the scope of this chapter to discuss profile analysis. Although there is "impressive consistency . . . in investigations of a wide variety of groups with *school-related* problems: mentally retarded, reading disabled, and learning disabled, . . . results of profile studies involving groups of children with . . . known *neurological* impairment have certainly been conflicting and inconclusive" (Kaufman, 1979a, p. 203). Unless a test can be shown to have equal biological relevance to all groups on which it is being used, it should not be interpreted within the medical assessment model as screening for biological functions. Three operational criteria are proposed.

1. Correlations with biological criteria should account for at least 10% of the variance for general population samples $(r > .31)$.

2. Validity coefficients should be of similar magnitude for all sociocultural groups.

3. The sociocultural characteristics of the populations on whom the measure is to be used should have minimal influence on the score. Any cutoff level is somewhat arbitrary, but variation within one standard error of measurement for a test seems permissible. Elsewhere (Mercer, 1979b), a 5% criterion was suggested $(r = .22)$. If sociocultural characteristics account for less than 5% of the variance in an individual's score, the impact of cultural factors would be considered negligible and the score could be interpreted transculturally. Occasionally, sociocultural characteristics may be associated, statistically, with certain pathological conditions, not because sociocultural characteristics *per se* are *causing* the pathological condition, but because both are correlated with some third factor or factors that are causing the condition. In such cases, it is important to recognize the operation of the intervening variable that is producing the spurious relationship between the sociocultural characteristics and the

pathological condition, and not to erroneously interpret the correlations as causation or to conclude that the measure does not meet the criterion for the medical model. For further discussion of this point, see Mercer (1979b), p. 42). Jensen is currently experimenting with the use of choice reaction time and evoked electrical potentials of the brain as alternative measures, which he perceives as relatively direct, culture-reduced organic techniques (see Jensen, 1980, p. 686 ff).

CRITERION 6: EQUAL CONTENT RELEVANCE

A second purpose of the comprehensive assessment described in the law is to determine a student's current functioning level in several areas; "academic performance," "communicative status," "speech and language disorders," and "adaptive behavior" are specifically mentioned in the guidelines (*Federal Register*, Section 121a.532 [f]; 121a.533 [a] [1]). Such tests are variously called *achievement tests, competency tests, diagnostic tests of academic performance, mastery tests, basic skills tests, adaptive behavior scales*, and so forth.

There are typically three general uses for assessments of current functioning:

1. Measures of current levels of knowledge or skill in an area can provide edumetric information (Carver, 1974) that can be used to develop an individual educational plan for the student in the area assessed. When used edumentrically, testing is ordinarily closely calibrated to a particular curriculum continuum and supplies continuous feedback on the student's progress through the curriculum, while providing information concerning the next logical step in the educational process. Teacher-constructed tests and published tests designed for "precision" teaching and "mastery" instruction are of this type.

2. Measures of current functioning level are also used to decide whether an individual has achieved sufficient mastery in the specified content areas to be awarded a diploma or other certificate of competency. This function is increasing in importance in public education as more states move to "minimum competency testing" to determine which students are eligible for the high school diploma.

3. Measures of current functioning are also important in determining whether a person has sufficient knowledge and/or skill in a particular field to be permitted to practice a profession or to go on to advanced training. The level of competency accepted as sufficient is

determined by those in control of the curriculum, the educational system, the profession, and so forth. There is, theoretically, no limit to the number of persons who can reach criterion performance.

Figure 1 presents in diagrammatic form the paradigm for determining content relevance when a test is being used for the purpose of evaluating an individual's current level of knowledge or skill. The first step is to decide, at the plane of theory, on the content or skill domains that are to be covered in the test. In Figure 1, the content domain has been divided into eight theoretical subdomains. Specifications for each subdomain are then defined clearly to provide a working definition of the content domain. Decisions are made about the relative weight to be given to each subdomain, the number of items in each domain, and the format of the items. The decision concerning the content domains to be covered is a sociopolitical decision based on the values of the persons conducting the assessment. If the purpose of the test is to measure the individual's understanding of a particular academic curriculum, then the content of that curriculum provides the cognitive map for describing the domains to be covered. If the purpose is to evaluate the individual's mastery of the knowledge and skills required for a particular profession, the "experts" in that professional field are usually asked to define the domains to be covered, and their specifications become the point of reference for content validation. If the purpose of the test is to assess minimum academic competency for receiving a high school diploma, those in political power in the educational system awarding diplomas decide on the domains to be covered and the minimal competency that is be considered acceptable. These decisions are not statistical or "scientific" in the usual sense in which these terms are applied.

After developing detailed test specifications, the next step is to create the items or tasks that will evaluate the person's knowledge

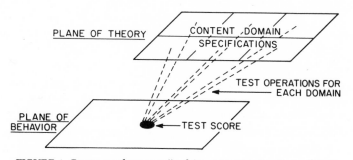

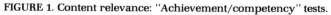

FIGURE 1. Content relevance: "Achievement/competency" tests.

or skill in each domain. In Figure 1, the procedures that are devised to operationalize the specifications that have been stated at the plane of theory are indicated by the broken lines. When individuals in the real world produce test scores at the plane of behavior, those test scores are interpreted as a direct reflection of the individual's mastery of the domains that the test presumably measures. The content-relevance questions are "How accurately do(es) the test score(s) reflect the content domain(s) specified at the plane of theory? Is there equal content relevance for all the groups on whom the test will be used?"

Procedures for determining content relevance are straightforward and can be illustrated by the process used in a recent content validation of the Multistate Bar Examination (Covington & Klein, 1980–1981). First, leading experts defined six subdomains of the law that they believed every qualified lawyer should have mastered: constitutional law, contracts, criminal law, evidence, real property, and torts. The content to be covered in each subdomain was carefully outlined. The percentage of the total score to be contributed by each subdomain was determined, together with the number of items needed for each subdomain. This set of specifications constituted the cognitive map at the plane of theory. Next, persons expert in each of the subdomains were asked to contribute questions written in a multiple-choice format, and the test was administered to candidates for the bar. The content validation consisted of asking a panel of nationally recognized legal experts, who were not involved in developing the test specifications or the items, to sort the items and their responses into the subdomains described in the test specifications. In short, test *makers* work from the content specification at the plane of theory down to the world of behavior. Test *validators* work up from the plane of behavior back to the plane of theory by sorting questions back into their content domains. The closeness of the match determines the content relevance of the test. Essentially the same procedures could be used in the content validation of any test that purports to measure the mastery of a body of knowledge or a set of skills. However, careful validation procedures such as those used in the Multistate Bar Examination are the exception rather than the rule.

Two points need to be emphasized. The fit between the test operations and the test specifications can be validated without reference to the nature of the individuals who will be taking the test. Second, the fact that one group may achieve an average score substantially higher than the average score of another group is not necessarily evidence that the test is discriminatory. For example, suppose that the purpose of a test is to evaluate a student's ability to read the English language. The fact that a group whose primary language is not English might score lower than a group whose primary language is English is not evidence of cultural discrimination because the students' skill in reading English is the "factor which the test purports to measure" (*Federal Register*, 121a.532 [c]). On the other hand, suppose that the purpose of the test is to evaluate a student's arithmetic competence and the questions are written in English, and once again, the students whose primary language is not English earn an average score substantially lower than the score of those whose primary language is English. If the nonnative speakers of English score lower because they have difficulty understanding the language in the questions but can, in fact, solve the arithmetic problems if presented in their own language, then the test is discriminatory. It is not measuring what it purports to measure, competence in arithmetic, but instead reflects the language competency of the student.

Similarly, a student with a visual handicap would be penalized on a paper-and-pencil test but might perform quite adequately if the testing materials were given orally. In such instances, it is the *form* of the testing procedures that produces the discriminatory impact rather than the content. Hence, those administering the tests must be sensitive to the possibility that the test format may interfere with an adequate assessment of mastery of the content or skills that the test is purportedly measuring.

Jensen (1980) mentioned content validity only briefly. He noted that

> most achievement tests, many Civil Service tests, and the state bar exams are all examples of tests that are justified by their content validity rather than by predictive validity. A test's content validity is determined by a consensus of experts in the particular content field covered by the test. (p. 420)

He did not deal with the issue of "bias" in achievement tests. Nevertheless, edumetric testing is currently the most important area of assessment in public education because it is used in educational programming, and it is growing rapidly. Many persons in the field of special education foresee the possibility that edumetric testing will eventually supplant so-called intelligence testing and make much of the current controversy about "bias" in measuring "general intelligence" obsolete (Hilliard, 1981).

CRITERION 7: EQUAL PRAGMATIC RELEVANCE

A third purpose for administering "mental" tests is strictly pragmatic: to improve predictions of future performance in some socially relevant role, for example, a profession, a job, or an educational program. This type of external relevance is variously called *pragmatic validity, predictive validity,* or *criterion validity.* The terms are used here interchangeably to describe pragmatic relevance as presented schematically in Figure 2. Pragmatic validity is totally atheoretical, hence the blank plane representing the level of theory: "Criterion-related validity . . . is simply the extent to which test scores are related to a socially important criterion measure" (Cleary *et al.,* 1975, p. 25). The test score, generated at the plane of behavior, is correlated with some criterion that is also generated at the plane of behavior. The psychometrist is interested primarily in the technical task of developing tools that will measure relationships between the "score on the test and significant criteria in a particular society" (p. 19).

Predictions are used to select persons for admission to jobs, to training programs, to graduate schools, and to special education programs. Any type of predictor may be used, alone or in combination with others—test scores, grade-point average, demographic characteristics such as sex, group membership, or age—so long as it accounts for a significant amount of the variance beyond that accounted for by other predictors. Correlation coefficients, either linear or multiple, are the basis for judging the percentage of reduction in error. In this context, they are called *validity coefficients.* Tests used for this purpose are typically norm-referenced to produce a neat, unambiguous rank order of status. The values and expectations of the social system are taken as a "given," and the technical task is simply to predict the criterion.

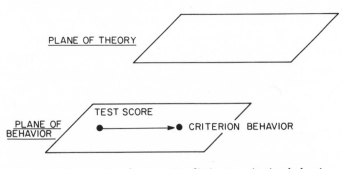

FIGURE 2. Pragmatic relevance: Prediction to criterion behavior.

The two main elements that need to be defined in Figure 2 are (1) the nature of the relationship between the test and the criterion that will be considered "unbiased," indicated by the arrow in Figure 2, and (2) the appropriate criterion measure when the purpose for testing is selection for a special education program that, presumably, is serving mentally retarded, learning-disabled, or other types of students. Each will be discussed in turn.

Definition of an "Unbiased" Prediction

Jensen (1980) presented a comprehensive explanation of the standard definition of predictive validity (Chapter 8) and a review of various perspectives and definitions of predictive test bias (Chapter 9). He proposed the standard regression model as the basis for determining whether predictions made from a test to a criterion are "unbiased": "A test with perfect reliability is a biased predictor if there is a statistically significant difference between the major and minor groups in the slopes b_{yx} or in the intercepts k, or in the standard error of estimates SE_y of the regression lines of the two groups" (p. 379). Because no test is perfectly reliable, Jensen suggested using estimated true scores or correcting for attenuation due to unreliability of measures when actually testing for bias in predictive validity. This definition provides an excellent method of detecting predictive bias and is proposed as the first component of the definition of *equal pragmatic relevance*.

Identification of an Appropriate Criterion

Jensen (1980) stated that

> the criterion performance may be measured by other tests (e.g., scholastic achievement tests and job-knowledge tests), by grades in courses, by supervisor's ratings of performance on the job, or by direct indices of work proficiency and productivity, such as the number of articles assembled per hour, number of sales per month, number of pages typed per hour, and the like. (p. 298)

When students are being selected for special education programs, ratings of job performance are obviously inappropriate, and they will not be discussed further here. This leaves us with the two remaining alternatives: "scholastic achievement tests" and "grades in courses" or some other type of teacher rating.

Jensen presented a large number of criterion validity studies in which some form of "achievement" test has been used as the criterion to validate an "intelligence" test. Such a procedure assumes that the two types of tests measure dimensions that are conceptually and operationally distinguishable. Yet, Jensen presented considerable evidence in his own review of the literature that such is not the case. He noted that the same items may appear in both types of tests. He reported correlations between the two types of tests that often run higher than correlations between subscales of the WISC-R and total scale scores on the WISC-R. For example, a study by Crano, Kenny, and Campbell (1972) is reported in Jensen's Figure 8.2 (p. 324). With a sample of 5,495 students, these authors found correlations between IQs and achievement test scores that ranged from .73 to .78. This correlation is only slightly lower than achivement–achievement correlations of .80 and IQ–IQ correlations of .83. Similarly high correlations are reported throughout Jensen's material. Even more enlightening are various factor analyses reported by Jensen in which "achievement" tests have loadings *as high or higher* on the first principal component—which he calls g and equates with "intelligence"—than do tests that purport to be measuring "intelligence." See, for example, Jensen's Table 11.3, which reports loadings for white and black students on 13 different tests. The three *highest* loadings on g were for the Wide Range Achievement Tests for spelling, reading, and arithmetic (.77–.79). Loadings for so-called intelligence scales ran markedly lower: .31 and .37 for WISC Coding; .47 and .49 for WISC Comprehension; and so forth. The two types of tests do not meet the criterion for discriminant validity, a form of construct relevance that is discussed in a later section of this paper.

Jensen (1980) recognized the situation when he stated, "'General achievement' is probably indistinguishable operationally (though not conceptually) from 'general intelligence.'" Although he argued that there are "important conceptual and theoretical" reasons for maintaining the aptitude–achievement distinction, such a distinction is not, in fact, supported by his own statistical evidence. Nevertheless, he continued to act as if the two are operationally distinguishable when he presented "empirical" evidence of the predictive validity of so-called intelligence tests by "validating" them with correlations to so-called achievement tests (p. 240).

It should be noted that Jensen's position is not widely shared by others in the field of testing. Wesman (1968) wrote:

> All ability tests—intelligence, aptitude, and achievement—measure what the individual *has* learned, and they often measure with similar content and similar process. . . . Such justification as we have for our labeling sys-

tem resides entirely in the *purpose* for which the test is used, not in the test document itself. (p. 269)

Cleary *et al.* (1975) reached the same conclusion:

> There are no differences in kind ... between intelligence and achievement, or between aptitude and achievement.... Just because differences among test items are quantitative and not qualitative, it is possible for one man's intelligence test to be another man's achievement test. Thus, Jensen categorized the National Merit Scholarship Examination as an intelligence test, but precisely the same items were used in the Iowa Tests of Educational Development for assessing achievement. (p. 21)

If "achievement" test scores cannot be operationally distinguished from "intelligence" test scores and are unacceptable for determining the pragmatic validity of tests for the purpose of selecting the mentally retarded, the learning disabled, and so forth, then we are left with the third criterion suggested by Jensen: some form of teacher grades or ratings. He discussed the problems that arise in using teacher data as the criterion variable. He argued that they are unreliable, that they include subjective factors other than the factors supposedly being rated, and that standards vary greatly from school to school. He presented only two and a half pages of material covering empirical studies of test bias in predicting scholastic performance for elementary-school children. Only one study was conducted on both black and white samples and included teacher data. The "intelligence" test was the Lorge–Thorndike (which is group-administered). The correlations were significantly lower between the test scores and the teachers' grades than they were between the test scores and the achievement tests. Additionally, there appears to be differential validity for black and white students. The correlations between teacher grades and Verbal IQ were .41 for whites and .26 for blacks. With Nonverbal IQ, they were .41 for whites and .25 for blacks. No information is given on the slopes or intercepts of the regression lines (Jensen, 1980, p. 473, Table 10.1).

Jensen noted that "the published evidence here is surprisingly meager" (p. 472). There are two additional analyses, done on the same data set, that were not cited by Jensen. Goldman and Hartig (1976) reported correlations of .25 ($p < .01$) between WISC full-scale IQs and GPAs for 234 white elementary-school students and correlations of .12 ($p <. 05$) for 211 Mexican-American children and .14 ($p < .01$) for 194 black children. The two latter correlations become .13 and .18 when corrected for the restricted range in the GPAs of minority children. The correlations were slightly higher when a teacher rating of competence, rather than a GPA, was the dependent variable. All validity coefficients are statistically significant, but the percentage of reduction in error is trivial: 6.3% for white, 1.7% for Mexican-American and 3.2% for black children. A reanalysis of the same general data set that was done at the request of the plaintiffs in Larry P. has been published (Mercer, 1979a) and yielded, of course, very similar results. The test has differential validity for the three groups. Reschly and Reschly (1980) used factor scores based on the Verbal Comprehension Factor and the Perceptual Organization Factor of the WISC-R, which was discussed earlier in this chapter. Using a stratified, random sample of 212 white, 189 black, and 184 Mexican-American chilren from the first, third, fifth, seventh, and ninth grades in the Pima County, Arizona schools, these authors correlated the factor scores with a 10-item rating of "academics" completed by a teacher of each student. For the white children, the authors reported correlations of .30 and .22 between "academic" ratings and the Verbal Comprehension and Perceptual Organization factors, respectively. The comparable correlations for the black students were .46 and .26, and those for the Mexican-American students were .32 and .27. All are statistically significant; however, none of the validity coefficients in any of these studies are very impressive.

This meager number of studies raises an obvious question: Why, if criterion validity is so important, have there been so few studies of elementary-school students in which a real-world criterion, not just another test score, has been used? Jensen (1980) hazarded a guess:

> [There are] probably two main reasons: (1) because tests are not generally used for selection in elementary grades (1 to 8), there has been little concern with their predictive validity, as compared with, say, college and vocational aptitude tests; and (2) teachers' marks in elementary school are not a very solid criterion for studies of predictive validity. (p. 472)

There is no arguing with the fact that teachers' marks are held in low repute as criterion variables and that researchers prefer a neat, reliable (albeit operationally indistinguishable) criterion like an achievement test score. But to say that pragmatic validity studies have not been done because tests "are not generally used for selection in elementary grades (1 to 8)" shows a profound ignorance of the assessment process in public education. "Mental" tests are used to select students for classes for the "mentally retarded," classes for the "learning-disabled," and classes for the "gifted," and to assign students to reading groups and arithmetic groups and to various curricula.

One of the primary functions of the educational system in American society has been to sort and categorize and select students for various roles and statuses, and the primary instruments for making those selections have been "mental" tests such as those described and defended in Jensen's book. Although school psychologists frequently protest that "intelligence" tests are not the chief or even the most important factor in selecting students for special education classes, such is not the case. See, for example, a recent, comprehensive analysis of the referral process in the Chicago public schools (Berk, Bridges, & Shih, 1981), which confirms conclusions that I had reached in a much earlier study (Mercer, 1973). These authors found that, holding constant a large number of variables, such as class of origin, race, referral reason, sex, language spoken in the home, family structure, and scores on a "social-misfit" index, IQ remained a critical causal variable in the placement process.

There are two other possible hypotheses that might explain the paucity of pragmatic validity studies: Educators may not, in fact, use "intelligence" tests to predict a student's future role performance in the same sense that employers use tests to predict future job performance or graduate schools use tests to predict performance in graduate school, or it may be that researchers have not addressed the difficult problem of identifying adequate criterion measures. Each hypothesis is discussed here briefly.

When psychologists and other educators interpret an "intelligence" test score, they do not discuss it as a predictor of future role performance. Rather, they discuss it as a measure of an abstract construct, "intelligence." Why would they use an IQ for prediction? If their purpose is primarily to predict which students are most likely to succeed or to fail in the following year, they already have a less expensive, better predictor than any IQ test: the student's current performance as judged by teacher grades or ratings. In an earlier study (Mercer, 1979b), we looked at the pragmatic validity of teacher grades, teacher ratings of competence, and the WISC in predicting teacher grades and teacher ratings in the following two years. Using a stepwise multiple-regression analysis in which teacher grades, teacher ratings, and the Verbal IQ (in that order) were entered as independent variables to predict teacher grades the following year, we found that teacher grades reduced the error by 46.47% for 425 white students in our sample. Adding the teacher rating to the equation improved the prediction by another 2.86%. Adding Verbal IQ improved the prediction by another .84%. For 142 black students, the error was reduced by 21.96% when we used the grades from the previous year. Adding a teacher rating improved the prediction by 4.68%, and adding the WISC Verbal score improved the prediction by only an additional .50%. The comparable percentages for 241 Hispanic students were 26.54% when grades alone were used as a predictor, an additional 5.33% when teacher ratings were added, and a trivial .06% when the Verbal IQ was added. Correlations with Performance IQ and full-scale IQ were much lower (Mercer, 1979b, Chapter 16). This analysis indicates that knowledge of a student's IQ adds nothing of any consequence to the prediction of that student's grades in school, once the student's grades for the prior year are known. It also indicates that there is almost complete covariance between whatever is being measured by the WISC-R and teacher grades and ratings. In fact, the validity coefficients yielded by the WISC-R alone are much lower than those for teacher grades alone. Knowledge of Verbal IQ reduces error by only 21.9% for white, 8.4% for black, and 4.8% for Hispanic students.

Teachers are very sensitive observers of student behavior. They are knowledgeable about the norms and expectations of the school. Consequently, they are more adept than any test in predicting which students will succeed or fail in the following years. Thus, we have the anomalous situation in which the schools are not really using the tests to "predict" future performance but to select students for handicapping conditions based on the belief that the tests have construct validity for identifying low "intelligence." Yet, the use of the tests in the schools is defended on the basis of their presumed predictive validity, which has not been fully verified. If the purpose for testing in school is to get the best prediction of future performance in school based on "a best-weighted composite score from a number of . . . predictor variables" (Jensen, 1980, p. 300), the clear choice would be to use teacher grades or ratings from prior years and to drop the IQ, because it does not "measure any appreciable part of the criterion-relevant abilities that are not already included in the first two predictors" (Jensen, 1980, p. 301).

The second hypothesis is related to the difficulty of finding an appropriate criterion measure when the purpose of testing is identification of the student as being educably mentally retarded or learning-disabled or as having another handicapping condition. Teachers' grades and ratings reveal a student's current functioning level in the school. However, identifying a student as educably mentally retarded or learning-disabled implies considerably more than simply having difficulty with schoolwork. What would be an appropriate criterion measure? The severely disabled, historically called idiots, imbeciles, and the feebleminded, were identified long before tests were invented and are still readily perceived as subnormal by laypersons without benefit of test scores. But the classifications "educably mentally retarded" and "learning-disabled" are, to a large extent, creations of the school and of the test itself. The category *moron* (an earlier term for the educably mentally retarded) was first invented by Goddard *after* "intelligence" testing was introduced (Doll, 1962). Most persons labeled educably mentally retarded or learning-disabled have no recognizable physical anomalies. They are not viewed as subnormal outside the school. Within the school, their "handicaps" are differentiated by their pattern of test performance. In general, an educable mental retardate is one who is failing academically and who has also failed an "intelligence" test. A learning-disabled student is one who is failing academically but who has passed the IQ test. When the categories themselves are creatures of the tests, how can there be an independent criterion for the category against which the test can then be validated?

These issues are not addressed in Jensen's book. They are conceptual questions rather than technical questions, but they cannot be brushed aside just because they are troublesome. The tests are currently being *used* for the purpose of supposedly identifying "handicaps," and their use in this fashion is being challenged, not only in the halls of academia, but in the courts. Taking the protestations of the testers at face value, the courts have simply asked for the evidence that the tests have been validated for that purpose. Judge Peckham stated the problem plainly:

> If defendants could somehow have demonstrated that the intelligence tests had been "validated" for the purpose of E.M.R. placement of black children, those tests could have been utilized despite their disproportionate impact. As discussed elsewhere in this opinion, however, defendants did not make these showings. (Peckham, Section VB)

In his remedy, he stated:

> In order to obtain court approval of the use of any standardized intelligence tests, the State Board of Education must take the following steps: . . . it must state whether the Board has determined that the tests or tests (a) are not radically and culturally discriminatory, (b) will be administered in a manner which is nondiscriminatory in its impact on black children, (c) have been validated for the determination of E.M.R. status or placement in E.M.R. classes. (Section VIB1)

The problem is that the testers have protested too much. They have argued that the tests have pragmatic validity for identifying handicapping conditions, but they have not devised and probably cannot devise acceptable criterion measures of the presence of those handicaps independent of the test scores themselves. Consequently, they are stymied when a judge ingenuously asks for evidence of such validation. The impasse might well have been avoided by recognizing that schools do not, in fact, interpret IQ as predictions of future performance and have better predictors at hand if they wish to make such predictions. The schools interpret IQ as measures of a construct, "intelligence," and the fundamental question when interpreted in this fashion is not predictive validity but construct validity.

Summary of Criterion 7: Equal Pragmatic Relevance

1. When a test or other measure is being used to predict performance in some social role, equal pragmatic relevance for two or more groups can be tested by means of the standard regression model to determine if the regression lines between test and criterion have similar slopes and similar intercepts and if the predictions have similar standard errors of estimate. When the avowed purpose for testing is prediction, the fact that the average scores for the groups being compared differ is not interpreted as a sign of bias if the other three criteria are met. A test can make equally accurate predictions for groups whose mean scores on the test are not the same.

2. The criterion measure used to establish pragmatic validity must be operationally distinguishable from the predictor. Consequently, the predictive validity of a "mental" test called an *intelligence test* cannot be established by correlating it with another "mental" test called an *achievement test*. Test–test correlations are a form of construct validity and do not qualify under the rubric of pragmatic validity.

3. The criterion measure must adequately reflect the actual criterion performance that is to be predicted. For example, when a test is used to predict future job performance, a supervisor's rating of that performance is usually used as the criterion. When a test is used to predict academic performance in graduate school or a professional school, professors' grades or ratings are used as the criterion. When a test is used to predict future performance in elementary school, a teacher's grades or ratings should be used as the criterion.

4. When a test is used to select persons for placement in programs for the handicapped, especially programs for the educably mentally retarded and the learning-disabled in which the test score itself is the major criterion for defining the handicap, predictive validity is not the appropriate standard. When it is used for this purpose, testers envision the score as measuring an abstract construct,

intelligence, and the test's construct validity for this purpose is the correct validity test. Construct validity is discussed in the following section.

5. If the major defense that can be made for the continued use of IQ tests in the public schools is based on their power as pragmatic predictors of future academic performance, the tests can be dispensed with on purely practical grounds. They are expensive to administer, their predictive powers are marginal, and their differential validity for various racial and ethnic groups is questionable. There are other predictors, such as prior school performance, that are inexpensive to secure and are at least twice as powerful as predictors. For the most part, "intelligence" tests are not used by the schools for purposes of prediction. Hence, pragmatic validity is not pertinent to most assessments conducted in elementary schools for the purposes of Public Law 94-142.

CRITERION 8: EQUAL CONSTRUCT RELEVANCE

Construct relevance is required when a test purports to measure an abstract construct or trait that presumably exists in the individual, such as introversion-extraversion, self-concept, anxiety, intelligence, and so forth. Such constructs are mental creations, abstractions used to organize existential phenomena so they can be comprehended and manipulated in thought. Constructs exist as ideas, as ways of classifying objects or behaviors in the real world. They are usually constructed by working up the abstraction ladder from concrete sensory experiences to higher and higher levels of classification in which fewer and fewer of the characteristics of the objects or behavior in the real world are used as the basis for grouping (Hayakawa, 1947). One perennial difficulty in working with constructs is the human tendency to reify them once they have been clearly conceptualized, that is, the tendency to treat the construct as if it existed as an entity in the existential world.

When testers declare that they are measuring "intelligence," "innate ability," "intellectual capacity," or similar constructs, the validity of their claim rests on the extent to which they can present a logically convincing argument that the procedures they are using adequately reflect whatever hypothetical trait they claim to be measuring. Jensen (1980) has stated this clearly:

> The validity of many tests does not or cannot depend on predictive validity. Often there is no single clear-cut external criterion for what the test is intended to measure. This is certainly true of intelligence tests, as intel-

ligence itself is a hypothetical construct that the test attempts to measure. It has no single objectively measurable external referent . . . an intelligence test *qua* a test of *intelligence* depends on *construct validity*, which is a complex, open-ended affair. (p. 420, emphasis in the original)

Citing Hebb (1949) and Vernon (1969), Jensen (1980) defined the construct "intelligence" by distinguishing logically between what he called Intelligence A, B, and C:

> *Intelligence A* refers to the individual's genotype, that is, the complement of genes, or the genetic blueprint, so to speak, that conditions the individual's intellectual development. The genotype is itself a theoretical construct. No one can look at a genotype for intelligence under a microscope or isolate it in a test tube. . . . The important point for our present purpose is to understand that Intelligence A is a theoretical construct and cannot be observed or measured directly. In other words, no test scores are measures of Intelligence A.
>
> *Intelligence B* is the individual's phenotypic intelligence. It is the final product, at any given time in the individual's life span, of the genotype and all the environmental factors that have interacted with the genotype from the moment of conception. The phenotype is not a constant value like the genotype, but is altered by constitutional and experiential factors. . . . Intelligence B is best regarded as an average of many measurements over a limited period of time, so as to average out momentary and idiosyncratic features of specific tests and situations. Intelligence B is the individual's *general* intelligence. . . .
>
> *Intelligence C* is the sample of "intelligent" behavior that we can actually observe and measure at a given point in time. Intelligence C is a sample of Intelligence B, or an imprecise estimate thereof. . . . Whenever we talk about a score on any particular intelligence test, we are talking about Intelligence C. (pp. 184–185)

In his Figure 6.2, Jensen depicted the three levels as a kind of layer cake. C, the lowest level, represents a specific test score. B, the middle level, represents a more stable general factor common to several specific test scores. The only difference between the two, conceptually, is that B is an "average" of C. Both reflect the phenotype, the product of the genotype and all environmental factors that have influenced its development. Both are generated at the level of behavior. Intelligence A, the top layer, is the theoretical construct, the genotype, which cannot be observed directly but must be inferred from the phenotypic behavior represented by B and C. It can be conceptualized as the proportion of Intelligence B and C "attributable to genotype."

Figure 3 presents a more general model of construct relevance that can be applied to the measurement of any hypothetical "trait." If we translate Jensen's definition into the schema for Figure 3, Intel-

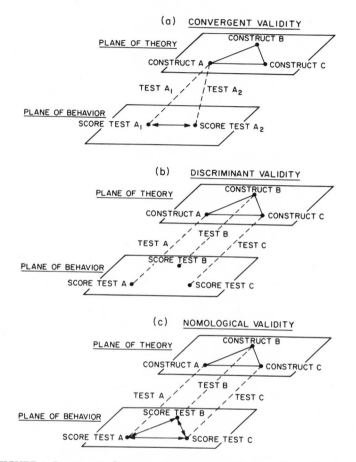

FIGURE 3. Construct relevance: Measurement of a hypothetical "trait."

ligence A would be the construct at the Plane of Theory. Intelligences B and C would be at the Plane of Behavior. C would be an individual test score, whereas B would be a combination of test scores. The broken lines are the operationalization of the construct, the set of procedures that the scientist has developed to reflect the construct. The questions in construct relevance are, How accurately do the operations reflect the construct that they purport to measure? Is there congruence between test score(s) and construct? Does the congruence hold across the various racial and ethnic groups on whom the test(s) are to be used?

Because the construct has "no clear-cut criterion" but is a hypothetical trait, tests of construct relevance are indirect, the conclusions are tenuous, and the issue is seldom definitively resolved to every-one's satisfaction. If the definition of the construct is modified, the linkage is altered. If different scientists operate from different defini-tions of the construct, consensus may be impossible to achieve. Lack of consensus does not necessarily imply that one position is correct and the other position in error. Each may be correct, given its defi-nition of the construct. The following discussion uses Jensen's layer-cake paradigm as the basis for discussion. There are three general strategies for establishing construct relevance: convergent validity, discriminant validity, and nomological validity. Jensen focused almost exclusively on convergent validity.

Convergent Validity

Figure 3a illustrates the general principle involved in convergent validity. A construct is defined at the plane of theory, and multiple measures of the construct are developed, indicated by the two bro-ken lines, Test A_1 and Test A_2: Different measures of the construct are administered to a sample of persons at the plane of behavior, and the results are correlated. If there is no correlation, that is strong evi-dence that there is a problem and that more work is needed either on the construct, the operations, or both. If there is a correlation, it is accepted as direct evidence that the tests probably measure the same dimension and as indirect evidence that the dimension is the construct as defined. The major difficulty with convergent validity is that neither Test A_1 nor Test A_2 may be a very adequate representa-tion of Construct A, and their correlation at the plane of behavior reveals nothing, directly, about the adequacy of the linkage.

Jensen (1980) noted that there have been numerous definitions of the construct "intelligence," but he pointed out broad similarities (pp. 170–171). After reviewing the array of different specific tests that have been devised to measure these constructs (Intelligence C), he called attention to the fact, first noted by Spearman, that the scores on many of these measures are intercorrelated. When the first prin-cipal component is extracted in a factor analysis, most tests, regard-less of the nature of the skill being measured, tend to load on that factor. Following Spearman's lead, Jensen called this factor g (Intel-ligence B). He continued by describing Thurstone's efforts to develop factor-pure tests, and he concluded that Thurstone's efforts were rel-atively unsuccessful because the "general factor worked against this dream." The persistence of the g factor, illustrated in numerous fac-tor analyses of a variety of tests, led Jensen to conclude that there is a fundamental dimension accounting for the shared variance in all of these tests and that that dimension is "intelligence":

> We identify intelligence with g. To the extent that a test orders individuals on g, it can be said to be a test of intelligence. Not all so-called intelligence tests meet this criterion equally well, and even the best tests can only approximate it, as g is a hypothetical construct and is not itself directly measurable. Yet IQ tests such as the Stanford-Binet and the Wechsler Scales would probably correlate between .8 and .9 with a hypothetical true scale of g in the normative population. (p. 224)

The correlation among test scores at the plane of behavior are presented as evidence that they must be measuring a hypothetical construct at the plane of theory, which Jensen has called "intelligence." There are at least four problems in this line of reasoning:

1. Intercorrelations among test scores at the plane of behavior do not, in any sense, prove that they have any necessary link with the construct at the plane of theory. Specifically, does Intelligence B, the g factor, adequately reflect Intelligence C, the construct at the plane of theory? To say simply that "intelligence is g" fails to recognize the distinction between the plane of theory and the plane of behavior and ignores the useful distinction made in his own layer-cake description of the various levels of "intelligence." This position is a more sophisticated version of the reductionism in the famous quotation by Boring (1923), "Measurable intelligence is simply what the tests of intelligence test." It abdicates responsibility for presenting a theoretical rationale for linking operations and construct by defining the construct as the operation. The chief difficulty in this type of abstracted empiricism is that it accepts the operations as given and precludes examination of the assumptions, the implicit world views, and the social values that may be imbedded in the measures themselves. It results in circular reasoning that makes it impossible to come to grips intellectually with the fundamental questions posed by cross-cultural assessment, because the construct "intelligence," which is transcultural, becomes inextricably bound up with tests that are not necessarily transcultural.

2. Another troublesome problem in defining "intelligence" as the first principal component is that the emergence of a principal factor depends on the type of factor analysis used. When a varimax rotation is used, as in Table 6, no principal factor emerges. Hence, the construct is built in by statistical definition if one insists, as Jensen has insisted, that investigators not "select the most popular computer program, Kaiser's varimax, for doing their factor analyses" because "this is flatly *wrong*, not mathematically, but psychologically and sci-

entifically" (p. 675). As mentioned earlier in this chapter, Jensen recommended either oblique rotations to permit the hierarchical extraction of g or the extraction of the first principal factor prior to rotation. As demonstrated in Table 6, the appearance of g is contingent on the factor-analytic approach used. It is not somehow inherent in the data. If one looks first only for the commonalities, one is bound to find the commonalities. If one insists that factors never be rotated until the general factor is first extracted, there will, of course, always be a general factor. What comes out of any factor analysis depends on what was put in and what procedures were used.

3. A very heterogeneous potpourri of tests emerges in the various factor analyses reported by Jensen because defining "intelligence" as the general factor emerging from an oblique rotation casts a very wide net. In addition to the tests that are ordinarily perceived as "intelligence" tests, the general factor includes a full assortment of "achievement" tests (Jensen's Table 6.11), tests of manual speed, hand steadiness, sonar pitch memory (Table 6.12), memory for shapes, writing speed, reaction time, weight discrimination, touch discrimination (Table 6.13), and tests of aiming and representational drawing (Table 6.14). To say that such skills are all aspects of g and that g is "intelligence" is not particularly informative. Gross, all-encompassing concepts are less useful, especially in educational assessment, than precise, clearly defined constructs that are theoretically focused and relevant to educational planning.

4. Assigning names to factors is a relatively arbitrary matter. The fact that Jensen has chosen to call the g factor "intelligence" reflects his disciplinary perspective. Persons trained in different disciplines perceive factors differently because each academic discipline has a set of constructs with which it works and builds theoretical models. Clusters of variables identified at the plane of behavior through factor analysis have no intrinsic meaning. The statistical procedures identify commonalities, but the scientist superimposes meaning and constructs, and names the factor accordingly. There is no single "correct" way to interpret or to label any factor. Because trait models have been popular in psychology, it is understandable that psychologists would perceive the commonalities as being the result of some trait residing in the individual. That this trait was named *intelligence* is probably an accident of history resulting from the fact that Binet elected to call his first test a measure of "intelligence" rather than calling it a test of "achievement," "current functioning level," or whatever.

The diffuse collections of knowledge and skills comprising the g factor have one thing in common: they are all responses that have been learned in a social setting. *Learned behavior, knowledge and skills, cognitive skills, Western civilization g,* and *achievement* are alternative labels that could have been applied. The fact that a general factor can be extracted from a variety of performances by the same individual does not in any sense prove that a trait called *intelligence* exists. It is only one hypothetical construct among the many that could be used to explain the clustering. The general factor may be picking up nothing more profound than the obvious fact that all the measures were taken on the same individual. Convergent validity is a very weak test of construct relevance and by itself, is never sufficient. It is simply one of several desirable criteria. For a test to be racially and culturally nondiscriminatory, it should have equivalent convergent validity for all the groups on which it is being used.

Discriminant Validity

Figure 3b depicts, schematically, the nature of discriminant validity. At the plane of theory, the investigator has two or more constructs that are conceptualized as distinct, independent dimensions: Construct A, Construct B, and Construct C. Operations are developed for each of these constructs: Test A, Test B, and Test C. At the plane of behavior, it is hypothesized that when the three tests are administered to a sample of individuals, the scores will be uncorrelated, an indication that they are indeed measuring distinguishable characteristics. As in the case of convergent validity, the finding of independent dimensions does not deal directly with the issue of linkage between test score and construct, but it does provide indirect evidence on this point because the scores are behaving as hypothesized.

Jensen (1980) did not pursue the issue of discriminant validity very extensively. As mentioned earlier, he made a conceptual distinction between so-called tests of intelligence and tests of achievement, but he readily admitted that the distinction collapses at the plane of behavior, and he presented factor analyses from numerous studies that demonstrate that the scores are factorially indistinguishable. He also made a distinction between "purely sensory or motor abilities or physical strength or endurance" and the concept of intelligence:

> Nowhere is a behavioral disability resulting from a sensory or a motor handicap thought of as a lack of intelligence. The deaf–mute is not thought of as "unintelligent," neither is the blind nor the physically dis-

abled. The idea of intelligence is clearly independent of sensory-motor
functions. (p. 171)

The American Association for Mental Deficiency (Heber, 1962;
Grossman, 1973) makes a conceptual distinction between "adaptive
behavior" and "intelligence" and requires that an individual be subnormal on both dimensions before she or he is regarded as mentally
retarded. Therefore, one way in which the discriminant validity of
the WISC-R could be tested would be to determine whether scores
on the WISC-R are independent of sensorimotor functions and of
adaptive behavior measures for the three ethnic groups in our samples. In addition to scores on the WISC-R, we also have student scores
on the Physical Dexterity Tasks (Mercer & Lewis, 1978) and the Adaptive Behavior Inventory for Children (ABIC) (Mercer & Lewis, 1977).
At the plane of theory, physical dexterity, adaptive behavior, and
cognitive skills are conceptualized as independent dimensions. If the
tests have discriminant validity, the scores on the three types of measures should be distinguishable at the plane of behavior.

Table 7 presents an orthogonal factor matrix using the Kaiser
varimax procedure for the six scales that comprise the ABIC, the six
scales which comprise the Physical Dexterity Tasks, and the Verbal
and Performance scales of the WISC-R. The number of factors was
not designated, and three distinct factors emerged, as predicted. The
Factor structures are very similar for each ethnic group. The ABIC,
the Physical Dexterity Scales, and the WISC-R appear to have been
distinguishable dimensions for all groups.

Table 7 also presents the first principal component when an
oblique rotation was used to determine whether there is a strong
general factor that can be used to represent the commonalities of the
three measures. The loadings are heavy for the ABIC scales but are
very small for the WISC-R and the Physical Dexterity Scales. In fact,
the oblique factor pattern yields three factors that are almost identical to those found by means of varimax procedures. There is no g
factor. The scales have discriminant validity, regardless of the procedure used. Therefore, they meet the second requirement of Criterion 8: The three measures are both conceptually and operationally
distinguishable.

Nomological Validity

Figure 3c depicts schematically the concept of nomological validity. In this approach, the investigator defines the concept at the plane
of theory and its theoretical characteristics relative to other con-

TABLE 7

Factor Analysis to Determine the Discriminating Power of the WISC-R for White, Hispanic, and Black Students in Relation to the Adaptive Behavior Inventory for Children and the Physical Dexterity Tasks in SOMPA with Varimax and Principal Component Procedures[a]

| | Orthogonal factor matrices | | | | | | | | | First principal component | | |
| | White | | | Hispanic | | | Black | | | | | |
	I	II	III	I	II	III	I	II	III	White	Hispanic	Black
Factor I: ABIC												
Family	.91	.00	.02	.91	.05	.07	.92	.06	.04	.90	.90	.92
Community	.89	.08	.03	.89	.05	.03	.87	.00	.07	.88	.88	.86
Peer	.72	.07	.17	.83	.10	.08	.79	.00	.13	.77	.83	.80
School	.84	.14	.05	.86	.10	.10	.89	.04	.05	.85	.87	.89
Earner/Consumer	.83	.00	.02	.86	.07	.03	.87	.01	.02	.81	.86	.86
Self-Maintenance	.88	.11	.12	.88	.13	.05	.88	.04	.10	.89	.89	.89
Factor II: WISC-R												
Verbal	.11	.84	.11	.17	.62	.11	.08	.82	.06	.25	.30	.11
Performance	.06	.60	.11	.08	.80	.18	.04	.72	.24	.17	.25	.09
Factor III: Physical Dexterity Tasks												
Placement	.03	.02	.58	.05	.00	.77	.03	.10	.48	.03	.04	.02
Ambulation	.14	.02	.44	.05	.18	.26	.12	.08	.48	.19	.11	.17
Involuntary Movement	.02	.07	.11	.11	.05	.26	.02	.04	.73	−.01	.14	.09
Fine Motor Sequence	.01	.16	.34	.04	.12	.30	.05	.11	.08	.07	.09	−.04
Equilibrium	.02	.04	.33	.04	.17	.22	.00	.09	.10	.06	.01	.02
Finger/Tongue Dexterity	.05	.13	.31	.02	.26	.17	.03	.15	.56	.10	.09	.09
Eigenvalue	4.5	1.3	.7	4.8	1.4	.7	4.6	.9	1.8	4.1	4.8	4.6
Percentage of variance	69	19	12	70	20	10	64	12	24	69	70	64

[a] Analyses conducted by means of the Statistical Package for Social Science (SPSS). Number of factors not designated. Pairwise deletion used.

structs. Measures are developed for the set of concepts, and their relationship to each other is tested at the plane of behavior to determine if the hypothetical relationships hold.

To test for the nomological validity of the WISC-R as a measure of "intelligence" requires that the concept be clearly defined and that the nature of its relationship to other critical variables be specified. The discussion here focuses on three formulations of the construct of "intelligence": Jensen's as presented in his book (1980), Wechsler's as presented in the WISC-R Manual (1974), and my own as presented in the *System of Multicultural Pluralistic Assessment (SOMPA): Technical Manual* (1979b). There are five points on which the three formulations appear to agree:

1. "Intelligence" is a hypothetical construct.
2. Test performance is not a direct measure of the hypothetical construct.
3. Therefore, "intelligence" must be inferred from the individual's present performance by comparing that performance with the performance of a normative population.
4. To have normative validity, the norm population must be of the same age as the individual to assure a "fair" comparison.
5. Tests currently used for measuring the individual's current "achievement" or functioning level, such as "intelligence" tests, are culturally loaded.

Although the language used is slightly different, the following quotations serve to document these five points of agreement. First, Wechsler (1974) provided the following statement of his theoretical construct:

> Intelligence is the overall capacity of an individual to understand and cope with the world around him. . . . (1) It (the definition) conceives of intelligence as an overall *global* entity; that is, a multidetermined and multifaceted entity rather than an independent, uniquely-defined trait. (2) It avoids singling out any ability, however esteemed (e.g. abstract reasoning), as crucial or overwhelmingly important. . . . Ultimately, intelligence is not a kind of ability at all, certainly not in the same sense that reasoning, memory, verbal fluency, etc., are so regarded. Rather *it is something that is inferred* [emphasis added] from the way these abilities are manifested under different conditions and circumstances. One can infer an individual's intelligence from how he thinks, talks, moves, almost from any of the many ways he reacts to stimuli of one kind or another. Indeed, historically, appraisal of such responses has been the usual way of judging intelligence. . . . [Inferences are made] by comparing each subject's test performance not with a composite age group but exclusively with the scores earned by individuals in a single (that is, his or her own) age group. . . . Each person tested is assigned an IQ which, at his age, represents his *relative* intelligence rating. This IQ, and all others similarly obtained, are deviation IQs since they indicate the amount by which a subject deviates above or below the average performance of individuals of his own age group. (pp. 3–5)

Wechsler was quite forthright in declaring that "no attempt has been made to define a priori the social and clinical significance of any given IQ" (p. 4). In short, no argument is made for the *predictive* validity of the test. The validity of the score derives from the logic of the inferences made on the basis of the individual's relative statistical rank when compared with others of the same age; this validity is the score's nomological validity. Finally, Wechsler recognized that a person's performance and, hence, the inferences that can be made from that performance are influenced by cultural and socioeconomic background. He emphasized the importance of "the examiner's awareness of the degree to which a subject's responses may be influenced or conditioned by his cultural and socioeconomic background" (p. 7), but he provided no procedure for estimating that influence or taking it into account in interpreting test scores.

Jensen (1980) discussed the issue of nomological validity in two related contexts. As mentioned earlier, he used the layer-cake analogy to differentiate Intelligence A, a "theoretical construct which cannot be observed or measured directly" (p. 184), from Intelligence B, which is the average performance on multiple tests, or g, and from Intelligence C, which is a specific test score. Both Intelligence B and Intelligence C are variables on the plane of behavior, whereas Intelligence A is on the plane of theory. The only difference between B and C is that B is conceptualized as more stable and general than C because it is based on multiple measures of current functioning. Elsewhere (p. 240), Jensen made a similar distinction but used the concept of *aptitude* to refer to the theoretical construct that is to be inferred on the plane of theory and *achievement* to refer to the measured functioning level. He also briefly elucidated the inferential paradigm for inferring "aptitude" from "achievement." Although he did not specifically mention the necessity of making proper age comparisons (that is taken for granted) he did mention other factors that must be equal if the inferences are to have normative validity: motivation, opportunity, formal education, and interest.

> The validity and importance of the aptitude-achievement distinction are conceptual and theoretical. Differences in aptitude are *inferred* [emphasis added] when individuals with roughly equal or equivalent experience, opportunity, and motivation to acquire some particular knowledge or skills, show marked difference in their rates of acquisition and level of performance after a given amount of exposure. A concept of aptitude is needed to account for the acquisition of a broad class of knowledge and skills in which the main sources of individual differences are not linked essentially to any particular sensory or motor capabilities.... A familiar formulation is *Aptitude* × *Motivation* × *Opportunity* = *Achievement*. (pp. 240–241)

In a similar vein, Jensen stated:

> Many formal definitions, and popular conceptions as well, suggest some kind of distinction between *intelligence* and *performance*. It is recognized that a highly intelligent person might also be very lazy and therefore never accomplish much. So there is an implied distinction between intelligence and achievement.... It is seldom the case that a lack of formal

education per se is equated with a lack of intelligence; opportunity and
interest are taken into account. (p. 171)

Jensen did not specify any procedures for taking differences in experience, opportunity, motivation, and interest into account so that one
can distinguish between "aptitude/intelligence" and "achievement/
performance," but like Wechsler, he clearly recognized the necessity
of doing so if the inferences drawn are to have construct relevance.

Jensen also asserted that tests have varying degress of cultural
loading and visualized two theoretical extremes on a continuum
extending from the least to the most "culturally specific" tests:

There is no definite point on the continuum that divides "culture loaded"
from "culture-free" tests. As we move in one direction along the continuum, tests become more "culture specific," and, as we move in the opposite direction, they become more "culture reduced." (p. 635)

He defined *cultural-reducedness,* however, entirely in terms of the
internal integrity of the test, not in terms of its *external* relevance.

Operationally, we can think of the degree of "culture reducedness" of a
test in terms of the "cultural distance" over which a test maintains substantially the same psychometric properties of reliability, validity, item-
total score correlation, and rank order of item difficulties. (p. 636)

Jensen also briefly alludes to the distinction between the two
purposes of testing and notes, as had been noted in this paper and
elsewhere (Mercer, 1973, 1975, 1978–1979, 1979a,b) that "the problem
of cross-cultural testing is made somewhat more tractable" when
one is

clear about whether one's purposes in testing involves *predictive* validity
or *construct* validity. If the problems of predictive validity increase arith-
metically as a function of cultural distance, the problems of construct
validity increase geometrically. A quite highly culture-specific test may
derive much of its validity for predicting a particular criterion from its
cultural specificity per se. . . . Demonstrating useful cross-cultural validity
for a particular educational or occupational criterion is invariably much
easier than establishing a test's construct validity across remote cultures.
Establishing the cross-cultural validity of a psychological construct . . .
involves much more than simply revamping an existing test. It calls for a
whole program of research. (pp. 636–637)

Jensen then proceeded to discuss various approaches that have been
used to develop "culture-reduced" tests, and he ranked tests according to his preception of their cultural specificity. Unlike Wechsler,
however, he concluded that ethnic and socioeconomic cultural factors have been overrated as factors in American society. He states:

> When tests that differ quite widely along the culture-reduced continuum
> are taken by various native-born ethnic minorities and different socioeco-
> nomic groups, there is remarkably little variation in any group's *mean
> score*, in relation to majority norms, across the more and less culture-
> reduced tests.

Note that he used the *mean score differences* as his indicator of
placement on the continuum. He concluded

> that practically all our present standardized tests, culture-reduced or not,
> span as wide or wider a range of cultural distance as is found among any
> native-born, English-speaking racial and socioeconomic groups within
> the United States today. The differences between the ordinary culture-
> loaded tests and the more culture-reduced tests, therefore, show up mark-
> edly only in foreign language groups and across quite remote cultures. (p.
> 642)

Hence, he postulated, in terms of his equation, that "motivation" and
"opportunity" have equal weights for all groups in American society; therefore, the equation Aptitude $\times$ Motivation $\times$ Opportunity =
Achievement reduces to Aptitude = Achievement.

My position on the nomological validity of inferring "intelli-
gence/aptitude" from measures of current "achievement/perfor-
mance" parallels that of Wechsler and Jensen except that, unlike Jensen, I cannot agree that all groups in American society have similar
"motivation" and "opportunity" to learn the materials in the test,
and consequently, I cannot agree that cultural loading in tests is a
trivial problem that can be ignored in assessment. The inferential
paradigm explicated in the pluralistic assessment model (Mercer,
1973; 1979b, Chap. 9) reasons that it is possible to make certain cau-
tious inferences about a child's "learning potential" (roughly equivalent to Jensen's Intelligence A, or *aptitude* and *intelligence*, as generally used in psychometric assessment), providing certain rigorous
assumptions have been met to control for differences in cultural
exposure. The persons whose current performance is being compared in order to make inferences about his or her relative "intelligence" must

1. have had equal opportunities to learn the materials in the test;
2. have had equal motivation to learn the materials in the test;
3. have had equal test-taking experience;
4. be equally free of anxieties, fears, or emotional disturbances
   that might interfere with learning or with test performance;
5. be equally free of physical, sensory, or motor disabilities that
   might interfere with learning or with test performance.

Whereas the traditional inferential paradigm controls only for age, the pluralistic paradigm argues that in a culturally complex society such as modern America, we cannot assume that the factors listed by Jensen—experience, opportunity, motivation, formal education, and interest—are equivalent for all "ethnic and socioeconomic cultural" groups. Therefore, to have nomological validity, the test must be normed not only for age but for sociocultural background factors. Otherwise, inferences about the hypothetical construct "intelligence" cannot be made, and the score must simply be treated as an indicator of present performance on a more-or-less culture-specific test. Four lines of evidence support the position that America is a socioculturally heterogeneous society and that cultural loading in test scores is a nontrivial factor that cannot be ignored when tests are used for the purpose of inferring "intelligence":

1. Measures of the characteristics listed by Jensen as influencing nomological validity, as well as other sociocultural measures, show both statistical and substantive differences across subgroups in American society. The mothers of the students in our samples were asked 38 questions concerning the social and cultural characteristics of their family, and the responses to 35 of these questions differed significantly across ethnic groups. The items were then factor-analyzed by means of varimax rotational procedures for each ethnic group. This procedure yielded 11 factors, 8 of which were identical across all three ethnic groups. The remaining three factors were similar for two of the three ethnic groups. We dropped 9 items that had commonalities of less than .40 and factor-analyzed the 29 remaining items, combining the three ethnic groups. The result was a 9-factor solution that permitted us to drop 4 more items. A second-order factor analysis resulted in four sociocultural scales, which we named Family Size, Family Structure, Socioeconomic Status, and Urban Acculturation. The questions cover the number of children in the family and the extended family living in the household; the marital status of the parents and whether the student is living with his or her biological parents; the occupational level of the head of the household and the source of family income; the sense of efficacy (which is a motivational variable), community participation, the formal education of the parents, the country or region in which parents were reared, and the language level of the respondent; and the urban-rural-migrant background of the parents.

Table 8 presents an analysis of variance across the three samples in our study for the sociocultural scales and the factors in each scale. The overall *F* ratios are all statistically significant, and most of them

TABLE 8

Analysis of Variance of Average Scores for the Sociocultural Scales and the Factors in Each Scale across Ethnic Group

Sociocultural scales and factors	Black (N = 696)		Hispanic (N = 690)		White (N = 699)		Overall F ratio	Scheffé
	Mean	SD	Mean	SD	Mean	SD		
Family size[a]	7.8	3.8	9.2	4.1	6.8	2.8	76.4**	W > B > H
Family structure	12.2	5.8	15.4	4.6	15.2	4.5	63.5**	WH > B
Parent–child relationship	1.7	.6	1.9	.4	1.8	.5	7.2**	H > B
Marital status	1.8	1.4	2.4	1.1	2.5	1.0	65.4**	WH > B
Socioeconomic status	4.8	3.4	5.1	2.8	8.1	2.8	230.0**	W > BH
Occupation of head of household	2.9	2.3	2.7	2.1	5.3	2.5	258.0**	W > BH
Source of income	2.1	1.3	2.5	1.0	2.8	.6	79.6**	W > H > B
Urban acculturation	53.4	14.3	38.9	21.4	66.1	12.8	433.7**	W > B > H
Sense of efficacy	2.2	1.0	2.0	1.1	2.7	.6	97.7**	W > B > H
Community participation	4.3	1.9	2.7	2.0	4.2	1.8	141.2**	WB > H
Anglicization	6.1	2.0	4.2	3.0	8.1	1.8	460.4**	W > B > H
Urbanization	3.9	1.8	3.7	1.7	3.9	1.7	3.5*	b

[a]Family Size is both a scale and a factor.
[b]Not statistically significant.
*Differences are significant at the .05 level.
**Differences are significant at the .01 level.

are very large. Sheffé tests pinpoint the locus of the differences (Mercer, 1979b, Chap. 6).

Even a cursory examination of Table 8 reveals large sociocultural differences. The Hispanic families were significantly larger than the black families, which, in turn, were significantly larger than the white families. The black students were less likely to be living with both biological parents. The white families had significantly higher socioeconomic status and higher urban acculturation than either the black or the Hispanic families. It is clear that we cannot assume these students came from a single population with a common lifestyle and a homogeneous cultural heritage. It should be noted that these samples consisted primarily of native-born students and were not from the "remote cultures" that Jensen has readily admitted may not be appropriately measured by culture-loaded tests.

2. Performance on the WISC-R and its subtests is consistently superior for the sample that has the most opportunity, motivation, and experience with the cultural materials in the test—as shown in Table 9, the white students. Table 9 presents a pattern that we would anticipate on the basis of our knowledge of the cultural differences in the three samples. The white students scored significantly higher on *every* scale and subtest of the WISC-R than either the black or the Hispanic students. In some cases, there were no differences between black and Hispanic students; in other cases, one group scored higher than the other. However, in *no* case do we have a reversal, in which white students scored lower.

Tables 10 and 11 provide an item analysis across ethnic groups for every item of each subtest in the WISC-R at the 6-, 8-, and 10-year age levels. If the analysis of variance indicated that the differences were not significant, NS is recorded on the table. When the overall F ratio was significant at the .05 level or beyond, Scheffé tests were conducted to identify the comparisons that were responsible for the significant differences. Table 10 reports the findings for the Verbal scales, and Table 11 reports the findings for the Performance scales. When items were so simple that everyone passed them or so difficult that few students could pass them, the differences were not significant across ethnic groups. The items that differentiated the groups were toward the middle of most of the scales and tended to move upward as the students got older. There are 540 analyses in the two tables, and 283 of them (52.4%) show statistically significant differences by ethnic group. Except two items where Hispanics were high, the white students scored significantly better than the black and/or the Hispanic students. There was little difference between the Verbal

TABLE 9
Analysis of Variance across Ethnic Group for WISC-R Scores

Scales and subtests	Black (N = 638)		Hispanic (N = 648)		White (N = 683)		Overall F ratio[a]	Scheffé
	Mean	SD	Mean	SD	Mean	SD		
Verbal Scale (IQ)	87.9	13.6	87.3	14.8	102.1	14.5	224.3	W > BH
Information	7.6	2.7	7.5	3.0	10.5	3.0	234.0	W > BH
Similarities	7.6	3.2	7.6	3.5	10.3	3.4	144.2	W > BH
Vocabulary	8.5	2.1	7.9	3.2	10.8	2.9	172.5	W > B > H
Comprehension	8.2	2.8	7.8	2.9	10.1	3.0	114.2	W > B > H
Arithmetic	8.4	2.7	8.7	2.9	10.3	2.9	82.1	W > BH
Digit Span	8.8	3.1	8.4	3.1	10.4	3.0	77.3	W > B > H
Performance Scale (IQ)	89.5	13.5	97.2	13.5	104.1	13.7	186.1	W > H > B
Picture Arrangement	8.0	2.9	9.1	3.0	10.3	2.9	96.8	W > H > B
Picture Completion	8.9	2.9	9.8	3.1	10.8	2.9	66.2	W > H > B
Block Design	8.3	2.8	9.7	2.7	10.8	2.8	141.7	W > H > B
Object Assembly	8.2	2.8	9.7	2.8	10.5	2.8	120.8	W > H > B
Mazes	8.7	3.1	10.0	3.2	11.2	3.1	103.2	W > H > B
Coding	9.1	3.3	9.7	3.2	10.6	3.2	36.4	W > H > B
Full-scale (IQ)	87.7	13.0	91.5	13.4	103.3	13.8	237.8	W > H > B

[a] All F ratios significant beyond the .001 level. Scheffé test reports differences beyond the .05 level.

TABLE 10
Item Analysis of Verbal Subscales on the WISC-R for Black, Hispanic, and White Students 6, 8, and 10 Years of Age: Direction of Significantly Different Responses

Item	Information[a]			Vocabulary[b]			Arithmetic		
	6	8	10	6	8	10	6	8	10
1	WB > H	B > H	NS	W > HB	W > B > H	NS	NS	NS	NS
2	NS	NS	NS	W > H	W > H	NS	NS	NS	NS
3	W > B	NS	NS	W > H	NS	NS	NS	NS	NS
4	WB > H	WB > H	WB > H	NS	W > H	NS	W > BH	NS	NS
5	W > HB	W > HB	W > HB	W > HB	W > H > B	NS	NS	W > B	NS
6	WB > H	B > H	NS	NS	W > H	NS	W > HB	NS	NS
7	W > B	W > HB	W > H	W > H	NS	NS	W > HB	NS	NS
8	W > HB	W > HB	W > H > B	W > HB	W > HB	NS	W > HB	NS	NS
9	W > HB	W > HB	W > HB	W > B > H	WB > H	WB > H	NS	W > HB	NS
10	W > HB	W > HB	W > HB	W > H	W > HB	W > H	NS	W > HB	W > HB
11	W > HB	W > HB	W > HB	W > HB	W > HB	W > H	NS	W > HB	W > B
12	W > B	W > HB	W > HB	W > HB	W > HB	W > HB	NS	NS	W > B
13	W > HB	W > HB	W > HB	W > HB	W > HB	W > HB	NS	W > B	W > HB
14	NS	W > HB	W > HB	W > HB	W > HB	W > H	NS	NS	W > HB
15	NS	NS	W > HB	W > HB	W > HB	W > HB	NS	NS	W > B
16	NS	NS	W > HB	NS	W > HB	W > HB	NS	NS	W > B
17	NS	W > H	W > B	W > HB	W > HB	W > HB	NS	NS	NS
18	NS	W > HB	W > B	NS	W > HB	W > HB	NS	NS	NS
19	NS	W > HB	W > HB	NS	W > HB	W > HB			
20	NS	W > B	W > HB	NS	NS	W > HB			
21	NS	NS	W > B	NS	W > HB	NS			
22	NS	NS	W > HB	NS	NS	NS			
23	NS	NS	W > HB	NS	NS	NS			
24	NS	NS	W > B	NS	NS	NS			
25	NS	NS	W > HB	NS	W > HB	W > B			
26	NS	NS	NS	NS	NS	NS			
27	NS	NS	W > B						

[a]W = White, H = Hispanic, B = Black. NS = not significant at the .05 level based on the Scheffé test, > = significantly greater than.
[b]Neither Information nor Vocabulary had any significantly different items beyond those reported in the table.

Comprehension			Similarities			Digit Span		
6	8	10	6	8	10	6	8	10
W > H	WB > H	W > H	W > H	NS	WH > B	W > H	NS	NS
NS	NS	NS	NS	NS	W > H	WB > H	W > H	NS
NS	NS	W > H	W > HB	W > H	NS	W > H	W > HB	W > H
W > H	W > H	NS	W > HB	W > H	W > HB	W > HB	W > H	W > B > H
H > BW	W > H	NS	W > HB	W > H	W > HB	NS	NS	W > HB
NS	NS	NS	W > HB	W > HB	W > H	NS	NS	W > H
W > HB	W > HB	W > HB	W > H	W > HB	NS	NS	NS	NS
W > HB	W > HB	W > HB	NS	W > H	W > H	W > HB	NS	NS
NS	W > HB	W > HB	W > HB	W > HB	W > HB	W > B	W > B	W > B
NS	NS	W > HB	W > HB	W > H	W > H	W > HB	NS	W > HB
W > H	W > HB	W > HB	W > HB	W > HB	W > H	NS	NS	W > B
NS	NS	W > HB	NS	W > HB	W > HB	NS	NS	W > B
NS	W > HB	W > HB	NS	NS	W > B	NS	NS	NS
NS	NS	W > HB	NS	NS	NS	NS	NS	NS
NS	NS	W > HB	NS	NS	W > HB			
NS	W > B	W > HB	NS	NS	W > H			
NS	NS	W > B	NS	NS	NS			

TABLE 11
Item Analysis of Performance Subscales of the WISC-R for Black, Hispanic, and White Students 6, 8, and 10 Years of Age: Direction of Significantly Different Responses[a]

Items	Picture Completion			Picture Arrangement			Block Design			Mazes			Object Assembly		
	6	8	10	6	8	10	6	8	10	6	8	10	6	8	10
1	NS	NS	NS	W > B	W > B	NS	W > B	NS	NS	W > B	NS	NS	W > HB	W > HB	WH > B
2	NS	NS	NS	W > HB	NS	NS	W > B	NS	NS	NS	NS	NS	W > H > B	W > HB	WH > B
3	WH > B	NS	NS	W > H > B	W > HB	WH > B	W > B	NS	NS	W > B	NS	WH > B	W > H > B	W > HB	W > HB
4	W > B	NS	NS	W > H > B	WH > B	NS	W > HB	W > HB	WH > B	W > HB	W > B	NS	W > H > B	W > B	WH > B
5	NS	NS	NS	W > B	W > B	NS	W > HB	NS	WH > B	WH > B	NS	NS			
6	NS	NS	NS	W > HB	W > B	W > B	W > HB	W > HB	WH > B	WH > B	H > BW	WH > B			
7	NS	NS	W > B	W > HB	WH > B	NS	W > B	W > B	W > B	WH > B	W > HB	WH > B			
8	WH > B	W > B	NS	W > HB	W > B	NS	W > B	NS	W > B	W > B	W > HB	W > B			
9	NS	NS	NS	NS	W > B	NS	NS	W > HB	W > B	NS	NS	W > B			
10	NS	NS	NS	NS	W > B	NS	NS	NS	WH > B						
11	NS	W > B	W > B	NS	NS	W > B	NS	NS	W > B						
12	NS	NS	W > B	NS	NS	NS									
13	W > B	NS	NS												
14	H > B	NS	NS												
15	NS	W > B	NS												
16	NS	NS	NS												
17	NS	W > B	W > B												
18	NS	W > B	WH > B												
19	H > B	NS	H > B												
20	NS	W > HB	NS												
21	NS	NS	NS												
22	W > B	W > B	W > HB												
23	W > B	W > B	W > B												
24	NS	W > B	WH > B												
25	NS	NS	NS												

[a]W = White, H = Hispanic, B = Black, NS = Not significant at the .05 level based on the Scheffé test, > = significantly greater than.

and Performance scales: 53.5% of the Verbal and 50.2% of the Performance items discriminated in favor of the white students. Following is a list of the individual subtests, rank-ordered by the percentage of items that favored the white students: Object Assembly, 100%; Similarities, 62.7%; Information, 61.7%; Block Design, 60.6%; Mazes, 59.3%; Vocabulary, 59.0%; Comprehension, 54.9%; Picture Arrangement, 50%; Digit Span, 45.2%; Picture Comprehension, 34.7%; and Arithmetic, 29.6%. The pattern of discrimination was consistent across age group and systematic across subtest. It is precisely the type of pattern that would be expected if performance is being uniformly depressed by sociocultural factors such as differences in the variables mentioned by Jensen: formal education, opportunity, motivation, and interest.

   3. Differences in average scores on the test and differences in sociocultural characteristics would not be relevant to nomological validity if the two were not linked. However, such is not the case. Table 12 presents the multiple-correlation coefficients when our sociocultural scales ·were used as independent variables predicting WISC-R scale scores and subtest scores. The findings in the first two columns are relevant to the issue of whether sociocultural differences in the total population can be regarded as trivial. They give the correlation coefficients and the percentage of the variance explained

TABLE 12

Multiple Correlation Coefficients Predicting WISC-R Scales and Subtest Scores from the Four Sociocultural Scales

	Total sample		Black		Hispanic		White	
Scales and subtests	r	% Variance	r	% Variance	r	% Variance	r	% Variance
Verbal Scale (IQ)	.52	27.4	.33	10.9	.47	22.5	.42	17.6
Similarities	.43	18.1	.27	7.0	.36	13.1	.32	10.2
Arithmetic	.34	11.3	.22	4.9	.31	9.7	.25	6.1
Vocabulary	.49	23.9	.30	8.8	.46	21.9	.34	11.8
Comprehension	.41	16.7	.24	5.7	.36	12.8	.35	12.1
Information	.51	25.8	.28	8.0	.48	23.0	.39	15.4
Digit Span	.37	14.0	.25	6.1	.39	15.1	.25	6.2
Performance Scale (IQ)	.37	13.6	.31	9.7	.23	5.2	.28	7.6
Picture Completion	.25	6.0	.23	5.2	.15	2.3	.15	2.2
Picture Arrangement	.29	8.4	.24	5.9	.21	4.6	.22	4.9
Block Design	.30	8.9	.20	3.8	.21	4.3	.21	4.6
Object Assembly	.28	7.6	.21	4.4	.22	4.8	.19	3.8
Coding	.22	4.9	.24	5.7	.09	.8	.18	3.2
Mazes	.23	5.2	.12	1.6	.16	2.7	.16	2.6
Full-scale IQ	.49	24.1	.36	12.8	.40	15.7	.40	15.9

when all three samples are included in the analysis. The results show that 27.4% of the variance in Verbal scores can be explained by sociocultural differences, as well as 13.6% of the variance in Performance scores, and 24.1 of the variance in full-scale scores. Individual subtests varied from a high of 25.8% of the variance in Information to a low of 4.9% of the variance in Coding. In general, the verbal subtests were more culture-loaded than the performance subtests. Except for Coding, all percentages exceed the 5% limit suggested earlier in this paper.

On first inspection, it may seem that 25% of the variance is minor until it is recognized that 25% of the variance is more than enough to "explain" the typical gap of 12–15 points between the average scores earned by minority groups and those earned by the majority, and that 25% can mean the difference between a student's being defined as mentally retarded or "normal."

Of course, the size of the multiple-correlation coefficients in any analysis is related to the heterogeneity or range of scores in the population. Hence, it has frequently been proposed that separate norms for each ethnic group would be sufficient to control for sociocultural variance. The separate analyses in Table 12 for each ethnic group show that a single, separate norm for each ethnic group would reduce the sociocultural variance in the scores, in several cases below the 5% of variance that we have proposed as an upper limit. The Performance subtests were, for the most part, within tolerable limits in our sample, but such was not the case for the Verbal subtests. The Verbal, Performance, and full-scale IQs still exceeded the limits. Although a single separate norm for each group would have greater nomological validity than a single norm for all groups, there is still considerable sociocultural variance within each ethnic population.

It seems clear from the above analyses (1) that there are large and statistically significant sociocultural differences in the three ethnic groups studied; (2) that the average scores on the WISC-R and the individual items consistently discriminate in favor of whites; and (3) that there is a significant amount of variance in the WISC-R scores, especially the Verbal subtests, that can be explained by sociocultural factors. Therefore, we conclude that the WISC-R, as traditionally used in psychological assessment for the purpose of inferring "intelligence," does not have normative validity, the type of nomological validity required when a test is used for this purpose on the socioculturally complex populations that comprise American society.

It is beyond the scope of this paper to discuss the various proposed solutions to this problem. In general, there have been four types of proposals:

1. Jensen and other defenders of the traditional psychometric belief-system have generally taken the position that there is no serious problem and that the test scores can be used to infer "intelligence," "aptitude," and similar constructs without reference to differences in experience, opportunity, motivation, and so forth.

2. At the other extreme, there are those who take the position that tests should not be used *at all* for the purpose of inferring "intelligence." They reason that the paradigm for inferring "intelligence" is so fragile and that the available measures are so culture-specific that the danger of making serious errors, especially in the assessment of minority persons, is too great to justify the continued use of the paradigm (Mercer, 1973, 1975, 1979a).

This was essentially the position taken by Cleary *et al.* (1975) when they proposed that test use be restricted to making predictions (pragmatic validity) and that psychologists abandon the practice of interpreting the scores as a measure of innate ability or similar constructs. This was also the position taken by Judge Peckham (*Larry P.* 1979), although he left open an opportunity for the State of California to present evidence to the court that it had established the validity of the test scores for inferring "intelligence" in the placement of the mentally retarded. To date, the state has not responded to Judge Peckham's query; Peckham's decision was upheld by the appellate court, and no further appeal has been filed by the state.

3. Others have proposed eliminating those tests that have high sociocultural variance from among the measures used to infer "intelligence" and treating them simply as measures of current functioning, or "achievement." Measures used to infer "intelligence" would be restricted to those that are "culture-reduced," measures similar to Coding, Mazes, and Picture Completion on the WISC-R. The Kaufmans (1983) have used this approach in the development of their new test, the Kaufman Assessment Battery for Children (K-ABC).

4. A fourth proposal has been to continue using the culture-specific tests now being employed and to maintain standard testing procedures and scoring, but to develop local, sociocultural norms for each subpopulation on which the test will be used for the purpose of inferring "intelligence." The assumption is that more rigorous norming procedures can control for most of the sociocultural variance and allow for making inferences that go beyond the student's current performance. This is the approach that I have used in devel-

oping a score called *estimated learning potential* (ELP) as part of the SOMPA (Mercer, 1979b, Chap. 17). This approach has several advantages. It uses testing procedures that are already developed and personnel already trained to administer those procedures. It is inexpensive. A five-minute interview with the parent provides all the background information needed. It takes about three minutes to calculate the ELP once the data are on hand. The scores generated meet the criteria for a racially and culturally nondiscriminatory inference concerning "intelligence." The means and the standard deviations for the scores are similar across the three groups and no longer systematically discriminate in favor of the white population. They meet the test for nomological validity as defined in this section of the paper.

Summary of Criterion 8: Equal Construct Relevance

When a test is being used to make inferences about constructs such as "intelligence," "aptitude," or "learning potential," it must have equal construct relevance for the groups on which it is being used if it is to be considered racially and culturally nondiscriminatory. Construct relevance has three components: convergent validity, discriminant validity, and nomological validity. The latter is the most crucial because the first two deal exclusively with relationships at the plane of behavior and do not address, directly, the linkage between test score and construct:

1. To have equal convergent validity, different measures that presumably measure the same construct should be similarly intercorrelated for the various groups on which they are being used.

2. To have equal discriminant validity, measures that presumably measure different constructs should be similarly uncorrelated for the various groups on which they are being used.

3. To have equal nomological validity, tests should have similar interrelationships with measures of other constructs as specified in the definition of the construct being measured. Specifically, when tests are being used to make inferences about "intelligence" or comparable constructs, they should have similar validity; that is, the cultural loading present in the measures should have been eliminated either by further refinements of the measures themselves or by statistical controls at the time of interpreting test scores by comparing individual performance only with others who have had similar "experience," "motivation," "opportunity," "formal education," and "interest" (Jensen, 1980, pp. 240–241). Depending on the procedure

used to achieve a racially and culturally nondiscriminatory inferential model, one or more of the following criteria should be met: (a) item analysis should demonstrate that item response patterns do not show evidence of systematically discriminating in favor of one or more of the groups; (b) correlations between test scores and measures of sociocultural background should be at a minimum: a standard of explaining less than 5% of the variance seems reasonable; and (c) the means and the standard deviations of the scores for the groups involved should be similar. Given that no test is completely reliable and that precise replication is unlikely, a tolerance range of one standard error of estimate overall difference between mean scores seems a reasonable standard.

SUMMARY

Jensen has provided the field with an encyclopedic review of the issues in test validity and "bias" from the traditional psychometric perspective. Unfortunately, he has not provided a conceptually crisp, theoretically consistent set of standards that can serve as the basis for public policy relating to racially and culturally nondiscriminatory assessment. Following is a recapitulation of the definition of testing procedures that are racially and culturally nondiscriminatory that was presented in the introduction to this chapter with brief statements of those issues where there is congruence and incongruence between Jensen's position and that taken in this paper.

To be racially and culturally nondiscriminatory, testing procedures must have (1) equal internal integrity and (2) equal external relevance to the groups on whom the procedures are to be used. There are four criteria for *equal internal integrity:*

Criterion 1 is that a test should have equivalent reliabilities. Our findings show that the WISC-R has equivalent reliabilities for the three groups studied. There is congruence between Jensen's position and that taken in this paper.

Criterion 2 is that a test should have equivalent stability. We have no data on the stability of the WISC-R for the group that we studied, and Jensen has presented no data on this point for minority populations. We agree that the criterion is important, but the research remains to be done.

Criterion 3 is equivalent item patterning. We found that the rank-order correlations of items on the WISC-R were very high across the groups studied and that there is equivalent item patterning. Jensen and his colleagues consider this a very important criterion. The position taken in this paper is that item patterning is related to factors that are not central to issues of test bias because it is almost inconceivable that item patterning would differ across groups except for tests administered under circumstances that violate accepted principles of good testing practice. Hence, although we are not opposed to using item patterning as a criterion, we regard it as an attribute of all tests and not particularly informative.

Criterion 4 is equivalent intercorrelational and/or factor patterns for all groups on whom the test is to be used. This is a standard test of internal consistency, and our findings support the view that the intercorrelational matrices and factor patterns for the WISC-R are similar across groups, regardless of whether varimax or oblique rotations are used. The major difference between Jensen's position and that taken in this paper is that Jensen has classified the internal factor patterning of a test as a form of construct validity. Because such analyses deal only with the internal characteristics of the test as a measurement instrument, I find it conceptually cleaner to classify factor analysis as another test of the internal integrity of the test.

Equal external relevance requires that a test be relevant to the purpose for which it is being used for all groups. Four purposes were identified and four forms of external relevance were described. The appropriate criterion to be applied in any particular case depends on the *purpose* for which the test is being used in that instance. To have internal integrity, all tests should meet all criteria; in examining external relevance, the criterion applied depends on the purposes under consideration.

Criterion 5 applies when a test is being used to measure organic functions. Because the WISC-R was not designed for organic testing, we did not apply this criterion to our data. Jensen has made no claim about the relevance of "mental tests" to organic screening. Hence, we are in essential agreement on this point.

Criterion 6 applies when the test is being used edumetrically to measure the level of knowledge or skill that the individual has in a particular area, and the appropriate criterion is content validity. Because "mental tests" are seldom used for such academic purposes, Jensen has dealt with issues of content validity only peripherally. We are in essential agreement that "intelligence" tests are not designed to measure academic competencies, and that content validity is not an appropriate criterion for such tests.

Criterion 7 deals with the issue of pragmatic validity, the ability of the test to make equally accurate predictions for members of different racial and ethnic groups. Jensen has focused primarily on pragmatic validity and has provided an excellent explanation of the rationale and statistical procedures. We are in agreement that, when a test is being used exclusively to predict some social behavior, pragmatic validity is the appropriate form. We differ with Jensen on his belief that validity can be determined by correlating so-called intelligence tests with so-called achievement tests, even though he has freely admitted that the two types of tests are statistically indistinguishable. The position taken in this chapter is that "intelligence" test–"achievement" test correlations are a form of convergent construct validity and do not qualify as a test of pragmatic validity in real-world situations. Rather, actual performance in the role being predicted should be the criterion. Jensen has reported very few studies in which role performances, as rated by a teacher, a supervisor, or other observer, have been the criterion and the subjects have been elementary-school students. This paper takes the position that pragmatic validity is not the primary issue in "intelligence" testing in any case, because schools do not, in fact, think of the scores as "predictors" but use them for the purpose of inferring "intelligence." If schools are concerned with making predictions of future scholastic performance, they have at hand other types of predictors that are much more powerful than "intelligence" tests.

Criterion 8 applies when tests are being used for the purpose of making inferences about an abstract construct. Construct relevance takes three forms: convergent validity, discriminant validity, and nomological validity. Jensen has placed great emphasis on the convergent validity of mental tests and has presented numerous studies showing high levels of intercorrelations among scores from various tests. His notion of "intelligence" is focused on the commonalities in such tests, the g factor. The position in this paper is that tests of convergent validity are of limited value. If there is no correlation, one can conclude that the tests lack construct validity. The converse, however, is not true. The fact that measures correlate with each other does not establish any necessary linkage to the construct at the plane of theory. Similarly, discriminant validity is of limited value. The fact that tests that supposedly measure separate constructs are not correlated establishes the fact that the scales probably do not measure the same construct, but it provides no information on the specific constructs that any of the scales do measure. Nomological validity is the crucial form of construct relevance for inferring intelligence.

In reviewing the statements of Weschler and Jensen and the position taken in this paper, we concluded that there were large areas of agreement concerning the measurement paradigm that is required for inferring "intelligence," a paradigm that we called *normative validity*. We noted general agreement on most elements of the nomological paradigm: that "intelligence" is a hypothetical construct; that the construct does not include experience, opportunity, motivation, formal education, or interest; that the construct cannot be measured directly but must be inferred from present performance; that age differences must be controlled in order to have normative validity; and that the tests now being used for this purpose have some cultural loading. The major disagreement centers on the extent to which the cultural loading in present tests violates the assumptions of the inferential model. Jensen has asserted that culture loading presents no problem as long as tests are administered to native-born individuals. We have presented data showing that the WISC-R discriminates systematically in favor of white students at the item level, the subtest level, and the scale level in three samples consisting mainly of native-born white, black, and Hispanic students. Hence, we reached the conclusion that inferences based on those test scores are racially and culturally discriminatory and that present procedures cannot be used without violating Public Law 94-142. Suggestions were presented for alternative approaches that would meet the standard for nomological validity: equivalent means and standard deviation, and/or equivalent or balanced item-response patterns, and/or minimal correlation between sociocultural background and test performance.

There are wide areas of agreement. It is my hope that stating explicitly a set of criteria for judging whether a test is racially and culturally discriminatory will focus the debate on those issues where there are fundamental disagreements and will eventually lead to a broader consensus on an acceptable set of standards for testing in a pluralistic society.

REFERENCES

Angoff, W. H., & Ford, S. F. Item-race interaction on a test of scholastic aptitude. *Journal of Educational Measurement*, 1973, *10*, 95–106.

Berk, R. A., Bridges, W. P., & Shih, A. Use of IQ scores for tracking mentally retarded. *American Sociological Review*, 1981, *46*, 58–71.

Boring, E. G. Intelligence as the tests test it. *New Republic*, 1923, *35*, 35–37.

Carver, R. Two dimensions of tests: Psychometric and edumetric. *American Psychologist*, 1974, *29*(7), 512–518.

Clarizio, H. F. In defense of the IQ test. *School Psychology Digest*, 1979, *8*, 79–88.

Cleary, T. A., & Hilton, T. L. An investigation of item bias. *Educational and Psychological Measurement*, 1968, *28*, 61–75.

Cleary, T. A., Humphreys, L. G., Kendrick, S. A., & Wesman, A. Educational uses of tests with disadvantaged students. *American Psychologist*, 1975, *30*, 15–41.

Covington, J. E., & Klein, S. P. Validity Study of the Multistate Bar Examination Conducted by an Independent Panel and Sponsored by the National Conference of Bar Examiners, Columbia, Missouri, 1980–1981, personal communication.

Crano, W. D., Kenny, D. A., & Campbell, D. T. Does intelligence cause achievement? A cross-lagged panel analysis. *Journal of Educational Psychology*, 1972, *63*, 258–275.

Doll, E. A. Historical survey of research and management of mental retardation in the U.S. In E. P. Trapp (Ed.), *Readings on the exceptional child*. New York: Appleton-Century-Crofts, 1962.

Federal Register, Tuesday, August 23, 1977: Part II, Department of Health, Education, and Welfare: Office of Education, Education of Handicapped Children: Implementation of Part B of the Education of the Handicapped Act. Vol. 42, No. 163, 42474–42518.

Figueroa, R. Progress Reports: The validation of the *System of Multicultural Pluralistic Assessment* (SOMPA). Department of Education, Grant 13.4430, 1979–1981 (unpublished).

Flaugher, R. L. The many definitions of test bias. *American Psychologist*, 1978, *33*, 671–679.

Goldman, R. D., & Hartig, L. K. The WISC may not be a valid predictor of school performance for primary-grade minority children. *American Journal of Mental Deficiency*, 1976, *80*(6), 583–587.

Gomez-Palacio, Margarita, Rangel-Hinojosa, Elena, Padilla, & Eligio. *Estandarización de la SOMPA en Mexico D.F.: Informe sobre teoria y resultados*. Dirección General de Educación Especial SEP-OEA Mexico, 1982.

Gomez-Palacio, Margarita, Padilla, Eligio, Roll, & Samuel. *WISC-R Mexicano: Manuel de aplicación adaptado*. Dirección de Educación Especial, SEP-OEA Mexico, 1982.

Gordon, R. A. Examining labeling theory: The case of mental retardation. In W. R. Gove (Ed.), *The labeling of deviance: Evaluating a perspective*. New York: Halsted Press, 1975.

Grossman, H. J. (Ed.). *Manual on terminology and classification in mental retardation*. Washington, D.C.: American Association on Mental Deficiency, 1973 (Special publication series No. 2.).

Hayakawa, S. I. *Language in action*. New York: Harcourt, Brace, 1947.

Hebb, D. O. *The organization of behavior: A neuropsychological theory*. New York: Wiley, 1949.

Heber, R. F. A manual on terminology and classification in mental retardation (2nd ed.). *American Journal of Mental Deficiency*, 1962 (Monograph Supplement 64).

Hilliard, A. G. Standardized testing and non standard populations. *The Generator: Division G, American Educational Research Association*, 1981, *11*(2).

Jensen, A. R. How biased are culture-loaded tests? *Genetic Psychology Monographs*, 1974, *90*, 185–244.

Jensen, A. R. *Bias in mental testing*. New York: Free Press, 1980.

Kaufman, A. S. *Intelligent testing with the WISC-R*. New York: Wiley, 1979. (a)

Kaufman, A. S. ISC-R research: Implication for interpretation. *The School Psychology Digest*, 1979, *8*, 5–27. (b)

Kaufman, A. S., & Kaufman, N. *Kaufman assessment battery for children (K-ABC)*. American Guidance Service, 1983.

Larry P. *et al.* v. Wilson Riles, Superintendent of Public Instruction for the State of California *et al.*, C 71 2270 RFP (United States District Court for the Northern District of California, Before the Honorable Robert F. Peckham, Chief Judge).

MacMillan, D. I., & Meyers, C. E. The nondiscriminatory testing provision of PL 94–142. *Viewpoints*. 1977, *53*(2), 39–56.

Mercer, J. R. *Labeling the mentally retarded*. Berkeley: University of California Press, 1973.

Mercer, J. R. Psychological assessment and the rights of children. In N. Hobbs (Ed.), *The classification of children* (Vol. 1). San Francisco: Jossey-Bass, 1975.

Mercer, J. R. Test "validity," "bias," and "fairness": An analysis from the perspective of the sociology of knowledge. *Interchange*, 1978–1979, *9*(1), 1–16.

Mercer, J. R. In defense of racially and culturally non-discriminatory assessment. *School Psychology Digest*, 1979, *8*, 89–115. (a)

Mercer, J. R. *System of multicultural pluralistic assessment (SOMPA): Technical manual*. New York: The Psychological Corporation, 1979. (b)

Mercer, J. R., & Lewis, J. F. *System of multicultural pluralistic assessment (SOMPA): Parent interview manual*. New York: The Psychological Corporation, 1977.

Mercer, J. R., & Lewis, J. F. *System of multicultural pluralistic assessment (SOMPA): Student assessment manual*. New York: The Psychological Corporation, 1978.

Messick, S. Test validity and the ethics of assessment. *American Psychologist*, November 1980, *35*.

Miele, F. Cultural bias in the WISC. *Intelligence*, 1979, *3*, 149–164.

Public Law 94-142. Amendment to the Education of the Handicapped Act, 94th Congress. S.6. November 29, 1975. 20 USC 1401.

Reschly, D. J. WISC-R factor structures among Anglos, blacks, Chicanos, and native American Papagos. *Journal of Consulting and Clinical Psychology*, 1978, *46*, 417–422.

Reschly, D. J., & Reschly, J. E. Validity of WISC-R factor scores in predicting teacher ratings of achievement and attention among four groups. *Journal of School Psychology*, 1980.

Sandoval, J. The WISC-R and internal evidence of test bias with minority groups. *Journal of Consulting and Clinical Psychology*, 1979, *47*(5), 919–927.

Senate Report (No. 94-168). Education for All Handicapped Children Act, June 2, 1975.

Vernon, P. E. *Intelligence and cultural environment*. London: Methuen, 1969.

Wechsler, D. *Manual for the Wechsler Intelligence Scale for Children—Revised*. New York: Psychological Corporation, 1974.

Wesman, A. G. Intelligent testing. *American Psychologist*, 1968, *23*(4), 267–274.

CHAPTER TEN

Digits Backward and the Mercer–Kamin Law

An Empirical Response to Mercer's Treatment of Internal Validity of IQ Tests

ROBERT A. GORDON

Jensen (e.g., 1980a) has grouped the various criteria for detecting bias in ability tests under two broad headings: internal and external. Studies under the first heading concern themselves with relations among the components of a test; those under the second are concerned with predictive relations between the test as a whole and outside variables. Mercer organized her chapter in this book to parallel Jensen's distinction, and my chapter parallels hers, but, because of space limitations, only the half of her chapter concerned with internal validity.

I give priority to internal validity because of the substantive challenge that Mercer's latest position may appear to represent, and because I have already discussed evidence that conflicts with results from her own single study of external validity (Gordon, 1980). Mercer essentially belittles, in her discussion of what she lists as "Criterion 3," the import of group-by-item interaction studies for the issue of IQ test fairness, whereas psychometricians regard such studies as indeed important (e.g., Berk, 1982). There is little likelihood that either Mercer or the psychometrician will be persuaded by the other's arguments as they now stand. Accordingly, I have taken as my

ROBERT A. GORDON ● Department of Sociology, Johns Hopkins University, Baltimore, Maryland 21218.

task the organization of a more effective, empirically based response
to Mercer's challenge, within the context of a discussion of internal
validity criteria generally. This response entails a lengthy and somewhat novel analysis of the performances of both blacks and whites
on digits-backward items over a 46.5-year period. It is hoped that
readers will bear with the necessity of explaining the many intrica-
cies of that analysis before I bring its results to bear on the "Mercer–
Kamin law," as clear an example of what I call the *diffusion-of-intelligence paradigm* as one could hope to find.

INTERNAL VALIDITY

Mercer lists four major empirical criteria that may reveal bias in
any specific comparison between a minority group and what is
loosely defined as the majority group. Although once it was possible
to define the majority group operationally as the population on
which an IQ test had been standardized, the inclusion of proportional minority samples in recent standardizations of the Stanford–
Binet (S-B) and the Wechsler Intelligence Scale for Children—Revised
(WISC-R) undercuts the utility of that designation. Equating the
majority group with the population displaying the highest average
on intelligence tests leads to the paradox that some familiar groups
outperform whites in general, although they are clearly minorities.
I have in mind the striking advantage of the American Jewish population on verbal tests, amounting to about 11 IQ points, and the
rather consistent and perhaps equally large advantage of Orientals,
here and in their country of origin, on nonverbal and mathematical
reasoning tests (see College Entrance Examination Board, 1982, p. 60;
Gordon & Rudert, 1979, p. 182; Hsia, 1980; Lynn, 1977, 1982; Lynn &
Dzioban, 1980; Rock & Werts, 1979, Fig. 4; Vernon, 1982).

Clearly, defining the population that is the prototypical carrier
of what Mercer (1979b, p. 17) termed the "Anglo core culture" is no
simple task. To proceed with the discussion, I shall ignore these
ambiguities of definition, although they are important for general
theoretical purposes. Criteria of bias can, of course, be applied to
comparisons between any two groups *a priori*, and so the methodology itself is not in question. However, the substantive and theoretical rationale employed by Mercer for her choice of comparisons—
which distinguishes them from being merely topical or pragmatic—
is in question. Despite her cultural orientation, Mercer has no way of
accounting for the fact that certain minorities have apparently been

more successful on average in appropriating IQ-relevant aspects of the "Anglo core culture" than those for whom that culture represents a long-standing heritage. Nor, for that matter, can she identify which minority groups will perform better on tests without depending on either the test outcomes themselves or their recognized surrogates. Her explanation of test differences between certain minorities and the majority relies, therefore, on unanalyzed stereotypes concerning the nature of cultural differences and their manner of persistence, rather than on any developed theory of cultural diffusion *per se.* I hope to make this last point more evident by the end of the discussion.

Briefly, the four internal criteria listed by Mercer require comparable results for both groups in (a) internal consistency reliability; (b) test–retest stability over time; (c) patterning of item difficulty; and (d) correlational or factorial structure among items, among subtests, and between both items and subtests on the one hand and total score on the other. Mercer concedes that empirical results, mainly her own, fail to reveal bias in the WISC-R for three of the criteria, but she states that there is little evidence concerning Criterion (b). Let us review the evidence too, including a considerable amount for Criterion (b), but in an order different from Mercer's. Because Criterion (c) constitutes my major topic, it is placed last—and only barely introduced at that—in the next major section, which is followed in turn by an extended analysis of digits-backward items, in preparation for the final section. Only after completing that do I return to Criterion (c) and group-by-item interaction, finally, to consider Mercer's position in depth.

A SUMMARY OF EVIDENCE CONCERNING INTERNAL VALIDITY

Reliability

Mercer's Table 1 displays internal consistency reliabilities of the same magnitude for white, Hispanic, and black elementary-school children in California, and her results are similar to those reported by Jensen (1980a, pp. 583–584) for the same populations on the Peabody Picture Vocabulary Test (PPVT) and Raven's Colored Progressive Matrices, and for blacks and whites on the Wonderlic Personnel Test; the results are also similar to those for blacks and whites on Raven's Standard Progressive Matrices and the PPVT reported by Scarr (1981, Table 13). As Mercer notes, the levels of reliabilities in her three WISC-R samples are comparable to those assembled for majority samples on numerous other tests by Jensen (1980a, Chap. 7). Consistent with these various demonstrations are the results of Rock and Werts (1979), who showed that the standard errors of measurement for subtests of the Scholastic Aptitude Test Verbal and Mathematics sections (SAT-V and -M) were equivalent across random samples of 500 college applicants drawn from each of the following six U.S. populations: American Indian, black, Mexican-American, Oriental, Puerto Rican, and white. Because the reliability of a test is a function of both its standard error of measurement and the heterogeneity of the sample in question, Rock and Werts noted that their approach is preferable when comparing the measurement accuracy of tests across populations whose variances differ on the trait of interest. Low-scoring minorities are especially apt to encounter "floor" effects on a test such as the SAT and to have their variance reduced in consequence. Hills and Stanley (1968, 1970), for example, showed that the SAT was often too difficult for black college applicants, producing many scores in the chance range, with some consequent lowering of predictive validity. Although the Rock and Werts study does not cover the full range of IQ, its finding of what amounts to equal reliability for six different populations, including two different Hispanic ones, is especially impressive.

Correlational Structure

In her Tables 3, 4, 5, and 6 Mercer shows that the correlational and factorial structure of the WISC-R and its subtests remains relatively invariant for the same three ethnic samples. Included in this invariance are loadings on the first principal component, which can be viewed as the best candidate for representing g as a general factor in any sample of cognitive tests. The first principal components for each of the three samples in Mercer's Table 6 are quite similar, with mean loadings for WISC-R subtests of .57, .59, and .59 for whites, Hispanics, and blacks, respectively. With sample sizes large and nearly equal, even the dispersions of loadings are similar; their standard deviations (SDs) are .11, .13, and .10, respectively. The correlations between each group's principal component loadings and the mean set of loadings are .98, .97, and .95, respectively.

Mercer's results concerning factorial invariance across populations are like those from other studies (Gutkin & Reynolds, 1980a, b; Jensen, 1980a, Chap. 11; 1980c; Jensen & Reynolds, 1982; Kaufman, 1979; Miele, 1979; Osborne, 1980, Table VII-L; Reschly, 1978; Reynolds, 1979; 1980; 1982, Table 4; Rock & Werts, 1979; Scarr, 1981). One of these, by Rock and Werts, includes a demonstration that regressions of observed scores on true scores are the same in all six of the populations named earlier.

Using test data for black sibs and white sibs, Jensen (1980a, pp. 546–548; 1980c, Tables 3 and 4) found invariance across race for all combinations of first principal components extracted from between family (BF) and within family (WF) correlation matrices within each race. Apparently, the g factor is not only the same between and within families in each race, it is also the same between families of one race and within families of the other. Jensen (1980c) reasoned:

> If variance in mental test scores were largely the result of differences in social class, cultural background, economic privilege, parental education, family values, and the like, as is often conjectured, then we should expect most of the significant intercorrelations among such tests to be BF rather than WF, and it would seem reasonable to expect different patterns (or factor structures) of BF and WF intercorrelations among various tests, and in different subpopulations. (p. 166)

Because the correlations computed within families essentially held constant the types of social background variables that Jensen listed, whereas the correlations computed between families would have exaggerated any effects other than those within families, the basis of the factor structure common to all of his first principal components must lie somewhere other than in family social background.

Stability

Now we come to the criterion for which Mercer claims a lack of evidence: equal stability over time. If we accept Mercer's characterization to mean there is not as much evidence as one would like, it is certainly possible to agree. Evidence is not altogether lacking. Mercer is correct in noting that Jensen did not present data on the stability of test scores for different ethnic groups in his recent book, but he has treated the stability of group means at some length in earlier publications (Jensen, 1974a, 1977a). Stability of means can be distinguished from stability of individual IQs, but these issues are not clearly separated by Mercer. Lability of the mean for blacks, especially in the upward direction, even in the presence of high test–retest correlations, would be an important indicator of potential bias in applied use. Although Mercer appears to note this fact, she does not make clear that the two types of stability, individual and group, are in principle potentially quite independent of each other.

Nichols (1970, Table 21) has reported correlations between Stanford–Binet IQ (short form) at age 4 and each of 13 other cognitive tests (including seven WISC subtests) at age 7 for large samples—more than 1,000 of each—of whites and blacks from the multicity Collaborative Study. The means (and SDs) of those 13 correlations for whites and blacks were .39 (.11) and .38 (.09), respectively. The cross-racial correlations between the two sets of 13 correlations was .95.

Although the Collaborative Study data do not stem from having used the same nominal test at the different ages, they do derive from a highly diverse set of both standard and less standard IQ and achievement tests, thus providing an indication of generalizability over the test domain. The comparability of the 13 correlations for each race between the two ages was consistent with the assumption that test–retest results for the same test would be comparable, too, for it must be remembered that even the same nominal test could not employ precisely the same items to test IQ at such widely separated chronological ages in early childhood. The high cross-racial correlation between the 13 correlations suggests that both races responded in a similar manner to whatever differences in length (i.e., reliability) and content were present among the 13 later tests.

Small samples of 80 whites and 48 blacks were followed from preschool through high school by Miele (1979, Table 8). Here, the same nominal IQ test was employed at each of four points in time and was always correlated against the same set of criterion measurements. At each of the four times of testing (preschool and first, third, and fifth grades), correlations of WISC Full-Scale IQ with high-school grade point average (GPA) did not differ significantly across race. This finding suggests that the WISC was not less stable at the individual level for blacks than for whites. As a matter of fact, the observed correlations for blacks at each time point were always higher than those for whites; however, this result could have reflected possible differences between races in the sample variances of IQ and GPA (which were not reported). Correlations for both races increased regularly and substantially over time as the interval between test and criterion decreased; once again, as in the Collaborative Study, we see that both races responded in parallel fashion to a common change in conditions.

Harris and Lovinger (1968, p. 63) have reported a correlation of .89 for WISC Full-Scale IQ administered at seventh and ninth grades, an average interval of about two and one-half years, to 80 disadvantaged students in New York City. Over 90% were black; the rest were Puerto Rican. The requirement that students must have had an unbroken record of tests from first grade on to be included resulted in this group's having an IQ mean that was about four IQ points higher than the average for their school; however, their WISC mean at seventh grade was still only 93.1 (SD = 11.6). Their reported stability correlation of .89 was comparable to those found for whites (see Table 1).

In Table 1, I have assembled other important test–retest correlations from one major study of blacks and two of whites. Kennedy's (1969) data are from six age cohorts of blacks tested at two points in time, whereas the two white studies involved single age cohorts tested repeatedly at different ages (Honzik, Macfarlane, & Allen, 1948; Bayley, 1949). The blacks were sampled in Florida and were found

TABLE 1
Comparisons of IQ Test–Retest Stability over Approximate Four-Year
Intervals among Blacks and Whites[a]

Age at first test:	6	7	8	9	10	11
Age at second test:	10	11	12	13	14	15
Black sample (Kennedy, 1969, Table 7)						
Test–retest r	.60	.86	.86	.74	.76	.76
First test mean IQ	81.2	77.8	81.4	76.9	78.9	79.1
First test SD	9.7	13.5	14.2	12.5	12.9	13.6
N	52	52	53	53	50	52
White sample (Honzik, Macfarlane, & Allen, 1948, Tables 2 and 3)[b]						
Test–retest r	.74	NA	.85	.84	.85	NA
First test mean IQ	118.6	NA	118.7	120.7	120.4	NA
First test SD	12.6	NA	17.2	18.2	17.1	NA
N (correlation only)	214	NA	199	97	107	NA
White sample (Bayley, 1949, Tables 1 and 7)						
Test–retest r	.90	.82	.91	.87	.92	.89
First test mean IQ	123.4	123.0	122.6	129.0	131.9	132.5
First test SD	15.6	15.1	20.1	22.2	23.6	22.1
N (correlation only)	46	44	42	36	36	38
Level of two-tailed significance of difference between black and white test–retest correlations[c]						
Kennedy vs. Honzik et al.	NS	—	NS	NS	NS	—
Kennedy vs. Bayley	.001	NS	NS	NS	.01	NS

[a] All testings involved versions of the Stanford–Binet except those at ages 13 and 15 of the Bayley study, which employed the Terman–McNemar, Forms C and D, respectively.
[b] NA = not available.
[c] NS = not significant.

to be representative of a larger black elementary-school sample regarded as typical of blacks in the southeastern United States that had been tested earlier by Kennedy, Van de Riet, and White (1963). Both white samples were from Berkeley, California, and consisted of children from families whose socioeconomic circumstances were well above average. The mean time interval between tests for the blacks, judging from the original reports, was approximately four and one-quarter years rather than the four years for whites because the first testing was spread over much of a school year, so that the interval for blacks ranged from 4.0 to 4.5 years. The test intervals for the blacks, tested originally as pupils in particular grades, were thus slightly longer than the intervals for the whites, whose testing dates in both studies were determined according to birthday. For the same reasons, the indicated ages are more approximate for the blacks than for the whites. As can be seen from the first note to Table 1, all but two of the testings employed versions of the Stanford–Binet.

Table 1 reveals only two significant differences between races in test–retest stability for individuals. One of those involves the relatively low correlation of .60 for blacks who were initially tested early in the fall of their first grade, and who were at that point presumably rather unfamiliar with school, strangers, and tests. Kennedy (1969, p. 27) suggested such an explanation for the fact that these black 6-year-olds had the lowest stability correlation of any cohort in his study. In contrast, both white samples had, in the course of research, been tested repeatedly before age 6, and most of Bayley's repeated testings were even done by the same person. Baughman and Dahlstrom (1968, p. 112) reported an equally low correlation of .62 for 29 black boys in the rural South who had also been tested with the Stanford–Binet for the first time in first grade during 1961–1962 and were then retested three years later. However, 28 black girls tested under the same circumstances produced a somewhat higher test–retest correlation of .77. In view of the lack of ease of such young children with examiners (e.g., Jensen, 1969a, p. 100)—the mean IQs of the black first-graders are actually equivalent in mental age to those of average whites at about age 5.5—it is probably wise, despite its statistical significance, to disregard the difference associated with black first-graders for general interpretive purposes not having to do with first-graders *per se*.

Even more important for understanding the differences between races in level of correlation in Table 1 are the large differences in IQ variance. Note that the correlations in the Honzik *et al.* study tended to be higher than those for the blacks, and those in the Bayley study were higher still. This happens to be the same order in which the IQ variance progressed from study to study. The Honzik *et al.* and Bayley samples were about 1.6 and 2.4 times as variable as the black samples. Greater variance was conducive to obtaining larger correlations even if the standard errors of measurement were always the same; the correlation of .93 between the standard deviations and the test–retest correlations in the six black age cohorts bears this out. The corresponding correlation among whites, .76, was also high. Substituting the average standard deviation from each white study into the simple regression equation for blacks that reflects the .93 correlation yields linear extrapolations of the test–retest correlation that are actually somewhat higher than the mean correlation in the corresponding white study. Apparently, the differences in IQ variance were more than sufficient to account for the average race difference in stability in Table 1. Both white samples appear to have been appreciably more variable in IQ than the 1937 Stanford–Binet standardization sample, which had an *SD* of 16.4 (Terman & Merrill, 1960, p. 18). Because the one other significant difference in Table 1 involves the Bayley age group with the largest *SD* in the entire table, it, too, should probably be discounted as evidence of race differences in test stability.

Given the small number of significant differences in Table 1, and the likelihood that they are best viewed as artifacts not intrinsic to the question of test stability, it seems fair to regard the data as consistent with equal stability for blacks and whites. Other analyses of mine parallel to those in Table 1, but using the five-year instead of the four-year test–retest interval from the two white studies, presented essentially the same picture. Of 10 possible differences, only one difference was significant. This analysis involved the 9–14 age group of Honzik *et al.*, whose correlation of .86 exceeded ($p < .05$) that of blacks in the 9–13 group.

The overall data show a pattern of equal stability for individuals of both races that extends throughout the range from age 4 to high school. This pattern emerged despite the fact that the whites and the blacks studied were not from the same segments of the IQ range and were known in many cases to differ in variability. Ideally, both segment of IQ range and variability should be held constant when comparing the two races for evidence of test bias, for the standard error of measurement is known to vary directly with magnitude of IQ (McNemar, 1942, Tables 17–19; Terman & Merrill, 1960, p. 10), and hence both factors can affect the size of stability correlations. In Table 1, the nature of the differences between races was such as to cause these two potential influences to work in opposing directions, although they were not necessarily equal in effect.

Now let us turn to stability of the group mean. Although this issue can be viewed both intra- and intergenerationally, the present discussion is confined to studies in the first category. In a longer work (in progress) from which the present chapter has been drawn, I show that there has been considerable stability in the mean IQ difference between blacks and whites over the historical period spanned by IQ testing, despite many substantial decreases in their relative social disadvantages and in their social separation. However, those results require too much introduction to be included here.

An especially important datum concerning the stability of the mean Stanford–Binet IQ of a black sample over a four-and-one-quarter-year interval has been provided by the Kennedy (1969, Table 3) test–retest study described earlier. On first testing, the mean IQ of the study's 312 elementary-school pupils was 79.2, and on second testing in 1965, their mean IQ was 79.4. A second important datum, from the Collaborative Study, probes the preschool years. By use of a graph, Nichols (1970, p. 99) reported the IQ means at ages 4 and 7 of over 1,000 singletons from each race born after 1959. The earlier IQ was based on the Stanford–Binet (short form) and the later one on the WISC. For the whites, the earlier and later IQ means were approximately 106 and 103, and for the blacks, 93 and 92. These changes over time are modest or negligible. One would have to consider the important Kennedy and Nichols studies to be in good agreement concerning stability of mean IQ among blacks. Together, they cover the age range from 4 (at first test) to 16 (at second test), with intervals between tests of three or four years.

Two other studies have yielded either similar or slightly mixed results. The 57 southern rural black children tested with the Stanford–Binet in first grade in the Baughman and Dahlstrom (1968, Table 6.1) study had a mean IQ of 83.7; when retested almost exactly three years later, their mean was 83.2. The net changes for boys and girls were trivial and in opposite directions. Earlier, Osborne (1960, Table 1) had reported data for 815 whites and 446 blacks from a single southern county whose IQs had been tested in Grades 6, 8, and 10 with the California Test of Mental Maturity (CTMM) during the years 1954, 1956, and 1958. At successive testings, the IQ means were 101.3, 100.6, and 102.3 for the whites and 78.8, 84.4, and 78.6 for the blacks. Except for the Grade 8 testing of blacks, where the mean was probably significantly different from the other two black means, Osborne's results show the usual stability over a four-year period.

For reasons unknown, however, the standard deviations decreased systematically by about the same amount in both races. Test–retest correlations were not reported. Because at Grade 10 the mean for blacks did return to its former level at Grade 6, it seems fair to regard Osborne's results as being generally in good agreement with the other three studies despite the presumably significant differences involving Grade 8.

Another significant difference ($p < .001$) appeared in Harris and Lovinger's (1968, Table 1) small study of 80 disadvantaged, predominantly black students in New York. The means at Grades 7 and 9 for WISC Full-Scale IQ were 93.1 and 96.2, showing a relatively modest gain. The authors themselves regarded all of their IQ means but one, from a variety of tests given at grades from the first on, as falling "within a relatively narrow range: 92.15–97.60" (p. 62). Because the use of so many different tests poses insuperable problems for interpreting differences in score level in only one race, I will not attempt to compare those other means further. The lack of a majority comparison group in this study also makes it impossible to rule out practice effects as the source of the 3-point gain in WISC IQ that was observed, but that the authors did not consider especially important.

Further evidence comes from a study by Jensen (1980a, Table 11.8), who furnished not the mean IQ for each race but the mean WISC Full-Scale IQ *difference* between samples of blacks and whites tested successively at ages 6, 7, 9 and 11. Such a difference is, of course, sensitive to changes in means within both races and somewhat less reliable than the mean of either. The samples, drawn from three Georgia counties, consisted initially of 163 whites and 111 blacks. Because there was attrition in the samples, some sampling variation was superimposed on the mean differences; Jensen reported that by age 11 there were 128 whites and 97 blacks remaining, or 21% fewer whites and 13% fewer blacks. The mean IQ differences, expressed as proportions of a 15-point *SD*, varied in the course of the four testings, but only over a range equivalent to 3.45 IQ points. A better measure, the *SD* of the mean differences, was equivalent to only 1.5 IQ points. Because of the sampling variability, this small *SD* understates the stability of the difference, which, in turn, understates the stability of the individual means.

Jensen's two studies (1974a, 1977a) of cumulative IQ deficit are also relevant to the question of mean stability because they address the hypothesis that IQs of black children decline with age. Note that there was no evidence of such a decline, which would imply a widening race difference with age, in any of the studies already reviewed, many of which were considered by Jensen (1974a). His method for detecting a cumulative IQ deficit entailed comparing older children with their younger full sibs.

The first study involved elementary-school children in California who had been tested with forms of the Lorge–Thorndike Intelligence Test appropriate for their grade. Within Jensen's (1974a) total sample of black sibs from 1,100 families, where the age difference between pairs averaged 2.05 years, the mean IQ difference was only .44 points in favor of the younger. Such a small difference can also be read as a lack of any signed difference in either direction, and therefore as evidence for stability generally. The mean absolute IQ differences within sib pairs were virtually identical: 13.20 for 2,074 white families and 13.16 for 1,100 black families. Jensen did find a slight, statistically significant decline of about 2–4 points in connection with some analyses involving measures of verbal IQ, but because no corresponding effect was apparent for nonverbal IQ, Jensen (p. 1018) suggested that this slight progressive decrement may have reflected reading comprehension skills needed for the verbal IQ section of the group test used, rather than intelligence *per se*.

Jensen's second study (1977a) was of black and white public-school children from a rural town in Georgia. IQ was tested with the CTMM. Here, for the first time in recent investigations, marked instability was observed in a black sample. This instability took the form of a fairly linear decrease in both verbal and nonverbal IQ between kindergarten and Grade 12 amounting to 14–16 IQ points. On average, the black younger sibs exceeded their older sibs by 3.31 IQ points at an average age difference of 2.48 years. Roughly that magnitude of IQ difference as a function of age was observed throughout the range of age differences. Verbal IQ, for example, declined an average of 1.62 points per year; nonverbal IQ, 1.19 points per year. No such effect appeared for the whites, whose average IQ was 102. The rate of decline in verbal IQ was comparable to the decline of 1.7 points per year from age 5.5 to age 9.5 in Stanford–Binet IQ observed among 75 pairs of older and younger black sibs in rural Texas during 1941–1942 by Tomlinson (1944, p. 477), and it was somewhat less than the declines of 1.9 and 2.0 IQ points per year observed in 1930 and 1940, respectively, on group tests among extremely rural white Tennessee mountain children by Wheeler (1942). However, the terminal IQ mean of 83.7 at age 9.5 in Tomlinson's study, unlike the one in Jensen's, did not extend below the IQ mean typical for blacks in general within the observed age range. Consequently, Tomlinson's data can also be interpreted as indicating a potential inflation of IQs at the earlier ages, thereby raising a somewhat different set of questions.

At least two considerations should be kept in mind when interpreting Jensen's second study of cumulative deficit. The first is that the method works: When the phenomenon was present, the method detected it. The second concerns the contribution of the observed effect to the familiar average IQ difference between blacks and whites that is conventionally described as 1 white *SD* or 15 or 16 IQ points. In the longer work from which this article has been drawn (in progress), I show that the race difference in representative samples typically amounts not to 1 *SD*, but to 18 IQ points nationally, and about 15–16 points in the North. In contrast, the mean IQ of the blacks in Jensen's study (1977a, p. 185) of cumulative deficit in the rural South was 71 (i.e., about 30 points below the general white mean) at the average age of 11.7 years, and the inverse linear trend with age that Jensen found would imply an average IQ at age 16 of about 65. Such a large difference certainly does not seem characteristic of all blacks, even in the rural South. The Stanford–Binet IQ of rural southern blacks in the large Kennedy *et al.* study (1963, Table 43) was 78.7 at mean age 8.9. If Jensen's linear trend for verbal IQ were operative, it would imply an IQ at age 11.7 of about 74.2 for the Kennedy *et al.* sample, which would still be 3.2 IQ points higher than the mean of Jensen's sample at that age. The 65 rural blacks (i.e., tantamount to southern rural) in the WISC-R standardization sample had an average IQ of 83.5, presumably at an average age of about 11.5 (Kaufman & Doppelt, 1976, Table 3). Because the mean IQ for blacks in the South as a whole is well below that of all U.S. blacks and about 19–21 IQ points below the mean for U.S. whites (Kaufman & Doppelt, 1976; Kennedy *et al.*, 1963, Table 38; Terman & Merrill, 1960, Figure 4), and because other investigations have failed to reveal signs of Jensen's effect outside the rural South (Jensen, 1977a; Kennedy, 1969), it is evident that the contribution of the cumulative deficit phenomenon to the black–white IQ difference conventionally conceived of as "one standard deviation" is practically nil, for that conventionalized difference understates the actual difference by an amount more than sufficient to accommodate the phenomenon, given our present understanding of its demographic and geographic limits. Although within its context the effect is strong, it is apparently too limited to account for a substantial share of the broader race difference in IQ.

A third consideration concerning the cumulative deficit phenomenon and its relevance to the question of test stability is that, except for Tomlinson's older, smaller, and less sophisticated Stanford–Binet study (1944), it has thus far been demonstrated only in connection with group tests, specifically the 1963 edition of the CTMM. The CTMM (short form, 1950 edition) was also the test that produced the perturbation at Grade 8 for blacks in the 1960 study by Osborne, although in that instance a rise from Grade 6 instead of a decline was observed. Because the location of Osborne's southern county on the rural-urban continuum was not reported, it is difficult to know in retrospect what trend to expect. Perhaps, it is merely a coincidence that the CTMM was involved both times, for both sets of CTMM data were generated in the course of a regular school testing-program mandated by the state (Georgia, apparently, in both cases).

In his own report, Osborne (1960, p. 234) remarked that different levels of the "California Test Battery" had been used for each race at Grade 10 in order to prevent floor effects for the blacks, a fact that complicates the task of interpreting the perturbation in his results at Grade 8. Both races may not have received the same IQ test at Grade 10, and if they had, the trend might have been different. When both blacks and whites had received the same advanced level at Grade 10 in a previous year, the test (whichever it was) had proved too difficult for the blacks and had resulted in scores that were "spuriously low" (p. 234). Unfortunately, it is not clear whether raw scores or IQs were intended, or whether the achievement or aptitude tests of the administered battery (which included the California Achievement Test) were implicated. Consequently, it is difficult to hypothesize what scoring mechanism would produce a lowering of scores.

However, there remains the real possibility that a too-difficult test would prove discouraging to black students, and that the inappropriateness for blacks of a group test keyed to grade levels—and hence the extent to which they experienced the test as discouraging—would be positively correlated with age. Often, black students need encouragement from others to attempt more items of multiple-choice tests, an encouragement necessitated by the fact that tests for their age level are usually far too difficult for a substantial fraction. For example, the fact that 29% of the black graduates of one of Baltimore's "magnet" high schools who took the SAT scored between 200 and 249 on SAT-V ("*Dunbar Report*," 1982, Table 2), essentially the range of scores obtainable by chance, suggests that putting forth a sustained effort to answer items correctly must be extremely unrewarding for an even larger percentage. According to Hills and Stanley (1970, p. 320), an expected chance score on the SAT would be in the neighborhood of 220 to 230, and, of course, there would be a chance distribution. Stanley and Porter (1967, p. 214) considered the

SAT-V "too difficult psychometrically for approximately 24% of the freshman entering the three predominantly Negro colleges [of Georgia] in the fall of 1964," a percentage similar to that at Baltimore's magnet high school. Nationally, in 1981, 19% of blacks taking the SAT-V scored between 200 and 249, as constrasted with 2% of their white age-peers (College Entrance Examination Board, 1982, pp. 41, 79).

Osborne's intriguing anecdote raises the question of whether Jensen's (1977a) later cumulative-deficit effect with the CTMM was not instead a "cumulative discouragement" effect, or some other function of the difficulty level of the test. Only 5% of the blacks in all three testings of Osborne's 1960 study scored above IQ 99. Adequate measurement of that sample's IQs with a group test would clearly depend on how much range the test made available for low scores, and on how well the sample persevered in the face of the test's inappropriate difficulty. As they stand, the IQs of blacks in Jensen's CTMM study were even lower on average than those in Osborne's. In contrast, the study by Baughman and Dahlstrom (1968) in rural North Carolina failed to show any appreciable IQ decline for blacks after an interval of three years with the individually administered Stanford–Binet. Clearly, a follow-up of Jensen's research in the rural South that employs an individual IQ test such as the Binet or the WISC is long overdue. The absence of such an investigation of the dramatic cumulative-deficit effect in Jensen's article (1977a), and of the causes and validity of the score changes that he identified, contrasts strangely with the attention that is now lavished on other methods of examining tests for possible bias, whose rapidly proliferating results have by now become predictable.

In summary, we have already seen that most of the existing evidence concerning the stability of individual IQs reveals no important differences between blacks and whites, and that the few differences that did appear in Table 1 could be attributed to well-understood artifacts. Now we see that aside from the unusual Jensen (1977a) study just discussed, there is also no recent evidence of race differences in mean stability within generations beyond what might reasonably be attributed to the normal vicissitudes of test–retest data. Osborne's 1960 results included a probably significant rise in mean CTMM IQ at Grade 8, but then a return at Grade 10 to the mean level that had been observed earlier at Grade 6. Harris and Lovinger (1968) reported a statistically significant increase in WISC IQ of about 3 points, but their sample was small and included 10% Puerto Ricans, whose initial proficiency in English was not reported. Moreover, practice effects could not be ruled out. Finally, the two authors themselves not only did not attach much importance to the small difference but regarded their various test results as falling within a narrow IQ band. Important studies by Kennedy (1969), Nichols, (1970), Baughman and Dahlstrom (1968) in the rural South, and Jensen (1974a, 1980a) have provided evidence that IQ means for blacks remained quite stable over intervals of two, three, four, and five years.

Group-by-Item Interaction

Although Mercer subtitles this criterion as *equivalent item patterning*, she explicitly acknowledges that she has group-by-item interaction in mind, and I prefer to use the more descriptive, statistical designation. As examples of the statistical procedures employed, Mercer cites correlations between the rank orders of item difficulty in majority and minority populations, item difficulty being measured by the percentage passing, and the correlations between the increments (or decrements) in the percentage passing adjacent items for majority and minority populations, the items being ordered according to their difficulty in the majority group. Jensen (1974b, 1977b, 1980a), for example, has employed these procedures, along with analysis of variance, to examine several tests for bias with respect to blacks and Mexican-Americans.

During her expert witness testimony in *Larry P.*—a trial in Federal District Court concerning the fairness of IQ tests in diagnosing mental retardation among black children in California public schools—Mercer (1977, p. 1704) was asked by plaintiffs' counsel, "Does Dr. Jensen have his own definition of bias?" and she responded, "Yes. Recently Dr. Jensen has proposed a definition of test bias which is different from either customary usage or the statistical usage." Although it certainly would not confuse persons familiar with the field, this practice of identifying the study of group-by-item interaction exclusively with Jensen could prove misleading to students.

I have called attention to this strategy before (Gordon, 1980, p. 190) in Mercer's work, where she dismissed internal validity as a useful consideration for assessing bias, characterized the opposing view as "unique to Jensen" (Mercer, 1979a, p. 93), and described Jensen as the "one defender of the psychometric knowledge system who bases his defense of the 'validity' of tests on measures of internal validity" (Mercer, 1978–1979, p. 10). Mercer's present discussion, although not as blatant, adheres to the strategy by maintaining the impression that Jensen is alone in considering group-by-item interaction a sensitive index of potential bias, an impression that may lead students who know of Jensen mainly through his less fair critics to suspect that the method is controversial or unorthodox.

I must emphasize, therefore, that the study of group-by-item interaction embraces an open-ended family of largely overlapping statistical and graphic procedures, each having its own particular combination of advantages and disadvantages. These procedures include delta plots (Angoff, 1972; Angoff & Ford, 1973), which Angoff (1982, pp. 96–97) traced back to Thurstone in 1925 and described as "essentially a graphical procedure for studying item-by-group interaction" (p. 106); latent-trait, log-linear, and chi-square methods, which Ironson (1982) described as "all fundamentally item-by-group interaction measures" (p. 154); the procedures already mentioned that have been used by Jensen and others; the discussion of item-by-sex interaction in the Stanford–Binet by McNemar (1942, p. 50) and also by Mercer's fellow witness for the plaintiffs, Kamin (1977, pp. 875–876), in *Larry P.*; and even, implicitly, any mention of particular items that, in the judgment of the speaker, stand out as likely examples of bias, as when Mercer (1977, p. 1616) herself quoted the information item "Who is Longfellow?" in her own *Larry P.* testimony.

The possibility exists that she may have intended to portray "Who is Longfellow?" as a typical item, but then, that would leave unexplained why she chose an example that would prove difficult even for whites, as it compares with actual items that fall well toward the end of the WISC-R Information subtest. Anyone familiar with recent criticism of IQ tests will recognize that such singling out of particular items plays a prominent role in that criticism (e.g., the "hit" item from the WISC). Although Mercer (1978–1979, pp. 14–15) elsewhere has used the Williams (1975) BITCH test of black slang, on which blacks score higher than whites, to illustrate "in reverse, the situation of the non-Anglo student taking a vocabulary test covering standard English" (p. 15), she fails to acknowledge that, if combined, the two tests would produce a strong group-by-item interaction, and that her juxtaposition of the two thus implicitly evokes the interaction construct. In short, the concept of interaction is central to most thinking about internal evidence of test bias, whether by critics or by defenders of tests. The interest of so many investigators in exploring different methods of studying group-by-item interaction as a potential indicator of bias testifies to the relevance and the importance of that form of internal validity. To help dispel the impression conveyed by Mercer, Gordon and Rudert (1979, p. 179) listed a number of others who have regarded and used group-by-item interaction as a test for bias, in some cases prior to Jensen (e.g., Angoff & Ford, 1973;

Chase & Pugh, 1971; Cleary & Hilton, 1968; Medley & Quirk, 1974; Stanley, 1969).

Although analysis of variance and hence the concept of interaction were not yet known in 1918 (Rucci & Tweney, 1980), one can also recognize the logic of interaction behind certain data analyses performed on subtests of the Army Alpha and Beta examinations and on items of the Stanford–Binet as long ago as World War I (Yerkes, 1921, pp. 738–741). For Alpha and Beta, internal validity was assessed by comparing correlations within each race between subtests and total scores, and interaction was assessed by comparing the relative difficulty of subtests for each race (Yerkes, 1921, Part III, Tables 277, 278). On Alpha, the mean correlations between eight subtests and total score for whites and blacks were .81 and .81; on Beta, for seven subtests, .73 and .80. The rank order of difficulty correlations across race for subtests in Alpha and Beta, as determined from tabulations of the percentage of zero scores, were .90 and .82, which are rather high when one recognizes that in designing a test the usual aim is to make all of the subtests about equally difficult in the normative group. The difference between the last two correlations is consistent with Yerkes' statement, "The general consensus seems to be that beta is not as satisfactory a test for illiterate negro recruits as it is for illiterate whites" (1921, p. 705). The problem with Beta for blacks was that it was still too hard, yielding too many zero scores.

In Table 2, I have reproduced what is very likely the earliest analysis of interaction with race at the item level on record. World War I U.S. Army psychologists calculated the percentage passing and the resultant difficulty rank within race of 25 items chosen for military use from the 1916 Stanford–Binet (Yerkes, 1921, Part III, Tables 274 and 275). Although originally no rank correlation was computed for these data either, the import of the analysis was evident from an inspection of the original tables, as it is in Table 2.

Three samples appear in Table 2. Two of them consist of whites and blacks referred for individual testing at Camp Funston (Kansas) because they had performed poorly on a group test, usually Beta. Combined, these two samples represented about 52% of all individual tests given at Camp Funston, which received a large number of blacks (Yerkes, 1921, p. 74). The average mental ages in the U.S. Army as a whole of all white draftees and all black draftees were estimated to be 13.08 and 10.37, respectively (Yerkes, 1921, Part III, Table 165). Note that the mental-age means of the two groups in Table 2 are considerably below those values, yet the two remain almost a year and a half apart and differ substantially from each other in their average percentages of items passed. Mental age, of course, was the only vehicle then available for conveying total test performance for adults so that it would be comparable to that of juveniles.

The third sample in Table 2 has been added from elsewhere in Yerkes' report (1921, Part II, Table 66) and consists of 486 white recruits tested at various camps, 324 of whom were relatively unselected (i.e., relatively representative); the 162 remaining were not clearly described (Yerkes, 1921, p. 407), but they may have been individuals who performed poorly on Alpha or Beta, which would account for the fact that the average mental age of the entire third group was somewhat below that of all white draftees. The difference of 4.51 years in average mental age between this white group and the blacks in Table 2 was considerably greater than the difference of 2.71 years between all white and all black draftees revealed by the means given above.

The correlations between rank orders of difficulty in Table 2, listed at the bottom, are all high: .97 between the very low-scoring groups of each race, .93 between very low-scoring blacks and the somewhat below-average (SBA) white group, and from .90 to .94 between the rank order of mental age in the 1916 Stanford–Binet standardization sample and the rank order of difficulty in each of the three samples. The small differences between the observed correlations and a perfect correlation of 1.0 summarize the minor amounts of group-by-item interaction in each pairing of groups. For further insight into the meaning of the correlations, let us proceed to the more detailed examination of the rankings that is made possible through the inclusion of 3 items among the 25 that share a highly structured form.

Despite the extreme diversity of item content—evident in the table but described more fully in Terman (1916)—and the large difference between races in average percentages passing, there are eight exact ties in rank between the low-scoring whites and blacks in Table 2. Three of them involve the short-term memory and mental manipulation task of repeating digits backward, each more difficult item in the series simply adding one more familiar digit. All persons credited with passing the easier "three digits backward" and "counting backward from 20 to 1," for example, were presumably well equipped to confront four and five digits backward from the standpoint of familiarity with digits alone. Because passing each digits-backward item required repeating correctly the numbers in merely one of three trials (with different digits) contained in the item, this formally simple task even provided some opportunity for practice.

TABLE 2

Rank Order of Difficulty of 25 1916 Stanford–Binet Items for Very-Low-Scoring Whites and Blacks Drafted in World War I and Tested Individually Because They Scored Low on Beta in 1918, and for Relatively Unselected but Somewhat-Below-Average (SBA) White Draftees[a]

Year, item	Item description	Percentage passing			Difficulty rank		
		Very low whites (N = 351)	Very low blacks (N = 938)	Somewhat low whites (N = 486)	Very low whites	Very low blacks	Somewhat low whites
VI, 1	Distinguishing right and left	99.4	98.3	99.6	2	1	1
VI, 2	Finding missing parts in pictures	92.9	77.5	96.3	5	6	5
VI, 3	Counting 13 pennies	99.7	92.9	98.8	1	2	2
VI, 4	Comprehension, second degree	96.6	85.2	97.5	3.5	4	3
VII, 2	Picture description	76.4	34.2	91.4	8.5	9	8.5
VII, 5	Giving differences between things	96.6	92.6	97.3	3.5	3	4
VII, 6	Copying a diamond	77.8	27.6	94.9	7	12	6
VII, Alt.	Repeating 3 digits backward	74.1	33.9	90.5	10	10	10
VIII, 1	Ball-and-field test	69.2	53.5	87.4	12	8	14
VIII, 2	Counting backward from 20 to 1	66.7	20.2	90.3	13	16	11
VIII, 3	Comprehension, third degree	92.3	79.2	94.4	6	5	7
VIII, 4	Giving similarities between two things	76.4	56.6	88.3	8.5	7	13
IX, 1	Giving the date	59.5	22.5	89.3	14	14	12
IX, 2	Arranging five weights	47.6	22.4	80.2	16	15	15
IX, 3	Making change	72.4	30.0	91.4	11	11	8.5

Item	Very low whites (% passing)	Very low blacks (% passing)	Somewhat low whites (% passing)	Very low whites (rank)	Very low blacks (rank)	Somewhat low whites (rank)
IX, 4 Repeating 4 digits backward	29.9	6.8	69.8	18	18	18
X, 2 Detecting absurdities	38.5	7.9	73.5	17	17	17
X, 3 Drawing designs from memory	16.2	1.5	58.4	20	22	19
X, 5 Comprehension, fourth degree	53.3	23.1	75.9	15	13	16
X, 6 Naming 60 words in 3 minutes	14.0	4.7	52.5	22	19	21
XII, 3 Ball-and-field test (superior plan)	18.8	3.1	56.0	19	21	20
XII, 5 Interpretation of fables	1.7	0.0	38.5	25	25	24
XII, 6 Repeating 5 digits backward	3.4	0.3	36.4	24	24	25
XII, 7 Interpretation of pictures	15.1	3.3	43.4	21	20	23
XII, 8 Giving similarities, three things	11.4	0.5	46.7	23	23	22
Mean percentage passing	56.0	35.1	77.6			
SD percentage passing	33.6	34.0	21.0			
Mental age, mean years	8.69	7.26	11.77			

Rank-order correlation (above diagonal):
Pearson correlation based on z or delta transformation (below diagonal):

	Very low whites	Very low blacks	Somewhat low whites
Very low whites	—	.97	.98
Very low blacks	.98	—	.93
Somewhat low whites	.98	.95	—
Rank-order correlation with mental-age year of items	.94	.90	.94

[a]From Yerkes (1921), Part III, Tables 274, 275, and Part II, Table 66.

The fortuitous presence of such a highly structured subset of items among the 25 permits us to use them as a natural yardstick of intuitive difficulty alongside which to set the other 22 items.

Although adjacent items within the digits-backward series are separated from each other in content by only a single digit—the minimum unit possible—they are widely separated in relative difficulty, ranking 10th, 18th, and 24th, respectively, in both low-scoring groups, and almost tying exactly with those two groups all three times again when the SBA whites are considered, too. The logic and sensitivity of the group-by-item interaction method is brought out by the fact that the numbers of preceding and intervening items were thus practically identical all three times in all three groups, despite the heterogeneity of the other items and the minute nature of the change in content represented by adding just a single digit each time to the highly structured and otherwise homogeneous items of the digits-backward series.

Judging from appearances, if any items at all had depended on cultural information or knowledge that was socially more available to one race than to the other, they were far more likely to be found among the other 22 than among the 3 digits-backward items. This judgment is supported, moreover, by the fact that much higher percentages of recruits than those connected with passing four and five digits backward had already exhibited sufficient familiarity with numbers to pass "three digits backward" and "counting backward . . .," and practically all had been credited with "counting 13 pennies" aloud before they reached any of the digits-backward items (see Table 2 and Yerkes, 1921, Part III, Tables 274, 275).

Knowledge of general cognitive strategies for solving certain kinds of problems is sometimes distinguished from knowledge of highly specific information. Hence, it could be hypothesized that digits-backward performance was potentially affected by differential knowledge of relevant cognitive strategies on the part of some groups, even if not by differential familiarity with numbers *per se*. In principle, such an argument is necessary to the view that digits-backward items were as susceptible to cultural bias as the remaining items, at least during that period in history (e.g., before dial telephones). The historical aspect can be checked by administering all 25 items to both races now, to see whether the digits-backward items have changed their relative difficulty levels, perhaps more for one race than for the other. In any case, research has produced little evidence that such general strategies normally account for the considerable differences between persons in repeating digits forward

(Dempster, 1981). Consequently, performances on the digits-backward items, and on the second and third of them especially (because more individuals than pass them have already passed the first), stand out as being relatively unsusceptible on their face to the kinds of cultural effects that might conceivably bias some of the remaining items. The second and third digits-backward items, of course, are the ones that define the harder ends of the two one-digit difficulty intervals.

Not only the *numbers* of other items distributed between and around the digit span items remain nearly identical from group to group in Table 2, so does the *content*. That is, the actual items that occupy slots within any segment of the range bounded by the digit items also overlap greatly from group to group. Because the segments below three and above five digits backward are open-ended (i.e., unbounded by other digits-backward items), let us attend to the two intervals we know to be exactly one digit wide in content difficulty. These are the intervals between three and four digits, and between four and five digits.

The first interval, bounded by the first and second digits-backward items at ranks 10 and 18, obviously contains 7 rank-order slots to be filled by specific items. For any two groups, there are thus 14 slots that must be filled by items that fall within a difficulty interval only one digit wide in content. Depending on how many such items are common to both groups, those 14 slots could be filled by a minimum of 7 and a maximum of 14 different items. With 7, the overlap between the two groups would be total; with 14, there would be no overlap at all in actual item content. It is meaningful to ask, therefore, how many of the available slots in an interval defined by a one-digit difference in content were occupied by items common to any pair of groups. In the second interval of interest, there are 10 such slots.

First, we compare the low-scoring whites and blacks in Table 2. Of the 14 slots between three and four digits backward, 12 were filled by items common to both groups (2.7 times chance expectation under the model of independence), and 10 of 10 were so filled between four and five digits (4.4 times chance expectation). Next, comparing the low-scoring blacks with the SBA whites, we find that 10 of 14 slots were filled by common items in the first interval (2.3 times chance expectation). Analysis of the second interval is complicated by the fact that the rank order of "five digits backward" differs by one in the two groups. However, the outcome is essentially the same as before: 5 items fill all 10 slots up to but not including rank 24 in both groups; that is, 10 out of 10 were filled by shared items. Thus, each possible comparison between races shows that 71%–86% of the slots in the first interval were filled by shared items, as were 100% of the slots in the second interval. Despite the heterogeneous content of the other 22 items, their seemingly greater susceptibility to purely cultural differences in availability of information, and the important differences in score level between the races, the very same items nearly always reappear within each one-digit interval for any racial pairing of groups. Overall, those slots are filled by shared items 87.5% of the time in the racial pairings. This outcome compares with 91.7% when both white groups are paired, which was equaled in the pairing of the two low-scoring groups of different race. We also know, from the high rank-order correlations in Table 2, that the missing items needed to complete the common matchings lie not many ranks away outside the intervals. Any attempt to defend allegations of bias by subsuming these uniformities into a model of cultural diffusion should be required to account satisfactorily for such details.

The intuitive appeal of the one-digit intervals as "natural units" of difficulty is upheld by the fact that the two intervals not only appear equal, but also scale as nearly equal to each other within each of the three groups. This means that, within the range of three to five digits backward, each added digit does represent a minimal and therefore roughly equal increment in difficulty for items of that type. The scaling depends not on psychological judgments of difficulty, but on actual performances, and it is accomplished as follows.

Under the assumption that the ability measured by the items is normally distributed, transforming the percentages passing (as areas under the normal curve) to their corresponding z scores (the abscissa of the unit normal distribution) yields an interval scale for the group in question (Jensen, 1980a, p. 439; see his Figure 4.9 for a distribution of forward-digit-span scores that is approximately normal). For the low-scoring whites and blacks and for the SBA whites, in that order, the differences in z values between three and four digits backward were 1.2, 1.1, and .8 units; group by group, each of those distances turns out to be close to the corresponding difference between four and five digits: 1.3, 1.3, and .9 units: "With the interval scale . . . the size of the difference between pairs of numbers has meaning, and corresponds to the distance . . . between the corresponding pairs of amounts of the property" (Torgerson, 1958, p. 16). Here, the near equality of the two intervals means that they represent nearly equal amounts of the operational property known as *difficulty*, which accords with the conspicuous fact that they represent exactly equal minimal increments in number of digits. On the average, the raw increments in difficulty defined by the second interval were only 13%

greater than the increments defined by the first interval. Put in terms of differences rather than proportions, the differences between the two intervals in these samples averaged only .13 units on an *SD* scale that has six units of range (practically speaking).

The transformation to an assumed interval scale does not guarantee that the intervals between any particular pairs of items will be equal; quite the contrary, they could display any relation whatever. The transformation simply enables us to see whether they are equal in fact, perhaps after having been hypothesized equal on prior grounds as in the present case. For the moment, I wish to emphasize the equality of the two intervals defined by the digits items, rather than the concomitant high degree of linearity between difficulty and number of digits that their equality implies for the range of three to five digits, because, as we shall see, there are no clear standards for distinguishing perfect linearity from merely very good approximations of linearity, which are always to be expected among monotonic transformations. What appears expectable is often dismissed hastily; there is less complacency to be overcome concerning the question of the equality of two intervals to each other because that phenomenon is less common than monotonicity. The equality is cogent evidence that the two intervals—and hence, the contents of the items—bear some common fundamental relation to each other in all three groups. This evidence makes particularly good sense in view of the way in which the difficulty of the items is increased, via definite quanta of digits.

However, the difference between the near-perfect linearity attained here and the extremely high degree of linearity to be expected whenever a straight line is fitted to only three pairs of observations already known to correlate perfectly in rank does deserve a comment. The rounded item distances given above for each sample indicate that the difficulty of the digits items correlates .999 (when rounded) with the number of digits backward in each sample. The closeness of fit revealed by these three extraordinarily high correlations merits a verbal description that distinguishes it from the merely extremely good linear fit of, say, any three items in general that happen to be ordered monotonically with the numbers 3, 4, and 5, and that might correlate with those numbers, say, only .98. Perhaps, the adjective *perfect* is not too strong. The Pearson correlations between the numbers of digits backward and the raw percentages passing in each group provide a doubly useful contrast because the three percentages meet the ordering requirement (but in reverse), and because the percentages are not assumed to be on an interval scale, so that the correlations also illustrate the advantage of the scaling procedure. For the low-scoring whites and blacks, and for the SBA whites, the three correlations between percentages and numbers of digits were $-.990$, $-.943$, and $-.991$. Clearly, these three correlations reveal what are conventionally regarded as very high approximations of linearity—but unlike the correlations of .999, they are far from perfect. Later, I shall return to the problem of discriminating perfect linearity from high approximations of linearity in imperfect data, but with the aid of three more samples.

The small differences in z-unit distances that are apparent among the groups for a given interval imply differences in their underlying SDs of mental ability, which were not reported but have been calculated (Table 4). The observed differences are consistent with the expectation that the SBA white group—in view of its suspected composition—might have had the largest SD, which it did. This source of differences between the groups in size of interval can be removed by standardizing the three digits-backward-item z scores for each of any two of the groups so that those scores have the same standard deviation as the corresponding three scores of the third (here, the SBA whites). When so standardized, the item distances in each interval turn out to be the same for all three groups (rounded to one decimal place): in the first interval, .8, .8, and .8, and in the second interval, .9, .9, and .9. The new, standardized values represent a major reduction in dispersion across groups within each interval, even if more decimal places were retained. Thus, the digits-backward items produce not only two nearly equal intervals in all three groups, but even the same-sized intervals when the underlying SDs of mental ability in the three World War I groups are controlled.

It would be difficult, if not impossible, to select another set of three items *a priori* from Table 2 that would space themselves so nearly equally when scaled in this manner. Even knowing the percentages passing in one of the groups would not help unless one were adroit at transforming them to unit normal deviates in one's head; neither the percentage differences nor the proportional relations between the percentages passing successive items offer any ready clues to their interval scale properties. Anyone who wishes can easily verify this statement by performing those calculations for the three digits-backward items using the percentages passing in Table 2.

The difficulty of selecting equally spaced items can be illustrated by picking a series of items that might offer some naive promise of being equally spaced because they happen to be equally spaced in mental age. Beginning at an arbitrary point, I chose five such items for closer examination from Table 2. Table 3 displays those five items, their percentages passing in the three World War I groups, their z transformations, and, in parentheses, the incremental differences between the z scores of adjacent items, that is, their interval widths. Note that there is no indication even within any single group—let alone all three—of nearly equal spacing between the five items or, for that matter, of any systematic linear relation between the spacing and increasing mental age other than the expectable inverse trends (Terman & Merrill, 1937, pp. 25–26; 1960, p. 14), which yield three consistently negative but ragged correlations with mental age ($-.27$, $-.51$, and $-.16$), one for each group. Some of the intervals are several times as large as others, and there is even one slight reversal of rank order. Note also that standardizing the z scores in terms of the SBA whites' digits-backward distribution does not improve matters; rather, it simply makes the absence of nearly equal intervals between the five items more evident because the items are now placed on the same metric as the digits items. There is nothing pathological about these five items, of course, as witnessed by the fact that their rank-order correlations are all very high, either .9 or 1.0. It is just that their contents do not have as fundamental and as highly predictable a relation to each other in all groups as the contents of the digits-backward items; hence, although they tend to fall in the same order, the five items do not fall at the same distances apart in every group to the very high degree that the digits items do once the transformation to a common interval scale is effected.

At the bottom, Table 3 also shows z transformation or delta correlations between the samples for two subsets of three items each. Because delta equals $4z + 13$, the correlations for z and delta—a conventionalized linear transformation found useful for studying group-by-item interaction because it is always positive (Angoff, 1982)—are always identical. These correlations are available for comparison with corresponding correlations among the three digits-backward items, to appear below in Table 8. Note that when perfect rank correlation is not present among the three items for all samples, as does happen, the correlations can fall sharply (see below the diagonal). When perfect rank correlation is preserved, the correlations can be extremely high (see above the diagonal); however, even so, two of the three correlations are "low" by digits-item standards. That is, two are lower than the lowest of 15 separate correlations among digits-item z scores in six different populations (including the three in Table 3) that appear below in Table 8. This is another indication of the spe-

TABLE 3
Demonstration of the Improbability of Picking Items Equally Spaced in Difficulty, Using Five 1916 Stanford–Binet Items Separated by Single Years of Mental Age

Year, item	Item description	Percentage passing			z transform (and intervals)			Standardized (to mean and SD of SBA whites) z transform (and intervals)[a]		
		Very low whites	Very low blacks	Somewhat low whites	Very low whites	Very low blacks	Somewhat low whites	Very low whites	Very low blacks	Somewhat low whites
VI, 2	Finding missing parts in pictures	92.9	77.5	96.3	-1.47 (.75)	-.76 (1.17)	-1.79 (.42)	-1.71 (.90)	-1.82 (1.20)	-1.59 (.76)
VII, 2	Picture description	76.4	34.2	91.4	-.72 (.29)	.41 (.42)	-1.37 (.07)	-.81 (.35)	-.62 (.43)	-.82 (.13)
VIII, 2	Counting backward from 20 to 1	66.7	20.2	90.3	-.43 (.49)	.83 (-.07)	-1.30 (.45)	-.47 (.59)	-.19 (-.07)	-.70 (.82)
IX, 2	Arranging five weights	47.6	22.4	80.2	.06 (.23)	.76 (.65)	-.85 (.22)	.12 (.28)	-.26 (.67)	.12 (.40)
X, 2	Detecting absurdities	38.5	7.9	73.5	.29	1.41	-.63	.40	.41	.52
	Pearson correlations for first three items (above diagonal) and for last three items (below diagonal):									
	Very low whites							—	.6810	1.0000
	Very low blacks							.9999	—	.6859
	Somewhat low whites							.9897	.9912	—

[a] To facilitate other comparisons, the mean and the SD of the SBA whites' digits-backward data have been used to standardize the entries in all three columns.

cial nature of the digits-backward items, especially in view of the fact that the items in Table 3, unlike items in general, were deliberately chosen to be evenly spaced in mental-age years. Usually, some items fall at the same mental-age year and are thus not well spaced in difficulty.

The unusual properties of the digits-backward items in these rare old data warrant expanding the analysis to include other major comparison samples; with their aid, a more definitive statistical analysis will be possible. That analysis will be concerned with the problem of detecting the presence of perfect linearity of item difficulty (the complement of ability). To the degree that its presence can be satisfactorily demonstrated, linearity holds profound implications for the topic of item–group interaction and for Mercer's arguments in the final section.

DIGITS BACKWARD, INTERVAL SCALES, AND NORMALITY

MORE DATA

One Additional Black Sample

Table 4 extends our exploration of the digits-backward items by scaling the performances of the 1,800 southern black elementary-school children tested with the 1960 Stanford–Binet in 1960 by Kennedy *et al.* (1963). Both sexes were equally represented. After second grade, and in the sample as a whole, the two intervals between the three items were again almost equal to each other. At and below second grade, of course, "five digits backward" was too difficult for the children for it to scale well.

What was mainly an assumption of the model earlier can be tested more adequately, because now we know the underlying *SD*s of general mental ability at the various elementary-school grades. Thus, from Grade 2 through Grade 6, and including the sample as a whole, we find that the correlation between the mean size of the two raw intervals and the *SD* of mental age was −.91, which was also the correlation between the *SD*s of the raw z scores and the *SD*s of mental age. When the variation between samples in interval size due to variation in the *SD*s of mental ability is removed by standardizing all of the z scores so that they have the *SD* (and, incidentally, the mean) of the z scores of SBA whites in World War I, we find that the intervals were the same size (to one decimal place) for all three World War I samples, for the 1960 black elementary-school sample

TABLE 4

Performance on Stanford–Binet Digits-Backward Items of Southern Black Elementary-School Children Tested in 1960 and of Three Samples of Army Draftees Tested in 1918[a]

	Grade 1 blacks (N = 300)		Grade 2 blacks (N = 300)		Grade 3 blacks (N = 300)		Grade 4 blacks (N = 300)		Grade 5 blacks (N = 300)		Grade 6 blacks (N = 300)		Grades 1–6 blacks (N = 1,800)		Very low white draftees (N = 351)		Very low black draftees (N = 938)		SBA white draftees (N = 486)	
	%	z	%	z	%	z	%	z	%	z	%	z	%	z	%	z	%	z	%	z
Number of digits backward																				
3	14.7	1.05	51.3	−.03	71.7	−.57	80.7	−.87	92.3	−1.43	94.7	−1.62	67.6	−.46	74.1	−.65	33.9	.41	90.5	−1.31
4	0.3	2.75	9.0	1.34	25.0	.67	41.7	.21	62.7	−.32	69.3	−.50	34.7	.39	29.9	.53	6.8	1.49	69.8	−.52
5	—	—	0.7	2.46	2.7	1.93	7.3	1.45	17.7	.93	28.3	.57	9.4	1.31	3.4	1.83	0.3	2.75	36.4	.35
Mean z score		1.90		1.26		.68		.27		−.27		−.52		.41		.57		1.55		−.49
SD, z score		1.20		1.25		1.25		1.16		1.18		1.10		.89		1.24		1.17		.83
Raw z distances between adjacent digits-backward items																				
3 to 4		1.70		1.37		1.24		1.08		1.11		1.12		.85		1.18		1.08		.79
4 to 5		—		1.12		1.26		1.24		1.25		1.07		.92		1.30		1.26		.87
Standardized z distances between adjacent digits-backward items (mean and SD of SBA whites)																				
3 to 4		Undefined[b]		.9		.8		.8		.8		.8		.8		.8		.8		.8
4 to 5		—		.7		.8		.9		.9		.8		.9		.9		.9		.9
Mental ability statistics																				
Mental-age mean (years)[c]		5.55		6.42		7.23		7.99		8.83		9.44		7.58		8.69		7.26		11.77
Mental-age SD (years)		.74		.91		.92		1.09		1.33		1.55		1.75		1.07[d]		.87[d]		3.24[d]
IQ mean		81.8		80.4		80.2		79.6		81.2		80.8		80.7		—		—		—
IQ SD		12.4		12.8		11.9		11.8		12.6		12.9		12.5		—		—		—

[a]From Kennedy, Van de Riet, and White (1963), Tables 38, 41, 45, 48 and 60 through 66; Yerkes (1921), Part III, Tables 274, 275, and Part II, Table 66.
[b]When there are only two items, the transformation to standardized distances always produces the same value.
[c]Mental ages measured with the 1960 Stanford–Binet may not be comparable to those measured with the 1916 Stanford–Binet.
[d]Sheppard's correction for coarse grouping was employed.

as a whole, and for Grades 4 and 5. The results for the other grades were not far off either; at two of them, the two intervals were exactly equal to each other. Table 4 shows, therefore, that the three digits-backward items scaled as far apart in difficulty among black elementary-school children tested in 1960 as they did among the three samples of adult draftees drawn from two races and tested 42 years earlier during World War I.

Two Additional White Samples

Table 5 extends the analysis to white children between the ages of 5.5 and 10 from the 1937 Stanford–Binet standardization sample, who had been tested circa 1930–1932, and to white children of selected ages from the 1916 Stanford–Binet standardization, who had been tested circa 1913–1914. Including older ages might be pointless, as can be seen from the two 10-year-old samples in Table 5, for beyond age 10 "three digits backward" may become too easy for that item to scale well. As not all three digits items were administered below age 10 in the course of the 1916 standardization, the 1916 10-year-olds are, in effect, the only age group available for a full comparison. Nevertheless, the 1916 9-year-olds have been included in the table in order to show how similar the available percentages are for both age groups in both standardizations, even though their testings occurred 17.5 years apart. Table 5 contains the first samples examined thus far that have not been below average in mean IQ. Both sexes were, of course, equally represented.

Once again, we find that the two raw z-score intervals are nearly equal to each other within every sample. When the z scores are scaled to match the SBA whites in dispersion (and, incidentally, in mean), the intervals are also nearly equal across samples. Again, testing the assumption that variation in raw interval size (or in SDs of raw z scores) across samples is due largely to variation in SDs of mental age, we find the correlation for ages 7–10 and in the 1937 sample as a whole to be $-.92$. Thus, Tables 4 and 5 provide good evidence that the rationale for standardizing the z scores of the three World War I samples was sound.

The average magnitudes of the first and second intervals across all 15 pairs of standardized z scores in Tables 4 and 5 are .83 and .83, with SDs of only .05 and .07, respectively. Plainly, the SDs show that increments in difficulty between adjacent digits-backward items have remained remarkably uniform across samples despite differ-

TABLE 5

Performance on Digits-Backward Items of White Children from the Standardization Samples of the 1937 Stanford–Binet, Tested Circa 1930–1932, and the 1916 Stanford–Binet, Tested Circa 1913–1914[a,b]

Number of digits backward	1937, age 5.5 (N = 110) %	z	1937, age 6 (N = 203) %	z	1937, age 7 (N = 202) %	z	1937, age 8 (N = 203) %	z	1937, age 9 (N = 204) %	z	1937, age 10 (N = 201) %	z	Ages 5.5–10 (N = 1,123) %	z	1916, age 9 (N = 113) %	z	1916, age 10 (N = 87) %	z
3 (Form M)	20	.84	34	.41	72	−.58	86	−1.08	93	−1.48	96	−1.75	70.7	−.54	90	−1.28	96	−1.75
4 (Form L)	3	1.88	6	1.56	26	.64	38	.31	61	−.28	79	−.81	38.2	.30	62	−.31	75	−.67
5 (Form L)	—	—	—	—	4	1.75	9	1.34	20	.84	39	.28	13.0	1.13	—	—	40	.25
Mean z score		1.36		.98		.60		.19		−.30		−.76		.30		−.79		−.72
SD, z score		.74		.81		1.17		1.21		1.16		1.02		.84		.69		1.00
Raw z distances between adjacent digits-backward items																		
3 to 4		1.04		1.15		1.22		1.39		1.20		.94		.84		.97		1.08
4 to 5		—		—		1.11		1.03		1.12		1.09		.83		—		.92
Standardized z distances between adjacent digits-backward items (mean and SD of SBA whites)																		
3 to 4		Undefined[c]		Undefined[c]		.9		.9		.9		.8		.8		Undefined[c]		.9
4 to 5		—		—		.8		.7		.8		.9		.8		—		.8
Mental ability statistics																		
Mental-age mean (years)		5.60		6.10		7.18		8.22		9.43		10.48		8.02		9.04		10.30
Mental-age SD (years)		.78		.77		1.11		1.25		1.49		1.62		1.97		1.12		1.26
IQ mean (L and M, 1937)		101.8		101.6		102.6		102.8		104.8		104.8		103.2		100.5		103.0
IQ SD (L and M, 1937)		14.2		12.8		15.9		15.6		16.6		16.2		15.4		12.4		12.2

[a] From McNemar (1942), Table 26; Terman and Merrill (1937), Tables 5 and 7; Terman, Lyman, Ordahl, Ordahl, Galbreath, and Talbert (1917), Appendix I.

[b] The 1937 Stanford–Binet contained only one digits-backward item three digits long, located in Form M, but two each at the four- and five-digit lengths, divided between Forms L and M. As there were some systematic differences in difficulty between the Form L and the Form M versions at four and five digits, the versions most similar in actual digits to the 1916 and the 1960 Stanford–Binet items have been used in this analysis. At three and four digits, these items correspond exactly to the 1960 versions; at five digits, two of the three trials correspond exactly, and the third involves only a permutation and change of one digit. Correspondence to the 1916 versions is almost as close: at three digits, two trials involve permutations and change of a single digit; at four digits, two trials are identical, and the third involves only a permutation; at five digits, two trials involve change in one digit, and the third is simply a permutation. As passing such items requires success on only one trial out of the three, even a total change in the digits of one of the trials does little to increase difficulty.

[c] When there are only two items, the transformation to standardized distances always produces the same value.

ences between them in race, IQ, age, sex, region of the country, and point in time of testing over a 46.5-year period.

The small residual differences across samples in interval size could well reflect minor departures from perfect normality in the samples; such departures are certain to be present. The IQ distribution of the 1,800 black elementary-school children in Table 4 from the study by Kennedy *et al.* (1963), for example, is known to be somewhat positively skewed (Jensen, 1980a, pp. 98–99); its moment coefficient of skewness is .37, and that of the sample's mental-age distribution over all six grades is .54. The manner in which it was generated, as well as the fact that its mean percentage passing in Table 2 is far above 50% and hence conducive to positive skewness (cf. Jensen, 1980a, p. 69), also suggests that the SBA white sample from World War I might exhibit positive skewness, and it does, with a coefficient of .41; the moment coefficients of skewness for the low-scoring white and low-scoring black draftees can be calculated, too, and are $-.22$ and .16, respectively (Sheppard's correction was applied; see Yule & Kendall, 1950, p. 158).

A Chi-Square Test for Relative Difficulty

With such valuable data in hand, obviously it would be desirable to be able to test the equalities of the intervals between digits items across samples, for the issue of whether a true interval scale can be detected among mental ability items has profound implications. One way to test the intervals would be to test the relative difficulties of the items, for if the boundaries of the intervals are equal, so are the intervals. Unfortunately, no satisfactory direct test of relative difficulties seems to be available. Jensen (1980a, pp. 440–441) has proposed a relevant chi-square test that would embody many elegant features if it were correct, but Darlington and Boyce (1982) have questioned Jensen's derivation of its standard error. The difficulty seems to be that Jensen's treatment assumed that z (or delta) transformations had been generated by sampling from some multiple of a unit normal distribution, whereas they are in fact generated from percentages passing. Readers who consult Jensen's proposed test should also be alerted that his formula (p. 461) for the standard error has the exponents misplaced in his book's first edition (Jensen agrees).

However, we can employ a conventional chi-square test of the equality of two percentages in a somewhat indirect manner for essentially the same purpose, although it will not embody some of the elegant statistical properties that Jensen sought with his test. In this application, the statistical test should be regarded as providing another heuristic framework for describing and interpreting the data. Interpretation rests on the pattern of results from 15 separate applications of the test to all pairings of six diverse samples; on a comparison of the outcomes from the three digits items with the outcomes after applying the test to a different set of three items; and on various supplementary statistical comparisons.

Like Jensen's test, the one to be used here assumes that differences between samples in means and *SD*s of z scores (or mental ability) are not at issue; hence, it is helpful to characterize it as a test for differences in *relative* difficulty. Samples must be standardized so that their z scores share a common mean and *SD*. For this purpose, we shall continue to use the mean and the *SD* of the SBA white draftees as the common basis for standardizing other samples. Once the z scores have been so standardized, they are converted to what I call *standardized percentages passing*. These standardized percentages represent predictions of the values that the percentages passing would have assumed if all of the groups had had the mental ability mean and the *SD* of the SBA whites, given the relative difficulties displayed by each sample's actually observed percentages passing. Simple chi-square tests can then be applied to the *standardized frequencies* implied by the standardized percentages passing of each item within the context of the sizes of each pair of samples. The test is applied only to the frequencies derived from the standardized percentages passing, and readers should not mistake observed percentages and standardized percentages in the tables to follow for the observed and expected frequencies of the chi-square test.

The most unorthodox aspect of the test is that it is applied to frequencies that, although empirically derived, have not actually been observed. However, the question of whether the differences in those frequencies between samples would have been significant had they been observed directly does provide a familiar framework, within which to consider rejecting or accepting the null hypothesis, that is not unlike that of testing a partial correlation or any controlled comparison. Comparison by inspection of the standardized percentages themselves across samples, as well as of the standardized z scores, should also prove informative.

An awkward aspect of the test is that its sensitivity varies somewhat according to the range in which the standardized percentages fall, and hence also according to the population selected to provide the basis for standardization. This variation effectively severs any simple connection between the sensitivities of the original and the standardized percentages, and it is one of the problems that Jensen sought to circumvent. Expressed in terms of a test based on the unit normal distribution that is the counterpart of our chi-square with one degree of freedom (Walker & Lev, 1953, p. 78), the percentage difference between any two samples tends to decrease, and the standard error tends to decrease also, as the standardization carries the percentages passing further from 50%. These changes tend to be offsetting, but not perfectly, and hence, the test yields somewhat higher chi squares at standardizations that produce standardized percentages passing nearer, on the average, to 50%. The presence of large samples, as can be seen in the case of our data, tends to be decisive, however, in determining whether the chi square, whatever its value, continues to exceed the critical values associated with conventional levels of significance regardless of standardization. Conceivably, always standardizing all of the distributions to some aptly chosen and well-explored standard z-score distribution—such as one with mean zero and a given small *SD*, for example—could lead to a reduction in the minor uncertainties surrounding probabilities that depend somewhat on the choice of population for standardization. However, this possibility has not been explored.

Another feature of the present test that Jensen sought to avoid is that the sensitivities of individual items within an analysis vary somewhat according to their own distances from a standardized value of 50%, as described above. However, this variation need be of concern only if one is comparing items with each other in searching for potentially biased items, which was Jensen's intention. In the present application, we are concerned not with which particular items within an analysis register statistical significance, but with whether any do and, if so, between which samples. This viewpoint distinguishes testing for potentially biased items from testing for interval scale properties across samples. It might be noted that the use of a conventional small *SD* in the z-score standardization, as mentioned above, could conceivably reduce differences between items in sensitivity because of their location in the percentage range; this possibility has not been explored either.

The Chi-Square Test Applied to Digits Items

Perhaps, the best way to learn more about the test at this point is to see it in action. Table 6 presents the outcomes of applying the chi-square test to the relative difficulties of the digits-backward items in six highly diverse populations spanning 46.5 years in time of test-

TABLE 6
Chi-Square Tests for Differences in Standardized Difficulties of Digits-Backward Items between Six Diverse Samples

	(1) 87 white S-B 10-year-olds		(2) 1,800 black grade school children		(3) 1,123 white 1937 S-B sample children		(4) 351 very low scoring white draftees		(5) 938 very low scoring black draftees		(6) 486 SBA white draftees		Row chi-square[b]	$p <$
Number of digits backward	Obs.%	Stand.%	Obs.%	Stand.%	Obs.%	Stand.%	Obs.%	Stand.%	Obs.%	Stand.%	Obs.%	Stand.%		
					Observed and standardized percentages passing[a]									
3	96.55	91.22	67.56	90.54	70.66	90.78	74.07	90.49	33.90	90.39	90.53	90.53	.14	NS
4	74.71	66.63	34.67	69.73	38.16	68.73	29.91	69.92	6.82	70.30	69.75	69.75	1.01	NS
5	40.23	38.15	9.44	36.44	13.00	36.97	3.42	36.34	.32	36.15	36.42	36.42	.26	NS
					z scores standardized to mean and SD of SBA white draftees									
3		−1.3545		−1.3127		−1.3271		−1.3098		−1.3040		−1.3126		
4		−.4296		−.5166		−.4881		−.5221		−.5331		−.5168		
5		.3016		.3467		.3327		.3493		.3544		.3468		
Mean z score		−.4942		−.4942		−.4942		−.4942		−.4942		−.4942		
SD, z score		.8299		.8299		.8299		.8299		.8299		.8299		

Chi squares for "three" (below diagonal) and "four" (above diagonal) digits backward, based on standardized frequencies[c]

Sample and testing date						
(1) 87 white children (1913–1914)	—	.38	.16	.35	.51	.34
(2) 1,800 black children (1960)	.04	—	.33	.01	.10	.00
(3) 1,123 white children (1930–1932)	.02	.05	—	.18	.59	.17
(4) 351 low white draftees (1918)	.04	.00	.03	—	.02	.00
(5) 938 low black draftees (1918)	.06	.02	.09	.00	—	.05
(6) 486 SBA white draftees (1918)	.04	.00	.02	.00	.01	—

Chi squares for "five" (below diagonal) and all (above diagonal) digits backward, based on standardized frequencies[c]

Sample and testing date						
(1) 87 white children (1913–1914)	—	.52	.23	.49	.71	.48
(2) 1,800 black children (1960)	.10	—	.46	.01	.14	.00
(3) 1,123 white children (1930–1932)	.05	.08	—	.26	.83	.23
(4) 351 low white draftees (1918)	.10	.00	.05	—	.02	.00
(5) 938 low black draftees (1918)	.14	.02	.15	.00	—	.07
(6) 486 SBA white draftees (1918)	.10	.00	.04	.00	.01	—

[a] Observed percentages passing reflect an attempt to reconstruct and undo rounding errors in original data of samples (1) and (3).

[b] Row chi-square tests have five degrees of freedom; to be significant at the .05 level, the chi square must equal or exceed 11.07.

[c] All four chi-square tests between pairs of samples (above and below diagonals) have one degree of freedom; to be significant at the .05 level, the chi square must equal or exceed 3.84.

ing. For ease of presentation, the various grades and ages of the 1960 black and 1937 white children's samples from Tables 4 and 5 have been combined into two major groupings. At the top are the observed percentages passing, and beside them are the standardized percentages passing derived from the standardized z scores immediately below. These z scores and standardized percentages have meaning in their own right, especially the z scores (whose differences between samples, if divided by the standardized *SD*, remain invariant), and should not be associated with the ambiguities concerning the exact level of significance of the chi-square test. Both standardized statistics reveal a highly uniform picture across samples. This uniformity indicates that, if all of the samples had the same mean and *SD* for mental ability, one would be able to predict the percentage passing of any one of the three digits items in a particular sample almost perfectly, simply by knowing the percentages passing in some other sample (as displayed below in Table 12). This relation holds across time of testing, across race, across age, and across sex composition.

The chi-square test represents a device for judging whether the minor departures from perfect prediction might safely be attributed to sampling fluctuations. For any pair of samples and a particular item, the standardized percentages passing and not passing define a two-by-two contingency table with one degree of freedom. The lower panels of Table 6 contain chi-square values for each such pairwise comparison among the six samples for tests of three, four, and five digits backward, respectively. There is also a test for all three items collectively, consisting of the sum of the three chi squares for individual items, which also has one degree of freedom in view of the imposition of a standardized mean and *SD*. Finally, there are three chi-square tests for each row of standardized percentages, which test all six samples simultaneously with respect to each single item.

Not 1 of the 60 different chi-square tests at the bottom of Table 6 exceeds or even approaches the critical value of 3.84 needed for significance at the .05 level, and none of the three row chi squares at the top approaches 11.07, the critical value at the .05 level when there are five degrees of freedom. For those curious, Jensen's chi-square test, which yields higher chi squares, also produced no significant findings when applied to the same original data. A "worst case" trial of the present test was also undertaken. This involved selecting as the basis for standardization the sample that would produce standardized percentages closer on the average to 50% than any other, and hence the highest chi squares. That sample happens to be the 1937 S-B whites. The chi square increased by only 5% on the average, and again, none of the 63 possible outcomes approached being significant. Because there are no significant differences for any of the three digits items in relative difficulty across the six samples, there are, by immediate implication, no significant differences in the size of either interval.[1] A cleaner result would be hard to imagine.

The Chi-Square Test Applied to Comparison Items

Questions concerning the meaning of a test and its power to detect differences are bound to arise whenever the acceptance of a potentially controversial null hypothesis is concerned. Such questions can be addressed in two complementary ways. First, attention can be directed to the large sizes of at least five of the six samples in Table 6. Second, we can compare the two sets of outcomes after applying the test to a different but otherwise largely equivalent set of three Stanford–Binet items to which the same populations have responded. This comparison would speak to the question of whether the null findings are due to special aspects of the digits items or to the statistical test itself. However, aside from the digits-backward items, there are relatively few items that have continued virtually unchanged through the various Stanford–Binet revisions. Obviously, comparisons of samples as widely separated in time as those in Table 6 require such items. Moreover, to remain comparable in gross formal structure to the three digits items, the new set of three would also have to have the same rank order of difficulty in all six populations. We have already witnessed how strong the effect can be on the z-score or delta correlation of slightly imperfect rank correlation among three items in Table 3, below the diagonal. The need for perfect concordance in rank order restricts further an already narrow choice from among the 25 items listed in Table 2. Nevertheless, constituting such a set did prove possible.

To meet the requirements, it was decided to include "four digits backward" as the second-ranking member of the new set of three items, with the first and third ranks being filled by "copying a diamond" and "drawing designs from memory" (the last involving complex designs). As items go, these three, like the digits items, make

[1]The slightly stricter test for this inference, which would involve the comparison of the difference between two within-sample differences between adjacent items for an interval (for any pair of samples), cannot be calculated for these data.

only the most minimal demands for information beyond what is present in the items themselves. The three are located at 1916 Stanford–Binet mental ages of VII, IX, and X, whereas the 1916, 1937, and 1960 revision mental ages of the three digits items were VII, IX, and XII. The 1916 mental ages of the first and second items of the new set hold across all three revisions, but on the 1937 and 1960 revisions, the third item, which there exists in two versions that differ only in the severity of scoring, must be taken from Year XI for it to be comparable to its 1916 version, which evidently was placed a year too low at that time (e.g., see Terman, 1916, p. 262). Although the spacing between the second and third items is thus slightly reduced in the new set, we should keep in mind that the digits items were not singled out on the basis of their mental-age locations, and because there is now no *a priori* reason to expect the two intervals in the new set to be equal to each other, the precise mental-age locations of the new items are immaterial. What is important is that perfect rank correlation among the six major samples be maintained. The same rank ordering of the new set also held throughout the six individual age levels of the 1937 Stanford–Binet sample listed in Table 5, and at all grades of the 1960 black sample in Table 4 except the first, where the second and third items were tied. Because relative difficulty takes both the z-score mean and *SD* into account and is thus a function of all of the items being considered, the inclusion of a digits item in the new set does not distort comparisons of the chi-square test between the two sets. Finally, 113 white 9-year-olds from the 1916 standardization sample had to be substituted for the 87 10-year-olds so as to make responses to all three new items available in every population. In order not to alter the power of the statistical tests, the size of this substitute sample from the same original population has been treated as though it, too, were 87. This change is noted where appropriate in the tables.

Table 7 repeats the analyses and chi-square tests for the new items that were reported in Table 6 for the digits items. To render the z scores and perhaps the significance tests more comparable to those for the digits items in Table 6, the z scores in Table 7 have been standardized to the mean and the *SD* of the z scores of the SBA whites' digits items instead of to the mean and the *SD* of the z scores of the SBA whites' new items. This decision proved to have no impact on the overall interpretation, although it did produce somewhat higher chi squares and five additional significant pairwise comparisons.

Table 7 contains numerous chi squares that now far exceed their critical values. Two of the three row tests are highly significant, involving the second and third items. Consistent with the row tests, none of the 15 pairwise comparisons for the first item proves significant, but 9 of 15 for the second item, 5 of 15 for the third item, and 10 of 15 for the pairwise comparisons of all three items, considered collectively, do. Of the 60 different pairwise comparisons, 24 are significant. Obviously, the picture is quite different now from that in Table 6 concerning the digits items, where there were no significant differences at all.

Interpreting Significant Chi Squares

The first matters to consider are the locations among items and among samples of the significant chi squares in Table 7. A caution against overinterpreting the locations of significant outcomes among items is immediately in order. This caution has its basis in two considerations, the first of which is largely an artifact of the relatively few items to which the test has here been applied, and the second of which is intrinsic to the analysis of relative difficulty in general. In preparation for a discussion of the artifacts, note that the number of significant outcomes for single items in Table 7 is related strongly and inversely to each item's average distance from the mean standardized z score in any sample. The closer to a z-score mean an item lies, the greater its number of significant outcomes; consequently, the middle item, "four digits backward," exhibits the greatest number of significant differences among samples: 9 out of 15 tests. This result may seem especially anomalous in view of the clean results for all three digits-backward items obtained earlier.

There is, however, a simple explanation. The constraint of a constant *SD* for all samples imposed when standardizing their z scores is equivalent to requiring that the sum of squares (of deviations from the mean) remains constant, and it is easy to see that the closer to the sample mean an item lies, the more it must change its position during standardization in response to changes in the locations of other items if the total sum of squares is to meet the constancy requirement. Conversely, a given adjustment of its contribution to the sum of squares can be satisfied by a much smaller change in standardized z the more distant an item lies from the mean of all three items. Because "four digits backward" is always the second-ranking item of three, and hence always the closest to the mean z score, it "travels" up and down the standardized z scale from sample to sample in

TABLE 7
Chi-square Tests for Differences in Standardized Difficulties of New Items between Six Diverse Samples

Observed and standardized (to SBA whites' digits items) percentages passing[a]

1916/1937/1960 Year, item, and content	(1) 113 white S-B 9-year-olds[b]		(2) 1,800 black grade school children		(3) 1,123 white 1937 S-B sample children		(4) 351 very low scoring white draftees		(5) 938 very low scoring black draftees		(6) 486 SBA white draftees		Row chi-square[c]	p <
	Obs.%	Stand.%	Obs.%	Stand.%	Obs.%	Stand.%	Obs.%	Stand.%	Obs.%	Stand.%	Obs.%	Stand.%		
VII,6/(L),VII,3/VII,3	93.81	92.30	60.94	90.35	68.34	90.44	77.78	92.24	27.61	91.29	94.86	92.40	3.41	NS
IX,9/(L),IX,6/IX,6	61.95	58.89	34.67	70.44	38.16	70.11	29.91	59.49	6.82	66.28	69.75	57.69	45.41	.001
X,3/(L),XI,1/XI,1	46.02	43.35	11.94	36.08	11.93	36.25	16.24	42.90	1.49	38.35	58.44	44.29	17.11	.005
	z scores standardized to mean and SD of SBA whites' digits-backward items													
Copy diamond		-1.4254		-1.3018		-1.3069		-1.4214		-1.3587		-1.4325		
Four digits backward		-.2246		-.5372		-.5277		-.2401		-.4202		-.1939		
Memory for designs		.1674		.3564		.3519		.1789		.2962		.1437		
Mean z score		-.4942		-.4942		-.4942		-.4942		-.4942		-.4942		
SD, z score		.8299		.8299		.8299		.8299		.8299		.8299		

Sample and testing date	Chi squares for first (below diagonal) and second (above diagonal) new items, based on standardized frequencies[d]					
(1) 87 white children (1913–1914)[b]	—	5.27	4.78	.01	1.93	.04
(2) 1,800 black children (1960)	.36	—	.04	16.36	4.99	28.47
(3) 1,123 white children (1930–1932)	.33	.01	—	13.77	3.47	23.44
(4) 351 low white draftees (1918)	.00	1.24	1.04	—	5.14	.27
(5) 938 low black draftees (1918)	.10	.64	.44	.30	—	10.18
(6) 486 SBA white draftees	.00	1.92	1.59	.01	.52	—

Sample and testing date	Chi squares for third (below diagonal) and all (above diagonal) new items, based on standardized frequencies[d]					
(1) 87 white children (1913–1914)[b]	—	7.52	6.86	.02	2.87	.07
(2) 1,800 black children (1960)	1.89	—	.06	23.45	6.99	41.36
(3) 1,123 white children (1930–1932)	1.75	.01	—	19.84	4.87	34.27
(4) 351 low white draftees (1918)	.01	5.85	5.03	—	7.65	.44
(5) 938 low black draftees (1918)	.84	1.36	.96	2.21	—	15.39
(6) 486 SBA white draftees (1918)	.03	10.97	9.24	.16	4.69	—

[a] Observed percentages passing reflect an attempt to reconstruct and undo rounding errors in original data of samples (1) and (3).
[b] In order not to alter the power of statistical tests, the sample (1) is treated as though its size were 87 in this table.
[c] Row chi-square tests have five degrees of freedom; to be significant at the .05 level, the chi square must equal or exceed 11.07.
[d] All four chi-square tests between pairs of samples (above and below diagonal) have one degree of freedom; to be significant at the .05 level, the chi square must equal or exceed 3.84.

response to relative changes in other items more than they do. In this sense, the three items form a "hydraulic" system; the inner item behaves like a piston with a smaller cross-sectional area than the pistons of the outer items, and hence, its displacement in response to any displacement in them is greater than theirs to the same displacement in it. Were there more than one item between the extremes, the compensating effect of a change in response to a change in relative difficulty in an extreme item could be spread over several central items without disturbing any one of them very much. This explanation, incidentally, also accounts for the fact that the sum of 15 chi squares was largest for "four digits backward" in the analysis of the three digits items in Table 6, even though none was significant. The absence of significance there despite the tendency of the statistical analysis to concentrate the chi square in the second-ranking of three items testifies further to the unusual generality of relative difficulty across samples in the case of the three digits items. The second-ranking item acts as bellwether in any set of three.

The artifact just described occurs at the standardized z-score stage before the transformation to standardized percentages, and it should not be confused with the tendency of the test to yield somewhat higher chi squares for items whose standardized percentages lie closer to 50% that was described earlier. The present artifact is peculiar to the situation when there are few items in the analysis, and it is the far more influential of the two phenomena. Both lead to differential sensitivity among items; again, such a differential is of no concern when the purpose of the analysis is to detect departures from interval scale properties rather than potentially biased items.

At this point, it is convenient to illustrate the relatively minor impact on interpretations of the differential sensitivity of items according to the distance of their percentages passing from 50% and, at the same time, to set to rest a question that might arise concerning the difference in results between the digits items and the new items. An inspection of the standardized percentages passing of the middle items ("four digits backward" in both cases) in Tables 6 and 7 shows that those percentages are closer to 50% in Table 7 four out of six times. Because the middle item in Table 7 also gave rise to more significant outcomes than the other two items put together, it is reasonable to ask whether the overall difference in significant outcomes can be explained by the difference in proximity to 50% rather than by a difference between the two sets of items. To answer this question, we need only refer to the analysis based on the alternative standardization that might well have been used in Table 7, that is, the standardization to the z-score mean and the *SD* of the SBA whites' new items rather than of their digits items. Vis-à-vis Table 6, that alternative but unreported standardization changes the order of closeness to 50% of the middle items so that the one in Table 6 is now closer in five out of six instances, with one tie, instead of only two out of six; however, the middle item in the new set still produces 6 significant outcomes in 15 comparisons, and the two row chi squares that were significant earlier, although lower in value, remain highly significant. Plainly, the overall difference between the two sets of items is no artifact of the choice of standardization. The impact of the choice of standardization, incidentally, is roughly proportional on all of the chi squares for a given item, although the proportion varies from item to item.

The second consideration to be kept in mind when interpreting the location among items of significant results from the chi-square test is one intrinsic to the study of relative difficulty; that is, the outcome for a particular item always depends on the nature of the other items tested with it because its difficulty is defined as relative to that of other items. Consequently, an item that is actually an extremely good one in the context of one subset of items may appear to be less adequate in a somewhat different context of items—witness "four digits backward." Jensen (1980a, p. 441) was undoubtedly aware of this when he suggested using relative difficulty on an assumed interval scale for detecting potential bias, but because he did not include an example with real data, the point may not have received sufficient emphasis. Instead, his discussion mentions, quite correctly, that the statistical significance of an item does not necessarily indicate that it is relatively more difficult for a minority group, for the item could be easier for that group (i.e., it could have a lower standardized z score or delta). In practice, significant differences in one direction tend to be accompanied by significant differences in the other direction for other items in any comparison of two samples. For example, in Table 7, the second item is often significantly easier for sample (2), whereas the third item is often significantly harder for sample (2), in relative terms. Thus, an item with unusually good attributes, such as "four digits backward," may be made to appear less good as the result of its having been placed among other items whose attributes are not as good as its own in some more general sense, such as in having true interval scale properties in at least some context. Not having been confronted with real examples, Jensen may have been too ready to label such counterbalancing but statistically significant items "biased." When the rank order of difficulty correlation is high, there-

fore, as it usually is, the investigator may wish to consider the possibility that significant but minor advantages in relative difficulty for
one group with respect to certain items are adequately offset by significant but minor advantages for the other group with respect to
other items (Jensen's recommendation notwithstanding), difficulty
being measured by standardized z or delta. The best overall summary measure of adequacy in this case may prove to be the level of
z-score or delta correlation between any two samples—which is not
affected by choice of standardization—interpreted in light of the
number of significant item outcomes, the power of the test, perhaps
the contingency or phi coefficients linked with each pairwise chi
square, and experience with other analyses. Finally, before concluding that an item is generally unsuitable in view of its performance
on a chi-square test of relative difficulty, one ought to investigate that
performance in the context of different items, preferably ones with
which it might have more in common, as in the case of "four digits
backward" and the other two digits items. Together, the three digits
items come closer to absolute perfection when subjected to certain
internal validity tests for potential bias than any other items now
known, as will become clearer from the next analysis in Table 8,
below, based on z or delta correlations.

Before proceeding to the next analysis, however, we must first
consider the location among samples of the significant outcomes in
Table 7. In the overall tests, the pattern—if, indeed, there is one—can
be summarized as follows: The two black samples are significantly
different from each other; both black samples are significantly different from three of the white samples, but not exactly the same three,
for a total of six out of eight possible comparisons across race; and
white samples are significantly different from other white samples
in three of six possible comparisons. With significant differences
within race about as common as significant differences between
race, there seems little reason to attribute the differences to racial
background *per se*. The differences in Table 7 are best viewed, therefore, simply as evidence that these data do not demonstrate a possession of true interval scale properties by the new set of three items,
rather than as evidence of bias against or between any particular
populations.

Linking the Chi-Square Test with z-Score Correlations

Now, let us turn to the next analysis concerning the digits-backward and new items, in Table 8. This analysis depends on comparisons among z-score (or delta) and other correlations involving the

two sets of three items in our six populations. Hypotheses concerning these correlations cannot be tested with the usual statistical formulas intended for correlations because those formulas assume that the number of cases and the number of data points are the same. Here, however, there are only three data points despite the extremely large numbers of cases. Three are too few to treat as though they were aggregate cases in the formulas, as is sometimes done under such circumstances. It was in order not to sacrifice or ignore the information in our large samples that the chi-square test was improvised earlier. However, now we can supplement the chi-square test, which was useful for comparing samples with each other, with nonparametric tests between sets of correlations, which capitalize on our having six independent samples to analyze simultaneously, but which cannot compare samples with other samples (except in the case of correlation with an external criterion, explained later).

Panel A of Table 8 contains two sets of z-score correlations among the six samples: one set for digits items and one set for the new items. By choice, no correlation in Table 8 has been rounded to 1.0000, no matter what the decimal places beyond the fourth contained. The set above the diagonal, with a mean of .9984 (SD = .0020), demonstrates the extraordinarily high level of correlation between the z scores of the digits-backward items. The lowest of the 15 digits correlations is .9942, and 6 of the 15 either round to or are greater than .9999 (if carried to more places). Among the five larger and hence more stable samples, the correlations are even more impressive: a mean of .9997 (SD = .0003), a lower bound of .9989, and 6 out of 10 either round to or exceed .9999. Moreover, all six of the correlations among the four samples that are both large and free of rounding errors in the original data (because frequencies rather than percentages were given) are .9999.[2] These four

---

[2]The data originally reported as simple percentages for samples (1) and (3) were first converted to the whole-number frequencies that would have rounded to the percentage in question, as the original frequencies could only have been whole numbers. However, there were often two adjacent whole numbers that could have rounded to a particular reported percentage, either upward or downward, in which case the two whole numbers were averaged, and a new percentage to two decimal places was determined for the average. The total frequencies for sample (3) were assembled from the frequencies determined in this manner for individual ages, whether whole numbers or averages of whole numbers, thus permitting errors in either direction an opportunity to cancel each other, and final percentages to two decimal places for the whole sample were calculated from the total frequencies, whether whole numbers or not, just as for the other samples.

TABLE 8

z-Score and Percentage-Passing Correlations for New Items and Digits-Backward Items, Correlations with Models of Digits-Item Difficulty, and Selected Tests of Significance

	(1)	(2)	(3)	(4)	(5)	(6)	Correlations between z scores of digits items and numbers:			First principal component, digits items
	1916 S-B whites (87)	1960 Blacks (1,800)	1937 S-B whites (1,123)	1918 Low whites (351)	1918 Low blacks (938)	1918 SBA whites (486)	(7) 3,4,5	(8) 9,16,25	(9) 6,24,120	(10)
A. z-score and other correlations for new items (below diagonal) and for digits items (above diagonal)										
(1) 1916 S-B whites (113)	—	.9959	.9981	.9953	.9942	.9959	.9977	.9903	.9032	.9972
(2) 1960 blacks	.9460	—	.9996	.9999	.9999	.9999	.9997	.9988	.9384	.9999
(3) 1937 S-B whites	.9492	.9999	—	.9994	.9989	.9996	.9999	.9969	.9277	.9999
(4) 1918 low whites	.9999	.9513	.9544	—	.9999	.9996	.9996	.9991	.9404	.9997
(5) 1918 low blacks	.9785	.9925	.9937	.9818	—	.9999	.9992	.9995	.9442	.9995
(6) 1918 SBA whites	.9994	.9346	.9381	.9987	.9710	—	.9997	.9988	.9385	.9999
Correlations between z scores of new items and numbers: 1,2,3	.9596	.9990	.9994	.9642	.9970	.9496				
B. Number of .9999 z-score correlations in row and column of sample										
Digits items	0	3	0	3	3	3				
New items	1	1	1	1	0	0				
C. Percentage passing and other correlations for new items (below diagonal) and for digits items (above diagonal)							Correlations between percentages passing of digits items and numbers:			First principal component, digits items
							3,4,5	9,16,25	6,24,120	
(1) 1916 S-B whites (113)	—	.9791	.9796	.9632			−.9917	−.9984	−.9696	.9820
(2) 1960 blacks	.9890	—	.9999	.9977			−.9971	−.9891	−.8995	.9999
(3) 1937 S-B whites	.9888	.9999	—	.9975			−.9973	−.9894	−.9006	.9999
(4) 1918 low whites	.9928	.9641	.9638	—			−.9897	−.9769	−.8680	.9966

(5) 1918 low blacks	.9903	.9589	.9586	.9998	.8901	−.9427	−.9163	−.7542	.9613
(6) 1918 SBA whites	.9997	.9850	.9847	.9955	—	−.9912	−.9981	−.9706	.9812
Correlations between percentages passing of new items and numbers:1,2,3	−.9820	−.9991	−.9992	−.9522	−.9769	−.9463	.9935	—	

D. Number of .9999 percentage passing correlations in row and column of sample

Digits items	1	1	1	0	1	0	0	1
New items	0	1	1	0	0	0	0	

E. Significance level of two-tailed Mann–Whitney tests between sets of 15 correlations[a]

	New items		Digits items	
	z score	% passing	z score	% passing
New items				
z score	—	NS	.0014	NOI
Percentage passing		—	.0008	NS
Digits items				
z score			—	.0008[b]
Percentage passing				—

F. Significance level of two-tailed Mann–Whitney tests between sets of six correlations[a]

	New items		Digits items			
	z score; 1,2,3	% passing; 1,2,3	z score; 3,4,5	z score; 9,16,25	% passing; 3,4,5	% passing; 9,16,25
New items						
z score; 1,2,3	—	NS	.016	NOI	NOI	NOI
Percentage passing; 1,2,3		—	.016	NOI	NS	NOI
Digits items						
z score; 3,4,5			—	.042[b]	.002[b]	.008[b]
z score; 9,16,25				—	NS	.026[b]
Percentage passing; 3,4,5					—	NS
Percentage passing; 9,16,25						—

[a] NOI indicates hypothesis not of interest.

[b] Row variable significantly higher in absolute value than column variable, rather than vice versa.

include the two black samples and white samples (4) and (6). Empirical correlations as high as these, even from aggregate data, are seldom seen.

The set of correlations below the diagonal in Panel A, for the new items, has a mean of .9726 (SD = .0247). As the mean indicates, the correlations in this set are also high by usual standards, but distinctly lower as a group than the correlations above the diagonal. Only two of the new set appear as .9999 (see Panel B). Although it may seem small, the difference between the two sets reflected in the means justifies the use of special terms for characterizing the upper set. Panel A in Table 8 demonstrates that although the precondition of perfect rank correlation of three items among samples virtually ensures a high linear correlation between the z scores of any two samples, it certainly does not guarantee an extraordinarily high correlation such as those for the digits items above the diagonal. According to the Mann–Whitney test (Walker & Lev, 1953), the two-tailed probability that the two sets of correlations represent the same statistical population is only .0014. The chi-square test, as we are now in a position to see, was also extremely sensitive to aspects of the difference between the two sets, as it yielded no significant differences for one, but 24 for the other.

Having witnessed that the chi-square test is extremely sensitive to the relatively small difference *between* correlation matrices above and below the diagonal in Table 8, it can now be shown that the test is also sensitive to variations in the strength of correlation *within* each of the two matrices. Not surprisingly, there is a strong association between the magnitudes of the correlations between samples in Panel A and the magnitudes of the overall pairwise chi squares between samples in Tables 6 and 7. Above the diagonal, the correlation between the correlations (despite their small SD) and the total chi squares in Table 6 is −.69; below the diagonal, it is −.82 with the total chi squares in Table 7. But for the fact that the chi square is a complex function involving sample size and choice of standardization, these cross-relations between the two statistics would be even stronger. In any case, they are strong enough to establish the relevance of both statistics to the interval scale question, for both statistics are obviously devices for assessing departures from perfect linearity. In samples as large as ours, the chi-square test can be understood, therefore, as one that discriminates extraordinarily high degrees from merely very high degrees of linearity.

Comparing the z versus Percentage Transformations for Evidence of Interval Scale Properties

Neither a significant chi square nor a low correlation necessarily proves that a set of items lacks interval scale properties, for a perfect interval scale can be obscured by, and a perfect correlation disrupted by, the impact of other variables on the observations. Such a configuration of statistics merely proves that the data depart sufficiently from perfect linearity so as not to constitute evidence for an interval scale as they stand. A replicable correlation of 1.0 and its accompanying chi square, on the other hand, do constitute sufficient proof of an interval scale as they stand, for such a correlation can appear only when interval scale properties are present in the measurements.

Social scientists are aware that monotonic, but not necessarily linear, transformations tend to correlate very highly with each other (Labovitz, 1970), and that awareness actually militates against their being sufficiently impressed by a particular high correlation to accept fully the existence of a true interval scale. Can there ever be a region of correlation short of 1.0 where it is warranted to dismiss that doubt? Given that empirical data can never reasonably be expected to yield perfect correlations of 1.0, the problem before us is that of deciding whether it can ever be appropriate to replace the idea of approximation with the idea of true functional fit and, if so, under what conditions. Not having often been faced with the problem, social scientists have no generally agreed-upon standards for accepting the hypothesis of perfect linearity, that is, really accepting it. Thus far, I have made a case that the correlations among the digits items are extraordinarily high—higher, in fact, than would be expected simply on the basis of perfect rank-order correlation among three data points, and significantly higher than corresponding correlations between comparable items in the same samples. Now let us see what other evidence is available among the remaining correlations in Table 8, as yet undiscussed.

Panel C of Table 8 contains correlations between samples for both sets of items that are based on the observed percentages passing instead of z transformations. Because the Panel C correlations also reflect perfect rank-order correlation among samples, they afford another opportunity to examine the extent to which that precondition alone is capable of producing extraordinarily high product–moment correlations when there are only three data points.

Above the diagonal in Panel C, the digits-backward items, whose correlations average .9686, now display only two correlations of

.9999; below the diagonal, the new items, whose correlations average .9843, display only one (see Panel D). Even these few examples of .9999 are due not simply to the precondition of perfect rank correlation, but to the fact that the pairs of samples in question just happen to have fairly similar mental-age means and SDs (see Tables 4 and 5 for these statistics). Counting on both sides of the diagonal, two of the three .9999 correlations occur for the same pair of samples, numbers (2) and (3). Their mental-age means and SDs are known and similar. The third .9999 correlation occurs between samples (1) and (6), above the diagonal. Their means are both known and similar. Moreover, the correlation below the diagonal between samples (1) and (6) is also unusually high, at .9997. When mental ability is normally distributed, and when two large and stable samples, such as numbers (2) and (3), have equal means and SDs, an interval scale will obviously lead to perfect correlations between both their z scores and their percentages passing. In Panel C, we are witnessing several cases that approximate such a condition, where the transformation with the higher correlation may simply be an accident of minor sampling fluctuations around a virtual tie.

Unlike the two correlations matrices based on z scores in Panel A, the two based on percentages in Panel C do not differ significantly from one another, according to the rather powerful Mann–Whitney test ($p = .25$, two-tailed test). This lack of difference is consistent with the interpretation that it is the z transformation that enables the interval scale properties of the digits items to become manifest.

An especially important comparison is that between each Panel C matrix and its z counterpart for the same set of items above in Panel A. If interval scale properties are present, and the z score is the correct transformation, that transformation rather than any other should allow the interval scale to emerge. To the extent that the z transformation is correct, therefore, other transformations may prove more incorrect than usual and hence, through a seesaw effect, may be more apt to yield relatively low correlations, especially when samples are as heterogeneous in their mental-age means and SDs as ours. A corollary compatible with, but independent of, the seesaw effect is that when one set of items embodies interval scale properties and an another set falls short, the choice of transformation should prove more critical for the first set. This, in fact, is what occurs in Table 8.

Thus, the Mann–Whitney test reveals a significant difference between the z score and the percentage-passing correlations of the digits items ($p = .0008$, two-tailed test), but no significant difference between the z-score and the percentage-passing correlations of the new items. In 13 of 15 comparisons, the z-score correlation of the digits items is larger than the corresponding percentage-passing correlation ($p = .008$, two-tailed sign test); the matrix of percentage-passing correlations for the digits items also has the lowest mean of the four matrices in Table 8, .9686, which would be consistent with a seesaw effect. The two exceptions in the 15 sign-test comparisons involve the pairs of samples with fairly similar mental-age means, and sometimes SDs, that were discussed earlier, and for which a special explanation was given. Each of the samples in those special pairs displays correlations with the remaining samples that are all enhanced by the z transformation, for a total of four of the five available comparisons. Even the few correlations that fail to be improved by the z transformation in the case of digits items, therefore, are neither truly exceptional nor characteristic of any particular sample, as they simply reflect the coincidences of similar means and SDs.

In short, the transformation to the abscissa of the normal distribution in combination with the digits items produces a correlation matrix significantly higher than either of the two matrices in which one or the other of these two factors is lacking or than the matrix in which both are lacking (test results appear in Panel E).[3] Before con-

---

[3]There are difficult philosophical problems surrounding my use of significance tests of the differences between correlation matrices in Panel E of Table 8. First of all, there is the problem of nonindependence between elements within each matrix, which the nonparametric test does not take into account. However, the samples for pairs of matrices, especially those pairs based on the same items, are not independent either, and hence, conditions certainly do not correspond to those for which the more sophisticated test of Jennrich (1970) is suited. Second, there is even a serious question of whether there is anything stochastic to be tested at all in the case of those matrices that differ only as the result of the nonlinear z transformation; if there is not, and the difference is merely a tautology, any difference is reliable, no matter how small. However, knowledge of the transformation is certainly not sufficient to predict the outcome *a priori*, as some of the comparisons demonstrate, especially the failure of the seesaw effect, below, and it does seem reasonable to regard the goodness of fit as subject to chance fluctuations in the data, by analogy with testing for curvilinearity of regression against linearity, where the two alternatives are also related by a transformation of the same data (but differ, note, by a degree of freedom in the simplest case, unlike here). The nonparametric test, in view of the second question, may be overly stringent, but it does lend security that correlations in two matrices are indeed specimens from different populations in the absence of any other way of knowing. The viewpoint taken is that the elements have been sampled from a larger population of potential pairings of samples otherwise meeting the conditions of each matrix. The idea of a larger population makes sense, as the rows and columns represent samples instead of variables. *A fortiori*, such considerations motivate the testing of matrices based on different items. The problem of independence among elements, however, remains unevaluated. I am indebted to James Fennessey for a helpful discussion of these perplexing issues.

sidering the important implications these data hold concerning the shape of the distribution of mental ability in all six samples, which many readers will have perceived for themselves by this point, we must return to Table 8 to discover what its remaining correlations have to say.

Relations with an Outside Criterion of Distance between Items

The correlations in Table 8 considered thus far hold no information concerning the relative sizes of the two intervals within any set of three items. They indicate only the degree to which the intervals between items, whatever their size relative to each other, are invariant across samples. Columns (7), (8), and (9) of Table 8, however, do contain sets of six correlations that bear on interval sizes within samples. These correlations are between the z scores (in Panel A) or the percentages passing (in Panel C) and numbers chosen to portray three alternative hypotheses concerning the manner in which digits-backward items increase in difficulty, that is, concerning the sizes of the intervals. The correlations in those columns also address the question of whether it is possible to discriminate among alternative *a priori* models of digits-item difficulty, given that all monotonic transformations of only three data points that are perfectly ordered are bound to correlate highly. Again, the statistical analysis depends on the presence of multiple samples.

The column (7) model, represented by the numbers 3, 4, and 5, views difficulty as increasing one unit for each additional digit, in accordance with the manifest structure of the items. This is the model with which the chi-square results thus far appear consistent. The column (8) model, represented by the numbers 9, 16, and 25, views difficulty as increasing linearly as the square of the number of digits backward. The column (9) model, represented by the numbers 3!, 4!, and 5!, or 6, 24, and 120, views difficulty as increasing as the number of permutations of the number of digits.[4] If scaled so as to have the same mean and *SD* as the first model, the second can be represented by the numbers 3.0441, 3.9169, and 5.0390, and the third by 3.2821, 3.5758, and 5.1422. When so transformed, it becomes evident that the second differs so slightly from 3, 4, and 5 that it is rea-

---

[4]The size of the total pool of potential content, such as all single digits or all letters of the alphabet, first suggested by Jacobs (1887, p. 75) as a factor in difficulty in simple or forward-memory span, does not seem to have any effect (Crannell & Parrish, 1957). Hence, the models do not reflect pool size.

sonable to wonder whether the chi-square test would be sensitive to the difference if the two models applied to different samples. However, we can address the problem of discriminating between such similar models by inspecting the sets of six correlations in columns (7), (8), and (9) that represent the models and also by using the Mann–Whitney U test to determine whether some are significantly better than others in fitting the observed measures of difficulty. The exact probabilities of the Mann–Whitney test for small samples are tabled in Siegel (1956).

Inspection of the permutation model in column (9) reveals it to be so inferior to the other two models in fitting either the z scores or the percentages passing that it need not be considered further. This leaves just two models. In Panel A, the correlations of the unit model in column (7) exceed those of the squared model in column (8) five out of six times, the single exception involving a small difference of only .0003. These two sets of correlations differ significantly (p = .042, two-tailed test). The corresponding sets in Panel C do not differ significantly from each other, but each Panel A set is significantly higher in absolute value than its corresponding Panel C set (see Panel F for probabilities). Such patterns add to the evidence in support of the z transformation as the proper metric for digits-item difficulty.

To assess further the extent to which monotonicity alone is responsible for the success of the unit model of digits difficulty in column (7), the digits 1, 2, and 3 (a linear transformation of 3, 4, and 5 used to reduce confusion) were correlated with the z scores and the percentages passing of the new items (see the last rows in Panels A and C), even though we have no a priori expectations concerning the relative sizes of the intervals between the new items. These two sets of correlations do not differ significantly from each other in absolute value, which indicates once again that the relation between the digits items and the z transformation holds special information not easily found among other items or other transformations. Both "1, 2, 3" sets are significantly lower in absolute value than the "3, 4, 5" set in column (7) of Panel A. These additional results mean that the unit model in conjunction with the z transformation of digits-item difficulty exhibits a significantly better fit than all seven other sets of six correlations in Panels A and C (see Panel F for probabilities for all but the obviously inferior permutations sets).

Now let us take a closer look at the correlations of our most successful model: z score with unit difficulty for digits-backward items. Five of the six correlations exceed .9990, and those five belong to the five large samples. Thus, the only discernible distinction among the samples appears to be a function not of mental ability level, age, race, sex composition, or time period, but simply of sample size.

The success of the model in column (7) of Panel A in passing such tests means that in addition to the evidence strongly indicative of an interval scale for the digits-backward items from the chi-square test, and from the extraordinarily high correlations among z scores of heterogeneous samples, we have now the extraordinarily high correlations between samples and an external criterion founded on the structural nature of the items. The last relationship can be summarized by the correlation between the numbers 3, 4, and 5 and the weighted averages of the z scores for digits items in Table 6, formed across samples. That correlation is .9998. The closeness of fit between the numbers of digits in an item and the relative difficulties derived from the performances of all 4,785 individuals can also be portrayed by standardizing the weighted z averages so that they have the mean and the *SD* of the numbers 3, 4, and 5; when this is done, the relative difficulties can be expressed by the numbers 3.01, 3.98, and 5.01, among which the intervals are very nearly perfectly equal.

Although it is not immediately visible, there is one final relation of interest concerning the z-score correlations for the digits items in Panel A. If the correlations between each of the six samples with other samples are summed—thus representing the total or average strength of association for each sample—and each sample's sum is correlated with the correlation between its z scores and the numbers 3, 4, and 5 in column (7), the resulting correlation equals .9910. Apparently, even the exceedingly small differences in degree to which the samples correlate with each other can be accounted for almost totally by the extent to which their z scores correlate with the unit model of digits-item difficulty. The better each sample fits the unit model, the more it correlates, on the average, with the other samples. In factor-analytic terms, the vector of six correlations between z scores and 3, 4, 5 represents "loadings" on the "3, 4, 5" factor, which is very nearly equivalent to the actual first principal component of the digits-item correlation matrix in Panel A. The actual first principal component accounts for 99.87% of the variance in that matrix and may be seen in column (10) of Panel A. The sum of squares of "loadings" on the "3, 4, 5" factor in column (7) indicates that it accounts for 99.86% of the variance. In contrast, loadings on the "1, 2, 3" factor account for only 95.72% of the variance in the matrix based on the three new items, and the first principal component of correlations based on digits-item percentages, in Panel C, accounts for only 97.40%.

One may be willing to grant that intriguing differences have been demonstrated between the two sets of items and between the z-score and the percentage-passing transformations and yet have reservations based on the following questions: To what extent are the new items typical of similarly ordered Stanford–Binet items in general? To what extent are the differences between the two sets due only to possible differences in reliability? To what extent are the digits-backward items typical of other digits-backward items, both within and beyond their range in length? Before attempting to harvest our interpretations, let us deal with these peripheral but important questions.

Examining a Wider Pool of Nondigits Items

Conceivably, the constraints discussed earlier on the choosing of three new items common to all six samples have led to an unfortunately atypical selection and thus a somehow flawed comparison. For example, the most difficult item in the new set was spaced one mental-age year closer to the next most difficult than strict correspondence with the digits items would require. Moreover, two of the items in the new set depend on the scoring of drawings (made from a simple model in one case, and from memory of complex models in the other), and such items may be less reliable than ones that are digital.[5] Even if they were well-founded, such conjectures would not make the chi-square test less sensitive, or necessarily detract from the properties of the digits items, although those properties might then be revealed to be more general than Tables 6–8 would suggest. The answers to the questions are clearly worth having, but as much for the light they can shed on other items—which constitute the preponderant content of the Stanford–Binet—as for what they reveal about the digits items themselves, for understanding of each kind of item can improve understanding of the other. Let us consider first the matter of the representativeness of the items analyzed thus far.

[5]"Copying a diamond" and "memory for designs" were listed by Terman (1918, Table 4) in the lower midrange of a group of items prone to scoring errors on the part of student examiners, but their error rates were modest. Digit span was not listed at all. Terman emphasized that his data did not necessarily bear on the intrinsic difficulty of scoring items, as they reflected the instructional preparation of those students. The scoring for the SBA whites included a small "doubtful" category, which I have treated as "failing," but the two nondigits new items received fewer doubtful scores than the digits-backward items (Yerkes, 1921, Part II, Table 66).

Recall that three of our larger and more heterogeneous samples, from 1918, were tested with 25 items from the same Stanford–Binet edition. Those items were listed in Table 2. We can extract all of the nondigits items that have exactly the same mental-age locations as the digits items, therefore, and examine their z-score and percentage-passing correlations between all pairings of the three samples. This procedure yields three qualifying items at each of the three mental ages VII, IX, and XII (Item XII, 5 having been dropped because it had a percentage passing of zero in one of the samples and hence an indeterminate z).[6] All combinations of three items consisting of one from each of the specified mental-age years yields 27 triplets of items. However, some of the triplets, because of item ties or inversions of order in one of the samples, fail to display percentages passing that are perfectly concordant in reversed order of magnitude with the order of the mental ages (z and the percentage passing are, of course, inversely related). Strict comparability demands perfect rank concordance, and so the number of actually concordant triplets for any pairing of samples is always somewhat less than 27. The discussion here focuses on correlations for the concordant triplets between each pairing of the three 1918 samples, and on their summary statistics. Like those in Table 8, these correlations reflect observed percentages passing that have been calculated to two decimal places. Whereas previous analyses enabled us to compare many pairings of samples with respect to just a few sets of items, we can now compare many sets of items with respect to just a few pairings of samples.

The statistics for all concordant triplets appear in Table 9, where they can be compared readily with correlations for the two sets of three items analyzed thus far, called *digits* and *new*, in the same pairings of samples. But because there are now only 3 of each, and those 3 correlations are not necessarily typical of all 15 in their Table 8 matrix, the comparisons with the digits and new items in Table 9 may seem of uncertain value. However, a brief introduction indicating the relation of each subset of 3 to the mean of the 10 corresponding correlations among the five large samples in Table 8 may increase their value and prevent misunderstandings. The five-sample means for digits items are .9997 and .9715 for z-score and percentage-passing correlations, respectively. The former is close to all three of its kind in Table 9, but the latter is close to only two of its

---

[6]For the calculation of the 25-item delta correlations in Table 2, this item was assigned the z score of 3.25, or the delta of 26, that is conventional in such cases (Jensen, 1980a, pp. 439–440).

TABLE 9
Comparisons between z-Score and Percentage-Passing Correlations for Concordant Triplets, Digits Items, New Items, and All 25 Available Items from the 1916 Stanford–Binet

	z score			Percentage passing			Difference		
	Low whites with low blacks A	Low blacks with SBA whites B	Low whites with SBA whites C	Low whites with low blacks D	Low blacks with SBA whites E	Low whites with SBA whites F	Low whites with low blacks A–D	Low blacks with SBA whites B–E	Low whites with SBA whites C–F
Review of correlations from Table 8 for these pairs of samples									
Digits items	.9999	.9999	.9999	.9807	.8901	.9620	.0192	.1098	.0379
New items	.9818	.9710	.9987	.9998	.9935	.9955	−.0180	−.0225	.0032
Concordant 1916 Stanford–Binet triplets from mental ages VII, IX, and XII									
Mean correlation	.9828	.9697	.9909	.9690	.9148	.9762	.0138	.0549	.0147
SD (of difference)	.0227	.0290	.0092	.0344	.0871	.0155	(.0384)	(.0334)	(.0113)
No. of triplets	24	21	24	24	21	24	—	—	—
No. equal to .9999	4	1	0	0	0	3	—	—	—
Mean of									
Lowest third	.9577	.9322	.9797	.9261	.8041	.9587	.0316	.1291	.0210
Middle third	.9914	.9804	.9941	.9844	.9444	.9787	.0070	.0360	.0154
Highest third	.9995	.9955	.9988	.9965	.9959	.9912	.0030	−.0004	.0076
No. of triplets where z score exceeds percentage passing r							15/24	14/21	21/24
Mann–Whitney test, one-tailed p =							.0317	.0758	.0007
Wilcoxon test, one-tailed p ≤							NS	.01	.005

(continued)

TABLE 9 (continued)

Comparisons between z-Score and Percentage-Passing Correlations for Concordant Triplets, Digits Items, New Items, and All 25 Available Items from the 1916 Stanford–Binet

	z score			Percentage passing			Difference		
	Low whites with low blacks	Low blacks with SBA whites	Low whites with SBA whites	Low whites with low blacks	Low blacks with SBA whites	Low whites with SBA whites	Low whites with low blacks	Low blacks with SBA whites	Low whites with SBA whites
	A	B	C	D	E	F	A–D	B–E	C–F
Mean correlation	.9838	.9741	.9917	.9711	.9317	.9786	.0127	.0424	.0131
SD	.0215	.0271	.0090	.0329	.0829	.0162	—	—	—
			Statistics for all 27 triplets from mental ages VII, IX, and XII						
Correlations between z score r and percentage passing r	.1645	.3739	.7128	—	—	—	—	—	—
			Statistics for all 25 1916 Stanford–Binet items from Table 2						
Correlation	.98	.95	.98	.90	.79	.97	.08	.16	.01

kind. However, the aberrant entry, in Column E, seems well-matched by its counterpart for concordant triplets, below, and hence comparisons of digits items with the concordant triplets benefit from the control on pairings of samples. The five-sample means for the new items are .9715 and .9803 for z scores and percentages passing, respectively; both means are a bit more than one point lower than the means for three correlations of their kind in Table 9. Although comparability between all of the correlations in Table 8 and their representatives in Table 9 may be lacking in certain fine details, the main facts are informative enough, especially when we keep in mind that comparisons between both sets of three items and the concordant triplets hold constant the pairings of samples involved, and hence at least some peculiarities, such as those affecting Column E, whatever their source.

The means of the z-score correlations for concordant triplets in Table 9 reveal those for the new items immediately above them to be quite typical of nondigits items in these pairings of samples (given the rank-order and mental-age preconditions); however, the mean percentage-passing correlations reveal those for the new items directly above to be higher than usual (and this applies to the five-sample mean, too, but not as strongly). The implication of these two comparisons concerning concordant triplets can be followed in the differences columns of Table 9, where we find that, given the preconditions, the z-score transformation actually does tend to improve the fit between samples even among nondigits items; that is, it produces correlations that tend to be higher than those calculated directly from percentages passing. However, the tendency is weaker among nondigits items than among digits items, for the mean difference between the two kinds of correlation for these pairs of samples is still only 50% as large as that produced by the digits items (cf. the differences columns in Table 9). Thus, the set of new items seems definitely to be atypical in not showing an advantage for the z transformation, and it is enlightening to realize this.

As for the digits items, their percentage-passing correlations now look quite typical of items in general in all three pairings (as does their corresponding five-sample mean), but their z-score correlations, at .9999, continue to stand out as being extraordinarily high (as does their corresponding five-sample mean). Although the difference between the two transformations clearly continues to matter more for the digits items, the data are no longer consistent with the hypothesis of a seesaw relation between the two types of correlation when the z-score version is extraordinarily high. The fact that the z transformation is "right" does not seem to make the other poorer than usual, after all. If the seesaw relation held over a broad range of z correlations, one would also expect a negative correlation between z-score and percentage-passing correlations over the same sets of triplets. However, Table 9 shows that the three such correlations between correlations there, calculated across all 27 triplets, are always positive (see the lower part of the table). If such positive correlations hold for items in general (i.e., without preconditions) and for all pairings of samples, as well they might, it would keep differences between the transformations consistent but small; hence, proof that the z transformation tends to yield the better fit between samples might require many more sets of results than are usually at hand. We have already seen that the difference between z and percentages in producing linearity is obscured when the samples are too similar in mean and *SD* of mental age. Perhaps these considerations explain, in part, the fact that I know of no publication that actually demonstrates the superiority of the z transformation or its derivative, delta, although several correctly regard z as the most appropriate function for expressing item difficulty (e.g., Angoff & Ford, 1973; Jensen, 1980a, p. 439). Whatever the reason, advocates of z rely on assumptions concerning the distribution of mental ability bolstered by references to the IQ distribution and to polygenic theory (Jensen, 1980a, pp. 80–81), which, as we shall see, some critics regard as unsatisfactory.

The extraordinary and improbable nature of correlations that equal .9999 or thereabouts, even in the case of only three monotonic data points, is now confirmed by the fact that, on the z-score side, only 5 of 69 correlations attain that value for concordant triplets, and on the percentage-passing side, only 3 of 69, for a total of 5.8%. The results suggest that among nondigits items the probability of obtaining three such correlations in three attempts, strictly by chance, is on the order of slightly less than .0004 for z scores, and slightly less than .0001 for percentages, even when 1916 mental-age separations correspond to those of the digits items exactly. Recall that the pairings of samples in question have not been selected for having .9999 digits correlations. Moreover, the few .9999 correlations that do appear among concordant triplets show no tendency to be associated with a particular constellation of items, for in no case does a given triplet produce a .9999 correlation in more than one pairing of samples (even when all 27 triplets are counted, at six correlations per triplet, whether z score or percentage passing). This failure of .9999 correlations to remain characteristic of particular triplets is in marked contrast to the digits items, whose extraordinary correlations replicate repeatedly across pairings of samples. The five-sample mean z correlation of the digits items, .9997, based on 10 correlations (two-thirds of the total in Table 8), is also higher than the mean of the highest third of the correlations from concordant triplets in any pairing of samples (see Table 9).

Table 9 reveals that, although the number of instances in which z scores yield higher correlations than percentages for a given concordant triplet is somewhat greater than perfect chance expectation in all three pairings, the superiority of the z transformation is not striking enough among nondigits items so that it could be said to leap out at one as it does for digits items. In fact, two different significance tests based on different nonparametric aspects of the data are required to demonstrate z-score superiority for all three pairings at conventional levels of probability: the Mann–Whitney test and the Wilcoxon signed-ranks test (Siegel, 1956). Whether the difference between the two transformations would tend to be as subtle as this among items in general is difficult to say on the basis of the data available here.

However, the means for each third of the distributions of correlations from concordant triplets indicate that the correlations produced by z scores and percentages differ most in their lower ranges; hence, the superiority of z scores in the case of nondigits items is most evident whenever percentages passing yield an especially poor correlational fit between samples. As we have seen, such a poor fit is more likely to be found in connection with pairs of samples that diverge in their means and/or SDs, for example, the pair in Columns B and E of Table 9. Those columns pair the low blacks and the SBA whites, two samples whose mental-age means and SDs diverge far more than those of blacks and whites in general, either in 1918 or now. The data suggest in various ways, therefore, that any run-of-the-mill contrast between the two transformations depending on samples much less different than those two, based mainly or entirely on typical intelligence-test items of the nondigits type, may well risk seeming inconclusive. The superiority of the z transformation may not be highly visible—however well-grounded it may be in theory— outside comparisons between extreme samples, and even such comparisons may not produce impressive differences in the case of many kinds of items. These lessons are borne out by the correlations to be discussed next.

Let us extend our comparisons so as to include the z-score and percentage-passing correlations for all 25 items from Table 2, which appear in the last row of Table 9. In certain important respects, these correlations are more like those usually seen, for they are based on many items instead of on triplets, with no precondition of perfect rank correlation across samples. Despite such major changes in fundamental composition, the 25-item correlations for z scores are only a shade lower than the corresponding correlations from triplets, concordant or not. This fact adds to the value of comparisons based on the triplets. The picture alters for the 25-item percentage-passing correlations; however, two of the pairings yield large differences between the two transformations, both involving blacks and whites. Not unexpectedly, Column E is again the locus of the largest difference. In contrast, the difference for the pairing of the two white samples is only .01, despite their large differences in mental age means and *SD*s (listed in Table 4). Evidently, the superiority of the z transformation is not visible in every pairing of samples, even when their parameters do differ considerably. This is understandable when we remind ourselves that our method of detecting that superiority depends on demonstrating a high order of linearity against a background having a high order of monotonicity.

Referring back to Table 2, we can also see that the z-score correlations barely exceed the 25-item rank-order correlations. Because the 25-item z-score correlations do not reach the striking level of perfection so often attained in the case of the digits-backward items, the hypothesis that an interval scale was present in those 25 items would not appear self-evident, and hence, it would have to compete with the alternative hypothesis that the very high, but not extraordinary, correlations were due simply to monotonicity in the majority of interitem orderings within any pair of samples. However, this alternative explanation has been ruled out entirely in the case of the digits items by the data in Tables 8 and 9.

Degradation of the z correlation by the usual disordinalities or imperfections in rank correlation among many items that are not all as widely separated in difficulty as our triplets undoubtedly contributes to the z correlation's falling enough short of perfection so as to obscure potential interval scale properties. However, as the 25-item z correlations in Table 9 are only slightly lower than those from concordant triplets, whose rank correlation is always controlled at 1.0, disordinalities of the usual sort are certainly not the whole story and, in fact, may not be nearly as important as one would expect. Note, for example, that the correlations of triplets containing disordinal and tied items actually exceed those based on strictly concordant triplets on the average in all three pairings of samples—as witnessed by the slightly higher mean correlations for all 27 triplets than for the subsets of concordant triplets (see Table 9). Even though this fact reflects in part the wide spacing of items in those triplets, it suggests that nondigits items in general produce slightly lower z correlations than the digits items because of their greater heterogeneity of content, and not simply because of imperfections in monotonicity, which to some extent can itself be attributed to heterogeneity in item components. This is a potentially vital clue for understanding why the two kinds of intelligence test item produce consistently different levels of z correlation even when both are ordered perfectly, and for understanding the relation of interval scale properties to both kinds of item, as we shall see.

The Question of Differential Reliability

Now, let us deal briefly with the question of whether the differences in level of correlation between the digits and the new items is due only to differences in the reliability of their z scores. Ideally, such reliabilities would be determined from correlations based on split halves of each sample, which are not available to us. However, we can approximate the ideal, and in a manner that answers our question adequately, by calculating the correlations between adjacent mental-age categories, ages, or grades within samples where they happen to be available. In principle, such pairs of categories sample exactly the same population, except for the slight difference in mental age. This use of adjacent categories within samples does not yield split halves in the literal sense, of course, but it does lead to a considerable reduction in the effects of any special differences among the six major samples that one might care to assume. Problems connected with the use of mental-age categories in such correlations, but deemed to be of minor relevance in this context, are discussed at a later point.

Note that an adequate answer to our question does not require the actual reliabilities for the two sets of three items, but only an indicator of their relative reliabilities. Because the correlations for both sets that we are considering have been obtained from the same adjacent categories, their relative magnitudes should testify to the relative reliabilities of the items under the reasonable assumption that homogeneity within samples is much greater than homogeneity between samples; thus, we can address the question of whether the somewhat lower z-score correlations of the new items in Table 8 are due simply to a greater instability of the new items than of the digits items within the six major samples, rather than to reliable differences between those samples that have a greater impact on the non-digits items.

Drawn from all samples except (1) and (5), nine sets of adjacent categories providing percentages passing for both sets of items are available. The sample sizes in these categories, identical for both sets of items, range from 75 to 300. The average correlation estimating reliability between categories is .9960 for the digits items and .9918 for the new items. In seven of the nine comparisons, the slightly higher correlation lies with the digits items, but the difference is not significant according to any of the three nonparametric tests tried. Thus, although there may possibly be a difference in reliability between the two sets of items, it is far too small to account for differences in level of correlation between samples. Recall that the five-sample means are .9997 for the digits items and .9715 for the new items. The mean correlation for the new items, therefore, despite the fact that the total samples are much larger in size than the adjacent categories and hence estimates based on the former are more reliable, is actually lower than our (under)estimate of those items' reliability. This comparison establishes beyond question that the sample differences reflected in lower z correlations for the new items are not due simply to differences in reliability between the z scores of the two sets of items (which is not to be confused with reliability at the level of individual responses, of course, although the two are undoubtedly related).

A positive correlation of .47 between the two sets of nine estimates indicates that both were responsive to a common influence, probably sample size. The correlation of .72 between the average correlation for both sets and the average sample size of both categories confirms this ($p < .05$, two-tailed test).

By allowing total samples to serve as one of the categories, despite some overlapping of membership, five additional comparisons can be mustered. If we take sample size and overlap into account, these five are quite typical of the nine discussed thus far. One of the five enables us to examine sample (5), the 1918 low blacks, where the overlap was minimal because the smaller category represents only 3.5% of the total sample. Here, the reliability for each set of items was quite similar to that based on adjacent categories drawn from the 1960 black sample 42 years later. For example, the reliability among blacks for digits items was .9991 in 1918 and .9990 for Grades 5 and 6 in 1960. No differences in reliability according to race can be discerned at any points in time, and there is no evidence of change over time within either race.

Other Digits Items of the Same Lengths

We turn finally to the last of the three questions that might engender reservations: To what extent are the digits-backward items that we have examined thus far typical of other such items, both within and beyond their range in length? The within-range aspect of this question is closely related to the issue of reliability just discussed, except that reliability is now defined operationally through the use of alternate forms of items instead of through split halves of samples.

The 1937 standardization and edition of the Stanford–Binet provided two forms of the test: Form L and Form M. Items in one form did not necessarily have a one-to-one correspondence in content with items in the other. Form L bore the greater resemblance to the original 1916 Stanford–Binet (Terman & Merrill, 1937, p. 3), but this generalization did not hold in every detail. Consequently, perusal of the digits-backward items reveals that those most similar, in the actual digits employed, to the items in earlier and later versions of the test are located in Forms M, L, and L for 3, 4, and 5 digits, respectively, and they are the digits items that have been used for sample (3) thus far (cf. the note to Table 5). Form M contained two additional digits-backward items at lengths 4 and 5, but there was no alternate item at length 3 anywhere in the test (this also applies to the single item at length 6).

Because a correlation with any meaning at all requires a minimum of three data pairs, we must employ the same item at length 3 in both test forms if we are to calculate a correlation for exactly the same individuals between the two sets of digits-backward items, that is, if we are to calculate what would ordinarily be a true alternate forms reliability coefficient. The effect of this expedient on the correlation is difficult to anticipate, but the result is bound to be suspect. Probably, the procedure is not as damaging as it might seem at first, as departure of the correlation from 1.0 reflects variation around the regression line (which is determined by all three item lengths) rather than variation between the members of a data pair. Conceivably, such double use of the same item could decrease the correlation as well as inflate it, depending on the true relation between the other two items from each form. Even though both sets contain one item in common, and that item is from Form M, it is convenient to distinguish the two sets of three digits items according to the form from which most of their items stem: Form L or Form M. Form L, therefore, is used here to refer to the set with which we are thus far acquainted.

Fortunately, we are not restricted to looking at just the suspect correlations in order to learn about the relative reliabilities of the two sets of digits items in the 1937 Stanford–Binet sample. The upper part of Table 10 presents the suspect correlations in the main diagonal, but it surrounds them with correlations between different age categories for each form. Form L correlations lie above the diagonal, Form M below. Although correlations within each form are based on the same items, they are not based on the same observations.

The results from the two forms are quite consistent with what we have already found, except in certain respects to be described shortly. The means of the six correlations above and the six below the diagonal—correlations based on totally independent observations—are identical for both forms, equaling .9972. This equality indicates that the two forms are equally reliable, and hence that different digits-backward items have the same amount of true score variance in their z scores. The rationale for these comparisons is essentially the same as that given before in connection with correlations between adjacent age categories for the digits items and the new items, except that now nonadjacent categories have been included. Because all of the comparisons now occur within only one of our major samples, the greater homogeneity makes the use of nonadjacent categories less problematic and thus enables us to increase the number of observed correlations.

Both forms correlate extraordinarily well with the numbers 3, 4, 5 (the unit model of digits-item difficulty), both at individual ages and with all ages combined (see Table 10). Let us concentrate on the combined ages 5.5–10. The correlations of Forms L and M with 3, 4, 5, .9999 and .9997, fall just to either side of that of Form L for all 4,785 individuals, namely, .9998. These correlations also imply similar reliability for the two forms and indicate similar loadings on the "3, 4, 5" factor. Comparable loadings for the other samples and the Form L set were presented in Table 8, above. Averaging the two forms does raise the correlations with the numbers 3, 4, 5, but only slightly, which suggests that the reliability of a single form is already so high that a two-thirds increase in the number of items has little impact (see Table 10).

Note that the suspect correlations on the diagonal in Table 10 do not seem to be out of line with other correlations in their rows and columns that are based instead on the approximation to split halves.

TABLE 10

Correlations between Forms L and M, and between Age Categories within Form, and with Unit Model, and z Scores for Three Digits Items from the 1937 Stanford–Binet Sample

	Age and sample size							r with 3, 4, 5		
	5.5 (110)	6 (203)	7 (202)	8 (203)	9 (204)	10 (201)	5.5 to 10 (1,123)	L	M	$\frac{L + M}{2}$
Alternate-forms correlations and z-score correlations between age categories, Form M (below diagonal) and Form L (above diagonal)										
Age										
7			.9982	.9989	.9998	.9968	.9996	.9994	.9997	.9999
8			.9997	.9967	.9978	.9919	.9971	.9966	.9999	.9990
9			.9993	.9999	.9999	.9982	.9999	.9999	.9999	.9999
10			.9968	.9945	.9930	.9983	.9987	.9990	.9946	.9974
5.5–10			.9999	.9996	.9992	.9969	.9995	.9999	.9997	.9999
z scores for Form L digits-backward items										
3(M,VII,4)	.8415	.4055	−.5834	−1.0786	−1.4679	−1.7250	−.5431			
4(L,IX,6)	1.9225	1.5418	.6433	.3003	−.2797	−.8014	.3008			
5(L,XII,4)	—	—	1.7272	1.3342	.8468	.2776	1.1265			
z scores for Form M digits-backward items										
3(M,VII,4)	.8415	.4055	−.5834	−1.0786	−1.4679	−1.7250	−.5431			
4(M,IX,6)	1.7945	1.3342	.5834	.0247	−.4918	−.9875	.1656			
5(M,XII,6)	—	—	1.8498	1.1241	.4370	.0748	.9400			
Form L z score minus Form M z score										
4	.1280	2.076	.0599	.2756	.2121	.1861	.1352			
5	—	—	−.1226	.2101	.4098	.2028	.1865			

Furthermore, the alternate forms correlation of .9995 for the total sample of 1,123 certainly does not overstate the reliability implied by the extraordinary correlations for large samples above the diagonal in Panel A of Table 8. There, the five-sample mean correlation is .9997. Recall that an obtained correlation cannot exceed the product of the square roots of the two reliabilities (e.g., Jensen, 1980a, p. 115), except by chance when the reliabilities do not come exactly from the sample in question. If both reliabilities are assumed to be the same, the obtained correlation itself represents a lower bound estimate for their values. Among the five large samples, many of the obtained z correlations for digits items in Table 8 that do not equal .9999 are, in fact, close to or greater than .9995; all of them, in fact, belong to the 1937 sample, whose own mean correlation with the other large samples equals .9994. Perhaps the suspect correlations need not be considered suspect, and hence, .9995 can be accepted as a reasonable estimate of the correlations between Forms L and M and as a lower bound for the absolute reliability of our large samples after all. Certainly, that value appears to make sense, its peculiar basis notwithstanding. Lower values elsewhere on the main diagonal in Table 10 point to the importance of large samples for studying relative difficulty. The lower correlations are often similar in magnitude to the z correlations for digits items of our smallest sample in Table 8.

As we see, digits items from both forms perform well in their present configurations, and hence, Form L is not unique. However, the z scores for both forms in Table 10 reveal a curious phenomenon. At length 4, all age levels—and at length 5 all age levels but one—show that Form M digits items are slightly easier than their Form L counterparts. Outside the range of ages in Table 10, the pattern continues uninterrupted through age 16 at length 4, and through age 18 with only five exceptions overall, mostly at later ages, at length 5 (McNemar, 1942, Table 26). As half of each age sample was given Form L first, and the other half Form M first (Terman & Merrill, 1937, p. 11), the rather consistent difference cannot be attributed to the order of the two forms. Unsuitable combinations of digits, such as familiar dates, repetitions, runs, and zeroes, were excluded from the test. Yet, beyond such material, nothing seems to be known about what would make one combination of digits systematically easier or harder than another of the same length. Because digits items offer three trials, each with different digits, only one combination would have to be easier to decrease difficulty, but all three might have to be more difficult to increase difficulty relative to another digits item of the same length. Depending on one's viewpoint about direction of change, and on how important the sheer number of trials is to success, any hypothesis based simply on the content of the digits fares better or worse.

The only real clue to this mystery, and it may be an important one, is that the easier form at lengths 4 and 5 also happens to be the one that includes a prior digits-backward item at length 3. Conceivably, the easy length-3 item provides an encouraging warm-up for tackling items of greater length. The unbroken sequence at 12 age levels from 5.5 to 16 for length 4, at which ages the M item is always easier than the L item (McNemar, 1942, Table 26), is consistent with such an interpretation, as length 4 in Form L would bear the brunt of its being the first digits-backward item encountered. A strength of the warm-up hypothesis is that the presence in Form M of a length-3 item could not be used to explain the difference had L been the easier form. The fact that half of the 1937 sample had no experience with "three digits backward" when given Form L, unlike all five other major samples, may account for its being the only large sample not to show any .9999 z correlations with other large samples in Table 8.

The warm-up hypothesis is by no means *ad hoc:* Modern investigators routinely schedule short warm-ups in memory span research (e.g., Case & Globerson, 1974, following a procedure of Jensen's; Dempster, 1978); modest practice effects on span have been noted within or after single sessions (Baumeister, 1974; Dempster, 1978; Mefferd, Wieland, & James, 1966); and whichever of Forms L and M was given last in the 1937 standardization produced an average gain of 2 IQ points between ages 5 and 16 (Terman & Merrill, 1937, p. 43).

The differences in difficulty between items from the two forms are modest in size: For the sample of 1,123, for example, they amount to 5.25% at length 4 and 4.36% at length 5, stated in percentages passing. On the z-score metric, the same differences amount to .1352 and .0513 SDs, which can be converted to mental-age units by multiplying them by the mental-age standard deviation of the 1937 sample in Table 5, 1.97. When so multiplied, the two differences equal .27 and .10 years of mental age, or 3.2 and 1.2 months. For IQ scoring, the items are each worth two months of mental age; depending on chronological age, 2 months would be worth 1–3 IQ points. However, the total impact of the practice effect on group means would not be detectable, because the two items are so far apart in mental age (3 years) that only rare individuals would benefit from the easier form of both, and only 4% or 5% benefit from either in any case.

The presence of slight differences in difficulty between the two forms makes it possible to rearrange the digits items so that their configuration is maximally unfavorable for obtaining a high correlation. Let us examine the resulting worst case made possible by the available data for our 1937 sample as a whole. Recall that the relevant correlation between forms in Table 10 was .9995. Suspect or not, that correlation qualifies as extraordinarily high. However, with items of equal length properly interchanged between forms, the z correlation between the two sets drops to .9862 (even though one observation is still common to both), which is well below all 15 digits correlations in Panel A of Table 8, and only slightly above the median z correlation there between new items. A correlation of .9862 is also below the means of the highest thirds of percentage-passing correlations for concordant triplets in Table 9, and barely above the mean percentage-passing correlation between new items, .9843, in Table 8. One would not claim, therefore, that a z correlation of .9862 was *prima facie* evidence for an interval scale.

The two perversely constituted digits sets also correlate only .9962 and .9968 with the numbers 3, 4, 5. These correlations are not horrendously low, but they are lower than the lowest of such loadings in Table 8, which is .9977, and they now fall within the range of correlations between percentages passing and the numbers 3, 4, 5 in Panel C of Table 8. Whereas the z-score average of the L and M Forms can be expressed by the numbers 3.005, 3.990, and 5.005 when transformed to the mean and *SD* of the numbers 3, 4, 5, and both forms individually fit the unit model just about as well as their average, the perversely composed sets yield 2.96, 4.09, and 4.95, or 3.05, 3.90, and 5.05. (The second perverse set correlates .9999 with the squared model of difficulty.)

Ideally, any combination of suitable digits items at lengths 3, 4, and 5 ought to perform as well as any other. The perversely constituted sets yield the only evidence thus far that seems at all inconsistent with earlier interpretations. At worst, however, that evidence indicates merely that interval scale properties may be present in only a subset of the possible configurations of digits items of the specified lengths, Forms L and M belonging to that subset, and the defining characteristics and extent of the subset being as yet quite unknown. This assessment certainly leaves the value demonstrated thus far of Forms L and M intact for present purposes, although it diminishes in a potentially important way the generality—and hence the depth—of the explanation of digits-item difficulty based on the manifest structure of the items.

However, we must keep in mind that the discordant evidence is modest in relation to the whole, that simply constituting such perverse configurations deliberately may capitalize disruptively on chance fluctuations, and that the interaction from differential practice with the length-3 item described earlier, now allocated maliciously to both sets of items, may actually explain the inconsistent results. When combined, the perverse sets are identical to the average of Forms L and M, which performs extraordinarily well. Thus, they illustrate the potential advantage of averaging the z scores of multiple items at each length, even in cases where separate configurations themselves may appear especially unpromising, as opposed to always depending on single items. As the perverse sets themselves demonstrate when combined, the use of multiple items may lead eventually to evidence that not only upholds the structural explanation represented by the unit model for the range of three to five digits backward but also places it on firmer ground.

Digits Items of Other Lengths and Possible Explanations of Their Behavior

There remains the question concerning digits items of lengths beyond what might conveniently be termed the moderately difficult range: How do they fit in? If the unit model of difficulty holds as well outside that range as it does within it, perfect fit by a true mathematical function that just happens to be a line—as distinct from merely excellent linear approximation—would be more firmly established. By locating themselves as precisely on the same line as the earlier ones, the additional data points would extend and thus confirm the function. The distinction between an approximation and a functional or lawful relationship is fundamental, but it is often difficult to resolve in favor of the latter (e.g., Scriven, 1961). Still, for many practical purposes, the resolution may not matter. Even functions can be limited in their domain and range of applicability, as any calculus textbook shows, and thus may not differ pragmatically in that respect from well-established empirical approximations known to hold within a particular range of interest.

Unfortunately for the purpose of confirming relationships, the range encompassed by three to five digits backward nearly exhausts the range of ability in ordinary human populations such as those assembled in Table 6. The average "spread" between the easiest and the hardest items in the table amounts to 55 percentage points. If centered in the distribution, that spread leaves only 22.5% to either side in which to add a digits item of another length. Although an addition is clearly possible for some one sample, the prospect for including more than three identical and consecutive lengths of digits items for all of the samples, when they differ as much in average mental age as those in Table 6, is not good. Some samples crowd 100% on one end and others zero on the other. Once the ceiling of zero is reached, additional discriminating items can only be easier ones, and the utility of digits-backward items below length 3 remains to be demonstrated. Wechsler (1939, p. 85) included length 2 in his IQ tests but warned that 90% of adults unable to pass three digits backward are found to be feebleminded. Apparently, almost no one fails length 2.

Because of the range problem and its influence on the choice of items often used, we have been compelled to work thus far with the bare minimum number of data points. However, the brighter side of the same coin is that, with only three items, we can reliably spread the aggregate responses of various samples as large as or larger than those usually used in national surveys by almost two central standard deviations (i.e., 55% versus 68%), which in certain cases would neatly divide a population into four nearly equal segments, in view of the intervals between our three items. By nonattitudinal-survey-item standards, such an even division in itself is no small accomplishment, not to mention the value of the stability over time of the intervals between the digits items, as well as the capability that the three items afford of scanning the full range of ability simply by sampling appropriate chronological-age categories (e.g., Tables 4 and 5).

There does exist, however, a scattering of data for other, longer item lengths, located in three of our samples: SBA whites, 1937 whites, and 1960 blacks. Such data require consideration in this treatment of digits backward, especially if they fail to present a neat picture. In each such sample, the data for longer items permit two different strategies of analysis. According to one strategy, the population of interest can be defined as the particular age level, grade level, or mental-age category that received the items. According to the other, it can be defined as the entire sample even though the vast bulk never saw all of the items now under consideration. Although I have employed both strategies thus far with respect to age and grade (e.g., Tables 4, 5, and 6), I have favored the more inclusive one for convenience, for the greater reliability of large samples, and because all three items of moderate difficulty had either been administered to the bulk of each sample or—in the case of the low black draftees, only 18.2% of whom reached "five digits backward"—

because I had no choice. Thus, in most cases, the favored strategy enjoyed the advantages of both.

It is true that the adult draftee samples are separately reported by mental-age categories, and so the first strategy would seem to be available for the low blacks. However, mental-age categories are utterly inappropriate for examining the z transformation *per se*, there being no possibility that mental ability is normally distributed within them if the total test score serves as a reasonable indicator of that ability. Even subsets of contiguous mental-age categories produce frequency distributions that are nearly rectangular and, in the case of the more difficult item lengths, often positively skewed as well. Moment coefficients of kurtosis for such distributions are typically below 2.0, in the range of values produced by perfect rectangularity, whereas the normal distribution has a kurtosis of 3.0.

Two such subsets of mental-age categories, from two of the draftee samples, were included knowingly in the study of relative reliability of digits and new items that was based on nine different sets of adjacent categories discussed earlier. That decision was taken because it doubled the number of our samples that could be included, and because there was no reason to anticipate that it might distort the conclusion, which it did not. Nevertheless, it is noteworthy that among the 4 z correlations added by the decision were the 3 lowest out of the 18 altogether. With those 4 correlations excluded, the estimates of relative reliability for the two sets of items would have been significantly different (Mann–Whitney test, two-tailed p = .026), but the difference between the digits items and the new items, whose mean correlations were now .9988 and .9935, would still have remained trivial. It is in that sense, of course, that the conclusion remained unaffected, but this example nevertheless indicates the inappropriateness of using mental-age categories for estimating absolute levels of z correlations.

With the reason for not subdividing the sample thus explained, we can examine the data in the entire SBA white draftee sample for digits-backward lengths 3 through 7. Here, the unit model (or any other that proves more correct) is especially handy because it furnishes a standard of comparison even in cases when data are available from just one sample. The correlation between the five z scores and the full set of five integers in the unit model is .9929, which is a bit low in comparison to correlations from just the first three digits items (see Table 8), but also absolutely higher than its percentage-passing counterpart with the unit model, −.9832. Standardized to the mean and the *SD* of the integers 3 through 7, the z-score fit can be

expressed as 2.9, 4.0, 5.2, 6.1, and 6.8. This fit to the unit model is neither especially good nor especially bad, and therefore, it is inconclusive as regards functional fit. The same holds for the slightly better
fit of just the first four digits lengths to the unit model, where the
correlations are .9977 for z scores and −.9946 for percentages. Naturally, it can be easier to fit four points than five and, by extension,
three than four. However, the ease of fitting three points with a
straight line as the explanation for the extraordinary correlations of
the three moderately difficult digits items has already been excluded
by extensive comparisons with nondigits sets of three Stanford–Binet
items. In the present case, the SBA white distribution is known to be
positively skewed (.41) in mental ability according to its mental-age
scores based on all 25 items, and that skewing could disturb the
results at the longer item lengths.

The 1937 Stanford–Binet sample contains analyzable percentages passing at ages 10 and 11 for digits lengths 3 through 6 on both
forms; that is, all individuals received all four items, and no item was
too easy or too difficult for either sample as a whole. Pooling the two
age categories yields a sample of 405. The resulting z scores from
Form M correlate .9928 with the unit model, and the Form M percentages passing only −.9795. From Form L, the corresponding two
correlations are .9975 and −.9891, respectively. Again, the fit is neither especially good nor especially bad. The z correlation between
this sample and the SBA whites for the four lengths in common is
fairly poor for Form M by Table 8 standards, namely .9826, but it
improves for Form L—which contains the digits items that are more
similar in actual content at all lengths for both samples—where it
reaches a respectable level, .9990. The low Form M correlation
would be about par for concordant triplets in Table 9 (I have not
explored concordant quadruplets). Both correlations may reflect the
known skew in the SBA white sample but, if so, apparently to different degrees.

If the 1937 data for the four lengths are merged experimentally
for all ages 5.5–11 ($N = 1,327$), some results are essentially similar,
but not all. Form L, for example, yields a z correlation of .9953 with
the unit model, and a corresponding percentage-passing correlation
of −.9916, but now a z correlation with the SBA whites of only .9865,
which is poorer than before for this form. The poorer correlation is
consistent with other data in this section that indicate the questionable nature of using entire samples, the bulk of which, below age 10
in this case, has not received all of the items, length 6 in this case.
Judging by outcomes, the first strategy appears to be the preferable

one when bulk coverage of the sample by all items is lacking. However, I cannot give a full rationale for that strategy beyond intuitive prudence, except to point to the outcomes and call attention to the reasonableness of sampling adequately the relevant ranges of difficulty without knowingly compromising the shape of the distribution. Fortunately, the z distances in Tables 4, 5, and 6 indicate that the issue of which strategy to pursue is not a vital one insofar as the analysis of the moderately difficult digits-backward items is concerned.

The last sample containing relevant digits lengths is that from the Kennedy *et al.* (1963, Table 66) study, in which three sixth-grade blacks did pass "six digits backward," an item located in the superior adult range. The z-score distance between that item and "five digits backward" turns out to be larger than the mean distance between the other adjacent digits items, whether scaled among the 300 sixth-graders (where it is 1.60 times too large) or among the entire sample of 1,800 blacks (where it is 1.83 times too large). Within that same item interval, an increase can also be observed for the 1937 white sample at ages 10 and 11 (approximately fourth and fifth grades, samples with an average mental age about 1.5 years greater than that of the sixth-grade blacks). Among the whites, that interval is too large by ratios of 1.58 in Form M and 1.33 in Form L. This elongation of the distance between lengths 5 and 6 in both children's samples does not appear for SBA white draftees; quite the contrary, there the later intervals decrease in size, to ratios of .74 and .55 after lengths 5 and 6, respectively. The SBA white sample is, of course, the only one to receive a length-7 digits-backward item, as that length was omitted from editions of the Stanford–Binet after 1916. The possible meaning, if any, of such partly agreeing and partly conflicting results at the higher lengths in these three samples is certainly not obvious as they stand.

However, the similar trend shared by the 1960 and the partial 1937 samples does lead to extraordinarily high z correlations between them for lengths 3 through 6 when Form M is employed for 1937: For just sixth-graders in 1960 it is .9999; for the entire sample, .9990. But parallel correlations for Form L, .9985 and .9954, remain in the inconclusive range.

The fit of the 1960 sample to the unit model when all four digits items are tested is expressed in the z correlations of .9923 for sixth-graders and .9867 for all grades. The first is inconclusive; the second is poor (which is consistent with preferring the former strategy for analysis). The sixth-grade z correlation fails to exceed its percentage-passing counterpart of $-.9958$, but the percentage correlation for the entire sample, $-.9735$, is so exceeded.

The results for longer digits items do nothing to advance the case for an interval scale in their range of difficulty, but neither do they detract, as they are borderline. In general, outcomes under the preferred strategy are mixed: A few are good, one is poor, and most reveal inconclusive correlations on the borderline between those for the three moderate digits items and those for the new items and the concordant triplets. The five z correlations with the unit model at various lengths beyond 5 range between .9923 and .9977, with a mean of .9946. The six-sample mean correlations with the unit model for digits items and new items in Table 8 were .9993 and .9781, respectively. Thus, the present mean is closer to that of the digits items, but the observations are more frequently overlapped by those for the new items, two of which were extraordinarily high with the 1, 2, 3 unit model in Table 8. Four of five z correlations with the unit model exceed their accompanying percentage-passing correlations, which looks reasonable. Between samples, z correlations (under the preferred strategy when available) averaged .9950, with one poor, one inconclusive, and two extraordinary (here, .9990 or above). This last mean is well above the six-sample mean for new items in Table 8, which was .9726, and well above the mean of .9816 for 69 concordant triplets in Table 9. Yet, it falls below the range of z correlations between the five large samples for digits items in Table 8, the lowest of which was .9989. Apparently, the digits items retain some advantage even at the greater difficulties over nondigits items, but on the average, it is a reduced advantage.

At present, I am inclined to regard digits-backward items beyond length 5 as *terra incognita* for two reasons. The first is that the more difficult items usually involve the upper tail of the distribution, where results become especially vulnerable to disturbances from skewness that may itself have resulted from sampling peculiarities. For calculating delta correlations, Angoff and Ford (1973) restricted themselves to items whose passing rates in both groups fell between 95% and 5%. True, samples (4) and (5) in Table 6 yielded good results for moderate items even though their percentages passing for "five digits backward" are only 3.42% and .32%, respectively. However, those two samples are rather symmetrical, with skewness coefficients of only $-.22$ and $.16$. Assuming the 1937 Stanford–Binet samples at ages 10 and 11 to be reasonably normal, the SBA whites and the 1960 blacks are left as our most (positively) skewed samples, with their long tails extending to the right—two of the three that enable us to examine item lengths over 5. Skewness cannot be calculated for the sixth-grade black subsample specifically, but as their grade displays the largest IQ *SD* of any in the 1960 sample (cf. Table 4), it may contain an accumulation of the low-IQ children retained in grade. The mental ages of retained children would not necessarily be extremely low (because they would be older), but they probably would be below average for the grade. "Six digits backward" was passed by only 1% of the black sixth-graders, and by only .17% of the entire 1960 black sample. As for whites, at ages 10 and 11, only 6.67% of the 1937 Stanford–Binet sample passed "six digits backward," and although 16.87% of the SBA white draftees passed "six digits backward," only 7.82% passed "seven digits backward." Although 16.87% is not an especially low percentage, the 1937 norms (McNemar, 1942, Table 26) indicate that a passing rate of 50% was expected of white 18-year-olds. At the higher mental ages of 16, 17, and 18, SBA white draftees actually exceeded the 1916 norms for length 6, having passing rates of 61%, 68% and 69% (Yerkes, 1921, Part II, Table 65). In addition to showing the greater vulnerability to skewness of longer items, these facts illustrate the peculiar heterogeneity of the SBA distribution: far below the norms as a whole for an adult sample, but considerably above the norms at the higher mental ages then assigned to the late adolescent years. The possible effect of such heterogeneity on the longer items emerges from the discussion of the second reason, below.

Besides skewing, the use of mnemonic strategies must be regarded as a potential source of disturbance for the more difficult lengths of digit item. Although general strategies under the selective control of the subject do not seem to contribute to individual (within-age) differences in simple memory span—as they are not used by some subjects and are neglected by others—at least some strategies can modestly facilitate digit span performance according to the comprehensive review by Dempster (1981). Grouping digits into clusters of three or four and meaningfully chunking such groupings by converting them into single multidigit numbers are two such strategies. However, because adults "nearly always group list items spontaneously ... grouping may not be a source of span differences between adults" (Dempster, 1981, p. 71). Instructions to group under conditions that permit grouping improves the performances of all individuals about equally, further indicating the negligible role of grouping in normal span differences between persons. Grouping and chunking probably increase with age (Dempster, 1981), however, and with list length (Brotemarkle, 1924, p. 232), and hence, researchers have anticipated an age-by-strategy interaction for tasks that lend themselves to the necessary recoding of input. Tasks with highly structured material, such as chess positions, seem conducive to the use of these strategies. Nevertheless, the interaction with age has proved difficult to demonstrate satisfactorily (Dempster, 1981).

Contrary to general impressions, chunking in particular is in doubt for digit span performance *per se* because the conventional rate of presentation and procedure for testing allow only minimal opportunity for recoding (Dempster, 1981, p. 77; Dempster & Zinkgraf, 1982). One could infer, therefore, as others have (e.g., Case, 1972, p. 301), that chunking for reverse digit span is even more unlikely because encoding, rehearsing, and then transforming the order of digits could interfere with each other (see, for example, the introspective reports of difficulty with forward digit span from college students in Brotemarkle, 1924). This leaves grouping as the more promising candidate.

Whatever the strategy involved, there is more than an outside chance that the elongation of distance in difficulty between lengths 5 and 6 in the two children's samples and the contraction of that same distance among the more sophisticated members of the SBA white sample, and of their next interval, too, is a reflection of the age-by-strategy interaction. The absence of any such interaction in the data for lengths 3 through 5 over all six of our samples is striking. However, the more difficult lengths may be the logical places for the strategy to flourish, especially when subjects are high in mental age. Those who dealt successfully with lengths 6 and 7 in the SBA sample were mostly at mental ages (on the 1916 scale) far above any members of the other five samples, and there is some evidence that, among adults, fast learners employ strategies more than slow learners when conditions are propitious (Dempster, 1981, p. 75).

When the percentage of a sample passing a difficult item is in excess of that required to satisfy the unit model, the interval preceding the item contracts. When the percentage is below that which the unit model would predict based on the responses of the sample to easier items (and the assumption of normality), yet over zero, the interval expands. Which occurs would depend on the proportion of strategy users in the sample, which, in turn, would depend on its age range and on the degree to which the strategy users extended the response range; thus, the basis for an age-by-strategy interaction would exist. Expansion may characterize the final interval if a digits series exhausts a sample's span capacity, and if the sample contains some individuals who are old enough to employ strategy, because then just a few atypical strategy-users would pass the very last item instead of simply supplementing those who pass that item normally without strategy.[7]

Because this is the only report I know of to scale relations between digits items of various lengths in several populations simultaneously, and because digits-backward frequency distributions for large, more-or-less naturally occurring samples are rare, the hypothesis concerning the age-by-strategy interaction must remain extremely tentative, for even the basic facts require replication. However, some additional evidence can be sought in digits-*forward* data from groups of relevant ages, for the strategies that lend themselves to backward span also facilitate forward span.

Evidence concerning Age-by-Strategy Interaction in Digits-Forward Data

Brotemarkle (1924, p. 252) published a frequency distribution for 1,263 college men and women that, when scaled, yields evidence of contracting interspan distances at the longer item lengths within yet another adult, brighter-than-average sample. Because z is indeterminate at 100% passing, and because 99.76% passing risks a floor effect, I omit consideration of digits-forward lengths 4 and 5 and begin with length 6, passed by 96.83%. Maximum forward spans under length 6 among college students between 20 and 21 in average age could well be due to extraneous influences anyway. Easier than the reverse task, forward-digit span can provide a more finely graded series of items within range of any one sample. We resort once again to comparing z scores with the unit model, which is now represented by the seven numerals 6 through 12 for Brotemarkle's study.

The z correlation with the unit model is .9982 (the percentage passing correlation is −.9902). An appropriate fund of comparative correlations for seven data points is difficult to define, but two single trials with seven different perfectly ordered items three items apart in Table 2, for the two different white samples, each yielded .97. The fit to the unit model in this study is better than the average unit

---

[7]Such potential interactions are difficult to detect through analyses based on means because they have little effect on the average score. For example, the mean backward-digit span of the SBA whites for lengths 3 through 7 would be 4.45 (SD = 1.20) for the distribution as observed, and 4.39 (SD = 1.08) if the distribution conformed to the unit model exactly (i.e., if every z interval were equal to that between lengths 3 and 4).

model correlation for three new items in Table 8, and better than the average fit between samples for concordant triplets in Table 9. Apparently, successive digits-forward lengths, too, are distributed rather evenly throughout the range of difficulty, as other unit model correlations bear out.

Transformed to have the mean and the *SD* of the unit model, the z scores for lengths 6 through 12 are expressed by 5.84, 6.99, 8.12, 9.13, 10.12, 10.97, and 11.84. If the expected strategies had been employed out of necessity on the more difficult items, so that more individuals passed them than otherwise would have according to the model, the intervals should contract as item length increases, which they do: 1.15, 1.13, 1.01, .99, .85, and .87. The strategy hypothesis for later items is also supported by introspective reports that Brotemarkle elicited from 14 individuals after they had attempted items at length 4 and then again at length 8. Four of these individuals mentioned using grouping, but in every instance it was in connection only with length 8.

A curious feature of the interval lengths within Brotemarkle's study is that they are nearly identical within consecutive pairs, as though an interval scale was present but had been broken into three-item or two-interval segments. Because three or four is about the optimal group size for aural presentation (Dempster, 1981, pp. 70–71, 73), the grouping strategy may result in the same number of groups of three or four digits, each being formed from neighboring items, which, after all, differ in length by only one digit. If so, the relative contribution of the grouping strategy to passing would alter in jumps every couple of items; for example, two groups might serve for lengths 7 and 8, three for lengths 9 and 10, and four for lengths 11 and 12. If different but adjacent item lengths thus shared the same modal number of groupings, they might also increase in difficulty in the same units as group span quanta were increasingly superimposed on digit span quanta in determining passing rates. This, essentially, would be an example in which factor structure shifted subtly with change in level of item difficulty, although the content domain of the items remained relatively constant, just as general intelligence suffices to predict elementary-school arithmetic performance, but for higher mathematics, we use the SAT-M rather than the SAT-V.

Exploring for the interaction's contrasting effect within younger samples using digits forward is limited by uncertainty about what age ranges are critical and by scarcity of data. Between ages 5 and 12, children apparently do not chunk, whereas beyond 12 they show an increasing tendency to do so (Dempster, 1981, p. 74). Because chunking is a more sophisticated strategy, age 12 is perhaps a significant point beyond which all strategies could be available. Spontaneous rehearsal, a relatively unsophisticated strategy, appears somewhere between the ages of 9 and 13 (Belmont & Butterfield, 1971, Figure 1). Hence, samples containing the transitional years may display the children's pattern, and samples entirely older than 12 may display the adult pattern. As to scarcity, there are fewer digits-forward data for any single group of subjects in the Stanford–Binet than one might expect: only lengths 3, 5, and 6 for the 1960 Form L-M blacks, and lengths 5, 6, 8, and 9 on Form L for ages 12 and 13 ($N = 406$) in the 1937 standardization sample. Thus, there is a gap in both series; the first definitely does not extend far enough in length because its terminal passing rate is 23.28%, and the second sample may well be entirely too old to display the children's pattern noted in the digits-backward data.

If one allows for the gaps by omitting the appropriate integers, the 1960 and 1937 data correlate .9995 and .9981 with the unit model, respectively. Both sets of data show a slight decrease in interval size at their later interval, thus resembling data for bright adults. However, more suitable data for a longer, uninterrupted series, ranging from length 4 through length 8 (the sample's empirical limit, apparently) were published by Viteles (1919, Tables 2 and 3). The subjects were 154 Jewish orphans with an average school retardation of over one year, a mean age of 12.3 ($SD = 3.0$), and a wide age range (6.2 to 17.2). Here, the five-item series has a z correlation of .9972 with its unit model and shows a decreasing trend in interval size that is terminated by an interval larger than any other. The final interval places this heavily preadolescent sample in the same category with the two digits-backward children's samples in pattern of intervals, and thus, it accords with age-by-strategy interaction as the hypothesized explanation of length discrepancies between longer items.

Lessons from the Longer Digits Lengths

Apart from finding that digits-forward z scores seem to correlate rather well with the unit model, too, in view of their four correlations ranging from .9972 to .9995 and averaging .9982, but not as extraordinarily well as the moderately difficult digits-backward items, what have we learned about digits-backward items? The most important insight, probably, is that the moderately difficult digits-backward items may be buffered against two potential sources of disturbance to interval scale properties that afflict such items at the longer lengths. First, they may often be somewhat sheltered from skewness when it occurs because most or all of the three moderate items fall in the range of difficulty between 2.5% and 97.5% passing (see Tables 4 and 5); this places them under or near the hump of the normal distribution rather than in the extreme tails. Second, because the moderate items manage to span a wide range of difficulty with relatively few items, they are unlikely to be differentially susceptible to strategies such as grouping into units of three or four. In this connection, the curious pairings of intervals from Brotemarkle's study of forward span are provocative. Even more important, the moderate items may consist of too few digits to benefit much from grouping in any case. The last point, especially, would account for the striking absence in the data for lengths 3 to 5 of known or suspected interactions involving strategy, such as that with age or, by extension, any with mental age, despite the extreme diversity of the six samples in those key respects.

Implications of the Absence of Interaction concerning Attentional Capacity

Memory span researchers draw a distinction between actual performance and an underlying attentional capacity that may increase with maturation and that may be rooted in biological structures (e.g., Dempster, 1981; Globerson, 1983). The distinction is as challenging empirically as it is valuable heuristically, for, despite much effort, a role for capacity in digit span performance has yet to be firmly established (Dempster, 1981, p. 87). However, the distinction creates the room needed for taking proper account of strategies and other artifacts that might recognizably improve performance without an accompanying improvement in span capacity. (Writing down digits would serve as an extreme fictional illustration.) The subtle shift in factor structure with level of item difficulty hypothesized earlier would be congruent with such a distinction, although neutral with respect to whether capacity was identifiable with one of the factors. To the extent that certain lengths of digit item are more immune to strategies and other perturbations than others, because they contain too few digits to show a strategy to advantage, but differ in difficulty nonetheless, they should come closer than other digits items to reflecting differences in the hypothetical underlying capacity. This argument is not a direct conclusion from the data but an inference concerning the potential explanation of the highly invariant relation among the three moderately long digits-backward items across such a heterogeneous group of samples and range of mental ages as those in Table 6. As the same or equivalent artifacts could hardly be present in all of the samples to the right degree to maintain the equal increments in difficulty between lengths 3 and 5, it is likely that those increments are maintained because they reflect universally equal increments in underlying structure, and little else. Needless to say, without additional data, the structure inferred from this absence of interaction is relatively neutral as regards the issue of its genetic and environmental bases.

According to strictly algebraic logic, an absence of statistical interaction does not of itself imply anything concerning the presence or absence of a main effect, and hence, there is no purely formal relation linking a structural explanation for equality of intervals (as above) with a structural explanation of mean differences between samples. In principle, a strategy artifact that was constant in its additive effect on all members of any one sample could contribute to mean differences between samples in passing rates or z scores. However, to the extent that such a nonspan artifact is likely to betray its presence by also producing interaction between digits items and samples, the absence of detectable interaction over a broad range of difficulty in diverse samples increases the *a priori* probability that mean differences, too, are the undisturbed reflections of the structural differences in capacity hypothesized by span researchers. I mention this merely as a matter of potential interest, for the eventual relevance of the moderate digits backward items to Mercer's position in no way depends on the question of hypothetical structural capacity. As we shall see, other knowledge concerning the highly interactive nature of cultural diffusion makes the inferential connection between the absence of interaction and the absence of cultural main effects even stronger in the case of Mercer's bias argument.

THE VALUE OF A SEGMENT OF INTERVAL SCALE

Even though it does not measure distance between cities well or that to the stars at all, a simple yardstick is an extremely useful instrument. So, too, with a limited segment of interval scale if that could be established among the moderately long digits-backward items. Let us review the evidence for such a scale and then consider the implications.

Review of Key Analyses concerning Digits-Backward Lengths 3 to 5

The original data come from six samples that probably differ more among themselves in important ways than those in any other study concerned with test bias between blacks and whites: chronological age, mental age, historical cohort and period, sex, race, and IQ all ranged freely. Yet, a sensitive chi-square test reveals no significant differences in percentages passing the three digits-backward items after these diverse samples have been standardized via the unit normal distribution for differences in means and *SD*s of the underlying ability (Table 6). Treated similarly, a different set of three Stanford–Binet items produces numerous significant chi squares (Table 7).

When based on the three digits-backward items, z-score correlations among the six samples and with the unit model often reach .9999 and are usually above .9990 (Table 8). Other Stanford–Binet items having comparable ordering and mental age characteristics yield discernibly and significantly lower correlations (Tables 8 and 9); those equaling .9999 are rare. Strong associations between the level of correlation and the significance of the chi-square test in the case of the digits items and new items (Tables 6, 7, and 8) make it evident that *many* of the concordant triplets of items (Table 9) would also produce significant chi squares for any single pairing of samples if submitted to test. Detailed inspection of the z correlations (and the correlations between z correlations, which were often low or negative) shows that not only many but *most* concordant triplets would produce a significant chi square for at least some pairing of samples, in that only 2 sets of triplets out of 21 yield z correlations greater than .9899 for all 3 pairings of 1918 samples; by contrast, the digits items always yield much higher z correlations for all 15 pairings of samples in Table 8. Plainly, the digits items are unusual, and their extraordinary correlations are not simply a reflection of monotonicity.

There is no indication that the higher correlations for digits items are due to greater reliability of those items. Estimates of the reliability of the z scores of digits items (Table 10) make it difficult to resist the conclusion that, if corrected for attenuation, the already extraordinarily high z correlations for digits items would be perfect, that is, equal to 1.0.

The z transformation produces significantly stronger correlations than do raw percentages passing among items in general (Table 9), but especially so in the case of digits items (Table 8). Thus, the moderately long digits items in combination with z transformation stand apart from other items and other metrics in giving evidence of interval scale properties.

That evidence rests mainly on the abundance of nearly perfect observed correlations and probably perfect corrected correlations among samples, as supported by the chi-square test. Correlations with the unit model for item lengths 3 to 5 provide a plausible basis— in view of the discrete quanta of content through which difficulty increases—for explaining the generality of high correlations among samples. Loadings on the "3, 4, 5" factor, for example, account for 99.86% of their variance (Table 8), almost exactly as much as loadings on the first principal component, which is the linear function that accounts for the maximum amount of variance. Because the unit model supplements the evidence for an interval scale without being essential (it represents only one special example of the form that an interval scale might take), it could be sacrificed if correlations between samples based on additional item lengths were to remain extraordinarily high while item difficulties diverged from the unit model in goodness of fit. Intervals can remain equal across samples without being equal between items. Currently, however, the unit model applies well within the range of 3 to 5 digits backward, and it very likely will continue to do so regardless of developments outside that range. Whenever it does apply, it bolsters the case for an interval scale by providing an independent reason for expecting the relationships among samples to be linear, that is, by providing a sufficient condition, but not a necessary one.

The unit model also provides a useful tool for examining scatterings of data based on combinations of backward digit-span items beyond length 5, but from only one sample, and miscellaneous runs of forward span items. Although the goodness of fit to the model seems to be somewhat poorer when backward lengths over 5 or long forward runs are included, it tends to be better than that for nondigits items (which should fit no better than monotonicity alone would dictate). Mean correlations with the model are .9946 and .9982 for such backward and forward span data, respectively. Thus, although backward lengths over 5 and the available forward-span data fail to extend and corroborate the model by registering extraordinary correlations, they do reveal that digits items in general tend to be spaced more evenly in difficulty, as measured by z score, than nondigits items, a finding that is provocative. Obviously, something internal must be involved in their spacing if certain spacings cannot occur (aside from floor or ceiling effects).

The poorer fit to the unit model when the more difficult digits-backward lengths are included could be due to skewness in the samples concerned or to the differential contribution of mnemonic strategy to passing those items. Some evidence was found in digits-forward data indicating that strategies such as grouping play a larger role in longer items, and that the effect of the grouping strategy on interval size may change every two intervals instead of every one. Hence, the unusual evidence of interval scale properties within the segment of digits-backward items ranging from lengths 3 to 5 may be due to some combination of buffering—from skewness effects, perhaps, because those items rarely land in the extreme tails of a distribution; from strategy, perhaps, because difficulty increases rapidly within a range of only a few digits, and because the short item lengths in combination with the demanding task of reversing digits renders strategy uneconomical (e.g., see Case, 1972, p. 301); and from sample-by-strategy interaction, perhaps, if strategy is present, because the two intervals, being adjacent, are equally affected by even varying amounts of grouping in all samples, grouping being the most promising candidate as strategy. However, these conjectures are based on relatively sparse and unsystematic data in no way comparable to the extensive evidence of interval scale properties among digits-backward items within the segment defined by lengths 3 through 5.

GENERAL IMPLICATIONS OF A PROVEN SEGMENT OF INTERVAL SCALE

Applications to the arguments of Mercer are reserved for a later section. Here, I consider only such matters as the immediate implications of the data concerning the shape of the distribution of mental ability, as well as the relation between digits and nondigits intelligence-test items. The discussion is developed for a "proven" segment of interval scale, regardless of whether the segment in question qualifies as such in the eyes of all readers. Reference is also made to a relaxed version of the argument concerning normality that depends merely on the observed findings. The alternative version may hold more appeal for those who are willing to grant that criteria for an interval scale have been well met by the data in hand for the segment of interest, but who are not yet convinced that the interval scale really exists.

Normality

The logical deduction that if mental ability is normally distributed, and if IQ (or test score) is normally distributed, it necessarily
follows that IQ constitutes an interval scale (e.g., Jensen, 1969a, pp.
21–22; 1969b, pp. 462–463; 1980a, p. 75) has generally been attacked
in two somewhat contradictory ways. According to one, IQ distributions are normal because test item difficulties and intercorrelations
are selected to force that outcome; according to the other, they are
not actually normal. In employing this classic deduction, Jensen has
responded to the first criticism by essentially conceding the point
(with some important qualifications), while shifting the emphasis
toward devising ways of testing the deduction independently by
showing that IQ behaves as does an interval scale. Those who dismiss Jensen's argument as "circular," therefore, seem to miss the
point of the independent test (e.g., Hunt, 1969, p. 283, who also found
"no serious fault" with Jensen's description of the IQ distribution;
Kempthorne & Wolins, 1982, p. 330). The last two authors took issue
with Jensen's use of the good fit between kinship correlations and
polygenic theory as one form of independent evidence, but their
objections depend mainly on their own opinion about how tenable
the assumptions of that theory are, and on its lack of experimental
verification in the case of human intelligence. In view of their object-
ing to one specific example of independent evidence, it is puzzling
that they should seem not to notice the role of the principle itself in
Jensen's argument. Thomas (1982) also failed to do justice to this
aspect, while quoting Jensen in a manner that oversimplifies his
positions.

Wahlsten (1980) and Vetta (1982) both questioned the normality
of empirical IQ but overlooked the fact that Jensen specified that IQ
distributions only approximate normality, with the fit being especially close within the IQ range from 60 to 150 that includes 98% of
whites (1980a, p. 84). Vetta (1982, p. 336) even cited one of the more
skewed examples in the literature as though it had not been depicted
and its author quoted by Jensen (1980a, p. 72) himself, who gave generally accepted reasons for expecting effects of skewness below IQ 60
(1969a, p. 25; 1980a, pp. 83–84). Large-sample chi-square tests rejecting normality of IQ performed by Dorfman (1978; see also McNemar,
1942, Tables 1 and 2) and cited by Wahlsten (p. 359) are irrelevant,
therefore, to the question of how good the fit is for some practical
purpose. In the course of describing the robustness of certain statis-

tical tests under departures from normality, Box (1953) once likened a sensitive test of assumptions to a rowboat, sent out to see whether it was safe for an ocean liner to leave port. The same might be said of the large-sample chi-square test. According to Yule and Kendall (1950),

> The normal form is reasonably close to many distributions of the humped type. If, therefore, we are ignorant of the exact nature of a humped distribution . . . we may assume as a first approximation that the distribution is normal and see where this assumption leads us. It is not infrequently found that a population represented in this way is sufficiently accurately specified for the purposes of the inquiry. (p. 188)

Interestingly enough, Vetta (1982) did concede that he was unable "to contemplate any distribution other than the normal for mental ability, as distinct from IQ" (p. 336).

Vetta (1980, p. 357) has correctly noted that one particular test for an interval scale proposed by Jensen, involving the correlation between sib means and sib differences, is not independent of the supposed imposition of normality on the IQ distribution, a criticism that Jensen (1980b, p. 362) accepted. This eliminates the simplest and least inferential test that Jensen has so far been able to suggest.

However, the fact that the z scores of the moderately long digits-backward items correlate so highly with each other across samples as to constitute a segment of interval scale represents now another kind of evidence. Here, one must keep in mind the 15 comparisons between samples, and not just the three data points. Constructing a physical analogy might proceed as follows: Imagine a ruler broken into two-inch segments, and each segment used to mark off two inches on one of six different boards; finally, imagine the marked sections of board being juxtaposed pairwise, and all found to be equal. Here, the different numbered inches would correspond to the different levels of z score generated by applying the scale (i.e., the digits items) to various samples differing in level and dispersion of mental ability.

Note that the argument at this point runs opposite in direction from the familiar one. We do not assume a normal distribution and then from that assumption infer that z scores provide an interval scale; rather, we observe a segment of interval scale based on z scores and infer that it could have arisen only from either a normal distribution or from some set of distributions that approximate normality closely enough not to disturb the interval scale.[8] This last stip-ulation reconciles the results with the fact that the mental age distri-butions of the present samples are known not to be exactly normal in every case, should that particular total score eventually be identi-fied with the mental ability on which passing digits backward depends. It also responds to Dorfman's point that if we accept the assertion that IQ is normally distributed within socioeconomic subgroups, then it is not likely that the distribution for the whole population is normal (cited in Vetta, 1982, p. 336, from a personal communication). Such arguments as Dorfman's, which Vetta consid-ers "excellent," address only the straw man view that the distribu-tion must be mathematically perfectly normal before we can use-fully apply the assumption of normality. Combining normal distributions, particularly when the centrally located ones are the most heavily populated, could very well yield a total distribution that adequately approximates normality, and Dorfman's assumption that the smaller subgroup distributions are perfect, whereas the larger total one is not, rather than the other way around, is simply gratuitous.

The fact that interval scale properties are well maintained by the digits-backward segment, wherever it falls within the various sam-ples' ranges of difficulty, helps to generalize the argument beyond the range the segment occupies in a particular sample. No assump-tion is required to transform a percentage to the normal curve func-tion z or to any other function, as the empirical test resides entirely in how well the particular transformation works for the correlations in which it later figures.

Regardless of whether one accepts that an interval scale has been proved for the digits-backward items, the empirical facts show that the transformation based on the normal function provides a markedly superior fit between samples and with the unit model over raw percentages passing (Table 8). To a lesser, but nevertheless sig-nificant, extent the z transformation also provides a better fit, on the average, between samples for nondigits items, too, as shown by the concordant triplets (Table 9). One need not accept the interval scale *per se* as proven in order to read these facts as evidence for the nor-mality or the near normality of the underlying mental ability. How-ever, to the extent that one accepts the evidence for normality as

---

[8]Obviously, it would be of interest to know more about just how much latitude this stipulation confers on the family of distributions, given the observed data.

stated, it becomes somewhat inconsistent not to accept the interval scale, as at that point the classic deduction would apply to the z transformation.

The Mental Ability in Question

Once we have argued the case for the normal or near-normal distribution of the mental ability underlying digits-backward performance, the logical next question must be: Is that mental ability the same as the mental ability underlying IQ items in general? Within the present data, as was noted earlier, the digits-backward items remain lodged at the same difficulty ranks among the 25 Stanford–Binet items in Table 2, regardless of mental age level and other differences among the 1918 samples, thus indicating that they covary with the other items. We have also seen that the SDs of the raw z scores of the digits-backward items are substantially negatively correlated with the SDs of mental age in the various subsamples in Tables 4 and 5, a finding that indicates that the dispersions of both mental abilities expand and contract together. Those correlations were $-.91$ and $-.92$ (the negative sign is to be expected, as z is in units of the unobserved underlying SD). Although one anomalous report of low negative correlations between forward digit span and SAT-V and -M exists (Chiang & Atkinson, 1976), Dempster and Cooney (1982) reported correlations with SAT-V and -M ranging from .69 to .77, and Dempster (1981, p. 65) cited correlations of .74–.81 between digit span (when reliably measured with many items or when corrected for attenuation) and various intelligence, aptitude, and achievement measures. Jensen and Figueroa (1975, Table 2) have shown that backward digit span correlates more highly than forward digit span with WISC-R Full-Scale IQ among both blacks and whites, and Globerson's (1983, Table 1) correlations with other measures of general intelligence reveal the same pattern among Israeli Jews. Using longitudinal data at four age levels, Jensen and Osborne (1979) found that forward and backward digit span formed two well-separated factors in both races, and that backward span usually loaded more highly than forward span on the first principal component of the WISC, despite instability from small samples. These facts all point to the conclusion that the mental abilities underlying digits-backward and other IQ items are largely if not entirely one and the same.

True, Jensen and Figueroa (1975, Table 3) did report a smaller race difference for backward digit span (.57 sigma) than Full-Scale IQ (1.15 sigma), which potentially suggests a difference between the two variables. However, if their difference in estimated reliability is taken into account, and both race differences are corrected by deducting the unreliable variance $(1 - r_{tt})$ from sigma squared (which represents the within-group variance), the two race differences reach roughly the same order of magnitude, 1.01 sigma and 1.18 sigma, respectively.[9] To the extent that backward digit span also draws independently on what Jensen (e.g., 1980a, p. 549) has called Level I (associative learning) ability, some difference between the race differences would be expected in view of his demonstrated interaction of Levels I and II (general intelligence) with race. The substrate ability underlying backward span would still be normally distributed, however, if its Level I and Level II components were normally distributed, and would not likely be so otherwise, for if two random variables are normal, so is their linear combination (Mood, Graybill, & Boes, 1974, p. 194). The substrate distribution would also reflect mainly the distribution of the dominant component, which seems to be Level II in the case of backward span, judging from the partial correlations reported by Jensen and Figueroa (1975, p. 885). To the extent that one component is known to be distributed normally, the other must be so if the digits-backward substrate is to remain normal and thus to conform with the data presented earlier. Jensen (1980a, Figure 4.9, citing Durning, 1968), in fact, presented a nearly normal distribution for forward-span performance, a prototypic measure of his Level I ability. The shape of the empirical forward-span distribution cannot be attributed to any juggling of items, deliberate or otherwise, as the only possible bases for selection in the case of digits items are in respect to range and uninterruptedness of lengths; departures from a wide range without gaps would seem forced and hence difficult to defend. Thus, once again, we infer that the Level II component must be at least nearly normal, even if there should be two major cognitive

[9]To estimate the reliability of WISC-R backward span, I follow Wechsler (1949, p. 14) and use Jensen and Figueroa's (1975, Table 6) correlation of .336 between it and forward span. As they gave only the correlations overall, race must be partialed out, a procedure that gives a within-groups estimate of .318 for reliability within race. The reliability of Full-Scale IQ has been taken as .95 (e.g., Wechsler, 1974, Table 9). Although this procedure for determining the reliability of backward span from its correlation with forward span may lead to an underestimate, the results need be only approximate to make the point. An alternative estimate, based on the reliability in the WISC standardization sample of a digit span test half as long as backward and forward span together (Wechsler, 1949, p. 13)—that is, .43—yields corrected race differences of .87 and 1.18 sigma for backward span and Full-Scale IQ.

components contributing to digits-backward performance instead of general intelligence alone.

Understanding the Two Kinds of Item and Their Relations to an Interval Scale

If, according to this reasoning, the segment of digits-backward items indicates that general intelligence is distributed normally or nearly so in the six samples, regardless of whether there is one underlying component or two, what does that tell us about items in general and their relation to an interval scale? The answer depends on the nature and the extent of the difference between the digits-backward and the nondigits items, as exhibited in the analyses thus far (as in Tables 8 and 9). Comprehending the nature depends on knowing the extent. Let us look, therefore, at two tables that address the question of extent.

One might suppose that the moderate digits-backward items, which fall at mental ages VII, IX, and XII in all Stanford–Binet revisions, just happen to be situated at the right mental ages to correlate extraordinarily well with the unit model, and that many other item triplets having that mental age composition would do as well. We have seen that this is not the case with respect to z correlations between samples (Table 9), and now we see in Table 11 that the same applies to z correlations with the unit model (based here on 1916 mental ages), which enable us to inspect the fit for one sample at a time.

Table 11 provides further evidence of the special nature of the digits-backward segment. The lower correlations of nondigits items with the unit model, as well as the fact that the digits item correlations consistently exceed almost all of the correlations between the model and the z scores of concordant triplets, show that the excellent fit of the digits items to the model is not simply the result of their being located at the right mental ages. Something beyond mental age is involved.

Some nondigits triplets fit consistently more poorly than others, and hence, despite the absolutely low SDs higher up in the table, two of the correlations between unit model correlations indicate the presence of some consistency in fit across samples (Table 11, bottom). Just three of the nine items in the pool from which the concordant triplets are formed account for 12 of the poorer model correlations (mean $= .9077$; $SD = .0156$), as well as for all six of the discordant

TABLE 11

Correlations with the Unit Model for Concordant Triplets, Digits-Backward Items, and New Items, and Correlations between Unit Model Correlations in Three 1918 Samples[a]

	Low whites (351)	Low blacks (938)	SBA whites (486)	Row mean
Concordant triplets				
Mean correlation	.9682	.9492	.9662	.9615
SD	.0385	.0378	.0328	—
Number of triplets	27	24	24	—
Review of correlations from Table 8				
Digits items	.9996	.9992	.9997	.9995
New items	.9642	.9970	.9496	.9703
Number of concordant triplet correlations exceeded by				
Digits items	24/27	23/24	23/24	93.3%
New items	7/27	21/24	6/24	45.3%

Correlations between unit model correlations for concordant triplets (and no. of triplets)

Low whites	—	.60[b]	.66[c]
Low blacks	(24)	—	.17
SBA whites	(24)	(21)	—

[a] According to the Mann–Whitney test, there are no significant differences between these samples in goodness of fit of concordant triplets to the unit model. In the lower panel, the difference between the two correlations .60 and .66 is not significant, when approximations are used as entries in the proper formula (Walker & Lev, 1953, p. 257).
[b] Significantly different from zero, $p < .01$.
[c] Significantly different from zero, $p < .001$.

triplets that have been excluded from analysis (IX, 3 when in combination with either VII, 2 or VII, 6; see Table 2 for their content).

The two high correlations in the lower panel are those involving low whites with each of the other two 1918 samples. The third correlation may be low because excluding the discordant triplets eliminates, in its case, all instead of just half of the item combinations that fit poorly even when they are not actually discordant. However, the correlational pattern can also be read as showing a consistency in fit across race and within race (for whites) that is diminished when mental age means and SDs become too different between samples, as in the case of low blacks and SBA whites, who differ that way far more than blacks and whites in general (see Table 4), and more than any other pairing of the three 1918 samples. Conceivably, this subtle form of consistency can survive substantial differences in mental age (e.g., low whites vs. SBA whites) or differences in race (e.g., low whites vs. low blacks), but not both at once; whatever the case, confounding makes it impossible to pursue the matter further, and we lack the mental age contrast within race for blacks. Note that all three samples fit the unit model equally well according to the Mann–Whitney test, and that the consistencies occur within a very narrow range of variation.

The essential difference between the two kinds of item does not depend on just a few combinations of nondigits items that fit especially poorly in more than one sample, or else the digits item correlations would not exceed so many of the unit model correlations involving concordant triplets in the same sample (i.e., 70 out of 75), despite sharing their mental age composition. Moreover, unlike the digits items, the five better fitting concordant triplets do not retain their exceptional fit in more than one sample, as defined by exceeding the lowest of the three digits correlations in Table 11, .9992. Thus, although there are some consistently ill-fitting combinations of nondigits items, there are no combinations that consistently are exceptionally good—the essential difference between the kinds of item is pervasive, therefore, as well as independent of mental age.

Table 12 describes the extent of the differences between item types in another way, one that will prove most relevant, at a later point, to Mercer's position. The top panel shows, for digits-backward items, that absolute differences between samples in standardized percentages passing average less than one percentage point: .87% for all six samples, and .40% for the five large samples. These magnitudes also represent the average absolute error if one were to predict the standardized percentage in one sample from that in another sample. The results are quite regular, even down to the modest effect of small sample size in the case of the 1916 Stanford–Binet whites.

Below the diagonal in the top panel are comparable entries for the three new items. As sample size seems to have no effect now within the context of greater variation from other sources, I give only the six-sample mean: 4.32%. This average absolute difference is 5 or 11 times larger than the corresponding figure for digits items (thus reflecting the difference between the two kinds of item), but nevertheless, it remains small as percentage differences go (thus lending perspective to the difference between the two kinds of item). The difference between item types is striking, but just as striking, certainly, is the fact that both kinds of item display rather small mean percentage differences despite the great heterogeneity of the samples in race, age, mental ability, sex composition, region, and location within a 46.5-year time interval. If we consider just the five large samples for simplicity, the differences between races are smaller on average (digits, .36; new, 4.33) than the differences among white samples (digits, .47; new, 5.72), and they are either the same as or only somewhat larger than the two single differences between black samples (digits, .37; new, 2.46). Essentially similar results obtain for all six samples (the actual figures are easily calculated from Table 12). Thus, the multisample data for both digits and new items reveal no indication of any uniquely racial effects *per se*, once the underlying mental ability has been standardized with respect to mean and *SD* (see also the earlier discussion of related chi-square results).

The middle panel of Table 12 shows the effect of item context and standardization on digits and new items, and it compares those items with all 25 Stanford–Binet items from Table 2. When placed among all 25 items, the especially good fit of the digits items across samples is obscured (just as that of "four digits backward" was among the new items in Table 7), although their fit seems to remain better than average. That of the new items actually improves slightly. The average fit across the three samples of all 25 items, as measured by the mean absolute difference of 3.49%, is quite comparable to that of new items in the context of either 3 or 25 items (a reassuring fact), and hence, it is rather good when viewed in the perspective of percentage differences in general. A close inspection of the results for new items and all 25 items in Table 12 suggests that the present mean absolute difference of 3.49% for 25 items in three samples would be a good approximation for their mean difference in all six samples, were the additional data available.

The right side of the middle panel qualifies the preceding statements slightly by exhibiting the differences produced by the "worst case," that is, the standardization yielding the largest differences in the case of all 25 items. The standardization target now turns out to be low whites, as their average raw passing rate was closest to 50% (cf. Table 2). Although this alternative standardization roughly doubles the mean absolute differences, those for digits items remain fairly small, and those for all 25 items are still not large as percentage differences go. Recall that absolute percentages are used because algebraic differences would tend to cancel out, leaving nothing to examine, and also indicating little net advantage in relative difficulty, as measured by passing rates, for any sample.

The correlations in the bottom panel of Table 12 provide a clue

TABLE 12

Absolute Differences between Samples, in Standardized Percentages Passing, Averaged over Items

Set of three new items (below diagonal) and set of three digits items (above diagonal)

	1916 S-B whites (87)	1960 blacks (1,800)	1937 S-B whites (1,123)	1918 low whites (351)	1918 low blacks (938)	1918 SBA whites (486)
1916 S-B whites (113)	—	1.83	1.24	1.94	2.17	1.85
1960 blacks	6.92	—	.59	.11	.37	.02
1937 S-B whites	6.73	.20	—	.70	.93	.61
1918 low whites	.37	6.55	6.36	—	.22	.10
1918 low blacks	4.47	2.46	2.26	4.10	—	.32
1918 SBA whites	.75	7.67	7.47	3.33	5.21	—

Three sets of items under two standardizations

Standardization to mean and SD of SBA whites			Standardization to mean and SD of low whites		
Low whites vs. low blacks	Low blacks vs. SBA whites	SBA whites vs. low whites	Low whites vs. low blacks	Low blacks vs. SBA whites	SBA whites vs. low whites

	Standardization to mean and SD of SBA whites			Standardization to mean and SD of low whites		
	Low whites minus low blacks	Low blacks minus SBA whites	SBA whites minus low whites	Low whites minus low blacks	Low blacks minus SBA whites	SBA whites minus low whites
Digits items (context of 3)	.22	.32	.10	—	—	—
New items (context of 3)	4.10	5.21	3.33	—	—	—
Digits items (context of 25)	2.20	2.60	.87	2.63	3.80	1.57
New items (context of 25)	3.37	5.20	2.03	6.57	10.90	4.67
All 25 S-B items						
Mean	2.90	4.87	2.70	5.06	8.30	4.04
SD	2.58	4.32	3.10	4.58	7.57	4.05

Correlations across 25 items between algebraic differences in standardized percentages for three pairs of samples

	Standardization to mean and SD of SBA whites			Standardization to mean and SD of low whites		
	Low whites minus low blacks	Low blacks minus SBA whites	SBA whites minus low whites	Low whites minus low blacks	Low blacks minus SBA whites	SBA whites minus low whites
Low whites minus low blacks	—			—		
Low blacks minus SBA whites	−.80[a]	—		−.80[a]	—	
SBA whites minus low whites	.33	−.83[a]	—	.33	−.83[a]	—

[a]Significantly different from zero, $p < .001$.

as to the nature of one component of the modest mean absolute differences. Although these correlations are conveniently invariant over choice of standardization, they must be interpreted carefully with regard to their signs, which are governed by the directions of subtraction in the differences between pairs of samples that were correlated. The key to interpretation is that each correlation involves a common sample and the algebraic differences from it of the other two samples. With this key, one can mentally recast the directions of subtraction listed in the table and reach the following conclusions for each correlation without regard to its tabled sign: First, the item differences between the low blacks and each of the two white groups covary directly, with a strength of .80; second, the item differences between the SBA whites and each of the two low groups covary directly, with a strength of .83; third, the item differences between each low group and the group next higher in mental age covary directly, with a nonsignificant correlation of .33.

The three sums of the mental age distances (see Table 2) from the common sample to each of the other two samples fall in the same order as the magnitudes of the correlations at the bottom of Table 12. This common ordering suggests that the minor group-by-item interaction in relative difficulty represented in the algebraic (as well as the absolute) differences between two samples widely separated in mental age, such as the low blacks and SBA whites, is to a considerable degree an interaction between mental ability level and items, as it can be paralleled fairly successfully with a third sample also distant from the common sample, regardless of race; the greater the average distance of the other two from the common sample in mental age, the greater the parallel. Such parallels would account for the fact that mean absolute differences are consistently somewhat larger between low blacks and SBA whites in Table 12 than between any other pairing of the 1918 samples. The rationale here is similar to that developed by Jensen (1974b, 1977b), when he demonstrated that, by substituting for a black group a pseudo-race group of whites matching the blacks in mental ability, he could reproduce a large amount of the small group-by-item interaction involving another group of whites, and that, by matching blacks with whites of the same mental ability, he could eliminate most of the interaction; he concluded, therefore, that the small amount of interaction reflected mental ability differences rather than cultural differences between races (see also Angoff & Ford, 1973). As individual scores are not available here, some technique other than Jensen's had to be devised for exploring the same issue.[10] If we regress the SBA white minus low black difference on the SBA white minus low white difference, in view of their .83 correlation, and calculate the mean and *SD* of the absolute residuals over all 25 items, we obtain 2.63 and 2.51, respectively. Having been thus corrected for interaction with level of ability, these values for the SBA white and low black pairing are now comparable to those for the low white and low black pairing in Table 12, which contains the samples closest in mental age.

Having seen that absolute differences per item in standardized percentages passing are rather modest in general, and that probably some part of them can be attributed to interactions with mental level, we can now turn with greater confidence to the question of why the digits items stand out as different. The answer need only account for a mean difference of about three to five standardized percentage points (depending on choice of standardization in Table 12), if some allowance is made for interaction with ability level in the case of low blacks and SBA whites (not a crucial point), and it must be applicable to all 22 nondigits items with no *a priori* basis for distinguishing among them (in view of the pervasiveness of the difference), yet it must also allow for variation in its effect that is not now predictable (an *SD* of three to five standardized percentage points).

The answer, of course, that could satisfy these requirements is the striking difference between digits and nondigits items in homogeneity of content and task, and hence in presumptive degree of unidimensionality. Only Binet's inspired recognition of an age scale could have led to such a jumble of items as those in Table 2, for with-

---

[10]By the same logic, it is reasonable to check for a positive correlation between size of mean absolute percentage difference in Table 12 and size of absolute mental age difference between samples according to Tables 4 and 5. However, all of the details are not fully predictable, and they must be interpreted tentatively and cautiously. The 1916 Stanford–Binet white sample cannot be included for digits items because of the obvious effect of sample size on its relatively large percentage differences. Excluding that sample leaves 10 percentage differences, which correlate $-.43$ (not significant [ns]) with their corresponding mental age gaps (i.e., which show the wrong sign). However, it may be unreasonable to expect a relation for digits items, whose percentage differences are miniscule, because it is argued next that they are less subject to interaction than nondigits triplets. The corresponding six-sample and five-sample-correlations for new items, on the other hand, are .41 (ns) and .57 ($p < .10$, two-tailed-test), respectively. Although these look supportive, there is sufficient uncertainty over the comparability of mental age means to warrant further caution. Those based on the 1916 Stanford–Binet may be only approximately comparable to those from other editions; moreover, some were derived as approximations from available IQ and age data.

out that discovery who, now starting afresh, would think to include them together in the same measure? The moderate digits-backward domain is unique, perhaps, in its capacity for generating items with minimal differences in secondary facets at different levels of difficulty. Even when drawn from a single nominal domain (an issue unexamined in this chapter), such as that of vocabulary or figural analogies, nondigits items seem more open to trivial forms of multidimensionality than digits items; those forms create opportunities for effects on item difficulty like those of the age-by-strategy interaction on some digits items. Vocabulary items, for example, can be difficult purely because of their rarity as well as because of their abstract complexity (Jensen, 1974b, p. 192). A clear understanding of the relative contributions of such influences, for example, as indicated by the size of the general factor in comparison to the residual variation, is always important.[11]

By usual psychometric standards, the extraneous variance due to such secondary sources is trivial, of course, and is far outweighed by the general factor in both minority and majority samples (see the earlier discussion of correlational structure). However, although diversity of item content is properly regarded as one of the strengths of individual IQ tests, the residual heterogeneity that it induces probably degrades z correlations of item triplets just enough to render them almost equivocal for the difficult purpose of discriminating segments of perfect linearity from merely monotonic ones, thereby spoiling their value as graphic evidence for interval scale properties in analyses of the sort undertaken here. Moreover, desirable or not, that source of variation may prove impossible to eradicate from nondigit item domains even by homogenizing them further, although the degree of success as gauged by this article's methods remains to be seen.

---

[11]After considering such terms as *specific factors* and *group factors*, I decided to use Guttman's deceptively simple concept of *facet* to make this point because he emphasized that it involves "the conceptual analysis of content" (Guttman, 1966, p. 495) and requires "the brains of the scientist" (p. 495). Guttman (1959, p. 130) viewed "dimension," "factor," "element," and so on as being related to but often radically different from "facet"; thus, my use of *dimensionality* within the same paragraph as *facet* represents a conscious decision to keep the heuristic implications as open as possible. The term *secondary facet* came to my attention when mentioned by Bert F. Green, Jr., in a lecture at Johns Hopkins University. Jensen and Reynolds (1982) presented a detailed comparison of general, group, and specific factors in the WISC-R for blacks and whites that complements my discussion nicely, but on the level of subtests rather than on the level of items.

Almost by definition, secondary facets would not be expected to match from item to item. Consequently, they are likely to generate small amounts of item–group interaction: first, through interacting separately with level of mental ability—that is, having item characteristic curves of their own with general ability that alter the overall curves of items in which they are embedded; second, through their varying sensitivity to special abilities of the sort contained in the highly stable cognitive profiles frequently found specific to particular ethnic groups (for further discussion of such profiles, see Gordon, 1975/1980, pp. 124–125; 1980, pp. 177–180).[12] Differences between groups in the relationship between a particular ability and the probability of answering an item correctly, depicted in their item characteristic curves, define internal bias (Ironson, 1982; Jensen, 1980a). Whether the differences are large enough and systematic enough to matter for practical purposes is quite another matter. For present theoretical purposes, however, differential susceptibility of items to such minor sources of interaction would seem quite sufficient for explaining the small mean differences in high z correlations and standardized percentages that distinguish digits backward from nondigits triplets of items in all six samples.

With the digits-backward segment providing independent evidence that general mental ability is approximated well by the normal curve, it automatically follows that if the distribution of IQ is also normal, however arrived at, IQ, too, constitutes an interval scale (e.g., Jensen, 1969a, pp. 21–22; 1980a, p. 262). This reversed form of the usual argument, based on observation rather than on "assumption" tested by observation, enables a score derived from the total test, such as IQ, to ride the coattails of the digits items in laying claim to interval scale properties.

A second, more inferential line of reasoning supports the same conclusion. Because the failure of nondigits triplets to produce *prima facie* evidence of an interval scale was laid to their contamination by numerous differing secondary facets, it would follow that the same interval scale lurks not far beneath their slightly noisy surface (in view of the principle demonstrated by the digits segment), and that the effects of the secondary facets, being largely unrelated to each

---

[12]Jensen (1980a, pp. 729–732) has provided an important critique of interpretations of profile studies, but none of his criticisms, in my opinion, invalidate evidence for stable profile differences relative to *some* set of reference tests originally equated in *some* reference population. My own arguments have always depended only on those minimal conditions.

other, would tend to average out in a total score based on many items. Hence, if z scores in general constitute a slightly noisy interval scale, a total score based on their sum in a representative sample of constant age would constitute a still less noisy interval scale. Except for some minor smoothing, as well as the use of point scales for entire subtests before converting to z scores and summing, this is essentially the way WISC IQ was derived (Wechsler, 1949, p. 15; Wechsler's, 1974, p. 21, discussion of WISC-R IQ is consistent, but slightly ambiguous in its use of the word *normalizing*). Stanford–Binet IQ follows a similar logic; although that test determines mental age before converting to z scores (Terman & Merrill, 1960, p. 27), the Guttman-like scaling features of IQ items mean that a total score based on the most difficult item answered correctly is largely equivalent in information contained to the sum of individual item scores (e.g., see the discussion in Jensen, 1980a, pp. 262–263 of a physical weight scale as an example of a Guttman scale).

Going in the other direction, the nondigits items also indicate something useful, if relatively uncontroversial, about the digits-backward items. As the two forms of item seem to measure the same mental ability on the aggregate level—and in both races, as well— the fact that essentially the same nondigits items reappear in the same intervals between digits items regardless of the varying difficulty of the latter over samples or race (Table 2) can be read as indicating that the substrate ability underlying digits-backward performance is probably continuous rather than discrete. That is, the difficulty of digits items may occur in quanta, but the ability to perform them does not. This evidence is consistent with Dempster's skepticism toward what he characterized as "the older 'slots' view" (1981, p. 87) of the capacity underlying memory span.

MERCER AND ITEM–GROUP INTERACTION

In this section, I first use statements by Mercer and by Kamin to place their cultural bias position within a broader diffusionist tradition concerning group differences in IQ. Then, I discuss their attempts to neutralize the bearing of item–group interaction studies on the plausibility of their variant of the diffusionist argument, which I label the *Mercer–Kamin law*. Next, I relate the unusual properties of the moderately long digits-backward items to the plausibility issue. Finally, I review how culture does diffuse.

The Diffusion-of-Intelligence Paradigm

This paradigm contains two key assumptions: One is that subcultures differ in important but alterable ways relevant to the measurement of IQ; the other is that IQ or rather its cultural basis diffuses from a dominant to a lower scoring subculture, so that the difference in their average IQs can be explained by imperfections in or incompleteness of the diffusion process. Hence, by intensifying exposure and accelerating diffusion, it should be possible to reduce the IQ difference. This chapter is concerned with the second assumption, which depends, in turn, on the first. The paradigm takes no position concerning the validity of scores, an issue that creates two subdivisions among its adherents.

Mercer and Kamin as Diffusionists

Now, let us consider the appropriate theoretical classification for Mercer and others like her who allege cultural bias in tests, that is, invalidity. To the extent that they purport to explain a mental condition or test performance that is also a changeable one within the lives of test respondents, and to the extent that any measurable special abilities that differ between populations in opposite directions are not fungible, those arguing cultural bias must adhere to the diffusion-of-intelligence paradigm.

Other forms of the culture bias argument are conceivable, but unstrategic, for unless invalidity is linked with a condition that is, in principle, alterable within lives, invalidity itself is called into question. It is difficult to allege score invalidity—and hence that a lower scoring population is functionally equivalent to a higher scoring one—without allowing for possibilities of score improvement. And unless special abilities are totally substitutable in some application (in which case, they might well be indistinguishable in the first place), so that a relative advantage on tests of one can cancel a disadvantage on tests of another, there can be no opening for a variant of the bias argument that would depend on mismeasurement of—as distinct from underestimation of—potential performance, thereby rendering the question of score improvability less crucial.

The dependence of invalidity on changeability for the practical purposes of argument distinguishes the cultural bias position from other forms of environmental explanation of group IQ differences that concede the validity of phenotypic scores, but that may or may not allow for their improvement in living individuals. Various hypotheses based, say, on nutrition could illustrate the remaining types. In view of its stand on cultural differences and its dependence on changeability, the cultural bias argument must be regarded as an example of the diffusion-of-intelligence paradigm—a classification made only the more plausible by the argument's position on invalidity.

Judging from their own words, there is little reason to suppose that Mercer and others would object to being classified as diffusionists. Mercer (1979b), for example, regards all tests as "measures of learning" and regards differences between majority and minority groups as reflections of "differences in the exposure of various groups to the materials in the test, differences in reinforcement for learning the material in the test, and differences in test-taking experience" (pp. 53–54); between-group differences are "an artifact of the cultural specificity of the test" (p. 54), whereas her pluralistic model "reveals potential masked by cultural differences" (p. 40); all tests, in fact, are "measures [of] an individual's acculturation to and familiarity with the American core culture" (p. 21).

Similarly, Kamin (1977) testified in *Larry P.* that "the very fact that the tests must depend upon the particular information that a child has acquired . . . means that they are bound to be culturally biased" (p. 930). According to Kamin, "IQ tests measure the familiarity of an individual with the particular bits of knowledge and content and some of the attitudes and approaches toward work of that sort" (p. 882). The phrases "bits of knowledge" and "bits of information" (p. 930) appear several times in the expert witness testimony that Kamin gave in both *Larry P.* and, three years later, in *PASE* (Kamin, 1980, pp. 44, 59, 63), its sister case against the Chicago school system. His "bits" phrases convey a view of what is tested as being fundamentally atomistic, separable, and independent in principle even if empirically correlated, in contrast, perhaps, to a mental construct of great generality.

It is highly instructive to contrast Kamin's description with that of another environmentalist critic of Jensen, a diffusionist from the other subdivision of the paradigm who does not question the validity of scores, and hence who can afford to acknowledge the coherence among items and its implications for validity:

> What seems to be behind each layer of tasks is one or more *cognitive structures*, or styles of abstraction and reasoning. Once a child learns to manage a given general cognitive structure . . . , he can usually solve or answer most of the tasks or test items using that cognitive structure. . . . There is a fair amount of evidence that such structures are well ordered,

so that a five year old average IQ score is rarely made up of a hash of questions at a four year old level and a fifteen year old level. Instead the normal five year old answers four year old and five year old questions. The six year old answers 4, 5, and 6 year old, etc. (Stinchcombe, 1969, p. 519)

The idiocy of rural life, the cognitive consequences of growing up in urban slums, the disparities of achievement among ethnic, religious, and social-class groups begin to make sense if we define civilization in terms of the densities or frequencies of use of intellectual structures at different levels. (Stinchcombe, 1969, p. 522)

The key difference here, of course, is sociologist Stinchcombe's use of *structures* where Kamin might use *bits*, for the two words have quite opposite implications for validity, without which the overly harsh judgment in Stinchcombe's final paragraph, quoted above, would be a *non sequitur*. (The *Communist Manifesto* is the origin for the "idiocy" phrase, of course.)

THE MERCER–KAMIN LAW

The fact that the rank order of difficulty and z-score or delta correlations between populations are high, and that the amount of item–group interaction measured in other ways is small, represents an additional specification of the data that any explanation of IQ differences between races must satisfy. As Jensen (1977b) put it, "The only way one could view these findings as being consistent with the hypothesis that [a test] is . . . culturally biased . . . would be to claim that culture bias depresses blacks' performance on all the test items to much the same degree" (p. 63). Although Jensen noted that this was "highly unlikely for cultural effects per se" (p. 63), he did not, in my opinion, develop the issue of plausibility to the extent that it deserves. Other psychometricians have treated the issue as though it were tacitly understood (but see Angoff, 1982, p. 102).

Accordingly, in preparing my own testimony for *Larry P.* (see Gordon, 1980), I gave thought to the implications of the item–group evidence for any explanation of group IQ differences that was based on cultural diffusion, and I later summarized my conclusions in print (Gordon & Rudert, 1979), pointing out that "such models must posit that information of a given difficulty among whites diffuses across the racial boundary to blacks in a solid front at all times and places, with no items leading or lagging behind the rest" (p. 180), and that "items of information must also pass over the racial boundary at all times and places in order of their level of difficulty among whites, which means that they must diffuse across race in exactly the same order in which they diffuse across age boundaries, from older to younger, among both whites and blacks" (p. 180). Focusing on Kamin's *Larry P.* testimony as an example, I stated:

> Note that it is precisely Kamin's "bits of knowledge" model that is rendered most implausible by the constraints imposed on any cultural diffusion process by the studies of internal validity. In order to accept Kamin's model, we must believe that "bits of knowledge" as divergent from each other as items on the nonverbal Raven's are from the vocabulary items on the Peabody, and as Performance items are from Verbal items on the WISC, diffuse across group boundaries in solid waves of equal difficulty, such that items of similar level of difficulty from tests of highly dissimilar content remain more closely linked with each other than with items of different difficulty but similar content from the same test. (Gordon & Rudert, 1979, p. 180)

In *PASE*, Mr. Patrick D. Halligan, a private attorney engaged by one of the defendants, confronted Kamin with the longer passages containing each of the two quotations above that precede the block quotation. Halligan (1982) later informed me that he had found the Gordon and Rudert article through library research. Each time, Kamin was asked whether he agreed with my passage, and each time, he stated that he disagreed (Kamin, 1980, pp. 115–116). The quotations may have taken Kamin off guard, for his disagreement was with statements that simply cast into bold relief certain empirical facts, the better to relate those facts to the diffusionist position. Given the ambiguities of oral cross-examination, however, in at least one of his two responses Kamin could have been disagreeing instead with my conclusion, also contained within the quoted text, that "such models" of diffusion were implausible, and this trend of thought may have carried over into his second response as well. In any case, at the end of his second response, Kamin (1980) made the necessary minimal concession to empirical reality, stating, "All that is being shown is what tends to be relatively difficult for whites also tends to be relatively difficult for blacks. . . . From that fact I cannot reach any of the conclusions which the authors of that article are obviously trying to reach" (p. 116).

It is worthwhile to ponder for a moment an additional interpretation of Kamin's testimony for what it may reveal about the diffusionist position. The question of plausibility of models aside, the item–group evidence confronts the diffusionist with a dilemma, one that Kamin may have recognized instantly with the very first question. The coherence among items across race that the interaction studies show, conceded freely by Stinchcombe, threatens the atomistic impression of items that Kamin had so consistently cultivated in his testimonies and, by implication, the presumption of invalidity. As the line between predictors and criteria can be located somewhat arbitrarily if one wishes, coherence among predictors implies coherence between predictors and criteria broadly, for predictors always represent a sampling of items, any of which can be used to predict the others. Thus, if one concedes too much coherence on the one side of the predictor–criterion equation in two populations, a judge is apt to conclude, correctly, that it very likely extends to the other side as well, making it hard for him to see in what sense a test could be biased *a priori.* It is difficult to conceive that heterogeneous items would be locked into such a mold, and not the criteria they are used to predict, even if the question must be settled empirically for any specific criterion. Indeed, Kamin's "bits" terminology encourages the impression that such a mold does not exist, and hence that empirical assessment in any given case may hardly be necessary.

If diffusionists try to counter the implication that their model is implausible by portraying the high rank order of difficulty correlations as truisms—that is, as entirely expectable, and hence trivial, empirical facts—they risk drawing attention to predictor–criterion coherence in general; but if they remain silent, they concede to the opposition its point concerning implausibility. This dilemma, therefore, also may account for Kamin's disagreeing with my formulation that highlighted the coherence among items, only to argue for a paler description of the same facts himself a moment later—as well as for the somewhat muted deployment of the truism argument by diffusionists in general whenever they also allege test invalidity. The problem confronting diffusionists is that it is difficult to assert the full coherence of items *and* their invalidity simultaneously and still to retain credibility for the model of diffusion that those propositions imply.

Turning now to Mercer's (1978–1979) own response to the item–group data, we find that her earlier argument that "it would be reasonable to expect that less exposure would more or less uniformly depress responses to all items" (p. 14) was applied to a vocabulary test rather than to all items of an omnibus test with miscellaneous content such as the WISC-R or the Stanford–Binet. Note that her argument treats a test as though it were based simply on freshly diffused materials whose relative difficulties have not changed since filtering across the group border. If correct responses to those materials were necessarily more-or-less uniformly depressed on first arrival—as Mercer would have us accept—they must have remained so when tested. But for how long? After all, once words and information have entered a minority culture, which like any other is capable of its own dynamics, they would be free to acquire new exposure frequencies and to adjust their difficulties to the needs of persons within that culture. To forestall this criticism, apparently, Mercer now asserts:

> Because the patterning of item difficulty is related to the cultural system covered in the test and not to the cultural background of persons taking the test, we would anticipate that item patterning for vocabulary and information type tests would remain relatively stabile, regardless of the background of the test-taker.

As nothing that we know about culture leads to such a static conception, we can only assume that it arises in response to an obvious need in Mercer's argument. The fact of the matter is that Mercer did not anticipate this stability in her published work on cultural bias prior to the studies of interaction by Jensen (1974b, 1977b). Moreover, we know that the very same items of the WISC-R are passed at higher percentages by older age cohorts of minority children than by younger age cohorts, and in many cases, the differences are as substantial as those depicted for digits-backward items in Table 4, where by Grade 5 two of them were passed by the overwhelming majority of blacks. It can hardly be claimed that the relevant content is not present in the black subculture. By as early as age 8, 45% of WISC-R items are passed by more than 50% of blacks, and similar statements would apply to Mexican-Americans.

In Chapter 9 of this book, Mercer develops her case against the interaction criterion further, concluding that "the correlations are so high that it raises the question of whether Criterion 3 contributes any information of value in assessing the internal integrity of a test across different ethnic groups." Her argument continues to be directed toward accounting for the order of difficulty within subtests of the WISC-R rather than over the entire test.

Thus, she attributes the rank order of difficulty of items to what she regards as its three major, but diagnostically trivial, determinants: (1) characteristics of the cultural system covered by the test, such as the frequency with which words, information, and concepts are used and hence encountered (e.g., Vocabulary, Information, Similarities, and Comprehension); (2) the hierarchical aspects of the knowledge system being covered, such as the order of learning arithmetic operations that places multiplying and dividing after adding and subtracting (e.g., Arithmetic); and (3) the number and complexity of elements to be processed (e.g., Block Design, Picture Arrangement, Object Assembly, and probably Digit Span). In view of its prior organization into relatively homogeneous subdomains of content, the WISC-R is an especially convenient target for Mercer's treatment, which does not generalize as readily to other tests, such as the Stanford–Binet.

There are two main points to be made concerning Mercer's argument against the item–group interaction criterion, both somewhat interrelated. First, her three mechanisms for explaining difficulty—and hence the absence of interaction—can themselves be arrayed according to the degree to which each depends on considerations extrinsic to, rather than intrinsic in, the items, and therefore it is reasonable to expect them to produce somewhat different results. Characteristics of the cultural system would fall at the extrinsic extreme, number and complexity of elements to be processed would fall at the intrinsic extreme, and hierarchical aspects of the knowledge would appear to fall between the other two. Consequently, even when her scheme is taken at face value (i.e., without questioning its adequacy as an account of difficulty within each of the content domains, some of which are homogeneous only in contrast to the total WISC-R), the scheme itself proclaims the susceptibility of items in different subtests to item–group interaction between them if, indeed, there are purely sociological obstacles to successful diffusion of the content in category (1), for there is little reason to suppose that difficulties in the less extrinsic categories would be affected to the same extent. Indeed, it is difficult to see that items in category (3) should be biased at all, as Mercer's account of their difficulties makes no mention of mechanisms relevant to cross-cultural diffusion. Interaction involving categories (1) and (3), therefore, seems especially likely under such conditions if cultural bias exists at all. Furthermore, category (2), at least as exemplified in the WISC-R Arithmetic subtest, ought to be far less subject to the vagaries of diffusion than category (1), as diffusion of arithmetic content is well standardized by the elementary-school curriculum. In short, Mercer's scheme implicitly favors the very conclusions arrived at by those who have used, for example, the difference in content between verbal and nonverbal items—on both of which blacks perform about equally far below whites (Jensen, 1969a, p. 81; 1973, p. 297; 1980a; McGurk, 1975; Shuey, 1966)—to question the plausibility of cultural bias that supposedly depends on imperfect diffusion across group boundaries.

In fact, Mercer's treatment of subtests in category (1) is modeled almost exactly after Jensen's own discussion (1974b, pp. 192–193) of the Peabody Picture Vocabulary Test (PPVT), which he described as "perhaps the most obviously culture-loaded test among the more widely used measures of IQ" (Jensen, 1980a, p. 570), in view of the close relation between its item difficulties and their Thorndike–Lorge word-frequency counts (in clusters of 15 items; see Jensen, 1974b, Figure 1). Jensen also contrasted the PPVT with the nonverbal Raven's, using a rationale similar to Mercer's distinction between categories (1) and (3), and he regarded the lack of interaction of the means of the two types of test with race as evidence against bias (1974b, Table 1).

Moreover, although the PPVT qualifies as a highly extrinsic test subject to Mercer's (1) mechanism, and the Raven's qualifies as a highly intrinsic test whose difficulties would be governed by Mercer's (3) mechanism, rank order of difficulty correlations across race of both are virtually identical (see Table 14, below). Apparently, the item contents of both types of test not only diffuse equally well as judged by mean scores in both races, they also diffuse in equal accordance with item difficulties among whites, thereby suggesting that only a single process may be operative after all, Mercer's three mechanisms notwithstanding. In view of the differences between types of subtests that her account of difficulty implies, it is puzzling that Mercer sees no need for explaining the parallel fact that in her own Table 2 the rank-order correlations at each age level for subtests falling in category (1) (e.g., Vocabulary; mean $r = .981$) are indistinguishable from those for subtests falling in category (3) (e.g., Block Design; mean $r = .987$), just as those for the Peabody are quite similar to those for the Raven. These results specify that a common fate is shared by both extrinsic and intrinsic materials in the course of cultural diffusion, but Mercer's separate mechanisms do not fully account for the extent of this empirical convergence, and they even seem to suggest that it should not occur.

From a diffusionist standpoint, one must also regard as miraculous the fact that rank-order correlations between blacks and Hispanics remain as high in her Table 2 as those between whites and each minority separately; one would anticipate some independence between the processes effecting diffusion into two separate minority cultures from a common source, if only because of entropy, as well as separate dynamics within each minority culture that would determine the fate of materials once they had arrived. Yet, for Vocabulary, for example, the average correlation between the two minorities over all ages is .980, whereas the average correlation between whites and either minority is .982. Even if the common source and its ordering of difficulty were the sole determinant of ordering between the two minorities, and there were no other disturbances, we would expect their correlation to be only .960, that is, the product of the two correlations with whites.[13]

As a matter of fact, the observed black–Hispanic correlations in Mercer's Table 2 exceed the value to be expected solely from the correlations of each with whites in 25 of the 33 instances ($p < .01$) created by the 11 WISC-R subtests and three age levels. The excess correlation observed between the minorities tends to be concentrated among subtests where it should be expected least, namely, those belonging in Mercer's extrinsic category (1), where 11 out of 12 instances show an excess. On four of the total occasions in which the expected correlation does match the observed, it is only because all of the correlations happen to equal 1.0, and the four involve either Digits Forward or Object Assembly, rather intrinsic subtests. Judged from these results, the WISC-R does measure more than "acculturation to and familiarity with the American core culture" (Mercer, 1979b, p. 21), as correlations between different minorities are consistently greater than can be accounted for on that basis alone.

Second, and perhaps ultimately more important, Mercer ignores rank order of difficulty correlations across entire tests, as well as the greater problem that they pose for the plausibility of diffusion models in view of the greater heterogeneity of their content. Table 13 summarizes Mercer's item-difficulty rank correlations within subtests from her Table 2 and compares them with similar correlations across nine WISC-R subtests (172 items) based on subsamples from her own sample at each age level (provided through courtesy of Jonathan Sandoval). As Digit Span and Object Assembly difficulties were not available in the data provided to me, I also summarize Mercer's data without those subtests. Although she did not include Mazes, I do (at .88, its correlation was one of the lowest within subtests between whites and blacks; see Sandoval, 1979, Table 3). Whichever way her data are summarized, the correlations across subtests are on a par with the mean within-subtest correlation, and always higher than the lowest within a subtest. Thus, there appears to be as little interaction across items of all subtests as there is within the average sub-

---

[13]Using the product of correlations in these analyses takes advantage of the fact that Spearman rank-order correlations are equivalent to product–moment correlations between ranks.

TABLE 13
A Comparison of Mercer's Rank Order of Item Difficulty Correlations between Anglos and Each of Two Minorities within WISC-R Subtests with Corresponding Correlations across the Varied Content of Nine WISC-R Subtests[a]

	6-year-olds		8-year-olds		10-year-olds	
	Black	M-A[b]	Black	M-A[b]	Black	M-A[b]
Range and mean of Mercer's 11 within-subtest rank order of difficulty correlations						
Range	.80–1.00	.93–1.00	.95–1.00	.88–1.00	.94–1.00	.95–1.00
Mean	.96	.96	.98	.97	.98	.98
Range and mean of Mercer's within-subtest rank order of difficulty correlations omitting Digit Span and Object Assembly						
Range	.94–.98	.93–1.00	.95–.99	.88–.99	.94–1.00	.95–1.00
Mean	.97	.97	.98	.97	.97	.98
Rank-order correlations across 9 WISC-R subtests (172 items), not including Digit Span and Object Assembly, but adding Mazes						
	.96	.97	.97	.97	.96	.96
Subsample size	(53)	(56)	(41)	(51)	(40)	(41)

[a]Mercer's correlations are from Table 2 of her article in the present volume, from her SOMPA standardization sample (Mercer, 1979b). The correlations across nine WISC-R subtests are from a subsample of Mercer's sample and were generously provided by Jonathan Sandoval. Anglo or white subsample sizes were 53, 51, and 53.
[b]Mexican-American.

test, an outcome that the bias type of diffusionist ought to find surprising, but for Mercer's claim that the ordering of items in all groups is determined *a priori* by her three mechanisms.

A priori arguments such as Mercer's seem more persuasive when items have been conveniently arranged in homogeneous subtests so that their order of difficulty is reasonably apparent from inspection. Ranking heterogeneous items by inspection when they lack Mercer's touchstones could prove more difficult. Consider the Stanford–Binet items in Table 2, for example. How would one know which items belonged between the digits-backward items? Achieving a rank correlation with the observed ordering as high as those in Table 13 (ca. .96) on an *a priori* basis might be similarly difficult if one were faced with 10 or 12 items drawn from each of the WISC-R subtests, even if they were representative in difficulty. Guessing the order of difficulty of Stanford–Binet items suitable for 4-year-olds so as to equal the empirical rank correlation of .99 between blacks and whites could also prove challenging (see Jensen, 1980a, Table 11.17).

Studies show that rational judgment is, in fact, a poor method for detecting differences between items in their differences in difficulty for minority and majority groups (Jensen, 1977b; Sandoval & Miille, 1980). In short, claims for the compelling nature of *a priori* determinants of difficulty rank need to be tested empirically, just as claims have been tested concerning certain supposed examples of extremely biased items (e.g., the "hit" item). Without such tests, we cannot be sure that we are not simply being presented with another form of *ad hoc* argument, one that states, in effect, that no matter what the empirical results show, that outcome was predicted by Mercer's theory all along.

Table 14 brings together all of the remaining rank order of difficulty correlations for whole tests that I have been able to locate. There is no indication of appreciably more interaction in those tests containing highly varied material (the Stanford–Binet, the WISC, and

TABLE 14

Rank Order of Item Difficulty Correlations across Varied Content of Entire or Almost Entire Tests, from Various Studies, Uncorrected for Attenuation

Study and test	Minority sample correlated with corresponding whites	
	Blacks	Mexican-Americans
Preschool		
Stanford–Binet for 4-year-olds[a]		
(16 items)	.99	—
Elementary School		
Peabody Picture Vocabulary Test[b]		
(150 items)	.98	.97
Colored Raven Matrices (35 items)[b]		
Study A	.98	.99
Study B	.96	.98
Nine WISC subtests (161 items)[c]		
Males	.96	—
Females	.95	—
Adult		
Wonderlic Personnel Test (50 items)[d]		
Sample 1	.93	—
Sample 2	.96	—

[a] From Jensen, 1980a, Table 11.17. Based on item percentages reported by Nichols, 1970, Tables 14 and 15.
[b] From Jensen, 1980a, Table 11.19.
[c] From Miele, 1979, p. 155.
[d] From Jensen, 1977b, Table 1.

the Wonderlic, a spiral omnibus test), which have a mean black–white correlation of .958, than in those that are more homogeneous (the Peabody and the Raven), where the mean correlation equals .973, even if one does not make any allowance for potential effects of special abilities (i.e., profile effects). The mean WISC-R correlation from the bottom of Table 13 is .965, which fits the pattern and also indicates that those results are typical for entire tests in general. The highest black–white correlation, of .99, in Table 14, which is based on over 2,500 children from each race, comes from the multicity Collaborative Study data reported by Nichols (1970) and involves items that Jensen (1980a) described as "probably more heterogeneous in form and content than the items in any other age range of the S-B or any set of the same number of consecutive items in any other standard test" (p. 564). Jensen determined that the correlations within each race were as high as the one between races in Nichols's data (.99), and that those within race in the Wonderlic study (all .98) were only slightly higher than those in Table 14 between race (Jensen, 1977b, p. 55). Thus, some part of the minuscule apparent interaction is probably due to sampling error rather than to race with items, and an appreciable part of that remaining, as we have seen, can be attributed to ability level with items. Jensen (1980a, p. 564) also deemed it noteworthy that the .99 correlation from Nichols's 4-year-olds was observed before any cultural differences between races were diluted by schooling, an observation consistent with the absence of trend across ages in Table 13.[14]

There is also an absence of historical trend that is surprising unless one holds to a remarkable view of the diffusion process in order to maintain one's commitment to a cultural explanation of group differences. Harking back to Table 2, above, we now see that the rank correlations of .93 and .97 between low blacks and the two white samples in 1918 are as high as those from contemporary samples in Tables 13 and 14. The 1918 delta correlations in Table 2 (of .95 and .98) also compare favorably with modern results. Among two samples each of blacks and whites taking the verbal part of the Preliminary Scholastic Aptitude Test, for example, delta correlations range from .93 to .95 (Angoff & Ford, 1973, Table 2).

---

[14]During his cross-examination in *PASE*, Kamin (1980) termed the finding of little race-by-item interaction in a study of college students irrelevant, and as "a very different kettle of fish than whether there is [such interaction] in the kinds of questions that are asked of a six and seven year old child" (p. 109). One wonders, therefore, what he would say about Table 13.

Rank correlations with item mental ages of the 1916 Stanford–Binet sample, using items up to the Year XII level, were also nearly equivalent in all three 1918 adult samples (see Table 2), although it is reasonable to suppose that by adulthood the easier items, at least, might no longer reflect the order of difficulty that they had had among very young white children originally. Items at Mental Ages VI and VII, for example, being almost equally distant from adult mental ages, ought to be about equally easy for adults. Hence, their ordering should become more arbitrary (i.e., show "local independence"), especially if adults on their own are able to master at least some of them after passing rates had been artificially depressed in the course of their diffusing to blacks. Yet, for the low blacks, the Year VI and VII items have exactly the same rank correlation between Stanford–Binet mental ages and passing rates as the Year X and XII items, namely, .65 (excluding XII, 5 because of its zero percentage). The levels of these correlations, of course, are lowered by the many tied ranks for mental age as well as by the limited range of difficulty when items from only two adjacent mental ages are used. What counts is their failure to be drastically different from each other; such a difference would have indicated a triple interaction between the two item–race interactions and the classification of items as to whether they were extremely easy or hard, that is, a special case of item–group interaction that would seem especially likely to appear if cultural effects were present.

Moreover, the easier set of eight items was passed by 67.8% of low blacks, on the average, but the harder set of eight by only 5.6%, on average. One set of correct answers, therefore, was about 12.1 times as available in the black subculture as the other, yet both reflected Stanford–Binet mental ages to the same degree in their passing rates. Apparently, even a large difference in availability as well as in difficulty has little impact on the order of passing rates.

Results such as these suggest that either internal cultural dynamics—and hence, cultural differences in general—have hardly any effect on item difficulty or the black culture is passive and static with respect to material once it has been received from the surrounding white culture. The second alternative is contrary to the literature on diffusion of ideas, which teaches that once an idea gains adherents in a system, local sources are widely available to persons who hear about the idea relatively late (Rogers, 1962, p. 104). The similar behavior of both sets of eight items—and in all three samples, as the other two reveal comparable rank correlations—would not be remarkable if item difficulty were determined simply by the ability level of the sample in question, however. In order to have an alternative to that conclusion, we must view culture as extremely regular in its manner of diffusion across social boundaries, and as extremely undynamic within subcultures once diffusion has begun.

If one attributes the lower average test performance of blacks generally to cultural differences, as both Mercer and Kamin do, the failure of culture to disturb the order of item difficulties in one way or another among the low blacks in Table 2 is especially difficult to comprehend, as their cultural distance from whites must have been far greater in 1918 than anything we can now imagine applying in the case of contemporary blacks. Not only was the estate of all blacks low in 1918, but relative to the rest, those in Table 2 must have stood close to the bottom. Their average mental age fell 3.1 years below that of the average black draftee, who, in turn, fell 2.71 years below the average white draftee (where the mental age SD for white draftees was 2.9 years), and so they most likely were drawn disproportionately from the lower social strata even of 1918 blacks. All black draftees averaged only 4.6 years of schooling, and those from the Deep South only 2.6 years (Yerkes, 1921, Part III, Tables 165, 303, and 304).

The fact that the World War I data do not show more item–group interaction than recent studies is consistent with evidence that I have reviewed showing little or no decrease in the mean difference on mental ability tests between races in the interim, despite major changes in the relative educational and socioeconomic standing of blacks. By 1970, for example, the median school years completed by young nonwhite adult males was in excess of 12. Considered together, such facts point to the conclusion that cultural differences between the two races have had no artificially depressing or disturbing effect on black IQ performance since as long ago as 1918.

Now, let us consider the meaning of these various results. Item–group interaction serves as an index of the extent to which items behave independently of one another, when their relation to each other within one population is used as the standard. If answering items correctly is influenced by the dynamics of cultural diffusion between populations, rather than by mental ability alone, correct answering should also prove to be subject to other aspects of cultural dynamics both within and between groups. To argue for the former without being able to produce evidence for the latter demands acceptance of a remarkably simple model of cultural process. Yet, wherever we have looked for likely signs of independence that would betray the responsiveness of items to such cultural processes, we have come away empty-handed. We have found no interaction with major content categories (even though Mercer's own mechanisms suggest its likelihood), no interaction with difficulty level (apart from floor and ceiling effects), no differential responsiveness to cultural processes according to the availability of material within the minority subculture, no trend with schooling, no trend historically, and no special amount of interaction involving a black sample that must have been far more isolated from white culture than any sample of modern American blacks. Finally, we have also seen in Mercer's own data that the order of difficulty asserts itself in minority groups that differ importantly from each other in mean scores and cultural background (Mercer, 1979b), so that they resemble each other in that respect more than would be expected simply on the basis of their rank correlations with whites. Jensen's data (1980a, Table 11.19) in Table 14 replicate that outcome for tests as different in cultural loading as the PPVT and Raven's, yet show no special distinction between the two tests: As can be seen from Table 14, the three black–Hispanic correlations to be expected on the basis of products are .95, .97, and .94, but Jensen observed higher black–Hispanic correlations of .98, .99, and .99 for the PPVT and two Raven's studies, respectively (not shown in the table). Despite the opportunity for items to respond independently to different subcultures, and thus to diverge in rank order, they behave as though they actually converge after diffusion.

Based on this examination of Mercer and Kamin's positions as constrained by the lack of interaction in the data, the following set of propositions ought to be known as the *Mercer-Kamin law*: (a) Materials of the same difficulty in the culture of origin diffuse to other subcultures at about the same rate, regardless of differences in their content; (b) the rate of diffusion includes an important component of delay due only to imperfect exposure when the receiving culture scores lower on tests; and (c) the order of diffusion conforms closely to the order of difficulty in the original culture. The proviso that materials, regardless of their nature, are never differentially affected by dynamics within the receiving culture might well be appended. The set of propositions should be known as a law because it embodies the major characteristics of scientific laws, namely, the expression of underlying regularities with completeness, precision, and simplicity (Achinstein, 1971, p. 13). If it is true, the law should be stated boldly and claimed by Mercer and Kamin, as its components represent statements of considerable consequence and as I know of no competing claims for priority in the literatures dealing with diffusion and culture. If, on the other hand, the law is not even plausible, then a certain mutedness in asserting it and reticence in claiming it would be understandable.

By treating the rank order of item difficulty within homogeneous subtests only, Mercer is able to sidestep temporarily the issues raised by proposition (a), especially, of the Mercer–Kamin law, which contains some of its most momentous implications. At worst, she need imply only a weaker form of proposition (a) to account for the rank correlations within the extrinsic subtests, such as Vocabulary, as their material is less heterogeneous by far than that of the entire test, although still not perfectly homogeneous by any means, except in respect to gross type of item. The extension of her account of difficulty rank to the entire WISC-R, with its more heterogeneous items, depends on the way the WISC-R happens to be organized. That organization enables Mercer, if her *a priori* mechanisms are granted, to account for the high rank correlation of the entire test, despite its heterogeneous content, somewhat derivatively and hence without having to state proposition (a) explicitly, which would invite attention to its plausibility. This comes about from the fact that most of the variance in the typical item–group analysis lies between items (i.e., the main effect for items is huge; see Jensen's 1980a, Table 11.11, analysis of variance). Because Mercer essentially stipulates via her three mechanisms that ordering within subtests is not eligible to contribute to interaction—and that its failure to do so is meaningless, therefore—that leaves only the unmentioned ordering between entire subtests as a remaining source. For it to depress the rank correlation between item difficulties in two groups, that source would have to be extremely productive, as the rank correlation reflects the ordering of the full set of items, both within subtests and between subtests, and in the case of the WISC-R, at least, most of the degrees of freedom lie within subtests.

In short, the rank correlation is the wrong statistic for examining the group-by-subtest interaction that Mercer has failed to account for with her three mechanisms; a better choice would be an analysis of variance that would isolate that component explicitly, and that then would enable us to compare its size with the corresponding component from an analysis based on two white groups, in the manner employed, for example, by Jensen (1974b, 1977b).

As an illustration, consider a nontrivial interaction created by setting the passing rates of blacks exactly equal to those of whites on all items within five of the nine WISC-R subtests involved in the rank correlations at the bottom of Table 13 (i.e., in all but the four most extrinsic tests). In effect, those five subtests would simulate the "Holy

Grail" of a valid test that also produces no race difference that has long been sought without success. My calculations show that such an adjustment would not even register on the rounded rank correlation of .96 between white and black 10-year-olds in Table 13, calculated over all 172 items. The interaction effect would be easily detectable by an appropriate analysis concerned with subtest means, however.

We see, therefore, that Mercer's argument, which is totally isomorphic with a weaker form of the Mercer–Kamin law within subtests of the extrinsic variety, is also capable of accounting for quite high rank correlations from entire tests in the absence of extraordinary amounts of group-by-subtest interaction, and consequently, she has found it possible to realize most of the benefits of the Mercer–Kamin law at its full strength without having to state it explicitly and thus expose it to scrutiny. However, the inability of investigators to demonstrate important race-by-subtest interactions via more sensitive statistics in the case of blacks and, above all, Jensen's (1980a, Chap. 11) ability to account for substantial amounts of what interaction there is by using the "weak form" of the Spearman hypothesis (Jensen & Reynolds, 1982)—that is, the hypothesis that white–black differences on WISC-R subtests are predominantly a positive function of the subtests' g loadings—continue to disconfirm the cultural bias argument with data from whole subtests, unless one invokes the Mercer–Kamin law explicitly, with all of its liabilities. Because once again there is little or no interaction to be explained, the cultural bias argument can be preserved only by an explanation of why there should be little or none despite the presence of cultural effects potent enough to produce large mean differences between groups—in the case of blacks and whites, a difference of 1.1 white SDs. The Mercer–Kamin law meets these specifications exactly, and it is clear now that Mercer needs that law to complete her account of item difficulty if heterogeneity in content is acknowledged even though it may not have seemed so necessary when attention was confined to the rank order of difficulty correlation only and to the WISC-R.

An Aside concerning Stable and Valid Profiles

Before going on to the next section, I want to acknowledge, as briefly as possible, that my discussion of group-by-subtest interaction in the case of blacks fails to address the question of what to make of the persistent interactions, often recognized outside the test fairness literature as profile differences, that appear in certain other ethnic

comparisons involving whole types of tests. Here, the substantial difference in WISC-R Verbal and Performance IQs exhibited by Mexican-Americans can serve as a specimen (e.g., the 10.2 IQ-point difference between the two in Mercer, 1979b, Table 43). Such interactions
pose a problem for Mercer, too, as they represent clear and sometimes substantial violations of the Mercer–Kamin law, showing that
it need not hold. Although interactions between whole tests might
tempt test critics to seize on them as evidence of cultural bias, these
critics would then have to forfeit their use of the Mercer–Kamin law
in the case of blacks or risk being accused of employing a double
standard.

Adhering to a single standard himself, Jensen (1974b, p. 240;
1980a, p. 605) has construed the Mexican-American profile on the
verbal PPVT and the nonverbal Raven as a sign of bias in the former,
due perhaps to bilingualism. Elsewhere (Gordon, 1975/1980, 1980), I
have called attention to an important ambiguity concerning causal
direction in such an interpretation, based on the following facts:
Robust profile differences between sexes and groups are the rule
rather than the exception; they do not always involve a depressed
score on a verbal test, even when that test is in a group's second language; the bias interpretation depends on unanalyzed assumptions
concerning how tests standardized to be equal in one gene pool
should behave in another gene pool; and finally, we have some evidence of independence between the genetic substrates for different
kinds of test, as witnessed by the large mean difference in Verbal and
Performance IQs of women with Turner's syndrome, amounting to
16–19 points. This was the discussion, incidentally, that has
prompted Mercer once again, in her present chapter, to refer ellip-
tically to my mentioning "verbal ability genes" and "nonverbal-abil-
ity genes," as she has on other occasions (Mercer, 1977, pp. 2173–
2175; 1979a, p. 97). The proper interpretation of well-established profile differences between groups with respect to test bias will have to
depend mainly on external validity and on item–group interaction
within tests; here, methods for assessing the validity of male and
female profiles on SAT-V and -M might serve as a model (e.g., Benbow & Stanley, 1982).

THE MODERATELY LONG DIGITS-BACKWARD ITEMS AS A PROBE FOR ASSESSING THE MERCER–KAMIN LAW AND THE DIFFUSIONIST POSITION IN GENERAL

We have seen that acceptance of Mercer's mechanisms would
deprive us explicitly of item–group interaction within subtests as an

assay for bias, and that, unless an extraordinary amount of group-by-subtest interaction were present, her mechanisms would place Mercer implicitly in agreement with the entire Mercer–Kamin law, because then they would also account for the high rank order of difficulty correlation over all items that only that law satisfactorily predicts, but that Mercer tacitly lets readers assume that her mechanisms have explained. Obviously, some explicit recognition of the law in addition to her mechanisms would be required to account for the absence of important race-by-subtest interaction. In view of Mercer's failure to exclude race-by-subtest interaction, rank correlations over whole tests as high as those in Tables 13 and 14—especially those based on heterogeneous tests without homogeneous subtests—are sufficient evidence in themselves that the entire law is being tacitly applied whenever mean differences between groups on those tests are attributed to cultural bias, because her mechanisms themselves depend on the law in a less sweeping form, and because only the law truly accounts for all of the lack of interaction. As it applies to all items regardless of their type of content, the law leaves no unexplained residue of coincidence surrounding the similar fates of different kinds of item.

My questioning of the law thus far has relied on its implausibility once it and its role in the cultural bias argument have been made explicit. This questioning was accompanied by an invitation to Mercer and Kamin to acknowledge the law frankly and so to take due credit for such an important generalization concerning cultural diffusion, if indeed it is true. Such a generalization would be at least as important as Grimm's law concerning linguistic diffusion, and it would fill an important vacuum in the theory of diffusion. If Mercer and Kamin rely on the law and believe in it, they should not hesitate to state it.

The *prima facie* plausibility of the law depends on what we know about cultural diffusion in general (which I review in the final section) and on how that knowledge might apply to test content. For example, should not an especially extrinsic item, such as one of vocabulary that is easy for whites, sometimes turn out to be uncharacteristically hard for minority group members, if their item difficulties do indeed reflect a substantial cultural influence as Mercer contends? Should there not be lacunae, in other words? The reverse situation is also a possible source for interaction, although perhaps a less fertile one. Cultural dynamics could make that situation fertile in specific instances, however. During the late 1950s, for example, a large black gang in Chicago took the incongruous name Conservative

Vice Lords, and within a few years, those words appeared often on walls in black neighborhoods (see the wall photograph in Keiser, 1969, p. 39, where the word is also misspelled "Consertive"). *Conservative* always struck me and others as an unusually difficult and uncommon word to be so prominent in the active speech of persons drawn from a larger black gang population whose average IQ tested at 79.9, but there it was, and they had a pretty good idea of what it meant in terms of personal style, manners, and dress (not that they emulated that idea in their behavior). According to Dawley's history of the Vice Lords (1973, p. 31), the term *conservative* had been added at the insistence of just one of the founding members; its rapid spread throughout black neighborhoods illustrates just how dynamic and idiosyncratic culture can be. Furthermore, not everything cognitive need originate from the white culture, even if it does find its way onto an intelligence test.

Its general plausibility or implausibility notwithstanding, Mercer's argument is a troublesome one from the standpoint of finding a truly crucial empirical test based on psychometric data as distinct from data concerned mainly with cultural issues. Let us now turn to the digits-backward data, therefore, recognizing that the facts in hand concern the black minority only. There are four aspects, not necessarily independent, of the digits data relevant for testing the cultural bias position. However, because each is not readily apparent from knowing the others, they must be developed individually.

The first places an additional constraint on the Mercer–Kamin law that renders it even less plausible. As implied and employed by Mercer and Kamin, the law (and Mercer's three mechanisms) need apply only to the *ordering* of items, which leaves a certain latitude for precise difficulties as a concession to the vicissitudes of cultural transmission. Table 12, however, reveals that the difficulties of the three digits items, after standardization for mean and variance, display not merely the same ranks in all six samples, but virtually the same passing rates exactly, to within less than one percentage point on average. Recall that the mean absolute difference was .87% for six samples, and .40% for the five large samples. Goodness of fit is a property of all three items together, as my discussion of the hydraulic model made clear, and so it is properly assessed by averaging over the three items. As the outcome depends slightly on the choice of target sample when standardizing, and the one chosen in Table 12 fell in the midrange of all six in the degree to which it favored small differences, it is useful to know the corresponding statistics from the "worst case": They are .91% and .43%, respectively, and thus minute under any standardization.

There is reason to believe, moreover, that even these minute residual differences are due, not to culture, but simply to unreliability, as the estimates of reliability in Table 10 are at such a level as to cause the residuals to vanish altogether if corrections for attenuation were to be applied to the z-score correlations in Table 8 (either before or after standardization). The chi-square results in Table 6 for the digits items and in Table 7 even for the new items, finally, give no sign that the size of residuals has any special relation to comparisons between race, which is where they would be expected most if the cultural hypotheses of Mercer and Kamin were correct. For the large samples, the actual magnitudes of the residuals, in Table 12, are smaller between race than within race.

The digits data require the Mercer–Kamin law to specify not only that items have about the same order of difficulty in various groups but, in their case, virtually the same passing rates exactly after standardization (a procedure familiar to sociologists in a variety of methodological settings). This requirement reduces the permissible role of culture merely to influencing somehow the mean difference between groups in z scores, and perhaps their variances. When one considers the range of differences among the six samples in respects that social scientists usually associate with "culture" in the descriptive sense, not to mention the historical intervals, the newly constrained Mercer–Kamin law becomes so overburdened with implausibility that it collapses of its own weight, leaving no role at all for culture as an explanation of differences among these six samples in digits-backward performance.

The second aspect, closely related to the first, adds to the severe constraints imposed by the first those imposed by the success of the z transformation in all six samples. Recall that the first principal component of the correlation matrix based on simple percentages passing, displayed in Panel C of Table 8, accounted for 97.40% of the variance, whereas the component extracted from its counterpart matrix based on the z transformation in Panel A accounted for 99.87%. (Judging from the reliabilities discussed earlier, the last figure could be raised to 100% by correcting the matrix in Panel A for attenuation.) The importance of adding such a small quantity to the variance, as the z transformation does with no increase in number of variables, depends on where in the range that increment falls. Here, it represents 95% of the residual variance, no small feat in any analysis. Such a high value makes it unlikely that any other transformation would do a better job. In addition, it represents an improvement on a situation where the advantages of perfect rank correlation and the chance benefits possible from having to fit only three data points in each pair of samples have already been realized; that is, it follows a tough act. In view of where it is coming from and going to, therefore, the 2.47% difference is a telling increment.

Substantively, the first principal component isolates the linear function that contributes the most variance to all of the samples, and in the case involving the z transformation, that component reflects a relation with the normal curve. The added variance, therefore, is a telltale indication that wherever they fall in the percentage range, the observed passing rates of the various samples in Table 6 behave with respect to each other as though they were ascending, descending, or straddling the humps of normal distributions, even though those distributions are entirely latent and not otherwise visible insofar as the digits data alone are concerned. This latency, in fact, insulates those distributions from the charge that their normality is somehow an artifact of test construction, for the three items alone could in no way reveal normality in each sample taken individually (unless we knew in advance that the outside criterion represented by the unit model was valid).

The additional consistency conferred on the digits data through allowing the latent normal distributions to express themselves via the z transformation, coupled with the differences between groups in observed passing rates, indicates that there are mean differences among the groups not merely in respect to passing digits items, but also in respect to the normally distributed latent trait that makes passing possible. Because what is normally distributed has been revealed by the digits items in conjunction with the z transformation, rather than being created by the items or their sum alone, and is otherwise without item content at this point, it cannot be subject to cultural bias unless in certain cases the observed passing rates of the digits items have been depressed, as discussed below. To the extent that the digits items themselves are free of cultural bias, therefore, the latent trait is also free. This line of reasoning establishes a context broader than that of digits items alone, potentially, for what is to be considered free from bias.

Demanding conditions would have had to be satisfied in order for the passing rates of individual digits items to have been artificially depressed in the case of blacks. The decrements would have had to be just those required not only to maintain or bring about the near-perfect correlations with z scores of white samples, in Table 8, but also to maintain or to bring about the relation to an underlying normal distribution. Cultural bias resulting from impediments to diffusion of knowledge cannot operate directly on the z score (which is a continuous variable like IQ); bias must be mediated through effects on individual items from changes in numbers or percentages of persons passing (a relatively discrete variable), as persons are the natural units of diffusion. To account for the digits data, any cultural interference with passing rates of individual items would not only have had to preserve the extraordinary fit between samples demonstrated by the absolute differences following standardization in Table 12, as discussed in connection with the first aspect above, it would also have had to respect the relations of the items to a latent normal distribution, or else the z transformation would not have improved the fit over percentages passing so successfully, quite aside from the actual goodness of that fit as reflected in Tables 8 and 12. It is quite a challenge to imagine how adjustments for the entire ensemble of three items could possibly have been coordinated so well for any particular black sample, as the hypothetical decrements in passing rates necessary to conserve normality would depend on where each rate fell in the percentage range and would thus have had to be individually tailored to each of the three digits items for any sample.

Take, for example, whites at age 10 from Table 5 and blacks in Grade 4 (approximately age 10) from Table 4, as illustrative of representative samples. To attribute the race difference in passing rates to cultural bias, we must assume decrements of 15.3%, 37.3%, and 31.7%, for each of the digits items, respectively. These varying effects not only preserve the fit between samples after standardization, as witnessed by the z correlation of .9999 between the two samples, but also conserve normality, as witnessed by the difference between the z correlation and the percentage-passing correlation of .9651.

As a matter of fact, the digits matrices in Table 8 show that cross-race and black–black correlations are improved by the z transformation even slightly more often than correlations within the white race. Comparing Panel A with Panel C shows eight of nine instances in which the former types improve, and five of six in which white–white correlations improve. As the correlations involving blacks are the cases in which the question of cultural bias arises, these results indicate that if the observed passing rates of blacks were indeed depressed by bias, some mysterious force must have seen to it that the decrement for each item constituted or reconstituted the indications of underlying normality that are also present in the passing rates of whites. Quite clearly, valid differences between groups on the latent trait would be a far more economical and plausible explanation of the precise contours shown by the digits data.

The third relevant aspect is that there is no indication in the digits data that the process of transmission across race is any noisier, even when samples are separated in time by decades, than the process of transmission within race across age levels at the same point in history. The means of the four adjacent grade and three adjacent age correlations, based on data in Tables 4 and 5, are .9991 for blacks and .9983 for whites, respectively. In comparison, the mean of the six cross-race correlations involving large samples from Table 8 (.9997) is actually higher, indicating less rather than more noise. The differences among these z correlations probably reflect only the differences in sample size and the rounding errors of the 1937 Stanford–Binet percentages. In any case, the correlations are similar enough to guarantee similar responsiveness to the linear transformations involved in standardizing for mean and variance, and hence little or no difference in goodness of fit measured by absolute differences between races and between age cohorts within race.

Such observations carry yet one step further the account given in Gordon and Rudert (1979), according to which items of information "must diffuse across race in exactly the same order in which they diffuse across age boundaries ... among both whites and blacks" (p. 180), for they enable us to see that the digits-backward items traverse both kinds of boundary not only in the same order, but also at virtually the same relative delta difficulties after standardization. Not only is there no plausible role for culture in accounting for differences between races in passing digits-backward items, as we have seen, but in addition, whatever does account for those differences is not detectably different from what accounts for differences in passing the items between adjacent ages. The kinds of differences in mental ability associated with maturation would seem to apply to both situations equally well.

The fourth and final aspect of the digits data relevant to assessing the Mercer–Kamin law concerns the extent to which interpretations based on those items apply to items in general. In an earlier section of this article, I reviewed evidence showing that digit span correlates highly with IQ, and that backward span does so more than forward span in both races; in another, I argued on the basis of my own evidence that digits items differ from other IQ items mainly in their lack of secondary facets, which enables the former to manifest interval scale properties obscured in the other items by the small amount of additional noise that such facets cause. Finally, although the data in

Table 12 show that mean absolute differences in fit between samples are poorer for nondigits items, and hence large enough, perhaps, to represent the noise expected from cultural interference, that noise is only slightly greater between samples of different race than between samples of the same race, besides which much of the slight excess noise could be accounted for in terms of an interaction of items with differences in mental age rather than with differences in culture or race. These considerations all point to the conclusion that other items are not much more subject to systematic cultural influences in the case of blacks than digits-backward items, and that they differ from digits items mainly, or perhaps merely, in their suitability for proving their lack of bias.

Now, however, in order to judge this issue further, I would like to refer back to my earlier discussion of the rank orders in Table 2, where I noted that, on average, 87.5% of the available rank-order slots between digits items were filled by common items when white and black samples were paired, which compared with 91.7% when the two white samples or the two low-scoring groups of different races were paired. Despite the minute difference between adjacent digits items in their actual task content, the very same nondigits items nearly always reappear in the same one-digit interval for both races.

We have seen that the three moderately long digits-backward items mark off two intervals of difficulty that are nearly exactly equal, and in fact, a strong case can be made that the items constitute a segment of interval scale in addition. The two nearly equal intervals, each within 6% of the length of the other when averaged over the full sample, represent two compartments of sharply defined relative difficulty embedded within a set of three items that qualifies as a homogeneous subtest of the highly intrinsic sort, according to Mercer's mechanisms.

Metaphorically, the two intervals are like two railroad cars coupled together that travel up and down the track of difficulty. Their precise location at any time depends on the sample under consideration, for they are not situated at the same points in the range of percentages passing for all samples. Let us imagine that the two intervals are gondola cars, which have low sides and are open at the top, and that the remaining 22 Stanford–Binet items used in World War I are the freight, carried either in one or the other of these two cars or in other cars elsewhere in the train. My examination of the rank-order slots shows that no matter where on the track the train travels (or in what sample), the freight is loaded in essentially the same way: practically the same items in each gondola car always and, located ahead or behind elsewhere on the train, practically the same items, too. This occurs despite the heterogeneous nature of the freight (which may bounce around somewhat), the higher extrinsic character of many of the nondigits items (see Table 2), and the extreme distance of the low blacks in 1918 from white culture according to conventional indices and historical accounts (Bond, 1934/1966).

Although the data in Table 2 exhibiting these relations apply only to the three 1918 samples, the rank-order and delta correlations for those samples enable one to generalize from 1918 with great confidence that the metaphor would hold in contemporary samples for items in use today, and with some confidence that it would hold even if the same items were to be employed again. For the correlations in 1918 are in every way comparable to those of today (Tables 13 and 14), and we have already seen that the interval scale properties of the digits items hold over time (Tables 6, 8, and 12). Thus, the challenges posed by the metaphor are not restricted to 1918.

Although differences between adjacent digits items may loom large on the scale of human affairs—witness the differences in their passing rates—their differences in content are so minimal that it would be difficult for a layperson to predict where many of the nondigits items would stand in relation to them. Yet, the two categories of item—one highly intrinsic, whose difficulties are governed according to Mercer by the number of elements, and the other often extrinsic, whose difficulties are governed by frequency of encounters according to Mercer—consistently display the same interrelations in the three 1918 samples. How can we account for this and still assign a major role to cultural interference and bias?

Certainly, it is not plausible that culture diffuses across group borders already packed in almost identical gondola car lots—and such miscellaneous lots at that! To remain consistent with both the bias argument and the data, diffusion of the car lots would also have to be impeded as units, or else their contents would not remain intact.

How, then, do the various items assume their rightful places on the train if not through the same process that governs the digits items? If, as we have seen, it is necessary for the proponents of bias to paint themselves into a corner of vanishingly small probability in order to account for the extraordinary fit and relation to normality of the digits items, where will they find room for the additional brushstrokes needed to account for the consistent intercalation of the two kinds of item? Certainly, there is no consolation for them in the fact that we cannot compartmentalize the full range of items with only three digits items as precisely as we can those in the two one-digit intervals, for the items that are so compartmentalized are various enough to represent items in general, besides which we realize that the train actually transports an infinite number and variety of items in addition to those on view in Table 2. New items, moreover, come constantly into being, yet find regular places on the train (e.g., "Name the last five presidents"). Specimens of virtually any type of good intelligence-test item can be found that, once loaded into the two well-defined compartments, would travel with the rest from then on in cross-racial comparisons.

Theoreticians of bias will recognize that, once others conclude that the issue of bias is simply too far-fetched in the case of the digits items, they are apt to progress easily to the recognition that the digits items serve as valid cross-cultural markers for the remaining items. Consequently, even if those other scientists do not move directly from the digits data to conclusions concerning the underlying distribution of ability along the lines reviewed in the paragraph that opens my discussion of the fourth aspect, they can still move to equally damaging conclusions concerning the lack of bias in the noisier types of items simply by taking the implications of the markers seriously. For they will see that the passing rates of nondigits items maintain a close relationship with the passing rates of the valid markers or anchor points, even to the extent of retaining the details of compartmentalization across groups. As the passing percentages of the markers rise or fall, so do those of the nondigits items contained within the compartments of difficulty that the markers define. This fact suffices to inform us about other items of the same type as those in the well-defined compartments.

There is no way that proponents of the bias position can treat the digits items separately from the nondigits items that they bracket so consistently. Exempting the digits items alone from the charge of bias would amount to conceding that they also measure valid group differences. Such a tack would succeed only if the digits items exhibited no differences between races, thereby contributing to a pronounced group-by-subtest interaction—but that is contrary to fact (see Tables 4, 5, and 6). Plainly, the theory of cultural bias cannot exempt the digits items and remain in business, and so it must attempt to subsume them by a yet more stringent and hence more improbable version of the Mercer–Kamin law.

In summary, the first and second aspects of the digits data demonstrate that test critics such as Mercer and Kamin must embrace a totally improbable approach to explaining why the relative difficulties of those items fit so perfectly across our six quite heterogeneous samples and conserve normality of the underlying ability as well. To remain consistent with the data and also to assign a major inhibitory role to cultural differences, the critics require a model of diffusion involving a concatenation of coincidences that defies belief, a model that I have called the *Mercer–Kamin law.*

Aspects two and three point to characteristics of the data quite apart from group differences in passing rates that are much better explained by group differences on a normally distributed latent ability, an ability that cannot be distinguished in the data from whatever determines mean differences between adjacent age categories within each race, usually referred to as *mental maturation.*

Aspect four reviews material relating digits-backward performance to IQ test performance in general and hence one kind of item to the rest, thus indicating that the ability in question is general intelligence. The discussion underscores that interpretation by demonstrating the inextricability of digits and nondigits items in the three 1918 samples, which also serves as a basis for concluding that the processes influencing the diffusion of one would influence the diffusion of the other, too. Reference was made to earlier analyses indicating that the two kinds of item differ mainly in their suitability for forcing the Mercer–Kamin law into untenable positions in order for it to accommodate the data; now, we see that arguing that the slight additional noise in nondigits items represents evidence of strong cultural interference becomes more difficult when the delicate structure of the digits items is so perfectly maintained from sample to sample. Finally, the material discussed under the fourth aspect leads to the conclusion that if one grants the failure of the bias argument in the case of the digits items, there is no way to salvage the argument for use with nondigits items.

How Does Culture Diffuse?

Here, only those aspects of the answer relevant to the bias issue need be considered. There are two major ones, closely related to each other, which I shall discuss in their order of increasing importance to the present issue rather than in their natural causal order. The first concerns internal cultural dynamics after borrowing from another culture, and the second concerns selection at the point of borrowing, which obviously controls the material available to internal influences. Usually, what we observe at any time is the resultant of both processes. However, unexpected juxtapositions and transformations found within a receiving culture are often considered under the heading of dynamics.

The intention here is not to provide a comprehensive discussion of cultural diffusion, but only to bring to the attention of psychologists well-known themes that are disregarded by proponents of the bias position when they dismiss the importance of there being so little item–group interaction, thereby acting as though they subscribe to the Mercer–Kamin law. As used here, *diffusion* includes processes of cultural transmission between groups that many anthropologists include under *acculturation* (e.g., Herskovits, 1938/1958, Chap. 1); all anthropologists recognize great overlap in the meaning of the two terms, however, and regard diffusion as the more general of the two (Beals, 1953; Herskovits, 1938/1958, pp. 10, 14–15; Linton, 1936, Chap. 19). The distinction between them is often based on the intensity and the continuity of contact between the two cultures—the former term implying more occasional and casual contact, the latter the degree of exposure attained when members of two cultures live among each other. Some writers also prefer the latter term when documentary data are available for study by historical methods (e.g., Herskovits, 1938/1958, p. 15). For present purposes, the two terms may be considered interchangeable.

Far from being static and passive in the acculturation process, the receiving culture is regarded by anthropologists as alive and dynamic. Mintz and Price (1976), for example, rejected the notion of "passive African recipients" (p. 18) and attributed to "early Afro-American cultures a fundamental dynamism, an expectation of cultural change as an integral feature of these systems" (p. 26). Internal dynamics in any one area of content, moreover, operate relatively independently from dynamics in other areas, as the following statement clearly implies:

> In terms of current knowledge, it seems reasonable to expect that almost any sub-system of an Afro-American culture—whether music, speech or religion—would be highly syncretistic in terms of its diverse African origins, as well as in terms of inputs from European (and often other) sources; and we must expect it to possess a built-in internal dynamism and a marked adaptiveness to changing social conditions as well. (Mintz & Price, 1976, p. 32)

Similarly, Herskovits (1941), writing of revivalism in religion, stated:

> Whether Negroes borrowed from whites or whites from Negroes, in this or any other aspect of culture, it must always be remembered that the borrowing was never achieved without resultant change in what was borrowed, and, in addition, without incorporating elements which orig-

inated in the new habitat that . . . give the new form its distinctive quality.
(p. 225)

Mintz and Price's (1976) comment on this passage is worth noting: "'borrowing' may not best express the reality at all—'creating' or 'remodelling' may make it clearer" (p. 44). Herskovits (1945b) himself used the phrase "reworking under diffusion" (p. 156).

Elsewhere, Herskovits (1945a) made clear that the situation of the black in the New World necessitated no exceptions to the general rule that diffusion is heavily accompanied by constant dynamic change:

> It is today clear that no two peoples have ever been in contact but that they have taken new ideas and new customs from each other, and this quite independently of whether that contact was friendly or hostile, whether it was between groups of the same size or of unequal size, whether differences of prestige existed between them or they met on a plane of equality.
>
> The conception of culture on which our hypotheses are based thus envisages the operation of the principle of constant change—through borrowing and internal innovation. (p. 18)

The complexity of the acculturation process is revealed in the following quotation describing culture contact in South Africa:

> As a result of these contacts, certain traits of culture formerly possessed by the BaKxatla have either disappeared completely or appear to be doing so, others have been much or only slightly modified, and still others appear to have remained largely intact. Other traits, again, have been taken over wholly or in part from Western civilization. Some have been widely accepted, others only to a limited extent. (Schapera, 1936, p. 227, after Herskovits, 1938/1958, p. 62)

The acceptance of European traits among the BaKxatla, even when they were accepted, was not uniform over persons, furthermore, "Some people are very conservative, while others have discarded many of the traditional customs and beliefs in favour of European institutions" (Schapera, 1936, p. 233).

All the preceding descriptions are of vigorous processes within receiving cultures that disrupt and rearrange whatever relations had existed among cultural contents in their group of origin prior to contact, and that give rise to novel juxtapositions, often involving entirely new material from the receiving culture. Some of the resulting effects are conveyed by the anthropologists' use of such terms as "amalgam of culture" (Herskovits, 1938/1958, p. 65), "syncretisms," and "substitutions" (Mintz & Price, 1976, pp. 29–30). These anthropological terms give recognition to what the psychologist would view as content–group interactions involving materials from both cultures. The internal processes, however, are clearly more general than that, for they entail the abundant formation of content–group interactions during diffusion that are either based on materials taken from both cultures or taken simply from either one alone. To the extent that test items are cultural elements, too, or draw on the content of cultural elements, whether from one or both cultures originally, the turbulence introduced into the diffusion process from such dynamic sources would inevitably be reflected in item–group interaction. The absence of important amounts of item–group interaction over heterogeneous contents would indicate either that the diffusion process had run its course with respect to the content of the items (i.e., that the culturally dependent aspects of the items had been assimilated), or that the items were not sensitive to purely cultural differences between the two groups in the first place.

These descriptions of internal dynamics underscore the significance that I attached earlier to the fact that minority–minority rank order of difficulty correlations, instead of being lower than those between each minority group and whites, were usually just as high, and instead of equaling or falling below the product of the correlations of each with whites, were significantly higher than those products. The active dynamic processes peculiar to each receiving culture would, in fact, lead us to expect minority–minority correlations to be even lower than the products if test performance reflected the effects of incomplete diffusion, that is, if bias were operative. One should not mistakenly judge this result, therefore, as though its importance were indicated by the small size of the differences between correlations that serve as tests of the theory underlying the bias position.

Selection is the other of the two major influences on how culture diffuses; as it is also the better known, only a few sample quotations are necessary. Herskovits (1945a), for example, recognized the complications caused by "the selective nature of borrowing" (p. 21) and stated, "Studies of cultural transmission in process have demonstrated that borrowing is never indiscriminate, but is selective" (1951, p. 637). Linton (1936) stated, "Because of . . . varying . . . receptivity, traits always spread from their origin points irregularly and certain traits may be diffused with amazing speed while others diffuse slowly, if at all" (p. 331); "It is easy to imagine situations in which . . . many elements from certain sections of a culture will have been presented and even accepted while few or none have been presented from other sections" (p. 337); "Even traits which originate in the same center spread irregularly and travel at different speeds" (p. 330).

The upshot of all of these descriptions of ways in which the distribution of the new contents in the receiving culture is affected by diffusion is depicted in Figure 1. There, using his ratings, I have graphed the locations of three Afro-American cultural groups on what Herskovits (1945a) conceived of as an African-European cultural "continuum" (p. 12), for each of 10 major areas of cultural content. Herskovits was, of course, the preeminent authority on the relative representation of African and European influences in the various cultures of New World blacks. In this study, he created a scale of intensity of Africanisms and rated each of 17 New World black populations on the extent of their maximum degree of African retention in each of the 10 domains of cultural content. To avoid a cluttered graph, I have presented the ratings for only the two United States groupings and, for contrast, one other.

To understand the graphed ratings fully, it is necessary to know what Herskovits intended, although their general import is apparent at a glance. Herskovits (1945a) explained:

> Since it is apparent that in every part of the New World where Negroes live, excepting only the Guiana Bush, class differences operate so as to make for variation in the number and intensity of Africanisms within each Negro group, our table will record only that degree of retention for each group which is closest to African custom. (p. 15)

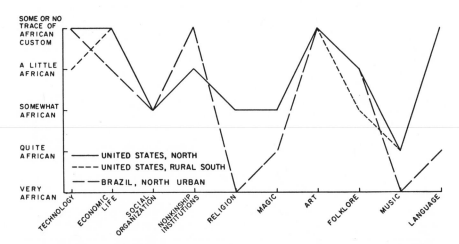

FIGURE 1. Differential diffusion, according to area of content, of European culture among three New World black populations, as shown by location on the African-European continuum. (Based on ratings by Herskovits, 1945a, Table I.)

One of the problems in making such ratings, of course, is in deciding whether they should reflect the central tendency or the extreme conditions in one of the tails of the distribution. Herskovits opted for the tail conditions, and so, his ratings can be characterized as reflecting the trailing edge of assimilation within each group over the various domains, rather than the average or the leading edge. Thus, he explained that Bahian blacks were rated most African in language because only they had retained certain African tongues intact, although in their daily speech they spoke the same Portuguese spoken by other Brazilians "with fewer elements of African vocabulary, pronunciation or grammar than is found in the speech of almost any other New World Negro group" (p. 15). If read in the upward direction, therefore, the graphed profiles can be interpreted as mappings of the maximum extent of diffusion of European traits to blacks in each of the domains, as indexed by the replacement of one culture by the other. The leading edge of assimilation, populated by certain blacks in each group, might well graph as parallel to the baseline, but at the top of the graph, had Herskovits provided the ratings. The modal or central tendency, therefore, would probably graph as a weighted compromise between the two extreme edges, that is, as roughly parallel to the trailing edge now plotted, but with its range of variations dampened somewhat. It is reasonable to assume, especially in view of the principles of diffusion just reviewed, not to mention Herskovits's own confidence in interpreting his results, that all of the various ways of indexing cultural diffusion would correlate substantially with each other and would tell essentially the same story, except for the leading edge, which may have no variance. These considerations should aid in reading Figure 1, which plainly indicates that all areas of content do not diffuse at the same rate, contrary to proposition (a) of the Mercer–Kamin law. This contradiction cannot be laid to differences in difficulty among the cultural areas, because the figure shows that the lines cross each other, so that there are not consistent differences in difficulty according to area.

My interpretations so far are consistent with Herskovits's own interpretations of his ratings:

> It cannot be too strongly stressed that in every area of the New World, except in the Guiana Bush, variation in African forms of behavior stretches from the point of greatest intensity indicated in our table to almost complete conformity with European ways of life. The problem thus becomes one of accounting for differing degrees of variability in the different populations studied. (Herskovits, 1945a, p. 15)
>
> Table I presents, then, those degrees of intensities of Africanisms, listed by aspect of culture and by region in terms of the most African-like

manifestation of a given cultural aspect or institution. (Herskovits, 1945a, p. 16)

Herskovits (1945a) remarked on the differing degree of variation over cultural aspects within the various black groups: "Turning now to consider the different degree to which differing elements in each of these cultures have responded to contact with non-African ways of life, we see that the carry-over of Africanisms *is anything but uniform over the individual cultures, being far greater in some aspects than in others*" (pp. 16–17, emphasis added); and on the differing degree of variation within particular aspects over the groups: "One further fact which emerges from our table is the differing variability, over the New World as a whole, of the several aspects of the cultures as these have been listed" (p. 17). Thus, as Figure 1 shows, differences in variability occur along two dimensions.

The point of Figure 1, of course, is not whether Herskovits's ratings accurately depict the locations of blacks today on the European-African cultural continuum, but that they testify to the great amount of interaction generated in the course of ongoing diffusion. The two components of variation in the variabilities that Herskovits commented on guarantee interaction, which is revealed by the contrast between the jaggedness of the profiles and the implicit flat line at the top of the graph that would represent Europeans. As that line would have little or no variance itself on the African-European continuum, its rank-order correlation with the degree of European culture among any group of blacks over the 10 cultural aspects would be virtually zero. Viewing the ratings as "passing rates" and the cultural aspects as 10 "items" or "subtests" enables us to quantify the considerable amount of interaction, for example, even between two black populations, in this case those labeled "United States, North" and "Brazil, North Urban" in Figure 1, neither of which has a totally flat and hence noncorrelating profile. In their case, the rank-order correlation is only .68, although the "passing rates" span the entire range and thus show plenty of variability. I mention such correlations only to orient the reader to certain parallels between item–group interaction and the diffusion data. The utility of correlation as an index of interaction in the case of Figure 1 is limited, because the diffusion data are expressed in a manner that totally obscures the difficulty dimension even among Europeans.

Just as there is an implicit flat line at the top of the graph that would represent Europeans, there is another at the bottom that would represent native Africans in their original setting. Herskovits

(1945a, p. 17) himself noted that his most African population, the Guiana Bush blacks, showed the least variation across the 10 cultural aspects (i.e., had the flattest profile). All 10 of their ratings would fall within the two lowermost scale positions in Figure 1.

We see, therefore, that jagged rather than flat profiles are characteristic of populations in which diffusion is incomplete and perhaps still in progress following contact with another culture. By definition, *cultural bias* also refers to a situation in which diffusion has begun but is incomplete, for the idea itself implies that it is possible for diffusion to proceed further and thus raise test scores. Because jagged and differing profiles represent conditions in which interaction is rife, the cultural bias situation is by definition one that occurs in a context typified by an abundance of content–group interaction. Consequently, the rank order of difficulty of items among whites would be especially likely to differ from their order among blacks if the differences between the races in passing items really reflected their differential familiarity with the cultural materials that display such jagged profiles in Figure 1. This makes the fact that their rank orders differ so little doubly meaningful (Tables 2, 13, and 14).

That Herskovits's data apply specifically to New World blacks and include those in the United States is simply an added fillip. Their main significance is as a demonstration, first, of the principles of diffusion described earlier; second, of the irregularity or content–group interaction that typically accompanies diffusion; and third, of the interesting fact that interaction is apt to be most intense (as measured by mean differences between content areas in two groups, as the rank correlation can be difficult to interpret in the absence of variation within fully European and African groups) when diffusion is well under way but incomplete. The third point is perhaps best left in its present crudely specified form, but that does not diminish the fact that its conditions obviously coincide with those in which the issue of cultural bias usually arises. Although only three populations are shown, the graph provides a good idea of both the great variability within typical New World black populations and the range of that variability, for the two United States black populations in Figure 1 rank only eleventh and twelfth in variability of profile of the 14 for which complete ratings were available, and the "Brazil, North Urban" population ranks first, yet all show considerable variation in their profiles, in contrast to what the Mercer–Kamin law would predict. As it would clearly be hazardous to predict the standing or rating on any one aspect from knowledge of a black population's absolute standing on any other aspect, but quite safe to do so for

Europeans, the data show precisely the lack of coherence in the receiving populations that Kamin seemed to imply with his "bits of knowledge" and "bits of information" phrases, thus indicating that even in his own mind Kamin may have found it difficult to conceive of cultural bias unattended by high degrees of interaction.

From a historical standpoint, it is of interest that the Herskovits data, which belong to the period circa 1945, are bracketed chronologically by measures of item–group interaction in Tables 2, 13, and 14 that show no trend between 1918 and the present, and by measures of the mean IQ difference between blacks and whites that also show no trend over time. According to Shuey's review (1966, p. 503), the race difference among elementary-school children was 1.0 white SDs in the period 1921–1944 and 1.1 white SDs between 1945 and 1965. Consequently, even if one were to suppose that cultural interaction due to diffusion had decreased among blacks in the United States since Herskovits made his ratings, in order to try to account for the lack of item–group interaction in recent data, the fact would remain that intelligence test items have shown no sensitivity to cultural interaction going back to 1918, when the amount must have been at least as great as that portrayed in Figure 1, if not greater.

CONCLUSION

The various criteria of internal validity reviewed in the first part of this article show no important differences between blacks and whites even in minute details of test performance, in accordance with the conclusions of Jensen (1980a) and many others, and thus no evidence of bias. However, the unusual cumulative deficit phenomenon, which does not figure in the conventional race difference, deserves further attention in view of its heuristic potential. Mercer generally agrees with the internal validity findings, but she refuses to interpret them as strong evidence that test bias is not present. In particular, she dismisses the implications of item–group interaction studies concerning the plausibility of the bias argument. Because that argument has long claimed that the substantial depression of item passing rates among certain minorities is simply an artifact of imperfect cultural diffusion, it has been embarrassed by the high rank order of difficulty correlations that have emerged subsequently, for those correlations reveal more regularity between groups across heterogeneous types of content than would square with the intuitions of many persons concerning the way in which culture normally diffuses.

Somewhat belatedly, Mercer now seeks to alter our expectations concerning the regularity and the predictability of cultural diffusion by assuring us that such regularity is to be expected. However, she herself has performed no new investigations of cultural diffusion in support of her assurance, and she cites no literature. Instead, she describes three mechanisms whose purpose it is to persuade us that high rank order of difficulty correlations are mere truisms.

On close inspection, these explicit mechanisms turn out to be little more than reassertions of her original implicit assurance, now tailored specifically to three sets of broad item domains. By thus dividing up the work and reducing the heterogeneity of content whose lack of interaction each mechanism must explain, Mercer essentially offers us a paler or weaker version of what I call the *Mercer–Kamin law*. Even at that, her mechanisms fail to account for the lack of group-by-subtest interaction, but this failure is obscured by the fact that the rank order of difficulty correlation is relatively insensitive to the presence or absence of that type of interaction. With this omission no longer glossed over, it is apparent that Mercer's account of item–group interaction does depend on the Mercer–Kamin law as I stated it earlier, after all.

Now let us turn to the role of that law in the bias argument. Philosophers of science recognize that no hypothesis is tested in isolation, that is, without depending on auxiliary hypotheses as premises to enable us to deduce testable consequences of the hypothesis of interest. A troublesome outcome of this circumstance is that unless the auxiliary hypotheses are firmly held or established (e.g., the laws of optics when examining a crucial slide under the microscope), they can be manipulated to protect the tested hypothesis from disconfirming evidence. This realization and the infinite regress it implies are sometimes known as the *Duhemian problem* (see Salmon, 1975). Here, testing the bias argument with measures of item–group interaction depends on auxiliary hypotheses concerning the manner in which culture is transmitted from one group to another by the processes that I have discussed under the heading of diffusion. The parts of the Mercer–Kamin law other than the proposition asserting bias, (b), represent the particular versions of those auxiliary hypotheses about diffusion that serve to protect (b) against disconfirmation by item–group studies that show no interaction of any consequence, as, in effect, they state that culture must diffuse in a manner that produces little or no interaction among intelligence test items.

In general, there is nothing objectionable about modifying auxiliary hypotheses in this manner as long as that modification is done explicitly, to alert others that crucial premises that they normally take for granted no longer apply. Accordingly, it is important to recognize that the cultural bias position of Mercer and Kamin is really represented by the *conjunction* of (b) and the other propositions of the Mercer–Kamin law and not just by (b) alone. For that reason, I placed (b), the claim of bias, within the body of the Mercer–Kamin law rather than stating it separately. Unless the modification of auxiliary hypotheses is explicit, there is nothing to restrain anyone from modifying them only implicitly to avoid paying the costs in plausibility usually associated with casually sacrificing principles that other scientists regard as too firmly established to be treated so cavalierly when no new evidence has been brought to bear. Of course, if Mercer and Kamin disagree with my assessment of the law's plausibility, they should show no reluctance in promulgating it.

Like many such conjunctions of threatened hypotheses and their specially modified protecting auxiliaries, the conjunction represented by the Mercer–Kamin law is less plausible than either hypothesis alone, especially the threatened one alone (e.g., my novel diagnosis of patient Jones is correct *and* the laws of optics fail when I examine his slide), because their probability is defined by the product of the probabilities of the conjuncts, assuming those probabilities are independent. Even if not independent, their joint probability is determined largely by the improbable auxiliary, whose low probability is not apt to be much influenced by assuming the other conjunct. Hence, it is essential that proponents of the bias position not be allowed the luxury of asserting each conjunct in relative isolation at different points in their argument, thereby taking advantage of the greater plausibility of each half when stated by itself.

In the present case, a considerable advantage in stating the conjuncts separately can be traced to the difficulty that we have in distinguishing the relevant components of variance clearly when we discuss the propositions of the Mercer–Kamin law in isolation from one another. To be meaningful, the discussion requires that the component of difficulty due to cultural bias be conceived of as orthogonal to the component of difficulty due to the intelligence that items require in order to be passed. Hence, to take the second conjunct as an example, when Kamin (1980, p. 116) and Mercer (1978–1979, p. 14) say, in effect, that it is reasonable for the order of item difficulties to be the same in both races, we must be careful not to find this assertion plausible for reasons having to do exclusively with intelligence.

To the extent that group differences in passing rates of items are shaped by intelligence, or by direct influences on the z score or the latent trait, those differences are valid. For this reason, I stated Table 12 in terms of absolute differences in standardized percentages passing, although technically its point could have been made with absolute differences in standardized z scores. However, the natural metric of diffusion to persons is in multiples of persons, not z scores, and standardized percentages help maintain the analytic distinction between differences that are due to culture on the one hand and differences that are due to intelligence on the other by representing the interaction data in the form more relevant to cultural diffusion in the broadest sense—that is, by representing the rate of diffusion regardless of the extent to which mental ability differences may be implicated. The cultural bias argument must properly be confined conceptually to group differences in passing rates that are independent of intelligence. This is one basic reason, incidentally, that interaction can serve as a useful index of such cultural differences, because item–group interaction is clearly orthogonal to the common g factor. Another is that diffusion is typically pregnant with interaction, as my review of internal dynamics and selection showed.

In light of the foregoing, the more correct and revealing statement by proponents of the bias position would run as follows: "The amount of variation in the order of items due to cultural differences is small in relation to the amount due to intelligence, *but* the amount of difference between groups in difficulty is large and entirely due to cultural differences." With the clauses in reverse order and minus the last six words, this is precisely the kind of statement that Jensen (1980a) has operationalized with his "group difference-interaction ratio" (p. 561). Jensen used his ratio to question whether cultural differences can account for the group difference, but in this chapter, I have explored the implications of framing the question in its other direction, not typically considered by psychologists, namely: Can large cultural differences be present without creating more interaction than we usually observe? To return to the first conjunct of the bias argument, the real problem is not whether there could be considerable cultural bias (a proposition that has some plausibility by itself, particularly if one imagines interaction simultaneously present), but whether there could be considerable cultural bias *without* more interaction, perhaps without *any*.

Logically, the answer to the last question is "yes" because, according to the mathematics alone, bias, as a main effect, can be present without interaction. However, it is a serious mistake to suppose that scientists depend on logic alone in resolving empirical controversies, without considering probability too. Hypotheses accepted by scientists depend on the fact that empirical phenomena leave diagnostic traces or signatures, even if those traces are relatively subtle in relation to the scale of the original event of interest. One of the more famous traces, for example, is that of the 3°K cosmic background radiation that informs cosmologists that the universe was at a much earlier time thousands of times smaller and hotter than it is now, thus leading to a resolution between the competing "steady-state" and "big-bang" hypotheses of its origin (Weinberg, 1977). The real scientific problem concerning bias, therefore, is whether an incomplete and energetic diffusion process could occur between entire cultures without leaving any special traces other than the undiagnostic test-score difference between races, which resembles other sources of differences, such as maturation, in its fine details.

To address this question more rigorously, I introduced in the middle section of this chapter an unusual triplet of test items that function as a segment of interval scale among whites (and blacks) and hence also as a far more refined and sensitive instrument for probing important theoretical questions than was hitherto available. This instrument, consisting of the three moderately long digits-backward items, was also used to enhance our understanding of the sources of noise in less sensitive items. To the extent that linearity and thus the evidence for an interval scale remained perfect in any two groups, item–group interaction would be absent.

The instrument successfully detected small effects attributable to the shape of the underlying distribution of ability that had been largely obscured for other items by their noisiness. When it was applied to the problem of seeking interactive traces of the diffusion processes supposedly underlying bias, however, in the final section of the chapter, none could be found. Other searches for small effects diagnostic of cultural diffusion, such as differences between minority–minority and majority–minority rank order of difficulty correlations, were equally unsuccessful. The delicate relation of the digits items to underlying normality within white samples was also surprisingly undisturbed in cross-racial comparisons. At the same time, evidence was presented that cultural diffusion is in general a highly interactive and noisy process, if not a turbulent one, that announces its presence with a profusion of strong content–group interactions. Taken together, these facts make it extremely difficult to assert the Mercer–Kamin law in the new and more sweeping fashion required to account both for the absence of item–group interaction in the digits data, which cannot be set apart from other items as exceptions in any way that would leave the bias argument intact, and for the consistent intercalation of the digits items with other items quite heterogeneous in content.

REFERENCES

Achinstein, P. *Law and explanation: An essay in the philosophy of science.* London: Oxford University Press, 1971.

Angoff, W. H. *A technique for the investigation of cultural differences.* Paper presented at the annual meeting of the American Psychological Association, Honolulu, September 1972. (ERIC Document Reproduction Service No. ED 069686.)

Angoff, W. H. Use of difficulty and discrimination indices for detecting item bias. In R. A. Berk (Ed.), *Handbook of methods for detecting test bias.* Baltimore: Johns Hopkins University Press, 1982.

Angoff, W. H., & Ford, S. F. Item-race interaction on a test of scholastic aptitude. *Journal of Educational Measurement,* 1973, *10,* 95–105.

Baughman, E. E., & Dahlstrom, W. G. *Negro and white children: A psychological study in the rural South.* New York: Academic Press, 1968.

Baumeister, A. A. Serial memory span thresholds of normal and mentally retarded children. *Journal of Educational Psychology,* 1974, *66,* 889–894.

Bayley, N. Consistency and variability in the growth of intelligence from birth to eighteen years. *Journal of Genetic Psychology,* 1949, *75,* 165–196.

Beals, R. Acculturation. In A. L. Kroeber (Ed.), *Anthropology today.* Chicago: University of Chicago Press, 1953.

Belmont, J. M., & Butterfield, E. C. What the development of short-term memory is. *Human Development,* 1971, *14,* 236–248.

Benbow, C. P., & Stanley, J. C. Consequences in high school and college of sex differences in mathematical reasoning ability: A longitudinal perspective. *American Educational Research Journal,* 1982, *19,* 598–622.

Berk, R. A. (Ed.). *Handbook of methods for detecting test bias.* Baltimore: Johns Hopkins University Press, 1982.

Bond, H. M. *The education of the Negro in the American social order.* New York: Octagon Books, 1966. (Originally published, 1934.)

Box, G. E. P. Non-normality and tests on variances. *Biometrika,* 1953, *40,* 318–335.

Brotemarkle, R. A. Some memory span test problems: An analytical study at the college-adult level. *Psychological Clinic,* 1924, *15,* 229–258.

Case, R. Validation of a neo-Piagetian mental capacity construct. *Journal of Experimental Child Psychology,* 1972, *14,* 287–302.

Case, R., & Globerson, T. Field independence and central computing space. *Child Development,* 1974, *45,* 772–778.

Chase, C. I., & Pugh, R. C. Social class and performance on an intelligence test. *Journal of Educational Measurement,* 1971, *8,* 197–202.

Chiang, A., & Atkinson, R. C. Individual differences and interrelationships among a select set of cognitive skills. *Memory and Cognition,* 1976, *4,* 661–672.

Cleary, T. A., & Hilton, T. L. An investigation of item bias. *Educational and Psychological Measurement,* 1968, *28,* 61–75.

College Entrance Examination Board. *Profiles, college-bound seniors, 1981.* New York: Author, 1982.

Crannell, C. W., & Parrish, J. M. A comparison of immediate memory span for digits, letters, and words. *Journal of Psychology,* 1957, *44,* 319–327.

Darlington, R. B., & Boyce, C. M. The validity of Jensen's statistical methods. *Behavioral and Brain Sciences,* 1982, *5,* 323–324.

Dawley, D. *A nation of lords: The autobiography of the Vice Lords.* Garden City, New York: Anchor Books, 1973.

Dempster, F. N. Memory span and short-term memory capacity: A developmental study. *Journal of Experimental Child Psychology,* 1978, *26,* 419–431.

Dempster, F. N. Memory span: Sources of individual and developmental differences. *Psychological Bulletin,* 1981, *89,* 63–100.

Dempster, F. N., & Cooney, J. B. Individual differences in digit span, susceptibility to proactive interference, and aptitude/achievement test scores. *Intelligence,* 1982, *6,* 399–416.

Dempster, F. N., & Zinkgraf, S. A. Individual differences in digit span and chunking. *Intelligence,* 1982, *6,* 201–213.

Dorfman, D. D. The Cyril Burt question: New findings. *Science,* 1978, *201,* 1177–1186.

"Dunbar Report" (untitled). Baltimore: Baltimore City Public Schools, 1982.

Durning, K. P. *Preliminary assessment of the Navy Memory for Numbers Test.* Unpublished master's thesis, San Diego State College, 1968.

Globerson, T. Mental capacity and cognitive functioning: Developmental and social class differences. *Developmental Psychology,* 1983, *19,* 225–230.

Gordon, R. A. Examining labelling theory: The case of mental retardation. In W. R. Gove (Ed.), *The labelling of deviance* (2nd ed.). Beverly Hills, Calif.: Sage Publications, 1980. (Originally published, 1975.)

Gordon, R. A. Labelling theory, mental retardation, and public policy: *Larry P.* and other developments since 1974. In W. R. Gove (Ed.), *The labelling of deviance* (2nd ed.). Beverly Hills, Calif.: Sage Publications, 1980.

Gordon, R. A., & Rudert, E. E. Bad news concerning IQ tests. *Sociology of Education,* 1979, *52,* 174–190.

Gutkin, T. B., & Reynolds, C. R. Factorial similarity of the WISC-R for Anglos and Chicanos referred for psychological services. *Journal of School Psychology,* 1980, *18,* 34–39. (a)

Gutkin, T. B., & Reynolds, C. R. *WISC-R factor equivalence across race: Examining the standardization sample.* Paper presented at the annual meeting of the American Psychological Association, Montreal, September 1980. (b)

Guttman, L. Introduction to facet design and analysis. *Proceedings of the Fifteenth International Congress of Psychology, Brussels, 1957.* Amsterdam: North-Holland Publishing, 1959.

Guttman, L. The nonmetric breakthrough for the behavioral sciences. *Proceedings of the Second National Conference on Data Processing.* Rehovot: Information Processing Association of Israel, 1966.

Halligan, P. D. Personal communication, January 19, 1982.

Harris, A. J., & Lovinger, R. J. Longitudinal measures of the intelligence of disadvantaged Negro adolescents. *School Review,* 1968, *76,* 60–66.

Herskovits, M. J. *The myth of the Negro past.* New York: Harper and Brothers, 1941.

Herskovits, M. J. Problem, method and theory in Afroamerican studies. *Afroamerica,* 1945, *1,* 5–24. (a)

Herskovits, M. J. The processes of cultural change. In R. Linton (Ed.), *The science of man in the world crisis*. New York: Columbia University Press, 1945. (b)

Herskovits, M. J. *Man and his works: The science of cultural anthropology*. New York: Knopf, 1951.

Herskovits, M. L. *Acculturation: The study of culture contact*. Gloucester, Mass.: Peter Smith, 1958. (Originally published, 1938.)

Hills, J. R., & Stanley, J. C. Prediction of freshman grades from SAT and from level 4 of SCAT in three predominantly Negro state colleges. *Proceedings of the 76th Annual Convention of the American Psychological Association*, 1968, 3, 241–242.

Hills, J. R., & Stanley, J. C. Easier test improves prediction of black students' college grades. *Journal of Negro Education*, 1970, 39, 320–324.

Honzik, M. P., Macfarlane, J. W., & Allen, L. The stability of mental test performance between two and eighteen years. *Journal of Experimental Education*, 1948, 17, 309–324.

Hsia, J. *Cognitive assessment of Asian Americans*. Paper presented at Symposium on bilingual research, sponsored by NIE-NCBR, Los Alamitos, Calif., September 3–5, 1980.

Hunt, J. McV. Has compensatory education failed? Has it been attempted? *Harvard Educational Review*, 1969, 39, 278–300.

Ironson, G. H. Use of chi-square and latent trait approaches for detecting item bias. In R. A. Berk (Ed.), *Handbook of methods for detecting test bias*. Baltimore: Johns Hopkins University Press, 1982.

Jacobs, J. Experiments on "prehension." *Mind*, 1887, 12, 75–79.

Jennrich, R. I. An asymptotic χ^2 test for the equality of two correlation matrices. *Journal of the American Statistical Association*, 1970, 65, 904–912.

Jensen, A. R. How much can we boost IQ and scholastic achievement? *Harvard Educational Review*, 1969, 39, 1–123. (a)

Jensen, A. R. Reducing the heredity-environment uncertainty: A reply. *Harvard Educational Review*, 1969, 39, 449–483. (b)

Jensen, A. R. *Educability and group differences*. New York: Harper & Row, 1973.

Jensen, A. R. Cumulative deficit: A testable hypothesis? *Developmental Psychology*, 1974, 10, 996–1019. (a)

Jensen, A. R. How biased are culture-loaded tests? *Genetic Psychology Monographs*, 1974, 90, 185–244. (b)

Jensen, A. R. Cumulative deficit in IQ of blacks in the rural South. *Developmental Psychology*, 1977, 13, 184–191. (a)

Jensen, A. R. An examination of culture bias in the Wonderlic Personnel Test. *Intelligence*, 1977, 1, 51–64. (b)

Jensen, A. R. *Bias in mental testing*. New York: Free Press, 1980. (a)

Jensen, A. R. Correcting the bias against mental testing: A preponderance of peer agreement. *Behavioral and Brain Sciences*, 1980, 3, 359–368. (b)

Jensen, A. R. Uses of sibling data in educational and psychological research. *American Educational Research Journal*, 1980, 17, 153–170. (c)

Jensen, A. R., & Figueroa, R. A. Forward and backward digit span interaction with race and IQ: Predictions from Jensen's theory. *Journal of Educational Psychology*, 1975, 67, 882–893.

Jensen, A. R., & Osborne, R. T. Forward and backward digit span interaction with race and IQ: A longitudinal developmental comparison. *Indian Journal of Psychology*, 1979, 54, 75–87.

Jensen, A. R., & Reynolds, C. R. Race, social class and ability patterns on the WISC-R. *Personality and Individual Differences*, 1982, *3*, 423–438.

Kamin, L. J. Expert witness testimony. *Larry P. et al. v. Wilson Riles et al.* Reporters' daily transcript, United States District Court, Northern District of California, 1977.

Kamin, L. J. Expert witness testimony. *Parents in Action on Special Education (P.A.S.E.) et al. v. Joseph P. Hannon et al.* Reporters' daily transcript, United States District Court, Northern District of Illinois, 1980.

Kaufman, A. S. WISC-R research: Implications for interpretation. *School Psychology Digest*, 1979, *8*, 5–27.

Kaufman, A. S., & Doppelt, J. E. Analysis of WISC-R standardization data in terms of the stratification variables. *Child Development*, 1976, *47*, 165–171.

Keiser, R. L. *The Vice Lords: Warriors of the streets*. New York: Holt, Rinehart and Winston, 1969.

Kempthorne, O., & Wolins, L. Testing reveals a big social problem. *Behavioral and Brain Sciences*, 1982, *5*, 327–336.

Kennedy, W. A. A follow-up normative study of Negro intelligence and achievement. *Monographs of the Society for Research in Child Development*, 1969, *34*(2, Serial No. 126).

Kennedy, W. A., Van de Reit, V., & White, J. C., Jr. A normative sample of intelligence and achievement of Negro elementary school children in the Southeastern United States. *Monographs of the Society for Research in Child Development*, 1963, *28*(6, Serial No. 90).

Labovitz, S. The assignment of numbers to rank order categories. *American Sociological Review*, 1970, *35*, 515–524.

Linton, R. *The study of man: An introduction*. New York: Appleton-Century, 1936.

Lynn, R. The intelligence of the Japanese. *Bulletin of the British Psychology Society*, 1977, *30*, 69–72.

Lynn, R. IQ in Japan and the United States shows a growing disparity. *Nature*, 1982, *297*, 222–223.

Lynn, R., & Dziobon, J. On the intelligence of the Japanese and other Mongoloid peoples. *Personality and Individual Differences*, 1980, *1*, 95–96.

McGurk, F. C. J. Race differences—Twenty years later. *Homo*, 1975, *26*, 219–239.

McNemar, Q. *The revision of the Stanford-Binet Scale: An analysis of the standardization data*. Boston: Houghton Mifflin, 1942.

Medley, D. M., & Quirk, T. J. The application of a factorial design to the study of cultural bias in general culture items on the National Teacher Examination. *Journal of Educational Measurement*, 1974, *11*, 235–245.

Mefferd, R. B., Jr., Wieland, B. A., & James, W. E. Repetitive psychometric measures: Digit span. *Psychological Reports*, 1966, *18*, 3–10.

Mercer, J. R. Expert witness testimony. *Larry P. et al. v. Wilson Riles et al.* Reporters' daily transcript, United States District Court, Northern District of California, 1977.

Mercer, J. R. Test "validity," "bias," and "fairness": An analysis from the perspective of the sociology of knowledge. *Interchange*, 1978–1979, *9*, 1–16.

Mercer, J. R. In defense of racially and culturally non-discriminatory assessment. *School Psychology Digest*, 1979, *8*, 89–115. (a)

Mercer, J. R. *SOMPA technical manual*. New York: Psychological Corporation, 1979. (b)

Miele, F. Cultural bias in the WISC. *Intelligence*, 1979, *3*, 149–164.

Mintz, S. W., & Price, R. *An anthropological approach to the Afro-American past: A Caribbean perspective*. Philadelphia: Institute for the Study of Human Issues, 1976.

Mood, A. M., Graybill, F. A., & Boes, D. C. *Introduction to the theory of statistics* (3rd ed.). New York: McGraw-Hill, 1974.

Nichols, P. L. *The effects of heredity and environment on intelligence test performance in 4 and 7 year old white and Negro sibling pairs.* Doctoral dissertation, University of Minnesota, 1970. (University Microfilms No. 71–18, 874.)

Osborne, R. T. Racial differences in mental growth and school achievement: A longitudinal study. *Psychological Reports,* 1960, *7,* 233–239.

Osborne, R. T. *Twins: Black and white.* Athens, Ga: Foundation for Human Understanding, 1980.

Reschly, D. J. WISC-R factor structures among Anglos, blacks, Chicanos, and native-American Papagos. *Journal of Consulting and Clinical Psychology,* 1978, *46,* 417–422.

Reynolds, C. R. The invariance of the factorial validity of the Metropolitan Readiness Tests for blacks, whites, males, and females. *Educational and Psychological Measurement,* 1979, *39,* 1047–1052.

Reynolds, C. R. Differential construct validity of a preschool battery for blacks, whites, males, and females. *Journal of School Psychology,* 1980, *18,* 112–125.

Reynolds, C. R. The problem of bias in psychological assessment. In C. R. Reynolds & T. B. Gutkin (Eds.), *The handbook of school psychology.* New York: Wiley, 1982.

Rock, D. A., & Werts, C. E. *Construct validity of the SAT across populations—An empirical confirmatory study* (RDR 78–79, No. 5). Princeton, N.J.: Educational Testing Service, 1979.

Rogers, E. M. *Diffusion of innovations.* New York: Free Press, 1962.

Rucci, A. J., & Tweney, R. D. Analysis of variance and the "second discipline" of scientific psychology: A historical account. *Psychological Bulletin,* 1980, *87,* 166–184.

Salmon, W. C. Confirmation and relevance. In G. Maxwell & R. M. Anderson, Jr. (Eds.), *Induction, probability, and confirmation.* Minnesota Studies in the Philosophy of Science (Vol. 6). Minneapolis: University of Minnesota Press, 1975.

Sandoval, J. The WISC-R and internal evidence of test bias with minority groups. *Journal of Consulting and Clinical Psychology,* 1979, *47,* 919–927.

Sandoval, J., & Miille, M. P. W. Accuracy of judgments of WISC-R item difficulty for minority groups. *Journal of Consulting and Clinical Psychology,* 1980, *48,* 249–253.

Scarr, S. The effects of family background: A study of cognitive differences among black and white twins. In S. Scarr (Ed.), *Race, social class, and individual differences in I.Q.* Hillsdale, N.J.: Erlbaum, 1981.

Schapera, I. The contributions of Western civilization to modern Kxatla culture. *Transactions of the Royal Society of South Africa,* 1936, *24,* 221–252.

Scriven, M. The key property of physical laws—inaccuracy. In H. Feigl & G. Maxwell (Eds.), *Current issues in the philosophy of science.* New York: Holt, Rinehart & Winston, 1961.

Shuey, A. M. *The testing of Negro intelligence* (2nd ed.). New York: Social Science Press, 1966.

Siegel, S. *Nonparametric statistics for the behavioral sciences.* New York: McGraw-Hill, 1956.

Stanley, J. C. Plotting ANOVA interactions for ease of visual interpretation. *Educational and Psychological Measurement,* 1969, *29,* 793–797.

Stanley, J. C., & Porter, A. C. Correlation of scholastic aptitude test score with college grades for Negroes versus whites. *Journal of Educational Measurement,* 1967, *4,* 199–218.

Stinchcombe, A. L. Environment: The cumulation of effects is yet to be understood. *Harvard Educational Review*, 1969, *39*, 511–522.

Terman, L. M. *The measurement of intelligence: An explanation of and a complete guide for the use of the Stanford revision and extension of the Binet-Simon Intelligence Scale*. Boston: Houghton Mifflin, 1916.

Terman, L. M. Errors in scoring Binet tests. *Psychological Clinic*, 1918, *12*, 33–39.

Terman, L. M., & Merrill, M. A. *Measuring intelligence: A guide to the administration of the new revised Stanford-Binet tests of intelligence*. Boston: Houghton Mifflin, 1937.

Terman, L. M., & Merrill, M. A. *Stanford-Binet Intelligence Scale: Manual for the Third Revision, Form L-M*. Boston: Houghton Mifflin, 1960.

Terman, L. M., Lyman, G., Ordahl, G., Ordahl, L. E., Galbreath, N., & Talbert, W. *The Stanford revision and extension of the Binet-Simon scale for measuring intelligence*. Baltimore: Warwick & York, 1917.

Thomas, H. IQ, interval scales, and normal distributions. *Psychological Bulletin*, 1982, *91*, 198–202.

Tomlinson, H. Differences between pre-school Negro children and their older siblings on the Stanford-Binet scales. *Journal of Negro Education*, 1944, *13*, 474–479.

Torgerson, W. S. *Theory and methods of scaling*. New York: Wiley, 1958.

Vernon, P. E. *The abilities and achievements of Orientals in North America*. New York: Academic Press, 1982.

Vetta, A. Correlation, regression and biased science. *Behavioral and Brain Sciences*, 1980, *3*, 357–358.

Vetta, A. IQ or intelligence? *Behavioral and Brain Sciences*, 1982, *5*, 336–337.

Viteles, M. S. The children of a Jewish orphanage. *Psychological Clinic*, 1919, *12*, 248–254.

Wahlsten, D. Race, the heritability of IQ, and the intellectual scale of nature. *Behavioral and Brain Sciences*, 1980, *3*, 358–359.

Walker, H. M., & Lev, J. *Statistical inference*. New York: Holt, 1953.

Wechsler, D. *The measurement of adult intelligence*. Baltimore: Williams & Wilkins, 1939.

Wechsler, D. *Wechsler Intelligence Scale for Children manual*. New York: Psychological Corporation, 1949.

Wechsler, D. *Wechsler Intelligence Scale for Children—Revised*. New York: Psychological Corporation, 1974.

Weinberg, S. *The first three minutes; A modern view of the origin of the universe*. New York: Basic Books, 1977.

Wheeler, L. R. A comparative study of the intelligence of East Tennessee mountain children. *Journal of Educational Psychology*, 1942, *33*, 321–334.

Williams, R. L. The BITCH-100: A culture-specific test. *Journal of Afro-American Issues*, 1975, *3*, 103–116.

Yerkes, R. M. (Ed.). *Psychological examining in the United States Army*. Memoirs of the National Academy of Sciences (Vol. 15). Washington, D.C.: Government Printing Office, 1921.

Yule, G. U., & Kendall, M. G. *An introduction to the theory of statistics* (14th ed.). New York: Hafner Publishing, 1950.

CHAPTER ELEVEN

Test Bias

Concepts and Criticisms

ARTHUR R. JENSEN

As one who has been reading about test bias now for over 30 years, I have noticed a quite dramatic change in this literature within just the last decade. This development was auspicious, perhaps even essential, for the production of my most recent book, *Bias in Mental Testing* (1980a). Developments in the last decade made it possible to present a fairly comprehensive and systematic treatment of the topic. Prior to the 1970s, the treatment of test bias in the psychological literature was fragmentary, unsystematic, and conceptually confused. Clear and generally agreed-upon definitions of bias were lacking, as was a psychometrically defensible methodology for objectively recognizing test bias. The study of test bias, in fact, had not yet become a full-fledged subject in the field of psychometrics. The subject lacked the carefully thought-out rationale and statistical methodology that psychometrics had long invested in such topics as reliability, validity, and item selection.

All this has changed markedly in recent years. Test bias has now become one of the important topics in psychometrics. It is undergoing the systematic conceptual and methodological development worthy of one of the most technically sophisticated branches of the behavioral sciences. The earlier scattered and inchoate notions about

Parts of this chapter are taken from "Précis of Bias in Mental Testing" by A. R. Jensen, *Behavioral and Brain Sciences*, 1980, *3*, 325–333.

ARTHUR R. JENSEN ● Institute of Human Learning, University of California, Berkeley, California 94720.

bias have been sifted, rid of their patent fallacies, conceptualized in objective terms, and operationalized by statistical methods. What is emerging is a theoretical rationale of the nature of test bias, some rather clearly formulated, mutually consistent definitions, and statistically testable criteria of bias. Moreover, a large fund of impressively consistent empirical evidence has been amassed in connection with this discipline, finally permitting objective, often definitive, answers to the long-standing question of racial-cultural bias in many of the standardized mental tests widely used in America today in schools, colleges, and the armed forces, and for job selection.

The editors have asked me to act as a commentator on all the preceding chapters in this volume. Before taking up the many specific points in this task, however, I should first present a succinct overview of the main concepts and findings in this field, as I see it. I have presented it all in much greater detail in *Bias in Mental Testing*.

NATURE OF MENTAL TESTS

Mental ability tests are a means of quantifying individual differences in a variety of capabilities classified as *mental*. *Mental* means only that the individual differences in the capabilities elicited by the test are not primarily the result of differences in sensory acuity or motor dexterity and coordination. *Ability* implies three things: (1) conscious, voluntary behavior; (2) maximum, as contrasted with typical, performance (at the time); and (3) an objective standard for rating performance on each unit or item of the test, such as correct versus incorrect, pass versus fail, or measurement of rate, such as number of test units completed per unit time or average time per unit. By *objective standard* one means that differences in performance on any unit of the test can be judged as "better than" or "worse than" with universal agreement, regardless of possible disagreements concerning the social value or importance that may be placed on the performance.

A mental test is composed of a number of items having these properties, each item affording the opportunity to the person taking the test to demonstrate some mental capability as indicated by his or her objectively rated response to the item. The total raw score on the test is the sum of the ratings (e.g., "pass" versus "fail" coded as 1 and 0) of the person's responses to each item in the test.

The kinds of items that compose a test depend on its purpose and on certain characteristics of the particular population for which its use is intended, such as age, language, and educational level. The set of items for a particular test is generally devised and selected in accordance with some combination of the following criteria: (1) a psychological theory of the nature of the ability the test is intended to measure; (2) the characteristics of the population for which it is intended; (3) the difficulty level of the items, as indicated by the proportion of the target population who "pass" the item, with the aim of having items that can discriminate between persons at every level of ability in the target population; (4) internal consistency, as indicated by positive intercorrelations among the items making up the test, which means that all the items measure some common factor; and (5) the "item characteristic curve," which is the function relating (a) the probability of an individual's passing a given item to (b) the individual's total score on the test as a whole (if a is not a monotonically increasing function of b, the item is considered defective). The individual items (or their common factors) are then correlated with external performance criteria (e.g., school grades, job performance ratings).

The variety of types of test items in the whole mental abilities domain is tremendous and can scarcely be imagined by persons outside the field of psychological testing. Tests may be administered to groups or individuals. They can be verbal, nonverbal, or performance (i.e., requiring manipulation or construction) tests. Within each of these main categories, there is a practically unlimited variety of item types. The great number of apparently different kinds of tests, however, does not correspond to an equally large number of different, measurable abilities. In other words, a great many of the superficially different tests—even as different as *vocabulary* and *block designs* (constructing designated designs with various colored blocks)—must to some extent measure the same abilities.

GENERAL INTELLIGENCE OR g

One of the great discoveries in psychology, originally made by Charles E. Spearman in 1904, is that, in an unselected sample of the general population, *all* mental tests (or test items) show nonzero positive intercorrelations. Spearman interpreted this fact to mean that every mental test measures some ability that is measured by all other mental tests. He labeled this common factor g (for "general factors"), and he developed a mathematical technique, known as *factor analysis*, that made it possible to determine (1) the proportion of the total variance (i.e., individual differences) in scores on a large collection of diverse mental tests that is attributable to individual variation in the general ability factor, or g, that is common to all of the tests, and (2) the degree to which each test measures the g factor, as indicated by the test's correlation with the g factor (termed the test's *factor loading*).

Later developments and applications of factor analysis have shown that in large, diverse collections of tests there are also other factors in addition to g. Because these additional factors are common only to certain groups of tests, they are termed *group factors*. Well-established group factors are verbal reasoning, verbal fluency, numerical ability, spatial-perceptual ability, and memory. However, it has proved impossible to devise tests that will measure only a particular group factor without also measuring g. All so-called factor-pure tests measure g plus some group factor. Usually, considerably more of the variance in scores on such tests is attributable to the g factor than to the particular group factor the test is designed to measure. The total score on a test composed of a wide variety of items reflects mostly the g factor.

Spearman's principle of the *indifference of the indicator* recognizes the fact that the g factor can be measured by an almost unlimited variety of test items and is therefore conceptually independent of the particular form or content of the items, which are merely vehicles for the behavioral manifestations of g. Spearman and the psychologists following him identify g with general mental ability or general intelligence. It turns out that intelligence tests (henceforth referred to as *IQ tests*), which are judged to be good indicators of intelligence by a variety of criteria other than factor analysis, have especially high g loadings when they are factor-analyzed among a large battery of diverse tests.

To gain some insight into the nature of g, Spearman and many others have compared literally hundreds of tests and item types in terms of their g loadings to determine the characteristics of those items that are the most and the least g-loaded. Spearman concluded that g is manifested most in items that involve "relation eduction," that is, seeing relationships between elements, grasping concepts, drawing inferences—in short, inductive and deductive reasoning and problem solving. "Abstractness" also enhances an item's g loading, such as being able to give the meaning of an abstract noun (e.g., *apotheosis*) as contrasted with a concrete noun (e.g., *aardvark*) when both words are equated for difficulty (i.e, percentage passing in the population). An item's g loading is independent of its difficulty. For example, certain tests of rote memory can be made very difficult, but they have very low g loadings. *Inventive* responses to novel situations are more highly g-loaded than responses that depend on recall or reproduction of past acquired knowledge or skill. The g factor is related to the *complexity* of the mental manipulations or transformations of the problem elements required for solution. As a clear-cut example, forward digit span (i.e., recalling a string of digits in the same order as the input) is less g-loaded than backward digit span (recalling the digits in reverse order), which requires more mental manipulation of the input before arriving at the output. What we think of as "reasoning" is a more complex instance of the same thing. Even as simple a form of behavior as *choice reaction time* (speed of reaction to either one or the other of two signals) is more g-loaded than is *simple reaction time* (speed of reaction to a single signal). It is a well-established empirical fact that more complex test items, regardless of their specific form or content, are more highly correlated with one another than are less complex items. In general, the size of the correlation between any two tests is directly related to the product of the tests' g loadings.

Tests that measure g much more than any other factors can be called *intelligence tests*. In fact, g accounts for most of the variance not only in IQ tests, but in most of the standardized aptitude tests used by schools, colleges, industry, and the armed services, regardless of the variety of specific labels that are given to these tests. Also, for persons who have been exposed to essentially the same schooling, the general factor in tests of scholastic achievement is very highly correlated with the g factor of mental tests in general. This correlation arises not because the mental tests call for the specific academic information or skills that are taught in school, but because the same g processes that are evoked by the mental tests also play an important part in scholastic performance.

Is the g factor the same ability that the layperson thinks of as "intelligence"? Yes, very largely. Persons whom laypeople generally recognize as being very "bright" and persons recognized as being very "dull" or retarded do, in fact, differ markedly in their scores on tests that are highly g-loaded. In fact, the magnitudes of the differences between such persons on various tests are more closely related to the tests' g loadings than to any other characteristics of the tests.

The practical importance of g, which is measured with useful accuracy by standard IQ tests, is evidenced by its substantial correlations with a host of educationally, occupationally, and socially valued variables. The fact that scores on IQ tests reflect something more profound than merely the specific knowledge and skills acquired in school or at home is shown by the correlation of IQ with brain size (Van Valen, 1974), the speed and amplitude of evoked brain potentials (Callaway, 1975), and reaction times to simple lights or tones (Jensen, 1980b).

CRITICISM OF TESTS AS CULTURALLY BIASED

Because IQ tests and other highly g-loaded tests, such as scholastic aptitude and college entrance tests and many employment selection tests, show sizable average differences between majority and minority (particularly black and Hispanic) groups, and between socioeconomic classes, critics of the tests have claimed that the tests are culturally biased in favor of the white middle class and against certain racial and ethnic minorities and the poor. Asians (Chinese and Japanese) rarely figure in these claims, because their test scores, as well as their performance on the criteria the tests are intended to predict, are generally on a par with those of the white population.

Most of the attacks on tests, and most of the empirical research on group differences, have concerned the observed average difference in performance between blacks and whites on virtually all tests of cognitive ability, amounting to about one standard deviation (the equivalent of 15 IQ points). Because the distribution of IQs (or other test scores) approximately conforms to the normal or bell-shaped curve in both the white and the black populations, a difference of one standard deviation between the means of the two distributions has quite drastic consequences in terms of the proportions of each population that fall in the upper and lower extremes of the ability scale. For example, an IQ of about 115 or above is needed for success in most highly selective colleges; about 16% of the white as compared with less than 3% of the black population have IQs above 115, that is, a ratio of about 5 to 1. At the lower end of the IQ distribution, IQs below 70 are generally indicative of mental retardation: Anyone with an IQ below 70 is seriously handicapped, educationally and occupationally, in our present society. The percentage of blacks with IQs below 70 is about six times greater than the percentage of whites. Hence blacks are disproportionately underrepresented in special classes for the academically "gifted," in selective colleges, and in occupations requiring high levels of education or of mental ability, and they are seen in higher proportions in classes for "slow learners" or the "educable mentally retarded." It is over such issues that tests, or the uses of tests in schools, are literally on trial, as in the well-known *Larry P.* case in California, which resulted in a judge's ruling that IQ tests cannot be given to blacks as a basis for placement in special classes for the retarded. The ostensible justification for this decision was that the IQ tests, such as the Stanford–Binet and the Wechsler Intelligence Scale for Children, are culturally biased.

The claims of test bias, and the serious possible consequences of bias, are of great concern to researchers in psychometrics and to all psychologists and educators who use tests. Therefore, in *Bias in Mental Testing*, I have tried to do essentially three things: (1) to establish some clear and theoretically defensible definitions of test bias, so we will know precisely what we are talking about; (2) to explicate a number of objective, operational psychometric criteria of bias and the statistical methods for detecting these types of bias in test data; and (3) to examine the results of applying these objective criteria and analytic methods to a number of the most widely used standardized tests in school, college, the armed services, and civilian employment.

TEST SCORES AS PHENOTYPES

Let me emphasize that the study of test bias *per se* does not concern the so-called nature–nurture or heredity–environment issue. Psychometricians are concerned with tests only as a means of measuring *phenotypes*. Test scores are treated as such a means. Considerations of their validity and their possible susceptibility to biases of various kinds in all of the legitimate purposes for which tests are used involve only the phenotypes. The question of the correlation between test scores (i.e., the phenotypes) and genotypes is an entirely separate issue in quantitative genetics, which need not be resolved in order for us to examine test bias at the level of psychometrics. It is granted that individual differences in human traits are a complex product of genetic and environmental influences; this product constitutes the *phenotype.* The study of test bias is concerned with bias in the measurement of phenotypes and with whether the measurements for certain classes of persons are systematically distorted by artifacts in the tests or testing procedures. Psychometrics as such is *not* concerned with estimating persons' genotypes from measurements of their phenotypes and therefore does not deal with the question of possible bias in the estimation of genotypes. When we give a student a college aptitude test, for example, we are interested in accurately assessing his or her level of developed ability for doing college work, because it is the student's developed ability that actually predicts his or her future success in college, and not some hypothetical estimate of what his or her ability *might* have been if he or she had grown up in different circumstances.

The scientific explanation of racial differences in measurements of ability, of course, must examine the possibility of test bias *per se.* If bias is not found, or if it is eliminated from particular tests, and a racial difference remains, then bias is ruled out as an adequate explanation. But no other particular explanations, genetic or environmental, are thereby proved or disproved.

MISCONCEPTIONS OF TEST BIAS

There are three popular misconceptions or fallacies of test bias that can be dismissed on purely logical grounds. Yet, they have all figured prominently in public debates and court trials over the testing of minorities.

Egalitarian Fallacy

This fallacy holds that any test that shows a mean difference between population groups (e.g., races, social class, sexes) is therefore necessarily biased. Men measure taller than women; therefore yardsticks are sexually biased measures of height. The fallacy, of course, is the unwarranted *a priori* assumption that all groups are equal in whatever the test purports to measure. The converse of this fallacy is the inference that the *absence* of a mean difference between groups indicates that the test is unbiased. It could be that the test bias is such as to equalize the means of groups that are truly unequal in the trait the test purports to measure. As scientifically egregious as this fallacy is, it is interesting that it has been invoked in most legal cases and court rulings involving tests.

Culture-Bound Fallacy

This fallacy is the mistaken belief that because test items have some cultural content they are necessarily culture-biased. The fallacy is in confusing two distinct concepts: *culture loading* and *culture bias.* (Culture-*bound* is a synonym for *culture-loaded.*) These terms do not mean the same thing.

Tests and test items can be ordered along a continuum of culture loading, which is the specificity or generality of the informational content of the test items. The narrower or less general the culture in which the test's information content could be acquired, the more culture-loaded it is. This can often be roughly determined simply by inspection of the test items. A test item requiring the respondent to name three parks in Manhattan is more culture-loaded than the question "How many 20-cents candy bars can you buy for $1?" To the extent that a test contains cultural content that is generally peculiar to the members of one group but not to the members of another group, it is liable to be culture-biased with respect to comparisons of the test scores between the groups or with respect to predictions based on their test scores.

Whether the particular cultural content actually causes the test to be biased with respect to the performance of any two (or more) groups is a separate issue. It is an empirical question. It cannot be answered merely by inspection of the items or subjective impressions. A number of studies have shown that although there is a high degree of agreement among persons (both black and white) when they are asked to judge which test items appear the most and the least *culture loaded*, persons can do no better than chance when asked to pick out the items that they judge will discriminate the most or the least between any two groups, say, blacks and whites. Judgments of *culture loading* do not correspond to the actual population discriminability of items. Interestingly, the test items most frequently held up to ridicule for being "biased" against blacks have been shown by empirical studies to discriminate less between blacks and whites than the average run of items composing the tests! Items judged as "most culture-loaded" have not been found to discriminate more between whites and blacks than items judged as "least culture loaded." In fact, one excellently designed large-scale study of this matter found that the average white–black difference is *greater* on the items judged as "least cultural" than on items judged "most cultural," and this remains true when the "most" and "least" cultural items are equated for difficulty (percentage passing) in the white population (McGurk, 1967).

STANDARDIZATION FALLACY

This fallacy is the belief that a test that was constructed by a member of a particular racial or cultural population and standardized or "normed" on a representative sample of that same population is therefore necessarily biased against persons from all other populations. This conclusion does not logically follow from the premises, and besides, the standardization fallacy has been empirically refuted. For example, representative samples of Japanese (in Japan) average about 6 IQ points higher than the American norms on the performance scales (nonverbal) of the Wechsler Intelligence Test, which was constructed by David Wechsler, an American psychologist, and standardized in the U.S. population. Arctic Eskimos score on a par with British norms on the Progressive Matrices Test, devised by the English psychologist J. C. Raven and standardized in England and Scotland.

THE MEANING OF BIAS

There is no such thing as test bias in the abstract. Bias must involve a specific test used in two (or more) specific populations.

Bias means *systematic* errors of measurement. All measurements are subject to *random* errors of measurement, a fact that is expressed in terms of the coefficient of *reliability* (i.e., the proportion of measurement) and the *standard error of measurement* (i.e., the standard deviation of random errors). *Bias*, or systematic error, means that an obtained measurement (test score) consistently *over*estimates (or *under*estimates) the true (error-free) value of the measurement for members of one group as compared with members of another group. In other words, a biased test is one that yields scores that have a different meaning for members of one group from their meaning for members of another. If we use an elastic tape measure to determine the heights of men and women, and if we stretch the tape every time we measure a man but do not stretch it whenever we measure a woman, the obtained measurements will be biased with respect to the sexes; a man who measures 5'6" under those conditions may actually be seen to be half a head taller than a woman who measures 5'6", when they stand back to back. There is no such direct and obvious way to detect bias in mental tests. However, there are many indirect indicators of test bias.

Most of the indicators of test bias are logically one-sided or nonsymmetrical; that is, statistical significance of the indicator can demonstrate that bias exists, but nonsignificance does not assure the absence of bias. This is essentially the well-known statistical axiom that it is impossible to prove the null hypothesis. We can only reject it. Unless a test can be shown to be biased at some acceptable level of statistical significance, it is presumed to be unbiased. The more diverse the possible indicators of bias that a test "passes" without statistical rejection of the null hypothesis (i.e., "no bias"), the stronger is the presumption that the test is unbiased. Thus, in terms of statistical logic, the burden of proof is on those who claim that a test is biased.

The consequences of detecting statistically significant bias for the practical use of the test is a separate issue. They will depend on the actual magnitude of the bias (which can be trivial, yet statistically significant) and on whether the amount of bias can be accurately determined, thereby permitting test scores (or predictions from scores) to be corrected for bias. They will also depend on the availability of other valid means of assessment that could replace the test and are *less* biased.

EXTERNAL AND INTERNAL MANIFESTATIONS OF BIAS

Bias is suggested, in general, when a test behaves differently in two groups with respect to certain statistical and psychometric features which are conceptually independent of the distributions of scores in the two populations. Differences between the score distributions, particularly between measures of central tendency, cannot themselves be criteria of bias, as these distributional differences are the very point in question. Other objective indicators of bias are required. We can hypothesize various ways that our test statistics should differ between two groups if the test were in fact biased. These hypothesized psychometric differences must be independent of distributional differences in test scores, or they will lead us into the egalitarian fallacy, which claims bias on the grounds of a group difference in central tendency.

Appropriate indicators of bias can be classified as *external* and *internal*.

EXTERNAL INDICATORS

External indicators are correlations between the test scores and other variables external to the test. An unbiased test should show similar correlations with other variables in the two or more populations. A test's *predictive validity* (the correlation between test scores and measures of the criterion, such as school grades or ratings of job performance) is the most crucial external indicator of bias. A significant group difference in validity coefficients would indicate bias. Of course, statistical artifacts that can cause spurious differences in correlation (or validity) coefficients must be ruled out or cor-

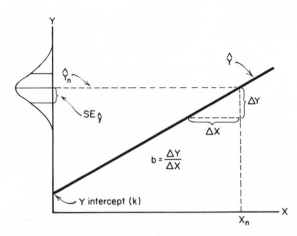

FIGURE 1. Graphic representation of the regression of criterion measurements (Y) on test scores (X), showing the *slope* (b) of the regression line $\hat{Y}$, the Y intercept (k), and the *standard error of estimate* ($SE_{\hat{Y}}$). A test score X_n would have a predicted criterion performance of $\hat{Y}_n$ with a standard error of $SE_{\hat{Y}}$. The regression line $\hat{Y}$ yields the statistically best prediction of the criterion Y for any given value of X. Biased prediction results if one and the same regression line is used to predict the criterion performance of individuals in majority and minority groups when, in fact, the regression lines of the separate groups differ significantly in intercepts, slopes, or standard errors of estimate. The test will yield unbiased predictions for all persons regardless of their group membership if these regression parameters are the same for every group.

rected—such factors as restriction of the "range of talent" in one group, floor or ceiling effects on the score distributions, and unequal reliability coefficients (which are *internal* indicators of bias). Also, the intercept and slope of the regression of criterion measures on test scores, and the standard error of estimate, should be the same in both populations for an unbiased test. The features of the regression of criterion measurements (Y) on test scores (X) are illustrated in Figure 1.

Another external indicator is the correlation of raw scores with age, during the period of mental growth from early childhood to maturity. If the raw scores reflect degree of mental maturity, as is claimed for intelligence tests, then they should show the same correlation with chronological age in the two populations. A significant difference in correlations, after ruling out statistical artifacts, would indicate that the test scores have different meanings in the two groups. Various kinship correlations (e.g., monozygotic and dizygotic twins, full siblings, and parent–child) should be the same in different groups for an unbiased test.

INTERNAL INDICATORS

Internal indicators are psychometric features of the test data themselves, such as the test's internal consistency reliability (a function of the interitem correlations), the factorial structure of the test or a battery of subtests (as shown by factor analysis), the rank order of item difficulties (percentage passing each item), the significance and magnitude of the items × groups interaction in the analysis of variance of the item matrix for the two groups (see Figure 2), and the relative "pulling power" of the several error "distractors" (i.e., response alternatives besides the correct answer) in multiple-choice test items. Each of these psychometric indicators is capable of revealing statistically significant differences between groups, if such differences exist. Such findings would indicate bias, on the hypothesis that

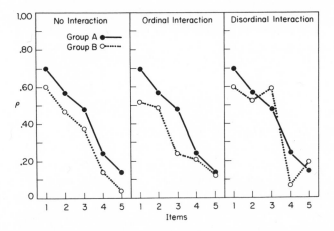

FIGURE 2. Graphic representation of types of items × groups interaction for an imaginary five-item test. Item difficulty (proportion passing the item) is shown on the ordinate; the five items are shown on the baseline. When the item difficulties for two groups, A and B, are perfectly parallel, there is no interaction. In *ordinal* interaction, the item difficulties of Groups A and B are not parallel but maintain the same rank order. In *disordinal interaction*, the item difficulties have a different rank order in the two groups. Both types of interaction are detectable by means of correlational analysis and analysis of variance of the item matrix. Significant items × groups interactions are internal indicators of test bias; that is, such interactions reveal that the test items do not show the same relative difficulties for both groups.

these essential psychometric features of tests should not differ between populations for an unbiased test.

UNDETECTABLE BIAS

Theoretically, there is a type of bias that could not be detected by any one or any combination of these proposed external and internal indicators of bias. It would be a *constant* degree of bias for one group that affects every single item of a test equally, thereby depressing all test scores in the disfavored group by a constant amount; and the bias would have to manifest the same relative effects on *all* of the external correlates of the test scores. The bias, in effect, would amount to subtracting a constant from every unit of measured performance in the test, no matter how diverse the units, and subtracting a constant from the test's external correlates for the disfavored group. No model of culture bias has postulated such a uniformly pervasive influence. In any case, such a uniformly pervasive bias would make no difference to the validity of tests for any of their usual and legitimate uses. Such an *ad hoc* hypothetical form of bias, which is defined solely by the impossibility of its being empirically detected, has no scientific value.

BIAS AND UNFAIRNESS

It is essential to distinguish between the concepts of *bias* and *unfairness.* Bias is an objective, statistical property of a test in relation to two or more groups. The concept of *unfairness* versus the *fair* use of tests refers to the way that tests are used and implies a philosophic or value judgment concerning procedures for the educational and employment selection of majority and minority groups. The distinction between bias and unfairness is important, because an unbiased test may be used in ways that can be regarded as fair or unfair in terms of one's philosophic position regarding selection strategies, for example, in the question of "color-blind" versus preferential or quota selection of minorities. A statistically biased test can also be used either fairly or unfairly. If one's selection philosophy permits identification of each individual's group membership, then a biased test can often be used fairly for selection, for example, by using separate (but equally effective) regression equations for majority and minority persons in predicting criterion performance, or by entering group membership (in addition to test scores) in the regression equation to predict future performance.

EMPIRICAL EVIDENCE ON EXTERNAL INDICATORS OF BIAS

The conclusions based on a preponderance of the evidence from virtually all of the published studies on each of the following external criteria of bias are here summarized for all tests that can be regarded as measures of general ability, such as IQ tests, scholastic aptitude, and "general classification" tests. This excludes only very narrow tests of highly specialized skills or aptitudes that have relatively small loadings on the general ability factor.

Most of the studies on test bias have involved comparisons of blacks and whites, although a number of studies involve Hispanics. I summarize here only those studies involving blacks and whites.

Test Validity

A test's predictive validity coefficient (i.e., its correlation with some criterion performance) is the most important consideration for the practical use of tests. A test with the same validity in two groups can be used with equal effectiveness in predicting the performance of individuals from each group. (The same or separate regression equations may be required for unbiased prediction, but that is a separate issue.)

The overwhelming bulk of the evidence from dozens of studies is that validity coefficients do not differ significantly between blacks and whites. In fact, other reviewers of this entire research literature have concluded that "differential validity is a nonexistent phenomenon." This conclusion applies to IQ tests for predicting scholastic performance from elementary school through high school; to college entrance tests for predicting grade-point average; to employment selection tests for predicting success in a variety of skilled, white-collar, and professional and managerial jobs; and to armed forces tests (e.g., Armed Forces Classification Test, General Classification Test) for predicting grades and successful completion of various vocational training programs.

The results of extensive test validation studies on white and black samples warrant the conclusion that today's most widely used standardized tests are just as effective for blacks as for whites in all of the usual applications of tests.

HOMOGENEITY OF REGRESSION

Criterion performance (Y) is predicted from test scores (X) by means of a linear regression equation $\hat{Y} = a + bX$, where a is the intercept and b is the slope (which is equal to the validity coefficient when X and Y are both expressed as standardized measurements).

An important question is whether one and the same regression equation (derived from either racial group or from the combined groups) can predict the criterion with equal accuracy for members of either racial group. There are scores of studies of this question for college and employment selection tests used with blacks and whites. If the white and black regression equations do not differ in intercept and slope, the test scores can be said to have the same predictive meaning for persons regardless of whether they are black or white.

When prediction is based on a regression equation that is derived on an all-white or predominantly white sample, the results of scores of studies show, virtually without exception, one of two outcomes: (1) Usually prediction is equally accurate for blacks and whites, which means that the regressions are the same for both groups; or (2) the criterion is *over*predicted for blacks; that is, blacks do not perform as well on the criterion as their test scores predict. This is shown in Figure 3. (This finding, of course, is the opposite of the popular belief that test scores would tend to *under*estimate the criterion performance of blacks.) This predictive bias would *favor* blacks in any color-blind selection procedure. Practically all findings of predictive bias are of this type, which is called *intercept bias*, because the intercepts, but not the slopes, of the white and black regressions differ. In perhaps half of all cases of intercept bias, the bias is elminated by using "estimated true scores" instead of obtained scores. This minimizes the effect of random error of measurement, which (again, contrary to popular belief) favors the lower scoring group in any selection procedure. Improving the reliability of the test reduces the intercept bias. Increasing the *validity* of the test in both groups also reduces intercept bias. Intercept bias is a result of the test's not predicting enough of the criterion variance (in either group) to account for all of the average group difference on the criterion. Intercept bias is invariably found in those situations where the test validity is only moderate (though equal for blacks and whites) and the mean difference between groups on the criterion is as large as or almost as large as the groups' mean difference in test scores. Therefore, a test with only moderate validity cannot predict as great a difference between blacks and whites on the criterion as it should. It comes as a surprise to most people to learn that in those cases where

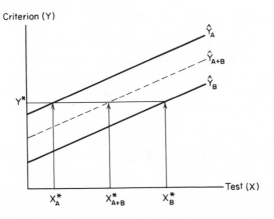

FIGURE 3. An example of the most common type of predictive bias: *intercept* bias. The major and minor groups (A and B, respectively) actually have significantly different regression lines $\hat{Y}_A$ and $\hat{Y}_B$; they differ in intercepts but not in slope. Thus, equally accurate predictions of Y can be made for individuals from either group, provided the prediction is based on the regression for the particular individual's group. If a common regression line ($\hat{Y}_{A+B}$) is used for all individuals, the criterion performance Y of individuals in Group A (the higher scoring group on the test) will be *under*predicted, and the performance of individuals in Group B (the lower scoring group) will be *over*predicted; that is, individuals in Group B will, on average, perform less well on the criterion than is predicted from the common regression line ($\hat{Y}_{A+B}$). The simplest remedy for intercept bias is to base prediction on each group's own regression line.

predictive bias is found, the bias invariably *favors* (i.e., *overestimates*) blacks. I have not come across a bona fide example of the opposite finding (Cleary, Humphreys, Kendrick, & Westman, 1975; Linn, 1973).

There are two mathematically equivalent ways to get around intercept bias: (1) Use separate regression equations for blacks and whites, or (2) enter race as a quantified variable (e.g., 0 and 1) into the regression equation. Either method yields equally accurate prediction of the criterion for blacks and whites. In the vast majority of cases, however, the intercept bias is so small (though statistically significant) as to be of no practical consequence, and many would advocate allowing the advantage of the small bias to the less favored group.

RAW SCORES AND AGE

During the developmental period, raw scores on IQ tests show the same correlation with chronological age and the same form of growth curves for blacks as for whites.

KINSHIP CORRELATIONS

The correlations between twins and between full siblings are essentially the same for blacks and whites in those studies that are free of artifacts such as group differences in ceiling or floor effects, restricted range of talent, or test reliability, which can spuriously make kinship correlations unequal.

EMPIRICAL EVIDENCE ON INTERNAL INDICATORS OF BIAS

RELIABILITY

Studies of the internal consistency reliability coefficients of standard tests of mental ability show no significant differences between whites and blacks.

FACTOR ANALYSIS

When the intercorrelations among a variety of tests, such as the 11 subscales of the Wechsler Intelligence Test, the Primary Mental Abilities Tests, the General Aptitude Test Battery, and other diverse tests, are factor-analyzed separately in white and black samples, the same factors are identified in both groups. Moreover, there is usually very high "congruence" (correlation between factor loadings) between the factors in the black and white groups. If the tests measured something different in the two groups, it would be unlikely that the same factor structures and high congruence between factors would emerge from factor analysis of the tests in the two populations.

SPEARMAN'S HYPOTHESIS

Charles Spearman originally suggested, in 1927, that the varying magnitudes of the mean differences between whites and blacks in standardized scores on a variety of mental tests were directly related to the size of the tests' loadings on g, the general factor common to all complex tests of mental ability. Several independent large-scale studies involving factor analysis and the extraction of a g factor from a number of diverse tests given to white and black samples show significant correlations between tests' g loadings and the mean white–black difference (expressed in standard score units) on the tests, thus substantiating Spearman's hypothesis. The average white–

black difference on diverse mental tests is interpreted as essentially a difference in Spearman's g, rather than as a difference in the more specific factors peculiar to any particular content, knowledge, acquired skills, or type of test.

Further support for Spearman's hypothesis is the finding that the average white–black difference in backward digit span (BDS) is about twice the white–black difference in forward digit span (FDS). BDS, being a cognitively more complex task than FDS, is more highly g-loaded (and so more highly correlated with IQ) than FDS. There is no plausible *cultural* explanation for this phenomenon (Jensen & Figueroa, 1975).

Because g is related to the cognitive complexity of a task, it might be predicted, in accordance with the Spearman hypothesis (that the white–black difference on tests is mainly a difference in g) that blacks would perform less well (relative to whites and Asians) on multiple-choice test items than on true-false items, which are less complex, having fewer alternatives to choose among. This prediction has been borne out in two studies (Longstreth, 1978).

ITEM × GROUP INTERACTION

This method detects a group difference in the relative difficulty of the items, determined either by analysis of the variance of the item matrix in the two groups or by correlation. The latter is more direct and easier to explain. If we determine the difficulty (percentage passing, labeled p) of each item of the test within each of the two groups in question, we can then calculate the correlation between the n pairs of p values (where n is the number of items in the test). If all the items have nearly the same rank order of difficulty in each group, the correlation between the item p values will approach 1.00.

The difficulty of an item is determined by a number of factors: the familiarity or rarity of its informational or cultural content, its conceptual complexity, the number of mental manipulations it requires, and so on. If the test is composed of a variety of item contents and item types, and if some items are culturally more familiar to one group than to another because of differential opportunity to acquire the different bits of information contained in different items, then we should expect the diverse items of a test to have different relative difficulties for one group and for another, if the groups' cultural backgrounds differ with respect to the informational content of the items. This, in fact, has been demonstrated. Some words in vocabulary tests have very different rank orders of difficulty for children in England from those for children in America; some words that are common (hence easy) in England are comparatively rare (hence difficult) in America, and vice versa. This lowers the correlation of item difficulties (p values) across the two groups. If the informational demands of the various items are highly diverse, as is usually the case in tests of general ability, such as the Stanford–Binet and Wechsler scales, it would seem highly unlikely that cultural differences between groups should have a *uniform* effect on the difficulty of every item. A cultural difference would show up as differences in the rank order of item difficulties in the culturally different groups. Thus, the correlation between the rank orders of item difficulties across groups should be a sensitive index of cultural bias.

This method has been applied to a number of tests in large samples of whites and blacks. The general outcome is that the order of item difficulty is highly similar for blacks and whites and is seldom less similar than the similarity between two random halves of either the white or the black sample or between males and females of the same race. The cross-racial correlation of item difficulties determined in large samples of whites and blacks for a number of widely used standardized tests of intelligence or general ability are as follows: Stanford–Binet (.98), Wechsler Intelligence Scale for Children (.96), Peabody Picture Vocabulary Test (.98), Raven's Progressive Matrices (.98), the Wonderlic Personnel Test (.95), and the Comprehensive Tests of Basic Skills (.94). The black–white correlation of item difficulties is very much lower in tests that were intentionally designed to be culturally biased, such as the correlation of .52 found for the Black Intelligence Test (a test of knowledge of black ghetto slang terms). Because of the extremely high correlations between item difficulties for all of the standard tests that have been subjected to this method of analysis, it seems safe to conclude that the factors contributing to the relative difficulties of items in the white population are the same in the black population. That *different* factors in the two groups would produce virtually the same rank order of item difficulties in both groups would seem miraculous.

AGE, ABILITY, AND RACE

It is informative to compare three types of correlations obtained within black and white populations on each of the items in a test: (1) correlation of the item with age (younger versus older children); (2) correlation of the item with ability in children of the same age as determined by total score on the test; and (3) correlation of the item with race (white versus black). We then obtain the correlations among 1, 2, and 3 on all items. This was done for the Wechsler Intelligence Scale for Children, the Peabody Picture Vocabulary Test, and Raven's Progressive Matrices, with essentially the same results in each case: (a) The items that correlate the most with age in the black group are the same ones that correlate the most with age in the white group; (b) in both groups, the items that correlate the most with age are the same ones that correlate the most with ability; and (c) the items that correlate the most with age and ability *within* each group are the same ones that correlate the most with race. In short, the most discriminating items in terms of age and ability are the same items *within* each group, and they are also the same items that discriminate the most *between* the black and white groups. It seems highly implausible that the racial discriminability of the items, if it was due to cultural factors, would so closely mimic the item's discriminabilities with respect to age (which reflects degree of mental maturity) and ability level (with age constant) *within* each racial group.

Sociologists Gordon and Rudert (1979) have commented on these findings as follows:

> The absence of race-by-item interaction in all of these studies places severe constraints on models of the test score difference between races that rely on differential access to information. In order to account for the mean difference, such models must posit that information of a given difficulty among whites diffuses across the racial boundary to blacks in a solid front at all times and places, with no items leading or lagging behind the rest. Surely, this requirement ought to strike members of a discipline that entertains hypotheses of idiosyncratic cultural lag and complex models of idiosyncratic cultural lag and complex models of cultural diffusion (e.g., "two-step flow of communication") as unlikely. But this is not the only constraint. Items of information must also pass over the racial boundary at all times and places in order of their level of difficulty among whites, which means that they must diffuse across race in exactly the same order in which they diffuse across age boundaries, from older to younger, among both whites and blacks. These requirements imply that diffusion across race also mimics exactly the diffusion of information from brighter to slower youngsters of the same age within each race. Even if one postulates a vague but broad kind of "experience" that behaves in exactly this manner, it should be evident that would represent but a thinly disguised tautology for mental functions that IQ tests are designed to measure. (pp. 179–180)

VERBAL VERSUS NONVERBAL TESTS

Because verbal tests, which, of course, depend on specific language, would seem to afford more scope for cultural influences than nonverbal tests, it has been commonly believed that blacks would score lower on verbal than on nonverbal tests.

A review of the entire literature comparing whites and blacks on verbal and nonverbal tests reveals that the opposite is true: Blacks score slightly better on verbal than on nonverbal tests. However, when verbal and nonverbal items are all perfectly matched for difficulty in white samples, blacks show no significant difference on the verbal and nonverbal tests. Hispanics and Asians, on the other hand, score lower on verbal than on nonverbal tests.

The finding that blacks do better on tests that are judged to be more culture-loaded than on tests judged to be less culture-loaded can be explained by the fact that the most culture-loaded tests are less abstract and depend more on memory and recall of past-acquired information, whereas the least culture-loaded tests are often more abstract and depend more on reasoning and problem solving. Memory is less g-loaded than reasoning, and so, in accord with Spearman's hypothesis, the white–black difference is smaller on tests that are more dependent on memory than on reasoning.

DEVELOPMENT TESTS

A number of tests devised for the early childhood years are especially revealing of both the quantitative and the qualitative features of cognitive development—such as Piaget's specially contrived tasks and procedures for determining the different ages at which children acquire certain basic concepts, such as the conservation of volume (i.e., the amount of liquid is not altered by the shape of its container) and the horizontality of liquid (the surface of a liquid remains horizontal when its container is tilted). Black children lag one to two years behind white and Asian children in the ages at which they demonstrate these and other similar concepts in the Piagetian tests, which are notable for their dependence only on things that are universally available to experience.

Another revealing developmental task is copying simple geometric figures of increasing complexity (e.g., circle, cross, square, triangle, diamond, cylinder, cube). Different kinds of copying errors are typical of different ages; black children lag almost two years behind white and Asian children in their ability to copy figures of a given level of complexity, and the nature of their copying errors is indistinguishable from that of white children about two years younger.

White children lag about six months behind Asians in both the Piagetian tests and the figure-copying tests.

Free drawings, too, can be graded for mental maturity, which is systematically reflected in such features as the location of the horizon line and the use of perspective. Here, too, black children lag behind the white.

A similar developmental lag is seen also in the choice of error distractors in the multiple-choice alternatives on Raven's Progressive Matrices, a nonverbal reasoning test. The most typical errors made on the Raven test systematically change with the age of children taking the test, and the errors made by black children of a given age are typical of the errors made by white children who are about two years younger.

In a "test" involving only preferences of the stimulus dimensions selected for matching figures on the basis of color, shape, size, and number, 5- to 6-year-old black children show stimulus-matching preferences typical of younger white children.

In summary, in a variety of developmental tasks, the performance of black children at a given age is quantitatively and qualitatively indistinguishable from that of white and Asian children who are one to two years younger. The consistency of this lag in capability, as well as the fact that the typical qualitative features of blacks' performance at a given age do not differ in any way from the features displayed by younger white children, suggests that this is a developmental rather than a cultural effect.

PROCEDURAL AND SITUATIONAL SOURCES OF BIAS

A number of situational variables external to the tests themselves, which have been hypothesized to influence test performance, were examined as possible sources of bias in the testing of different racial and social class groups. The evidence is wholly negative for every such variable on which empirical studies are reported in the literature. That is to say, no variables in the test situation have been identified that contribute significantly to the observed average test-score differences between social classes and racial groups.

Practice effects in general are small, amounting to a gain of about 5 IQ points between the first and second test, and becoming much less thereafter. Special coaching on test-taking skills may add another 4–5 IQ points (over the practice effect) on subsequent tests if these are highly similar to the test on which subjects were coached. However, neither practice effects nor coaching interacts significantly with race or social class. These findings suggest that experience with standard tests is approximately equal across different racial and social class groups. None of the observed racial or social class differences in test scores is attributable to differences in amount of experience with tests *per se.*

A review of 30 studies addressed to the effect of the race of the tester on test scores reveals that this is preponderantly nonsignificant and negligible. The evidence conclusively contradicts the hypothesis that subjects of either race perform better when tested by a person of the same race than when tested by a person of a different one. In brief, the existence of a race of examiner × race of subject interaction is not substantiated.

The language style or dialect of the examiner has no effect on the IQ performance of black children or adults, who do not score higher on verbal tests translated and administered in black ghetto dialect than on those in standard English. On the other hand, all major *bilingual* populations in the United States score slightly but significantly lower on verbal tests (in standard English) than on nonverbal tests, a finding suggesting that a specific language factor is involved in their lower scores on verbal tests.

The teacher's or tester's expectation concerning the child's level of ability has no demonstrable effect on the child's performance on IQ tests. I have found no bona fide study in the literature that shows a significant expectancy (or "Pygmalion") effect for IQ.

Significant but small "halo effects" on the *scoring* of subjectively scored tests (e.g., some of the verbal scales of the Wechsler) have been found in some studies, but these halo effects have not been found to interact with either the race of the scorer or the race of the subject.

Speeded versus unspeeded tests do not interact with race or social class, and the evidence contradicts the notion that speed or time pressure in the test situation contributes anything to the average test-score differences between racial groups or social classes. The same conclusion is supported by evidence concerning the effects of varying the conditions of testing with respect to instructions, examiner attitudes, incentives, and rewards.

Test anxiety has not been found to have differential effects on the test performances of blacks and whites. Studies of the effects of achievement motivation and self-esteem on test performance also show largely negative results in this respect.

In summary, as yet no factors in the testing procedure itself have been identified as sources of bias in the test performances of different racial groups and social classes.

OVERVIEW

Good tests of abilities surely do not measure human worth in any absolute sense, but they do provide indices that are correlated with certain types of performance generally deemed important for achieving responsible and productive roles in our present-day society.

Most current standardized tests of mental ability yield unbiased measures for all native-born English-speaking segments of American society today, regardless of their sex or their racial and social class background. The observed mean differences in test scores between various groups are generally not an artifact of the tests themselves but are attributable to factors that are causally independent of the tests. The constructors, publishers, and users of tests need to be concerned only about the psychometric soundness of these instruments and must apply appropriate objective methods for detecting any possible biases in test scores for the groups in which they are used. Beyond that responsibility, the constructors, publishers, and users of tests are under no obligation to explain the *causes* of the statistical differences in test scores between various subpopulations. They can remain agnostic on that issue. Discovery of the causes of the observed racial and social-class differences in abilities is a complex task calling for the collaboration of several specialized fields in the biological and behavioral sciences, in addition to psychometrics.

Whatever may be the causes of group differences that remain after test bias is eliminated, the practical applications of sound psychometrics can help to reinforce the democratic ideal of treating every person according to the person's *individual* characteristics, rather than according to his or her sex, race, social class, religion, or national origin.

SECOND THOUGHTS ON *BIAS IN MENTAL TESTING*

More than 100 reviews, critiques, and commentaries have been addressed to my *Bias in Mental Testing* since its publication in January 1980. (A good sampling of 27 critiques, including my replies to them, is to be found in the "Open Peer Commentary" in *Brain and Behavioral Sciences*, 1980, *3*, 325–371.) It is of considerable interest that not a single one has challenged the book's main conclusions, as summarized in the preceding section. This seemed to me remarkable, considering that these conclusions go directly counter to the prevailing popular notions about test bias. We had all been brought up with the conviction that mental ability tests of nearly every type are culturally biased against all racial and ethnic minorities and the poor and are slanted in favor of the white middle class. The contradiction of this belief by massive empirical evidence pertinent to a variety of criteria for directly testing the cultural bias hypothesis has revealed a degree of consensus about the main conclusions that seems unusual in the social sciences: The observed differences in score distributions on the most widely used standardized tests between native-born, English-speaking racial groups in the United States are not the result of artifacts or shortcomings of the tests themselves; they represent real differences—*phenotypic* differences, certainly— between groups in the abilities, aptitudes, or achievements measured by the tests. I have not found any critic who, after reading *Bias in Mental Testing*, has seriously questioned this conclusion, in the sense of presenting any contrary evidence or of faulting the essential methodology for detecting test bias. This is not to suggest that there has been a dearth of criticism, but criticisms have been directed only at a number of side issues, unessential to the cultural bias hypothesis, and to technical issues in factor analysis and statistics that are not critical to the main argument. But no large and complex work is unassailable in this respect.

Of all the criticisms that have come to my attention so far, are there any that would cause important conceptual shifts in my thinking about the main issues? Yes, there are several important points that I am now persuaded should be handled somewhat differently if I were to prepare a revised edition of *Bias*.

GENERALIZABILITY OF PREDICTIVE VALIDITY

The belief that the predictive validity of a job selection test is highly specific to the precise *job*, the unique *situation* in which the workers must perform, and the particular *population* employed has been so long entrenched in our thinking as to deserve a special name. I shall call it the *specificity doctrine*. This doctrine has been incorporated as a key feature of the federal "Uniform Guidelines on

Employee Selection Procedures" (Equal Employment Opportunity Commission, 1978), which requires that where tests show "adverse impact" on minority hiring or promotion because of average majority–minority differences in test scores, the predictive validity of the tests must be demonstrated for each and every job in which test scores enter into employee selection. In *Bias*, I had given rather uncritical acceptance to this doctrine, at least as it regards job specificity, but I have since learned of the extremely important research of John E. Hunter and Frank L. Schmidt and their co-workers, cogently demonstrating that the specificity doctrine is false (e.g., Schmidt & Hunter, 1977). This doctrine gained currency because of failure to recognize certain statistical and psychometric artifacts, mainly the large sampling error in the many typical small-sample validity studies. When this error-based variability in the validity coefficients for a given test, as used to predict performance in a variety of jobs in different situations in different populations, is properly taken into account, the specificity doctrine is proved false. Most standard aptitude tests, in fact, have the same true validity across many jobs within broad categories of situations and subpopulations. Schmidt and Hunter (1981) based their unequivocal conclusions on unusually massive evidence of test validities for numerous jobs. They stated, "The theory of job specific test validity is false. Any cognitive ability test is valid for any job. There is no empirical basis for requiring separate validity studies for each job" (p. 1133).

In *Bias*, I also gave too much weight to the distinction between test validity for predicting success in job training and later actual performance on the job. But this turns out to be just another facet of the fallacious specificity doctrine. Again, a statistically proper analysis of the issue led Schmidt and Hunter (1981) to this conclusion:

> Any cognitive test valid for predicting performance in training programs is also valid for predicting later performance on the job . . . when employers select people who will do well in training programs, they are also selecting people who will do well later on the job. (p. 1133)

DIFFERENTIAL VALIDITY FOR MAJORITY AND MINORITY GROUPS

Although the vast majority of studies of the predictive validity of college entrance tests and personnel selection tests shows nonsignificantly different validity coefficients, regressions, and standard errors of estimate in white and black and Hispanic samples, there are occasionally statistically significant differences between the groups in these parameters. I now believe I did not go far enough in putting these relatively few deviant findings in the proper perspective, statistically. To do so becomes possible, of course, only when a large number of studies is available. Then, as Hunter and Schmidt (e.g., 1978) have pointed out repeatedly in recent years, we are able to estimate the means and standard deviations of the various validity parameters over numerous studies in the majority and the minority, and by taking proper account of the several statistical artifacts that contribute to the between-studies variability of these parameters, we can better evaluate the most deviant studies. Such meta-analysis of the results of numerous studies supports an even stronger conclusion of the general absence of bias in the testing of minorities than I had indicated in my book. When subjected to meta-analysis, the few deviant studies require no special psychological or cultural explanations; they can be interpreted as the tail ends of the between-studies variation that is statistically assured by sampling error and differences in criterion reliability, test reliability, range restriction, criterion contamination, and factor structure of the tests. Taking these sources of variability into account in the meta-analysis of validity studies largely undermines the supposed importance of such moderator variables as ethnic group, social class, sex, and geographic locality. I hope that someone will undertake a thorough meta-analysis of the empirical studies of test bias, along the lines suggested by Hunter and Schmidt (e.g., Schmidt, Hunter, Pearlman, & Shane, 1979). Their own applications of meta-analysis to bias in predictive validities has led to very strong conclusions, which they have clearly spelled out in the present volume. When applied to other types of test bias studies, such as groups-by-items interaction, I suspect it will yield equally clarifying results. These potentially more definitive meta-analytic conclusions are latent, although not objectively explicit, in my own summaries of the evidence in *Bias*, which in some ways probably *understated* the case that most standard tests are culturally unbiased for American-born racial and ethnic minorities.

BILINGUALISM AND VERBAL ABILITY

A recent article by sociologist Robert A. Gordon (1980), which appeared after *Bias*, is one of the most perceptive contributions I have read in the test bias literature. One point in Gordon's article (pp. 177–180) especially gave me pause. Until I read it, I had more or less taken for granted what seemed the commonsense notion that *verbal* tests are biased, or at least highly suspect of that possibility, for any bilingual person, particularly if the verbal test is in the person's second language. But Gordon pointed out that bilingualism and low verbal ability (relative to other abilities), independent of any specific language, may covary across certain subpopulations merely by happenstance, and that not all of the relative verbal-ability deficit is causally related to bilingualism *per se*. The educational disadvantage of bilingualism may be largely the result of lower verbal aptitude *per se* than of a bilingual background. Admittedly, it is psychometrically problematic to assess verbal ability (independently of general intelligence) in groups with varied language backgrounds. But Gordon has made it clear to me, at least, that we cannot uncritically assume that bilingual groups will necessarily perform below par on verbal tests, or that, if they do, the cause is necessarily their bilingualism. Gordon noted some bilingual groups that perform better, on the average, on verbal tests *in their second language* than on nonverbal reasoning tests. Samples from certain ethnic groups that are entirely monolingual, with no exposure to a second language, nevertheless show considerable differences between levels of verbal and nonverbal test performance. Gordon hypothesized that acquisition of English would proceed most rapidly among immigrant groups natively high in verbal ability, which would lead eventually to a confounding between low verbal ability and bilingual handicap. He noted, for example, that verbal IQ had no relation to degree of bilingualism among American Jews, once the children were several years in public school. Such findings would seem to call for a more thorough and critical assessment of the meaning of lower verbal test scores in today's predominant bilingual groups in America.

Interpretation of Groups × Item Interaction as a Detector of Cultural Bias

The statistical interaction of group × item in the analysis of variance (ANOVA) of the total matrix of groups, subjects, and items has been one of the most frequently used means of assessing item bias in tests. The method is very closely related to another method of assessing item bias, the correlation (Pearson r) between the item p values (percentage of each group passing each item) of the two population groups in question. A perfect correlation between the groups' p values is the same as a group × item interaction of zero, and there is a perfect inverse relationship between the size of the correlation between groups' p values and the size of the group × item interaction term in the complete ANOVA of the group × item × subject matrix. The advantage of the correlation method is that it yields, in the correlation coefficient, a direct indication of the degree of similarity (with respect to both rank order and interval properties) of the item p values in the two groups, for example, whites and blacks. The advantage of the ANOVA group × item interaction method is that it provides a statistical test of the significance of the group difference in the relative difficulties of the items.

Applications of both methods to test data on whites and blacks have generally shown very high correlations ($r > .95$) between the groups' p values. The group × item interaction is usually very small relative to other sources of variance (usually less than 1% or 2% of the total variance), but it is often statistically significant when the sample size is large ($N > 200$). It has also been observed that if the comparison groups (usually blacks and whites) are composed of subjects who are specially selected on the basis of total scores so as to create black and white groups that are perfectly matched in overall ability, the correlation between the matched groups' p values is even higher than the correlation for unmatched groups, and (in the ANOVA of the matched groups) the group × item interaction is appreciably reduced, usually to nonsignificance.

Some critics have interpreted this finding as an indication that the black and white groups that are matched on overall ability (e.g., total test score) show a smaller group × item interaction because they have developed in culturally more similar backgrounds than the unmatched samples. However, this is not necessarily so. There is no need to hypothesize cultural differences to explain the observed effects—at least, no cultural factors that would cause significant group × item interaction. The observed group × item interaction, in virtually all cases that we have examined, turns out to be an artifact of the method of scaling item difficulty. Essentially, it is a result of the nonlinearity of the item-characteristic curve. As I failed to explain this artifact adequately in my treatment of the group × item method in *Bias in Mental Testing*, I will attempt to do so here.

A hypothetical simplest case is shown in the item-characteristic curves (ICC) of Figure 4. Assume that the ICC of each item, i and j, is *identical* for the two populations, A and B. The ICC represents the percentage of the population passing a given item as a function of the overall ability (X) measured by the test as a whole. If an item's ICC is identical for the two populations, it means that the item is an unbiased measure of the same ability in both groups; that is, the item is related to ability in the same way for members of both groups. When two groups' ICCs are the same, individuals of a given level of

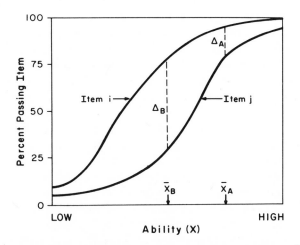

FIGURE 4. Hypothetical item-characteristic curves (ICC) for items i and j, illustrating the typically nonlinear relationship between probability of a correct response to the test item and the ability level of persons attempting the item.

ability X will have the same probability of passing a given item, regardless of their group membership. This is one definition of an unbiased item. Therefore, in our simple example in Figure 4, both items, i and j, are unbiased items. Yet, they can be seen to show a significant group $\times$ item interaction. But this interaction is an artifact of the nonlinearity of the ICCs. The ICC is typically a logistic or S-shaped curve, as shown in Figure 4. If the means, $\overline{X}_A$ and $\overline{X}_B$, of two groups, A and B, are located at different points on the ability scale, and if any two items, i and j, have different ICCs (as is always true for items that differ in difficulty), then, the difference Δ_A between the percentage passing items i and j in group A will differ from the difference Δ_B between the percentage passing items i and j in Group B. This, of course, is what is meant by a group $\times$ item interaction; that is, Δ_B is significantly greater than Δ_A. If the ordinate (in Figure 4) were scaled in such a way as to make the two ICCs perfectly linear and parallel to one another, there would be no interaction. There could be no objection to changing the scale on the ordinate, as p (percentage passing) is just an arbitrary index of item difficulty. It can be seen from Figure 4 that matching the groups on ability so that $\overline{X}_A = \overline{X}_B$ will result in exactly the same Δ for both groups (i.e., no group $\times$ item interaction).

The practical implication of this demonstration for all data that now exist regarding group $\times$ item interaction is that the small but significant observed group × item interactions would virtually be reduced to nonsignificance if the artifact due to ICC nonlinearity were taken into account. It is likely that the correct conclusion is that in most widely used standard tests administered to any American-born English-speaking populations, regardless of race or ethnic background, group × item interaction is either trivially small or a nonexistent phenomenon.

This conclusion, however, does not seem to me to be a trivial one, as Jane Mercer claims. The fact that item-characteristic curves on a test like the Scholastic Aptitude Test (SAT) are the same (or nonsignificantly different) for majority and minority groups in the United States runs as strongly counter to the cultural-bias hypothesis as any finding revealed by research. To argue otherwise depends on the implausible hypothesis that the cultural difference between, say, blacks and whites affects every item equally, and that the cultural disadvantage diffuses across all items in a uniform way that perfectly mimics the effects on item difficulty of differences in ability level *within* either racial group, as well as differences in chronological age *within* either racial group. A much more plausible hypothesis is that either (1) the cultural differences between the racial groups are so small as not to be reflected in the item statistics, or (2) the items composing most present-day standardized tests have been selected in such a way as not to reflect whatever differences in cultural backgrounds may exist between blacks and whites. If test items were typically as hypersensitive to cultural differences (real or supposed) as some test critics would have us believe, it is hard to imagine how such a variety of items as is found in most tests would be so *equally* sensitive as to show Pearsonian correlations between blacks and white item difficulties (*p* values) in the upper .90s. And even these very high correlations, as explained previously, are attenuated by the nonlinearity of the ICCs. The total evidence on item bias, in numerous well-known tests, gives no indication of a distinctive black culture in the United States.

METHODS OF FACTOR ANALYSIS

Because all the intercorrelations among ability tests, when obtained in a large representative sample of the general population, are *positive*, indicating the presence of a general factor, I believe that it is psychologically and theoretically wrong to apply any method of factor analysis in the abilities domain that does not permit estimation of the general factor. Methods of factor analysis involving orthogonal rotation of the factor axes, which submerges the general factor, may make as much sense mathematically as any other methods of factor analysis, but they make much less sense psychologically. They ignore the most salient feature of the correlation matrix for ability tests: positive manifold.

In *Bias*, I considered various methods of extracting g and the group factors. This is not the appropriate place to go into all of the technical details on which a comparison of the various methods must depend. But now, I would emphasize, more than I did in *Bias*, that in my empirical experience, the g factor is remarkably robust across different methods of extraction on the same set of data, and it is also remarkably robust across different populations (e.g., male and female, and black and white). The robustness, or invariance, of g pertains more to the *relative* magnitudes and rank order of the individual tests' g loadings than to the absolute amount of variance accounted for by the g factor. The first principal component accounts for the most variance; the first principal factor of a common factor analysis accounts for slightly less variance; and a hierarchical or second-order g, derived from the intercorrelations among the obliquely rotated first-order factors, accounts for still less of the total variance. But the rank orders of the g loadings are highly similar, with congruence coefficients generally above .95, among all three methods of g extraction. This has been found in more than two dozen test batteries that I have analyzed, each test by all three methods. This outcome, however, is not a mathematical necessity. Theoretically, collections of tests could be formed that would yield considerably different g factors by the different methods. This would occur when a particular type of ability test is greatly overrepresented in the battery in relation to tests of other abilities. The best insurance against this possible distortion of g is a hierarchical analysis, with g extracted as a second-order factor.

Rotation of factor axes is often needed for a clear-cut interpretation of the factors beyond the first (which is usually interpreted as g). In *Bias* (p. 257), I suggested taking out the first principal factor and then orthogonally rotating the remaining factors (plus one additional factor), using Kaiser's varimax criterion for approximating simple structure. This suggested method is inadequate and will be deleted in subsequent printings and editions of *Bias*. A mathematically more defensible method, and one that I find empirically yields much clearer results, had already been devised (Schmid & Leiman, 1957; and Wherry, 1959, using a different computational routine leading to the same results). The Schmid–Leiman method is hierarchical; it extracts first-order oblique factors, and from the intercorrelations among these, it extracts a second-order (or other higher order) g factor; and then the first-order oblique factors are "orthogonalized"; that is, with the g removed to a higher level, the first-order factors are left uncorrelated (i.e., orthogonal). The Schmid–Leiman transformation, as it is known, now seems to me to result in the clearest, theoretically most defensible, factor-analytic results in the ability domain. Like all hierarchical solutions, the Schmid–Leiman transformation is probably more sensitive to statistical sampling error than are principal components and common factor analysis, and so its wise use depends on reasonably large samples. The Schmid–Leiman transformation warrants greater recognition and use in the factor analysis of ability tests. In the study of test bias, it seems an optimal method for comparing the factor structures of a battery of tests in two or more subpopulations, provided the sample sizes are quite large ($N > 200$).

GENOTYPES AND PHENOTYPES

I stated in the preface of *Bias*, and again in my final chapter, that the study of test bias is *not* the study of the heredity–environment question, and that the findings on bias cannot explain the cause of group differences, except to rule out test bias itself as a possibile cause. I emphasized that all that tests can measure directly are phenotypes: *All test scores are phenotypes.* The chief aim of the study of test bias is to determine whether the measurements of phenotypic differences are biased. That is, are they an artifact of the measurement technique *per se*, or do they reflect real phenotypic differences in a broader sense, with implications beyond the test scores themsleves? My analysis of the massive evidence on this issue led me to conclude in *Bias*, "The observed mean differences in test scores between various [racial and social class] groups are generally not an artifact of the tests themselves, but are attributable to factors that are causally independent of the tests" (p. 740).

Despite my clearly stated position regarding the study of test bias in relation to the heredity–environment question, a number of critics and reviewers, in this volume and elsewhere (e.g., "Open Peer Commentary," 1980), have insisted on discussing heredity–environment in the context of test bias. It makes me think that perhaps I have not stated my thoughts on this matter strongly and fully enough in *Bias*. I will try to do so here.

Misunderstandings on this issue fall into two main categories: (a) Nonbiased test scores mean genetic differences, and (b) if group differences are not proved to be genetic, they are not really important. Both propositions are clearly false, but we must examine them more closely to see why.

a. First, let us look at the belief that if a test has been shown to be unbiased, any group difference in test scores must be due to genetic factors. The primary fallacy here is the implicit assumption that a test's bias (or absence of bias) applies to *every* criterion that the test might conceivably be used to predict. A test score (X) is said to be biased with respect to two (or more) groups if it either overpredicts or underpredicts a criterion measurement (Y) for one group when prediction is based on the common regression of Y on X in the two (or more) groups. But there is nothing in the logic of psychometrics or statistical regression theory that dictates that a test that is biased (or unbiased) with respect to a particular criterion is necessarily biased (or unbiased) with repsect to some other criterion. Whether a test is or is not biased with respect to some other criterion is a purely empirical question. It is merely an empirical fact, not a logical or mathematical necessity, that a test that is found to be an unbiased predictor of one criterion is also generally found to be an unbiased predictor of many other criteria—usually somewhat similar criteria in terms of their factorial composition of requisite abilities. But the genotype is conceptually quite different from the criteria that test scores are ordinarily used to predict—such criteria as school and college grades, success in job-training programs, and job performance. Some critics have been overly defensive about the general finding of nonbias in so many standard tests for blacks and whites with respect to the criterion validity and other external correlates of the test scores, which they have apparently viewed as presumptive evidence that the scores are probably also unbiased estimators of intelligence genotypes in different racial groups. This may seem a plausible inference; it is certainly not a logical inference. The issue is an empirical one. I have not found any compelling evidence marshaled with respect to it. As I have explained in greater detail elsewhere (Jensen, 1981), answers to the question of the relative importance of genetic and nongenetic causes of the average differences between certain racial groups in test performance (and all the correlates of test performance) at present unfortunately lie in the limbo of mere plausibility and not in the realm of scientific verification. Without a true genetic experiment, involving cross-breeding of random samples of racial populations in every race $\times$ sex combination, as well as the cross-fostering of the progeny, all currently available types of test results and other behavioral evidence can do no more than enhance the plausibility (or implausibility) of a genetic hypothesis about any particular racial difference. Whatever social importance one may accord to the race–genetics question regarding IQ, the problem is scientifically trivial, in the sense that the means of answering it are already fully available. The required methodology is routine in plant and animal experimental genetics. It is only because this appropriate well-developed methodology must be ruled out of bounds for social and ethical reasons that the problem taxes scientific ingenuity and may even be insoluble under these constraints.

Although it is axiomatic that test scores are measures of the phenotype only, this does not preclude the *estimation* of individuals' genotypes from test scores, given other essential information. One can see the logic of this estimation, using the simplest possible quantitative-genetic model:

$$P = G + E$$

where P is the individual's phenotypic deviation from the mean, $\overline{P}$, of all the individual phenotypic values in the population of which the individual is a member; G is the individual's genotypic deviation from the mean genetic effect in the population; and E is the individual's deviation from the mean environmental effect in the population. The (broad) *heritability*, h^2, of P in the population is defined as the squared correlation between phenotypic and genotypic values, that is, $h^2 = r^2_{PG}$. Methods of quantitative genetics, using a variety of kinship correlations, can estimate h^2. (For mental test scores, most estimates of h_2 in numerous studies fall in the range from .50 to .80). If we assume, for the sake of expository simplicity, that h^2 can be determined without sampling error, then it follows from our statistical model that we can obtain an estimate, $\hat{G}$, of an individual's genotypic value, G, given P for that individual: $G = h^2P$. The $\hat{G}$, of course, has a standard error of estimate, just as any other value estimated from a regression equation. In this case, the error of estimate for $\hat{G}$ is $\sigma_P h \sqrt{1 - h^2}$, where σ_P is the standard deviation of P in the population.

It is seen that all the parameters involved in this estimation procedure are specific to the population of which the individual is a member. Therefore, although the statistical logic of G estimation permits us to compare the $\hat{G}$ values of individuals from the same population, and to test the difference between individuals for statistical significance at some specified level of confidence, it cannot logically justify the comparison of $\hat{G}$ values of individuals from *different* populations, even if h^2 is identical *within* each of the two populations. In other words, the logic of estimation of G from this model *within* a given population cannot be extended to the mean difference *between* two populations. Here is why: If $\overline{P}_C$ = the mean of two populations, A and B, combined and $\overline{P}_A$ and $\overline{P}_B$ are the deviations of the population means (on the phenotype) from the composite mean, $\overline{P}_C$, then the calculation of $\hat{G}_A$ or $\hat{G}_B$ from the model described above would be $\hat{G}_A = h^2\overline{P}_A$ and $G_B = h^2\overline{P}_B$. But in this case, the required h^2 is *not* the h^2 *within* each population (or *within* the combined populations), as in estimating G for individuals; what is required is the heritability of the difference *between* the two populations. But we have no way of determining h^2 *between* populations, short of a true genetic experiment involving random cross-breeding and cross-fostering of the two populations. Thus, if the means, $\overline{P}_A$ and $\overline{P}_B$, of two populations, A and B, differ on a given scale, we cannot infer whether it is because $G_A \neq G_B$, or $E_A \neq E_B$, or some weighted combination of these component differences, and this limitation is as true of measurements of height or weight or any other physical measurements as it is of mental test scores: They are all just *phenotypes*, and the logic of quantitative genetics applies equally to all metric traits. If you believe that Watusis are taller than Pygmies because of genetic factors, it is only because this belief seems plausible to you, not because there is any bona fide genetic evidence for it. We are in essentially the same position regarding racial differences in mental test scores. The mistake is to assume, in the absence of adequate evidence, that either the plausible or the opposite of the plausible is true. All that we mean by *true* in the scientific sense is that the evidence for a given conclusion is deemed adequate by the current standards of the science. By the standards of genetics, adequate evidence for a definitive conclusion regarding the race–genetics mental ability question is not at hand. In the absence of adequate evidence, the only defensible posture for a scientist is to be openly agnostic. Unfortunately, it is often more dangerous to be openly agnostic about the race–IQ–genetics question than to be loudly dogmatic on the environmentalist side.

The fact that a genetic difference between two populations cannot properly be inferred on the basis of estimates of h^2 in both populations, however, should not be misconstrued, as it so often is, to mean that the heritability of a trait *within* each of two groups has no implication whatsoever with respect to the causes of the mean difference *between* the groups. To make the explanation simple, consider the case of complete heritability ($h^2 = 1$) *within* each of two groups for which the distributions of measurable phenotypes have different means. The fact is that $h^2 = 1$ severely constrains the possible explanations of the causes of the mean difference between the groups. It means that none of the environmental (or nongenetic) factors showing variation *within* the groups could be the cause of the group difference if the groups are, in fact, not genetically different. It would mean either (a) that the groups differ genetically or (b) that the group difference is the result of some nongenetic factor(s) not varying among individuals within either group, or both (a) and (b). To the extent that the heritability within groups increasingly exceeds zero, heritability implies some increasing constraint on the environmental explanation of a difference between the groups, the degree of constraint also being related to both the magnitude of the mean difference and the amount of overlap of the two phenotypic distributions. Within-group heritability *per se*, whatever its magnitude, of course, could never demonstrate heritability between groups. But no knowledgeable person has ever claimed that it does.

b. If a phenotypic difference between groups cannot be attributed to genetic factors, or if its cause is unknown, is it therefore unimportant? Not at all. There is no necessary connection at all between the individual or social importance of a phenotypic trait and its degree of heritability. The importance of variation on any trait or behavior must be judged in terms of its practical consequences for the individual and for society, regardless of the causes of such variation. For many years now, there has been a very broad consensus that the IQ deficit of black Americans is important—not because performance on an IQ test *per se* is important, but because of all of the "real-life" behavioral correlates of the IQ that are deemed important by society, and these correlations are largely the same for blacks as for whites. The complete disappearance of mental tests would not in the least diminish all of the educational, occupational, and economic consequences of the fact that, at this time, black Americans, on average, are about one standard deviation below the white and Asian populations in general mental ability. The immediate practical consequences of this deficit are the same, whether or not we understand its cause. What we *do* know, at present, is that mental tests are not the cause of the deficit, but merely an accurate indicator of it.

Lloyd Humphreys (1980a) has written tellingly on this point. He concluded:

> The phenotypic difference is important, not trivial. It is real, not ephemeral. It is not a spurious product of the tests and the test-taking situation

but extends to classrooms and occupations. Today the primary obstacle to the achievement by blacks of proportional representation in higher education and in occupations is not the intelligence test or any of its derivatives. Instead, it is the lower mean level of black achievement in basic academic, intellectual skills at the end of the public school period. It is immaterial whether this mean deficit is measured by an intelligence test, by a battery of achievement tests, by grades in integrated classrooms, or by performance in job training. The deficit exists, it is much broader than a difference on tests, and there is no evidence that , even if entirely environmental in origin, it can be readily overcome. From this point of view it is immaterial whether the causes are predominantely genetic or environmental. (pp. 347–348)

COMMENTARY ON PREVIOUS CHAPTERS

From here on, I will comment on specific points that have especially attracted my attention in the other contributions to this volume, taking the chapters in alphabetical order by first author. Naturally, I have the most to say about those chapters in which I find some basis for disagreement. I see little value in noting all the points of agreement.

BERNAL

Bernal's main argument is that something he refers to as the "total testing ambience" has the effect of depressing the test performance of minority subjects. Although the meaning of *testing ambience* is not made entirely clear, it presumably involves certain attitudes and skills that are amenable to teaching or to an experimental manipulation of the test situation. It is not a novel idea, and there is a considerable empirical literature on it. The best studies I could find in the literature are reviewed in Chapter 12 ("External Sources of Bias") in *Bias in Mental Testing*. The reviewed studies have taken account of practice effects on tests, interpersonal effects (race, attitude, expectancy, and dialect of examiner), manner of giving test instructions, motivating and rewarding by the examiner, individual and group administration, timed versus untimed tests, and the effects of classroom morale and discipline on test performance. The overwhelming conclusion from all these studies is that these "ambience" variables make a nonsignificant and negligible contribution to the observed racial and social class differences in mean test scores on standardized tests. If there are published studies that would lead to a contrary conclusion, I have not been able to find them, and Bernal has not cited them.

Bernal states, "As in his previous works, Jensen continued to use selected studies to broaden the data base that supports his basic contentions" (Chap. 5, p. 172). Actually, in *Bias*, I was not selective of the studies I cited; I tried to be as comprehensive as feasibly possible in reviewing relevant studies. If I have overlooked relevant studies, then these should be pointed out, with a clear explanation of how their results would alter my conclusions based on the studies I reviewed. In all the reviews and critiques of *Bias* since its publication two years ago, I have not seen any attempt to bring forth any evidence that I may have overlooked and that would contradict any of my main conclusions. If Bernal (and Hilliard) know of any such evidence, they have kept it a secret.

Elsewhere (Jensen, 1976), I have explained why it is logically fallacious to infer either test bias or the absence of genetic effects from the presence or absence of training effects on test performance. The demonstration of a training effect on a particular trait or skill is not at all incompatible either with nonbias in the test measuring the skill (before *or* after training) or with a high degree of genetic determination of individual or group differences. An experiment involving a group $\times$ training design does not logically permit conclusions concerning the genetic or nongenetic causes of the main effect of the group difference or their interaction with treatments, nor can such a design reflect on the culture-fairness of the measuring instrument. But this restriction of inference about bias applies only to training subjects in the ability, knowledge, or skill measured by the test itself. It should not apply to the testing ambience, which includes the instructions for taking the test and the atmosphere in which it is administered. It is important that all subjects understand the instructions and the sheer mechanics of taking the test. When these situational factors have been experimentally manipulated, however, they have generally shown small but statistically significant main effects of the experimental treatment, but they have not shown significant interactions with race or social class (see Jensen, 1980a, pp. 611–615). We shall see if Bernal's own experiment is an exception to this general finding.

But first, two other more general observations are called forth by Bernal's chapter.

Bernal refers mainly to children in test situations, for it is in this age group that lack of sophistication in test taking is most likely. But the white–black differences in test performance observed among elementary-school children are no greater, in standard score units, than the racial differences seen between much older groups that have become much more test-wise, after completing 12 years of public school, or 4 years of college, or an additional 3 or 4 years of post-graduate professional school. Yet, differences of one standard deviation or more are found between whites and blacks on the Armed-Forces Qualification Test, on college entrance exams such as the SAT, on the Graduate Record Exam (taken after college graduation), on the Law School Admission Test and the Medical College Aptitude Test (taken after prelaw and premedical college programs), and on state bar exams (taken after graduation from law school), which, according to the National Bar Association, are failed by three out of four black law school graduates—a rate two to three times that of their white counterparts. Data provided by the test publishers on these various post-high-school tests, based on nationwide test scores obtained in recent years, are summarized in Table 1 in terms of the mean difference between the white and minority groups, expressed in standard deviation units (i.e., the mean difference divided by the

TABLE 1

Mean Difference (in Standard Deviation Units) between Whites and Blacks (W–B) and Whites and Chicanos (W-C) on Various College and Postgraduate Level Tests[a]

| | Difference in *SD* units | |
Test	W–B	W–C
Scholastic Aptitude Test—Verbal	1.19	0.83
Scholastic Aptitude Test—Math	1.28	0.78
American College Test	1.58	1.22
National Merit Qualifying Exam.	1.11	
Graduate Record Exam—Verbal	1.43	0.81
Graduate Record Exam—Quantitative	1.47	0.79
Graduate Record Exam—Analytical	1.61	0.96
Law School Admission Test	1.55	1.62

	Minorities[b]
Medical College Admission Test	
Verbal	1.01
Quantitative	1.01
Information	1.00
Science	1.27

[a]From statement submitted by Educational Testing Service (Princeton, N.J.) to the U.S. House of Representatives Subcommittee on Civil Service, in a hearing on May 15, 1979.
[b]Differences here are smaller than those typically found for blacks and larger than those typically found for Chicanos, reflecting the fact that the minority data reported here are based on both blacks ($N = 2406$) and Chicanos ($N = 975$).

average of the *SDs* of the two groups being compared). The groups taking these tests are all self-selected persons at advanced levels of their education who have already had considerable experience in taking tests in school and presumably understand their reasons for taking these admissions tests. And they surely appreciate the importance of scoring well on them. Hence, it is hard to put much stock in Bernal's claim that minority persons perform less well on tests because they are less sophisticated about them and that they "are being 'put on the spot' to perform like whites on tasks that are of no relevance to them." Is the bar exam of no relevance to a person who has completed 12 years of public school, 4 years of college, and 3 years of law school, and who wants to practice law?

Bernal's "test ambience" theory also seems an inadequate explanation of why some tests show larger white–black differences than others—even tests as similar as the forward and backward digit-span test of the Wechsler Intelligence Scales. The white–black difference is about twice as great (in *SD* units) for backward as for forward digit span, even though both tests are given in close succession in the same "ambience." But backward digit span is more highly correlated with the IQ and the g factor than is forward digit span, and this is true within each racial group (Jensen & Figueroa, 1975).

A difference in motivation remains a highly dubious explanation of majority–minority differences. For one thing, there is simply no good evidence for it. In general, motivation, in the sense of making a conscious, voluntary effort to perform well, does not seem to be an important source of variance in IQ. There are paper-and-pencil tests and other performance tasks that do not superficially look very different from some IQ tests and that can be shown to be sensitive to motivational factors, by experimentally varying motivational instructions and incentives, and that show highly reliable individual differences in performance but show no correlation with IQ. And minority groups do not perform differently from whites on these tests. Differences in IQ are not the result of some persons' simply trying harder than others. In fact, there is some indication that, at least under certain conditions, low scorers try harder than high scorers. Ahern and Beatty (1979), measuring the degree of pupillary dilation as an indicator of effort and autonomic arousal when subjects are presented with test problems, found that (a) pupillary dilation was directly related to the level of problem difficulty (as indexed both by the objective complexity of the problem and the percentage of subjects giving the correct answer), and (b) subjects with higher psychometrically measured intelligence showed less pupillary dilation to problems at any given level of difficulty. (All the subjects were university students.) Ahern and Beatty concluded,

> These results help to clarify the biological basis of psychometrically-defined intelligence. They suggest that more intelligent individuals do not solve a tractable cognitive problem by bringing increased activation, "mental energy" or "mental effort" to bear. On the contrary, these individuals show less task-induced activation in solving a problem of a given level of difficulty. This suggests that individuals differing in intelligence must also differ in the efficiency of those brain processes which mediate the particular cognitive task. (p. 1292)

Bernal's experiment was intended to test his ambience theory. Essentially, four groups of eighth-graders were given two brief cognitive tests (number series and letter series). The groups were white (W), black (B), monolingual English-speaking Mexican-Americans (M1) and bilingual Mexican-Americans (M2). A random half of each group was tested under standard conditions (control), and the other half (experimental) of each group was tested under special conditions of instruction, prior practice on similar test items, and so on, intended to improve test performance. The control groups were tested by a white examiner, the experimental groups by examiners of the same minority ethnic background as the subjects. In addition, Bernal states that the "facilitation condition combined several facilitation strategies designed to educe task-related, problem-solving mental sets that cannot be assumed to occur spontaneously in all subjects ... and that seem to assist in concept attainment." The exact nature of these "facilitation conditions" is not described. Hence, if they produced significant results, other investigators would be at a loss in their attempts to replicate the study. Whether the experimental treatment was in any way importantly different from those in other studies that have manipulated instructions, coaching, practice, examiner's demeanor, and so on, prior to the actual test, cannot be determined from Bernal's account. But a plethora of other studies in this vein have yielded preponderantly negative results with respect to Bernal's hypothesis, that such facilitating treatment should have a greater advantageous effect on blacks and Mexican-Americans' test performance than on whites' performance.

The results of Bernal's experiment can be seen most easily when presented graphically. Figures 5 and 6 show the mean scores of the four ethnic groups under the experimental and control conditions for the letter series and the number series tests. Figure 7 shows the mean difference (on each test) between the experimental and control conditions for each ethnic group.

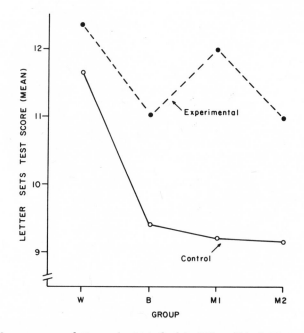

FIGURE 5. Mean scores on letter series test of white (W) and black (B), English-speaking (M_1) and bilingual (M_2) Mexican-Americans, under the control (standard test instructions) and experimental (facilitating pretest experience) conditions.

Bernal commits an unfortunately rather common error in statistical logic in interpreting his results.[1] It has been termed a *Type III error:* testing an inappropriate hypothesis that is mistaken for the intended one. Bernal performed ANOVA separately on the control condition and found that the ethnic groups differed significantly (p = .04 for the letter series and p = .006 for the number series). Then, he did an ANOVA separately on the experimental condition and found that the ethnic groups did not differ significantly (p = .483 for the letter series and p = .24 for the number series). He then concluded that his "ambience" hypothesis is substantiated because the four ethnic groups differed significantly under the standard test administration condition and differed nonsignificantly under the

---

[1]Three months or so before writing this commentary, I personally spoke to Dr. Bernal about this statistical faux pas and suggested that he might wish to emend his paper accordingly, so that I wouldn't have to devote any of my commentary to criticizing his analysis on this point. I have since received no communication about this matter from Dr. Bernal. I have asked the editors to solicit a reply to my comments from Dr. Bernal, to be appended to this chapter.

test-facilitating condition. But this reasoning is a Type III error—an error in statistical logic—because it does not provide a test of the essential question: Did the ethnic groups differ significantly in the difference between the experimental and the control conditions? That is, do the data points in Figure 7 differ significantly among the ethnic groups?

Of what interest is the hypothesis that the significance level of the difference between ethnic groups under the control condition is different from that under the experimental condition? If that were really the hypothesis of interest, then we should be presented with a significance test of the difference between the p values for the ethnic groups' main effect under the experimental (E) and control (C) conditions. But that is not the question we want to have answered. What we really want to know is whether the experimental treatment had significantly different effects (i.e., Experiment − Control; E-C) on the various ethnic groups.

Fortunately, Bernal, apparently unknowingly, provides the proper test of this hypothesis in the ANOVAs of his Tables 5 and 6, in which the interaction of treatment × race (A × B in Bernal's tables) is the proper test of the hypothesis. He notes, correctly, that

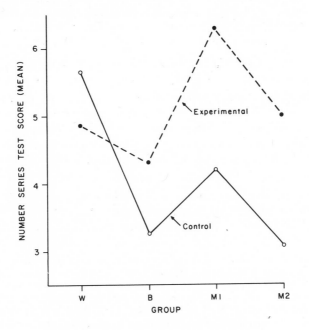

FIGURE 6. Mean scores on number series test.

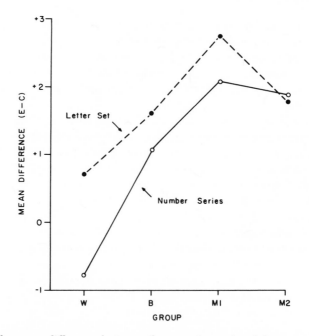

FIGURE 7. The mean difference between the experimental and the control conditions for each ethnic group on the letter series and number series tests. The differences between ethnic groups on the E-C differences (for each test) are what constitute the group × treatment interaction. It is nonsignificant for both the letter series ($F = .67$, $df = 3{,}168$, $p = .575$) and the number series ($F = 2.17$, $df = 3{,}168$, $p = .092$).

these interactions are nonsignificant by the usual criteria (for the number series, $p = .092$; for the letter series, $p = .575$). (*Post hoc* Scheffé tests of the contrasts between the E-C difference for the white group and the overall mean E-C difference of the three minority groups are, of course, also nonsignificant for both the letter series and the number series. In other words, the effect of the treatment was not significantly greater for the minorities than for the whites.) The smaller p of .092 for the number series, as we can see in Figure 7, depends mainly on the anomalous condition that the treatment effect resulted in *lower* test scores in the white group. It also seems unexpected that the M_1 group (monolingual English-speaking Mexican-Americans) showed a greater enhancement of test scores by the treatment than did the bilingual Mexican-Americans (Group M_2). Of course, the similarity in configuration of the group mean E-C differences shown in Figure 7 for the two tests does not carry the same significance as if the two tests were based on independent groups.

Because the same subjects took both tests, which were undoubtedly correlated, sampling errors would produce similar profiles of group means for both tests. Because both tests were intended to measure the common factor found in intelligence tests, it would have been a stronger design to have combined the two test scores (after conversion to standard scores) for each subject. This procedure would have minimized test-specific variance and maximized (for the given data) the common-factor variance, making the results potentially of more general interest. Considering the unimpressive significance levels of the group × treatment interactions for the separate tests, however, it is unlikely that the combined scores would appreciably enhance the significance of the interaction.

In summary, the result of Bernal's experiment, when correctly interpreted, does not statistically substantiate his "test ambience" hypothesis; instead, it is quite in line with the preponderance of many other experiments in the same vein, which have similarly yielded nonsignificant treatment × race (and treatment × social class) interactions (see Jensen, 1980a, Chap. 12).

EYSENCK

Eysenck has presented a comprehensive and well-balanced review of the main lines of contemporary thinking and empirical evidence bearing on the causes of the observed differences in mental test scores (and all their socially important correlates) among various populations. As I find practically nothing in Eysenck's presentation to which I would take exception, and as I have fully spelled out my own views in this area in my latest book (Jensen, 1981), I will here comment only on a point that seems perpetually to confuse many readers of this literature and to which Eysenck does not point with sufficient warning. It all falls under the heading of what I once labeled the *sociologist's fallacy* (Jensen, 1973, p. 235) because I came across it most often in the writings of sociologists. As I point out in my comments on Mercer's work, the sociologist's fallacy seems to be one of the main pillars of her advocacy of tests with pluralistic norms.

In its simplest form, the sociologist's fallacy consists of attributing an exclusively causal role to socioeconomic status (SES). SES is usually indexed by a host of variables, in some weighted combination, such as occupational prestige; amount and sources of income; amount of formal education; size, condition, and neighborhood of the home; reading material and other amenities in the home; and membership in civic, cultural, and social organizations. These indices are all highly intercorrelated, so the measurement of any one of them pulls along with it all the others to a large extent.

Eysenck points out that many studies show that when blacks and whites are equated on one of the standard composite indices of SES, the mean black–white IQ difference is generally reduced by something like one-third of a standard deviation. This assertion is factually true. But then readers should immediately beware of making any causal inference, lest they fall into the sociologist's fallacy. For unless we already know that SES is one of the causal factors in IQ variance and that IQ is *not* a causal factor in SES variance, then the interpretation of the reduction in the black–white IQ difference when the groups are equated (either by direct matching or by statistical regression) on SES is at risk for the sociologist's fallacy. Without the prior knowledge mentioned above, the reduction in IQ difference must be interpreted as the maximum IQ difference between the races that could be attributed to the causal effect of the fact that the races differ, on average, in SES. It is logically possible that equating the racial groups on SES could reduce the IQ difference to zero, and yet, not one bit of the IQ difference would be causally attributed to SES. As Eysenck points out, the one inference that we are logically justified in drawing from IQ studies that equate blacks and whites (or any other groups) on SES is that the reduction in the mean IQ difference (generally 3–5 IQ points of the 15-point overall mean black–white difference) is the largest part of the race difference that could be causally attributed to all the variables subsumed in the SES index. The evidence thus clearly shows that the race difference in IQ cannot be explained entirely in terms of the SES difference. And because we know from other evidence[2] that, within each race, IQ has a stronger causal relationship to SES than SES has to IQ, whatever reduction in the black–white IQ difference results from equating the two groups on SES is a considerable overestimate of the effect of SES on the IQ difference.

The few simple path diagrams in Figure 8 shows the most obvious possibilites for the causal connections among race, SES, and

[2]For example, the correlation between individuals' IQs and the SES of the parental homes in which the individuals are reared is much lower than the correlation between individuals' IQs and the SES that they themselves attain as adults. Also, on average, persons who are brighter than their parents (or siblings) attain higher SES as adults than that of their parents (or siblings). Thus, high IQ is causally related to upward SES mobility, and low IQ is causally related to downward SES mobility.

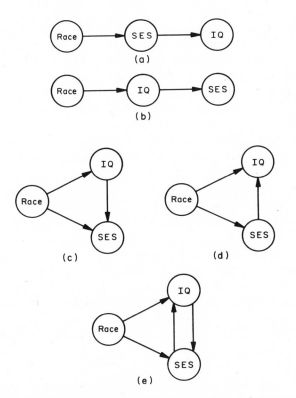

FIGURE 8. Path models illustrating possible forms of causal connections (arrows) among race, social class (SES), and IQ.

IQ. There is no implication in any of these path models that any of these three variables is exclusively the cause of any of the others. IQ and SES are multiply determined by many factors, both environmental and genetic. In each model, the arrows represent the direction of the causal connections between variables.

Model (a) is the implicit assumption underlying all the varied manifestations of the sociologist's fallacy. If this model were indeed correct, we would be justified in matching races on SES when comparing their IQs, or in partialing SES out of any correlations between race and IQ. But this model is clearly contradicted by evidence that shows that there is not just a one-way causal connection going from SES to IQ. The arrow from race to SES in this model would be due to racial discrimination, unequal educational and employment opportunities, and any other racial-cultural factors (other than IQ) that might affect social mobility. Readers should especially note that the genetic question *per se* is not addressed by any of these models. *Race* in these models denotes all characteristics associated with race, except the variables subsumed under the SES index, regardless of whether they are genetic or cultural in origin.

Model (b) has been much less frequently considered than Model (a), and there is much less good evidence pertaining to it, other than correlational data.

Model (c) seems more realistic than Model (a) or (b), but it is probably too simple in omitting any causality from SES to IQ, although the extent of that causality is not at all well established by empirical evidence. It was on this very point that the necessity of discarding Burt's (1921) questionable (probably fraudulent) "data" on monozygotic twins reared apart constituted the greatest loss to our knowledge on this matter.

Model (d) is inadequate because there is good evidence that, in adults, SES attainment is caused to some extent by IQ.

Model (e) is probably the most appropriate, as it expresses all of the empirically known and plausible relationships, particularly the two-way interaction between IQ and SES. Perhaps, someone will collect all the relevant empirical data and, using the method of path analysis, determine which of these several models (or possibly others) shows the best fit to all the data.

Eysenck mentions still another approach to the study of the connection between race and SES with respect to mental ability differences. This involves an examination of the *profile* of race differences and of SES differences across a number of tests of various abilities. If the profiles of race and SES differences are dissimilar, this dissimilarity is strong evidence that the causal factors in the race difference are not the same as the causes of the SES differences observed within each race.

In this connection, I refer to the study by Reynolds and Jensen (1980; 1983) discussed by Eysenck. Blacks and whites (270 of each) from the national standardization sample of the WISC-R were perfectly matched on full-scale IQ, and a comparison was made from the profiles of the two groups on the 12 subscales of the WISC-R. It was found that whites and blacks differed significantly on certain subscales, even when they were perfectly equated on overall IQ. As the white subjects were specially selected to match the black subjects in IQ, and the mean of the white IQ distribution is about one standard deviation higher than the black mean, we are faced with possible regression artifacts in the profile of subtest scores of the selected white group. As these subjects were selected largely from the lower half of the white IQ distribution, their scores on the 12 subscales would be expected to regress upward (toward the white mean) by varying amounts, depending on the reliability of the subscales and on their degree of correlation with the full-scale IQ. Therefore, the method used in this study, based on matched groups, could produce results that are simply artifactual if the regression effects are large enough.

Fortunately, there is a better method for comparing the black and white subtest profiles when the groups are, in effect, equated on full-scale IQ. Reynolds and I have now applied this method, using the *entire* national standardization sample of 1,868 whites and 305 blacks (Jensen & Reynolds, 1982). The sampling method for obtaining these groups ensures that they are highly representative of the white and black populations in the United States.

We used the point-biserial correlation (r_{pb}) as the measure of the average white–black difference. (Whites are coded 1, blacks are coded 0, in computing the point-biserial r, so that a *positive* r_{pb} indicates that whites score *higher* than blacks, and a *negative* r_{pb} indicates that whites score *lower* than blacks). The r_{pb} has a perfect monotonic relationship to the mean group difference expressed in standard score units, and within the range of mean differences found in this study, the relationship between r_{pb} and the mean difference is almost perfectly linear, so the relative differences among the various subtests are not distorted by the r_{pb} scale as an index of the racial difference. To show the profile of racial differences when the groups are equated on full-scale IQ (FSIQ), one simply partials out the FSIQ from the race $\times$ subscale r_{ps}. Figure 9 shows the results of this analysis. We see that partialing out full-scale IQ reduced most of the point-biserial correlations between race and subtests to near zero; but with such a large number of subjects, five of the partial correlations were significant at the .05 level (indicated by asterisks). When whites and blacks were statistically equated for FSIQ, the whites significantly exceeded blacks on Comprehension, Block Designs, Object Assembly, and Mazes. The latter three subtests (BD, OA, and M) appear to represent a spatial visualization factor. (Other studies, too, have shown that blacks perform relatively poorly on spatial ability tests, which are invariably the low points in the average ability profiles of blacks.) The difference on the Comprehension test cannot be attributed to the g factor (which was partialed out via the FSIQ) or to a verbal factor *per se*, as three other tests that are highly loaded on the verbal factor showed negligible differences. In fact, the best measure of the verbal factor, Vocabulary, showed zero difference between IQ-equated whites and blacks. When equated with the

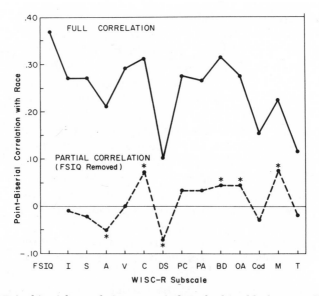

FIGURE 9. Point-biserial correlation as an index of white–black mean difference on full-scale IQ and on each of 13 subtests of the WISC-R (Wechsler Intelligence Scale for Children–Revised). The upper profile shows the actual group differences. (All are statistically significant.) The lower profile shows the white–black differences on the 13 subtests after full-scale IQ has been partialed out, in effect equating the racial groups on general intelligence. Those differences that are significant beyond the .05 level are indicated by asterisks. (I—Information, S—Similarities, A—Arithmetic, V—Vocabulary, C—Comprehension, DS—Digit Span, PC—Picture Completion, PA—Picture Arrangement, BD—Block Designs, OA—Object Assembly, Cod—Coding [Digit Symbol], M—Mazes, T—Tapping [Knox Cubes].)

whites for IQ, the blacks performed significantly better than the whites on Arithmetic and Digit Span. These subtests, along with Coding and Tapping (on which blacks also excelled) are the only WISC-R tests that are loaded on a short-term memory factor, which can be classed as a Level I ability (Jensen, 1974; Jensen & Figueroa, 1975; Vernon, 1981).

The profile of the partial correlations is correlated .96 with the profile of mean differences (in standard score units) obtained by direct matching of whites and blacks in the analysis by Reynolds and Jensen (1980). Apparently, the possible regression effects due to matching subjects from populations with different means did not result in much, if any, distortion of the white–black differences in subtest profiles.

The same correlation analysis (using Pearson r) was performed with respect to SES (rated on a 5-point scale) in the white sample (N = 1,895). That is, full-scale IQ was partialed out of the correlations between SES and each of the subtests. The profile of partial correlations (indicating the size of the SES difference on each of the subtests) looks quite different from the corresponding profile for white–black differences. The correlation between the SES and race profiles is *negative:* − .45. In other words, the pattern of ability differences between whites and blacks was quite different—almost the opposite—from the pattern of differences associated with SES. The black–white differences, therefore, cannot be interpreted as an SES difference.

The pattern of nonpartialed correlations (representing white–black differences) in Figure 9 is also relevant to the Spearman hypothesis, which states that the magnitudes of white–black differences on various tests are directly related to the g loadings on the tests (Spearman, 1927, p. 379). The WISC-R for the total sample (N = 2,173) was subjected to a hierarchical factor analysis, using the Schmid–Leiman (1957) procedure, to yield a second-order g factor. As a test of the Spearman hypothesis, the g loadings of the 13 subtests were correlated with the profile of r_{pb}'s (the upper profile in Figure 9), giving a Pearson r of $+ .76$, $df = 12$, $p < .01$, which more or less bears out Spearman's hypothesis. But in evaluating this correlation of +.76, one must take into account the *profile reliabilities* of the g loadings and of the white–black differences (r_{pb}). This was done by splitting the sample randomly in half and performing the same analysis separately in both halves. When the profile reliabilities are taken into account, so as to correct the correlation between g loadings and white–black differences for attenuation, the corrected correlation is +.84. Thus, the Spearman hypothesis is clearly supported, at least in the sense that g is the most important factor in the race difference. But it is not the only factor contributing to the difference. As indicated by the analysis in Figure 9, the groups also differed, albeit slightly, on other ability factors independent of g, particularly spatial ability (in favor of whites) and short-term memory (in favor of blacks).

HARRINGTON

Before looking at Harrington's major thesis, a number of side issues raised in his chapter call for comment. Some are misleading.

Harrington states, "A test is considered biased if and only if the effects of such interaction [i.e., group × item interaction] lead to group differences in means, in predictive validities, or in standard errors of estimate of the test (Jensen, 1980)" (Chap. 3, p. 110). The reference to *Bias* would make it appear that this is a paraphrase of something I have said, but the fact is, I have never said anything of the kind and, in fact, have said exactly the opposite. What I have said in *Bias* is as follows:

> It should be kept in mind that a significant and large group × items interaction can exist even though the groups do not differ at all in their overall mean test score. This means that, according to the criterion of a group × items interaction, a test may be markedly biased without there being an iota of difference between the group means. (p. 435) A test in which item biases with respect to different subpopulations are "balanced out" is still regarded as a biased test from a psychometric standpoint. (p. 455)

The determination of test bias does not hinge on whether two (or more) subpopulations do or do not show significant differences in mean test scores. If a test does not behave the same *internally* in the various groups—that is, if there are differences in the reliability, factor structure, and rank order of item difficulties (i.e., group × item interaction)—then the test's construct validity is suspect as an unbiased measure of ability across the various groups.

Harrington describes hypothetical methods by which test items *could* be selected that would ensure creation of a biased test, in terms of the several standard criteria of bias explicated in *Bias in Mental Testing* (Chap. 9). No one questions that biased tests *can* be constructed, if one wishes to work at it. But that is not how real tests are actually constructed. If one believes that the mean white–black difference on virtually all cognitive tests is the result of bias in item selection, it should be possible to demonstrate that it is possible to *reverse* the direction of the white–black difference in mean test scores by making some other biased selection from a pool of items that measure g, that is, that involve some form of relation eduction, for that is the essence of the g factor common to all cognitive tests, and it is the largest factor in the white–black difference. No one has claimed that whites and blacks differ, or differ in one direction only, on all conceivable behavioral measurements. The claim is made only about intelligence or cognitive ability tests insofar as these are loaded on the g factor common to the vast majority of such tests. So far, no one has been able to devise a cognitive test that reverses the white–black difference, despite numerous intensive efforts to do so (reviewed in *Bias*). The so-called "chitlin" test of knowledge of black ghetto slang, or the very similar Black Intelligence Test, or the BITCH test, does not qualify as a successful attempt in this vein, as none of them has demonstrated construct validity of any kind, or factorial validity for any mental abilities, or predictive validity for any practical criteria. At most, these "tests" can claim only face validity, as measures of knowledge of black ghetto argot, and there is not even evidence that they are psychometrically adequate measures of that. Scores on these tests are most probably *negatively* correlated with the kind of upward socioeconomic mobility that is the proclaimed goal of the black leadership in the United States.

It would be surprising, of course, if these tests of black argot, like all vocabulary tests, did not also have some g loading within the group that uses this particular argot. But the extreme subcultural specificity of such tests makes them unsuitable as measures of any broad cognitive abilities, such as g and verbal ability, even among black Americans. The BITCH test, for example, has shown correlations of $-.04$ with the Wechsler Adult Intelligence Scale (WAIS) Verbal IQ, $+.13$ with Performance IQ, $+.04$ with full-scale IQ, and a correlation of $-.33$ with level of education in a black sample averaging two and one-half years of college (Matarazzo & Wiens, 1977).

Harrington states: "It is possible that whatever intelligence tests measure is devoid of evolutionary significance or survival value" (Chap. 3, p. 130). Yes, "possible," but most *improbable*. The one feature that most distinguishes the human species from the rest of the animal kingdom is humans' superior intelligence, made possible by the biological evolution of a large and complex cerebrum. The cerebrum has tripled in size in the course of human evolution, despite the fact that there are many anatomical and perinatal disadvantages to increased brain and cranial size. The only selective advantage in the evolution of greater brain size is the more complex behavioral capacities that it confers. The greatest development of the brain has been of the neocortex, especially those areas serving speech and manipulation. Tools found with fossil remains indicate that increasing brain size was accompanied by the increasing complexity of tools, and along with the development of complex tools are also found artistic drawings on the walls of caves. In the last 1 or 2 million years, the strongest selection pressure in humans has been for behavioral traits of increasing complexity, accompanied by the increasing size and complexity of the cerebrum. Konrad Lorenz (1973), the first behavioral scientist to win a Nobel prize, has expounded the thesis that the evolution of the complex functions of the human brain that make possible such intelligent operations as comparing, analyzing, separating, seeing relationships, classifying, counting, abstracting, conceptualizing, recalling, imagining, planning, and the like came about from selection by environmental demands acting directly on the behaviors made possible by increasingly complex nervous functions. These are the behavioral capacities that, in large part, are measured by our present tests of mental ability, in which the largest unidimensional part of the individual differences variance is termed the g factor. Independent evidence that our present most g-loaded tests tap an ability that has undergone directional selection in the course of human evolution is the presence of genetic dominance deviation, revealed in quantitative-genetic analyses of test data. Dominance effects are revealed especially in studies of inbreeding depression, which is found for IQ as well as for certain physical traits. Stature, for example, has also increased in the course of evolution and also shows genetic dominance (Jensen, 1978). Genetic dominance (and other nonadditive effects of genes) increases, as a result of selection, for those traits that are advantageous in the species' struggle for survival.

Harrington suggests that the reason that the observed racial group differences on tests remain even when a test shows identical predictive validity for both racial groups is that the measurement of the criterion is itself as biased as the predictor test. One explanation for bias in the criterion measurement, he hypothesizes, is that the same biased test-item selection procedures that are used in the construction of the predictor test are also used in the construction of the criterion test, making it equally biased.

There is nothing we know that would *a priori* rule out this possibility for some particular rare tests and the criteria on which their validity is based. But I believe that the hypothesis is of very limited generality and cannot be accepted as an explanation of the typical majority–minority differences in test scores or the typical finding that the test scores are unbiased predictors of educational and occupational criteria. First of all, there is no general evidence (aside from Harrington's experiment) that the usual item-selection procedures used in test construction will automatically bias a test against a minority group. Second, not all validity studies are based on correlating a predictor test with a similarly constructed criterion test (e.g., a standardized scholastic achievement test). The criterion measure is often an actual work sample, an objective productivity measure, performance ratings, or course grades. Often, when the criterion measure is a test score, it is from an informally constructed test, such as most teacher-made tests, examinations in college courses, and specific job-knowledge tests—none of them based on the classical techniques of item selection. Yet, scores on these tests and all the other types of criterion measures also show majority–minority differences and are predicted with equal validity in majority and minority groups by standard aptitude tests. The tremendous variety of criteria that are predicted by aptitude tests and the many hundreds of studies that have failed to show significant differential validity for whites, blacks, and Hispanics render highly improbable the hypothesis that congruent biases in predictor tests and criteria account for the group differences and the absence of differential validity.

Harrington's main thesis is based on an interesting experiment with six genetically different inbred strains of laboratory rats. They were given multiple learning trials in a set of mazes with varied stimulus attributes and problem configurations in which the rats' performance was scoreable, analogous to the items of a psychometric test. From the total set of all possible scoreable units ("items") of learning performance in these mazes, tests were made up by selecting a subset of "items," by the use of one of the classical selection criteria in psychometric practice: the item–test correlation. Different proportions of the various genetic strains of rats were included in the "standardization sample" on which the subset of "items" was selected. It was then found that the mean test scores (based on the selected subset of "items") differed across the various strains. The mean scores were directly related to the proportional representation of each strain in the "standardization sample." From these results of the experiment, Harrington has drawn the following generalizations:

> First, the mean performance of homogeneous groups on tests tends to vary directly with the extent of representation of the groups in the population used for psychometric construction of the tests.
> Second, the predictive validity of tests for members of homogeneous groups tends to vary directly with representation of the groups in the population used for psychometric construction of the tests. . . .
> The data of this research program provide one explanation of minority group differences in test performance. The results are applicable to all forms of tests. They imply a general tendency for tests to be biased against minorities and to have less validity when used with minorities. (Chap. 3, p. 134)

I have no complaint with Harrington's effort as a contribution to experimental behavioral genetics. The result is indeed interesting. But it seems to me that it merely poses a problem. It does not answer any question about human minority-group test-performance. What needs to be explained is why, with these particular inbred strains of rats, one finds the interesting phenomenon described above, which, for brevity, I shall dub the *Harrington effect*. And why are data on humans so lacking in evidence of this phenomenon?

The Harrington effect is interesting in its own right, as a demonstration of genetic differences in the factors involved in maze learning in strains of rats. But I see no justification or need to generalize the conclusions from strains of rats to races of humans—the species of practical concern with regard to test bias. We already have much direct evidence, based on humans, that the Harrington effect cannot be generalized to human racial differences in test performance (e.g., see Reynolds, 1982). No amount of experimentation with *rats* can possibly nullify all the evidence based on *human* test results that goes directly contrary to the generalizations from Harrington's rat experiment.

For example, Asians and Jews are minorities in America that score as high as or higher than the majority on majority-standardized IQ tests and college entrance exams. Japanese in Japan, on the average, outperform American whites on the U.S. norms of the Performance Scale of the Wechsler IQ test. Arctic Eskimos perform on a par with British and American norms on the British-standardized Raven's Matrices Test. We have recently discovered that Chinese children in Hong Kong outperform white children of the same age in California on the Raven. African infants score higher on the American-standardized Bayley Infant Scales of Development than do the middle-class white American infants on whom the test was originally developed.

Still more direct counterevidence to the Harrington effect in human populations is found in the application of one of the methods described in *Bias* (pp. 580–583) for detecting biased items: the item selection method. Subtests are made up by selecting items from a large pool of items according to the usual psychometric criteria for item selection, on samples from the two (or more) subpopulations in question. The method was applied separately to large samples of blacks and whites by Green and Draper (see Jensen, 1980a, pp. 581–583), creating somewhat different subtests, each derived by the same item selection procedures in the different racial groups. The items thus selected in each subtest are the "best" selection of items for each group, according to common psychometric criteria. This procedure would seem to provide a direct test of Harrington's hypothesis on human subjects. When the two subtests were given to blacks and whites, the average white–black difference (in standard deviation units) on the white-derived subtest was 0.78σ; it was 0.85σ on the black-derived subtest. (Both differences are in favor of whites.) The authors of this study concluded:

> The amount of relative improvement in score that a minority group could expect to gain by using tests built with tryout groups like itself does not appear to be very large. The relative improvement is most unlikely to overcome any large discrepancy between typical test scores in that group and those in more favored groups. (Green & Draper, 1972, p. 13)

Another direct test of Harrington's hypothesis was the construction of the Listening Comprehension Test (LCT) by the American Institutes of Research (which is fully described in Jensen, 1980a, pp. 678–679). The LCT was devised completely within a low-SES black population, following all of the usual psychometric procedures of test construction. After the test was developed entirely on blacks, it was tried on other samples of blacks and whites of middle and low SES levels. In every comparison, whites scored higher than blacks. Although the test was devised on low-SES blacks, that group scored 1.32σ lower than middle-SES whites. Moreover, the LCT had equally good validity for blacks and whites as a predictor of scores on a standard test of verbal ability. Thus, a number of studies contradict the Harrington hypothesis with human samples. On the other hand, I can find no study in the psychometric literature that affords any support to Harrington's hypothesis. It seems strange that when biological psychologists like Harrington urge such extreme caution about generalizing, say, the results of heritability studies from one human racial group to another, they nevertheless show no hesitation in generalizing experimental results directly from rats to humans!

Finally, Harrington argues that, because he finds little or no evidence of a general ability factor in the maze performance of rats, this lack of evidence somehow brings into question the g factor in the test performance of humans. Because the rat behavior appears to be highly "multifactorial," Harrington concludes:

> To suggest that such results are true only for animals and not for humans is to argue that the rat is intellectually a much more complicated creature than is the human being. Yet this, it seems to me, is the implication of the g hypothesis. (Chap. 3, p. 130)

Harrington's conclusion, however, is a sheer *non sequitur*. It rests on a confusion of complexity of mental processes with factorial complexity. The factors of factor analysis depend on covariation among various tests of abilities. In principle, there is no necessary connection between the complexity of the cognitive processes involved in any of the tests and the degree of covariance among the tests—the covariance that gives rise to factors. Whether there is any connection between the cognitive complexity of the processes required by the various tests entering into a factor analysis and the degree of simplicity or complexity (i.e., the number of factors) of the emergent factor structure is a strictly empirical question. The number of factors emerging from n tests of abilities carries no necessary or logical implication about the complexity of behaviors or inferred cognitive functions involved in the test performance. However, as pointed out in Chapter 6 of *Bias*, there is now considerable evidence, from human test data, that the factor analysis of tests involving relatively more cognitive complexity yields a smaller ratio of factors to tests than the factor analysis of relatively simple tests. Clark L. Hull (1928) made this important observation more than half a century ago, in factor-analyzing a large collection of tests including tests of sensorimotor skills, coordination, reaction time, rhythm, balancing, memory, tapping, card sorting, and verbal and nonverbal intelligence tests of various types. He concluded that

> The highly complex intellectual activities correlate highly with each other, the less complex correlate with each other to an intermediate degree, and the relatively simple motor activities correlate with each other only slightly. (p. 215)

Many more recent studies fully substantiate Hull's observation (see *Bias*, pp. 213–222; 229–233), and it is the g factor that is loaded most heavily in the relatively more complex tests, especially those calling for some form of relation eduction, as Spearman (1927) noted. Thus, a very large g factor and relatively large, but few, group factors, in addition to g, are empirically associated with the greater cognitive complexity involved in the tests subjected to factor analysis. The highly multifactorial nature of the behaviors that Harrington noted in his rats' maze-learning activity is much what one would expect from the factor analysis of relatively simple sensorimotor abilities, even in humans. Thus, Harrington's interesting finding is not at all in conflict with the g theory of intelligence and even seems to confirm it.

HILLIARD

Like all the other critics who have disliked *Bias in Mental Testing*, Hilliard steers clear of the book's main findings and conclusions. Instead of challenging these, he takes up a number of side issues and alludes to supposedly germane research that the book failed to include. But it must be outstandingly apparent to readers that Hilliard never summons any empirical evidence or closely reasoned arguments based thereon that would support a position on test bias contrary to that expounded in my book. He writes as though there exists some body of evidence that would comfort those who dislike my book's conclusions, but that I have chosen to ignore, and that, if I properly considered it, would overturn the book's main conclusions based on the massive evidence reviewed in the book. But he does not tell us what this contrary evidence is or how it is supposed to contradict all the other evidence that has been brought to bear on the issue of test bias. Hilliard characterizes my book as a review of "highly selected empirical research," whereas, in fact, I tried my best to include everything I could find in the research literature on test bias, and certainly nothing else comes near my book in comprehensiveness on this topic. It was never intended to be, as Hilliard claims, "an exhaustive review of all the relevant literature that pertains to the IQ argument." And certainly, neither I nor anyone else, to my knowledge, has ever had the fatuous thought that it is "the book for the century," as Hilliard suggests. *Bias* was intentionally quite narrowly focused on those aspects of psychometric theory and research most relevant to the problem of test bias. (However, my latest book—Jensen, 1981—gives a much more comprehensive overview of what Hilliard terms the "IQ argument.") Of course, anyone who wishes to argue that my coverage of the research on test bias is itself a biased selection (which I deny) is free to review whatever other evidence bears on the issue and to explain how it would alter the conclusions based on the evidence that I have presented. In view of Hilliard's claim, we might reasonably have expected him to do just that in his present chapter. But neither Hilliard nor any other critic of *Bias*, out of some 100 published critiques, so far, has attempted to do so. I suspect they would if they could. There has not been a scarcity of ideologically or emotionally hostile criticisms, but all of it is substantively innocuous.

Hilliard seems to be arguing that cultural differences between blacks and whites are chiefly responsible for the typical white–black differences in test scores. But as I have pointed out earlier in this chapter, the results of our studies of black and white test performances, at every level of psychometric analysis, from single test items to broad factors, indicate that the cultural differences between whites and blacks in the present-day United States have been grossly exaggerated by those who would insist on a purely cultural explanation of the racial difference in test performance. Analyses of test data in terms of both internal and external criteria of bias yield results that are quite incompatible with the hypothesis of large cultural or experiental differences between blacks and whites, at least as these affect test performance. I will not belabor this point further. The evidence is there for all to see (*Bias*, especially Chaps. 10 and 11).

Hilliard emphasizes linguistic differences as a chief source of cultural bias and argues that the field of linguistics somehow contains the antidote to what he views as the current unpalatable psychometric conclusions about the absence of cultural bias in widely used standardized tests. But theoretical psychometricians as well as pragmatic users of tests are quite unimpressed by the linguistic arguments, in view of the well-established finding that the black deficit is no greater on tests of verbal abilities than on wholly nonverbal and performance tests. When the general factor is extracted from a large and diverse battery of verbal and nonverbal tests, we find that blacks and whites differ almost entirely on the g factor and not at all on the verbal factor, least of all on vocabulary, after g is partialed out (see Figure 9). Chapter 9 of *Bias* reviews the many attempts to vary the familiarity of the test contents, with the consistent result that the white–black differences remain fully constant across all these test variations. Only tests of rote memory and motor skills show negligible differences. On all other types of tests, the race differences are substantial. But when g is partialled out, hardly any test shows an appreciable difference between blacks and whites. The racial difference is a difference in g and not just a linguistic difference or a difference dependent on any special type of item content. Hilliard comes down especially hard on vocabulary tests, as they would appear to be the most quintessentially cultural of all test types. But the lower scores of blacks on the vocabulary subtests of standard scales such as the Stanford–Binet and the Wechsler probably do not underestimate black children's functional vocabulary, whether estimated by their use of standard English or of their own patios—what Hilliard would call the "normal vocabulary" of a particular cultural group. In a study by langauge experts in Detroit, tape recordings were made of black children's speech, and it was discovered that their vocabulary contains only about half as many words as white children's (Silberman, 1964, p. 283). A comprehensive review of research pertaining to the cultural-linguistic hypothesis of the black IQ deficit concluded there was no evidence that supports it and that the explanation of the black IQ deficit must be sought elsewhere (Hall & Turner, 1971).

Hilliard objects to a social definition of race instead of a strictly biological criterion and asks how IQ researchers select "black" or "white" samples for comparison. The answer is, of course, that they do it in the same was as those who assess racial balance in the public schools, or the proportions of different racial groups in special classes, or an institution's conformity to federal guidelines for affirmative action, or for trying court cases of racial discrimination. Although there is a high correlation between the ordinary socially recognized categories of races in the United States and strictly biological criteria of classification, involving a host of visible physical characteristics as well as blood groups[3] and biochemical factors, it is only the social and cultural definition of race that is actually relevant to the study of test bias as it concerns all the practical uses of tests. Moreover, if the observed test-score differences between racial groups are due only to social-cultural factors, as Hilliard claims, then the social definition of race should be quite adequate and, in fact, should be the only appropriate definition. If it is argued that two socially defined racial groups that differ in mean IQ are not racially "pure," by strictly biological criteria, and that one or both groups have some genetic admixture of the other, it can mean only that the biological racial aspect of the IQ difference, if such exists, has been *under*estimated by comparing socially, rather than genetically, defined racial groups.

The chapter by Lloyd Humphreys should provide adequate background for evaluating Hilliard's claim that intelligence "has no common definition among the community of scholars who study it." In fact, there is high agreement among the experts about what they mean by the term *intelligence*. The issue has been the subject of an empirical investigation. Yale psychologist Robert Sternberg devised an elaborate questionnaire intended to assess people's conceptions of the meaning of *intelligence* and the specific types of behavior that they recognize as instances of whatever they mean by *intelligence*. The questionnaire was sent to a representative sample of Ph.D. psychologists who do research and teach courses in the area of human abilities. The questionnaire was also given to laypeople. Sternberg,

---

[3]Today, the average percentage of Caucasian genes in persons who are socially identified as black and who so identify themselves, in America, is estimated, on the basis of blood group analysis, at something close to 25%, with a standard deviation of about 14%. The frequency of genes of African origin among persons socially identified as white is estimated at less than 1%. (A detailed discussion of this research, with complete references, is to be found in Jensen, 1973, Chap. 9.)

Conway, Ketron, and Bernstein (1980) reported a very high degree of concordance between psychologists and laypeople about the meaning of *intelligence*. This remarkably high consensus among experts and laypeople as to the subjective meaning of *intelligence* and the recognition of its behavioral manifestations clearly contradicts the notion that *intelligence* is an esoteric technical concept or that there is little agreement among persons concerning its manifest characteristics.

How valid is Hilliard's claim that IQ tests differ widely and bear merely an association with each other? It is granted that the specific item content differs greatly among IQ tests. But the truly remarkable fact is that despite the great variation in types of item content, all IQ tests measure much the same mental factors, especially the g factor, which is predominant in all such tests. To get some idea of how widely IQ tests differ, I have determined the average intercorrelation among 30 different published IQ tests, gathered from various studies reported in the literature. I determined the median correlation for each test of all its correlations with other tests. The mean of these median correlations for all 30 tests is .77. But the average reliability of all of the tests is .90, and so we must correct the mean correlation of .77 for attenuation, which brings the true correlation among the tests up to about .86. The median correlation between the Stanford–Binet and the WISC in 47 studies is .80 (or .85 when correlated for attenuation). This is indeed a high degree of agreement among different IQ tests, considering the great variety of samples used in those studies, with widely varying degrees of restrictions of range, and considering the fact that there is some amount of "method variance" among all these tests, which include group paper-and-pencil tests, individual tests, and verbal, nonverbal, and performance tests. The fact that their true-score intercorrelations average about .86 in a wide variety of samples indicates that a large common factor, namely g, runs throughout all of these IQ tests. This clearly belies the essence of Hilliard's claim that "IQ tests differ widely."

An important criterion of the absence of test bias, for Hilliard, is evidence that "the same mental process is being measured in two or more cultural groups whose standardized IQ test scores are being compared." One way of examining the test performance of different groups for an answer to this question is by looking at the degree of similarity of the factor structures and factor loadings on the various scorable parts of a test for the two groups in question. C. R. Reynolds and I have recently done this. We subjected the WISC-R national standardization data to a hierarchical factor analysis (Schmid & Leiman,

1957)[4] separately in the white and black samples, with numbers of 1,868 and 305, respectively. (See the chapter by Humphreys for a description of this type of factor analysis, which he deems the most satisfactory method for extracting the general factor, g.) We found that both the factor structure and the factor loadings of the 13 subtests of the WISC-R standardization edition (the 12 subtests of the WISC plus a Tapping subtest later deleted from the WISC-R) were virtually identical in the white and black samples, despite the difference of 15.8 points between the group means on the full-scale IQ. The coefficient of congruence (an index of factor similarity, on a sacle from 0 to 1) was computed between blacks and whites for each of the four WISC-R factors: general factor (g) = 1.00, Verbal factor = .99, Performance factor = .98, Memory factor = .98. If Hilliard knows of any bona fide evidence that blacks and whites differ in the types of mental processes that they bring to bear on standard IQ tests, he should bring it to light. We are not aware of any such evidence.

Now, two minor points:

First, the test bias issue does not in the least hinge on settling the question of the true form of the distribution of intelligence in the population. Moreover, I have never claimed that scores on any particular type of test, such as information or vocabulary, should be assumed to have a normal distribution. I have said that many psychologists, for a number of statistical, genetic, biologically analogical, and scientifically heuristic reasons, have explicitly assumed that the latent trait of general intelligence is normally distributed, and that this theoretical assumption is reflected in most IQ scales and derived scores on other cognitive tests standardized on the general population.

Second, Sir Cyril Burt, whom Hilliard refers to as a politician, was never a politician in any sense of the word. In fact, many of his long-time close associates were totally unaware of his very private political views. (His sympathies were with the socialist Labor Party of Britain.) Interestingly, as also noted by Reynolds and Brown in this volume, Burt (1921) was one of the first psychologists to draw attention to the problem of test bias, with respect to social class differences, not long after the publication of the first Binet intelligence scales. (My final conclusions regarding the notorious scandal surrounding Burt's data on identical twins are detailed elsewhere; see Jensen, 1981.)

---

[4]We are grateful to Professor John Schmid for doing these factor analyses for us.

Finally, the present massive research on our standard mental tests, their associated group differences and all their educationally, occupationally, and socially significant correlates, and the consistent failure to demonstrate by means of any objective evidence that the tests are biased against blacks, constitute an impressive and important body of evidence for psychometric theory and practice. Humphreys (1980b) has summarized the implications very well:

> The measured differences in intelligence are real barriers to equal access by the majority of blacks to higher education, to skilled occupations, and to the professions. The measured differences are causally related to high levels of unemployment and to below average incomes for blacks. The differences and their direct effects are also indirectly related to such social pathologies as higher rates of delinquency and crime in the black population. (p. 55)

To pretend that these conclusions can be likened to the "emperor's new clothes" is, I suspect, only wishful denial—an ineffectual and fatuous response to the reality and the import of the evidence. If there is anything as truly unsubstantial as the "emperor's new clothes" in the IQ cultural bias debate, it is probably the evidence that Hilliard seems to imagine would contradict the main conclusions of *Bias in Mental Testing*.[5] If Hilliard claims to disagree with my definitions of test bias, or with the proposed methods of objectively recognizing bias, or with the empirical evidence on which my conclusions, within this framework, are based, then I think he is obligated to state an alternative definition of bias, to formulate other explicit methods by which one can detect bias, and to cite evidence that specifically contradicts my conclusions. Hilliard has done nothing of the kind. Nor, to my knowledge, has anyone else.

HUMPHREYS

Humphreys's chapter is one of the most lucid and enlightening essays on intelligence that I have come across in my wide reading in this field. It merits thoughtful reading by everyone with an interest in this topic.

[5]Jensen, 1980a, p. 740: "The observed mean differences in test scores between various [racial and social-class] groups are generally not an artifact of the tests themselves, but are attributable to factors that are causally independent of the tests. . . . The present most widely used standardized tests can be used just as effectively for blacks as for whites in all of the usual applications of tests."

The only point on which I have any serious reservations may or may not be a fundamental one—I am not sure. It involves Humphreys's formal definition of intelligence. Not that anyone could sensibly disagree with it, as far as it goes, but it does not go far enough, in my opinion. In one way, it is not sufficiently precise, and in another way, it is not sufficiently open-ended. But before proceeding further, I should restate Humphreys's definition:

> Intelligence is defined as the entire repertoire of acquired skills, knowledge, learning sets, and generalization tendencies considered intellectual in nature that are available at any one period of time. An intelligence test contains items that sample the totality of such acquisitions. . . . The definition of intelligence here proposed would be circular as a function of the use of intellectual if it were not for the fact that there is a consensus among [cognizant] psychologists as to the kinds of behaviors that are labeled intellectual. Thus, the Stanford–Binet and the Wechsler tests can be considered examples of this consensus and define the consensus. (Chap. 7, pp. 243–244)

First of all, there is no hint in this statement that, among all the "repertoire of acquired skills" and so on, some things might be weighted differently from others in the degree to which they represent intelligence. Einstein never knew how to drive an automobile, but he had mastered tensor calculus, an abstruse branch of mathematics. Are we to assign these skills equal (negative and positive) weights in forming a judgment of Einstein's intelligence? I dislike the idea of leaving the relative weights to be assigned to these skills up to the subjective judgment of any one psychologist or any collection of psychologists, cognizant or not. A consensus of expert judgment, it seems to me, is a weak basis for scientific theory. The overthrow of expert consensus is a prominent feature in the history of science. Thanks to Spearman, Burt, Thurstone, and others, we now have a set of tools—namely, factor analysis—for dealing more objectively with the weighting problem. I think that this was the essential contribution of the now-classic paper by Spearman (1904). It seems a reasonable guess that if we included skill in driving an automobile and skill in tensor calculus among the "entire repertoire" referred to by Humphreys, and if we analyzed the whole works, tensor calculus would have a higher g loading than automobile driving. Value judgments, academic snobbery, and the like would not enter into this conclusion, as they might do in a mere consensus among Ph.D.'s.

The definition refers to "acquired skills, knowledge," and so on. This definition does not take care of types of behavior that cannot be construed as learned (at least as far as the source of individual differences is concerned) and that may not be deemed "intellectual" by any expert consensus, but that are nevertheless found to be g-loaded when factor-analyzed along with other types of performance deemed "intellectual." I have in mind, for example, choice reaction time, which is not a learned skill and which under some experimental conditions shows no learning or practice effects whatever; yet, it is correlated with Stanford–Binet and Wechsler IQs (Jensen, 1982b). Clearly, IQ tests measure something *more* than just learned skills and bits of knowledge, although these may serve as adequate vehicles for measuring whatever it is that the test measures, which is something more, and different from, the vehicle itself. If that were not so, why should the verbal subtests of the Wechsler correlate .80 with the performance subtests, with which they have virtually nothing in common at the "phenotypic" level of item contents, knowledge, and skills? No, I think our intelligence-test scores are only the tip of the iceberg.

So, I think we need a deeper conception of intelligence than that suggested by Humphreys's definition; which seems to imply that intelligence consists of no more than what we can readily see with the unaided eye at a given point in time. It also seems to be merely whatever we *say* it is, albeit said by a consensus of the cognoscenti, instead of a wondrous phenomenon, the full nature of which still awaits discovery by scientific means. Everyone knows in general what *universe* means, although astronomers and cosmologists know more about it than laypeople. By rough analogy, Humphreys defines intelligence much as if we said that the universe is simply the myriad specks of light that we all can see when we look up at the sky on any given night. With this approach, what would be the incentive to build a telescope or, if we already had a telescope, to want a more powerful one? When astronomers obtain a more powerful telescope and other instruments for the analysis of starlight, they discover things that were in neither their observations nor their imaginations before. We must presume, if we are not completely solipsistic, that this is so because there is indeed a reality out there, referred to as the *universe*, and that it amounts to a great deal more than our present conceptions of it. It is still being discovered, and there is still much to be understood scientifically about what has already been discovered. I think much the same sort of thing is true of the concept of intelligence. Is there anything in Humphreys's definition, for example, that could have led anyone to expect, much less look for, a correlation between IQ and the frequency and amplitude of evoked electrical potentials in the brain? I believe that there *is* some "nature" underlying our observations and test measurements of what we call *intelligence*. To use the word *entity*, as Humphreys does, to describe the "nature" or "reality" underlying our measurements (and factors) is to set up a straw man, if by *entity* he implies some "thing"—a single cause, anatomical structure, physiological mechanism, or biochemical substance.[6] If I really thought that there was nothing more to intelligence than the IQ test scores and more of the same kinds of things we already know about them, I would change my field of research immediately and take up something scientifically more interesting.

Because I do think that there is more to intelligence than merely the behavioral vehicles by which it can be expressed or measured, I think it is theoretically important to retain the ability–achievement distinction, although from that point on, I would agree with everything else that Humphreys says about it.

Humphreys's definition of intelligence seems to be in the tradition of the strictest logical positivism. This philosophy of science, which once had great appeal to me, now seems to me less convincing, and it is my impression that it has already lost favor, generally, in the most advanced physical sciences. Whereas Humphreys insists on an aseptically explicit operational definition of the concept of intelligence, I tend to regard it more as an open-ended theoretical construct still in the process of being explored and more fully understood scientifically. I am reminded of a modern philosopher of science, Yehuda Elkana, who, in the frontispiece of his book on the discovery of the conservation of energy (1974), quoted a statement by H. A. Kramers, which, at several points in his book, he referred to as being of key significance in scientific progress: "In the world of human thought generally and in physical science particularly, the most fruitful concepts are those to which it is impossible to attach a well-defined meaning." I think intelligence is such a concept.

Fortunately, at least from my own standpoint, everything else that Humphreys says in his chapter does not seem to hinge at all on his formal definition of *intelligence*. My own "working definition" of *intelligence* is the general factor of a large and diverse battery of cog-

---

[6]Elsewhere (Jensen, 1982a), I have written, "It is a mistake to waste time arguing about the definition of *intelligence*, except to make sure everyone understands that the term does not refer to a 'thing,'" and elsewhere, we should heed Miles' (1957) advice: 'The important point is not whether what we measure can appropriately be labelled 'intelligence,' but whether we have discovered something worth measuring. And this is not a matter that can be settled by an appeal to what is or is not the correct use of the word 'intelligent.'"

nitive tests, and this definition does not seem to conflict with anything I find in Humphreys's paper.

Whatever may be the conception of intelligence that actually guides Humphreys's thinking and research in this field, it obviously has not hindered his continuing to make creative and important contributions to our understanding of the nature and the measurement of intelligence, of which we are presented a good sample in his present chapter. We all can learn from it.

HUNTER, SCHMIDT, AND RAUSCHENBERGER

In their chapter, these investigators present an excellent summary of their many important original contributions to the study of test bias, particularly as it concerns the use of tests in personnel selection. Probably, no one else in the field has done more than these researchers to dispel the twin illusions of situational specificity of test validity and differential validity for majority and minority populations. The type of meta-analysis of the mountains of validity data that led to their conclusions is one of the signal contributions to both the methodology and the substantive knowledge of psychometrics and personnel psychology. In addition, they have highlighted more explicitly and rigorously than has anyone else the practical consequences—in terms of work productivity and dollars and cents—of test validity, various personnel selection models, and minority quotas. These objective cost–benefit analyses may come as a shocking surprise to many of those who would belittle the practical importance of mental tests or who imagine the world would be better off without them.

MANNING AND JACKSON

The chapter by Manning and Jackson is an extremely valuable, empirical, research-based defense of the Scholastic Aptitude Test (SAT) and other advanced educational aptitude tests developed by the Educational Testing Service. Comprehensive and detailed documentation of Manning and Jackson's claim of equal validity of the SAT for white and minority populations in predicting academic performance in college can be found in Breland (1979).

The Educational Testing Service (ETS) is the developer and publisher of the College Entrance Examination Board's SAT, which has practically preempted the field of college aptitude testing. Partly as a result, the ETS in recent years has been assailed by critics from out-

side the psychological and educational testing discipline. The attacks
on the ETS have resulted not because anyone has been able to show
that their tests are technically substandard or that they are not as
valid for racial minorities as for whites, but mainly because the ETS
tests are virtually unassailable by these criteria and hence reveal all
too clearly unwelcome and disturbing facts about inequalities in the
distribution of mental abilities in the nation's population—particularly those developed abilities that are necessary (although not sufficient) for academic attainment beyond high school.

From a strictly psychometric standpoint, the ETS has no real
problem countering its critics: High-powered technical expertise and
all the statistical evidence are on its side. But I think the ETS repeatedly displays a sorry spectacle in its squirming to offer excuses for
the unwelcome social realities that its tests so soundly reveal. We see
more examples of it in Manning and Jackson's chapter. But my complaint is not limited to the ETS; other test publishers, in my observation, are in the same straits. Of course, one may easily sympathize
with the predicament of a commercial establishment trying to maintain good public relations and avoid controversy. But it seems to me
that the ETS and other test publishers have chosen the wrong stance
to avoid the heat.

The same good science that is found in the research and test
development of the major test publishers should also be evinced in
their public statements about socially touchy issues, the main one
being, of course, the need they feel for an explanation of the lower
average test scores of blacks, if, as the ETS claims, the tests are not
culturally biased or unfair to minority students. Typically, escape-
hatch explanations take the form of blame. Because the tests have
been exculpated, blame is now redirected elsewhere, and in the ETS
litany, the public schools, as usual, unfairly receive the brunt: "public miseducation," "failures of education," "teacher expectancy," and
"caste and class barriers" to educational opportunity, along with
"segregation" and "poverty." I have no way of knowing if this limited explanatory repertoire, which I have repeatedly encountered in
the ETS's public statements, reflects an official doctrine of the ETS or
merely a coincidental likeness of minds among those who speak for
the enterprise.

Whatever faults one may legitimately point out in the public
schools, the causation of the black IQ deficit certainly is not one of
them. The typical one-standard-deviation mean difference between
blacks and whites on tests of general intelligence or scholastic aptitude is full blown by the age of school entry, and it does not change

(relative to individual variability within the populations) from kindergarten to Grade 12. The schools, therefore, are not in any degree to blame for the observed social differences in scholastic aptitude. But should the schools be held culpable for not *overcoming* the difference? In the past 25 years, many millions of dollars of federal funds have been expended for numerous and massive attempts to overcome the difference, with apparently unimpressive success. The mean mental-test-score difference (in standard score units) between black and white youths is the same today as it was 75 years ago, at the time of World War I, when, for the first time, large samples of the nation's young men were given mental tests.

A standard individual or group test of general intelligence is an unbiased predictor of scholastic performance for blacks and whites, and it has proved no easier to raise intelligence and its correlated academic achievement by an appreciable amount for black children than for white children. We can safely say that, up to the present time, researchers have not yet discovered any educational prescription feasibility within the power of the schools that can substantially and permanently raise the general intelligence of black children *or* of white children. In this respect as in many others, the IQ difference between the races behaves very much as do the IQ differences among individuals of the same race. I have found no compelling evidence that the group differences are essentially different in nature from individual differences. The failure to discover any important race $\times$ treatment interactions (independent of IQ) in the educative process would seem consistent with this observation.

As for poverty and the other explanatory factors mentioned by Manning and Jackson, they should be viewed in the light of the available facts about the ETS tests: Less than 10% of the variance in SAT scores is *associated* with (not necessarily *caused* by) differences in family income; black students from the highest family-income level, on average, obtain SAT (and GRE, LSAT, MCAT) scores that fall at least half a standard deviation below the white average; and within any given level of measured aptitude, a higher percentage of blacks than of whites go to college.

Thus, these explanations in terms of popular clichés only lead eventually to embarrassment under critical scrutiny of the evidence. They are wholly out of keeping with the scientifically impeccable manner in which the ETS has treated the evidence pertaining directly to the tests themselves.

What would I suggest instead? Certainly, pusilanimous pussyfooting about the issue deserves no more to be condoned than propounding scientifically unfounded explanations. The simplest, most completely defensible course is the only scientifically honest one: *open agnosticism*. On this point I repeat what I said in *Bias:*

> The observed racial group differences are *real* in the sense that they are not merely an artifact of the measuring instruments. Once that point has been determined for any standard test . . . and the proper uses and limitations of the test are duly noted, the psychopsychometricians and the test publishers should be under no obligation to *explain* the causes of the statistical differences between groups. The problem of explaining the causes of group differences, aside from possible psychometric artifacts, is not the . . . responsibility of the constructors, publishers, or users of tests. The search for causes is an awesomely complex task calling for the collaborative endeavor of at least several specialized fields of science in addition to psychometrics. The state of our scientific knowledge on these matters at present only justifies an agnostic stance on the part of psychometricians, publishers, and users of tests, whatever else their personal sentiments may dictate. (p. 737)

MERCER

As I am told that Robert Gordon's chapter[7] is mainly addressed to an analysis of Mercer's position, I will only briefly indicate my views on a few key points of her paper.

Mercer's case, I believe, is built on what I have already referred to as the *sociologist's fallacy*, namely, the assumption of causality on the basis only of correlation. The whole notion of pluralistic population norms for tests of intelligence or scholastic aptitude is the full flowering of the sociologist's fallacy. Such norms are derived, essentially, by statistically adjusting the actually obtained test scores in terms of a number of their socioeconomic and cultural *correlates,* so that the derived scores for various subpopulations will be more nearly equal. The rationale for this procedure is based on the assumption that the subpopulations in question do not "truly" differ in whatever ability the test purports to assess, and that the observed differences in test scores merely reflect cultural differences. Minority groups obtain lower scores because of the "Anglocentric" bias of the tests. (Nothing is said about why Asians perform on a par with whites on these "Anglocentric" tests.)

If the usual standardized IQ test scores, instead of the pluralistically normed scores, are shown to be unbiased predictors of scholas-

---

[7]Editors' note: Gordon's chapter was written after Jensen's was completed; therefore, Jensen was unable to comment on Gordon's contribution.

tic achievement for majority and minority groups, then the derived scores from pluralistic norms are bound to be biased predictors. The preponderance of the present evidence indicates that the unadjusted IQs are unbiased predictors of scholastic achievement, whether measured by objective achievement tests or by teacher ratings. Where significant predictive bias has been found, it results in an *over*estimate of the actual performance of minority pupils (Messé, Crano, Messé, & Rice, 1979; Reschly & Sabers, 1979; Reynolds & Gutkin, 1980; Svanum & Bringle, 1982).

Mercer argues that the predictive validity of IQ for scholastic performance can be legitimately determined only from teacher ratings or graders, rather than from scores on achievement tests. The argument for this condition is that the correlation between IQ and achievement test scores is spuriously inflated by "common method" variance, because both measures are derived from tests. But it is hard to see that there could be much common method variance between an individually administered IQ test like the WISC or the Stanford–Binet and a paper-and-pencil scholastic achievement test. The lower correlation between IQ and teacher ratings of achievement than between IQ and scores on standardized achievement tests is explainable by (1) the lower reliability of teacher ratings and (2) the coarse scale, usually of only 3 to 5 points, on which teacher ratings or grades are assigned. This precludes as high a correlation as can be obtained between continuous variables measured on a fine-grained scale such as exists for IQ and standard achievement tests.

Under equal opportunity to learn, cognitive scholastic subject matter, after a course of instruction, will show individual differences that are highly correlated with scores on tests of general intelligence. This does not mean that a measure of scholastic achievement and an IQ measure of intelligence are one and the same thing. The contents and skills involved in the two tests may be "phenotypically" quite different. For example, proficiency in high school algebra is correlated with IQ, even though the IQ test items contain nothing resembling algebra and the IQ is measured before the pupils have taken a course in algebra or know anything at all about algebra.

The notion that we cannot make both a theoretical and a practical distinction between aptitude and achievement is nonsense. One of the more striking bits of evidence requiring such a distinction, which I have come across recently, is the finding by Carlson and Jensen (1981) of a correlation of $-.71$ between intraindividual (trial-to-trial) variability in choice reaction time (RT) and scores on one type of scholastic achievement: the Reading Comprehension test (Comprehensive Test of Basic Skills) among ninth-graders.[8] Where is the common method variance in this correlation? Or the common skills and knowledge? (Interestingly, the same RT measure was also correlated −.71 with scores on Raven's Progressive Matrices, a highly g-loaded nonverbal test.) A scientific explanation for such findings would not only justify but necessitate a distinction between ability and achievement. The fact that two classes of tests traditionally labeled *ability* (or *aptitude*) *tests*, on the one hand, and *achievement tests*, on the other, may in some cases be indistinguishable in appearance or, because of their high intercorrelation, can be used interchangeably for some purposes is beside the point. *Ability* and *achievement* are not different kinds of things, but different levels of analysis. The performances or achievements measured by all behavioral tests of whatever label are direct observations; abilities are inferred theoretical constructs needed to explain the observed covariation among a variety of performances and achievements.

"Edumetric" testing may supplant intelligence testing in schools, but I doubt that this substitution would make the controversy about bias in measuring general intelligence obsolete, as Mercer suggests. Instead, it will merely displace the controversy onto edumetric or scholastic achievement tests, because the largest part of the variance in these tests is identified by factor analysis as the g that is also measured by intelligence tests. The controversy over test bias will wane as educators and school psychologists gain greater understanding of the proper uses of intelligence tests and achievement tests and of the objective methods of assessing test bias. The largest study of item bias in scholastic achievement tests (Comprehensive Tests of Basic Skills), by Arneklev (1975), is reviewed in *Bias* (pp. 575–578). Out of 183 achievement test items were found a total of only 15 that met a statistical criterion of bias in large samples of black and white schoolchildren. Of these 15 biased items, 12 were biased in the direction that "disfavors" whites, and only 3 were biased in the direction that "favors" whites, in the effect of the item bias on the total score. Therefore, elimination of the biased items would slightly increase the average white–black difference.

In case anyone overlooks it, I should note the fact that the data in Mercer's Tables 6 and 9 can be used to examine Spearman's hypothesis of a correlation between tests' g loadings and the magni-

---

[8]An intriguing and researchable question is: Would the Reading Comprehension scores show the same or different regressions on the RT measures in white and minority groups?

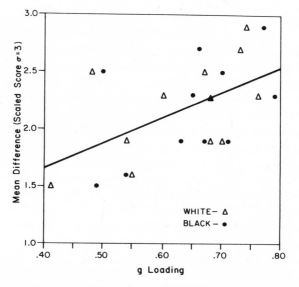

FIGURE 10. Mean white–black difference on 12 WISC-R subtest scores plotted as a function of the subtests' g loadings (corrected for attenuation) in Mercer's white ($N = 683$) and black ($N = 638$) samples.

tudes of the mean white–black difference on the various tests. The first principal component (Mercer's Table 6) is a good estimate of the WISC-R subtests' g loadings. These loadings are highly similar for blacks and whites, as indicated by a coefficient of congruence of .998 between the two sets of g loadings. For testing the Spearman hypothesis, these g loadings should be corrected for attenuation,[9] which I have done, using the reliabilities of the subscales based on the national standardization sample ($N = 2,200$). In Figure 10, the mean white–black differences (in scaled score units) on the WISC-R subtests are shown plotted as a function of the attenuation-corrected g loadings for whites and blacks. The correlation between the mean differences and average g loadings of blacks and whites is $+.55$, $df = 11$, $p < .05$. This correlation should be evaluated in light of the fact that in the national standardization data, the split-half sample reliability of the profile of white–black differences on the various subtests is only .83, and the corresponding split-half sample reliability of the g loadings is about .96. If these figures are used to correct the correla-

[9]This correction, however, makes little difference for these data, the correlations between the corrected and the uncorrected g loadings being .99 for whites and .97 for blacks.

tion of $+.55$ for attenuation, it becomes $+.62$. A significant positive correlation is consistent with the Spearman hypothesis, if the hypothesis is interpreted only as meaning that g is the most discriminating factor, racially. Similar data supporting the Spearman position that differences in g are primarily responsible for black–white differences on mental tests are reported by Reynolds and Gutkin (1981) and Jensen and Reynolds (1982). The obtained correlation of $+$ .62 suggests that these two racial groups must also differ to some degree on other factors besides g.

EPILOGUE

The popular belief that all mental tests are necessarily culturally biased against racial minorities is well entrenched and of long standing. It remains to be seen how much longer this prevailing belief among nonspecialists in psychometrics will withstand contradiction by objective psychometric and statistical evidence and analysis. The words of Sir Francis Galton, generally considered the father of mental measurement and differential psychology, seem most appropriate here:

> General impressions are never to be trusted. Unfortunately when they are of long standing they become fixed rules of life and assume a prescriptive right not to be questioned. Consequently those who are not accustomed to original inquiry entertain a hatred and horror of statistics. They cannot endure the idea of submitting their sacred impressions to cold-blooded verification. But it is the triumph of scientific men to rise superior to such superstitions, to desire tests by which the value of beliefs may be ascertained, and to feel sufficiently masters of themselves to discard contemptuously whatever may be found untrue.[10]

REFERENCES

Ahern, S., & Beatty, J. Pupillary responses during information processing vary with Scholastic Aptitude Test scores. *Science*, 1979, *205*, 1289–1292.

Arneklev, B. L. *Data related to the question of bias in standardized testing.* Tacoma, Wash.: Office of Evaluation, Tacoma Public Schools, 1975.

Breland, H. M. *Population validity and college entrance measures* (Research Monograph No. 8). New York: The College Board, 1921.

Burt, C. *Mental and scholastic tests* (3rd ed.). London: P. S. King, 1921.

---

[10]This quotation appears on the frontispiece of every issue of the *Annals of Human Genetics*, which Galton founded in 1909.

Callaway, E. *Brain electrical potentials and individual psychological differences.* New York: Grune & Stratton, 1975.

Carlson, J. S., & Jensen, M. *Reaction time, movement time, and intelligence: A replication and extention.* Paper presented at the annual meeting of the American Educational Research Association, Los Angeles, Calif., April 1981.

Cleary, T. A., Humphreys, L. G., Kendrick, S. A., & Wesman, A. Educational uses of tests with disadvantaged students. *American Psychologist,* 1975, *30,* 15–41.

Elkana, Y. *The discovery of the conservation of energy.* Cambridge: Harvard University Press, 1974.

Equal Employment Opportunity Commission. Uniform guidelines on employment selection procedures. *Federal Register,* 1978, *43* (166).

Gordon, R. A. Labeling theory, mental retardation, and public policy: *Larry P.* and other developments since 1974. In W. R. Gove (Ed.), *The labeling of deviance: Evaluating a perspective* (2nd ed.). Beverly Hills, Calif.: Sage Publications, 1980.

Gordon, R. A., & Rudert, E. E. Bad news concerning IQ tests. *Sociology of Education,* 1979, *52,* 174–190.

Green, D. R., & Draper, J. F. *Exploratory studies of bias in achievement tests.* Presented at annual meeting of American Psychological Association, Honolulu, September 1972.

Hall, V. C., & Turner, R. R. Comparison of imitation and comprehension scores between two lower-class groups and the effects of two warm-up conditions on imitation of the same groups. *Child Development,* 1971, *42,* 1735–1750.

Hull, C. L. *Aptitude testing.* New York: World, 1928.

Humphreys, L. G. Intelligence testing: The importance of a difference should be evaluated independently of its causes. *Behavioral and Brain Sciences,* 1980, *3,* 347–348.(a)

Humphreys, L. G. Race and intelligence re-examined. *The Humanist,* 1980, *40,* 52–55.(b)

Jensen, A. R. *Educability and group differences.* New York: Harper & Row, 1973.

Jensen, A. R. Interaction of Level I and Level II abilities with race and socioeconomic status. *Journal of Educational Psychology,* 1974, *66,* 99–111.

Jensen, A. R. Race differences, strategy, training, and improper inference. *Journal of Educational Psychology,* 1976, *68,* 130–131.

Jensen, A. R. Genetic and behavioral effects of nonrandom mating. In R. T. Osborne, C. E. Noble, & N. Weyl (Eds.), *Human variation: Psychology of age, race, and sex.* New York: Academic Press, 1978.

Jensen, A. R. *Bias in mental testing.* New York: Free Press, 1980.(a)

Jensen, A. R. Chronometric analysis of mental ability. *Journal of Social and Biological Structures,* 1980, *3,* 103–122.(b)

Jensen, A. R. *Straight talk about mental tests.* New York: Free Press, 1981.

Jensen, A. R. The chronometry of intelligence. In R. J. Sternberg (Ed.), *Recent advances in research on intelligence.* Hillsdale, N.J.: Lawrence Erlbaum, 1982.(a)

Jensen, A. R. Reaction time and psychometric g. In H. J. Eysenck (Ed.), *A model for intelligence.* New York: Springer, 1982.(b)

Jensen, A. R., & Figueroa, R. A. Forward and backward digit span interaction with race and IQ: Predictions from Jensen's theory. *Journal of Educational Psychology,* 1975, *67,* 882–893.

Jensen, A. R., & Reynolds, C. R. Race, social class and ability patterns on the WISC-R. *Personality and Individual Differences,* 1982, *3,* 423–438.

Linn, R. L. Fair test use in selection. *Review of Educational Research,* 1973, *43,* 139–161.

Longstreth, L. E. Level I-Level II abilities as they affect performance of three races in the college classroom. *Journal of Educational Psychology,* 1978, *70,* 289–297.

Lorenz, K. *Die Ruchseite des Spiegels: Versuch einer Naturgeschichte menschlichen Erkennens.* Munich: R. Piper Verlag, 1973.

Matarazzo, J. D., & Wiens, A. N. Black Intelligence Test of Cultural Homogeneity and Wechsler Adult Intelligence Scale scores of black and white police applicants. *Journal of Applied Psychology,* 1977, *62,* 57–63.

McGurk, F. C. J. The culture hypothesis and psychological tests. In R. E. Kuttner (Ed.), *Race and modern science.* New York: Social Science Press, 1967.

Messé, L. A., Crano, W. D., Messé, S. R., & Rice, W. Evaluation of the predictive validity of tests of mental ability for classroom performance in elementary grades. *Journal of Educational Psychology,* 1979, *71,* 233–241.

Miles, T. R. Contributions to intelligence testing and the theory of intelligence: I. On defining intelligence. *British Journal of Educational Psychology,* 1957, *27,* 153–165.

Open peer commentary. *Behavioral and Brain Sciences,* 1980, *3,* 325–371.

Reschly, D. J., & Sabers, D. L. An examination of bias in predicting MAT scores from WISC-R scores for four ethnic-racial groups. *Journal of Educational Measurement,* 1979, *16,* 1–9.

Reynolds, C. R. The problem of bias in psychological assessment. In C. R. Reynolds and T. B. Gutkin (Eds.), *The handbook of school psychology.* New York: Wiley, 1982.

Reynolds, C. R., & Gutkin, T. B. A regression analysis of test bias on the WISC-R for Anglos and Chicanos referred to psychological services. *Journal of Abnormal Child Psychology,* 1980, *8,* 237–243.

Reynolds, C. R., & Gutkin, T. B. A multivariate comparison of the intellectual performance of blacks and whites matched on four demographic variables. *Personality and Individual Differences,* 1981, *2,* 175–180.

Reynolds, C. R., & Jensen, A. R. *Patterns of intellectual abilities among blacks and whites matched on g.* Paper presented at the annual meeting of the American Psychological Association, Montreal, 1980.

Reynolds, C. R., & Jensen, A. R. WISC-R subscale patterns of abilities of blacks and whites matched on Full Scale IQ. *Journal of Educational Psychology,* 1983, *75,* 207–214.

Schmid, J., & Leiman, J. M. The development of hierarchical factor solutions. *Psychometrika,* 1957, *22,* 53–61.

Schmidt, F. L., & Hunter, J. E. Development of a general solution to the problem of validity generalization. *Journal of Applied Psychology,* 1977, *62,* 529–540.

Schmidt, F. L., & Hunter, J. E. Moderator research and the law of small numbers. *Personnel Psychology,* 1978, *31,* 215–232.

Schmidt, F. L., & Hunter, J. E. Employment testing. *American Psychologist,* 1981, *36,* 1128–1137.

Schmidt, F. L., Hunter, J. E., Pearlman, K., & Shane, G. S. Further tests of the Schmidt-Hunter Bayesian validity generalization procedure. *Personnel Psychology,* 1979, *32,* 257–281.

Silberman, C. E. *Crisis in black and white.* New York: Random House, 1964.

Spearman, C. "General intelligence," objectively determined and measured. *American Journal of Psychology,* 1904, *15,* 201–292.

Spearman, C. *The abilities of man.* New York: Macmillan, 1927.

Sternberg, R. J., Conway, B. E., Ketron, J. L., & Bernstein, M. People's conceptions of intelligence. Technical Report No. 28, October, 1980, and *Journal of Personality and Social Psychology: Attitudes and Scoial Cognition,* 1981, *41,* 37–55.

Svanum, S., & Bringle, R. G. Race, social class, and predictive bias: An evaluation using the UISC, WRAT, and Teacher Ratings. *Intelligence,* 1982, *6,* 275–286.

Van Valen, L. Brain size and intelligence in man. *American Journal of Physical Anthropology*, 1974, *40*, 417–423.

Vernon, P. A. Level I and Level II: A review. *Educational Psychologist*, 1981, *16*, 45–64.

Wherry, R. J. Hierarchical factor solutions without rotation. *Psychometrika*, 1959, *24*, 45–51.

Postscript
Bernal Replies

ERNEST M. BERNAL

I wish to thank Professor Jensen for his lesson in statistics and hypothesis testing. I am sorry, however, that he apparently missed one of the key points of my study.

Notice, for example, Jensen's Table 1, which summarizes white–black and white–Chicano differences on SAT, ACT, GRE, LSAT, and MCAT test scores. These data are quite similar to those presented in many other studies over the last 60 years or so, studies that support the propositions of the heritability of g and of the average intellectual superiority of whites over blacks and certain other minority ethnic groups in the United States. The data in my own Tables 1 and 2 are part of this set, for whites (W) score significantly higher than blacks (B), Mexican-American English-speaking monolinguals (M1), and Mexican-American English-Spanish bilinguals (M2) under standard test administration (control) conditions on both the Number Series Test (NST) and the Letter Sets Test (LST), even though socioeconomic status was controlled.

But my research also presented evidence that under an alternative testing condition (experimental treatment), the tested group differences—so clearly evident under standard testing conditions—virtually disappear. The data in my Tables 3 and 4 are not tractable to analysis through the heritability index, as the significance of the differences can no longer be detected, not between nor among the several groups.

ERNEST M. BERNAL ● School of Education and Human Development, California State University, Fresno, California 93740.

The investigations on training effects that Jensen cited in *Bias in Mental Testing*, he concludes, "have generally shown small but statistically significant main effects." In those instances where whites were included in these studies, however, they maintained a reliable performance advantage over minority subjects. Also, the interventions in which the minority groups participated involved considerably longer periods of time than the one I employed. In this respect, my study appears to be a rare but not necessarily unique exception to this literature.

Jensen objects to my observation that he utilizes studies that support his contentions on the heritability of g and the general superiority of whites on such tests. I have ended this postscript with a brief bibliography of some selected references for his perusal, including several studies on the coachability of the SAT. The problem, however, seems to lie in Jensen's perception of the meaning or applicability of the literature, for its difficult to believe that Jensen could have read so many of the relevant studies and still make such artless remarks as those found in his chapter. In the studies that I previously cited, for example, Burger (1972) discussed the issues in educing verbal responses from Hispanic children, findings with clear implications for individually administered IQ tests. Matluck and Mace (1973) brought other linguistic analyses to bear on the assessment of Mexican-American children with various language characteristics. Katz, Epps, and Axelson (1964), Prehm (1966), Rapier (1967), and Zimmerman and Rosenthal (1972) have addressed the testing situation in one way or another to suggest, variously, a differential readiness of minority subjects to engage in different tasks under different circumstances, the importance of pretraining, and the effects of expected comparisons to whites on minority examinees.

It does not follow logically that because students select themselves for graduate school or the state bar examination that they are equally well prepared to take the entrance examinations or the licensing tests. Nor does the fact that two subtests of the WISC-R are administered sequentially ensure that the same testing conditions obtain in the mind of the person tested. It is facile to think that motivation alone can account for much of the difference in tested levels of performance between groups, and it is naive to believe that the sequence and shift of tasks (such as the shift from digits forward to digits backward) could not possibly be perceived as highly novel or threatening by one group but not by another.

Jensen believes that "other investigators would be at a loss to replicate [my] study." The processes involved, I think, should be clear enough to the many professionals who can administer group tests well and who possess even a fairly high degree of interpersonal spontaneity and social skills. Ethnic matching of examiner and students, small-group settings, informal attire and introductions, linguistically appropriate dialogue, test practice, feedback and the ability to elicit student explanations of the correct choice are the only requirements. I know dozens of clinicians, school counselors, linguists, teachers, anthropologists, and—yes—even a few research psychometricians who would not find these conditions to be beyond their understanding or management. Nevertheless, Jensen has a point: These conditions require certain intuitions that are difficult to articulate and that certainly need further explication and specification. My study was, after all, admittedly based not only on a search of the literature but also on a surmise; it properly constitutes an initial effort to explore gross effects. In the future, experiments along this line might investigate the efficiency of the factors that comprise this treatment, singly and in combination, in an effort to isolate the most important ones and to optimize the mix for all groups in the experiment. Also, an ethnographic component of such research might yield further insights into how the subjects perceive the treatments as well.

Jensen criticized my test of the hypothesis that the testing ambience is largely responsible for the noted ethnic group differences and my hypothesis that tests, as we now understand them, do not satisfactorily tap the true abilities of many minority groups. He pointed out that, as the treatment × ethnicity interaction terms in my Tables 5 and 6 were not significant, "the effect of the treatment was not significantly greater for the minorities than for the whites." In this statement, however, he would seem to be only partly correct. I will proceed to explain why.

As Jensen recognizes that my purpose initially was to test the "*differences* between the experimental and control conditions," I should like to take the liberty of presenting two planned comparisons of this hypothesis now, instead of using a more conservative *post hoc* test such as Tukey's or the general Scheffé procedure that Jensen mentions. Although these belated studies are subject to the criticism that they should have been conducted before the data were examined, these *a priori* tests nonetheless constitute a more exact examination of the ambience hypothesis than the overall interaction term, because planned comparisons specify the exact contrasts to be made. Using the notations E for "experimental" and C for "control," the equation would read:

$$\psi = [M_{E(W)} - M_{C(W)}]$$
$$- \left[\frac{(M_{E(M1)} - M_{C(M1)}) + (M_{E(M2)} - M_{C(M2)}) + (M_{E(B)} - M_{C(B)})}{3} \right]$$

Table 1 presents the contrasts for both the NST and the LST. The comparison for the NST, then, is

$$\psi_1 = (1)(4.88) + (-\tfrac{1}{3})(4.33) + (-\tfrac{1}{3})(6.29) + (-\tfrac{1}{3})(5.00)$$
$$+ (-1)(5.67) + (\tfrac{1}{3})(3.25) + (\tfrac{1}{3})(4.21) + (\tfrac{1}{3})(3.08) = -2.484$$

and

$$w_1 = \frac{1}{24} \left[1 + \frac{1}{9} + \frac{1}{9} + \frac{1}{9} + 1 + \frac{1}{9} + \frac{1}{9} + \frac{1}{9} \right] = \frac{1}{9}$$

so

$$SS\psi_1 = \frac{\psi_1^2}{w_1} = \frac{-2.484^2}{\frac{1}{9}} = 55.532$$

and

$$F = \frac{MS_\psi}{\text{Residual}} = \frac{55.532}{9.584} = 5.79$$

The probability for F (with 1 and 168 df) $< .02$. The null hypothesis is then rejected, and it appears that for the NST the effects of the experimental treatment were indeed different for the minority groups than for the whites. Figure 1 illustrates this result.

TABLE 1
Planned Comparison of NST and LST for Experimental and Control Groups

H_0: Experimental minus control differences between w groups are the same as E minus C differences between the minority groups combined

Comparison	E(W)	E(B)	E(M1)	E(M2)	C(W)	C(B)	C(M1)	C(M2)
1 (NST)	1	$-\tfrac{1}{3}$	$-\tfrac{1}{3}$	$-\tfrac{1}{3}$	-1	$\tfrac{1}{3}$	$\tfrac{1}{3}$	$\tfrac{1}{3}$
	4.88	4.33	6.29	5.00	5.67	3.25	4.21	3.08
2 (LST)	1	$-\tfrac{1}{3}$	$-\tfrac{1}{3}$	$-\tfrac{1}{3}$	-1	$\tfrac{1}{3}$	$\tfrac{1}{3}$	$\tfrac{1}{3}$
	12.38	11.04	12.00	11.00	11.67	9.42	9.21	9.17

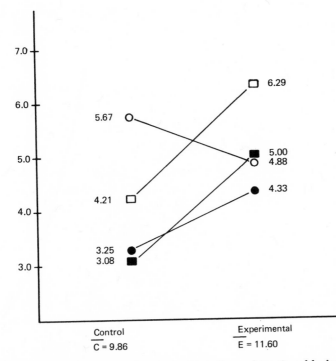

FIGURE 1. Results of the Number Series Test: ○ = white; ● = black; □ = Mexican-American English monolingual; ■ = Mexican-American English-Spanish bilingual.

A similar study of the LST, however, failed to yield significance ($F = 1.30$), so the test of the "ambience hypothesis" is verified only in that comparison where the whites demonstrated slightly (and insignificantly) lower performance from control to experimental conditions. Figure 2 illustrates the results for the LST.

The results of the hypothesis that the testing ambience itself explains much of the white–minority differences in test performance, then, are ambiguous. The trends in the data, however, merit further investigation, perhaps through a longer intervention.

The consistently higher scores made by the minority groups on both tests and the lack of significant ethnic differences (including, of course, white–minority differences) under the experimental treatment have important implications for the hereditarian position. We have demonstrated the possibility that hereditary differences in g may actually be more amenable to environmental effects than was heretofore believed or that tests developed by, for, and with whites

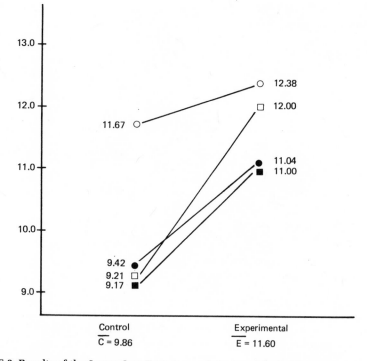

FIGURE 2. Results of the Letter Sets Test: ○ = white; ● = black; □ = Mexican-American English monolingual; ■ = Mexican-American English-Spanish bilingual.

may not be as cross-culturally applicable as we have presumed. Were hereditarians like Jensen faced with more data such as those derived from the experimental condition, they might not be able to support their conclusions about white–black and white–Mexican-American differences in higher order intellectual functions.

REFERENCES

Burger, H. G. "Ethno-lematics": Evoking "shy" Spanish-American pupils by cross-cultural mediation. *Adolescence*, 1972, *6*, 61–76.

Jensen, A. R. *Bias in mental testing.* New York: Free Press, 1980.

Katz, I., Epps, E. G., & Axelson, L. J. Effect upon Negro digit-symbol performance of anticipated comparison with Whites and other Negroes. *Journal of Abnormal and Social Psychology*, 1964, *69*, 77–83.

Matluck, J. H., & Mace, B. J. Language characteristics of Mexican American children: Implications for assessment. *Journal of School Psychology*, 1973, *11*, 365–386.

Prehm, H. J. Concept learning in culturally disadvantaged children as a function of verbal pretraining. *Exceptional Children*, 1966, *32*, 599–604.

Rapier, J. L. Effects of verbal mediation upon the learning of Mexican American children. *California Journal of Educational Research*, 1967, *18*, 40–48.

Zimmerman, B. J., & Rosenthal, T. L. Observation, repetition, and ethnic background in concept attainment and generalization. *Child Development*, 1972, *43*, 605–613.

BIBLIOGRAPHY

Cohen, R. A. Conceptual styles, culture conflict, and nonverbal tests of intelligence. *American Anthropologist*, 1969, *71*, 828–856.

De Avila, E. A., & Havassy, B. Piagetian alternatives to IQ: Mexican American study. In N. Hobbs (Ed.), *Issues in the classification of exceptional children*. San Francisco: Jossey-Bass, 1975.

Dickie, J., & Bagur, J. S. Considerations for the study of language in low-income minority group children. *Merrill-Palmer Quarterly of Behavior and Development*, 1972, *18*, 25–38.

Ferrell, G. *Development and use of a test of test-wiseness*. Paper presented at the annual meeting of the Western College Reading Association, Denver, March–April 1977. (ERIC Document Reproduction Service No. ED 154 374)

Gage, N. L. I. Q. heritability, race differences, and educational research. *Phi Delta Kappan*, 1972, *53*, 308–312.

García, A. B., & Zimmerman, B. J. The effect of examiner ethnicity and language on the performance of bilingual Mexican American first graders. *Journal of School Psychology*, 1972, *87*, 3–11.

van Hekken, S. The influence of verbalization on observational learning in a group of mediating and a group of non-mediating children. *Human Development*, 1969, *12*, 204–213.

Kleinfeld, J. S. Intellectual strengths in culturally different groups: An Eskimo example. *Review of Educational Research*, 1973, *43*, 341–359.

Oakland, T. The effects of test-wiseness materials on standardized test performance of preschool disadvantaged children. *Journal of School Psychology*, 1972, *10*, 355–360.

Pike, L. *Short-term instruction, test-wiseness, and the SAT: A literature review with research recommendations*. New York: The College Board, 1979.

Pike, L. *Implicit guessing strategies of GRE-Aptitude examinees classified by ethnic group and sex: GRE Board professional report* No. 75-10P. Princeton, N.J.: Educational Testing Service, 1980.

Pike, L., & Evans, F. *CEEB research report no. 1: Effects of specific instruction for three kinds of mathematics aptitude items*. New York: College Entrance Examination Board, 1972.

Sarason, S. B. Anxiety and learning. In W. B. Waetjen (Ed.), *Human variability and learning: Papers and reports from the Fifth Curriculum Research Institute*. Washington, D.C.: Association for Supervision and Curriculum Development, National Education Association, 1961.

Author Index

Subject Index